BARRON'S
BUSINESS
TRAVELERS

SPANISH
FOR THE
BUSINESS
TRAVELER

T. Bruce Fryer
Professor of Spanish
Department of Spanish, Italian, and Portuguese
University of South Carolina, Columbia

Hugo J. Faría
Instituto de Estudios Superiores de Administración
IESA
Caracas, Venezuela

BARRON'S

All inquiries should be addressed to:
Barron's Educational Series, Inc.
250 Wireless Boulevard
Hauppauge, NY 11788

Library of Congress Catalog Card No. 93-23414

International Standard Book No. 0-8120-1773-0

Library of Congress Cataloging-in-Publication Data

Fryer, T. Bruce.
    Spanish for the business traveler / by T. Bruce Fryer, Hugo J. Faría.
    — 2nd ed.
        p. cm. — (Barron's bilingual business guides)
    Prev. ed. cataloged under the title: Talking business in Spanish.
    ISBN 0-8120-1773-0
        1. Business—Dictionaries. 2. English language—Dictionaries—Spanish.
3. Business—Dictionaries—Spanish. 4. Spanish language—Dictionaries—
English. I. Faría, Hugo J. II. Fryer, T. Bruce. Talking business in Spanish.
III. Title. IV. Series.
HF1002.F79   1994   93-23414
650′.03—dc20   CIP

PRINTED IN THE UNITED STATES OF AMERICA
4567   9692   9876543

CONTENTS

PREFACE

It is the nature of business to seek out new markets for its products, to find more efficient ways to bring its goods to more people. In the global marketplace, this often means travel to foreign countries, where language and customs are different. Even when a businessperson knows the language of the host country, the specific and often idiosyncratic terminology of the business world can be an obstacle to successful negotiations in a second language. Pocket phrase books barely scratch the surface of these problems, while standard business dictionaries prove too cumbersome.

Now there is a solution—*Barron's Spanish for the Business Traveler*. Here is the essential pocket reference for all international business travelers. Whether your business be manufacturing or finance, communications or sales, this three-part guide will put the right words in your mouth and the best expressions in your correspondence. It is a book you'll carry with you on every trip and take to every meeting. But it is also the reference you'll keep on your desk in the office. This is the business dictionary for people who do business in Spanish.

Barron's Spanish for the Business Traveler offers you the following features:

- a 6,000-entry list of basic business terms, dealing with accounting, advertising and sales, banking, computers, export/import, finance and investment, labor relations, management. manufacturing, marketing, retail and wholesale sales, and more;
- 1,000-word vocabulary listing of terms related to specific industries;
- a quick guide to basic terms and expressions for getting by when you don't know the language;
- a pronunciation guide for speaking the language;
- a comprehensive list of common business abbreviations;
- reference words for numbers and amounts, days of the week, months and seasons of the year;
- conversion tables for metric and customary measurements;
- lists of major holidays, annual trade fairs, travel times between cities, average temperatures throughout the year;
- information on international currencies, country and city telephone codes, useful addresses in the foreign countries;
- a hotel and restaurant guide for the major cities in selected Spanish-speaking countries.

This book is one of a new series of business dictionaries. We welcome your comments on additional phrases that could be included in future editions.

Acknowledgments

We would like to thank the following individuals and organizations for their assistance on this project:

John Downes, Business Development Consultant, Office for Economic

Development, New York City; Frank Medley, West Virginia University; Peter McWilliam of Unibanco, New York City; Susana Sarago of Extebank, New York City; José Bertran, Embassy of Spain, New York City; and Milan Skacel, Latin American Chamber of Commerce, New York City.

We are also grateful to the following people and organizations for supplying us with information on services in their countries:

Liliana A. de Alfaro, Commercial Attaché, Embassy of the Republic of Argentina; Joaquín de la Infiesta, Commercial Counselor, Embassy of Spain; Eduardo M. Perez-Vizcarrondo, Executive Vice-President, Puerto Rican Chamber of Commerce in the United States; Miguel Sebastia, Executive Director, Spain–U.S.A. Chamber of Commerce. We are also grateful to Mr. Dominguez of the Mexican Institute for Foreign Trade; to the Colombia Information Service; to Professor Nestor A. Moreno, Francisca Jimenez, Silvia Milian, Martina M. Isaac, and Jesús Salamanca of the University of South Carolina; and to David Frankel for assembling the materials.

Portions of Part I of this book are reprinted with permission from *Spanish at a Glance*, by Heywood Wald, and from *Travel Diary: Spanish*, both published by Barron's Educational Series, Inc.

I. PRONUNCIATION GUIDE

This book assumes you are already somewhat familiar with the basic pronunciation rules of Spanish, but for those whose knowledge is a little rusty, here are some tips.

Spanish contains three additional letters not found in English: *ch*, *ll*, and *ñ*. All letters are pronounced, with the exception of *h*; the letters *v* and *b* are most often both pronounced like the English *b*.

Words ending in a vowel, an *n*, or an *s* are stressed on the next-to-last syllable—*casa* (KAH-sah). Words ending in a consonant (other than *n* or *s*) are stressed on the last syllable—*general* (hehn-eh-RAHL). A written accent is required on any words which break either of these rules—*lápiz* (*LAH*-pees).

NOTE: When pronouncing the words in the following examples, stress the syllables that appear in CAPITAL letters.

Consonants

SPANISH LETTER(S)	SOUND IN ENGLISH	EXAMPLES
c before (*a*, *o*, *u*)	hard k sound (*c*at)	campo (KAHM-poh) cosa (KOH-sah) Cuba (Koo-bah)
c (before *e*, *i*)	soft s sound (*c*ent)	central (sehn-TRAHL) cinco (SEEN-koh)
cc	hard and soft cc (ks sound) (a*cc*ept)	acción (ahk-see-OHN)
ch	hard ch sound (*ch*air)	muchacho (moo-CHAH-choh)
g (before *a*, *o*, *u*)	hard g (*g*o)	gafas (GAH-fahs) goma (GOH-mah)
g (before *e*, *i*)	breathy h (*h*ot)	general (hehn-eh-RAHL)
h	always silent	hasta (AHS-tah)
j	breathy as in h sound (*h*ot)	José (ho-SAY)
l	English l sound (*l*amp)	lámpara (LAHM-pahr-ah)
ll	as in English y (*y*es)	pollo (POH-yoh)
n	English n (*n*o)	naranja (nah RAHN-ha)

SPANISH LETTER(S)	SOUND IN ENGLISH	EXAMPLES
ñ	English ny (ca*n*yon)	señorita (seh-nyoh-REE tah)
qu	English k (*k*eep)	que (kay)
r	trilled once	caro (KAH-roh)
rr (or r at beginning of word)	trilled strongly (operator saying th*ree*)	rico (RREE-koh) perro (PEH-rroh)
s	English s (*s*ee)	rosa (ROH-sah)
v	Approximately as in English b (*b*ook)	primavera (pree-mah BEHR-ah)
x	English s, ks (*s*ign, so*cks*)	extra (ES-trah) examinar (ek-sah-mee NAHR)
y	English y (*y*es) (by itself y = i)	yo (yoh) y (ee)
z	English s	zapato (sah-PAH toh)

Castilian pronunciations, spoken in parts of Spain, are as follows:

SPANISH LETTER(S)	SOUND IN ENGLISH	EXAMPLES
ll	ly sound as in million	llamo (LYAH-moh)
c (before *e* or *i*)	a *th* sound	gracias (GRAH-thee-ahs)
z	instead of an *s* sound	lápiz (LAH-peeth)

Vowels

SPANISH LETTER(S)	SOUND IN ENGLISH	EXAMPLES
	Vowels	
a	ah (*ya*cht)	taco (TAH-koh)
e	ay (d*ay*)	mesa (MAY-sah)
	eh (p*e*t)	perro (PEH-rroh)
i	ee (m*ee*t)	libro (LEE-broh)
o	oh (*o*pen)	foto (FOH-toh)
o	oo (t*oo*th)	mucho (MOO-choh)

SPANISH LETTER(S)	SOUND IN ENGLISH	EXAMPLES
Common Vowel Combinations (Dipthongs)		
au	ow (c*ow*)	causa (COW-sah) auto (OW-toh)
ei	ay (d*ay*)	aceite (ah-SAY-tay)
ai	y (t*y*pe)	baile (BY-lay)
ie	yeh (*ye*t)	abierto (ah-BYEHR-toh)
ue	weh (*we*t)	bueno (BWEH-noh)

II. INTRODUCTION

DOING BUSINESS IN SPANISH-SPEAKING COUNTRIES

Doing business with another culture and in another language can be a difficult and mystifying experience. Customs and procedures may be quite different from what is perceived as the "normal" way of conducting oneself in a business circumstance.

In this introduction, some of the customs and economic aspects of Spanish-speaking countries are outlined, in order to assist you in effectively conducting business in these areas. Basic knowledge of these factors will help in becoming more accustomed to the business situation of the Spanish-speaking world.

SPAIN

By I. Febrer, Vice President of the Spanish Trade Center in New York City

Usual Hours of Operation

Monday to Friday   8:00 AM to 1:00 PM & 3:00 PM to 7:00 PM
Saturday   8:00 AM to 1:00 PM (Sales premises only)

Business Customs

- Spanish businessmen tend to be rather formal and conservative on first occasions, loosening up and becoming very friendly as the relationship develops.
- Go slowly in establishing a relationship. Never take the lead in calling your foreign counterpart by his or her first name. Always begin speaking by using the third person "Usted"; the other person may ask you to call him "tú," by saying "me puedes tutear," otherwise stick to the "usted."
- Don't rush things. Be patient. This is probably the most important advice one can give to an American in adapting to the style of other cultures. To Americans, who are accustomed to doing things on the old adage, "Time is money," this may not be easy at first. Business people want to establish rapport and size you up before they do business with you.
- Remember to shake hands when meeting someone and also when taking leave.
- It is customary to do business while dining in a regional restaurant. Spaniards are very proud of the regions where they were born and where they live.
- Exercise caution in discussing delicate topics such as politics or religion before you learn what are acceptable topics of conversation in that culture.
- Talking about family, friendship, and other personal matters is considered normal at a business meal. Spaniards enjoy talking while having coffee after the meal; it is then that business is at its best.

General Government Policy and Economic Situation

(Statistics given in this section are generally accurate through 1992.)

The Spanish economic framework is that of an industrialized country. The major contributor to the economy is the service sector, followed by industry.

The area of Spain is a little more than 500,000 square kilometers. The country is divided into 17 autonomous regions, each with its own government. The capital is Madrid. The stock exchanges are located in Madrid, Barcelona, Bilbao, and Valencia. The main ports are Barcelona, Bilbao, and Valencia. The Spanish economy combines free enterprise and some nationalized companies, such as railroads, telephone, and energy. The currency is the peseta. 116 ptas = approximately US $1.

Structure of GDP (% of total)

SECTORS	1980	1984	1992
Farming	7.4	6.7	6.0
Industry	28.7	28.6	23.0
Construction	7.7	6.7	7.0
Services	56.2	58.0	60.0

(INE National Statistics Institute, 1992)

Future Development in Trade Policies

In January 1986, Spain joined the EEC; since then, it has steadily been incorporating its trade policies, including custom duties, foreign exchange control, and foreign investment policies.

Principal trading partners: United States, France, Germany, United Kingdom
Inflation rate: 5%
Population: 39.6 million
Religion: Roman Catholic (90%)
Language: Castilian, Catalan, Basque, Galician, and several dialects
GDP: 36 billion pesetas
Average exchange rate: 139
Prime rate: 7.5%

When doing business in Spain it is advisable to seek the help of an agent. Negotiations are done at a slow pace and patience is required. As in any other country, courtesy goes a long way; if you are going to be late, a telephone call is expected.

It is also a very good idea to fax your messages immediately following telephone conversations. Don't count on the spoken word; back up verbal agreements with written statements.

LATIN AMERICA

By Milan B. Skacel, award-winning writer specializing in international affairs and president of the Chamber of Commerce of Latin America in the United States, Inc.

Latin America is not a monolith, but the countries south of the Rio Grande share many economic problems and national characteristics and idiosyncrasies.

Most Latin American countries are heavily in debt, their economic growth is sluggish and uneven, and cold statistics seem to discourage even guarded optimism about the future. At the end of 1992, the major Latin American countries—Argentina, Brazil, Chile, Colombia, Mexico, Peru, and Venezuela—together owed more than $400 billion to foreign leaders, including U.S. banks. Interest payments alone consumed more than 40 percent of their export revenues, and total debt service—even when repayment of capital was "rescheduled"—equaled close to 60 percent of earnings.

Despite all of the above, with the signing of NAFTA with Mexico and ratification of the GATT, the horizon looks very promising for Latin America, in general, and, in particular, for Mexico, Colombia, Argentina, and Chile, who have signed agreements of their own that will no doubt increase imports and exports, paving the way for American business to boom. There is a great deal of activity at the present time in this respect and many American companies are actively seeking participation of these markets.

In addition, many Latin American countries are changing their political and economic policies and, as a result, are coming out of the stagnation in which they have been for so long. Our advice, therefore, is to look very closely for new opportunities; certainly the privatization of many of the government agencies in most Latin countries has opened many opportunities for foreign companies and investors who are trying to get a share of the business.

Business is generally conducted in a more leisurely way than in the United States. The word here is patience, for negotiations, by U.S. standards, may seem to drag on forever. Younger technocrats and business people, however, tend to be somewhat more direct; some of them have been schooled and trained in the United States and have adopted many American business practices. Still, government contracts and joint ventures involve extensive red tape, and delays are common.

Proficiency in Spanish is a distinct asset. Even if you do not speak the language fluently, a few words are appreciated. For business discussions, an interpreter versed in your business is often indispensable; do not expect to conduct the conversation in English, even if the other person speaks it. As interpreter you can use your local representative or, failing that, ask U.S. embassy or consulate officials to recommend a reputable interpreter.

If you choose an interpreter, make sure the individual is briefed on the subject of the conversation or negotiation. You might have selected a very reputable interpreter in economics and politics, etc. but that interpreter might not be familiar with the intricate vocabulary of computers, the petroleum industry, or electronic equipment; don't assume that interpretation is just a matter of words, there is a great deal more going into it, ask for someone familiar with your business. Beware of obtaining a referral from your business counterpart on the other side of the negotiation: his or her translations may be subtly biased in ways you are not able to detect, even if you have studied the language.

Many Latin American businessmen, however, know English and enjoy using it, the problem is that they don't speak "our" English—the melange of slang, business and technical jargon, colloquialisms, sports expressions, military metaphors, and local humor that constitutes the daily vernacular of commerce in the United States. What's more, some of the words we use can have entirely different meanings from those of other cultures, further complicating the communication process for Americans abroad. So speak plainly, clearly, and slowly in meetings with those who speak English as a second language. Try to keep as many Americanisms and slang expressions as possible out of your conversation. Most Latin Americans have learned proper English or textbook English, and they simply won't understand you if you depart too radically from what they have learned.

Remember also that, if you know Spanish, you have probably studied Castilian Spanish in school. Should you, however, go to Mexico, you will find that there are major differences in Spanish pronunciation and vocabulary, as well as differences in cultural attitudes. Writing or speaking in one regional variation of a language to someone in another region can actually end up in insulting those for whom the messages were intended.

Business hours vary from country to country, even from company to company. The best time to telephone for an appointment is around 10 AM— before the executive or government official begins his or her daily routine. Unless your Spanish is good, do not place the call yourself; have your representative or interpreter set the appointment. Afternoon siesta is still a tradition with many, but less so with the younger generation.

Latin Americans are conscious of their dignity. Do not try using first names unless the initiative comes from the other person. Address people by title or surname. (Most Latins have at least three names, the "last" name usually being his mother's maiden name. E.g., Juan Martínez Romero should be addressed as Señor Martínez.)

Punctuality is not a Latin American strong point, yet foreigners are expected to be on time. Never mention the other person's tardiness, even in a joking way. Being late is not deliberate rudeness, merely an ingrained habit. Shaking hands on arrival and departure is common, but wait for the person to extend his or her hand first. The ritual of "abrazo"—a symbolic hug—is reserved for friends or close associates; if the other person initiates it, it is a sign of favor.

An invitation to a person's home is a privilege and can lead to useful contacts and even business deals. Do not, however, talk business unless your host broaches the subject. You may simply be there "on approval"—with your host and others trying to make up their minds as to whether you are the kind of person they want to do business with.

If you have a business representative, that person should lay the groundwork for your visit and make appointments in advance. If this is your first visit, do not be discouraged if few tangible results come of it. Establishing personal contact and getting a firsthand feeling of the country often later lead to translating your objectives into reality. The word, again, is patience.

General Information

(Statistics given in this section are generally accurate through 1992.)

Argentina: Democratic rule returned in 1983. The military, discredited in the 1982 war over the British Falkland Islands, nevertheless remains a major force and could seize power again, if Argentina's deep-seated economic problems generate wider discontent and attendant unrest. Economic planning is hampered by public opposition to austerity measures and by powerful labor unions, largely controlled by ideological followers of the late Juan Perón, which share the blame for seemingly unending inflationary pressures.

Main imports: Nonelectrical machinery, petroleum and petroleum products, cast-iron and steel products; also electrical machinery, road vehicles and transport equipment, plastics and artificial resins, chemicals.

Main exports: Foodstuff for animals, vegetables, grains and cereals, meat and meat preparations, hides and skins, vegetable oils, fats and waxes.

Principal trading partners: United States, Russia, Brazil, Germany, the Netherlands, China, Japan, Italy.

Population: 33 million.

Religion: Roman Catholic (92%).

GDP: 79 billion (U.S.).

Unemployment rate: 8%.

Bolivia: The country's chronically volatile political situation, with five coups during the past five years, is compounded by depressed world prices for tin.

Main imports: Capital goods, including transport equipment and raw materials.

Main exports: Tin, natural gas, coffee, sugar, wood.

Principal trading partners: United States, Argentina, Brazil, Japan, Mexico, the Netherlands.

Population: 7.9 million.

Religion: Roman Catholic (94%).

GDP: $4.2 billion (U.S.).

Unemployment rate: 11%.

Chile: Headed by President Eduardo Frei Ruiz-Tagle, former president Pinochet remains as commander-in-chief of the army.

Main imports: Machinery, variety of consumer and capital goods, petroleum.

Main exports: Mining products including copper and nickel, fruits and vegetables, fish meal.

Principal trading partners: United States, Japan, Venezuela, Argentina, Brazil, Germany, Britain, France.

Population: 13.7 million.

Religion: Roman Catholic (80%); Protestant (6%).

GDP: $31 billion (U.S.).

Unemployment rate: 15%.

Colombia: Although it has a functioning, democratically elected government, there are guerillas operating in the countryside. However, President César Gaviria has succeeded in negotiating with the guerrillas and, with the recent "disappearance" of Pablo Escobar, the head of the Medellín cartel, the outlook for Colombia is very encouraging.

Despite Colombia's bad reputation for violence, Colombians have not had one single year of recession since 1948. While its neighbors spent most of the 1980s negotiating foreign debt and controlling hyperinflation, Colombia increased its per capita to 15%, and the economic and political outlook is very promising.

Main imports: Machinery, equipment, chemicals, crude petroleum and petroleum products, base metals and metal manufactures, paper and paper products.

Main exports: Coffee, crude petroleum and petroleum products, bananas, fresh-cut flowers, cotton.

Principal trading partners: United States, European Union countries, Venezuela, Ecuador, Peru, Japan.

Population: 34.8 million.

Religion: Roman Catholic (97%).

GDP: $43 billion (U.S.).

Unemployment rate: 8.1%.

Costa Rica: Representative government; no standing army. Latin America's longest continuously functioning democracy.

Main imports: Machinery, including telecommunications equipment, paper and paper products, iron and steel, chemicals, petroleum.

Main exports: Coffee, bananas, chemical products including pharmaceuticals, beef.

Principal trading partners: United States, Germany, Japan, Venezuela, Mexico, Guatemala, El Salvador, Nicaragua.

Population: 3 million.

Religion: Roman Catholic (92%).

GDP: $3.1 billion (U.S.).

Unemployment rate: 10%.

Dominican Republic: Representative government since 1970. Continued depressed world prices have affected the main export commodity, sugar.

Main imports: Crude petroleum and petroleum products, machinery, foodstuffs, chemicals, iron, steel.

Main exports: Raw sugar, gold alloy, ferronickel, coffee, cacao.

Principal trading partners: United States, Venezuela, Mexico, Japan, Switzerland, Canada, Puerto Rico, the Netherlands.

Population: 7.6 million.

Religion: Roman Catholic (98%).

GDP: $9.7 billion (U.S.).

Unemployment rate: 26%.

Ecuador: Peaceful transition from military to civilian rule took place in 1979. For the past 14 years the country's economy has revolved around its petroleum exports; with sharply lower oil prices, there have been severe economic problems.

Main imports: Chemical products, machinery, food products, transportation equipment.

Main exports: Crude petroleum, fish products, coffee, bananas.

Principal trading partners: United States, Japan, Germany, Italy, Brazil, Panama, Colombia.

Population: 10.4 million.
Religion: Roman Catholic (91%).
GDP: $12.2 billion (U.S.).
Unemployment rate: 6.3%.

El Salvador: The newly elected president will hopefully bring this troubled country to the end of its civil war and new business opportunities.
Main imports: Chemical products, crude petroleum, food products including dairy products and wheat, electrical machinery and appliances.
Main exports: Coffee, refined sugar, shrimp, cotton and cotton products.
Principal trading partners: United States, Guatemala, Mexico, Venezuela, Costa Rica, Japan, Germany.
Population: 5.6 million.
Religion: Roman Catholic (96%).
GDP: $3.3 billion (U.S.).
Unemployment rate: 40%.

Guatemala: The country has returned to democratic rule, but the armed forces remain a major force. There has been extensive guerrilla activity since 1975.
Main imports: Chemical products, mineral fuels and lubricants, machinery, transport equipment.
Main exports: Coffee, sugar, cotton, bananas.
Principal trading partners: United States, El Salvador, Germany, Honduras, Costa Rica, Mexico, Netherlands Antilles.
Population: 10 million.
Religion: Roman Catholic (80%), Protestant (18%).
GDP: $9 billion (U.S.).
Unemployment rate: 21%.

Honduras: An elected civilian government took power in 1982. Substantial U.S. aid has been helping the economy, but severe problems remain. The armed forces, which have launched several coups over the past 20 years, are still a force to be reckoned with in case of popular unrest.
Main imports: Chemical products, mineral fuels and lubricants, food products, machinery, transport equipment.
Main exports: Bananas, coffee, wood, shrimp and lobsters, refined sugar, lead and zinc.
Principal trading partners: United States, Venezuela, Guatemala, Costa Rica, Trinidad and Tobago, Japan, Germany, Belgium.
Population: 5.6 million.
Religion: Roman Catholic (94%).
GDP: $3.1 billion (U.S.).
Unemployment rate: 27%.

Mexico: President Salinas de Gortari has brought Mexico to new economic and political heights. Certainly the signing of the NAFTA agreement with the United States and Canada is making this country a haven for new business, both for imports and exports, and the now famous *maquiladoras*. Many

American companies have opened branches in Mexico City, as well as other major cities, and business prospects are excellent.

Main imports: Unprocessed agricultural products including maize, sorghum and soybean seed, metal-working equipment, chemicals, transportation and communication equipment, electrical machinery, petrochemicals.

Main exports: Crude petroleum, petroleum products, automobile motors, coffee, silver bars, frozen shrimp.

Principal trading partners: United States, Spain, Germany, Japan, Canada.

Population: 83 million.

Religion: Roman Catholic (92%), Protestant (6%).

GDP: $195 billion (U.S.).

Unemployment rate: 10%.

Panama: Although the new president of Panama is struggling with the economic problems, all indications are that, with the help of the United States, Panama may eventually overcome its present situation. Panama's high unemployment and economic stagnation, however, have caused some Latin American experts to consider it a time bomb.

Main imports: Crude petroleum, machinery, and transport equipment, chemical products, food products.

Main exports: Bananas, shrimp, sugar, leather products, coffee, cocoa.

Principal trading partners: United States, Mexico, Venezuela, Germany, Ecuador, Japan.

Population: 2.1 million.

Religion: Roman Catholic (89%), Protestant (5%), Muslim (4%).

GDP: $3.9 billion (U.S.).

Unemployment rate: 10.8%.

Paraguay: Paraguay is enjoying a healthy economy with the new president and the country is negotiating free market treaties with Chile, Uruguay, and Argentina. It has always been a very peaceful country and, for business or pleasure, it's a very nice place to visit.

Main imports: Fuels and lubricants, machines and engines, food and foodstuffs.

Main exports: Cotton fibers, soybeans, timber, animal fodder, tobacco.

Principal trading partners: Brazil, Argentina, Algeria, Germany, the Netherlands, United States.

Population: 3.7 million.

Religion: Roman Catholic (97%).

GDP: $5 billion (U.S.).

Unemployment rate: 31%.

Perú: President Alberto Fugimori is bringing this country out of its many problems with the guerilla terrorists known as Sendero Luminoso (Shining Path). The economy is progressing and much of the capital that had been taken out is now coming back. Many American companies are looking into business again in Peru with the privatization of many government-controlled businesses. Caution should, however, be exercised before going to Peru, unless you already have connections and reliable representatives.

Main imports: Capital goods, food items including wheat.

Main exports: Petroleum, copper, zinc, lead, silver.
Principal trading partners: United States, Japan, Argentina, Germany, Brazil, Belgium-Luxembourg, Great Britain.
Population: 21 million.
Religion: Roman Catholic (93%).
GDP: $18.9 billion (U.S.).
Unemployment rate: 9.9%.

Uruguay: The country's elected government is fragile, with the military still the power in the background. Once a model democracy with a high standard of living, Uruguay has had a succession of coups, and its economy is in dire straits.
Main imports. Machinery and appliances, mineral products, chemical products, synthetic plastic, resins and rubber.
Main exports: Animals and live animal products, hides and skins, textiles.
Principal trading partners: Nigeria, Brazil, Argentina, United States, Mexico, Germany, Russia.
Population: 3.7 million.
Religion: Roman Catholic (60%), Protestant (4%).
GDP: $7 billion (U.S.).
Unemployment rate: 15%.

Venezuela: Since 1959 the country has enjoyed progressive, democratically elected governments. During most of the 1970's ambitious programs modernized and partially diversified Venezuela's economy. Sharp decline in oil prices, however, has caused much of the task to remain unfinished.
Main imports: Machinery, road motor vehicles, iron and steel, chemicals, cereals and cereal preparations.
Major exports: Petroleum and crude oils, petroleum products.
Principal trading partners: United States, Japan, Germany, Canada, Netherlands Antilles.
Population: 18.1 million.
Religion: Roman Catholic (92%).
GDP: $79 billion (U.S.).
Unemployment rate: 15%.

BEFORE YOU GO...

Passports

All permanent U.S. residents must carry a valid passport in order to travel to, from, and within Europe. In recent years most South American countries require passports and visas before allowing a person to board a plane. Many of the visas are issued at the airport; to be on the safe side, however, it is better to call the consulate of the country you are traveling to and inquire about the requirements. Many consulates require you to show the ticket before issuing the visa.

Application for a passport should be made by mail or in person at least eight and preferably twelve weeks in advance to either: (1) a U.S. Passport Agency office located in twelve major cities and the District of Columbia; (2) designated U.S. post offices throughout the country; or (3) state and Federal courthouses.

Visas

No visas are required by Spain for travelers with U.S. passports whose stay does not exceed three months. If planning to stay longer, contact the consulate or national tourist organization of the country in the nearest major city or in New York City or ask your travel agency or international airline office about visa applications.

No visas are required by Caribbean or Central American countries. Check the South American countries you plan to visit for visa requirements.

Immunizations

There are no immunization requirements for entry into western Europe and most Latin American countries, or for return to the U.S. However, if you plan to visit Latin America or the Caribbean, consult your doctor or the nearest U.S. Public Health Service office for recommended inoculations.

Customs and Currency Regulations

In general, American travelers to Europe and Latin America are allowed to bring in fairly generous amounts of duty-free items for their own *personal use*. These items include tobacco, alcohol, and perfume and are typically allowed in the following quantities (despite local variation):

200 cigarettes or 50 cigars or 250 grams of tobacco (about 1/2 lb.)
2 liters of wine
1 liter of liquor
2 ounces of perfume

If you are not well in excess of these amounts, a simple statement of "nothing to declare" will be respected by most customs officials.

If you are traveling to Colombia, Venezuela, Brazil, Perú, or Bolivia there are restrictions as to the amount of cash you can bring into the country. Check with the local consulate; you do not want to be accused of laundering money.

For gifts whose final destination is the country you are entering, the rules are a bit stricter and vary greatly among the different countries. It would be wise to check on the duty-free limits beforehand and to declare whatever is in excess.

For personal valuables like jewelry or furs and foreign-made items like watches, cameras, computers, or tape recorders (acquired before your trip) you should have proof of prior possession or register with U.S. Customs before departure. This will ensure that they are not subject to duty either by the United States upon return or by any country you visit.

Upon return to the United States each person has a duty-free allowance of $400, including 100 cigars and 1 carton of cigarettes. Each adult may bring in only 1 liter of wine or other liquor duty-free. Gifts worth $50 or less may be sent home subject to certain restrictions. For further up-to-date details, ask your travel agent or airline to provide a copy of U.S. customs regulations.

There are no restrictions on the amounts of *foreign currency* (or checks) that foreign nationals may bring into western Europe, but if in doubt, consult a travel agent.

Traveler's Checks, Credit Cards, Foreign Exchange

All major international traveler's checks and credit cards are accepted by most of the hotels, restaurants, and shops. The most recognized are: American Express, Barclays, Visa, Citibank, and Bank of America. The cards most acceptable are: American Express, MasterCard, Visa, Diners Club.

However, be advised that the exchange rate on dollar traveler's checks is almost always disadvantageous. If you want, you can buy foreign currency checks and/or actual currency in the United States before leaving at rates equivalent to or better than the bank rate you will get over there. Currency or checks may be purchased from retail foreign currency dealers.

A warning to credit card users: When charging, make sure that the following information appears on the original and all copies of your bill: the correct date; the type of currency being charged (*francs*, *marks*, *pesos*, etc.), the official exchange rate for that currency on that date (if possible); and the total amount of the bill. Without this information, you may end up paying at an exchange rate less favorable to you and more favorable to your foreign host, and for a larger bill than you thought!

Drivers' Licenses

A valid American (state) license is usually respected. However, if you have time, and want to avoid language problems on the road, it is a good idea to get an international driver's document through the AAA or a local automobile club.

Electrical Appliances

If you plan to bring along any small electrical appliances for use without batteries, be aware that Europe's (and parts of Latin America's) system of electric current and voltage differs from ours. If your appliance has no special internal adapters or converters made especially for use abroad, you will have to supply your own. For most appliances, you will need plug adapters that provide the proper number and shape prongs to fit foreign outlets.

Spain—220 V AC 50 Hz. Two-pin round plug.
Mexico—110/120 V AC 60 Hz. Two-pin flat plug.
Mexico City—125 V AC 60 Hz.
Argentina—220 V AC 60 Hz. Two-pin flat plug (American three-pin flat plug in some new buildings).
Colombia—110/220 V AC 60 Hz. Two-pin flat plug. 150 V AC 60 Hz in parts of Bogotá.
Peru—220 V AC 60 Hz. Two-pin round plug.
Uruguay—220 V AC 50 Hz. Two-pin round plug.
Venezuela—110 V AC 60 Hz. Two-pin flat plug.
Puerto Rico—110 V AC 60 Hz. Two-pin flat plug.

Different American-made appliances (irons, hair dryers, razors, radios, battery rechargers, etc.) need either *adapters or converters* to transform voltage and frequency levels.

III. BASIC WORDS AND PHRASES

Fundamental Expressions

Yes.	Sí. (see)
No.	No. (noh)
Maybe.	Quizás. (kee-SAHS)
Please.	Por favor. (pohr-fah-BOHR)
Thank you very much.	Muchas gracias. (MOO-chahs GRAH-see-ahs)
Excuse me.	Perdón. (pehr-DOHN) Con permiso. (kohn pehr-MEE-soh)
I'm sorry.	Lo siento. (loh see-EHN-toh)
Just a second.	Un momento. (oon moh-MEN-toh)
That's all right.	Está bien. (eh-STAH byehn)
It doesn't matter.	No importa. (noh eem-PORT-ah)
Sir	Señor (seh-NYOHR)
Madame	Señora (seh-NYOHR-ah)
Miss	Señorita (seh-nyohr-EE-tah)
Good morning.	Buenos días. (bway-nohs DEE-ahs)
Good afternoon.	Buenas tardes. (bway-nahs TAHR-dehs)
Good evening (night).	Buenas noches. (bway-nahs NOH-chehs)
Good-bye.	Adiós. (ah-DYOHS)
See you later (so long).	Hasta la vista. (AH-stah lah BEE-stah) Hasta luego. (AH-stah loo-AY-goh)
See you tomorrow.	Hasta mañana. (AH-stah mah-NYAH-nah)
How are you?	¿Cómo está usted? (KOH-moh ehs-TAH oos-TEHD)
How's everything?	¿Qué tal? (kay tahl)
Very well, thanks.	Muy bien, gracias. (mwee byehn GRAH-see-ahs)
And you?	¿Y usted? (ee oos-TEHD)
My name is ____ .	Me llamo ____ . (may YAH-moh)
What's your name?	¿Cómo se llama usted? (KOH-moh say YAH-mah oos-TEHD)
How do you do (Glad to meet you).	Mucho gusto (en conocerle). (MOO-choh GOOS-toh [ehn koh-noh-SEHR-lay])

How do you do (The pleasure is mine).

El gusto es mío. (ehl GOOS-toh ehs MEE-oh)

Where are you from?

¿De dónde es usted? (day DOHN-day ehs oos-tehd)

At what hotel are you staying?

¿En qué hotel está? (ehn kay oh-TEL ehs-TAH)

How long will you be staying?

¿Cuánto tiempo va a quedarse? (KWAHN-toh tee-EHM-poh bah ah kay-DAHR-say)

Here's my telephone number (address).

Aquí tiene mi número de teléfono (mi dirección). (ah-KEE tee-EH-nay mee NOO-mehr-oh day tel-EH-foh-noh [mee dee-rehk-SYOHN])

Communications

Do you speak English?

¿Habla usted inglés? (ah-blah oos-TEHD een-GLAYS)

I speak (a little) Spanish.

Hablo español (un poco). (AH-bloh ehs-pah-NYOHL) ([oon POH-koh])

I don't speak Spanish.

No hablo español. (noh AH-bloh ehs-pah-NYOHL)

Is there anyone here who speaks English?

¿Hay alguien aquí que hable inglés? (AH-ee AHL-ghee-EHN ah-KEE kay AH-blay een-GLAYS)

Do you under-stand?

¿Comprende usted? (kohm-PREHN-day oos-tehd)

I understand.

Yo comprendo. (yoh kohm-PREHN-doh)

What does this mean?

¿Qué quiere decir esto? (kay kee-YEH-ray day-SEER ehs-toh)

What? What did you say?

¿Cómo? (KOH-moh)

How do you say _____ in Spanish?

¿Cómo se dice _____ en español? (KOH-moh say DEE-say _____ ehn ehs-pah-NYOHL)

Please speak slowly.

Hable despacio, por favor. (AH-blay dehs-PAH-see-oh pohr fah-BOHR)

Please repeat.

Repita, por favor. (ray-PEE-tah pohr fah-BOHR)

Common Questions and Phrases

Where is _____?	¿Dónde está _____?(DOHN-day ehs-TAH)
When?	¿Cuándo? (KWAHN-doh)
How?	¿Cómo? (KOH-moh)
How much?	¿Cuánto? (KWAHN-toh)
Who?	¿Quién? (key-EN)
Why?	¿Por qué? (pohr-KAY)
Which?	¿Cuál? (kwal)
Here it is.	Aquí está. (ah-KEE eh-STAH)
I (don't) know.	Yo (no) sé. (yoh [noh] say)

Useful Nouns

address	la dirección (lah dee-rehk-SYOHN)
amount	el monto, la suma (ehl MOHN-toh) (lah SOO-ma)
appointment	la cita (lah SEE-tah)
bill	la cuenta (lah KWEHN-tah)
business	el negocio (ehl neh-GOH-syoh)
car	el automóvil (ehl ow-toh-MOH-beel)
cashier	el cajero (ehl kah-HEH-roh)
check	el cheque (ehl CHEH-keh)
city	la ciudad (lah syoo-DAHD)
customs	la aduana (lah ah-DWAH-nah)
date	la fecha (lah FEH-chah)
document	el documento (ehl doh-koo-MEHN-toh)
elevator	el ascensor (ehl ahs-sehn-SOHR)
flight	el vuelo (ehl BWEH-loh)
friend	el amigo, la amiga (ehl ah-MEE-goh) (lah ah-MEE-gah)
hanger	la percha (lah PEHR-chah)
key	la llave (lah YAH-beh)
list	la lista (lah LEES-tah)
magazine	la revista (lah reh-BEES-tah)
maid	la camarera (lah kah-mah-REH-rah)
manager	el gerente, la gerente (ehl heh-REHN-teh), (lah heh-REHN-teh)
map	el mapa (ehl MAH-pah)
mistake	el error (ehl ehr-ROHR)
money	el dinero (ehl dee-NEH-roh)
name	el nombre (ehl NOHM-breh)
newspaper	el periódico, el diario (ehl peh-RYOH-dee-koh), (ehl dee-AHR-ee-oh)
office	la oficina (lah oh-fee-SEE-nah)

package	el paquete (ehl pah-KEH-teh)
paper	el papel (ehl pah-PEHL)
passport	el pasaporte (ehl pah-sah-POHR-teh)
pen	la pluma (lah PLOO-mah)
pencil	el lápiz (ehl LAH-pees)
porter	el maletero (ehl mah-leh-TEHR-oh)
post office	la oficina de correos (lah oh-fee-SEE-nah deh kohr-REH-ohs)
postage	la estampilla, el sello (lah ehs-tahm-PEE-yah)(ehl SEH-yoh)
price	el precio (ehl PREH-syoh)
raincoat	el impermeable (ehl eem-pehr-meh-AH-bleh)
reservation	la reservación (lah reh-sehr-bah-SYOHN)
restroom	la sala de descanso (lah SAH-lah deh des-kahn-soh)
restaurant	el restaurante (ehl rehs-tow-RAHN-teh)
road	la carretera, el camino (lah kahr-reh-TEH-rah) (ehl kah-MEE-noh)
room	la habitación (lah ah-bee-tah-SYOHN)
shirt	la camisa (lah kah-MEE-sah)
shoes	los zapatos (lohs sah-PAH-tohs)
shower	la ducha (lah DOO-chah)
store	el almacén (ehl ahl-mah-SEHN)
street	la calle (lah KAH-yeh)
suit	el traje (ehl TRAH-heh)
suitcase	la maleta (lah mah-LEH-tah)
taxi	el taxi (ehl TAHK-see)
telegram	el telegrama (ehl teh-leh-GRAH-mah)
telephone	el teléfono (ehl teh-LEH-foh-noh)
terminal	la estación (lah eh-stah-SYOHN)
ticket	el boleto (ehl boh-LEH-toh)
time	el tiempo (ehl TYEHM-poh)
tip	la propina (lah proh-PEE-nah)
train	el tren (ehl trehn)
trip	el viaje (ehl BYAH-heh)
umbrella	el paraguas, la sombrilla (ehl pah-RAH-gwahs) (lah sohm-BREE-yah)
waiter	el mozo, el mesero (ehl MOH-soh) (ehl meh-SEHR-oh)

| watch | el reloj (ehl reh-LOH) |
| water | el agua (ehl AH-gwah) |

Useful Verbs (infinitive forms)

accept	aceptar (ah-sehp-TAHR)
answer	responder (rehs-pohn-DEHR)
arrive	llegar (yeh-GAHR)
ask	preguntar (preh-goon-TAHR)
assist	ayudar (ah-yoo-DAHR)
be	ser, estar (sehr) (ehs-TAHR)
begin	comenzar (koh-mehn-SAHR)
bring	traer (trah-EHR)
buy	compar (kohm-PAHR)
call	llamar (yah-MAHR)
carry	llevar (yeh-BAHR)
change	cambiar, trocar (kahm-BYAHR) (tro-KAHR)
close	cerrar (sehr-RAHR)
come	venir (beh-NEER)
confirm	confirmar (kohn-feer-MAHR)
continue	continuar (kohn-tee-NWAHR)
cost	costar (kohs-TAHR)
deliver	entregar (ehn-treh-GAHR)
direct	dirigir (dee-ree-HEER)
do	hacer (ah-SEHR)
eat	comer (koh-MEHR)
end	terminar (tehr-mee-NAHR)
enter	entrar (ehn-TRAHR)
examine	examinar (ehk-sah-mee-NAHR)
exchange	cambiar (kahm-BYAHR)
feel	sentir (sehn-TEER)
finish	completar (kohm-pleh-TAHR)
fix	arreglar (ahr-reh-GLAHR)
follow	seguir (seh-GHEER)
forward	expedir, remitir (ehk-speh-DEER) (reh-mee-TEER)
get	procurar (proh-koo-RAHR)
give	dar (dahr)
go	ir (eer)
hear	oir (oh-EER)
help	ayudar (ah-yoo-DAHR)
keep	guardar (gwahr-DAHR)
know	saber, conocer (sah-BEHR) (koh-noh-SEHR)
learn	aprender (ah-prehn-DEHR)
leave	salir (sah-LEER)
like	gustar (goos-TAHR)
listen	escuchar (ehs-koo-CHAHR)
look	mirar (mee-RAHR)

lose	perder (pehr-DEHR)
make	hacer (ah-SEHR)
mean	significar (seeg-nee-fee-KAHR)
meet	encontrar (ehn-kohn-TRAHR)
miss	perder (pehr-DEHR)
need	necesitar (neh-seh-see-TAHR)
open	abrir (ah-BREER)
order	pedir (peh-DEER)
park	parquear (pahr-keh-AHR)
pay	pagar (pah-GAHR)
prefer	preferir (preh-feh-REER)
prepare	preparar (preh-pah-RAHR)
present (be)	presenciar (preh-sehn-SYAHR)
prove	probar (proh-BAHR)
pull	halar (ah-LAHR)
purchase	comprar (kohm-PRAHR)
push	empujar (em-poo-HAHR)
put	poner (poh-NEHR)
read	leer (leh-EHR)
receive	recibir (reh-see-BEER)
recommend	recomendar (reh-koh-mehn-DAHR)
remain	quedar (keh-DAHR)
repair	reparar (reh-pah-RAHR)
repeat	repetir (reh-peh-TEER)
rest	descansar (dehs-kahn-SAHR)
return	volver (bohl-BEHR)
run	correr (kohr-REHR)
say	decir (deh-SEER)
see	ver (behr)
send	enviar (ehn-BYAHR)
show	mostrar (mohs-TRAHR)
sit	sentar (se) (sehn-TAHR [seh])
speak	hablar (ah-BLAHR)
stand	estar de pie (ehs-STAHR deh pyeh)
start	comenzar (koh-mehn-SAHR)
stop	parar (pah-RAHR)
take	tomar (toh-MAHR)
talk	conversar (kohn-behr-SAHR)
tell	decir (deh-SEER)
think	pensar (pehn-SAHR)
try	probar (proh-BAHR)
turn	volver, doblar (bohl-BEHR) (doh-BLAHR)
use	usar (oo-SAHR)
visit	visitar (bee-see-TAHR)
wait	esperar (ehs-peh-RAHR)
walk	andar (ahn-DAHR)
want	querer (keh-REHR)

wear	llevar (yeh-BAHR)
work	trabajar (trah-bah-HAHR)
write	escribir (ehs-kree-BEER)

Useful Adjectives and Adverbs

above/below	arriba/abajo (ahr-REE-bah/ah-BAH-hoh)
ahead/behind	adelante/detrás (ah-deh-LAHN-teh/deh-TRAHS)
best/worst	el mejor/el peor (ehl meh-HOHR/ehl peh-OHR)
big/small	grande/pequeño (GRAHN-deh/peh-KEHN-yoh)
early/late	temprano/tarde (tehm-PRAH-noh/TAHR-deh)
easy/difficult	fácil/difícil (FAH-seel/dee-FEE-seel)
few/many	pocos/muchos (POH-kohs/MOO-chohs)
first/last	primero/último (pree-MEH-roh/OOHL-tee-moh)
front/back	delantero/trasero (deh-lahn-TEH-roh/trah-SEHR-oh)
full/empty	completo/vacío (kohm-PLEH-toh/bah-SEE-oh)
good/bad	bueno/malo (BWEH-noh/MAH-loh)
high/low	alto/bajo (AHL-toh/BAH-hoh)
hot/cold	caliente/frío (kah-LYEHN-teh/FREE-oh)
inside/outside	dentro/fuera (DEHN-troh/FWEH-rah)
large/small	grande/pequeño (GRAHN-deh/peh-KEHN-yoh)
more/less	más/menos (mahs/MEH-nohs)
near/far	cercano/lejos (sehr-KAH-noh/LEH-hohs)
old/new	viejo/nuevo (BYEH-hoh/NWEH-boh)
open/shut	abierto/cerrado (ah-BYEHR-toh/sehr-RAH-doh)
right/wrong	correcto/falso (koh-REHK-toh/FAHL-soh)
slow/fast	lento/de prisa (LEHN-toh/deh PREE-sah)
thin/thick	delgado/grueso (dehl-GAH-doh/grew-EH-soh)

Other Useful Small Words

a, an	un, una (oon) (OO-nah)
about	alrededor de (ahl-reh-deh-DOHR deh)
across	a través (ah trah-BEHS)
after	después (dehs-PWEHS)
again	otra vez (OH-trah behs)
all	todo (TOH-doh)
almost	casi (KAH-see)
also	también (tahm-BYEHN)
always	siempre (SYEHM-preh)
among	entre (EHN-treh)
and	y (ee)
another	otro (OH-troh)
any	alguno (ahl-GOO-noh)
around	alrededor (de) (ahl-reh-deh-DOHR [deh])
at	en (ehn)
away	ausente (ow-SEHN-teh)
back	atrás (ah-TRAHS)
because	porque (pohr-KEH)
before	antes de (AHN-tehs deh)
behind	detrás de (deh-TRAHS deh)
between	entre (EHN-treh)
both	ambos, uno y otro (AHM-bos) (oo-noh ee OH-troh)
but	pero (PEH-roh)
down	abajo (ah-BAH-hoh)
each	cada (KAH-dah)
enough	bastante (bahs-TAHN-teh)
even	unido, igual (oo-NEE-doh) (ee-GWAL)
every	cada (KAH-dah)
except	excepto (ehk-SEHP-toh)
few	pocos (POH-kohs)
for	para (PAH-rah)
from	de (deh)
however	sin embargo (seen ehm-BAHR-goh)
if	si (see)
in	en (ehn)
instead	en vez de (ehn BEHS deh)
into	en (ehn)
maybe	quizá (kee-SAH)
more	más (mahs)
much	mucho (MOO-choh)
next (to)	próximo (PROHK-see-moh)
not	no (noh)
now	ahora (ah-OHR-ah)

of	de (deh)
often	a menudo (ah meh-NOO-doh)
only	sólo (SOH-loh)
or	o (oh)
other	otro (OH-troh)
perhaps	quizá (kee-SAH)
same	mismo (MEES-moh)
since	desde (DEHS-deh)
some	alguno (ahl-GOO-noh)
still	todavía (toh-dah-BEE-ah)
that (close by)	eso (EH-soh)
that (far away)	aquello (ah-KEH-yoh)
these	estos (EH-stohs)
this	esto (EH-stoh)
those (close by)	esos (EH-sohs)
those (far away)	aquellos (ah-KEH-yohs)
to	a (ah)
unless	a menos que (ah MEH-nohs keh)
until	hasta (AHS-tah)
very	muy (mwee)
with	con (kohn)

Directions

North	el norte (ehl NOHR-teh)
South	el sur (ehl soor)
East	el este (ehl EHS-teh)
West	el oeste (ehl oh-EHS-teh)
around the corner	a la vuelta (ah lah BWHEL-tah)
straight ahead	derecho (deh-REH-choh)
left	a la izquierda (ah lah ees-KYEHR-dah)
right	a la derecha (ah lah deh-REH-chah)

Days of the Week

Sunday	domingo (doh-MEEN-goh)
Monday	lunes (LOO-nehs)
Tuesday	martes (MAHR-tehs)
Wednesday	miércoles (MYEHR-koh-lehs)
Thursday	jueves (HWEH-behs)
Friday	viernes (BHYEHR-nehs)
Saturday	sábado (SAH-bah-doh)
What day is today?	¿Qué día es hoy? (kay DEE-ah ehs oy)
Today is _____ .	Hoy es _____ .(oy ehs)
yesterday	ayer (ah-YEHR)
the day before yesterday	anteayer (ANT-eh-ah-YEHR)
tomorrow	mañana (mahn-YAH-nah)

the day after tomorrow	pasado mañana (pah-SAH-doh mahn-YAH-nah)
last week	la semana pasada (lah seh-MAH-nah pah-SAH-dah)
next week	la semana próxima (lah seh-MAH-nah PROHK-see-mah)
tonight	esta noche (EHS-tah noh-chay)
last night	anoche (ah-NOH-chay)
next month	el mes próximo (ehl mehs PROHK-see-moh)
this weekend	este fin de semana (EHS-teh feen deh seh-MAH-nah)

Months of the Year

January	enero (ay-NEHR-oh)
February	febrero (fay-BREH-roh)
March	marzo (MAHR-soh)
April	abril (ah-BREEL)
May	mayo (MAH-yoh)
June	junio (HOO-nee-oh)
July	julio (HOO-lee-oh)
August	agosto (ah-GOHS-toh)
September	septiembre (sep-tee-EHMB-ray)
October	octubre (ohk-TOO-bray)
November	noviembre (noh-bee-EHMB-ray)
December	diciembre (dee-SYEHM-bray)
this month	este mes (EHS-tay mehs)
last month	el mes pasado (ehl mehs pah-SAH-doh)
next month	el mes próximo (ehl mehs PROHK-see-moh)
last year	el año pasado (ehl AHN-yoh pah-SAH-doh)
next year	el año que viene (ehl AHN-yoh kay bee-EN-ay)
What's today's date?	¿Cuál es la fecha de hoy? (kwahl ehs lah FAY-chah day oy)
Today is August _____ .	Hoy es _____ de agosto. (oy ehs day ah-GOHS-toh)

The first of the month is *el primero* (an ordinal number). All other dates are expressed with cardinal numbers.

first	el primero (ehl pree-MEHR-oh)
second	el dos (ehl dohs)
fourth	el cuatro (ehl KWAH-troh)
25th	el veinticinco (ehl bayn-tee-SEEN-koh)

May 1, 1876	El primero de mayo de mil ochocientos setenta y seis (ehl pree-MEHR-oh day MAH-yoh day meel oh-choh-SYEHN-tohs say-TEN-tah ee SAYS)
July 4, 1994	El cuatro de julio de mil novecientos noventa y cuatro (ehl KWAH-troh day HOO-lyoh day meel noh-bay-SYEHN-tohs noh-BEHN-tah ee KWAH-troh)

The Four Seasons

spring	la primavera (lah pree-mah-BEHR-ah)
summer	el verano (ehl beh-RAH-noh)
fall	el otoño (ehl oh-TOH-nyoh)
winter	el invierno (ehl eem-BYEHR-noh)

Time

What time is it?	¿Qué hora es? (kay OH-rah ehs)

When telling time in Spanish, *It is* is expressed by **Es la** for 1:00 and **Son las** for all other numbers.

It's 1:00	Es la una (ehs lah OO-nah)
It's 2:00	Son las dos (sohn lahs dohs)
It's 3:00	Son las tres (sohn lahs trehs)

The number of minutes after the hours is expressed by adding **y** (and) followed by the number of minutes.

It's 4:10	Son las cuatro y diez (sohn lahs KWAH-troh ee dyehs)
It's 5:20	Son las cinco y veinte (sohn lahs SEEN-koh ee BAYN-tay)

A quarter after and half past are expressed by placing **y cuarto** and **y media** after the hour.

It's 6:15	Son las seis y cuarto (sohn lahs sayss ee KWAHR-toh)
It's 7:30	Son las siete y media (sohn lahs SYEH-tay ee MEH-dyah)

After passing the half-hour point on the clock, time is expressed in Spanish by *subtracting* the number of minutes from the next hour.

It's 7:35	Son las ocho menos veinticinco (sohn lahs OH-choh meh-nohs bayn-tee-SEEN-koh)
It's 8:50	Son las nueve menos diez (sohn lahs NWEH-bay meh-nohs dyehs)
At what time?	¿A qué hora? (ah kay OH-rah)
At 1:00	A la una (ah lah OO-nah)
At 2:00 (3:00, etc.)	A las dos (tres, etc.) (ah lahs dohs[trehs])
A.M.	de la mañana
(in the morning)	(day lah mahn-YAH-nah)
P.M.	de la tarde
(in the afternoon)	(day lah TAHR-day)
(at night)	de la noche (day lah NOH-chay)
It's noon	Es mediodía (ehs meh-dyoh-DEE-ah)
It's midnight	Es medianoche (ehs MEH-dee-ah-NOH-chay)
It's early (late)	Es temprano (tarde) (ehs temp-RAH-noh [TAHR-day])

Arrival/Hotel

My name is _____ .	Me llamo _____ . (may YAH-moh)
Here is (are) my _____ .	Aquí tiene mi _____ (ah-KEE tee-EHN-eh mee)
• passport	• pasaporte (pah-sah-POHR-teh)
• business card	• tarjeta de presentación (tahr-HEH-tah deh preh-sehn-tah-SYOHN)
I'm on a business trip.	Estoy en un viaje de negocios. (ehs-TOY ehn oon BYAH-heh deh neh-OH-syohs)
I'd like to go to the _____ Hotel.	Quisiera ir al Hotel _____ . (kee-SYEH-rah eer ahl oh-TEL)
Where can I get a taxi?	¿Dónde puedo tomar un taxi? (dohn-deh pweh-doh toh-mahr oon TAHK-see)

I'd like a single (double) room for tonight.

Quisiera una habitación con una sola cama (con dos camas) para esta noche. (kee-SYEHR-ah OO-nah ah-bee-tah-SYOHN kohn OO-nah SOH-lah KAH-mah [kohn dos KAH-mahs] pah-rah EHS-tah NOH-chay)

I (don't) have a reservation.

(No) tengo reservación ([noh] ten-goh reh-sehr-bah-SYOHN)

Could you call another hotel to see if they have something?

¿Podría llamar a otro hotel para ver si tienen algo? (poh-DREE-ah yah-MAHR ah OH-troh o-TEL pah-rah behr see tee-yen-ehn AHL-goh)

May I see the room?

¿Podría ver la habitación? (poh-DREE-ah behr lah ah-bee-tah-SYOHN)

The room is very nice. I'll take it.

La habitación es muy bonita. Me quedo con ella (lah ah-bee-tah-SYOHN ehs mwee boh-NEE-tah) (may KAY-doh kohn EH-ya)

I'll be staying here for _____ .

Me quedaré aquí _____. (may kay-dahr-AY ah-KEE)

• one night

• una noche (oo-nah NOH-chay)

• a few nights

• unas noches (oo-nahs NOH-chayes)

• one week

• una semana (oo-nah seh-MAH-nah)

Where is the elevator?

¿Dónde está el ascensor? (DOHN-deh ehs-TAH ehl ahs-sehn-SOHR)

Please send a bottle of mineral water to my room.

Haga el favor de mandar una botella de agua mineral a mi habitación. (HAH-gah ehl fah-BOHR deh mahn-DAHR oo-nah boh-TEH-yah deh AH-gwah mee-neh-RAHL ah mee ah-bee-tah-SYOHN)

Please wake me tomorrow at _____ .

¿Puede despertarme mañana a _____? (PWEH-deh dehs-pehr-TAHR-meh mahn-YAH-nah ah)

Are there any messages for me?

¿Hay recados para mí? (AH-ee reh-KAH-dohs PAH-rah MEE)

I'd like to leave this in your safe.	Quisiera dejar esto en su caja fuerte. (kee-SYEHR-ah deh-HAHR EHS-toh ehn soo kah-hah FWEHR-teh)
Will you make this call for me?	¿Podría usted hacerme esta llamada? (poh-DREE-ah oo-STEHD ah-SEHR-meh EHS-tah yah-MAH-dah)
Please send someone up for the baggage.	Haga el favor de mandar a alguien para recoger el equipaje. (AH-ga ehl fah-BOHR deh mahn-DAHR ah AHL-gyen PAH-rah reh-koh-HEHR ehl eh-kee-PAH-heh)
I'd like the bill please.	Quisiera la cuenta, por favor. (kee-SYEHR-ah lah KWEHN-tah pohr fah-BOHR)

Transportation

bus	el autobús (ehl ow-toh-BOOS)
train	el tren (ehl trehn)
subway	el metro (ehl MEH-troh)
ticket	el billete (ehl bee-YEH-teh)
station	la estación (lah ehs-tah-SYOHN)
Where is the closest subway (underground) station?	¿Dónde está la estación más cercana? (DOHN-day EHS-tah lah ehs-tah-SYOHN mahs sehr-KAH-nah)
How much is the fare?	¿Cuánto es la tarifa? (KWAHN-toh ehs lah tah-REE-fah)
Where can I buy a token (ticket)?	¿Dónde puedo comprar una ficha (un billete)? (DOHN-day PWEH-doh kohm-PRAHR oo-nah FEE-chah [oon bee-YEH-teh])
Does this train go to _____?	¿Va este tren a _____? (bah ehs-teh trehn ah)
Please tell me when we get there.	Haga el favor de avisarme cuando lleguemos. (AH-gah ehl fah-BOHR day ah-bee-SAHR-may KWAHN-doh yeh-GAY-mohs)

Please get me a taxi.	¿Puede usted conseguirme un taxi, por favor? (PWEH-day oos-TEHD kohn-say-GHEER-may oon TAHK-see pohr fah-BOHR)
Where can I get a taxi?	¿Donde puedo tomar un taxi? (DOHN-day PWEH-doh toh-MAHR oon TAHK-see)
Take me (I want to go) _____ .	Lléveme (Quiero ir) _____ . (YEHV-eh-may [kee-EHR-oh eer])
• to the airport	• al aeropuerto (ahl ah-ehr-oh-PWEHR-toh)
• to this address	• a esta dirección (ah ehs-tah dee-rehk-SYOHN)
• to the hotel	• al hotel (ahl o-TEL)
Where can I rent a car?	¿Dónde puedo alquilar un coche? (dohn-day PWEH-doh ahl-kee-LAHR oon KOH-chay)
How much does it cost _____?	¿Cuánto cuesta _____ ? (KWAHN-toh KWEHS-tah)
• per day	• por día (pohr DEE-ah)
• per week	• por semana (pohr seh-MAHN-ah)
• per kilometer	• por kilómetro (pohr kee-LOH-meht-roh)
• for unlimited mileage	• con kilometraje ilimitado (kohn kee-loh-may-TRAH-hay ee-lee-mee-TAH-doh)
How much is the insurance?	¿Cuánto es el seguro? (KWAHN-toh ehs ehl seh-GOOR-oh)
Is the gas included?	¿Está incluída la gasolina? (ehs-TAH een-kloo-EE-dah lah gahs-oh-LEEN-ah)
Do you accept credit cards?	¿Acepta usted tarjetas de crédito? (ah-sehp-tah oos-TEHD tahr-HAY-tahs day KREH-dee-toh)
Here's my driver's license.	Aquí tiene mi carnet de conducir. (ah-KEE tee-EH-nay mee kahr-NE day kohn-doo-SEER)
Where is there a gas station?	¿Dónde hay una estación de gasolina? (DOHN-day AH-ee oo-nah ehs-tah-SYOHN day gahs-oh-LEE-nah)

Fill it up with _____ .	Llénelo con _____. (YAY-nay-loh kohn)

- diesel
- regular (90 octane)
- super (96 octane)
- extra (98 octane)

- diesel (dee-EH-sel)
- normal (nohr-MAHL)
- super (SOO-pehr)
- extra (EHS-trah)

Please check _____ .	¿Quiere inspeccionar _____ ? (kee-YEHR-ay eens-pehk-syohn-AHR)

- the battery
- the carburetor

- the oil
- the spark plugs
- the tires

- the tire pressure

- the antifreeze

- la batería (lah bah-tehr-EE-ah)
- el carburador (ehl kahr-boor-ah-DOHR)
- el aceite (ehl ah-SAY-tay)
- las bujías (lahs boo-HEE-ahs)
- los neumáticos, las llantas, las ruedas (lohs neh-oo-MAH-tee-kohs), (lahsYAHN-tahs), (RWAY-dahs)
- la presión de las llantas (lah preh-SYOHN day lahs YAHN-tahs)
- el agua del radiador (ehl ah-GWAH del rah-dee-ah-DOHR)

My car has broken down.	Mi coche se ha averiado. (mee KOH-chay say ah ah-behr-ee-AH-doh)

Drivers should be familiar with these universal road signs:

Guarded railroad crossing

Yield

Stop

Right of way

Dangerous intersection ahead

Gasoline (petrol) ahead

Parking

No vehicles allowed

Dangerous curve

Pedestrian crossing

Oncoming traffic
has right of way

No bicycles allowed

No parking allowed

No entry

No left turn

No U-turn

No passing

Border crossing

Traffic signal ahead

Speed limit

Traffic circle
(roundabout) ahead

Minimum speed limit

All traffic turns left

End of no passing zone

One-way street

Detour

Danger ahead

Entrance to expressway

Expressway ends

When is there a flight to _____?	¿Cuándo hay un vuelo a _____? (KWAHN-doh AH-ee oon BWEHL-oh ah)
I would like a _____ ticket.	Quisiera un billete _____ . (kee-see-YEHR-ah oon bee-YEH-tay)
• round trip	• de ida y vuelta (day EE-dah ee BWEHL-tah)
• one way	• de ida (day EE-dah)
• tourist class	• en clase turista (ehn KLAH-say toor-EES-tah)
• first class	• en primera clase (ehn pree-MEHR-ah KLAH-say)
When does the plane leave (arrive)?	¿A qué hora sale (llega) el avión? (ah kay oh-ra SAH-lay [YEH-gah] ehl ah-BYOHN)
When must I be at the airport?	¿Cuándo debo estar en el aeropuerto? (KWAHN-doh deh-boh ehs-TAHR en ehl ah-ehr-oh-PWEHR-toh)
What is my flight number?	¿Cuál es el número del vuelo? (kwahl ehs ehl NOO-mehr-oh dehl BWEH-loh)
What gate do we leave from?	¿De qué puerta? (day kay PWEHR-tah)

I want to confirm (cancel) my reservation for flight _____ .

Quiero confirmar (cancelar) mi reservación para el vuelo _____ . (kee-YEHR-oh kohn-feer-MAHR [kahn-say-LAHR] mee reh-sehr-bah-SYOHN pah-rah ehl BWEH-loh)

I'd like to check my bags.

Quisiera facturar mis maletas. (kee-SYEHR-ah fahk-too-RAHR mees mah-LEH-tahs)

I have only carry-on baggage.

Tengo solo equipaje de mano. (TEN-goh so-loh ay-kee-PAH-hay day MAH-noh)

Leisure Time

Let's go to a nightclub.

Vamos a un cabaret. (BAH-mohs ah oon kah-bah-REH)

Is a reservation necessary?

¿Hace falta una reserva? (ah-say FAHL-tah oo-nah reh-SEHR-bah)

Is there a minimum (cover) charge?

¿Hay un mínimo? (AH-ee oon MEE-nee-moh)

Where is the checkroom?

¿Dónde está el guardarropa? (DOHN-day eh-STAH ehl gwahr-dah-ROH-pah)

I'd like to watch a soccer match.

Quisiera ver un partido de fútbol. (kee-SYEHR-ah behr oon pahr-TEE-doh day FOOT-bohl)

Where's the stadium?

¿Dónde está el estadio? (DOHN-day ehs-TAH ehl ehs-TAH-dee-oh)

What teams are going to play?

¿Qué equipos van a jugar? (kay eh-kee-pohs bahn ah hoo-GAHR)

I'd like to see a jai alai match.

Me gustaría ver un partido de pelota. (may goos-tahr-EE-ah behr oon par-TEE-doh day pel-OH-tah)

Where is the jai alai court?

¿Dónde está el frontón? (DOHN-day ehs-TAH ehl frohn-TOHN)

Do you play tennis?

¿Sabe usted jugar al tenis? (SAH-bay oos-TEHD hoo-GAHR ahl TEN-ees)

Where is a safe place to run?

¿Dónde hay un sitio seguro para correr? (DOHN-day AH-ee oon SEE-tee-oh seh-GOOR-oh pah-rah kohr-EHR)

Is there a golf course?	¿Hay un campo de golf? (AH-ee oon KAHM-poh day gohlf)
Can one rent clubs?	¿Se puede alquilar los palos? (say PWEH-day ahl-kee-LAHR lohs PAH-lohs)

Restaurants

breakfast	desayuno (deh-sah-YOO-noh)
lunch	almuerzo (ahl-MWHER-soh)
dinner	cena (SEH-nah)
Do you have a good restaurant?	¿Conoce usted un buen restaurante? (koh-NOH-say oos-TEHD oon bwehn rehs-tah-oo-RAHN-tay)
Is it very expensive?	¿Es muy caro? (ehs mwee KAH-roh)
A table for two, please.	Una mesa para dos, por favor. (oon-nah MAY-sah pah-rah dohs pohr fah-BOHR)
Waiter!	¡Camarero! (kah-mah-REHR-oh)
Miss!	¡Señorita! (sen-yohr-EE-tah)
We'd like to have lunch now.	Queremos almorzar ahora. (kehr-AY-mohs ahl-mohr-SAHR ah-OHR-ah)
The menu, please.	La carta, por favor. (lah KAHR-tah pohr fah-BOHR)
What's today's special?	¿Cuál es el plato del día de hoy? (KWAHL ehs ehl PLAH-toh del DEE-ah day oy)
What do you recommend?	¿Qué recomienda usted? (kay reh-koh-mee-EHN-dah oos-TEHD)
What's the house specialty?	¿Cuál es la especialidad de la casa? (KWAHL ehs lah ehs-peh-see-ah-lee-DAHD day lah KAH-sah)
Do you have a house wine?	¿Tiene un vino de la casa? (tee-YEHN-ay oon BEE-noh day lah KAH-sah)
I'd like to order now.	Me gustaría ordenar ahora. (may goos-tahr-EE-ah ohr-den-AHR ah-OHR-ah)
Waiter, we need _____ .	Camerero, necesitamos _____ . (kah-mah-REHR-oh neh-seh see-TAH-mohs)
• a knife	• un cuchillo (oon koo-CHEE-yoh)

- a fork
- un tenedor (oon ten-eh-DOHR)

- a spoon
- una cuchara (oo-nah koo-CHAHR-ah)

- a teaspoon
- una cucharita (oo-nah koo-chahr-EE-tah)

- a soup spoon
- una cuchara de sopa (oo-nah koo-CHAHR-rah day SOH-pah)

- a glass
- un vaso (oon BAH-soh)
- a cup
- una taza (oo-nah TAH-sah)
- a saucer
- un platillo (oon plah-TEE-yoh)

- a plate
- un plato (oon PLAH-toh)
- a napkin
- una servilleta (oo-nah sehr-bee-YEH-tah)

- a toothpick
- un palillo (oon pahl-EE-yoh)

Shopping

Where can I find _____ ?
¿Dónde se puede encontrar _____ ? (DOHN-day say pweh-day ehn-kohn-TRAHR)

Can you help me?
¿Me podría ayudar? (may poh-DREE-ah ah-yoo-DAHR)

Do you take credit cards?
¿Acepta tarjetas de crédito? (ah-SEP-tah tahr-HAY-tahs day KRED-ee-toh)

Can I pay with a traveler's check?
¿Puedo pagar con un cheque de viajero? (PWEH-doh pah-GAHR kohn oon CHEH-kay day bee-ah-HEHR-oh)

I'd like to see _____ .
Quisiera ver _____ . (kee-SYEHR-ah behr)

How much is it?
¿Cuánto vale? (KWAHN-toh BAH-lay)

Do you carry English newspapers (magazines)?
Tiene usted periódicos (revistas) en inglés? (tee-YEHN-ay oos-TEHD peh-ree-OH-dee-kohs [ray-BEES-tahs] en een-GLAYS)

I'd like to buy some (picture) postcards.
Quisiera comprar postales (ilustradas). (kee-SEYHR-ah kohm-PRAHR pohs-TAHL-ays [ee-loos-TRAH-dahs])

Do you have stamps?
¿Tiene sellos? (tee-YEHN-ay SEH-yohs)

Medical Care

Where is the nearest (all-night) pharmacy?	¿Dónde está la farmacia (de guardia) más cercana? (DOHN-day ehs-TAH lah fahr-MAH-see-ah [day GWAHR-dee-ah] mahs sehr-KAH-nah)
I need something for _____ .	Necesito algo para _____ . (neh-seh-SEE-toh AHL-go pah-rah)
• a cold	• un catarro (oon kah-TAH-roh)
• constipation	• el estreñimiento (ehl ehs-trayn-yee-MYEHN-toh)
• a cough	• la tos (lah-tos)
• diarrhea	• la diarrea (lah dee-ahr-RAY-ah)
• a headache	• un dolor de cabeza (oon doh-LOHR day kah-BAY-sah)
• insomnia	• el insomnio (ehl een-SOHM-nee-oh)
• a toothache	• un dolor de muelas (oon doh-LOHR day MWEH-lahs)
• an upset stomach	• la indigestión (lah een-dee-hes-TYOHN)
I don't feel well.	No me siento bien. (noh may SYEYN-toh BYEHN)
I need a doctor.	Necesito un médico. (neh-seh-SEE-toh oon MEH-dee-koh)
Do you know a doctor who speaks English?	¿Conoce un médico que hable inglés? (koh-NOH-say oon MEH-dee-koh kay ah-blay een-GLAYS)
I feel dizzy.	Estoy mareado. (ehs-TOY mahr-ay-AH-doh)
I feel weak.	Me siento débil. (may SYEHN-toh DAY-beel)
I have a pain in my chest.	Tengo dolor en el pecho. (TEN-goh doh-LOHR ehn ehl PAY-choh)
I had a heart attack _____ year(s) ago.	Tuve un ataque al corazón hace _____ año(s). (TOO-bay oon ah-TAH-kay ahl kohr-ah-SOHN ah-say _____ ahn- yoh[s])
Can you recommend a dentist?	¿Puede recomendar un dentista? (PWEH-day reh-koh-men-DAHR oon den-TEES-tah)

I have a toothache.	Tengo un dolor de muela. (TEN-goh oon doh-LOHR day MWEH-lah)
Can you repair these glasses (for me)?	¿Puede usted arreglar (me) estas gafas? (PWEH-day oos-TEHD ah-ray-GLAHR [may] ehs-TAHS GAH-fahs)

Telephone

Where is a public telephone?	¿Dónde hay un teléfono público? (DOHN-day AH-ee oon tel-EHF-oh-noh POO-blee-koh)
• a telephone directory	• una guía telefónica (oo-nah GHEE-ah tel-eh-FOHN-ee-kah)
Do I need tokens for the phone?	¿Necesito fichas para el teléfono? (neh-seh-SEE-toh FEE-chahs pah-rah ehl tel-EHF-oh-no)
How do I get the operator?	¿Cómo puedo conseguir la central? (KOH-moh PWEH-doh kon-seh-GHEER lah sehn-TRAHL)
My number is ____ .	Mi número es ____ . (mee NOO-mehr-oh ehs)
May I speak to ____ ?	¿Puedo hablar con ____ ? (PWEH-doh ah-BLAHR kohn)
Who is this?	¿Con quién hablo? (kohn kee-YEHN AH-bloh)
Don't hang up.	No cuelgue. (noh KWEHL-gay)
I was cut off.	Me han cortado. (may ahn kohr-TAH-doh)

Postal Service

a letter	una carta (oo-nah KAHR-tah)
an insured letter	una carta asegurada (oo-nah KAHR-tah ah-say-goor-AH-dah)
a registered letter	una carta certificada (oo-nah KAHR-tah sehr-teef-ee-KAH-dah)
a special delivery letter	una carta urgente (oo-nah KAHR-tah oor-HEN-tay)
a package	un paquete postal (oon pah-KAY-tay pohs-TAHL)

a postcard	una postal (oo-nah pohs-TAHL)
I want to mail a letter.	Quiero echar una carta al correo. (kee-YEHR-oh ay-CHAHR OO-NAH KAHR-tah ahl kohr-AY-oh)
Where's the post office?	¿Dónde está el correo? (DOHN-day ehs-TAH ehl kohr-AY-oh)
Where's a mailbox?	¿Dónde hay un buzón? (DOHN-day AH-ee oon boo-SOHN)
Are there any letters for me? My name is _____ .	¿Hay cartas para mí? Me llamo _____ . (AH-ee KAHR-tahs pah-rah mee may YAH-moh)
I need to send a telex (fax).	Tengo que enviar un telex, fax. (TEN-goh kay ehm-bee-AHR oon TEL-eks [fahks])

Signs

Se Alquila	For Rent
Se Vende	For Sale
Ascensor	Elevator
Cuidado	Caution
Peligro	Danger
Prohibido el Paso	Do Not Enter
Entrada	Entrance
Salida	Exit
Señoras, Damas	Ladies, Women
Hombres, Caballeros	Men, Gentlemen
Ocupado	Occupied
Libre	Empty
Abierto	Open
Cerrado	Closed
Privado	Private
Empuje	Push
Tire	Pull
Prohibido Estacionarse	No Parking
Prohibido Fumar	No Smoking
No Pisar el Césped	Keep Off the Grass
No Beba el Agua	Don't Drink the Water
Sala de Espera	Waiting Room
Información	Information

Numbers

Cardinal Numbers

Numerals of more than three figures have a period in Spanish, instead of a comma. Thus, 1,000 will appear as 1.000.

0	cero (SEHR-oh)
1	uno (OO-noh)
2	dos (dohs)
3	tres (trehs)
4	cuatro (KWAH-troh)
5	cinco (SEEN-koh)
6	seis (sayss)
7	siete (SYEH-teh)
8	ocho (OH-choh)
9	nueve (NWEH-bay)
10	diez (dyess)
11	once (OHN-say)
12	doce (DOH-say)
13	trece (TREH-say)
14	catorce (kah-TOHR-say)
15	quince (KEEN-say)
16	diez y seis OR dieciséis (dyeh-see-SAYSS)
17	diez y siete OR diecisiete (dyeh-see-SYEH-tay)
18	diez y ocho OR dieciocho (dyeh-see-OH-choh)
19	diez y nueve OR diecinueve (dyeh-see-NWEH-bay)
20	veinte (BAYN-tay)
21	veintiuno (bayn-tee-OO-noh)
22	veintidós (bayn-tee-DOHS)
23	veintitrés (bayn-tee-TREHS)
24	veinticuatro (bayn-tee-KWAH-troh)
25	veinticinco (bayn-tee-SEEN-koh)
26	veintiséis (bayn-tee-SAYSS)
27	veintisiete (bayn-tee-SYEH-tay)
28	veintiocho (bayn-tee-OH-choh)
29	veintinueve (bayn-tee-NWEH-bay)
30	treinta (TRAYN-tah)
40	cuarenta (kwahr-EHN-tah)
50	cincuenta (seen-KWEHN-tah)
60	sesenta (seh-SEHN-tah)
70	setenta (seh-TEHN-tah)
80	ochenta (oh-CHEHN-tah)
90	noventa (noh-BEHN-tah)
100	cien(to) (syen[toh])

101	ciento uno (SYEHN-toh OO-noh)
102	ciento dos (SYEHN-toh DOHS)
200	doscientos (as) (dohs-SYEHN-tohs[tahs])
300	trescientos(as) (trehs-SYEHN-tohs[tahs])
400	cuatrocientos(as) (kwah-troh-SYEHN-tohs[tahs])
500	quinientos(as) (kee-NYEHN-tohs[tahs])
600	seiscientos(as) (sayss-SYEHN-tohs[tahs])
700	setecientos(as) (seh-teh-SYEHN-tohs[tahs])
800	ochocientos(as) (oh-choh-SYEHN-tohs[tahs])
900	novecientos(as) (noh-beh-SYEHN-tohs[tahs])
1.000	mil (meel)
2.000	dos mil (dohs meel)
3.000	tres mil (trehs meel)
4.000	cuatro mil (KWAH-troh meel)
5.000	cinco mil (SEEN-koh meel)
6.000	seis mil (sayss meel)
7.000	siete mil (SYEH-tay meel)
8.000	ocho mil (OH-choh meel)
9.000	nueve mil (NWEH-bay meel)
10.000	diez mil (dyess meel)
20.000	veinte mil (BAYN-tay meel)
30.000	treinta mil (TRAYN-tah meel)
40.000	cuarenta mil (kwahr-EHN-tah meel)
50.000	cincuenta mil (seen-KWEHN-tah meel)
60.000	sesenta mil (seh-SEHN-tah meel)
70.000	setenta mil (seh-TEHN-tah meel)
80.000	ochenta mil (oh-CHEHN-tah meel)
90.000	noventa mil (noh-BEHN-tah meel)
100.000	cien mil (syehn meel)
200.000	doscientos mil (dohs-SYEHN-tohs meel)
300.000	trescientos mil (trehs-SYEHN-tohs meel)
400.000	cuatrocientos mil (kwah-troh-SYEHN-tohs meel)

500.000	quinientos mil (kee-NYEHN-tohs meel)
600.000	seiscientos mil (sayss-SYEHN-tohs meel)
700.000	setecientos mil (seh-teh-SYEHN-tohs meel)
800.000	ochocientos mil (oh-choh-SYEHN-tohs meel)
900.000	novecientos mil (noh-beh-SYEHN-tohs meel)
1.000.000	un millón (oon mee-YOHN)
2.000.000	dos millones (dohs mee-YOHN-ays)
10.000.000	diez millones (dyess mee-YOHN-ays)
1.000.000.000	mil millones (meel mee-YOHN-ays)

Years

1900	mil novecientos (meel NOH-beh-SYEHN-tohs)
1989	mil novecientos ochenta y nueve (meel noh-beh-SYEHN-tohs oh-CHEHN-tah ee NWEH-bay)
1992	mil novecientos noventa y dos (meel noh-beh-SYEHN-tohs noh-BEHN-tah ee dohs)
1993	mil novecientos noventa y tres (meel noh-beh-SYEHN-tohs noh-BEHN-ta y trehs)
1994	mil novecientos noventa y cuatro (meel noh-beh-SYEHN-tohs noh-BEHN-tah ee KWAH-troh)
1995	mil novecientos noventa y cinco (meel noh-beh-SYEHN-tohs noh-BEHN-tah ee SEEN-koh)

Ordinal Numbers

1°	primero(a) (pree-MEH-roh[rah])
2°	segundo(a) (seh GOON-doh[dah])
3°	tercero(a) (tehr-SEH-roh[rah])
4°	cuarto(a) (KWAHR-toh[tah])
5°	quinto(a) (KEEN-toh[tah])
6°	sexto(a) (SEHS-toh[tah])
7°	séptimo(a) (SEHT-tee-moh[mah])
8°	octavo(a) (ohk-TAH-boh[bah])
9°	noveno(a) (noh-BAY-noh[nah])

10°	décimo(a) (DEH-see-moh[mah])
last	último(a) (OOL-tee-moh[mah])
once	una vez (OO-nah behs)
twice	dos veces (dohs BEH-sehs)
three times	tres veces (trehs BEH-sehs)

Fractions

half of _____ .	la mitad de _____ (lah mee-TAHD day)
• half (of) the money	• la mitad del dinero (lah mee-TAHD del dee-NEH-roh)
half a _____ .	medio _____ . (MEH-dyoh)
• half a kilo	• medio kilo (MEH-dyoh KEE-loh)
a fourth (quarter)	un cuarto (oon KWAHR-toh)
a dozen _____ .	una docena de _____ (OO-nah doh-SAY-nah day)
• a dozen oranges	• una docena de naranjas (OO-nah doh-SAY-nah day nah-RAHN-hahs)
100 grams	cien gramos (syehn GRAH-mohs)
200 grams	doscientos gramos (dohs SYEHN-tohs GRAH-mohs)
350 grams	trescientos cincuenta gramos (trehs-SYEHN-tohs seen-KWEHN-tah GRAH-mohs)
a pair (of) _____ .	un par de _____ . (oon pahr day)
• a pair of shoes	• un par de zapatos (oon pahr day sah-PAH-tohs)

Spanish Abbreviations

apdo.	apartado	post office box
Av. Avda.	avenida	avenue
C., Cia.	compañía	company
c	calle	street
D.	don	title of respect used before a masculine first name: don Pedro
Da., Dª	doña	title of respect used before a feminine first name: doña María
EE.UU.	los Estados Unidos	United States (U.S.)

F.C.	ferrocarril	railroad
Hnos.	hermanos	brothers
N°, num.	número	number
1°	primero	first
pta.	peseta	peseta (Spanish monetary unit)
RENFE	Red Nacional de Ferrocarriles	Spanish National Railroad System
2°	segundo	second
S., Sta.	San, Santa	Saint
S.A.	Sociedad Anónima	Inc.
Sr.	Señor	Mr.
Sra.	Señora	Mrs.
Sres., Srs.	Señores	Gentleman
Srta.	Señorita	Miss
Ud., Vd.	Usted	You (polite singular)
Uds., Vds.	Ustedes	You (polite and familiar plural)

IV. BUSINESS DICTIONARY

A

abandon (v)	abandonar	*ah-bahn-doh-'nahr*
abandonment	el abandono	*ehl ah-bahn-'doh-noh*
abatement	la disminución, la rebaja	*lah dees-mee-noo-see-'ohn, lah reh-'bah-hah*
ability-to-pay concept	el concepto de la capacidad de pago	*ehl kohn-'sehp-toh deh lah cah-pah-see-'dahd deh 'pah-goh*
above par	por encima de la par, sobre la par	*pohr ehn-'see-mah deh lah pahr, 'soh-breh lah pahr*
above-mentioned	antedicho	*ahn-teh-'dee-choh*
above-the-line	sobre la línea	*'soh-breh lah 'lee-neh-ah*
absentee ownership	la ausencia de los propietarios	*lah ow-'sehn-see-ah deh lohs proh-pee-eh-'tah-ree-ohs*
absenteeism	el ausentismo	*ehl ow-sehn-'tees-moh*
absolute (adj)	absoluto	*ahb-soh-'loo-toh*
absorb (v)	absorber	*ahb-sohr-'behr*
absorb the loss (v)	absorber la pérdida	*ahb-sohr-'behr lah 'pehr-dee-dah*
absorption costing	la absorción de costos	*lah ahb-sohr-see-'ohn deh 'kohs-tohs*
abstract of title	el resumen del título	*ehl reh-'soo-mehn dehl 'tee-too-loh*
abundant (adj)	abundante	*ah-boon-'dahn-teh*
accelerated depreciation	la depreciación acelerada	*lah deh-preh-see-ah-see-'ohn ah-seh-leh-'rah-dah*
acceleration clause	la cláusula para el vencimiento anticipado de una deuda	*lah 'clow-soo-lah 'pah-rah ehl vehn-see-mee-'ehn-toh ahn-tee-see-'pah-doh deh 'oo-nah deh-'oo-dah*
acceleration premium	la prima escalonada	*lah 'pree-mah ehs-kah-loh-'nah-dah*
accept (v)	aceptar	*ah-'sehp-tahr*

acceptable quality level	el nivel de calidad aceptable	*ehl nee-'behl deh kah-'lee-dahd ah-sehp-'tah-bleh*
acceptance	la aceptación	*lah ah-sehp-tah-see-'ohn*
acceptance agreement	el convenio de aceptación	*ehl kohn-'beh-nee-oh deh ah-sehp-tah-see-'ohn*
acceptance bill	la letra aceptada	*lah 'leh-trah ah-sehp-'tah-dah*
acceptance credit	el crédito de aceptación	*ehl 'kreh-dee-toh deh ah-sehp-tah-see-'ohn*
acceptance house	la casa de aceptaciones	*lah 'kah-sah deh ah-sehp-tah-see-'oh-nehs*
acceptance sampling	la muestra de aceptación	*lah 'mweh-strah de ah-sehp-tah-see-'ohn*
acceptance test	la prueba de aceptación	*lah proo-'eh-bah deh ah-sehp-tah-see-'ohn*
acceptor	el aceptante	*ehl ah-sehp-'tahn-teh*
access	acceso	*ahk-'seh-soh*
accession rate	la tasa de aumento	*lah 'tah-sah deh ow-'mehn-toh*
accidental damage	el daño accidental	*ehl 'dah-nyoh ahk-see-'dehn-tahl*
accommodation bill	la letra a favor	*lah 'leh-trah ah fah-'bohr*
accommodation credit	el crédito de firma por aval	*ehl 'creh-dee-toh deh 'feer-mah pohr ah-'bahl*
accommodation endorsement	el endoso de favor	*ehl ehn-'doh-soh deh fah-'bohr*
accommodation paper	el documento avalado	*ehl doh-koo-'mehn-toh ah-ba-'lah-doh*
accommodation parity	la conveniencia paritaria	*lah kohn-beh-nee-'ehn-see-ah pah-ree-'tah-ree-ah*
accompanied goods	la mercadería acompañada, los bienes acompañados	*lah mehr-kah-deh-'ree-ah ah-kohm-pah-'nyah-dah, lohs bee-'eh-nehs ah-kohm-pah-'nyah-dohs*
account	la cuenta	*lah 'kwehn-tah*
account balance	el saldo de la cuenta	*ehl 'sahl-doh deh la 'kwehn-tah*
account day	el día de liquidación en bolsa	*ehl 'dee-ah deh lee-kee-dah-see-'ohn ehn 'bohl-sah*
account executive	el ejecutivo de cuentas	*ehl eh-heh-koo-'tee-boh deh 'kwehn-tahs*

account for (v)	contabilizar	*kohn-tah-bee-lee-'zahr*
account number	el número de cuenta	*ehl 'noo-meh-roh deh 'kwehn-tah*
account period	el período contable	*ehl peh-'ree-oh-doh kohn-'tah-bleh*
accountability	la responsabilidad	*lah reh-spohn-sah-bee-lee-'dahd*
accountant	el contable, el contador	*ehl kohn-'tah-bleh, ehl kohn-tah-'dohr*
accounting department	el departamento de contabilidad	*ehl deh-pahr-tah-'mehn-toh deh kohn-tah-bee-lee-'dahd*
accounting method	el método de contabilidad	*ehl 'meh-toh-doh deh kohn-tah-bee-lee-'dahd*
accounting period	el ejercicio o período contable	*ehl eh-hehr-'see-see-oh oh ehl peh-'ree-oh-doh kohn-'tah-bleh*
accounting ratio	el índice contable	*ehl 'een-dee-seh kohn-'tah-bleh*
accounts payable	las cuentas a pagar	*lahs 'kwehn-tahs ah pah-'gahr*
accounts receivable	las cuentas por cobrar	*lahs 'kwehn-tahs pohr koh-'brahr*
accretion	acreción, el aumento	*ah-kreh-see-'ohn, ehl ow-'mehn-toh*
accrual	la acumulación	*lah ah-koo-moo-lah-see-'ohn*
accrue (v)	acumular	*ah-koo-moo-'lahr*
accrued assets	los activos acumulados	*lohs ahk-'tee-bohs ah-koo-moo-'lah-dohs*
accrued depreciation	la depreciación acumulada	*lah deh-preh-see-ah-see-'ohn ah-koo-moo-'lah-dah*
accrued expenses	los gastos acumulados por pagar	*lohs 'gah-stohs ah-koo-moo-'lah-dohs pohr pah-'gahr*
accrued interest	el interés acumulado	*ehl 'een-teh-rehs ah-koo-moo-'lah-doh*
accrued method	el método de acumulacíon	*ehl 'meh-toh-doh deh ah-koo-moo-lah-see-'ohn*
accrued revenue	los ingresos acumulados	*lohs een-'greh-sohs ah-koo-moo-'lah-dohs*

accrued taxes	los impuestos acumulados	*lohs eem-'pweh-stohs ah-koo-moo-'lah-dohs*
accumulated depreciation	la depreciación acumulada	*lah deh-preh-see-ah-see-'ohn ah-koo-moo-'lah-dah*
acetate	el acetato	*ehl ah-seh-'tah-toh*
acetic acid	el ácido acético	*ehl 'ah-see-doh ah-'seh-tee-koh*
acetone	la acetona	*lah ah-seh-'toh-nah*
acid	el ácido	*ehl 'ah-see-doh*
acid content	el contenido acídico	*ehl kohn-teh-'nee-doh ah-'see-dee-koh*
acid rain	lluvia ácida	*'yoo-bee-ah 'ah-see-dah*
acid test	la prueba de fuego	*lah proo-'eh-bah deh fweh-go*
acknowledge (v)	reconocer, acusar	*reh-koh-noh-'sehr, ah-koo-'sahr*
acknowledge receipt of (v)	acusar recibo de	*ah-koo-'sahr reh-'see-boh deh*
acknowledgment	el reconocimiento, el agradecimiento	*ehl reh-koh-noh-see-mee-'ehn-toh, ehl ah-grah-deh-see-mee-'ehn-toh*
acoustic coupler	el acoplador acústico	*ehl ah-koh-plah-'dohr ah-'koos-tee-koh*
acquire (v)	adquirir	*ahd-kee-'reer*
acquired rights	los derechos adquiridos	*lohs deh-'reh-chohs ahd-kee-'ree-dohs*
acquisition	la adquisición	*lah ahd-kee-see-see-'ohn*
acquisition profile	el perfil de aquisición	*ehl pehr-'feel deh ah-kee-see-see-'ohn*
acre	el acre (0.4047 hectáreas)	*ehl 'ah-kreh (0.4047 ehk-'tah-reh-ahs)*
acreage allotment	la asignación de terreno	*lah ah-seeg-nah-see-'ohn deh teh-'reh-noh*
acronym	el acrónimo	*ehl ah-'kroh-nee-moh*
across-the-board settlement	el acuerdo integral, el ajuste lineal	*ehl ah-'kwehr-doh een-teh-'grahl, ehl ah-'hoos-teh lee-neh-'ahl*
across-the-board tariff negotiation	las negociaciones arancelarias lineales	*lahs neh-goh-see-ah-see-'oh-nehns ah-rahn-seh-'lah-ree-ahs lee-neh-'ah-lehs*
act of God	la fuerza mayor	*lah 'fwehr-sah mah-'yohr*

action research	la investigación aplicada	*lah een-behs-tee-gah-see-'ohn ah-plee-'kah-dah*
active account	la cuenta activa	*lah 'kwehn-tah ahk-'tee-bah*
active assets	los activos productivos	*lohs ahk-'tee-bohs proh-dook-'tee-bohs*
active debts	las deudas activas	*lahs dee-'ooh-dahs ahk-'tee-bahs*
active trust	el fideicomiso activo	*ehl fee-deh-ee-koh-'mee-soh ahk-'tee-boh*
activity chart	el cuadro de actividades	*ehl -kwah-droh deh ahk-tee-bee-'dah-dehs*
actual cash value	el valor verdadero en efectivo	*ehl bah-'lohr behr-dah-'deh-roh ehn eh-fehk-'tee-boh*
actual cost	el costo real, el costo verdadero	*ehl 'kohs-toh reh-'ahl, ehl-'kohs-toh behr-dah-'deh-roh*
actual income	los ingresos verdaderos	*lohs een-'greh-sohs behr-dah-'deh-rohs*
actual liability	el pasivo verdadero	*ehl pah-'see-boh behr-dah-'deh-roh*
actual market volume	el volumen verdadero del mercado	*ehl boh-'loo-mehn behr-dah-'deh-roh dehl mehr-'kah-doh*
actual total loss	la pérdida total efectiva	*lah 'pehr-dee-dah toh-'tahl eh-fehk-'tee-bah*
actuals	las disponibilidades	*lahs dees-poh-nee-bee-lee-'dah-dehs*
actuary	el actuario	*ahk-too-'ah-ree-oh*
add-on-sales	las ventas adicionales	*lahs 'behn-tahs ah-dee-see-oh-'nah-lehs*
addendum	el anexo	*ehl ah-'nehk-soh*
adjudge (v)	adjudicar	*ahd-hoo-dee-'kahr*
adjudication	el juicio, la adjudicación	*ehl 'hoo-ee-see-oh, lah ahd-hoo-dee-kah-see-'ohn*
adjust (v)	ajustar	*ah-hoo-'stahr*
adjustable peg	el tipo de cambio fijo ajustable	*ehl 'tee-poh deh 'kahm-bee-oh 'fee-hoh ah-hoo-'stah-bleh*
adjusted CIF price	el precio ajustado de costo, seguro y flete	*ehl 'preh-see-oh ah-hoo-'stah-doh deh 'koh-stoh, seh-'goo-roh ee 'fleh-teh*

A

adjusted earned income	los ingresos ajustados	*lohs een-'greh-sohs ah-hoo-'stah-dohs*
adjusted rate	la tasa ajustada	*lah 'tah-sah ah-hoo-'stah-dah*
adjusting entry	el asiento de ajuste	*ehl ah-see-'ehn-toh deh ah-'hoo-steh*
adjustment process	el proceso de ajuste	*ehl proh-'seh-soh deh ah-'hoo-steh*
adjustment trigger	el iniciador de ajustes	*ehl ee-nee-see-ah-'dohr deh ah-'hoo-stehs*
administration	la gerencia	*lah heh-'rehn-see-ah*
administration (handling of)	el manejo	*ehl mah-'neh-hoh*
administrative expense	los gastos administrativos	*lohs 'gah-stohs ahd-mee-nee-strah-'tee-bohs*
administrator	el administrador	*ehl ahd-mee-nee-strah-'dohr*
administratrix	la administradora	*lah ahd-mee-nee-strah-'doh-rah*
advance (v)	anticipar, adelantar	*ahn-tee-see-'pahr, ah-deh-lahn-'tahr*
advance freight	el flete pagado	*ehl 'fleh-teh pah-'gah-doh*
advance notice	el aviso anticipado	*ehl ahn-tee-see-'pah-doh*
advance payment	el pago por adelantado	*ehl 'pah-goh pohr ah-deh-lahn-'tah-doh*
advance refunding	las devoluciones por adelantado	*lahs deh-boh-loo-see-'oh-nehs pohr ah-deh-lahn-'tah-doh*
adverse balance	el balance desfavorable	*ehl bah-'lahn-seh dehs-fah-boh-'rah-bleh*
advertising	la publicidad	*lah poo-blee-see-'dahd*
advertising agency	la agencia de publicidad	*lah ah-'hehn-see-ah deh poo-blee-see-'dahd*
advertising budget	el presupuesto de publicidad	*ehl preh-soo-'pwehs-toh deh poo-blee-see-'dahd*
advertising campaign	la campaña de publicidad	*lah kahm-'pah-nyah deh poo-blee-see-'dahd*
advertising drive	la campaña para conseguir anunciadores	*lah kahm-pah-nyah 'pah-rah kohn-seh-'geer ah-noon-see-ah-'doh-rehs*

advertising expenses	los gastos de publicidad	*lohs 'gahs-tohs deh poo-blee-see-'dahd*
advertising manager	el gerente de publicidad	*ehl heh-'rehn-teh deh poo-blee-see-'dahd*
advertising media	los medios de publicidad	*lohs 'meh-dee-ohs deh poo-blee-see-'dahd*
advertising research	la investigación publicitaria	*lah een-behs-tee-gah-see-'ohn poo-blee-see-'tah-ree-ah*
advice notice	el aviso de expedición	*ehl ah-'bee-soh deh ehks-peh-dee-see-'ohn*
advise (v)	aconsejar	*ah-kohn-seh-'hahr*
advisory council	el consejo asesor	*ehl kohn-'seh-hoh ah-seh-'sohr*
advisory funds	los fondos de asesoramiento	*lohs 'fohn-dohs deh ah-seh-soh-rah-mee-'ehn-toh*
advisory service	el servicio consultivo	*ehl sehr-'bee-see-oh kohn-sool-'tee-boh*
affidavit	el afidávit	*ehl ah-fee-'dah-beet*
affidavit entry	la declaración jurada	*lah deh-klah-ra-see-'ohn hoo-'rah-dah*
affiliate	el asociado, el afiliado	*ehl ah-soh-see-'ah-doh, ehl ah-fee-lee-'ah-doh*
affiliate (local)	afiliado local	*ah-fee-lee-'ah-doh loh-'kahl*
affiliate (international)	afiliado internacional	*ah-fee-lee-'ah-doh een-tehr-nah-see-oh-'nahl*
affiliate (v)	afiliar	*ah-fee-lee-'ahr*
affirmative action	las medidas para la protección de los derechos personales	*lahs meh-'dee-dahs 'pah-rah lah proh-tehk-see-'ohn deh lohs deh-'reh-chohs pehr-soh-'nah-lehs*
affreightment	el fletamento	*ehl fleh-tah-'mehn-toh*
afloat	a flote	*ah 'floh-teh*
after-sales-service	el servicio de post-venta	*ehl sehr-'bee-see-oh deh pohst-'behn-tah*
after-sight	posterior a la fecha de presentación	*pohs-teh-ree-'ohr ah lah 'feh-cha deh preh-sehn-tah-see-'ohn*
after-tax real rate of return	la tasa de retorno real después de impuestos	*lah tah-sah deh reh-'tohr-noh reh-'ahl dehs-'pwehs deh ihm-'pwehstos*

afterdate	después del día de vencimiento	*dehs-'pwehs dehl 'dee-ah deh behn-see-mee-'ehn-toh*
against all risks	a todo riesgo	*ah 'toh-doh ree-'ehs-goh*
agency	la agencia	*lah ah-'hehn-see-ah*
agency bank	la agencia bancaria	*lah ah-'hehn-see-ah bahn-'kah-ree-ah*
agency fee	los honorarios de agencia	*lohs oh-noh-'rah-ree-ohs deh ah-'hehn-see-ah*
agenda	la agenda	*lah ah-'hehn-dah*
agent	el agente	*ehl ah-'hehn-teh*
agent bank	el banco representante	*ehl 'bahn-koh reh-preh-sehn-'tahn-teh*
aggregate demand	la demanda agregada	*lah deh-'mahn-dah ah-greh-'gah-dah*
aggregate risk	el riesgo agregado	*ehl ree-'ehs-goh ah-greh-'gah-doh*
aggregate supply	la oferta agregada	*lah oh-'fehr-tah ah-greh-'gah-dah*
aging	el envejecimiento	*ehl ehn-beh-heh-see-mee-'ehn-toh*
agreed and satisfied	acordado y satisfecho	*ah-kohr-'dah-doh ee sah-tees-'feh-choh*
agreement	el pacto, el acuerdo, el convenio	*ehl 'pahk-toh, ehl ah-'kwehr-doh, ehl kohn-'beh-nee-oh*
agricultural paper	las obligaciones agrícolas, los efectos agrícolas	*lahs ohb-lee-gah-see-'ohn-ehs ah-'gree-koh-lahs, lohs eh-'fehk-tohs ah-'gree-koh-lahs*
agricultural products	los productos agrícolas	*lohs proh-'dook-tohs ah-'gree-koh-lahs*
agriculture	la agricultura	*lah ah-gree-kool-'too-rah*
air compressor	compresor del aire	*kohm-preh-'sohr dehl 'ah-ee-reh*
air express	el correo aéreo	*ehl koh-'rreh-oh ah-'eh-reh-oh*
air filter	el filtro de aire	*ehl 'feel-troh deh 'ah-ee-reh*
air freight	el flete aéreo	*ehl 'fleh-teh ah-'eh-reh-oh*
air shipments	los embarques aéreos	*lohs ehm-'bahr-kehs ah-'eh-reh-ohs*

A

alcoholic content	el contenido alcohólico, el porcentaje de alcohol	*ehl kohn-teh-'nee-doh ahl-koh-'oh-lee-koh, ehl pohr-sehn-'tah-heh deh ahl-koh-'ohl*
algae	las algas (f)	*lahs 'ahl-gahs*
algorithm	el algoritmo	*ehl ahl-goh-'reet-moh*
algorithmic language	el lenguaje algorítmico	*ehl lehn-'gwah-heh ahl-goh-'reet-mee-koh*
alien corporation	la compañía extranjera	*lah kohm-pah-'nyee-aha ehks-trahn-'heh-rah*
all or none	todo o nada	*'toh-doh oh 'nah-dah*
all-in-cost	el costo total	*ehl 'koh-stoh toh-'tahl*
allocation of costs	la asignación de costos	*lah ah-seeg-nah-see-'ohn deh 'koh-stohs*
allocation of responsibilities	la asignación de responsabilidades	*lah ah-seeg-nah-see-'ohn deh reh-spohn-sah-bee-lee-'dah-dehs*
allonge	el añadido	*ehl ah-nyah-'dee-doh*
allot (v)	asignar	*ah-seeg-'nahr*
allotment letter	la notificación de reparto	*lah noh-tee-fee-kah-see-'ohn deh reh-'pahr-toh*
allow (v)	permitir	*pehr-mee-'teer*
allowance	la asignación, la concesión, la rebaja	*lah ah-seeg-nah-see-'ohn, lah kohn-seh-see-'ohn, lah reh-'bah-hah*
alloy steel	la aleación de acero	*lah ah-leh-ah-see-'ohn deh ah-'seh-roh*
alongside (nautical)	al costado de	*ahl koh-'stah-doh deh*
alteration	el cambio, la alteración	*ehl 'kahm-bee-oh, lah ahl-teh-rah-see-'ohn*
alternating current	la corriente alterna	*lah koh-rree-'ehn-teh ahl-tehr-nah*
alternative order	la orden alternativa	*lah 'ohr-dehn ahl-tehr-nah-'tee-bah*
amalgamation	la fusión	*lah foo-see-'ohn*
amend (v)	enmendar, reformar	*ehn-mehn-'dahr*
amendment	la enmienda	*lah ehn-mee-'ehn-dah*
ammonia	el amoníaco	*ehl ah-moh-'nee-ah-koh*

amortization	la amortización	*lah ah-mohr-tee-zah-see-'ohn*
amount	la suma	*lah 'soo-mah*
amount due	el importe debido, el importe vencido	*ehl eem-'pohr-teh deh-bee-doh, ehl eem-'pohr-teh behn-'see-doh*
ampere	el amperaje	*ehl ahm-peh-'rah-heh*
amphibians	anfibios	*ahm-'fee-bee-ohs*
amplifier	el amplificador	*ehl ahm-plee-fee-kah-'dohr*
amplitude modulation (AM)	la amplitud modulada, la modulación de amplitud	*lah ahm-plee-tood moh-doo-'lah-dah, lah moh-doo-lah-see-'ohn*
analgesic	el analgésico	*ehl ah-nahl-'heh-see-koh*
analogue computer	la computadora análoga	*lah kohm-poo-tah-'doh-rah ah-'nah-loh-gah*
analysis	el análisis	*ehl ah-'nah-lee-sees*
analyst	el analista	*ehl ah-nah-'lees-tah*
analytic chemistry	la química analítica	*lah 'kee-mee-kah ah-nah-'lee-tee-kah*
anchorage (dues)	los derechos de anclaje	*lohs deh-'reh-chohs deh ahn-'klah-heh*
ancillary	auxiliar, equipo auxiliar	*owk-see-lee-'ahr, eh-'kee-poh owk-see-lee-'ahr*
ancillary operations	las operaciones auxiliares	*lahs oh-peh-rah-see-'oh-nehs owx-see-lee-'ah-rehs*
anesthetic	el anestético	*ehl ah-neh-'steh-tee-koh*
angle of incidence	el ángulo de incidencia	*ehl 'ahn-goo-loh deh enn-see-'dehn-see-ah*
animal kingdom	el reino animal	*ehl 'reh-ee-noh ah-nee-'mahl*
annealing	el recocido	*ehl reh-koh-'see-doh*
annual	anual	*ah-noo-'ahl*
annual accounts	las cuentas anuales	*lahs 'kwehn-tahs ah-noo-'ah-lehs*
annual audit	la auditoría anual	*lah ow-dee-toh-'ree-ah ah-noo-'ahl*
annual report	el informe anual	*ehl een-'fohr-meh ah-noo-'ahl*

annuity	la anualidad	*lah ah-noo-ah-lee-'dahd*
anti-dumping duty	el impuesto anti-dumping, el derecho protector contra importación a precios arbitrarios	*ehl eem-'pwehs-toh ahn-tee-'doom-peeng, ehl deh-'reh-choh proh-tehk-'tohr 'kohn-trah eem-pohr-tah-see-'ohn ah 'preh-see-ohs ahr-bee-'trahr-ree-ohs*
anti-inflammatory	el antiinflamatorio	*ehl ahn-tee-een-flah-mah-'toh-ree-oh*
anticholinergic	el anticolinérgico	*ehl ahn-tee-koh-lee-'nehr-hee-koh*
anticoagulant	el anticoagulante	*ehl ahn-tee-koh-ah-goo-'lahn-teh*
antique authenticity certificate	el certificado de antigüedad auténtica	*ehl sehr-tee-fee-'kah-doh deh ahn-tee-gweh-'dahd ow-'tehn-tee-kah*
antitrust laws	las leyes antimonopolio	*lahs 'leh-yehs ahn-tee-moh-noh-'poh-lee-oh*
apparel	el vestido, la indumentaria	*ehl behs-'tee-doh, lah een-doo-mehn-'tah-ree-ah*
application form	el formulario de solicitud, la solicitud	*ehl fohr-moo-'lah-ree-oh deh soh-lee-see-'tood, lah soh-lee-see-'tood*
applied proceeds swap	el apoyo recíproco del producto aplicado	*ehl ah-'poh-yoh reh-'see-pree-koh dehl proh-'dook-toh ah-plee-'kah-doh*
appointment (engagement)	el nombramiento, la cita	*ehl nohm-brah-mee-'ehn-toh, lah 'see-tah*
appraisal	la tasación	*lah ta-sa-'see-ohn*
appraiser	el tasador, el valuador	*ehl tah-sah-'dohr, ehl bah-loo-ah-'dohr*
appreciation	la revalorización, el alza	*lah reh-bah-loh-ree-sah-see-'ohn, ehl 'ahl-sah*
apprentice	el aprendiz	*ehl ah-prehn-'dees*
appropriation	la consignación, la asignación	*lah kohn-seeg-nah-see-'ohn, la ah-seeg-nah-see-'ohn*
approval	la aprobación	*lah ah-proh-bah-see-'ohn*
approve (v)	aprobar	*ah-proh-'bahr*
approved delivery facility	la localidad de reparto aprobada	*lah loh-kah-lee-'dahd deh reh-'pahr-toh ah-proh-'bah-dah*

approved securities	las valores aprobados	*lahs bah-'loh-rehs ah-proh-'bah-dohs*
arbitrage	el arbitraje	*ehl ahr-bee-'trah-heh*
arbitration	el arbitrage	*ehl ahr-bee-'trah-heh*
arbitration agreement	el convenio de arbitraje	*ehl kohn-'beh-nee-oh deh ahr-bee-'trah-heh*
arbitrator	el árbitro	*ehl 'ahr-bee-troh*
area manager	el gerente de zona	*ehl heh-'rehn-teh deh 'soh-nah*
arithmetic mean	la media aritmética	*lah 'meh-dee-ah ah-reet-'meh-tee-kah*
armaments	los armamentos	*lohs ahr-mah-'mehn-tohs*
arms	las armas	*lahs 'ahr-mahs*
arm's length	las empresas vinculadas a otras que operan como si no lo fueran	*lahs ehm-'preh-sahs been-koo-'lah-dahs ah 'oh-trahs keh oh-'peh-rahn 'koh-moh see noh loh 'fweh-rahn*
arrears	los atrasos	*lohs ah-'trah-sohs*
as if and when	siempre y cuando	*see-'ehm-preh ee 'kwahn-doh*
as per advice	según aviso	*seh-'goon ah-'bee-soh*
as soon as possible	cuanto antes, lo más pronto posible	*'kwahn-toh 'ahn-tehs, loh mahs prohn-tow poh-see-bleh*
as-is goods	los bienes así como así	*lohs bee-'eh-nehs ah-'see 'koh-moh ah-'see*
ASCII	código utilizado como estándard en los EE.UU. para el intercambio de información entre sistemas de procesamiento de datos	*'koh-dee-goh oo-tee-lee-'sah-doh 'koh-moh ehs-'tahn-dahrd ehn lohs eh-'stah-dohs oo-'nee-dohs 'pah-rah ehl een-tehr-'kahm-bee-oh deh een-fohr-mah-see-'ohn 'ehn-treh sees-'teh-mahs deh proh-seh-sah-mee-'ehn-toh deh 'dah-tohs*
asking price	el precio de venta	*ehl 'preh-see-oh deh 'behn-tah*
aspirin	la aspirina	*lah ahs-pee-'ree-nah*
assay	el ensayo, la prueba	*ehl ehn-'sah-yoh, lah proo-'eh-bah*

assemble (v)	ensamblar, montar	*ehn-sahm-'blahr, mohn-'tahr*
assembly	la asamblea	*lah ah-sahm-'bleh-ah*
assembly line	la línea de ensamblaje, la línea de montaje, la producción en cadena	*lah 'lee-neh-ah deh ehn-sahm-'lah-heh, lah 'lee-neh-ah deh mohn-'tah-heh, lah proh-dook-see-'ohn ehn kah-'deh-nah*
assess (v)	avaluar, tasar	*ah-bah-loo-'ahr, tah-sahr*
assessed valuation	el valor imponible	*ehl bah-'lohr eem-poh-'nee-bleh*
assessment	la tasación	*lah tah-sah-see-'ohn*
asset turnover	la rotación del activo	*lah roh-tah-see-'ohn dehl ahk-'tee-boh*
asset value	el valor del activo, según los libros	*ehl bah-'lohr dehl ahk-'tee-boh, seh-'goon lohs 'lee-brohs*
assets	el activo	*ehl ahk-'tee-boh*
assign (v)	asignar	*ah-seeg-'nahr*
assignee	el asignatario, el cesionario	*ehl ah-seeg-nah-'toh-ree-oh, ehl seh-see-oh-'nah-ree-oh*
assigner	el cedente, el asignador	*ehl seh-'dehn-teh, ehl ah-seeg-nah-'dohr*
assistant	el asistente	*ehl ah-sees-'tehn-teh*
assistant general manager	el gerente general asistente	*ehl heh-'rehn-teh heh-neh-'rahl ah-sees-'tehn-teh*
assistant manager	el gerente asistente	*ehl heh-'rehn-teh ah-sees-'tehn-teh*
associate company	la compañía asociada	*lah kohm-pah-'nyee-ah*
assumed liability	el pasivo asumido	*ehl pah-'see-boh ah-soo-'mee-doh*
at and from	en y desde	*ehn ee 'dehs-deh*
at best	en el mejor de los casos	*ehn loh meh-'hohr deh lohs 'kah-sohs*
at call	disponible, a la vista	*dees-poh-'nee-bleh, ah lah 'bees-tah*
at or better than (market price)	al precio (del mercado) o mejor	*ahl 'preh-see-oh (dehl mehr-'kah-doh) oh meh-'hohr*

at par	a la par	*ah lah 'pahr*
at sight	a la vista	*ah lah 'bees-tah*
at the close	al cierre	*ahl see-'eh-reh*
at the market	en el mercado	*ehn ehl mehr-'kah-doh*
at the opening	a la apertura	*ah lah ah-pehr-'too-rah*
atmosphere	la atmósfera	*lah aht-'mohs-feh-rah*
atom	el átomo	*ehl 'ah-toh-moh*
atomic (adj)	atómico	*ah-'toh-mee-koh*
attach (v)	adjuntar	*ahd-hoon-'tahr*
attaché case	el maletín ejecutivo, el maletín, la cartera de papeles	*ehl mah-leh-'teen eh-heh-koo-'tee-boh, ehl mah-leh-'teen, lah kahr-'teh-rah deh pah-'peh-lehs*
attended time	el tiempo concurrido	*ehl tee-'ehm-poh kohn-koo-'ree-doh*
attestation	la atestación	*la ah-tehs-tah-see-'ohn*
attorney	el abogado	*ehl ah-boh-'gah-doh*
attrition	el agotamiento	*ehl ah-goh-tah-mee-'ehn-toh*
auction market	subasta, puja	*soo-'bah-stah, 'poo-hah*
audit (v)	controlar, inspeccionar, auditorear	*kohn-troh-'lahr, een-spehk-see-oh-'nahr, ow-dee-toh-reh-'ahr*
audit trail	la pista de auditoría	*lah 'peehs-tah deh ow-dee-toh-'ree-ah*
auditing balance sheet	la auditoría del balance general	*lah ow-dee-toh-'ree-ah heh-neh-'rahl*
auditor	el auditor	*ehl ow-dee-'tohr*
autarchy	la autarquía	*lah ow-tahr-'kee-ah*
authenticity (gold)	la autenticidad (de oro)	*lah ow-tehn-tee-see-dahd (deh 'oh-roh)*
authorize (v)	autorizar	*ow-toh-ree-'sahr*
authorized dealer	el concesionario autorizado	*ehl kohn-seh-see-oh-'nah-ree-oh ow-toh-ree-'sah-doh*
authorized shares	las acciones autorizadas	*lahs ahk-see-'oh-nehs ow-toh-ree-'sah-dahs*
authorized signature	la firma autorizada	*lah 'feer-mah ow-toh-ree-'sah-dah*

automatic	automático	*ow-toh-'mah-tee-koh*
automatic gearshift	el cambio automático de velocidades	*ehl 'kahm-bee-oh ow-toh-'mah-tee-koh deh beh-loh-see-'dah-dehs*
automation	el automatización	*lah ow-toh-mah-tee-sah-see-'ohn*
automotive worker	el obrero automotriz	*ehl oh-'breh-roh ow-toh-moh-'trees*
autonomous	autónomo	*ow-'toh-noh-moh*
available	disponible	*dees-poh-'nee-bleh*
average	el promedio	*ehl proh-'meh-dee-oh*
average cost	el costo promedio	*ehl 'koh-stoh proh-'meh-dee-oh*
average life	la vida promedio	*lah 'bee-dah proh-'meh-dee-oh*
average price	el precio promedio	*ehl 'preh-see-oh proh-'meh-dee-oh*
average unit cost	el costo unitario promedio	*ehl 'koh-stoh oo-nee-'tah-ree-oh proh-'meh-dee-oh*
averaging	el proceso de promediar	*ehl proh-'seh-soh deh proh-meh-dee-'ahr*
avoidable costs	los costos evitables	*lohs 'koh-stohs eh-bee-'tah-blehs*

B

back date	la fecha previa	*lah 'feh-chah 'preh-bee-ah*
back date (v)	atrasar la fecha	*ah-trah-'sahr lah 'feh-chah*
back order	el pedido previo pendiente de entrega	*ehl peh-'dee-doh 'preh-bee-oh pehn-dee-'ehn-teh deh ehn-'treh-gah*
back selling (v)	vender nuevamente a quienes compramos	*behn-'dehr noo-eh-bah-'mehn-teh ah kee-'ehn-ehs kohm-'prah-mohs*
back taxes	los impuestos atrasados	*lohs eem-'pweh-stohs ah-trah-'sah-dohs*
back-to-back credit	el crédito al fabricante con respaldo de un crédito exterior	*ehl 'kreh-dee-toh ahl fah-bree-'kahn-teh kohn reh-'spahl-doh deh oon 'kreh-dee-toh ehx-teh-ree-'ohr*

back-to-back loan	el préstamo subsidiario	*ehl 'preh-stah-moh soob-see-dee-'ah-ree-oh*
back-up bonds	los bonos de respaldo	*lohs 'boh-nohs deh reh-'spahl-doh*
backed note	el pagaré a respaldo	*ehl pah-gah-'reh a reh-'spahl-doh*
backing and filling	el respaldo y la satisfacción	*aehl reh-'spahl-doh ee lah sah-tees-fahk-see-'ohn*
backing support	el respaldo y soporte	*ehl reh-'spahl-doh ee soh-'pohr-teh*
backlog	los pedidos pendientes	*lohs peh-'dee-dohs pehn-dee-'ehn-tehs*
backspace	retroceder en una unidad	*reh-troh-seh-'dehr ehn 'oo-nah oo-nee-'dahd*
backup	copia física que se hace del contenido de un disco o una cinta	*'koh-pee-ah 'fee-see-kah keh seh 'ah-seh dehl kohn-teh-'nee-doh deh oon 'dees-koh oh 'oo-nah 'seen-tah*
backwardation	la diferencia entre precios de entrega inmediata y futuro	*lah dee-feh-'rehn-see-ah 'ehn-treh 'preh-see-ohs deh ehn-'treh-gah een-meh-dee-'ah-tah ee foo'too-roh*
backwash effect	las consecuencias de una ocurrencia, la disminución de la producción para el interior en favor de la exportación en naciones subdesarrolladas	*lahs kohn-seh-'kwehn-see-ahs deh 'oo-nah oh-koo-'rehn-see-ah, lah dees-mee-noo-see-'ohn deh lah proh-dook-see-'ohn 'pah-rah ehl een-teh-ree-'ohr ehn fah-'bohr deh lah ehx-pohr-tah-see-'ohn ehn nah-see-see-'oh-nehs*
bad debt	la deuda incobrable	*lah deh-'oo-dah een-koh-'brah-bleh*
balance (economic)	el equilibrio	*ehl eh-kee-'lee-bree-oh*
balance of an account	el saldo	*ehl 'sahl-doh*
balance of payments	la balanza de pagos	*lah bah-'lahn-sah deh 'pah-gohs*
balance of trade	la balanza comercial	*lah bah-'lahn-sah koh-mehr-see-'ahl*
balance ratios	los índices del balance	*lohs 'een-dee-sehs dehl bah-'lahn-seh*

balance sheet	el balance general, el estado financiero	*ehl bah-'lahn-seh heh-neh-'rahl, ehl ehs-'tah-doh fee-nahn-see-'eh-roh*
bale capacity	la capacidad de empaquetar	*lah kah-pah-see-'dahd deh ehm-pah-keh-'tahr*
bale cargo	la carga de fardos	*lah 'kahr-gah deh 'fahr-dohs*
ballast bonus	el bono de lastre	*ehl 'boh-noh deh 'lah-streh*
balloon note	la nota de pago grande generalmente al final	*lah 'noh-tah deh 'pah-goh 'grahn-deh heh-neh-rahl-'mehn-teh ahl fee-'nahl*
balloon payment	pago global, el pago grande generalmente al final	*'pah-goh gloh-'bahl, ehl 'pah-goh 'grahn-deh heh-neh-rahl-'mehn-teh ahl fee-'nahl*
bank	el banco	*ehl 'bahn-koh*
bank (commercial)	banco comerciales	*'bahn-koh koh-mehr-see-'ah-lehs*
bank (investment)	banco inversionistas	*'bahn-koh een-behr-see-oh-'nees-tahs*
bank acceptance	la aceptación bancaria	*lah ah-sehptah-see-'ohn bahn-'kah-ree-ah*
bank account	la cuenta bancaria	*lah 'kwehn-tah bahn-'kah-ree-ah*
bank balance	el saldo bancario	*ehl 'sahl-doh bahn-'kah-ree-oh*
bank carnet	la identificación bancaria	*lah ee-dehn-tee-fee-kah-see-'ohn bahn-'kah-ree-ah*
bank charges	los cargos bancarios	*lohs 'kahr-gohs bahn-'kah-ree-ohs*
bank check	el cheque bancario	*ehl 'cheh-keh bahn-'kah-ree-oh*
bank deposit	el depósito bancario	*ehl deh-'poh-see-toh bahn-'kah-ree-oh*
bank draft	el giro bancario	*ehl 'hee-roh bahn-'kah-ree-oh*
bank examiner	el inspector bancario	*ehl een-spehk-'tohr bahn-'kah-ree-oh*
bank exchange	el intercambio bancario	*ehl een-tehr-'kahm-bee-oh bahn-'kah-ree-oh*
bank holiday	el día feriado bancario	*ehl 'dee-ah feh-ree-'ah-doh bahn-'kah-ree-oh*

B

bank letter of credit	la carta de crédito bancaria	*lah 'kahr-tah deh 'kreh-dee-toh bahn-'kah-ree-ah*
bank loan	el préstamo bancario	*ehl 'preh-stah-moh bahn-'kah-ree-oh*
bank money order	el giro bancario	*ehl 'hee-roh bahn-'kah-ree-oh*
bank note	la nota bancaria	*lah 'noh-tah bahn-'kah-ree-ah*
bank rate	el tipo de interés bancario	*ehl 'tee-poh deh een-teh-'rehs bahn-'kah-ree-oh*
bank release	la exoneración bancaria	*lah ehks-'oh-neh-rah-see-'ohn bahn-'kah-ree-ah*
bank statement	el estado de cuenta bancaria	*ehl eh-'stah-doh deh 'kwehn-tah bahn-'kah-ree-ah*
banking industry	la industria bancaria	*lah een-'doos-tree-ah*
bankruptcy	la quiebra, la bancarrota	*lah kee-'eh-brah, lah bahn'kah-'rroh-tah*
barbiturates	los barbitúricos	*lohs bahr-bee-'too-ree-kohs*
bareboat charter	la carta de fletamiento sin tripulación ni combustible	*lah 'kahr-tah deh fleh-tah-mee-'ehn-toh seen tree-poo-lah-see-'ohn nee kohm-boo-'stee-bleh*
bargain (sale)	la ganga	*lah 'gahn-gah*
bargain	el convenio, el pacto	*ehl kohn-'beh-nee-oh, ehl 'pahk-toh*
bargaining power	el poder para negociar	*ehl poh-'dehr 'pah-rah neh-goh-see-'ahr*
barrel	el barril	*ehl bah-'rreel*
barrier	la barrera	*lah bah-'rreh-rah*
bars	las barras	*lahs 'bah-rrahs*
barter (v)	permutar	*pehr-moo-'tahr*
bartering	el trueque, la permuta	*ehl tro-'eh-keh, lah pehr-'moo-tah*
base	la base	*lah 'bah-seh*
base currency	la base monetaria	*lah 'bah-seh moh-neh-'tah-ree-ah*
base price	el precio base	*ehl 'pree-see-oh 'bah-seh*
base rate	el tipo base	*ehl 'tee-poh 'bah-seh*
base year	el año base	*ehl 'ah-nyoh 'bah-seh*

basin	la cuenca	*lah 'kwehn-kah*
basin (marine)	cuenca marina	*'kwehn-kah mah-'ree-nah*
basis point (1/100%)	el punto de base	*ehl 'poon-toh deh 'bah-seh*
batch	grupo, el lote, la serie	*'groo-poh, ehl 'loh-teh, lah 'seh-ree-eh*
batch processing	el procesamiento en función al orden de llegada	*ehl proh-seh-sah-mee-'ehn-toh ehn foonk-see-'ohn ahl 'ohr-dehn deh yeh-'gah-dah*
batch production	la producción en lote	*lah proh-dook-see-'ohn ehn 'loh-teh*
baud	baudio, unidad de velocidad de transmisión de información	*'bah-oo-dee-oh, oo-nee-'dahd deh beh-loh-see-'dahd deh trahns-mee-see-'ohn deh een-fohr-mah-see-'ohn*
beach	la playa	*lah 'plah-yah*
beam	el rayo	*ehl 'rah-yoh*
bear	el especulador sobre la baja del mercado, el bajista	*ehl ehs-peh-koo-lah-'dohr 'soh-breh lah 'bah-hah dehl mehr-'kah-doh, ehl bah-'hees-tah*
bear market	el mercado bajista	*ehl mehr-'kah-doh bah-'hees-tah*
bearer	el portador, el tenedor	*ehl pohr-tah-'dohr, ehl teh-neh-'dohr*
bearer bond	el bono al portador, el título al portador	*ehl 'boh-noh ahl pohr-tah-'dohr, ehl 'tee-too-loh ahl pohr-tah-'dohr*
bearer security	el valor al portador	*ehl bah-'lohr ahl pohr-tah-'dohr*
beaver	el castor	*ehl kahs-'tohr*
bell-shaped curve	la curva de campana	*lah 'koor-bah deh kahm-'pah-nah*
below par	bajo-par, por debajo de la par	*'bah-hoh pahr, pohr deh-'bah-hoh deh lah pahr*
below the line	por debajo de la línea	*pohr deh-'bah-hoh deh lah 'lee-neh-ah*
belt	el cinturón, el cinto	*ehl seen-too-'rohn, ehl 'seen-toh*
belt (automobile)	la correa	*lah koh-'rreh-ah*

B

beneficiary	el beneficiario	*ehl beh-neh-fee-see-'ah-ree-oh*
benzene	el benceno	*ehl behn-'seh-noh*
bequest	la donación, el legado	*lah doh-nah-see-'ohn, ehl leh-'gah-doh*
berth terms	las condiciones de atraque y muellaje	*lahs kohn-dee-see-'oh-nehs deh ah-'trah-keh ee mweh-'yah-heh*
bid and asked price	el precio de compra y venta	*ehl 'preh-see-oh deh 'kohm-prah ee 'behn-tah*
bidder	el subastador	*ehl soo-bah-stah-'dohr*
bill	el giro, la factura, la letra de cambio	*ehl 'hee-roh, lah fahk-'too-rah, lah 'leh-trah de 'kahm-bee-oh*
bill broker	el corredor de valores	*ehl koh-rreeh-'dohr deh bah-'loh-rehs*
bill of exchange	la letra de cambio	*lah 'leh-trah deh 'kahm-bee-oh*
bill of lading	el conocimiento de embarque	*ehl koh-noh-see-mee-'ehn-toh deh ehm-'bahr-keh*
bill of sale	el comprobante de venta, la factura de venta	*ehl kohm-proh-'bahn-teh deh 'behn-tah, lah fahk-'too-rah deh 'behn-tah*
bill of sight	la declaración provisional	*lah deh-klah-rah-see-'ohn proh-bee-see-oh-'nahl*
billboard	la cartelera	*lah kahr-teh-'leh-rah*
billets	los lingotes	*lohs leen-'goh-tehs*
billfold	el billetero, la cartera	*ehl bee-yeh-'teh-roh, lah kahr-'teh-rah*
binary (adj)	binario	*bee-'nah-ree-oh*
binary code	el código binario	*ehl 'koh-dee-goh bee-'nah-ree-oh*
binary notation	la notación binaria	*lah noh-tah-see-'ohn bee-'nah-ree-ah*
binder	el recibo para pago preliminar	*ehl reh-'see-boh 'pah-rah 'pah-goh preh-lee-mee-'nahr*
biochemistry	la bioquímica	*lah bee-oh-'kee-mee-kah*
biodiversity	la biodiversidad	*lah bee-oh-dee-behr-see-'dahd*

biological diacidizing	la diacidificación biológica	*lah dee-ah-see-dee-fee-kah-see-'ohn bee-oh-'loh-hee-kah*
biological function	la función biológica	*lah foonk-see-'ohn bee-oh-'loh-hee-kah*
biologist	el biólogo	*ehl bee-'oh-loh-goh*
biology	la biología	*lah bee-oh-loh-'hee-ah*
birds	los aves, los pájaros	*los 'ah-behs, 'los pah-hah-rohs*
bit	bit, unidad elemental de información del sistema binario, el dígito binario	*beet, oo-nee-'dahd eh-leh-mehn-'tahl de een-fohr-mah-see-'ohn dehl sees-'teh-mah bee-'nah-ree-oh, ehl 'dee-hee-toh bee-'nah-ree-oh*
black and white (adj)	blanco y negro	*'blahn-koh ee 'neh-groh*
black market	el mercado negro	*ehl mehr-'kah-doh 'neh-groh*
blanket bond	la fianza general	*lah fee-'ahn-sah heh-neh-'rahl*
blanket order	la orden general	*lah 'ohr-dehn heh-neh-'rahl*
blast furnace	el alto horno	*ehl 'ahl-toh 'ohr-noh*
blazer	la chaqueta deportiva	*lah chah-'keh-tah deh-pohr-'tee-bah*
bleed (v) (in printing)	desteñir	*dehs-teh-'nyeer*
bleed (v)	sangrar	*sahn-'grahr*
blend (v)	mezclar	*mehs'klahr*
block	bloque (m)	*'bloh-keh*
blockage	bloqueo	*bloh-'keh-oh*
blockage of funds	el bloqueo de fondos	*ehl bloh-'keh-oh deh 'fohn-dohs*
blocked currency	la moneda bloqueada	*lah moh-'neh-dah bloh-keh-'ah-dah*
blood	la sangre	*lah 'sahn-greh*
blotter	el secante	*ehl seh-'kahn-teh*
blouse	la blusa	*lah 'bloo-sah*
blowup (v)	ampliar	*ahm-plee-'ahr*

blue chip stock	el valor de la más alta categoría	*ehl bah-'lohr deh lah mahs 'ahl-tah kah-teh-goh-'ree-ah*
blue collar worker	el obrero	*ehl oh-'breh-roh*
blueprint	la heliografía, el plano	*lah eh-lee-oh-grah-'fee-ah, ehl 'plah-noh*
board meeting	la reunión de la junta	*lah reh-oo-nee-'ohn deh lah 'hoon-tah*
board of directors	la junta directiva	*lah 'hoon-tah dee-rehk-'tee-bah*
board room	la sala de conferencias	*lah 'sah-lah deh kohn-feh-'rehn-see-ahs*
board of supervisors	las junta de inspectores	*lahs 'hoon-tah deh een-spehk-'toh-rehs*
body	el cuerpo	*ehl 'kwehr-poh*
body (in winemaking)	el sabor	*ehl sah-'bohr*
bodywork	la carrocería	*lah kah-rroh-seh-'ree-ah*
boiler plate (contract)	la copia literal de contratos legales pasados	*lah 'koh-pee-ah lee-teh-'rahl deh kohn-'trah-tohs leh-'gah-lehs pah-'sah-dohs*
boldface	la negrita	*lah neh-'gree-tah*
bond	el bono, la obligación hipotecaria, obligación	*ehl 'boh-noh, lah ohb-lee-gah-see-'ohn ee-poh-teh-'kah-ree-ah, oh-blee-gah-see-'ohn*
bond areas	las áreas de obligación	*lahs 'ah-reh-ahs deh ohb-lee-gah-see-'ohn*
bond issue	la emisión de bonos	*lah eh-mee-see-'ohn deh 'boh-nohs*
bond power	el título poder	*ehl 'tee-too-loh poh-'dehr*
bond rating	la clasificación de bonos	*lah klah-see-fee-kah-see-'ohn deh 'boh-nohs*
bond value	el valor de la obligación	*ehl bah-'lohr deh lah oh-blee-gah-see-'ohn*
bonded carrier	el transportista asegurado	*ehl trahns-pohr-'tees-tah ah-seh-goo-'rah-doh*
bonded goods	los bienes afianzados	*lohs bee-'eh-nehs ah-fee-ahn-'sah-dohs*

bonded warehouse	el almacén afianzado	*ehl ahl-mah-'sehn ah-fee-ahn-'sah-doh*
bone china	la porcelana traslúcida	*lah pohr-'seh-'lah-nah trahs-loo-'see-dah*
bonus (premium)	la prima	*lah 'pree-mah*
book	el libro	*ehl 'lee-broh*
book inventory	el inventario según libros	*ehl een-behn-'tah-ree-oh seh-'goon 'lee-brohs*
book value	el valor según libros	*ehl bah-'lohr seh-'goon 'lee-brohs*
book value per share	el valor según libros por acción	*ehl bah-'lohr seh-'goon 'lee-brohs pohr ahk-see-'ohn*
bookkeeping	la contabilidad	*lah kohn-tah-bee-lee-'dahd*
boom	la prosperidad repentina, la bonanza	*lah prohs-peh-ree-'dahd reh-pehn-tee-nah, lah boh-'nahn-sah*
boot shop	la zapatería	*lah sah-pah-teh-'ree-ah*
bootmaker	el zapatero	*ehl sah-pah-'teh-roh*
boots	las botas	*lahs 'boh-tahs*
border	la frontera	*lah frohn-'teh-rah*
border tax adjustment	el ajuste de los impuestos fronterizos	*ehl ah-'hoo-steh deh lohs eem-'pweh-stohs frohn-teh-'ree-sohs*
borrow (v)	pedir prestado	*peh-'deer preh-'stah-doh*
botany (n)	la botánica	*lah boh-'tah-nee-kah*
bottle	la botella	*lah boh-'teh-yah*
bow tie	la corbata de lazo	*lah kohr-'bah-tah deh 'lah-soh*
bowl	el plato hondo, el cuenco, la escudilla	*ehl 'plah-toh 'hon-doh, ehl 'kwehn-koh, lah ehs-koo-'dee'yah*
boycott	el boicot	*ehl boh-ee-'coht*
brainstorming	la inspiración, la repartición grupal de sugerencias para creer ideas generales	*lah een-spee-rah-'syohn, lah reh-pahr-tee-'syohn groo-pahl deh soo-heh-'rehn-syahs pah-rah-kreh-ahr ee-'dey-ahs heh-neh-'rah-lehs*
brake	los frenos	*lohs 'freh-nohs*

brake pedal	el pedal de freno	*ehl peh-'dahl deh 'freh-noh*
branch office	la sucursal	*lah soo-koor-'sahl*
branching	bifurcaciones	*bee-foor-kah-see-'oh-nehs*
brand	la marca de fábrica	*lah 'mahr-kah deh 'fah-bree-kah*
brand acceptance	la aceptación de marca	*lah ah-sehptah-see-'ohn deh 'mahr-kah*
brand image	la imagen de la marca	*lah ee-'mah-hehn deh lah 'mahr-kah*
brand loyalty	la lealtad a la marca	*lah leh-ahl-'tahd ah lah 'mahr-kah*
brand manager	el gerente de marca	*ehl heh-'rehn-teh deh 'mahr-kah*
brand recognition	el reconocimiento de marca	*ehl reh-koh-noh-see-mee-'ehn-toh deh 'mahr-kah*
breadbasket	la panera	*lah pah-'neh-rah*
break even (v)	salir sin ganar ni perder	*sah-'leer seen gah-'nahr nee pehr-'dehr*
breakdown	avería	*ah-beh-'ree-ah*
breakeven analysis	el análisis del punto donde los ingresos son iguales a los egresos	*ehl ah-'nah-lee-sees dehl 'poon-toh 'dohn-deh lohs een-'greh-sohs sohn ee-'gwah-lehs ah lohs eh-'greh-sohs*
breakeven point	el punto donde los ingresos son iguales a los egresos	*ehl 'poon-toh 'dohn-deh lohs een-'greh-sohs sohn ee-'gwah-lehs ah lohs eh-'greh-sohs*
breakpoint	punto de interrupción	*'poon-toh deh een-teh-roop-see-'ohn*
briefcase	la cartera, el maletín, el portafolio	*lah kahr-'teh-rah, ehl mah-leh-'teen, ehl pohr-tah-'foh-lee-oh*
broadcast (v)	transmitir (TV), emitir (radio)	*trahns-mee-teer (TV) eh-mee-'teer (radio)*
broken lot	la partida incompleta, menos de cien acciones	*lah pahr-'tee-'dah een-kohm-'pleh-tah, 'meh-nohs deh see-ehn ahk-see-'oh-nehs*
broken stowage	el abarrote, la estiba con vacíos	*ehl ahl-bah-'rroh-teh, lah ehs-'tee-bah kohn bah-'see-ohs*

broker	el corredor, el intermediario	*ehl koh-rreh-'dohr, ehl een-tehr-meh-dee-'ah-ree-oh*
budget	el presupuesto	*ehl preh-soo-'pwehs-toh*
budget appropriation	la asignación presupuestaria	*lah ah-seeg-nah-see-'ohn preh-soo-pwehs-'tah-ree-ah*
budget forecast	el presupuesto estimado, el proyecto de presupuesto	*ehl preh-soo-'pwehs-toh ehs-tee-'mah-doh, ehl proh-'yehk-toh deh preh-soo-'pwehs-toh*
bug (defect in computer program)	error, el defecto en el programa de computación, avería (máquina)	*eh-'rrohr, ehl deh-'fehk-toh ehn ehl proh-'grah-mah deh kohm-poo-tah-see-'ohn, ah-beh-'ree-ah ('mah-kee-nah)*
bull	el alcista	*ehl ahl-'sees-tah*
bull market	el mercado de alcistas	*ehl mehr-'kah-doh deh ahl-'sees-tahs*
bumper	el parachoques, la defensa	*ehl pah-rah-'choh-keh, lah deh-'fehn-sah*
burden rate	la carga promedia	*lah 'kahr-gah proh-'meh-dee-ah*
bureaucrat	el burócrata	*ehl boo-'roh-krah-tah*
buret	la bureta	*lah boo-'reh-tah*
burning	incineración	*een-see-neh-rah-see-'ohn*
business activity	la actividad comercial	*lah ahk-tee-bee-'dahd koh-mehr-see-'ahl*
business card	la tarjeta comercial	*lah tahr-'heh-tah koh-mehr-see-'ahl*
business cycle	el ciclo económico	*ehl 'see-kloh eh-koh-'noh-mee-koh*
business failure	la quiebra, la bancarrota	*lah kee-'eh-brah, lah bahn-kah-'rroh-tah*
business management	la gerencia de negocios	*lah heh-'rehn-see-ah deh neh-'goh-see-ohs*
business plan	el plan comercial	*ehl plahn koh-mehr-see-'ahl*
business policy	la política comercial	*lah poh-'lee-tee-kah koh-mehr-see-'ahl*
business risk	el riesgo económico	*ehl ree-'ehs-goh eh-koh-'noh-mee-koh*

business strategy	la estrategia comercial	*lah ehs-trah-'teh-gee-ah koh-mehr-see-'ahl*
business success	el éxito comercial	*ehl 'ehk-see-toh koh-mehr-see-'ahl*
butter dish	la mantequillera	*lah mahn-teh-kee-'yeh-rah*
button	el botón	*ehl bah-'tohn*
buttonhole	el hojal	*ehl oh-'hahl*
buy at best	la compra al mejor	*lah 'kohm-prah ahl meh-'hohr*
buy back (v)	rescatar	*rehs-kah-'tahr*
buy back	la recompra	*lah reh-'kohm-prah*
buy on close	comprar al cierre	*kohm-'prahr ahl see-'eh-rreh*
buy on opening	comprar a la apertura	*kohm-'prahr ah lah ah-pehr-'too-rah*
buy out (v)	comprar la parte de	*kohm-'prahr lah 'pahr-teh deh*
buyer	el comprador	*ehl kohm-prah-'dohr*
buyer credit	el crédito del comprador	*ehl 'kreh-dee-toh dehl kohm-prah-'dohr*
buyers' market	el mercado de compradores	*ehl mehr-'kah-doh deh kohm-prah-'doh-rehs*
buyers option	la opción del comprador	*lah 'ohp-see-ohn dehl kohm-prah-'dohr*
buyer's premium	la prima del comprador	*lah 'pree-mah dehl kohm-prah-'dohr*
buyer's responsibility	la responsabilidad del comprador	*lah reh-spohn-sah-bee-lee-'dahd dehl kohm-prah-'dohr*
by-laws	los estatutos	*lohs ehs-tah-'too-tohs*
by-product	el subproducto	*ehl soob-proh-'dook-toh*
byte	el byte, el carácter de memoria	*ehl bah-eet, ehl kah-'rahk-tehr deh meh-'moh-ree-ah*

C

cable	el cable	*ehl 'kah-bleh*
cable television	la televisión por cable	*lah teh-leh-bee-see-'ohn pohr kah-bleh*
cable transfer	la transferencia cablegráfica	*lah trahns-feh-'rehn-see-ah kah-bleh-'grah-fee-kah*
calcium	el calcio	*ehl 'kahl-see-oh*
calculator	la calculadora	*lah kahl-koo-lah-'doh-rah*
calfskin	el cuero de becerro	*ehl 'kweh-roh deh beh-'seh-rroh*
call (v) (a meeting)	convocar junta	*kohn-boh-'kahr 'hoon-tah*
call (v) (in money)	pedir la devolución de dinero	*peh-'deer lah deh-boh-loo-see-'ohn deh dee-'neh-roh*
call (v) (the debt)	rescatar anticipadamente	*reh-skah-'tahr ahn-tee-see-pah-dah-'mehn-teh*
call (v) a strike	declarar una huelga	*deh-klah-'rahr 'oo-nah 'wel-gah*
call back (v)	retirar	*reh-tee-'rahr*
call feature	el reembolso a la vista	*ehl reh-ehm-'bohl-soh ah lah 'bees-tah*
call loan	el préstamo reembolsable a la vista	*ehl 'prehs-tah-moh reh-ehm-bohl-'sah-bleh ah lah 'bees-tah*
call money	el dinero a la vista	*ehl dee-'neh-roh ah lah 'bees-tah*
call option	la opción de retiro (bono) anticipadamente	*lah ohp-see-'ohn deh reh-'tee-roh ('boh-noh) ahn-tee-see-pah-dah-'mehn-teh*
call price	el precio de amortización de valores (los bonos antes de vencimiento)	*ehl 'preh-see-oh deh ah-mohr-tee-sah-see-'ohn deh bah-'loh-rehs (lohs 'boh-nohs 'ahn-tehs dehl behn-see-mee-'ehn-toh)*
call protection	la protección contra la exigibilidad a la vista	*lah proh-tehk-see-'ohn 'kohn-trah lah ehs-ee-hee-bee-lee-'dahd ah lah 'bees-tah*

call rate	el tipo de interés para préstamos diarios	*ehl 'tee-poh deh een-teh-'rehs 'pah-rah 'prehs-tah-mohs dee-'ah-ree-ohs*
call rule	la norma para poder ejercer la exigibilidad a la vista	*lah 'nohr-mah 'pah-rah poh-'dehr eh-hehr-'sehr lah eks-ee-hee-bee-lee-'dahd ah lah 'bees-tah*
camel's hair	el pelo de camello	*ehl 'peh-loh deh kah-'meh-yoh*
campaign productivity	la productividad de la campaña	*lah proh-dook-tee-bee-'dahd deh lah kahm-'pah-nyah*
camshaft	el eje de leva	*ehl 'eh-heh deh 'leh-bah*
cancel (v)	cancelar	*kahn-seh-'lahr*
cancelled check	el cheque cancelado	*ehl 'cheh-keh kahn-seh-'lah-doh*
candlestick	la vela	*lah 'beh-lah*
capacity	la capacidad de refinación, la capacidad	*lah kah-pah-see-'dahd deh reh-fee-nah-see-'ohn, lah kah-pah-see-'dahd*
capital (city)	la capital	*lah kah-pee-tahl*
capital (letter)	la mayúscula	*lah mah'yoos-koo-lah*
capital (money)	el capital	*ehl kah-pee-'tahl*
capital account	la cuenta de capital	*lah 'kwehn-tah deh kah-pee-'tahl*
capital allowance	la asignación por depreciaciones de capital	*lah ah-seeg-nah-see-'ohn pohr deh-preh-see-ah-see-'oh-nehs deh kah-pee-'tahl*
capital asset	el activo fijo	*ehl ahk-'tee-boh 'fee-hoh*
capital budget	el presupuesto de gastos de capital	*ehl preh-soo-'pwehs-toh deh 'gah-stohs deh kah-pee-'tahl*
capital expenditure	los gastos de capital	*lohs 'gah-stohs deh kah-pee-'tahl*
capital expenditure appraisal	la evaluación de gastos de capital	*lah eh bah-loo-ah-see-'ohn deh 'gah-stohs deh kah-pee-'tahl*
capital exports	las exportaciones de capital	*lahs ehks-pohr-tah-see-'oh-nehs deh kah-pee-'tahl*

capital gains (losses)	las ganancias (las pérdidas) de capital	*lahs gah-'nahn-see-ahs (lahs 'pehr-dee-dahs) deh kah-pee-'tahl*
capital goods	los bienes de capital	*lohs bee-'eh-nehs deh kah-pee-'tahl*
capital increase	el aumento de capital	*ehl ow-'mehn-toh deh kah-pee-'tahl*
capital market	el mercado de capital	*ehl mehr-'kah-doh deh kah-pee-'tahl*
capital spending	los gastos de capital	*lohs 'gah-stohs deh kah-pee-'tahl*
capital stock	capital social	*kah-pee-'tahl soh-see-'ahl*
capital structure	la estructura de capital	*lah ehs-trook-'too-rah deh kah-pee-'tahl*
capital surplus	el excedente de capital	*ehl ehks-seh-'dehn-teh deh kah-pee-'tahl*
capital-output ratio	la relación capital-producto	*lah reh-lah-see-'ohn kah-pee-'tahl proh-'dook-toh*
capitalism	el capitalismo	*ehl kah-pee-tah-'lees-moh*
capitalization	la capitalización	*lah kah-pee-tah-lee-sah-see-'ohn*
car	el carro	*ehl 'kah-rroh*
carbon	el carbón	*ehl kahr-'bohn*
carbon monoxide	el monóxido de carbono	*ehl moh-'nohk-see-doh deh kahr-'boh-noh*
carbon steel	el acero al carbono	*ehl ah-'seh-roh ahl kahr-'boh-noh*
card case	el tarjetero	*ehl tahr-heh-'teh-roh*
career	la profesión	*lah proh-feh-see-'ohn*
cargo	el cargamento, la carga	*ehl kahr-gah-'mehn-toh, lah 'kahr-gah*
carload	la vagonada	*lah bah-goh-'nah-dah*
carnet	el carnet	*ehl kahr-'neht*
carrier	el transportador	*ehl trahns-pohr-tah-'dohr*
carrier's risk	el riesgo del transportador	*ehl ree-'ehs-go dehl trahns-pohr-tah-'dohr*
carry back (v)	devolver, transferir al pasado	*deh-bohl-'behr, trahns-feh-'reer ahl pah-'sah-doh*
carrying value	el valor de acarreo	*ehl bah-'lohr deh ah-kah-'rreh-oh*

carryover	la suma pasada al frente	*lah 'soo-mah pah-'sah-dah ahl 'frehn-teh*
carryover (v)	arrastrar un saldo al siguiente período	*ah-rrah-'strahr oon 'sahl-doh ahl see-gee-'ehn-teh peh-'ree-oh-doh*
cartel	el cartel	*ehl kahr-'tehl*
carving knife	el trinchador, el cuchillo de trinchar	*ehl treen-chah-'dohr*
case (of wine)	la caja	*lah 'kah-hah*
cash	el efectivo	*ehl eh-fehk-'tee-boh*
cash (v)	hacer efectivo	*ah-'sehr eh-fehk-'tee-boh*
cash balance	el saldo de caja	*ehl 'sahl-doh deh 'kah-hah*
cash basis	en efectivo, al contado	*ehn eh-fehk-'tee-boh, ahl kohn-'tah-doh*
cash before delivery	el pago en efectivo antes de la entrega	*ehl 'pah-goh ehn eh-fehk-'tee-boh 'ahn-tehs deh lah ehn-'treh-gah*
cash book	el libro de caja	*ehl 'lee-broh deh 'kah-hah*
cash budget	el presupuesto de caja	*ehl preh-soo-'pwehs-toh deh 'kah-hah*
cash delivery	la entrega al momento y pago en efectivo	*lah ehn-'treh-gah ahl moh-'mehn-toh y 'pah-goh ehn eh-fehk-'tee-boh*
cash discount	el descuento en efectivo, descuento por pronto pago	*ehl dehs-'kwehn-toh ehn eh-fehk-'tee-boh, dehs-'kwehn-toh pohr 'prohn-toh 'pah-goh*
cash dividend	el dividendo en efectivo	*ehl dee-bee-'dehn-doh ehn eh-fehk-'tee-boh*
cash entry	el asiento de caja, la entrada de efectivo	*ehl ah-see-'ehn-toh deh 'kah-hah, lah ehn-'trah-dah deh eh-fehk-'tee-boh*
cash flow	el flujo de caja	*ehl 'floo-hoh deh 'kah-hah*
cash flow statement	el estado de flujo de caja	*ehl ehs-'tah-doh deh 'floo-hoh deh 'kah-hah*
cash in advance	el efectivo pagado por adelantado	*ehl eh-fehk-'tee-boh pah-'gah-doh pohr ah-deh-lahn-'tah-doh*
cash management	el manejo de caja	*ehl mah-'neh-hoh deh 'kah-hah*

cash on delivery	el pago de efectivo contra entrega	*ehl 'pah-goh deh eh-fehk-'tee-boh 'kohn-trah ehn-'treh-gah*
cash surrender value	el valor de rescate (póliza de seguros)	*ehl bah-'lohr deh rehs-'kah-teh ('poh-lee-sah deh seh-'goo-rohs)*
cash-and-carry	el sistema de pago al contado con el transporte pagado por el comprador	*ehl sees-'teh-mah deh 'pah-goh ahl kohn-'tah-doh kohn ehl trahns-'pohr-teh pah-'gah-doh pohr ehl kohm-prah-'dohr*
cashier's check	el cheque de gerencia	*ehl 'cheh-keh deh heh-'rehn-see-ah*
cashmere	la cachemira	*lah kah-cheh-'mee-rah*
cask (225 litres)	el tonel, el barril	*ehl toh-'nehl, ehl bah-'rreel*
cassette	el casette, la cinta magnetofónica	*ehl kah-'seh-teh, lah 'seen-tah mahg-neh-toh-'foh-nee-kah*
cast iron	el hierro fundido	*ehl 'yeh-rroh foon-'dee-doh*
casualty insurance	los seguros contra accidentes	*lohs seh-'goo-rohs 'kohn-trah ahk-see-'dehn-tehs*
catalogue	el catálogo	*ehl kah-'tah-loh-goh*
catalyst	el catalizador	*ehl kah-tah-lee-sah-'dohr*
cathode	el cátodo	*ehl 'kah-toh-doh*
ceiling	el techo	*ehl 'teh-choh*
cellular phone	el teléfono celular	*ehl teh-'leh-foh-noh seh-loo-'lahr*
census	el censo	*ehl 'sehn-soh*
census (to take the)	levantar el censo	*leh-bahn-'tahr ehl 'sehn-soh*
central bank	el banco central	*ehl 'bahn-koh sehn-'trahl*
central processing unit (computers)	la unidad procesadora central	*lah oo-nee-'dahd proh-seh-sah-'doh-rah sehn-trahl*
central rate	la tasa central	*lah 'tah-sah sehn-'trahl*
centralization	la centralización	*lah sehn-trah-lee-sah-see-'ohn*
certificate	el certificado	*ehl sehr-tee-fee-'kah-doh*
certificate of deposit	el certificado de depósito	*ehl sehr-tee-fee-'kah-doh deh deh-'poh-see-toh*

C

C

certificate of incorporation	la escritura de constitución (de una sociedad anónima)	*lah ehs-kree-'too-rah deh kohn-stee-too-see-'ohn (deh oo-nah soh-see-eh-'dahd ah-'noh-nee-mah)*
certificate of origin	el certificado de origen	*ehl sehr-tee-fee-'kah-doh deh oh-'ree-hehn*
certified check	el cheque certificado	*ehl 'cheh-keh sehr-tee-fee-'kah-doh*
certified public accountant (C.P.A.)	el contador público	*ehl kohn-tah-'dohr 'poo-blee-koh*
chain of command	la cadena de mando (la jerarquía)	*lah kah-'deh-nah deh 'mahn-doh (lah heh-rahr-'kee-ah*
chain store	la cadena de tiendas	*lah kah-'deh-nah deh tee-'ehn-dahs*
Chairman of the Board	el presidente de la junta directiva	*ehl preh-see-'dehn-teh deh lah 'hoon-tah dee-rehk-'tee-bah*
chamber of commerce	la cámara de comercio	*lah 'kah-mah-rah deh koh-'mehr-see-oh*
champagne glass	el vaso de champaña, la copa de champaña	*ehl 'bah-soh deh chahm-'pah-nyah, lah 'koh-pah deh chahm-'pah-nyah*
channel	el canal	*ehl kah-'nahl*
channel of distribution	el canal de distribución	*ehl kah-'nahl deh dees-tree-boo-see-'ohn*
chapter	el capítulo	*ehl kah-'pee-too-loh*
character	la cualidad, la condición	*lah kwah-lee-'dahd, lah kohn-dee-see-'ohn*
charge account	la cuenta de crédito	*lah 'kwehn-tah deh 'kreh-dee-toh*
charge chrome	la carga de cromo	*lah 'kahr-gah deh 'kroh-moh*
charge-off	el descargo	*ehl dehs-'kahr-goh*
charges	los cargos	*lohs 'kahr-gohs*
charter	el permiso legal para constituir una compañía	*ehl pehr-'mee-soh leh-'gahl 'pah-rah kohn-stee-too-eer 'oo-nah kohm-pan-'nyee-ah*
chartered accountant	el contador público	*ehl kohn-tah-'dohr 'poo-blee-koh*

charterparty agent	el agente de póliza de fletes	*ehl ah-'hehn-teh deh 'poh-lee-sah deh 'fleh-tehs*
chassis	el bastidor	*ehl 'bah-stee-dohr*
chattel mortgage	la hipoteca sobre bienes muebles	*lah ee-poh-'teh-kah 'soh-breh bee-'eh-nehs moo-'eh-blehs*
chattels	los bienes muebles	*lohs bee-'eh-nehs moo-'eh-blehs*
cheap	barato	*bah-'rah-toh*
check	el cheque	*ehl cheh-keh*
check (v)	investigar, verificar	*een-behs-tee-'gahr, beh-ree-fee-'kahr*
checking account	la cuenta corrienté	*lah 'kwehn-tah koh-rree-'ehn-teh*
checklist	la lista de verificación	*lah 'lee-stah deh beh-ree-fee-kah-see-'ohn*
cheese tray	la bandeja para queso	*lah bahn-'deh-hah 'pah-rah 'keh-soh*
chemical	químico	*'kee-mee-koh*
chemical (adj)	químico	*'kee-mee-koh*
chemistry	la química	*lah 'kee-mee-kah*
chief accountant	el jefe contador	*ehl 'heh-feh kohn-tah-'dohr*
chief buyer	el jefe de compras	*ehl 'heh-feh deh 'kohm-prahs*
chief executive	el director ejecutivo, el presidente ejecutivo	*ehl dee-rehk-'tohr eh-heh-koo-'tee-boh, ehl preh-see-'dehn-teh eh-heh-koo-'tee-boh*
china	la porcelana, la loza	*lah pohr-seh-'lah-nah, la 'loh-sah*
chip	el micrológico, el circuito integrado, el chip (m)	*ehl mee-kroh-'loh-hee-koh, ehl seer-koo-'ee-toh een-teh-'grah-doh, ehl cheep*
chloride	el cloruro	*ehl kloh-'roo-roh*
chloroform	el cloroformo	*ehl kloh-roh-'fohr-moh*
chromium	el cromo	*ehl 'kroh-moh*
cigarette case	la pitillera	*lah pee-tee-'yeh-rah*
circuit	el circuito	*ehl seer-koo-'ee-toh*
civil action	la acción civil	*lah ahk-see-'ohn see-'beel*

civil engineering	la ingeniería civil	*lah een-heh-nee-eh-'ree-ah*
claim	la reclamación	*lah reh-klah-mah-see-'ohn*
classified ad	el aviso clasificado	*ehl ah-'bee-soh klah-see-fee-'kah-doh*
classified sparkling wine	el vino espumoso clasificado	*ehl 'bee-noh ehs-poo-'moh-soh klah-see-fee-'kah-doh*
clean document	el documento limpio	*ehl doh-koo-'mehn-toh 'leem-pee-oh*
clear (v)	borrar	*boh-'rrahr*
clearing	la clarificación	*lah klah-ree-fee-kah-see-'ohn*
clearinghouse	la cámara de compensación	*lah 'kah-mah-rah deh kohm-pehn-sah-see-'ohn*
climate	el clima	*ehl 'klee-mah*
closed account (accounting)	la cuenta saldada	*lah 'kwehn-tah sahl'dah-dah*
closely held corporation	la compañía cerrada	*lah kohm-pah-'nyee-ah seh-rah-dah*
closing entry (accounting)	el asiento de cierre	*ehl ah-'see-ehn-toh deh see-'eh-reh*
closing price	el precio de cierre	*ehl 'preh-see-oh deh see-'eh-reh*
clothing	el vestido	*ehl beh-'stee-doh*
clouds	las nubes	*lahs 'noo-behs*
clutch	el embrague	*ehl ehm-'brah-geh*
clutch pedal	el pedal de embrague	*ehl peh-'dahl deh ehm-'brah-gue*
co-insurance	el coaseguro	*ehl koh-ah-seh-'goo-roh*
co-ownership	la copropiedad	*lah koh-proh-pee-eh-'dahd*
coal	el carbón	*ehl kahr-'bohn*
coast	la costa	*lah 'koh-stah*
coastal (adj)	costeño	*koh-'steh-nyoh*
coat	el abrigo, el saco	*ehl ah-'bree-goh, ehl 'sah-koh*
coated paper	el papel cuché, el papel revestido	*ehl pah-'pehl koo-'cheh, ehl pah-'ehl reh-vehs-'tee-doh*
coaxial cable	el cable coaxial	*ehl 'kah-bleh koh-ahks-ee-'ahl*

codicil	el codicilo	*ehl koh-dee-'see-loh*
coffee break	el descanso	*ehl dehs-'kahn-soh*
coffeepot	la cafetera	*lah kah-feh-'teh-rah*
coil	el serpentín	*ehl sehr-pehn-'teen*
cold rolling	el laminado en frío	*ehl lah-mee-'nah-doh ehn 'free-oh*
collar	el cuello	*ehl 'kweh-yoh*
collateral	el colateral	*ehl koh-lah-teh-'rahl*
colleague	el colega	*ehl koh-'leh-gah*
collect on delivery	cobrar a la entrega	*koh-'brahr ah lah ehn-'treh-gah*
collection period	el período de cobro	*ehl peh-'ree-oh-doh deh 'koh-broh*
collective agreement	el convenio de trabajo colectivo	*ehl kohn-'beh-nee-oh deh trah-'bah-hoh koh-lehk-'tee-boh*
collective bargaining	el contrato colectivo, el convenio colectivo	*ehl kohn-'trah-toh koh-lehk-'tee-boh, ehl kohn-'beh-nee-oh koh-lehk-'tee-boh*
collector of customs	el administrador de aduanas	*ehl ahd-mee-nee-strah-'dohr de ah-'dwah-nahs*
colloquium	el coloquio	*ehl koh-'loh-kee-oh*
column	la columna	*lah koh-'loom-nah*
combination	la combinación	*lah kohm-bee-nah-see-'ohn*
combination duty	el gravamen combinado, el arancel combinado	*ehl grah-'bah-mehn kohm-bee-'nah-doh, ehl ah-rahn-'sehl kohm-bee-'nah-doh*
command	el mando	*ehl 'mahn-doh*
commerce	el comercio	*ehl koh-'mehr-see-oh*
commercial ad	el anuncio publicitario	*ehl ah-'noon-see-oh poo-blee-see-'tah-ree-oh*
commercial bank	el banco comercial	*ehl 'bahn-koh koh-mehr-see-'ahl*
commercial draft	letras de cambio comerciales	*'leh-trahs deh 'kahm-bee-oh koh-mehr-see-'ah-lehs*
commercial grade	la calidad comercial	*lah kah-lee-'dahd koh-mehr-see-'ahl*
commercial invoice	la factura comercial	*lah fahk-'too-rah koh-mehr-see-'ahl*

commercial paper	el pagaré financiero	*ehl pah-gah-'reh fee-nahn-see-'eh-roh*
commission (agencies)	la junta	*lah 'hoon-tah*
commission (agency)	el organismo	*ehl ohr-gah-'nees-moh*
commission (fee)	la comisión	*lah koh-mee-see-'ohn*
commitment	el compromiso	*ehl kohm-proh-'mee-soh*
commodity	la mercancía	*lah mehr-kan-'see-ah*
commodity exchange	la bolsa, el comercio mercantil	*lah 'bohl-sah, ehl koh-'mehr-see-oh mehr-kahn-'teel*
common carrier	la empresa de transporte	*lah ehm-'preh-sah deh trahns-'pohr-teh*
Common Market	el Mercado Común	*ehl mehr-'kah-doh koh-'moon*
common stock	las acciones ordinarias, las acciones comunes	*lahs ahk-see-'oh-nehs ohr-dee-'nah-ree-ahs, lahs ahk-see-'oh-nehs koh-'moo-nehs*
communication link	enlace de comunicación, vínculo de comunicación	*ehn-'lah-seh deh koh-moo-nee-kah-see-'ohn, 'been-koo-loh deh koh-moo-nee-kah-see-'ohn*
communism	el comunismo	*ehl koh-moo-'nees-moh*
compact disk	el disco compacto	*ehl 'dees-koh kohm-'pahk-toh*
company	la compañía	*lah kohm-pa-'nyee-ah*
company (nationalized)	la compañía nacionalizada	*lah kohm-pah-'nyee-ah nah-see-oh-nah-lee-'sah-dah*
company (state-owned)	la compañía estatal	*lah kohm-pah-'nyee-ah eh-stah-'tahl*
company (privately-owned)	la compañía privada	*lah kohm-pah-'nyee-ah pree-'bah-dah*
company (privatized)	la compañía privatizada	*la kohm-pah-'nyee-ah pree-'bah-tee-'sah-dah*
company goal	el objetivo de la compañía	*ehl ohb-heh-'tee-boh deh lah kohm-pa-'nyee-ah*
company policy	la política de la compañía	*lah poh-'lee-tee-kah deh lah kohm-pa-'nyee-ah*

compensating balance	el saldo compensatorio	*ehl 'sahl-doh kohm-pehn-sah-'toh-ree-oh*
compensation	la indemnización	*lah een-dehm-nee-sah-see-'ohn*
competition	la competencia	*lah kohm-peh-'tehn-see-ah*
competitive advantage	la ventaja competitiva	*lah behn-'tah-hah kohm-peh-teh-'tee-bah*
competitive edge	la ventaja competitiva	*lah behn-'tah-hah kohm-peh-teh-'tee-bah*
competitive price	el precio competitivo	*ehl 'preh-see-oh kohm-peh-teh-'tee-boh*
competitive strategy	la estrategia competitiva	*lah ehs-trah-'teh-hee-ah kohm-peh-teh-'tee-bah*
competitor	el competidor	*ehl kohm-peh-tee-'dohr*
competitor analysis	el análisis de la competencia	*ehl ah-'nah-lee-sees deh lah kohm-peh-'tehn-see-ah*
complimentary copy	el ejemplar gratuito	*ehl eh-hehm-plahr grah-too-'ee-toh*
component	el componente	*ehl kohm-poh-'nehn-teh*
composite index	el índice compuesto	*ehl 'een-dee-seh kohm-'pwehs-toh*
composition	la composición	*lah kohm-poh-see-see-'ohn*
compound	el compuesto	*ehl kohm-'pweh-stoh*
compound (chemical)	el compuesto químico	*ehl kohm-'pweh-stoh 'kee-mee-koh*
compound interest	el interés compuesto	*ehl een-teh-'rehs kohm-'pwehs-toh*
compounding intervals	el período de capitalización	*ehl peh-'ree-oh-doh deh kah-pee-tah-lee-sah-see-'ohn*
comptroller	el contralor	*ehl kohn-trah-'lohr*
computer	la computadora, el ordenador (Spain)	*lah kohm-poo-tah-'doh-rah, ehl ohr-deh-nah-'dohr*
computer bank	el banco de datos	*ehl 'bahn-koh deh 'dah-tohs*
computer center	el centro de computación	*ehl 'sehn-troh deh kohm-poo-tah-see-'ohn*
computer input	los datos-entrada a la computadora	*lohs 'dah-tohs-ehn-'trah-dah ah lah kohm-poo-tah-'doh-rah*
computer language	el lenguaje de computación	*ehl lehn-'gwah-heh deh kohm-poo-tah-see-'ohn*

computer memory	la memoria de la computadora	*lah meh-'moh-ree-ah deh la kohm-poo-tah-'doh-rah*
computer output	la salida de información de la computadora	*lah sah-'lee-dah deh een-fohr-mah-see-'ohn deh lah kohm-poo-tah-'doh-rah*
computer program	la programación de computadora	*lah proh-gah-mah-see-'ohn deh kohm-poo-tah-'doh-rah*
computer storage	el almacenaje de la computadora	*ehl ahl-mah-seh-'nah-heh deh la kohm-poo-tah-'doh-rah*
computer terminal	el terminal de computadora	*ehl tehr-mee-'nahl deh kohm-poo-tah-'doh-rah*
concentration	la concentración	*lah kohn-sehn-trah-see-'ohn*
concentration bank	el banco de centralización	*ehl 'bahn-koh deh sehn-trah-lee-sah-see-'ohn*
condensor	el condensador	*ehl kohn-dehn-sah-'dohr*
conditional acceptance	la aceptación condicional	*lah ah-sehp-tah-see-'ohn kohn-dee-see-oh-'nahl*
conditional sales contract	el contrato de ventas condicional	*ehl kohn-'trah-toh deh 'behn-tahs kohn-dee-see-oh-'nahl*
conductor	el conductor	*ehl kohn-dook-'tohr*
conference room	la sala de conferencias	*lah 'sah-lah deh kohn-feh-'rehn-see-ahs*
confidential	confidencial	*kohn-fee-dehn-see-'ahl*
confirmation of order	la confiscación de pedido	*lah kohn-fees-kah-see-'ohn deh peh-'dee-doh*
conflict of interest	el conflicto de intereses	*ehl kohn-'fleek-toh deh een-teh-'reh-sehs*
conglomerate	el conglomerado	*ehl kohn-gloh-meh-'rah-doh*
connecting rod	la biela	*lah bee-'eh-lah*
conservation	la conservación	*lah kohn-sehr-bah-see-'ohn*
consideration (bus. law)	la deliberación	*lah deh-lee-beh-rah-see-'ohn*
consignee	el consignatario	*ehl kohn-seeg-nah-'toh-ree-oh*
consignment	la consignación	*lah kohn-seeg-nah-see-'ohn*
consignment note	la carta de consignación	*lah 'kahr-tah deh kohn-seeg-nah-see-'ohn*

consolidated financial statement	el estado financiero consolidado	*ehl ehs-'tah-doh fee-'nahn-see-eh-roh kohn-soh-lee-'dah-doh*
consolidation	la consolidación	*lah kohn-soh-lee-dah-see-'ohn*
consortium	el consorcio	*ehl kohn-'sohr-see-oh*
consular invoice	la factura consular	*lah fahk-'too-rah kohn-soo-'lahr*
consultant	el consultor	*ehl kohn-sool-'tohr*
consumer	el consumidor	*ehl kohn-soo-mee-'dohr*
consumer acceptance	la aceptación por parte de los consumidores	*lah ah-seh-tah-see-'ohn pohr 'pahr-teh deh lohs kohn-soo-mee-'doh-rehs*
consumer credit	el crédito al consumidor	*ehl 'kreh-dee-toh ahl kohn-soo-mee-'dohr*
consumer goods	los bienes de consumo	*lohs bee-'eh-nehs deh kohn-'soo-moh*
consumer price index	el índice de precios al consumidor	*ehl 'een-dee-seh deh 'preh-see-ohs ahl kohn-soo-mee-'dohr*
consumer research	la investigación acerca de los hábitos de consumo	*lah een-behs-tee-gah-see-'ohn ah-'sehr-kah deh lohs 'ah-bee-tohs deh kohn-'soo-moh*
consumer satisfaction	la satisfacción del consumidor	*lah sah-tees-fahk-see-'ohn dehl kohn-soo-mee-'dohr*
consuming center	el centro de consumo	*ehl 'sehn-troh deh kohn-'soo-moh*
consumption (of provisions) (animal)	el consumo animal	*ehl kohn-'soo-moh ah-nee-'mahl*
consumption (of provisions) (human)	el consumo humano	*ehl kohn-'soo-moh oo-'mah-noh*
consumption reduction	la reducción en el consumo	*lah reh-dook-see-'ohn ehn ehl kohn-'soo-moh*
container	el envase	*ehl ehn-'bah-seh*
contaminate (v)	contaminar	*kohn-tah-mee-'nahr*
content	el contenido	*ehl kohn-teh-'nee-doh*
contingencies	las contingencias	*lahs kohn-teen-'hehn-see-ahs*

contingency fund	el fondo de contingencia	*ehl 'fohn-doh deh kohn-teen-'hehn-see-ah*
contingent liability	el pasivo contingente	*ehl pah-'see-boh kohn-teen-'hehn-teh*
continuous caster	el laminador continuo	*ehl lah-mee-nah-'dohr kohn-'tee-noo-oh*
continuous compounding	la capitalización continua gestión	*lah kah-pee-tah-lee-sah-see-'ohn kohn-'tee-noo-ah hehs-tee-'ohn*
contract	el contrato	*ehl kohn-'trah-toh*
contract carrier	la empresa de transporte por contrato	*lah ehm-'preh-sah deh trahs-'pohr-teh pohr kohn-'trah-toh*
contract month	el mes de la entrega	*ehl mehs deh lah ehn-'treh-gah*
control	el control	*ehl kohn-'trohl*
controllable costs	los gastos controlables	*lohs 'gah-stohs kohn-troh-'lah-blehs*
controller	el contralor	*ehl kohn-trah-'lohr*
controlling interest	el interés predominante	*ehl een-teh-'rehs preh-doh-mee-'nahn-teh*
conversion price	el valor de conversión	*ehl bah-'lohr deh kohn-behr-see-'ohn*
convert (v)	transformar	*trans-fohr-'mahr*
convertible debentures	las obligaciones convertibles	*lahs ohb-lee-gah-see-'oh-nehs kohn-behr-'tee-blehs*
convertible preferred stocks	las acciones preferidas convertibles	*lahs ahk-see-'oh-nehs preh-feh-'ree-dahs kohn-behr-'tee-blehs*
conveyor	el transportador	*ehl trahns-pohr-tah-'dohr*
conveyor belt	la correa transportadora	*lah koh-'rreh-ah trans-pohr-tah-'doh-rah*
cooperation agreement	el acuerdo de cooperación	*ehl ah-'kwehr-doh deh koh-oh-peh-rah-see-'ohn*
cooperative	la cooperativa	*lah koh-oh-peh-rah-'tee-bah*
cooperative advertising	la publicidad cooperativa	*lah poo-blee-see-'dahd koh-oh-peh-rah-'tee-bah*
copper	el cobre	*ehl 'koh-breh*
copy (v)	copiar, reproducir datos	*koh-pee-'ahr, reh-proh-doo-'seer 'dah-tohs*

copy (text)	el ejemplar	*ehl eh-hehm-'plahr*
copy testing	la prueba de copia	*lah proo-'eh-bah deh 'koh-pee-ah*
copyright	los derechos de autor	*lohs deh-'reh-chohs deh ow-'tohr*
coral reef	el arrecife de coral	*ehl ah-rreh-'see-feh deh koh-rahl*
cork	el corcho	*ehl 'kohr-choh*
corkscrew	el sacacorchos	*ehl sah-kah-'kohr-chohs*
corporate growth	el crecimiento corporativo	*ehl kreh-see-mee-'ehn-toh kohr-poh-rah-'tee-boh*
corporate image	la imagen corporativa	*lah ee-'mah-gen kohr-poh-rah-'tee-bah*
corporate planning	la planificación corporativa	*lah plah-nee-fee-kah-see-'ohn kohr-poh-rah-'tee-bah*
corporate structure	la estructura corporativa	*lah ehs-trook-'too-rah kohr-poh-rah-'tee-bah*
corporation	la corporación, la sociedad anónima	*lah kohr-poh-rah-see-'ohn, lah soh-see-eh-'dahd ah-'noh-nee-mah*
corporation tax	el impuesto a la corporación	*ehl eem-'pwehs-toh ah lah kohr-poh-rah-see-'ohn*
corpus	los bienes tangibles	*lohs bee-eh-nehs tahn-'hee-blehs*
correspondence	la correspondencia	*lah koh-rreh-spohn-'dehn-see-ah*
correspondent bank	el banco corresponsal	*ehl 'bahn-koh koh-rreh-spohn-'sahl*
cortisone	la cortisona	*lah kohr-tee-'soh-nah*
cost	el costo, el coste	*ehl 'koh-stoh, ehl 'koh-steh*
cost (v)	costear	*koh-steh-'ahr*
cost accounting	la contabilidad de costos	*lah kohn-tah-bee-lee-'dahd deh 'koh-stohs*
cost analysis	el análisis de costos	*ehl ah-'nah-lee-sees deh 'koh-stohs*
cost and freight	el costo y flete	*ehl koh-'stoh ee 'fleh-teh*
cost control	el control de costos	*ehl kohn-'trohl deh 'koh-stohs*

cost factor	el factor de costo	*ehl fahk-'tohr deh 'koh-stoh*
cost of capital	el costo de capital	*ehl 'koh-stoh deh kah-'ee-'tahl*
cost of goods sold	el costo de ventas	*ehl 'koh-stoh deh 'behn-tahs*
cost of living	el costo de vida	*ehl 'koh-stoh deh 'bee-dah*
cost reduction	la reducción de costos	*lah reh-dook-see-'ohn deh 'koh-stohs*
cost-benefit analysis	el análisis de costos y beneficios	*ehl ah-'nah-lee-sees deh 'koh-stohs ee beh-neh-'fee-see-ohs*
cost-effective (adj)	costo efectivo	*'koh-stoh eh-fehk-'tee-boh*
cost-plus contract	el contrato de costo más tanto fijo	*ehl kohn-'trah-toh deh 'koh-stoh mahs 'tahn-toh 'fee-hoh*
cost-price squeeze	la diferencia entre precio y costo tan pequeña que puede originar la quiebra	*lah dee-feh-'rehn-see-ah 'ehn-treh 'preh-see-oh ee 'koh-stoh tahn peh-'keh-nyah keh 'pweh-deh oh-ree-hee-'nahr lah kee-'eh-brah*
cotton	el algodón	*ehl ahl-goh-'dohn*
cough (v)	toser	*toh-'sehr*
cough drop	la pastilla para la tos	*lah pahs-'tee-yah 'pah-rah lah tohs*
cough syrup	el jarabe para la tos	*ehl hah-'rah-beh 'pah-rah lah tohs*
counter check	el talón bancario	*ehl tah-'lohn bahn-'kah-ree-oh*
counterfeit	la falsificación	*lah fahl-see-fee-kah-see-'ohn*
countervailing duty	el arancel compensatorio	*ehl ah-rahn-'sehl kohm-pehn-sah-'toh-ree-oh*
country	el país	*ehl pah-'ees*
country of origin	el país de origen	*ehl pah-'ees deh oh-'ree-hehn*
country of risk	el país de riesgo	*ehl pah-'ees deh ree-'ehs-goh*
coupon (bond interest)	el cupón	*ehl koo-'pohn*

courier service	el servicio de correo, el servicio de mensajero	*ehl sehr-'bee-see-oh deh koh-'rreh-oh, ehl sehr-'bee-see-oh deh mehn-sah-'heh-roh*
covariance	modelo de equilibrio	*moh-'deh-loh deh eh-kee-'lee-bree-oh*
covenant (promises)	el acuerdo	*ehl ah-'kwehr-doh*
cover	la cubierta	*lah koo-bee-'ehr-tah*
cover charge	el cargo de admisión	*ehl 'kahr-goh deh ahd-mee-see-'ohn*
cover letter	la carta con anexos, la carta de transmisión	*lah 'kahr-tah kohn ah-'nehk-sohs, lah 'kahr-tah deh trans-mee-see-'ohn*
cover ratio	el porcentaje de cobertura	*ehl pohr-sehn-'tah-heh deh koh-behr-'too-rah*
coverage	la cobertura	*lah koh-behr-'too-rah*
cowhide	el cuero de vaca	*ehl 'kweh-roh deh 'bah-kah*
cracking	el craqueo	*ehl krah-'keh-oh*
crane	la grúa	*lah 'groo-ah*
crane (revolving)	grúa giratoria	*'groo-ah hee-rah-'toh-ree-ah*
crankshaft	el cigüeñal	*ehl see-gweh-'nyahl*
crawling peg	la paridad móvil	*lah pah-ree-'dahd 'moh-beel*
credit	el crédito	*ehl 'kreh-dee-toh*
credit (v)	acreditar	*ah-kreh-dee-'tahr*
credit balance	el saldo crediticio	*ehl 'sahl-doh kreh-dee-'tee-see-oh*
credit bank	el crédito bancario	*ehl 'kreh-dee-toh bahn-'kah-ree-oh*
credit bureau	la oficina de crédito	*lah oh-fee-'see-nah deh 'kreh-dee-toh*
credit card	la tarjeta de crédito	*lah tahr-'heh-tah deh 'kreh-dee-toh*
credit control	el control de crédito	*ehl kohn-'trohl deh 'kreh-dee-toh*
credit insurances	los seguros de créditos	*lohs seh-'goo-rohs deh 'kreh-dee-tohs*
credit line	la línea de crédito	*lah 'lee-neh-ah deh 'kreh-dee-toh*

credit management	la gerencia de crédito	*lah heh-'rehn-see-ah deh 'kreh-dee-toh*
credit note	la nota de crédito	*lah 'noh-tah deh 'kreh-dee-toh*
credit rating	la clasificación de créditos	*lah klah-see-fee-kah-see-'ohn deh 'kreh-dee-tohs*
credit reference	la referencia de crédito	*lah reh-feh-'rehn-see-ah deh 'kreh-dee-toh*
credit terms	las condiciones de crédito	*lahs kohn-dee-see-'oh-nehs*
credit union	la unión crediticia	*lah oo-nee-'ohn kreh-dee-'tee-see-ah*
creditor	el acreedor	*ehl ah-kreh-eh-'dohr*
critical path analysis	el análisis del camino crítico	*ehl ah-'nah-lee-sees dehl kah-'mee-noh 'kree-tee-koh*
crop	la cosecha	*lah koh-'seh-chah*
crop rotation	la rotación de las cosechas	*lah roh-tah-see-'ohn deh lahs koh-'seh-chahs*
crop rotation (improper)	la rotación impropia de las cosechas	*lah roh-tah-see-'ohn eem-'proh-pee-ah deh lahs koh-'seh-chahs*
cross-licensing	la concesión recíproca de licencias	*lah kohn-see-see-'ohn reh-'see-proh-koh deh lee-'sehn-see-ahs*
crosscheck	el control cruzado	*ehl kohn-'trohl kroo-'sah-doh*
crucible	el crisol	*ehl kree-'sohl*
crude (adj)	crudo	*'kroo-doh*
crude oil	crudo, bruto, aceite bruto, petróleo crudo	*'kroo-doh, 'broo-toh, ah-'see-ee-teh 'broo-toh, peh-'troh-leh-oh 'kroo-doh*
crude oil (excess)	crudo en exceso	*'kroo-doh ehn ehk-'seh-soh*
crystal glass manufacturing	la manufactura de vasos de cristal, la fabricación de vasos de cristal	*lah mah-noo-fahk-'too-rah deh 'bah-sohs deh kree-'stahl, lah fah-bree-kah-see-'ohn deh 'bah-sohs deh kree-'stahl*
crystallization	la cristalización	*lah krees-tah-lee-sah-see-'ohn*
cuff link	los gemelos, los yugos	*lohs heh-'meh-lohs, lohs 'yoo-gohs*

cultural export permit	el permiso de exportación cultural	*ehl pehr-'mee-soh deh ehks-pohr-tah-see-'ohn kool-too-'rahl*
cultural property	las propiedades culturales	*lahs proh-pee-eh-'dah-dehs kool-too-'rah-lehs*
cum dividend	el dividendo incluso	*ehl dee-bee-'dehn-doh een-'kloo-soh*
cumulative	acumulativo	*ah-koo-moo-lah-'tee-boh*
cumulative preferred stocks	las acciones preferentes acumulativas	*lahs ahk-see-see-'oh-nehs preh-feh-'rehn-tehs ah-koo-moo-'lah-tee-bahs*
cup	la taza	*lah 'tah-sah*
cupola	el horno de ladrillo	*ehl 'ohr-noh deh lah-'dree-yoh*
currency	el dinero en circulación	*ehl dee-'neh-roh ehn seer-koo-lah-see-'ohn*
currency band	el bono pagadero en moneda nacional	*ehl 'boh-noh pah-gah-'deh-roh ehn moh-'neh-dah nah-see-oh-'nahl*
currency clause	la cláusula monetaria	*lah 'klow-soo-lah moh-neh-'tah-ree-ah*
currency conversion	la conversión monetaria	*lah kohn-behr-see-'ohn moh-neh-'tah-ree-ah*
currency exchange	el intercambio monetario	*ehl een-tehr-'kahm-bee-oh moh-neh-'tah-ree-oh*
current, electrical	la corriente	*lah koh-rree-'ehn-teh*
current (up to date)	actual	*ahk-too-ahl*
current account	la cuenta corriente	*lah 'kwehn-tah koh-rree-'ehn-teh*
current asset	el activo circulante	*ehl ahk-'tee-boh seer-koo-'lahn-teh*
current liabilities	los pasivos circulantes	*lohs pah-'see-bohs seer-koo-'lahn-tehs*
current ratio	el coeficiente de solvencia	*ehl koh-eh-fee-see-'ehn-teh deh sohl-'behn-see-ah*
current yield	el rendimiento corriente	*ehl rehn-dee-mee-'ehn-toh koh-rree-'ehn-teh*
cursor	el cursor	*ehl koor-'sohr*
customer	el cliente	*ehl klee-'ehn-teh*
customer service	el servicio al cliente	*ehl sehr-'bee-see-oh ahl klee-'ehn-teh*

customs	la aduana	*lah ah-'dwah-nah*
customs broker	el agente de aduana	*ehl ah-'hehn-teh deh ah-dwah-nah*
customs duty	el derecho de aduana	*ehl deh-'reh-choh deh ah-dwah-nah*
customs entry	la entrada de aduana	*lah ehn-'trah-dah deh ah-dwah-nah*
customs union	la unión aduanera	*lah oo-nee-'ohn ah-dwah-'neh-rah*
cut (v)	cortar	*kohr-'tahr*
cutback	el recorte, la reducción de gastos	*ehl reh-'kohr-teh, lah reh-dook-see-'ohn deh 'gah-stohs*
cutlery	los cubiertos, la cuchillería	*lohs koo-bee'ehr-tohs, la koo-chee-yehr-'ee-ah*
cycle	el ciclo	*ehl 'see-kloh*
cycle (biological)	ciclo biológico	*'see-kloh bee-oh-'loh-hee-koh*
cycle billing	la facturación cíclica	*lah fahk-too-rah-see-'ohn 'see-klee-kah*

D

daily	el diario	*ehl dee-'ah-ree-oh*
daily newspaper	el periódico, el diario	*ehl peh-ree-'oh-dee-koh, ehl dee-'ah-ree-oh*
dairy products	los productos lácteos	*lohs proh-'dook-tohs 'lahk-teh-ohs*
dam	la represa	*lah reh-'preh-sah*
damage	los daños y perjuicios	*lohs 'dah-nyohs ee pehr-hoo-'ee-see-ohs*
damage (environmental)	daño	*'dah-nyoh*
danger	el peligro	*ehl peh-'lee-groh*
data	los datos, la información particular a computadoras	*lohs 'dah-tohs, lah een-fohr-mah-see-'ohn pahr-tee-koo-'lahr ah kohm-poo-tah-'doh-rahs*
data acquisition	la adquisición de datos	*lah ahd-kee-see-see-'ohn deh 'dah-tohs*

data bank	el banco de datos	*ehl 'bahn-koh deh 'dah-tohs*
data base	la base de datos	*lah 'bah-seh deh 'dah-tohs*
data entry	la entrada de datos	*la ehn-'trah-dah deh 'dah-tohs*
data processing	la elaboración de los datos, el procesamiento de datos	*lah eh-lah-boh-rah-see-'ohn deh lohs 'dah-tohs, ehl proh-seh-sah-mee-'ehn-toh deh 'dah-tohs*
data storage	el almacenamiento de datos	*ehl alh-mah-seh-nah-mee-'ehn-toh deh 'dah-tohs*
date of delivery	la fecha de entrega	*lah 'feh-chah deh ehn-'treh-gah*
day loan	el préstamo diario	*ehl 'preh-stah-moh dee-'ah-ree-oh*
day order (stock market)	la orden que caduca después de un día	*lah 'ohr-dehn keh kah-'doo-kah dehs-'pwehs deh oon 'dee-ah*
dead freight	el falso flete	*ehl 'fahl-soh 'fleh-teh*
dead rent	la parte de renta reservada para uso futuro	*lah 'pahr-teh deh 'rehn-tah reh-sehr-'bah-dah 'pah-rah 'oo-soh foo-'too-roh*
deadline	el plazo, el término	*ehl 'plah-soh, ehl 'tehr-mee-noh*
deadlock	el estancamiento, el impase	*ehl ehs-tahn-kah-mee-'ehn-toh, ehl eem-'pah-seh*
deal	el negocio	*ehl neh-'goh-see-oh*
deal (v)	comerciar	*koh-mehr-see-'ahr*
dealer	el comerciante, el detallista, el negociante	*ehl koh-mehr-see-'ahn-teh, ehl deh-tah-'yees-tah, ehl neh-goh-see-'ahn-teh*
dealership	el comercio, el negocio	*ehl koh-'mehr-see-oh, ehl neh-'goh-see-oh*
death rate	la mortalidad	*lah mohr-tah-lee-'dahd*
death rate (infant)	mortalidad infantil	*mohr-tah-lee-'dahd een-fahn-'teel*
debentures	las obligaciones (sinónimo genérico de deuda)	*lahs ohb-lee-gah-see-'oh-nehs*
debit	el cargo, el débito	*ehl 'kahr-goh, ehl 'deh-bee-toh*
debit entry	el asiento en el debe, el débito	*ehl ah-see-'ehn-toh ehn ehl 'deh-beh, ehl 'deh-bee-toh*

D

debit note	la nota de débito	*lah 'noh-tah deh 'deh-bee-toh*
debt	la deuda	*lah deh-'oo-dah*
debug (v)	corregir	*koh-reh-'heer*
decanter	el decantador	*ehl deh-kahn-tah-'dohr*
deceit	el engaño	*ehl ehn-'gah-nyoh*
deck	la cubierta	*lah koo-bee-'ehr-tah*
deck (lower)	la cubierta inferior	*lah koo-bee-'ehr-tah een-feh-ree-'ohr*
deck (middle)	la cubierta intermedia	*lah koo-bee-'ehr-tah een-tehr-'meh-dee-ah*
deck (top, main)	la cubierta superior	*lah koo-bee-'ehr-tah soo-peh-ree-'ohr*
deductible	deducible	*deh-doo-'see-bleh*
deduction	la deducción	*lah deh-dook-see-'ohn*
deed	la escritura	*lah ehs-kree-'too-rah*
deed of sale	el contrato de ventas	*ehl kohn-'trah-toh deh 'behn-tahs*
deed of transfer	el contrato de traspaso	*ehl kohn-'trah-toh deh trahs-'pah-soh*
deed of trust	la escritura de fideicomiso	*lah ehs-kree-'too-rah deh fee-deh-ee-koh-'mee-soh*
default (v)	faltar, incumplir	*fahl-'tahr, een-koom-'pleer*
defective	defectuoso	*deh-fehk-too-'oh-soh*
deferred annuities	las anualidades diferidas	*lahs ah-noo-ah-lee-'dah-dehs dee-feh-'ree-dahs*
deferred assets	los cargos diferidos, los activos diferidos	*lohs 'kahr-gohs dee-feh-'ree-dohs, lohs ahk-'tee-bohs dee-feh-'ree-dohs*
deferred charges	los cargos diferidos	*lohs 'kahr-gohs dee-feh-'ree-dohs*
deferred deliveries	las entregas diferidas	*lahs ehn-'treh-gahs dee-feh-'ree-dahs*
deferred income	los ingresos diferidos	*lohs een-'greh-sohs dee-feh-'ree-dohs*
deferred liabilities	los pasivos diferidos	*lohs pah-'see-bohs dee-feh-'ree-dohs*
deferred taxes	los impuestos diferidos	*lohs eem-'pweh-stohs dee-feh-'ree-dohs*

D

deficit	el déficit	*ehl 'deh-fee-seet*
deficit financing	el financiamiento mediante déficit	*ehl fee-nahn-see-ah-mee-'ehn-toh meh-dee-ahn-teh 'deh-fee-seet*
deficit spending	los gastos deficitarios	*lohs 'gah-stohs deh-fee-see-'tah-ree-ohs*
deflation	la deflación	*lah deh-flah-see-'ohn*
defoliating agent	agente desfoliante (m)	*ah-'hehn-teh dehs-foh-lee-'ahn-teh*
deforestation	deforestación, despoblación forestal	*deh-foh-reh-stah-see-'ohn, dehs-poh-blah-see-'ohn foh-reh-'stahl*
defroster	el descongelador	*ehl dehs-kohn-heh-lah-'dohr*
degree	el grado	*ehl 'grah-doh*
delay	el retardo, la demora	*ehl reh-'tahr-doh, lah deh-moh-rah*
delete (v)	eliminar	*eh-lee-mee-'nahr*
delinquent account	la cuenta atrasada	*lah 'kwehn-tah ah-trah-'sah-dah*
delivery	la entrega	*lah ehn-'treh-gah*
delivery date	la fecha de entrega	*lah 'feh-chah deh ehn-'treh-gah*
delivery notice	el aviso de entrega	*ehl ah-'bee-soh deh ehn-'treh-gah*
delivery points	los puntos de entrega	*lohs 'poon-tohs deh ehn-'treh-gah*
delivery price	el precio de entrega	*ehl preh-see-oh deh ehn-'treh-gah*
demand	la demanda	*lah deh-'mahn-dah*
demand (v)	demandar	*deh-mahn-'dahr*
demand deposit	el depósito a la vista	*ehl deh-'poh-see-toh ah lah 'bee-stah*
demand line of credit	la línea de crédito a la vista	*lah 'lee-neh-ah deh 'kreh-dee-toh ah la 'bee-stah*
demographic	demográfico	*deh-moh-'grah-fee-koh*
demotion	el degrado, el descenso	*ehl deh-'grah-doh, ehl deh-'sehn-soh*
demurrage	la demora, los gastos de estadía	*lah deh-'moh-rah, lohs 'gah-stohs deh eh-stah-'dee-ah*

D

density	la densidad	*lah dehn-see-'dahd*
department	el departamento	*ehl deh-pahr-tah-'mehn-toh*
department store	el gran almacén, la tienda por departamentos	*ehl grahn ahl-mah-'sehn, lah tee-'ehn-dah pohr deh-pahr-tah-'mehn-tohs*
depletion accounting	la contabilidad de agotamiento	*lah kohn-tah-bee-lee-'dahd deh ah-goh-tah-mee-'ehn-toh*
depletion control	el control de agotamiento	*ehl kohn-'trohl deh ah-goh-tah-mee-'ehn-toh*
deposit	el depósito	*ehl deh-'poh-see-toh*
deposit account	la cuenta de depósito	*lah 'kwehn-tah deh deh-'poh-see-toh*
depository	la depositaria	*lah deh-poh-see-'tah-ree-ah*
depreciation	la depreciación	*lah deh-preh-see-ah-see-'ohn*
depreciation allowance	la provisión para depreciación, la reserva para depreciación	*lah proh-beeh-see-'ohn pah-rah deh-preh-see-ah-see-'ohn, lah reh-'sehr-bah 'pah-rah deh-preh-see-ah-see-'ohn*
depreciation of currency	la depreciación de la moneda	*lah deh-preh-see-ah-see-'ohn deh lah moh-'neh-dah*
depression	la depresión	*lah deh-preh-see-'ohn*
depth analysis	el análisis del puntal de arqueo	*ehl ah-'nah-lee-sees dehl poon-'tahl deh ahr-'keh-oh*
deputy chairman	el presidente delegado	*ehl preh-see-'dehn-teh deh-leh-'gah-doh*
deputy manager	el asistente al gerente	*ehl ah-sees-'tehn-teh ahl heh-'rehn-teh*
derrick	la torre de perforación (f)	*lah 'toh-rreh deh pehr-foh-rah-see-'ohn*
desert	el desierto	*ehl deh-see-'ehr-toh*
desertification	la desertificación	*lah deh-sehr-tee-fee-kah-see-'ohn*
design (v)	diseñar	*dee-seh-'nyahr*
design engineering	la ingeniería de diseño	*lah een-heh-nee-eh-'ree-ah deh dee-'seh-nyoh*
designer	el diseñador	*ehl dee-seh-nyah-'dohr*

D

desktop publishing	la editorial de despacho, editorial de sobremesa	*lah eh-dee-toh-ree-'ahl deh dehs-'pah-choh, eh-dee-toh-ree-'ahl deh soh-breh-'meh-sah*
dessert plate	el plato de postre	*ehl 'plah-toh deh 'poh-streh*
destruction	la destrucción	*lah deh-strook-see-'ohn*
detector	el detector	*ehl deh-tehk-'tohr*
deterioration	el deterioro	*ehl deh-teh-ree-'oh-roh*
devaluation	la devaluación	*lah deh-bah-loo-ah-see-'ohn*
develop (v)	desarrollar	*dehs-ah-rroh-'yahr*
developed (adj)	desarrollado	*dehs-ah-rroh-'yah-doh*
developing (adj)	en vías de desarrollo	*ehn 'bee-ahs deh dehs-ah-'rroh-yoh*
development	el desarrollo	*ehl deh-sah-'rroh-yoh*
development (economic)	el desarrollo económico	*ehl deh-sah-'rroh-yoh eh-koh-'noh-mee-koh*
development (urban)	el desarrollo urbano	*ehl deh-sah-'rroh-yoh oor-'bah-noh*
device	el dispositivo, el montaje	*ehl dees-poh-see-'tee-boh, ehl mohn-'tah-heh*
diabetes	la diabetis	*lah dee-ah-'beh-tees*
dictionary	el diccionario	*ehl deek-see-oh-'nah-ree-oh*
differential tariffs	las tarifas diferenciales	*lahs tah-'ree-fahs dee-feh-rehn-see-'ah-lehs*
digital (adj)	digital	*dee-hee-'tahl*
digital computer	la computadora digital	*lah kohm-poo-tah-'doh-rah dee-hee-'tahl*
digitalis	la digitalla	*lah dee-hee-'tahl*
dilution	la dilución	*lah dee-loo-see-'ohn*
dinner plate	el plato	*ehl 'plah-toh*
diode	el diodo	*ehl dee-'oh-doh*
direct access storage	el almacenaje por acceso directo	*ehl ahl-mah-seh-'nah-heh pohr ahk-'seh-soh dee-'rehk-toh*
direct cost	el costo directo	*ehl 'koh-stoh dee-'rehk-toh*
direct current	la corriente directa	*lah koh-rree-'ehn-teh dee-'rehk-tah*

D

direct expenses	los gastos directos	*lohs 'gah-stohs dee-'rehk-tohs*
direct investments	las inversiones directas	*lahs een-behr-see-see-'oh-nehs dee-'rehk-tahs*
direct labor (accounting)	la mano de obra directa	*lah 'mah-noh deh 'oh-brah dee-'rehk-tah*
direct mail	el correo directo	*ehl koh-'rreh-oh dee-'rehk-toh*
direct paper	el documento directo	*ehl doh-koo-'mehn-toh dee-'rehk-toh*
direct quotation	la cotización directa	*lah koh-tee-sah-see-'ohn dee-'rehk-tah*
direct selling	la venta directa	*lah 'behn-tah dee-'rehk-tah*
director	el director	*ehl dee-rehk-'tohr*
directory	el directorio	*ehl dee-rehk-'toh-ree-oh*
disadvantage	la desventaja	*lah dehs-behn-'tah-hah*
disappearance	la desaparición	*lah dehs-ah-pah-ree-see-'ohn*
disbursement	el desembolso, el egreso	*ehl dehs-ehm-'bohl-soh, ehl eh-'greh-soh*
discharge (v)	descargar, despedir	*dehs-kahr-'gahr, dehs-peh-'deer*
discount	el descuento	*ehl dehs-'kwehn-toh*
discount rate	el tipo de descuento	*ehl 'tee-poh deh dehs-'kwehn-toh*
discount securities	las valores descontados	*lohs bah-'loh-rehs dehs-kohn-'tah-dohs*
discounted cash flow	el flujo de caja descontado	*ehl 'floo-hoh deh 'kah-hah dehs-kohn-'tah-doh*
discounting	el proceso de descontar	*ehl proh-'seh-soh deh dehs-kohn-'tahr*
discretionary account	la cuenta discrecionaria	*lah 'kwehn-tah dees-kreh-see-oh-'nah-ree-ah*
discretionary order	la orden discrecionaria	*lah 'ohr-dehn dees-kreh-see-oh-'nah-ree-ah*
disease	la enfermedad	*lah ehn-fehr-meh-dahd*
disease (contagious)	la enfermedad contagiosa	*lah ehn-fehr-meh-dahd kohn-tah-hee-'oh-sah*
disease (deadly)	la enfermedad mortal	*lah ehn-fehr-meh-dahd mohr-'tahl*

disease (respiratory)	la enfermedad respiratoria	*lah ehn-fehr-meh-dahd reh-spee-rah-'toh-ree-ah*
dish	el plato	*ehl 'plah-toh*
dishonor (as a check)	no aceptar	*noh ah-sehp-'tahr*
disincentive	el desincentivo, la falta de incentivo	*ehl dehs-een-sehn-'tee-boh, lah 'fahl-tah deh een-sehn-'tee-boh*
disk drive	el dispositivo de disco, el impulsor de disco	*ehl dees-poh-see-'tee-boh deh 'dees-koh, ehl eem-pool-'sohr deh 'dees-koh*
disk	el disco, el disquete	*ehl 'dees-koh, ehl dees-keh-teh*
diskette	el disco flexible de capacidad pequeña	*ehl 'dees-koh flehk-'see-bleh deh kah-pah-see-'dahd peh-'keh-nyah*
dispatch	el envío, el mensaje	*ehl ehn-'bee-oh, ehl mehn-'sah-heh*
disposable income	los ingresos disponibles	*lohs een-'greh-sohs dees-poh-'nee-blehs*
dispute	el debate, el pleito, la discusión	*ehl deh-'bah-teh, ehl pleh-'ee-toh, lah dees-koo-see-'ohn*
dispute (v)	debatir, discutir, disputar	*deh-bah-'teer, dees-koo-'teer, dees-poo-'tahr*
distillation	la destilación	*lah dehs-tee-lah-see-'ohn*
distillation plant	la instalación de destilación	*lah een-stah-lah-see-'ohn deh dehs-tee-lah-see-'ohn*
distribute	distribuir	*dees-tree-boo-'eer*
distribution	la distribución	*lah dees-tree-boo-see-'ohn*
distribution costs	los costos de distribución	*lohs 'koh-stohs deh dees-tree-boo-see-'ohn*
distribution network	la red de distribución	*lah rehd deh dees-tree-boo-see-'ohn*
distribution policy	la política de distribución	*lah poh-'lee-tee-kah deh dees-tree-boo-see-'ohn*
distributor	el distribuidor	*ehl dees-tree-boo-ee-'dohr*
diuretic	el diurético	*ehl dee-oo-'reh-tee-koh*
diversification	la diversificación	*lah dee-behr-see-fee-kah-see-'ohn*
diversion	el desvío	*ehl dehs-'bee-oh*

D

divestment	el despojamiento	*ehl dehs-poh-hah-mee-'ehn-toh*
dividend	el dividendo	*ehl dee-bee-'dehn-doh*
dividend yield	el rendimiento del dividendo, rentabilidad por dividendos	*ehl rehn-dee-mee-'ehn-toh dehl dee-bee-'dehn-doh, rehn-tah-bee-lee-'dahd pohr dee-bee-'dehn-dohs*
division of labor	la división del trabajo	*la dee-bee-see-'ohn dehl trah-'bah-hoh*
dock (ship's receipt)	el muelle (el recibo de muelle)	*ehl moo-'eh-yeh (ehl reh-'see-boh de moo-'eh-yeh)*
dock handling charge	el cargo de muelle por desembarco	*ehl 'kahr-goh deh moo-'eh-yeh pohr dehs-ehm-'bahr-koh*
document	el documento	*ehl doh-koo-'mehn-toh*
documentation	la documentación	*lah doh-koo-mehn-tah-see-'ohn*
dollar cost averaging	el promedio de costo en dólares	*ehl proh-'meh-dee-oh deh 'koh-stoh ehn 'doh-lah-rehs*
dolphin	el delfín (m)	*ehl dehl-'feen*
domestic bill	la letra sobre el interior	*lah 'leh-trah 'soh-breh ehl een-teh-ree-'ohr*
domestic corporation	la compañía doméstica	*lah kohm-pah-'nyee-ah doh-'mehs-tee-kah*
door-to-door (sales)	de puerta en puerta (ventas)	*deh 'pwehr-tah ehn 'pwehr-tah ('behn-tahs)*
dosage	la dosis	*lah 'doh-sees*
dose	la dosis	*lah 'doh-sees*
dot matrix printer	la impresora por matriz de puntos	*lah eem-preh-'soh-rah pohr mah-'trees deh 'poon-tohs*
double dealing	el engaño	*ehl ehn-'gah-nyoh*
double taxation	la tributación doble	*lah tree-boo-tah-see-'ohn 'doh-bleh*
double time	el tiempo cortado a la mitad	*ehl tee-'ehm-poh kohr-'tah-doh ah lah mee-'tahd*
double-entry bookkeeping	el mantenimiento de libros por partida doble, la contabilidad de partida doble	*ehl mahn-teh-nee-mee-'ehn-toh deh 'lee-brohs pohr pahr-'tee-dah 'doh-bleh, lah kohn-tah-bee-lee-dahd deh pahr-'tee-dah 'doh-bleh*

double-pricing	el precio doble	*ehl 'preh-see-oh 'doh-bleh*
down payment	el pago inicial	*ehl 'pah-goh ee-nee-see-'ahl*
down period	el período de baja	*ehl peh-'ree-oh-doh deh 'bah-hah*
down the line	en el futuro	*ehl ehl foo-'too-roh*
downgraded (adj)	reducido	*reh-doo-'see-doh*
downloading	la conversión descendente	*lah kohn-behr-see-'ohn deh-sehn-'dehn-teh*
downswing	la fase descendente	*lah 'fah-seh dehs-sehn-'dehn-teh*
downtime	el tiempo improductivo, el tiempo muerto, el período, de paralización	*ehl tee-'ehm-poh eem-proh-dook-'tee boh, ehl tee-'ehm-poh 'mwehr-toh, ehl peh-'ree-oh-doh deh pah-rah-lee-sah-see-'ohn*
downturn	el receso ecónomico	*ehl reh-'seh-soh eh-koh-'noh-mee-koh*
draft	la letra de cambio	*lah 'leh-trah deh 'kahm-bee-oh*
drape (v)	cubrir con colgaduras	*koo-'breer kohn kohl-gah-'doo-rahs*
draw off (v)	sacar	*sah-'kahr*
drawback	el descuento, la rebaja	*ehl dehs-'kwehn-toh, lah reh-'bah-hah*
drawee	el girado, el librado	*ehl hee-'rah-doh, ehl lee-'brah-doh*
drawer (of a check)	el girador, el librador	*ehl hee-rah-'dohr, ehl lee-brah-'dohr*
drayage	el carretaje, el acarreo	*ehl kah-rreh-'tah-heh, el ah-kah-'rreh-oh*
dregs	las heces	*lahs 'eh-sehs*
dress	el vestido	*ehl beh-'stee-doh*
dressing (bandage)	el vendaje	*ehl behn-'dah-heh*
drilling rig	la plataforma de perforación	*lah plah-tah-'fohr-mah deh pehr-foh-rah-see-'ohn*
drink (v)	beber	*beh-'behr*
drive (computer)	la unidad que gobierna el soporte	*lah oo-nee-'dahd keh goh-bee-'ehr-nah ehl soh-'pohr-teh*

D

driver	el conductor, el chófer	*ehl kohn-dook-'tohr, ehl 'choh-fehr*
drop	la gota	*lah 'goh-tah*
drop shipment	el despacho directo del fabricante al detallista	*ehl dehs-'pah-choh dee-'rehk-toh dehl fah-bree-'kahn-teh ahl deh-tah-'yees-tah*
dropout	la omisión, la eliminación	*lah oh-mee-see-'ohn, lah eh-lee-mee-nah-see-'ohn*
drought	sequía	*seh-'kee-ah*
drug	la droga	*lah 'droh-gah*
drugstore	la farmacia	*lah fahr-'mah-see-ah*
dry (adj)	seco	*'seh-koh*
dry cargo	la carga seca	*lah 'kahr-gah 'seh-kah*
dry goods	las mercancías secas o finas	*lahs mehr-kahn-'see-ahs 'seh-kahs oh 'fee-nahs*
dry wine	el vino seco	*ehl 'bee-noh 'seh-koh*
dummy	la maqueta	*lah mah-'keh-tah*
dumping goods in foreign markets	la inundación del mercado con precios por debajo del costo	*lah ee-noon-dah-see-'ohn dehl mehr-'kah-doh kohn 'preh-see-ohs deh-'bah-hoh dehl 'koh-stoh*
dunnage	el abarrote	*ehl ah-bah-'rroh-teh*
duopoly	el duopolio	*ehl doo-oh-'poh-lee-oh*
durable goods	los bienes durables	*lohs bee'-eh-nehs doo-'rah-blehs*
duress	la compulsión	*lah kohm-pool-see-'ohn*
duties	los derechos, los impuestos	*lohs deh-'reh-chohs, lohs eem-'pweh-stohs*
duty	el arancel	*ehl ah-rahn-'sehl*
duty ad valorem	los impuestos ad valorem	*lohs eem-'pweh-stohs ahd bah-'loh-rehm*
duty free	libre de impuestos	*'lee-breh deh eem-'pweh-stohs*
dye (v)	teñir	*teh-'nyeer*

E

earmark (v)	reservar	*reh-sehr-'bahr*
earnings	las ganancias, las utilidades	*lahs gah-'nahn-see-ahs, lahs oo-tee-lee-'dah-dehs*
earnings on assets	las ganancias sobre los activos	*lahs gah-'nahn-see-ahs 'soh-breh lohs ahk-'tee-bohs*
earnings per share	la utilidad por acción	*lah oo-tee-lee-'dahd pohr ahk-see-'ohn*
earnings performance	el comportamiento de las ganancias	*ehl kohm-pohr-tah-mee-'ehn-toh deh lahs gah-'nahn-see-ahs*
earnings report	el informe de ganancias	*ehl een-'fohr-meh deh gah-'nahn-see-ahs*
earnings yield	el rendimiento de las ganancias	*ehl rehn-dee-mee-'ehn-toh deh lahs gah-'nahn-see-ahs*
Earth	Tierra	*tee-'eh-rrah*
earthenware	la alfarería, los objetos de barro	*lah ahl-fah-reh-'ree-ah, lohs ohb-'heh-tohs deh 'bah-rroh*
earthquake	el temblor	*ehl tehm-'blohr*
econometrics	la econometría	*lah eh-koh-noh-meh-'tree-ah*
economic	económico	*eh-koh-'noh-mee-koh*
economic indicators	los indicadores económicos	*lohs een-dee-kah-'doh-rehs eh-koh-'noh-mee-kohs*
economic life	la vida económica	*lah 'bee-dah eh-koh-'noh-mee-koh*
economic order quantity	el lote ordenado económico	*ehl 'loh-teh ohr-deh-'nah-doh eh-koh-noh-mee-koh*
economics	la economía	*lah eh-koh-noh-'mee-ah*
economy of scale	la economía de escala	*lah eh-koh-noh-'mee-ah deh ehs-'kah-lah*
ecosystem	ecosistema	*eh-koh-sees-'teh-mah*
edit (v)	editar	*eh-dee-'tahr*
editing of input	la redacción de los datos de entrada	*lah reh-dahk-see-'ohn deh lohs 'dah-tohs deh ehn-'trah-dah*
edition	la edición	*lah eh-dee-see-'ohn*

editor	el editor	*ehl eh-dee-'tohr*
effective yield	el rendimiento efectivo	*ehl rehn-dee-mee-'ehn-toh eh-fehk-'tee-boh*
efficiency	la eficiencia	*lah eh-fee-see-'ehn-see-ah*
eject (v)	expulsar	*ehs-pool-'sahr*
electric arc furnace	el horno de arco voltaico	*ehl 'ohr-noh deh 'ahr-koh bohl-tah-'ee-koh*
electrical engineering	la ingeniería eléctrica	*lah een-heh-nee-eh-'ree-ah*
electricity	la electricidad	*lah eh-lehk-tree-see-'dahd*
electrode	el electrodo	*ehl eh-lehk-'troh-doh*
electrolysis	la electrólisis	*lah eh-lehk-'troh-lee-sees*
electrolytic process	el proceso electrolítico	*ehl proh-'seh-soh eh-lehk-troh-'lee-tee-koh*
electromagnetics	electromecánica	*eh-lehk-troh-meh-'kah-nee-kah*
electron	el electrón	*ehl eh-lehk-'trohn*
electronic (adj)	electrónico	*eh-lehk-'troh-nee-koh*
electronic mail	correo electrónico	*koh-'rreh-oh eh-lehk-'troh-nee-koh*
electronic whiteboard	el pizarrón electrónico	*ehl pee-sah-'rrohn eh-lehk-'troh-nee-koh*
electrostatic	la electroestática	*lah eh-lehk-troh-eh-'stah-tee-kah*
element	el elemento	*ehl eh-leh-'mehn-toh*
elephant	el elefante (m)	*ehl eh-leh-'fahn-teh*
elevator	el montecargas (m)	*ehl mohn-teh-'kahr-gahs*
elevator shaft	la caja del ascensor	*lah 'kah-hah dehl ah-sehn-'sohr*
embargo	el embargo	*ehl eem-'bahr-goh*
embezzlement	el desfalco	*ehl dehs-'fahl-koh*
emissions	las emisiones	*lahs eh-mee-see-'oh-nehs*
emissions (toxic)	las emisiones tóxicas	*lahs eh-mee-see-'oh-nehs 'tohk-see-kahs*
employee	el empleado	*ehl ehm-pleh-'ah-doh*
employee counseling	la asesoría de empleados	*lah ah-seh-soh-'ree-ah deh ehm-pleh-'ah-dohs*

employee relations	las relaciones entre empleados	*lahs reh-lah-see-'oh-nehs 'ehn-treh ehm-pleh-'ah-dohs*
employment agency	la agencia de colocaciones	*lah ah-'hehn-see-ah deh koh-loh-kah-'syoh-nehs*
encode (v)	codificar	*koh-dee-fee-'kahr*
encumbrance	el gravamen	*ehl grah-'bah-mehn*
end	el fin	*ehl feen*
end of block	el fin de bloque	*ehl feen deh 'bloh-keh*
end of data	el fin de datos	*ehl feen deh 'dah-tohs*
end of job	el fin de trabajo	*ehl feen deh trah-'bah-hoh*
end of periods	el final del período	*ehl fee-'nahl dehl peh-'ree-oh-doh*
end product	el producto final	*ehl proh-'dook-toh fee-'nahl*
endorsee	el endosatario	*ehl ehn-doh-sah-'tah-ree-oh*
endorsement	el endoso	*ehl ehn-'doh-soh*
endowment	la dotación	*lah doh-tah-see-'ohn*
end-use certificate	el certificado de uso final	*ehl sehr-tee-fee-'kah-doh deh 'oo-soh fee-'nahl*
energy	la energía	*lah eh-nehr-'hee-ah*
energy mix	la mezcla de recursos de energía	*lah 'mehs-klah deh reh-'koor-sohs deh eh-nehr-'hee-ah*
energy sources	las fuentes (f) de energía	*lahs 'fwehn-tehs deh eh-nehr-'hee-ah*
engine	el motor	*ehl moh-'tohr*
engineer	el ingeniero	*ehl een-heh-nee-'eh-roh*
engineering	la ingeniería	*lah een-heh-nee-eh-'ree-ah*
engineering and design department	el departmento de ingeniería y diseño	*ehl deh-pahr-tah-'mehn-toh deh een-heh-nee-eh-'ree-ah ee dee-'seh-nyoh*
engrave (v)	grabar	*grah-'bahr*
enlarge (v)	ampliar	*ahm-plee-'ahr*
enter (v)	dar entrada, entrar	*dahr ehn-'trah-dah, ehn-'trahr*
enterprise	la empresa	*lah eem-'preh-sah*
entitlements	los derechos económicos	*lohs deh-'reh-chohs eh-koh-'noh-mee-kohs*

entrepreneur	el empresario	*ehl eem-preh-'sah-ree-oh*
entry	la entrada	*lah ehn-'trah-dah*
entry permit	el permiso de declaración, el permiso de entrada	*ehl pehr-'mee-soh deh deh-klah-rah-see-'ohn, ehl pehr-'mee-soh deh ehn-'trah-dah*
environment	el medio ambiente (m), el hábitat (m)	*ehl 'meh-dee-oh ahm-bee-'ehn-teh, ehl 'ah-bee-taht*
enzyme	la enzima	*lah ehn-'see-mah*
equal pay for equal work	a igual trabajo - igual salario	*ah ee-'gwahl trah-'bah-hoh – ee-'awahl sah-'lah-ree-oh*
equipment	el equipo	*ehl eh-'kee-poh*
equipment leasing	el alquiler de equipo	*ehl ahl-kee-'lehr deh eh-'kee-poh*
equity	el capital propio, el valor líquido, los recursos propios	*ehl kah-pee-'tahl 'proh-pee-oh, ehl bah-'lohr 'lee-kee-doh, lohs reh-'koor-sohs 'proh-pee-ohs*
equity investment	la inversión en acciones	*lah een-behr-see-'ohn ehn akh-see-'oh-nehs*
equity share	la participación accionaria	*lah pahr-tee-see-pah-see-'ohn ahk-see-oh-'nah-ree-ah*
ergonomics	la ergonomía	*lah ehr-goh-noh-'mee-ah*
erosion	la erosión	*lah eh-roh-see-'ohn*
error	el error	*ehl eh-'rrohr*
error checking	la verificación de errores	*lah beh-ree-fee-kah-see-'ohn deh eh-'rroh-rehs*
escalator clause	la cláusula sobre el tipo móvil de salario, alquiler, etc.	*lah 'klow-soo-lah 'soh-breh ehl 'tee-poh moh-beel deh sah-'lah-ree-oh, ahl-kee-'lehr*
escape clause	la cláusula de escape	*lah 'klow-soo-lah deh ehs-'kah-peh*
escheat	la confiscación	*lah kohn-fees-kah-see-'ohn*
escrow account	la cuenta de plica	*lah 'kwehn-tah deh 'plee-kah*
espresso cup	la taza de café expreso, el pocillo	*lah 'tah-sah deh kah-'feh ehk-'spreh-soh, ehl poh-'see-yoh*

E

estate	el patrimonio, la fortuna, la herencia	*ehl pah-tree-'moh-nee-oh, lah fohr-'too-nah, lah eh-'rehn-see-ah*
estate (or chateau)	la estancia, la viña	*lah ehs-'tahn-see-ah, lah 'bee-nyah*
estate agent	el corredor de bienes raíces	*ehl koh-rreh-'dohr deh bee-'eh-nehs rah-'ee-sehs*
estate tax	el impuesto sucesorio	*ehl eem-'pweh-stoh soo-seh-'soh-ree-oh*
estate-bottled	el envasado en la viña	*ehl ehn-bah-'sah-doh ehn lah 'bee-nyah*
estimate	la estimación	*lah ehs-tee-mah-see-'ohn*
estimate (v)	estimar	*ehs-tee-'mahr*
estimated price	el precio estimado	*ehl 'preh-see-oh ehs-tee-'mah-doh*
estimated time of arrival	el tiempo estimado (la hora estimada) de llegada	*ehl tee-'ehm-poh ehs-tee-'mah-doh (lah 'oh-rah ehs-tee-'mah-dah) deh yeh-'gah-dah*
estimated time of departure	el tiempo estimado (la hora estimada) de salida	*ehl tee-'ehm-poh ehs-tee-'mah-doh (lah 'oh-rah ehs-tee-'mah-dah) deh sah-'lee-doh*
ethane	el étano	*ehl 'eh-tah-noh*
ethanol	el etanol (m)	*ehl eh-tah-'nohl*
ether	el éter	*ehl 'eh-tehr*
Eurobond	el eurobono	*ehl eh-oo-roh-'boh-noh*
Eurocurrency	la euromoneda	*lah eh-oo-roh-moh-'neh-dah*
Eurodollar	el eurodólar	*ehl ee-oo-roh-'doh-lahr*
evaluation	la evaluación	*lah eh-bah-loo-ah-see-'ohn*
ex dividend	sin dividendo	*seen dee-bee-'dehn-doh*
ex dock	franco en el muelle, puesto en el muelle	*'frahn-koh ehn ehl 'mweh-yeh pweh-stoh ehn ehl 'mweh-yeh*
ex factory	franco en fábrica	*'frahn-koh ehn 'fah-bree-kah*
ex mill	en fábrica	*ehn 'fah-bree-kah*
ex mine	en la mina	*ehn lah 'mee-nah*
ex rights	sin derechos	*seen deh-'reh-chohs*
ex ship	puesto en buque, ex buque	*'pweh-stoh ehn 'boo-keh, ehks 'boo-keh*

E

ex warehouse	franco en almacén	*'frahn-koh ehn ahl-mah-'sehn*
excess population	exceso de población	*ehk-'seh-soh deh poh-blah-see-'ohn*
exchange	el cambio	*ehl 'kahm-bee-oh*
exchange (v)	cambiar, intercambiar	*kahm-bee-'ahr, een-tehr-kahm-bee-'ahr*
exchange control	el control de cambio	*ehl kohn-'trohl deh 'kahm-bee-oh*
exchange discount	el descuento cambiario	*ehl dehs-'kwehn-toh kahm-bee-'ah-ree-oh*
exchange loss	la pérdida por conversión de moneda	*lah 'pehr-dee-dah pohr kohn-behr-see-'ohn deh moh-'neh-dah*
exchange rate	el tipo de cambio	*ehl 'tee-poh deh 'kahm-bee-oh*
exchange risk	el riesgo de cambio	*ehl ree-'ehs-goh deh 'kahm-bee-oh*
exchange value	el valor de cambio	*ehl bah-'lohr deh 'kahm-bee-oh*
excise duties	los impuestos indirectos	*lohs eem-'pweh-stohs een-dee-'rehk-tohs*
excise license	el permiso impositivo	*ehl pehr-'mee-soh eem-poh-see-'tee-boh*
excise tax	el impuesto al consumo, el impuesto sobre ventas	*ehl eem-'pweh-stoh ahl kohn-'soo-moh, ehl 'eem-'pweh-stoh 'soh-breh 'behn-tahs*
executive	el ejecutivo	*ehl eh-heh-koo-'tee-boh*
executive board	la junta ejecutiva	*la 'hoon-tah eh-heh-koo-'tee-bah*
executive committee	el comité ejecutivo	*ehl kom-mee-'teh eh-heh-koo-'tee-boh*
executive compensation	la compensación del ejecutivo	*lah kohm-pehn-sah-see-'ohn dehl eh-heh-koo-'tee-boh*
executive director	el director ejecutivo	*ehl dee-rehk-'tohr eh-heh-koo-'tee-boh*
executive search	la búsqueda de ejecutivos	*lah 'boos-keh-dah deh eh-heh-koo-'tee-bohs*
executive secretary	el secretario ejecutivo	*ehl seh-kreh-'tah-ree-oh eh-heh-koo-'tee-boh*

E

executor	el ejecutor testamentario	*ehl eh-heh-koo-'tohr tehs-tah-mehn-'tah-ree-oh*
exemption	la exención	*lah ehks-ehn-see-'ohn*
exhaust	el escape (m), la descarga	*ehl eh-'skah-peh, lah dehs-'kahr-gah*
exhaust (v)	agotar	*ah-goh-'tahr*
exhausted (adj)	agotado	*ah-goh-'tah-doh*
exit (v)	salir	*sah-'leer*
expected results	los resultados esperados	*lohs reh-sool-'tah-dohs ehs-peh-'rah-dohs*
expenditure	la erogación	*lah eh-roh-gah-see-'ohn*
expense account	la cuenta de gastos	*lah 'kwehn-tah deh 'gah-stohs*
expenses	los gastos	*lohs 'gah-stohs*
experiment	el experimento	*ehl lah ehks-peh-ree-'mehn-toh*
expiry date	la fecha de vencimiento	*lah 'feh-chah deh behn-see-mee-'ehn-toh*
exploration	la exploración	*lah ehks-ploh-rah-see-'ohn*
exploration (local)	exploración doméstica	*ehks-ploh-rah-see-'ohn doh-'mehs-tee-kah*
exploration site	el sitio de exploración	*ehl 'see-tee-oh deh ehks-ploh-rah-see-'ohn*
explore	explorar	*ehks-ploh-'rahr*
export (v)	exportar	*ehks-pohr-'tahr*
export agent	el agente de exportaciones	*ehl ah-'hehn-teh deh ehks-pohr-tah-see-'oh-nehs*
export credit	el crédito de exportación	*ehl 'kreh-dee-toh deh ehks-pohr-tah-see-'ohn*
export duty	el impuesto de exportación, los derechos de exportación	*ehl eem-'pweh-stoh deh ehks-pohr-tah-see-'ohn, los deh-'reh-chohs deh ehks-pohr-tah-see-'ohn*
export entry	la declaración de exportaciones	*lah deh-klah-rah-see-'ohn deh ehks-pohr-tah-see-'oh-nehs*
export house	la casa exportadora	*lah 'kah-sah deh ehks-pohr-tah-'doh-rah*
export manager	el gerente de exportaciones	*ehl heh-'rehn-teh deh ehks-pohr-tah-see-'oh-nehs*

E

export middleman	el intermediario de exportaciones	*ehl een-tehr-meh-dee-'ah-ree-oh deh ehks-pohr-tah-see-'oh-nehs*
export permit	el permiso de exportación	*ehl pehr-'mee-soh deh ehks-pohr-tah-see-'ohn*
export quota	la cuota de exportación	*lah 'kwoh-tah deh ehks-pohr-tah-see-'ohn*
export regulations	las regulaciones de exportación	*lahs reh-goo-lah-see-'ohnehs deh ehks-pohr-tah-see-'ohn*
export sales contract	el contrato de venta de las exportaciones	*ehl kohn-'trah-toh deh 'behn-tah deh lahs ehks-pohr-tah-see-'oh-nehs*
export taxes	los impuestos de exportación	*lohs eem-'pweh-stohs deh ehks-pohr-tah-see-'ohn*
export-import bank	el banco de exportaciones-importaciones	*ehl 'bahn-koh deh ehks-pohr-tah-see-'oh-nehs-eem-pohr-tah-see-'oh-nehs*
expropriation	la expropriación	*lah ehks-proh-pree-ah-see-'ohn*
extinction	la extinción	*lah ehk-steenk-see-'ohn*
extra dividends	los dividendos extras	*lohs dee-bee-'dehn-dohs 'ehks-trahs*
eyedrop	la gota para los ojos	*lah 'goh-tah 'pah-rah lohs 'oh-hohs*
eyeglass case	el estuche de espejuelos, el estuche de gafas	*ehl eh-'stoo-cheh deh ehs-peh-'weh-lohs, ehl eh-'stoo-cheh deh gah-fas*

F

fabric	la tela	*lah 'teh-lah*
face value	el valor nominal	*ehl bah-'lohr noh-mee-'nahl*
facilities	las instalaciones	*lahs een-stah-lah-see-'oh-nehs*
fact sheet	la hoja de acontecimientos	*lah 'oh-hah deh ah-kohn-teh-see-mee-'ehn-tohs*
factor	el factor	*ehl fahk-'tohr*
factor (v)	factorizar	*fahk-toh-ree-'sahr*
factor, load	el factor de carga	*ehl fahk-'tohr deh 'kahr-gah*

factor analysis	el análisis de factores	*ehl ah-'nah-lee-sees deh fahk-toh-rehs*
factor cost	el costo de factores	*ehl 'koh-stoh deh fahk-'toh-rehs*
factor rating	la clasificación según factores	*lah klah-see-fee-kah-see-'ohn seh-'goon fahk-'toh-rehs*
factoring	factorización	*fahk-toh-ree-sah-see-'ohn*
factory	la fábrica	*lah 'fah-bree-kah*
factory overhead	los gastos generales de fabricación	*lohs 'gah-stohs heh-neh-'rah-lehs deh fah-bree-kah-see-'ohn*
fail (v)	fracasar	*frah-kah-'sahr*
failure	el fracaso	*ehl frah-'kah-soh*
fair market value	el justo valor de mercado	*ehl 'hoo-stoh vah-'lohr deh mehr-'kah-doh*
fair return	el retorno razonable	*ehl reh-'tohr-noh rah-soh-'nah-bleh*
fair trade	las prácticas comerciales justas	*lahs 'prahk-tee-kahs koh-mehr-see-'ah-lehs 'hoo-stahs*
farm out (v)	subcontratar	*soob-kohn-trah-'tahr*
farming	cultivo	*kool-'tee-boh*
fashion	la moda	*lah 'moh-dah*
fashionable	de moda	*deh 'moh-dah*
fauna and flora	fauna y flora	*'fah-oo-nah ee 'floh-rah*
fax	el facsímil, el fax	*ehl fahk-'see-meel, ehl fahks*
feed (v)	alimentar	*ah-lee-mehn-'tahr*
feed ratio	la relación de alimentación	*lah reh-lah-see-'ohn deh ah-lee-mehn-tah-see-'ohn*
feedback	realimentación, retroalimentación	*reh-ah-lee-mehn-tah-see-'ohn, reh-troh-ah-lee-mehn-tah-see-'ohn*
felling (of a tree)	la tala	*lah 'tah-lah*
fellow man, fellow creature	los prójimos	*lohs 'proh-hee-mohs*
fender	el guardabarros, el guardafangos	*ehl gwahr-dah-'bah-rrohs, ehl gwar-dah-'fahn-gohs*
ferroalloys	las ferroaleaciones	*lahs feh-rroh-ah-leh-ah-see-'oh-nehs*

F

fertilizer	fertilizante (m)	*fehr-tee-lee-'sahn-teh*
fidelity bond	la fianza de fidelidad	*lah fee-'ahn-sah deh fee-deh-lee-'dahd*
fiduciary	el fiduciario	*ehl fee-doo-see-'ah-ree-oh*
fiduciary issue	la emisión fiduciaria	*lah eh-mee-see-'ohn fee-doo-see-'ah-ree-ah*
fiduciary loan	el préstamo fiduciario	*ehl 'preh-stah-moh fee-doo-see-'ah-ree-oh*
field	el campo	*ehl 'kahm-poh*
field warehousing	el almacenaje provisorio	*ehl ahl-mah-seh-'nah-heh proh-bee-'soh-ree-oh*
file	archivo, fichero	*ahr-'chee-boh, fee-'cheh-roh*
file protection	la protección de un fichero	*lah proh-tehk-see-'ohn deh oon fee-'cheh-roh*
filter	el filtro	*ehl 'feel-troh*
finalize (v)	finalizar	*fee-nah-lee-'sahr*
finance (v)	financiar	*fee-nahn-see-'ahr*
finance company	la compañía financiera	*lah kohm-pah-'nyee-ah*
financial analysis	el análisis financiero	*ehl ah-'nah-lee-sees fee-nahn-see-'eh-roh*
financial appraisal	el avalúo financiero	*ehl ah-bah-'loo-oh fee-nahn-see-'eh-roh*
financial control	el control financiero	*ehl kohn-'trohl fee-nahn-see-'eh-roh*
financial director	el director financiero	*ehl dee-rehk-'tohr fee-nahn-see-'eh-roh*
financial highlights	los elementos sobresalientes financieros	*lohs eh-leh-'mehn-tohs soh-breh-sah-lee-'ehn-tehs fee-nahn-see-'eh-rohs*
financial incentive	el incentivo financiero	*ehl een-sehn-'tee-boh fee-nahn-see-'eh-roh*
financial lease	arrendamiento financiero	*ah-rrehn-dah-mee-'ehn-toh fee-nahn-see-'eh-roh*
financial leverage	el aplancamiento financiero	*ehl ah-plahn-kah-mee-'ehn-toh fee-hahn-see-'eh-roh*
financial management	la gerencia financiera	*lah heh-'rehn-teh fee-nahn-see-'eh-roh*

F

financial period	el ejercicio (periódo) financiero	*ehl eh-hehr-'see-see-oh (peh-'ree-oh-doh) fee-nahn-see-'eh-roh*
financial planning	la planificación financiera	*lah plah-nee-fee-kah-see-'ohn fee-nahn-see-'eh-rah*
financial services	los servicios financieros	*lohs sehr-'bee-see-ohs fee-nahn-see-'eh-rohs*
financial statement	el estado financiero	*ehl eh-stah-doh fee-nahn-see-'eh-roh*
financial year	el ejercicio financiero	*ehl eh-hehr-'see-see-oh fee-nahn-see-'eh-roh*
find (oil)	descubrimiento de (aceite)	*dehs-koo-bree-mee-'ehn-toh deh ah-'seh-ee-teh*
fine	la multa	*lah 'mool-tah*
finished goods inventory	el inventario de bienes terminados	*ehl een-behn-'tah-ree-oh deh bee-'eh-nehs tehr-mee-'nah-dohs*
finished products	los productos terminados	*lohs proh-'dook-tohs tehr-mee-'nah-dohs*
finishing mill	la fábrica de terminación	*lah 'fah-bree-kah deh tehr-mee-nah-see-'ohn*
fire (v)	despedir del trabajo	*dehs-peh-'deer dehl trah-'bah-hoh*
firm	la empresa, la firma	*lah ehm-'preh-sah, lah 'feer-mah*
firmness	la firmeza	*lah feer-'meh-sah*
first in-first out	el primero que entra-el primero que sale	*ehl pree-'meh-roh keh 'ehn-trah-ehl -pree-'meh-roh keh 'sah-leh*
first preferred stocks	las acciones preferidas de primera	*lahs ahk-see-'oh-nehs preh-feh-'ree-dahs deh pree-'meh-rah*
fiscal agent	el agente fiscal	*ehl ah-'hehn-teh fees-'kahl*
fiscal year	el año fiscal	*ehl 'ah-nyoh fees-'kahl*
fish	los peces (m), el pez (sing.)	*lohs 'peh-sehs, ehl pehs*
fixed assets	el activo fijo	*ehl ahk-'tee-boh 'fee-hoh*
fixed capital	el capital fijo	*ehl kah-pee-'tahl 'fee-hoh*
fixed charges	los cargos fijos	*lohs 'kahr-gohs 'fee-hohs*
fixed costs	los costos fijos	*lohs 'koh-stohs 'fee-hohs*
fixed expenses	los gastos fijos	*lohs 'gah-stohs 'fee-hohs*

F

fixed income	la renta fija	*la'rehn-tah 'fee-hah*
fixed investment	la inversión fija	*lah een-behr-see-'ohn 'fee-hah*
fixed liabilities	los pasivos a largo plazo	*lohs pah-'see-bohs ah 'lahr-goh 'plah-soh*
fixed rate of exchange	el tipo de cambio fijo	*ehl 'tee-poh deh 'kahm-bee-oh 'fee-hoh*
fixed term	el plazo fijo	*ehl 'plah-soh 'fee-hoh*
fixture (on balance sheet)	el préstamo a plazo fijo	*ehl 'preh-stah-moh ah 'plah-soh 'fee-hoh*
flat bond	el bono sin intereses	*ehl 'boh-noh seen een-teh-reh-sehs*
flat car	el vagón batea	*ehl bah-'gohn bah-'teh-ah*
flat rate	la tasa uniformal	*lah 'tah-sah oo-nee-fohr-'mahl*
flat yield	el rendimiento fijo (uniforme)	*ehl rehn-dee-mee-'ehn-toh 'fee-hoh (oo-nee-'fohr-meh)*
flats products	las planchuelas rectangulares de hierro o acero	*lahs plahn-choo'eh-lahs rehk-tahn-goo-'lah-rehs deh 'yeh-roh oh ah-'seh-roh*
fleet policy	la póliza de flotilla	*lah 'poh-lee-sah deh floh-'tee-yah*
flexible tariff	la tarifa flexible	*lah tah-'ree-fah flek-'see-bleh*
float (outstanding checks)	los cheques cobrados y no abonados	*lohs 'cheh-kehs koh-'brah-dohs ee noh ah-boh-'nah-dohs*
float (rates)	variar	*bah-ree-'ahr*
float (v) (issue stock)	emitir valores	*eh-mee-'teer bah-'loh-rehs*
floater	la póliza que protege contra pérdidas	*lah 'poh-lee-sah keh proh-'teh-heh 'kohn-trah 'pehr-dee-dahs*
floating asset	el activo flotante	*ehl ahk-'tee-boh floh-'tahn-teh*
floating charge	el cargo variable	*ehl 'kahr-goh bah-ree-'ah-bleh*
floating debt	la deuda flotante	*lah deh-'oo-dah floh-'tahn-teh*

floating exchange rate	el tipo de cambio flotante	*ehl 'tee-poh deh 'kahm-bee-oh floh-'tahn-teh*
floating rate	la tasa flotante	*lah 'tah-sah floh-'tahn-teh*
floating rates	los tipos variables	*lohs 'tee-pohs bah-ree-'ah-bleh*
floor (of exchange)	la sala de operaciones de bolsa	*lah 'sah-lah deh oh-peh-rah-see-'oh-nehs deh 'bohl-sah*
floppy disk	el disco flexible	*ehl 'dees-koh flek-'see-bleh*
flowchart	el diagrama de flujo (m)	*ehl dee-ah-'grah-mah deh 'floo-hoh*
flute (arquit.)	la acanaladura, la estria	*lah ah-kah-na-lah-'doo-rah, lah ehs-'tree-ah*
folio	la página	*leh 'pah-hee-nah*
follow up (v)	seguir	*seh-'geer*
follow-up order	la continuación del pedido	*lah kohn-tee-noo-ah-see-'ohn dehl peh-'dee-doh*
font	el tipo de letra	*ehl tee-poh deh 'leh-trah*
foodstuffs	los productos alimenticios	*lohs proh-'dook-tohs ah-lee-mehn-'tee-see-ohs*
footage	la longitud	*lah lohn-hee-'tood*
footing (accounting)	el total de una columna	*ehl toh-'tahl deh 'oo-nah koh-'loom-nah*
for export	para exportar, para la exportación	*'pah-rah ehks-pohr-'tahr, 'pah-rah lah ehks-pohr-tah-see-'ohn*
for forwarding	para la entrega futura	*'pah-rah lah ehn-'treh-gah foo-'too-rah*
force majeure	la fuerza mayor	*lah foo-'ehr-sah mah-'yohr*
forecast	el pronóstico, la estimación	*ehl proh-'noh-stee-koh, lah ehs-tee-mah-see-'ohn*
forecast (v)	estimar, pronosticar	*eh-stee-'mahr, proh-noh-stee-'kahr*
foreign bill of exchange	las letras de cambio extranjeras	*lahs 'leh-trahs deh 'kahm-bee-oh ehks-trahn-'heh-rahs*
foreign corporation (to country)	la compañía extranjera	*lah kohm-pah-'nyee-ah ehks-trahn-'heh-rah*

F

foreign corporation (to region)	la compañía foránea	*lah kohm-pan-'nyee-ah foh-'rah-neh-ah*
foreign currency	la moneda extranjera	*lah moh-'neh-dah ehks-trahn-'heh-rah*
foreign debt	la deuda extranjera	*lah deh-'oo-dah ehks-trahn-'heh-rah*
foreign exchange	el cambio exterior, la moneda extranjera, las divisas	*ehl 'kahm-bee-oh ehks-teh-ree-'ohr, lah moh-'neh-dah ehks-trahn-'heh-rah, lahs dee-'bee-sahs*
foreign exchange market	el mercado de divisas	*ehl mehr-'kah-doh deh dee-'bee-sahs*
foreign securities	las valores extranjeros	*lohs bah-'loh-rehs ehks-trahn-'heh-rohs*
foreign tax credit	la deducción por impuestos pagados en el exterior	*lah deh-dook-see-'ohn pohr eem-'pweh-stohs pah-'gah-dohs ehn ehl ehks-teh-ree-'ohr*
foreign trade	el comercio exterior	*ehl koh-'mehr-see-oh ehks-teh-ree-'ohr*
foreman	el capataz	*ehl kah-pah-'tahs*
forgery	la falsificación	*lah fahl-see-fee-kah-see-'ohn*
fork	el tenedor	*ehl teh-neh-'dohr*
form letter	la carta modelo	*lah 'kahr-tah moh-'deh-loh*
format	el formato	*ehl fohr-'mah-toh*
format (v)	dar formato	*dahr fohr-'mah-toh*
fortune	la fortuna	*lah fohr-'too-nah*
forward contract	el contrato a futuro	*ehl kohn-'trah-toh ah foo-'too-roh*
forward cover	la cobertura a futuro	*lah koh-behr-'too-rah ah foo-'too-roh*
forward exchange rate	el tipo de cambio	*ehl 'tee-poh deh 'kahm-bee-oh*
forward margin	el margen al futuro	*ehl 'mahr-hehn ahl foo-'too-roh*
forward market	el mercado futuro	*ehl mehr-'kah-doh foo-'too-roh*
forward purchase	la compra a futuro	*lah 'kohm-prah ah foo-'too-roh*

F

forward shipment	el embarque futuro	*ehl ehm-'bahr-keh foo-'too-roh*
forwarding agent	el agente expedidor	*ehl ah-'hehn-teh ehks-peh-dee-'dohr*
foul bill of lading	el conocimiento de embarque con reservas	*ehl koh-noh-see-mee-'ehn-toh deh ehm-'bahr-keh kohn reh-'sehr-bahs*
foundry	la fundición	*lah foon-dee-see-'ohn*
four-color	los cuatro colores	*lohs 'kwah-trohs koh-'loh-rehs*
four-cylinder engine	el motor de cuatro cilíndros	*ehl moh-'tohr deh 'kwah-troh see-'leen-drohs*
fox	la zorra	*lah 'soh-rrah*
franchise	la franquicia, la licencia	*lah frahn-'kee-see-ah, lah lee'sehn-see-ah*
fraud	el engaño, el fraude	*ehl ehn-'gah-nyoh, ehl 'frow-deh*
free alongside ship	libre al costado del vapor	*'lee-breh ahl koh-'stah-doh dehl bah-'pohr*
free and clear	libre de gravamen	*'lee-breh deh grah-'bah-mehn*
free enterprise	la libre empresa	*lah 'lee-breh ehm-'preh-sah*
free list (commodities without duty)	la lista de artículos exentos de derechos	*lah 'lee-stah deh ahr-'tee-koo-lohs ehks-'ehn-tohs deh deh-'reh-chohs*
free market	el mercado libre	*ehl mehr-'kah-doh 'lee-breh*
free market industry	la industria del mercado libre	*lah een-'doo-stree-ah dehl mehr-'kah-doh 'lee-breh*
free of particular average	libre de avería particular	*'lee-breh deh ah-beh-'ree-ah pahr-tee-koo-'lahr*
free on board	franco a bordo	*'frahn-koh ah 'bohr-doh*
free on rail	libre sobre carril	*'lee-breh 'soh-breh kah-'rreel*
free port	el puerto libre	*ehl 'pwehr-tah 'lee-breh*
free time	el tiempo libre	*ehl tee-'ehm-poh 'lee-breh*
free trade	el libre comercio	*ehl 'lee-breh koh-'mehr-see-oh*
free trade zone	la zona de libre cambio	*lah 'soh-nah deh 'lee-breh 'kahm-bee-oh*
freeboard	la obra muerta	*lah 'oh-brah 'mwehr-tah*

F

freelance	trabajar independientemente	*trah-beh-'hahr een-deh-pen-dee-ehn-teh-'mehn-teh*
freelancer	el hombre independiente	*ehl 'ohm-breh een-deh-pehn-dee-'ehn-teh*
freight	el flete	*ehl 'fleh-teh*
freight all kinds (v)	fletar todas las especies	*fleh-'tahr 'toh-dahs lahs eh-'speh-see-ahs*
freight allowed to...	porte a... incluso	*'pohr-teh ah . . . een-'kloo-soh*
freight collect	el flete por cobrar	*ehl 'fleh-teh pohr koh-'brahr*
freight forwarder	el expedidor de fletes, la empresa de transporte	*ehl ehks-peh-dee-'dohr deh 'fleh-tehs, lah ehm-'preh-sah deh trahns-'pohr-teh*
freight included	el flete incluído	*ehl 'fleh-teh een-kloo-'ee-doh*
freight prepaid	el flete pagado por adelantado	*ehl 'fleh-teh pah-'gah-doh pohr ah-deh-lahn-'tah-doh*
French cuff	el puño francés	*ehl 'poo-nyoh frahn-'sehs*
frequency curve	la curva de frecuencia	*lah 'koor-bah deh freh-'kwehn-see-ah*
frequency modulation (FM)	la modulación de frecuencia	*lah moh-doo-lah-see-'ohn deh freh-'kwehn-see-ah*
fringe benefits	los beneficios adicionales al sueldo, las prestaciones adicionales al sueldo	*lohs beh-neh-'fee-see-ohs ah-dee-see-oh-'nah-lehs ahl 'swehl-doh, lahs preh-stah-see-'oh-nehs ah-dee-see-oh-'nah-lehs*
fringe market	el mercado marginal	*ehl mehr-'kah-doh mahr-hee-'nahl*
front-end fee	el cobro adelantado	*ehl 'koh-broh ah-deh-lahn-'tah-doh*
front-end financing	el financiamiento adelantado	*ehl fee-nahn-see-ah-mee-'ehn-toh ah-deh-lahn-'tah-doh*
front-end loading	el cargamento por la puerta delantera	*ehl kahr-gah-'mehn-toh pohr lah 'pwehr-tah deh-lahn-'teh-rah*
front-wheel drive	la tracción delantera	*lah trahk-see-'ohn*
frosts	las heladas	*lahs eh-'lah-dahs*

frozen assets	los activos congelados	*lohs ahk-'tee-bohs kohn-heh-'lah-dohs*
fruity	el sabor a frutas	*ehl sah-'bohr ah 'froo-tahs*
fuel	el combustible, la gasolina	*ehl kohm-boo-'stee-bleh, lah gah-soh-'lee-nah*
fuel (aviation)	la gasolina de aviación	*lah gah-soh-'lee-nah deh ah-bee-ah-see-'ohn*
fuel (motor)	el combustible para motores	*ehl kohm-boo-'stee-bleh 'pah-rah moh-'toh-rehs*
fueling pit	el foso de abastecimiento de combustibles	*ehl 'foh-soh deh ah-bah-steh-see-mee-'ehn-toh deh kohm-boo-'stee-blehs*
full settlement	el pago total, el arreglo total	*ehl 'pah-goh toh-'tahl, ehl ah-'rreh-gloh toh-'tahl*
functional analysis	el análisis funcional	*ehl ah-'nah-lee-sees foon-see-oh-'nahl*
fund	el fondo	*ehl 'fohn-doh*
funded debt	la deuda consolidada, la deuda con vencimiento de más de un año	*lah deh-'oo-dah kohn-soh-lee-'dah-dah, lah deh-'oo-dah kohn behn-see-mee-'ehn-toh deh mahs deh oon 'ah-nyoh*
fungible goods	los bienes fungibles	*lohs bee-'eh-nehs foon-'hee-blehs*
furnace	el horno	*ehl 'ohr-noh*
future generations	las generaciones futuras	*lahs heh-neh-rah-see-'oh-nehs foo-'too-rahs*
futures	los futuros	*lohs foo-'too-rohs*
futures option	la opción a futuro	*lah ohp-see-'ohn ah foo-'too-roh*

G

galley proof	la galerada	*lah gah-leh-'rah-dah*
galvanizing	el galvanizado	*gahl-bah-nee-'sah-doh*
garbage	la basura	*lah bah-'soo-rrah*
garment bag	la bolsa para ropa, la maleta para ropa	*lah 'bohl-sah 'pah-rah 'roh-pah, lah mah-'leh-tah 'pah-rah 'roh-pah*

garnishment	el emplazamiento	*ehl ehm-plah-sah-mee-'yehn-toh*
gas	el gas (m)	*ehl gahs*
gas (liquid petroleum)	el gas líquido	*ehl gahs 'lee-kee-doh*
gas (natural)	el gas natural	*ehl gahs nah-too-'rahl*
gas consumption	el consumo de gasolina	*ehl kohn-'soo-moh deh gah-soh-'lee-nah*
gas pedal	el pedal de gasolina, el acelerador	*ehl peh-'dahl deh gah-soh-'lee-nah, ehl ah-seh-leh-rah-'dohr*
gasoline (regular)	la gasolina normal	*lah gah-soh-'lee-nah nohr-'mahl*
gasoline (super grade)	la gasolina super	*lah gah-soh-'lee-nah soo-'pehr*
gasoline tank	el tanque de gasolina	*ehl 'tahn-keh deh gah-soh-'lee-nah*
gearing	el ratio de deuda con interés fijo a intereses más la deuda	*ehl 'rah-tee-oh deh deh-'oo-dah kohn een-teh-rehs 'fee-hoh ah een-teh-'reh-sehs mahs lah deh-'oo-dah*
gearless	sin cambios	*seen 'kahm-bee-ohs*
gearshift	el cambio de velocidades	*ehl 'kahm-bee-oh deh beh-loh-see-'dah-dehs*
general acceptance	la aceptación general	*lah ah-seht-tah-see-'ohn heh-neh-'rahl*
general average loss	la pérdida general promedio	*lah 'pehr-dee-dah heh-neh-'rahl proh-'meh-dee-oh*
general manager	el gerente general	*ehl heh-'rehn-teh heh-neh-'rahl*
general meeting	la reunión general	*lah reh-oo-nee-'ohn heh-neh-'rahl*
general partnership	la sociedad general (en nombre colectivo)	*lah soh-see-eh-'dahd heh-neh-'rahl (ehn 'nohm-breh koh-lehk-'tee-boh)*
general strike	la huelga general	*lah 'wehl-gah*
generator	el generador	*ehl heh-neh-rah-'dohr*
gentleman's agreement (verbal)	el acuerdo de caballeros (verbal)	*ehl ah-'kwehr-doh deh kah-bah-'yeh-rohs (behr-'bahl)*

gilt (British govt securities)	los bonos de Tesorería Británica	*lohs 'boh-nohs deh teh-soh-reh-'ree-ah bree-'tah-nee-kah*
glass	el vaso, la copa	*ehl 'bah-soh, lah 'koh-pah*
global warming	el calentamiento global	*ehl kah-lehn-tah-mee-'ehn-toh gloh-'bahl*
glossy (adj)	lustroso, glaseado	*loos-'troh-soh, glah-see'ah-doh*
gloves	los guantes	*lohs 'gwahn-tehs*
glut	la inundación, la saturación	*lah een-oon-dah-see-'ohn, lah sah-too-rah-see-'ohn*
go around (v)	dar la vuelta	*dahr lah 'bwehl-tah*
go public (v)	abrir la compañía	*ah-'breer lah kohm-pah-'nyee-ah*
going concern value	el valor de la empresa en marcha	*ehl bah-'lohr deh lah ehm-'preh-sah ehn 'mahr-chah*
going rate (or price)	el precio actual	*ehl 'preh-see-oh ahk-too-'ahl*
gold clause	la cláusula de oro	*lah 'clow-soo-lah deh 'oh-roh*
gold price	el precio del oro	*ehl 'preh-see-oh dehl 'oh-roh*
gold reserves	las reservas de oro	*lahs reh-'sehr-bahs deh 'oh-roh*
gold standard	el patrón oro	*ehl pah-'trohn 'oh-roh*
good delivery (securities)	la buena entrega (de valores)	*lah 'bweh-nah ehn-'treh-gah (deh bah-'loh-rehs)*
good will	el crédito mercantil	*ehl 'kreh-dee-toh mehr-kahn-'teel*
goods	las mercancías, los bienes	*lahs mehr-kahn-'see-ahs, lohs bee-'eh-nehs*
government	el gobierno	*ehl goh-bee-'ehr-noh*
government agency	la agencia gubernamental	*lah ah'gehn-see-ah*
government bank	el banco gubernamental	*ehl 'bahn-koh goo-behr-mehn-'tahl*
government bonds	los bonos del gobierno	*lohs 'boh-nohs dehl goh-bee-'ehr-noh*
grace period	el período de gracia	*ehl peh-'ree-oh-doh deh 'grah-see-ah*
graft	el soborno	*ehl soh-'bohr-noh*

G

grain	el grano	*ehl 'grah-noh*
gram	el gramo	*ehl 'grah-moh*
grant an overdraft (v)	conceder un sobregiro	*kohn-seh-'dehr oon soh-breh-'hee-roh*
grape	la uva	*lah 'oo-bah*
grape bunch	el racimo de uvas	*ehl rah-'see-moh deh 'oo-bahs*
grape harvest	la vendimia, la cosecha de uvas	*lah behn-'dee-mee-ah, lah koh-'seh-chah deh 'oo-bahs*
graph	la gráfica, el diagrama	*lah 'grah-fee-kah, ehl dee-ah-'grah-mah*
gratuity	la propina	*lah proh-'pee-nah*
gravitation of earth	la gravitación terrestre	*lah grah-bee-tah-see-'ohn teh-'rreh-streh*
gravy boat	la salsera	*lah sahl-'seh-rah*
gray market	el mercado gris	*ehl mehr-'kah-doh grees*
green revolution	la revolución verde	*lah reh-boh-loo-see-'ohn 'behr-deh*
grid	la cuadrícula	*lah kwah-dree-'koo-lah*
grievance procedure	el manejo de quejas	*ehl mah-'neh-hoh deh 'keh-hahs*
grille	la rejilla del radiador	*lah reh-'hee-yah dehl rah-dee-ah-'dohr*
grinding	el molido, el esmerilaje	*ehl moh-'lee-doh, ehl ehs-meh-ree-'lah-heh*
gross domestic product	el producto territorial bruto	*ehl proh-'dook-toh teh-rree-toh-ree-'ahl 'broo-toh*
gross income	los ingresos brutos	*lohs een-'greh-sohs 'broo-tohs*
gross investment	la inversión bruta	*lah een-behr-see-'ohn 'broo-toh*
gross loss	la pérdida bruta	*lah 'pehr-dee-dah 'broo-tah*
gross margin	el beneficio bruto, el margen bruto	*ehl beh-neh-'fee-see-oh 'broo-toh, ehl 'mahr-hehn 'broo-toh*
Gross National Product (G.N.P.)	el producto nacional bruto	*ehl proh-'dook-toh nah-see-oh-'nahl 'broo-toh*
gross price	el precio bruto	*ehl 'preh-see-oh 'broo-toh*

G

gross profit	la utilidad bruta, el beneficio bruto	*lah oo-tee-lee-'dahd 'broo-tah, ehl beh-neh-'fee-see-oh 'broo-toh*
gross sales	las ventas brutas	*lahs 'behn-tahs 'broo-tahs*
gross spread	la diferencia bruta	*lah dee-feh-'rehn-see-ah 'broo-tah*
gross weight	el peso bruto	*ehl 'peh-soh 'broo-toh*
gross yield	el rendimiento bruto	*ehl rehn-dee-mee-'ehn-toh 'broo-toh*
ground (adj)	molido	*moh-'lee-doh*
group account	la cuenta colectiva, la cuenta mancomunada	*lah 'kwehn-tah koh-lehk-'tee-bah, lah 'kwehn-tah mahn-koh-moo-'nah-dah*
group dynamics	la dinámica de grupo	*lah dee-'nah-mee-kah deh 'groo-poh*
group insurance	los seguros colectivos	*lohs seh-'goo-rohs koh-lehk-'tee-bohs*
growing (adj)	creciente	*kreh-see-'ehn-teh*
growth	el crecimiento	*ehl kreh-see-mee-'ehntoh*
growth index	el índice de crecimiento	*ehl 'een-dee-seh deh crecimiento*
growth industry	la industria creciente	*lah een-'doos-tree-ah kreh-see-'ehn-teh*
growth potential	el potencial para crecimiento	*ehl poh-tehn-see-'ahl 'pah-rah crecimiento*
growth stocks	las acciones de crecimiento	*lahs ahk-see-'oh-nehs deh crecimiento*
guanaco	el guanaco	*ehl gwah-'nah-koh*
guarantee	la garantía	*lah gah-rahn-'tee-ah*
guarantee (v)	garantizar	*gah-rahn-tee-'sashr*
guaranteed classified vintage	la cosecha clasificada garantizada	*lah koh-'seh-chah klah-see-fee-'kah-dah gah-rahn-tee-'sah-dah*
guaranty bond	la fianza	*lah fee-'ahn-sah*
guaranty company	la compañía de fianzas	*lah kohm-pah-'nyee-ah deh fee-'ahn-sahs*
guessmate	la estimación aproximada	*lah ehs-tee-mah-see-'ohn ah-prohk-see-'mah-dah*
guidelines	las direcciones, las indicaciones	*lahs dee-rehk-see-'oh-nehs, lahs een-dee-kah-see-'oh-nehs*

G

H

half-life (bonds)	el período medio	*ehl peh-'ree-oh-doh 'meh-dee-oh*
hand-blown glass	el vidrio soplado, el cristal soplado	*ehl 'bee-dree-oh soh-'plah-doh, ehl kree-'stahl soh-'plah-doh*
hand-painted	pintado a mano	*peen-'tah-doh ah 'mah-noh*
handbag	el bolso de mano, la cartera de mano	*ehl 'bohl-soh deh 'mah-noh, lah kahr-'teh-rah deh 'mah-noh*
handicap	el obstáculo, la desventaja	*ehl ohb-'stah-koo-loh, lah dehs-behn-'tah-hah*
handkerchief	el pañuelo	*ehl pah-nyoo-'eh-loh*
handler	el manejador	*ehl mah-neh-hah-'dohr*
harbor dues	los derechos portuarios	*lohs deh-'reh-chohs pohr-too-'ah-ree-ohs*
hard copy	la copia dura, la copia de tapa dura, salida impresa	*lah 'koh-pee-ah 'doo-rah, lah 'koh-pee-ah deh 'tah-pah 'doo-rah, sah-'lee-dah eem-'preh-sah*
hard currency	la moneda estable, la moneda fraccionaria	*lah moh-'neh-dah ehs-'tah-bleh, lah moh-'neh-dah frahk-see-oh-'nah-ree-ah*
hard sell	la venta atosigante	*lah 'behn-tah ah-toh-see-'gahn-teh*
hardcover	la carpeta dura	*lah kahr-'peh-tah 'doo-rah*
hardness	la dureza	*lah doo-'reh-sah*
hardware	la circuitería física	*lah seer-koo-ee-teh-'ree-ah 'fee-see-kah*
hardware (computer)	las máquinas, los equipos	*lahs 'mah-kee-nahs, lohs eh-'kee-pohs*
head office	la casa matriz	*lah 'kah-sah mah-'trees*
headhunter	el reclutador de ejecutivos, la selección de directivos de otras empresas	*ehl reh-kloo-tah-'dohr deh eh-heh-koo-'tee-bohs, lah seh-lehk-see-'ohn deh dee-rehk-'tee-bohs deh 'oh-trahs ehm-'preh-sahs*
headline	el titular	*ehl tee-too-'lahr*
headload	la carga delantera	*lah 'kahr-gah deh-lahn-'teh-rah*

headquarters	la casa matriz, la oficina principal	*lah 'kah-sah mah-'trees, lah oh-fee-'see-nah preen-see-'pahl*
heat	el calor	*ehl kah-'lohr*
heavy industry	la industria pesada	*lah een-'doos-tree-ah peh-'sah-dah*
heavy lift charges	los recargos por bultos pesados	*lohs reh-'kahr-gohs pohr 'bool-tohs peh-'sah-dohs*
hectare	la hectárea (2.47 acres)	*lah ehk-'tah-reh-ah*
hedge (v)	evitar las pérdidas ocasionadas por las fluctuaciones de precios	*eh-bee-tahr lahs 'pehr-dee-dahs oh-kah-see-oh-'nah-dahs pohr lahs flook-too-ah-see-'oh-nehs deh 'preh-see-ohs*
hem	el dobladillo	*ehl doh-blah-'dee-yoh*
hexachlorophene	el hexaclorofeno	*ehl ehk-sah-kloh-roh-'feh-noh*
hidden assets	los activos escondidos	*lohs ahk-'tee-bohs ehs-kohn-'dee-dohs*
high fashion designer	el diseñador de alta costura	*ehl dee-seh-nyah-'dohr deh 'ahl-tah koh-'stoo-rah*
high fidelity	la alta fidelidad	*deh 'ahl-tah fee-deh-lee-'dahd*
high technology firm	la empresa de alta tecnología	*lah ehm-'preh-sah deh 'ahl-tah tehk-noh-loh-'hee-ah*
highest bidder	el mejor postor	*ehl meh-'hohr pohs-'tohr*
highlight	el realce acentuado	*ehl reh-ahl-'seh ah-sehn-too-'ah-doh*
hire (v)	contratar	*kohn-trah-'tahr*
hoard (v)	atesorar	*ah-teh-soh-'rahr*
holder in due course	el tenedor legítimo	*ehl teh-neh-'dohr leh-'hee-tee-moh*
holder of negotiable instruments	el portador	*ehl pohr-tah-'dohr*
holding company	la compañía matriz, la sociedad inversionista controladora	*lah kohm-pan-'nyee-ah mah-'trees, lah soh-see-eh-'dahd een-behr-see-oh-'nista kohn-troh-lah-'doh-rah*
holding period	el período de posesión	*ehl peh-'ree-oh-doh deh poh-seh-see-'ohn*

H

hole	agujero	*ah-goo-'heh-roh*
holster (gun)	la pistolera, la funda de pistola	*lah pees-toh-'leh-rah, lah 'foon-dah deh pees-'toh-lah*
home heating	la calefacción casera	*lah kah-leh-fahk-see-'ohn kah-'seh-rah*
home market	el mercado doméstico	*ehl mehr-'kah-doh doh-'mehs-tee-koh*
homogeneity	la homogeneidad	*lah oh-moh-heh-neh-ee-'dahd*
hood	la capucha	*lah kah-'pooh-chah*
hormone	la hormona	*lah ohr-'moh-nah*
horsepower	los caballos de fuerza	*lohs kah-'bah-yohs deh 'fwehr-sah*
hot money	el dinero muy realizable	*ehl dee-'neh-roh moo-ee-reh-ah-lee-'sah-bleh*
hot rolling	el laminado en caliente	*ehl lah-mee-'nah-doh ehn kah-lee-'ehn-teh*
hourly earnings	los ingresos por hora	*lohs een-'greh-sohs pohr 'oh-rah*
housing authority	la autoridad de vivienda	*lah ow-toh-ree-'dahd deh bee-bee-'ehn-dah*
human resources	el personal, los recursos humanos	*ehl pehr-soh-'nahl, lohs reh-'koor-sohs oo-'mah-nohs*
hunting	la caza	*lah 'kah-sah*
hunting (excessive)	caza excesiva	*'kah-hah ehk-seh-'see-bah*
hybrid computer	la computadora híbrida	*lah kohm-poo-tah-'doh-rah 'ee-bree-dah*
hydrocarbon	el hidrocarburo	*ehl ee-droh-kahr-'boo-roh*
hydrocarbons	los hidrocarburos	*lohs ee-droh-kahr-'boo-rohs*
hydrochloric acid	el ácido clorhídrico	*ehl 'ah-see-doh kloh-'ree-dree-koh*
hydrolysis	la hidrólisis	*lah ee-'droh-lee-sees*
hydrosulfate	el hidrosulfato	*ehl ee-droh-sool-'fah-toh*
hypertension	la hipertensión	*lah ee-pehr-tehn-see-'ohn*
hyphenate (v)	meter guión para separar sílabas	*meh-'tehr gee-'ohn 'pah-rah seh-pah-'rahr 'see-lah-bahs*
hypothecation	la hipoteca	*lah ee-poh-'teh-kah*

I

icon	el icono	*ehl ee-'koh-noh*
idle capacity	la capacidad ociosa	*lah kah-pah-see-'dahd oh-see-'oh-sah*
ignition	la ignición, el encendido	*lah eeg-nee-see-'ohn, ehl ehn-sehn-'dee-doh*
illegal	ilegal	*ee-leh-'gahl*
illegal shipments	los embarques ilegales	*lohs ehm-'bahr-kehs ee-leh-'gah-lehs*
imbalance	el desequilibrio	*ehl dehs-eh-kee-'lee-bree-oh*
imitation	la imitación	*lah ee-mee-tah-see-'ohn*
impact on (v)	impactar	*eem-pahk-'tahr*
impending changes	los cambios inminentes	*lohs 'kahm-bee-ohs ee-mee-'nehn-tehs*
implication	la implicación	*lah eem-plee-kah-see-'ohn*
implied agreement	el acuerdo implícito	*ehl ah-'kwehr-doh eem-'plee-see-toh*
import	la importación	*lah eem-pohr-tah-see-'ohn*
import (v)	importar	*eem-pohr-'tahr*
import declaration	la declaración de importación	*lah deh-klah-rah-see-'ohn deh eem-pohr-tah-see-'ohn*
import deposits	los depósitos de importación	*lohs deh-'poh-see-tohs deh eem-pohr-tah-see-'ohn*
import duty	el arancel de importación	*ehl ah-rahn-'sehl deh eem-pohr-tah-see-'ohn*
import entry	el asiento de importación	*ehl ah-see-'ehn-toh deh eem-pohr-tah-see-'ohn*
import license	la licencia de importación	*lah lee-'sehn-see-ah deh eem-pohr-tah-see-'ohn*
import quota	la cuota de importación	*lah 'kwoh-tah deh eem-pohr-tah-see-'ohn*
import regulations	las regulaciones de importación	*lah reh-goo-lah-see-'oh-nehs deh eem-pohr-tah-see-'ohn*
import tariff	el arancel de importación	*ehl ah-rahn-'sehl deh eem-pohr-tah-see-'ohn*
import tax	el impuesto de importación	*ehl eem-'pweh-stoh deh eem-pohr-tah-see-'ohn*

I

importer of record	el importador vigente	*ehl eem-pohr-tah-'dohr bee-'hehn-teh*
impound (v)	incautar	*een-kow-'tahr*
improve upon (v)	mejorar	*meh-hoh-'rahr*
improvements	las mejoras	*lahs meh-'hoh-rahs*
impulse buying	la compra impulsiva	*lah 'kohm-prah eem-pool-'see-bah*
impurity	la impureza	*lah eem-poo-'reh-sah*
imputed	imputado	*eem-poo-'tah-doh*
in reply to	en respuesta a	*ehn reh-'spoo-ehs-tah ah*
in the red	endeudado	*ehn-deh-oo-'dah-doh*
in transit	en tránsito	*ehn 'trahn-see-toh*
inadequate	insuficiente	*een-soo-fee-see-'ehn-teh*
incentive	el incentivo	*ehl een-sehn-'tee-boh*
inch	la pulgada	*lah pool-'gah-dah*
inchoate interest	el interés incoado	*ehl een-teh-'rehs een-koh-'ah-doh*
incidental expenses	los gastos menudos	*lohs 'gah-stohs meh-'noo-dohs*
incinerator	el incinerador	*ehl een-see-neh-rah-'dohr*
income	los ingresos, la renta	*lohs een-'greh-sohs, lah 'rehn-tah*
income account	la cuenta de ingreso	*lah 'kwehn-tah deh een-'greh-soh*
income bonds	los bonos de ganancias	*lohs 'boh-nohs deh gah-'nahn-see-ahs*
income bracket	el tramo de ingresos	*ehl 'trah-moh deh een-'greh-sohs*
income statement	el estado de ganancias y pérdidas	*ehl eh-'stah-doh deh gah-'nahn-see-ahs*
income tax	el impuesto sobre la renta	*ehl eem-'pweh-stoh 'soh-breh lah 'rehn-tah*
income yield	el rendimiento de las ganancias	*ehl rehn-dee-mee-'ehn-toh deh lahs gah-'nahn-see-ahs*
incorporate (v)	constituir, incorporar	*kohn-stee-too-'eer, een-kohr-poh-'rahr*
increase	el aumento	*ehl ow-'mehn-toh*

I

increase (demographic)	el crecimiento demográfico	*ehl kreh-see-mee-'ehn-toh deh-moh-'grah-fee-koh*
increase (economic)	el crecimiento económico	*ehl kreh-see-mee-'ehn-toh eh-koh-'noh-mee-koh*
increase (v)	incrementar	*een-kreh-mehn-'tahr*
increased costs	los costos incrementados	*lohs 'koh-stohs een-kreh-mehn-'tah-dohs*
indebtedness	el endeudamiento	*ehl ehn-deh-oo-dah-mee-'ehn-toh*
indemnity	la indemnización	*lah een-dehm-nee-sah-see-'ohn*
indenture	el documento	*ehl doh-koo-'mehn-toh*
index (indicator)	el índice	*ehl 'een-dee-seh*
index option	la opción de índice	*lah ohp-see-'ohn deh 'een-dee-seh*
index-linked guaranteed minimum wage	el salario mínimo garantizado por indexación	*ehl sah-'lah-ree-oh 'mee-nee-moh gah-rahn-tee-'sah-doh pohr een-dehk-sah-see-'ohn*
indexing	la indexación, modificación por índice	*lah een-dehk-sah-see-'ohn, moh-dee-fee-kah-see-'ohn pohr 'een-dee-seh*
indirect claim	el reclamo indirecto	*ehl reh-'klah-moh een-dee-'rehk-toh*
indirect cost	el costo indirecto	*ehl 'koh-stoh een-dee-'rehk-toh*
indirect expenses	los gastos indirectos	*lohs 'gah-stohs een-dee-'rehk-tohs*
indirect labor	la mano de obra indirecta	*lah 'mah-noh deh 'oh-brah een-dee-'rehk-tah*
indirect tax	el impuesto indirecto	*ehl eem-'pweh-stoh een-dee-'rehk-toh*
induction furnace	el horno de inducción	*ehl 'ohr-noh deh een-dook-see-'ohn*
industrial accident	el accidente industrial	*ehl ahk-see-'dehn-teh een-doo-stree-'ahl*
industrial arbitration	el arbitraje industrial	*ehl ahr-bee-t-'trah-heh een-doo-stree-'ahl*
industrial engineering	la ingeniería industrial	*lah een-heh-nee-eh-'ree-ah een-doo-stree-'ahl*
industrial goods	los bienes industriales	*lohs bee-'eh-nehs een-doo-stree-'ah-lehs*

I

industrial insurance	el seguro industrial	*ehl seh-'goo-roh een-doo-stree-'ahl*
industrial planning	la planificación industrial	*lah plah-nee-fee-kah-see-'ohn een-doo-stree-'ahl*
industrial relations	las relaciones industriales	*lahs reh-lah-see-'oh-nehs een-doo-stree-'ah-lehs*
industrial union	el sindicato industrial	*ehl seen-dee-'kah-to een-doo-stree-'ahl*
industry	la industria	*lah een-'doos-tree-ah*
industry-wide	por toda la industria	*pohr 'toh-dah lah een-'doos-tree-ah*
inefficient	ineficiente	*een-eh-fee-see-'ehn-teh*
inelastic demand or supply	la demanda o oferta inelástica	*lah deh-'mahn-dah oh oh-'fehr-tah een-eh-'lahs-tee-kah*
infant industry	la industria naciente	*lah een-'doos-tree-ah nah-see-'ehn-teh*
inflation	la inflación	*lah een-flah-see-'ohn*
inflation rate	la tasa de inflación	*lah 'tah-sah deh een-flah-see-'ohn*
inflationary	inflacionista	*een-flah-see-oh-'nees-tah*
information	la información	*lah een-fohr-mah-see-'ohn*
infrastructure	la infraestructura	*lah een-frah-ehs-trook-'too-rah*
ingot mold	la lingotera	*lah leen-goh-'teh-rah*
ingots	los lingotes	*lohs leen-'goh-tehs*
inheritance tax	el impuesto sucesorio	*ehl eem-'pweh-stoh soo-seh-'soh-ree-oh*
injection	la inyección	*lah een-yehk-see-'ohn*
injunction	la prohibición judicial	*lah proh-ee-bee-see-'ohn hoo-dee-see-'ahl*
ink	la tinta	*lah 'teen-tah*
inland bill of lading	el conocimiento de transporte interior	*ehl koh-noh-see-mee-'ehn-toh deh trahns-'pohr-teh een-teh-ree-'ohr*
innovation	la innovación	*lah een-noh-bah-see-'ohn*
inorganic chemistry	la química inorgánica	*lah 'kee-mee-kah een-ohr-'gah-nee-kah*
input	el insumo, la entrada	*ehl een-'soo-moh, lah ehn-'trah-dah*

input-output analysis	el análisis de entradas y salidas	*ehl ah-'nah-lee-sees deh ehn-'trah-dahs ee sah-'lee-dahs*
insert	el entredós, el encarte	*ehl ehn-treh-'dohs, ehl ehn-'kahr-teh*
insolvent	insolvente	*eeh-sohl-'behn-teh*
inspection	la inspección	*lah een-spehk-see-'ohn*
inspector	el inspector	*ehl een-spehk-'tohr*
instability	la inestabilidad	*lah een-ehs-tah-bee-lee-'dahd*
installment credit	el crédito a plazos	*ehl 'kreh-dee-toh ah 'plah-sohs*
installment plan	el plan de venta a plazos	*ehl plahn deh 'behn-tah ah 'plah-sohs*
institutional advertising	la publicidad institutional	*lah poo-blee-see-'dahd een-stee-too-see-oh-nahl*
institutional investor	el inversionista institutional	*ehl een-behr-see-oh-'neesta een-stee-too-see-oh-nahl*
instrinsic value	el valor intrínsico	*ehl bah-'lohr een-'treen-see-koh*
instruct	instruir	*eens-troo-'eer*
instrument	el documento, el instrumento	*ehl doh-koo-'mehn-toh, ehl een-stroo-'mehn-toh*
insulator	el aislador	*ehl ah-ee-slah-'dohr*
insulin	la insulina	*lah een-soo-'lee-nah*
insurance	los seguros	*lohs seh-'goo-rohs*
insurance broker	el corredor de seguros	*ehl koh-rreh-'dohr deh seh-'goo-rohs*
insurance company	la compañía aseguradora	*lah kohm-pah-'nyee-ah ah-seh-goo-rah-'doh-rah*
insurance fund	el fondo de seguros	*ehl 'fohn-doh deh seh-'goo-rohs*
insurance policy	la póliza de seguros	*lah 'poh-lee-sah deh seh-'goo-rohs*
insurance premium	la prima de seguros	*lah 'pree-mah deh seh-'goo-rohs*
insurance underwriter	el asegurador	*ehl ah-seh-goo-rah-'dohr*
intangible asset	el activo intangible	*ehl ahk-'tee-boh een-tahn-'hee-bleh*

I

integrated circuit	el circuito integrado	*ehl seer-koo-'ee-toh een-teh-'grah-doh*
integrated management system	el sistema gerencial integrado	*ehl sees-'teh-mah heh-rehn-see-'ahl een-teh-'grah-doh*
interact (v)	obrar recíprocamente	*oh-'brahr reh-'see-proh-kah-mehn-teh*
interactive (adj)	interactivo	*een-tehr-ahk-'tee-boh*
interbank	entre bancos	*'ehn-treh 'bahn-kohs*
interest	el interés	*ehl een-teh-'rehs*
interest arbitrage	el arbitraje de interés	*ehl ahr-bee-'trah-heh deh een-teh-'rehs*
interest expenses	los gastos de interés	*lohs 'gah-stohs deh een-teh-'rehs*
interest income	los ingresos por intereses	*lohs een-'greh-sohs pohr een-teh-'reh-sehs*
interest parity	la paridad de interés	*lah pah-ree-'dahd deh een-teh-'rehs*
interest period	el período de interés	*ehl peh-'ree-oh-doh deh een-teh-'rehs*
interest rate	la tasa de interés	*lah 'tah-sah deh een-teh-'rehs*
interface	el interfaz, acoplamiento mutuo, la junción	*ehl een-tehr-'fahs, ah-koh-plah-mee-'ehn-toh 'moo-too-oh, lah hoonk-see-'ohn*
interface (v)	comunicar	*koh-moo-nee-'kahr*
interim	el interino, provisional	*ehl een-tehe-'ree-noh, proh-bee-see-oh-'nahl*
interim budget	el presupuesto provisional	*ehl preh-soo-'pweh-stoh proh-bee-see-oh-'nahl*
interim statement	el estado intermedio	*ehl eh-'stah-doh een-tehr-'meh-dee-oh*
interlocking directorate	el directorio entrelazado	*ehl dee-rehk-'toh-ree-oh ehn-treh-lah-'sah-doh*
intermediary	el intermediario	*ehl een-tehr-meh-dee-'ah-ree-oh*
intermediary goods	los bienes intermedios	*lohs bee-'eh-nehs een-tehr-'meh-dee-ohs*
internal (adj)	interior, interno	*een-teh-ree-'ohr, een-'tehr-noh*

internal audit	la auditoría interna	*lah ow-dee-toh-'ree-ah een-'tehr-nah*
internal funding	la financiación interna	*lah fee-nahn-see-see-'ohn een-'tehr-nah*
internal rate of return (IRR)	la tasa interna de rentabilidad, la tasa interna de retorno	*lah 'tah-sah een-'tehr-nah deh rehn-tah-bee-lee-'dahd, lah 'tah-sah een-'tehr-nah deh reh-'tohr-noh*
investment grade	la inversión cualificada	*lah een-behr-see-'ohn kwah-lee-fee-'kah-dah*
International Date Line	la Línea de Fecha International	*lah 'lee-neh-ah deh 'feh-chah een-tehr-nah-see-oh-'nahl*
interpreter	el intérprete	*ehl een-'tehr-preh-teh*
interstate	interestatal	*een-tehr-ehs-tah-'tahl*
interstate commerce	el comercio interestatal	*ehl koh-'mehr-see-oh een-teh-reh-stah-'tahl*
intervene (v)	intervenir	*een-tehr-beh-'neer*
interview	la entrevista	*lah ehn-treh-'bee-stah*
intestate	sin testar	*seen tehs-'tahr*
invalidate (v)	invalidar	*een-bah-lee-'dahr*
inventory	el inventario	*ehl een-behn-'tah-ree-oh*
inventory control	el control del inventario	*ehl kohn-'trohl dehl een-behn-'tah-ree-oh*
inventory turnover	la rotación del inventario	*lah roh-tah-see-'ohn dehl een-behn-'tah-ree-oh*
invertebrate	invertebrado	*een-behr-teh-'brah-doh*
inverted market	el mercado invertido (inverso)	*ehl mehr-'kah-doh eeh-behr-'tee-doh (een-'behr-soh)*
invest (v)	invertir	*een-behr-'teer*
invested capital	el capital invertido	*ehl kah-pee-'tahl een-behr-'tee-doh*
investment	la inversión	*lah een-behr-see-'ohn*
investment adviser	el consejero sobre inversiones	*ehl kohn-seh-'heh-roh 'soh-breh een-behr-see-'oh-nehs*
investment analysis	el análisis de inversiones	*ehl ah-'nah-lee-sees deh een-behr-see-'oh-nehs*
investment appraisal	el avalúo de inversiones	*ehl ah-bah-'loo-oh deh een-behr-see-'oh-nehs*

I

investment bank	el banco inversionista	*ehl 'bahn-koh een-behr-see-oh-'nees-tah*
investment budget	el presupuesto de inversión, el presupuesto inversonista	*ehl preh-soo-'pwehs-toh deh een-behr-see-'ohn, ehl preh-soo-'pwehs-toh een-behr-see-oh-'nees-tah*
investment company	la compañía inversionista	*lah kohm-pah-'nyee-ah een-behr-see-oh-'nees-tah*
investment credit	el crédito para gastos de capital	*ehl 'kreh-dee-toh 'pah-rah 'gah-stohs deh kah-pee-'tahl*
investment criteria	el criterio para invertir	*ehl kree-'teh-ree-oh 'pah-rah een-behr-'teer*
investment grade	la inversión cualificada	*lah een-behr-see-'ohn kwah-lee-fee-'kah-dah*
investment letter	la carta de inversión	*lah 'kahr-tah deh een-behr-see-'ohn*
investment policy	la política de inversión	*lah poh-'lee-tee-kah deh een-behr-see-'ohn*
investment program	el programa de inversión	*ehl proh-'grah-mah deh een-behr-see-'ohn*
investment strategy	la estrategia inversionista	*lah ehs-trah-'teh-hee-ah een-behr-see-oh-'nees-tah*
investment trust	la compañía de inversiones	*lah kohm-pah-'nyee-ah deh een-behr-see-'oh-nehs*
investor relations	las relaciones con inversionistas	*lahs reh-lah-see-'oh-nehs kohn een-behr-see-oh-'nees-tahs*
investors	los inversores	*lohs een-behr-'soh-rehs*
invisible	invisible	*eem-bee-'see-bleh*
invitation to bid	la invitación a concurso	*lah een-bee-tah-see-'ohn ah kohn-'koor-soh*
invoice	la factura	*lah fahk-'too-rah*
invoice cost	el costo según factura	*ehl 'koh-stoh seh-'goon fahk-'too-rah*
iodine	el yodo	*ehl 'yoh-doh*
iron	el hierro	*ehl 'yeh-roh*
iron ore	el mineral de hierro	*ehl mee-neh-'rahl deh 'yeh-roh*
irrigation	el riego	*ehl ree-'eh-goh*
isotope	el isótopo	*ehl ee-'soh-toh-poh*

issue (stock)	la emisión	*lah eh-mee-see-'ohn*
issue (v)	emitir	*eh-mee-'teer*
issue price	el precio de emisión	*ehl 'preh-see-oh deh eh-'mee-see-'ohn*
issued shares	las acciones emitidas	*lahs ahk-see-'oh-nehs eh-mee-'tee-dahs*
italic (adj)	cursiva	*koor-'see-bah*
item	la partida	*lah pahr-'tee-dah*
itemize (v)	detallar, pormenorizar	*deh-tah-'yahr, pohr-meh-noh-ree-'sahr*
itemized account	la cuenta detallada	*lah 'kwehn-tah deh-tah-'yah-dah*

J

---

jacket (book)	la sobrecubierta	*lah soh-breh-koo-bee-'ehr-tah*
jacket (coat)	la chaqueta	*lah chah-'keh-tah*
Jason Clause	la cláusula que cubre las pérdidas por defectos propios del buque o mercancías	*lah 'clow-soo-lah keh 'koo-breh lahs 'pehr-dee-dahs pohr deh-'fehk-tohs dehl 'boo-keh*
jawbone (economics)	la economía de aficionados	*lah eh-koh-noh-'mee-ah deh ah-fee-see-oh-'nah-dohs*
jet lag	el cansancio debido al vuelo	*ehl kahn-'sahn-see-oh deh-'bee-doh ahl 'bweh-loh*
jig (production)	el guía para fabricar piezas idénticeas	*ehl 'gee-ah 'pah-rah fah-bree-'kahr pee-eh-'sahs ee-'dehn-tee-seh-ahs*
job	el trabajo	*ehl trah-'bah-hoh*
job analysis	la valoración, el análisis del trabajo	*lah bah-loh-rah-see-'ohn, ehl ah-'nah-lee-sees dehl trah-'bah-hoh*
job description	la descripción del trabajo	*lah dehs-kreep-see-'ohn dehl trah-'bah-hoh*
job evaluation	la evaluación del trabajo	*lah eh-bah-loo-ah-see-'ohn dehl trah-'bah-hoh*
job hopper	el trabajador que cambia de un puesto a otro	*ehl trah-bah-hah-'dohr keh 'kahm-bee-ah deh oon 'pweh-stoh ah 'oh-troh*
job lot	la partida a precio gobal	*lah pahr-'tee-dah ah 'preh-see-oh gloh-'bahl*

J

job performance	el rendimiento en el trabajo	*ehl rehn-dee-mee-'ehn-toh en ehl trah-'bah-hoh*
job search (v)	buscar trabajo	*boos-'kahr trah-'bah-hoh*
jobber	el comerciante, el mayorista	*ehl koh-mehr-see-'ahn-teh, ehl mah-yoh-'rees-tah*
jobber's turn	el curso del comerciante	*ehl 'koor-soh dehl koh-mehr-see-'ahn-teh*
joint account	la cuenta mancomunada (en participación)	*lah 'kwehn-tah mahn-koh-moo-'nah-dah (ehn pahr-tee-see-pah-see-'ohn*
joint cost	el costo colectivo	*ehl 'koh-stoh koh-lehk-'tee-boh*
joint estate	los bienes raíces comuneros	*lohs bee-'eh-nehs rah-'ee-sehs koh-moo-'neh-rohs*
joint liability	la responsabilidad mancomunada, la responsabilidad solidaria	*lah reh-spohn-sah-bee-lee-'dahd mahn-koh-moo-'nah-dah, lah reh-spohn-sah-bee-lee-'dahd soh-lee-'dah-ree-ah*
joint owner	el coproprietario	*ehl koh-pro-pee-eh-'tah-ree-oh*
joint ownership	la propiedad conjunta	*lah pro-pee-eh-'dahd kohn-'hoon-tah*
joint stock company	la sociedad en comandita por acciones	*lah soh-see-eh-'dahdehn koh-mahn-'dee-tah pohr ahk-see-'oh-nehs*
joint venture	el negocio en participación	*ehl neh-'goh-see-oh ehn pahr-tee-see-pah-see-'ohn*
journal	el diario	*ehl dee-'ah-ree-oh*
journeyman	el artesano, el jornalero	*ehl ahr-teh-'sah-noh, ehl hohr-nah-'leh-roh*
joy ride	la excursión de placer	*lah ehkx-koor-see-'ohn deh plah-'sehr*
joystick	la palanca de juego	*lah pah-'lahn-kah deh hoo-'eh-goh*
junior partner	el socio menor	*ehl 'soh-see-oh meh-'nohr*
junior security	el valor secundario	*ehl bah-'lohr seh-koon-'dah-ree-oh*
jurisdiction	la jurisdicción	*lah hoo-rees-deek-see-'ohn*
justification (margin)	la alineación	*lah ah-lee-neh-ah-see-'ohn*
justify (v)	justificar	*hoos-tee-fee-'kahr*

J

K

keep posted (v)	mantener al corriente	*mahn-teh-'nehr ahl koh-rree-'ehn-teh*
key case	la funda de las llaves	*lah 'foon-dah deh lahs 'yah-behs*
key exports	las exportaciones esenciales	*lahs ehks-pohr-tah-see-'oh-nehs eh-sehn-see-'ah-lehs*
keyboard	el teclado	*ehl teh-'klah-doh*
key-man insurance	el seguro que cubre los riesgos de un directivo	*ehl seh-'goo-roh keh 'koo-breh lohs ree-'ehs-gohs deh oon dee-rehk-'tee-boh*
Keynesian economics	la economía keynesiana	*lah eh-koh-noh-'mee-ah keh-ee, neh-see-'ah-nah*
keypunch (v)	teclar (la computadora)	*teh-'klahr (lah kohm-poo-tah-'doh-rah)*
kickback	el pago ilegal para incumplir algunas condiciones de un contrato	*ehl 'pah-goh ee-leh-'gahl 'pah-rah een-koom-'pleer ahl-'goo-nahs kohn-dee-see-'oh-nehs deh oon kohn-'trah-toh*
kidskin	la cabritilla	*lah kah-bree-'tee-yah*
kiting checks (banking)	la circulación de cheques en descubierto	*lah seer-koo-lah-see-'ohn deh 'cheh-kehs ehn dehs-koo-bee-'ehr-toh*
knife	el cuchillo	*ehl koo-'chee-yoh*
knot (nautical)	el nudo	*ehl 'noo-doh*
know-how	los conocimientos técnicos especializados	*lohs koh-noh-see-mee-'ehn-tohs 'tehk-nee-kohs ehs-peh-see-ah-lee-'sah-dohs*
knowledge	el conocimiento	*ehl koh-noh-see-mee-'ehn-toh*

L

label	la etiqueta	*lah eh-tee-'keh-tah*
labor	el labor, el trabajo	*ehl lah-'bohr, ehl trah-'bah-hoh*
labor code	la legislación del trabajo, el código de trabajo	*lah leh-hee-slah-see-'ohn dehl trah-'bah-hoh*

labor dispute	la discusión laboral	*lah dees-koo-see-'ohn lah-boh-'rahl*
labor force	la fuerza laboral	*lah 'fwehr-sah lah-boh-'rahl*
labor freeze	el conflicto laboral	*ehl kohn-'fleek-toh lah-boh-'rahl*
labor law	la ley del trabajo	*lah leh dehl trah-'bah-hoh*
labor leader	el líder laboral	*ehl 'lee-dehr lah-boh-'rahl*
labor market	el mercado laboral	*ehl mehr-'kah-doh lah-boh-'rahl*
labor relations	las relaciones laborales	*lahs reh-lah-see-'oh-nehs lah-boh-'rah-lehs*
labor turnover	la rotación de personal	*lah roh-tah-see-'ohn deh pehr-soh-'nahl*
labor union	el sindicato laboral	*ehl seen-dee-'kah-toh lah-boh-'rahl*
laboratory	el laboratorio	*ehl lah-boh-rah-'toh-ree-oh*
laboratory technician	el técnico de laboratorio	*ehl 'tehk-nee-koh deh lah-boh-rah-'toh-ree-oh*
laborer	el obrero, el trabajador	*ehl oh-'breh-roh, ehl trah-bah-hah-'dohr*
labor-intensive	trabajo-intensivo	*trah-'bah-hoh-een-tehn-'see-boh*
labor-saving	que ahorra trabajo	*keh ah-'oh-rrah trah-'bah-hoh*
lace	el encaje	*ehl ehn-'kah-heh*
lagging indicator	el indicador de rezago	*ehl een-dee-kah-'dohr deh reh-'sah-goh*
lagoon	la laguna	*lah lah-'goo-nah*
laissez-faire	dejar hacer	*deh-'hahr ah-'sehr*
lake	el lago	*ehl 'lah-goh*
lamb	el cordero	*ehl kohr-'deh-roh*
land	las tierras, terreno	*lahs tee-'eh-rrahs, teh-'rreh-noh*
land grant	la concesión de tierras	*lah kohn-seh-see-'ohn deh tee-'eh-rrahs*
land reform	la reforma agraria	*lah reh-'fohr-mah ah-'grah-ree-ah*
land taxes	los impuestos sobre tierras	*lohs eem-'pweh-stohs 'soh-breh tee-'eh-rrahs*

landed costs	el costo descargado	*ehl 'koh-stoh dehs-kahr-'gah-doh*
landing certificate	el certificado de desembarque	*ehl sehr-tee-fee-'kah-doh deh dehs-ehm-'bahr-keh*
landing charges	los cargos de desembarco	*lohs 'kahr-gohs deh dehs-ehm-'bahr-koh*
landing costs	los costos de desembarco	*lohs 'koh-stohs deh dehs-ehm-'bahr-koh*
landowner	el terrateniente	*ehl teh-rrah-teh-nee-'ehn-teh*
language (mode of speech)	el lenguaje	*ehl lehn-'gwah-heh*
language (national)	la lengua	*lah lehn-gwah*
large-scale	en gran escala	*ehn grahn- eh-'skah-lah*
laser disk	el disco láser	*ehl 'dees-koh 'lah-sehr*
laser printer	la impresora láser	*lah eem-preh-'soh-rah 'lah-sehr*
lash	el latigazo	*ehl lah-tee-'gah-soh*
last in-first out	el inventario a costos más viejos, últimas entradas-primeras salidas	*ehl een-behn-'tah-ree-oh ah 'koh-stohs mahs bee-'eh-hohs, 'ool-tee-mahs ehn-'trah-dahs-pree-'meh-rahs sah-'lee-dahs*
law	la ley	*lah leh*
law of diminishing returns	la ley de rendimientos decrecientes	*lah leh deh rehn-dee-mee-'ehn-tohs deh-kreh-see-'ehn-tehs*
lawsuit	el juicio, el pleito legal	*ehl hoo-'ee-see-oh, ehl pleh-'ee-toh leh-'gahl*
lawyer	el abogado	*ehl ah-boh-'gah-doh*
laxative	el laxante	*ehl lahk-'sahn-teh*
lay days	los días de estadía	*lohs 'dee-ahs deh eh-stah-'dee-ah*
lay time	los días de estadía	*lohs 'dee-ahs deh eh-stah-'dee-ah*
lay up (v)	acumular	*ah-koo-moo-'lahr*
lay-off	el despido	*ehl deh-'spee-doh*
layout	la composición, diseño, la organización, el trazado	*lah kohm-poh-see-see-'ohn, dee-'seh-nyoh, lah ohr-gah-nee-sah-see-'ohn, ehl trah-'sah-doh*

lead (metal)	el plomo	*ehl 'ploh-moh*
lead time	el tiempo de anticipación	*ehl tee-'ehm-poh deh ahn-tee-see-pah-see-'ohn*
leader	el jefe, el líder	*ehl 'heh-feh, ehl 'lee-dehr*
leading indicator	el indicador anticipado	*ehl een-dee-kah-'dohr ahn-tee-see-'pah-doh*
leads and lags	los adelantos y retrasos	*lohs ah-deh-lahn-'tah-dohs ee reh-'trah-sohs*
leaf	la hoja	*lah 'oh-hah*
leakage	la filtración	*lah feel-trah-see-'ohn*
learning curve	la curva del aprendizaje	*lah 'koor-bah dehl ah-prehn-dee-'sah-heh*
lease	el alquiler, el arrendamiento	*ehl ahl-kee-'lehr, ehl ah-rrehn-dah-mee-'ehn-toh*
leased department	el departamento arrendado	*ehl deh-pahr-tah-'mehn-toh ah-rrehn-'dah-doh*
leather	la piel, el cuero	*lah pee-'ehl, ehl 'kweh-roh*
leather goods	los artículos de piel, los artículos de cuero	*lohs ahr-'tee-koo-lohs dee pee-'ehl, lohs ahr-'tee-koo-lohs deh 'kweh-roh*
leather jacket	la chaqueta de piel, la chaqueta de cuero	*lah chah-'keh-ta deh pee-'ehl, lah chah-'keh-tah deh 'kweh-roh*
leave of absence	la ausencia por permiso	*lah ow-'sehn-see-ah pohr pehr-'mee-soh*
ledger	el libro mayor	*ehl 'lee-broh mah-'yohr*
ledger account	la cuenta del mayor	*lah 'kwehn-tah dehl mah-'yohr*
ledger entry	la entrada en el libro mayor, el asiento del mayor	*lah ehn-'trah-dah ehn ehl 'lee-broh mah-'yohr, ehl ah-see-'ehn-toh dehl mah-'yohr*
legacy	el legado	*ehl leh-'gah-doh*
legal capital	el capital legal	*ehl kah-pee-'tahl leh-'gahl*
legal entity	la persona jurídica	*lah pehr-'soh-nah hoo-'ree-dee-kah*
legal holiday	el día festivo legal	*ehl 'dee-ah fehs-'tee-boh leh-'gahl*
legal investment	la inversión legal	*lah een-behr-see-'ohn leh-'gahl*

legal monopoly	el monopolio legal	*ehl moh-noh-'poh-lee-oh leh-'gahl*
legal tender	la moneda de curso legal, el billete de moneda de curso legal	*lah moh-'neh-dah deh 'koor-soh leh-'gahl, ehl bee-'yeh-teh deh moh-'neh-dah deh 'koor-soh leh-'gahl*
lending firm	la institución prestamista, la empresa de crédito	*lah een-stee-too-syohn-preh-stah-mee-stah, lah ehm-'preh-sah deh 'kreh-dee-toh*
lending margin	el margen de prestación	*ehl 'mahr-hehn deh prehs-tah-see-'ohn*
less-than-a-carload	menos que un vagón completo	*'meh-nohs keh oon bah-'gohn kohm-'pleh-toh*
less-than-a-truckload	menos que un camión completo	*'meh-nohs keh oon kah-mee-'ohn kohm-'pleh-toh*
lessee	el arrendatario	*ehl ah-rrehn-dah-'toh-rree-oh*
lessor	el arrendador	*ehl ah-rrehn-dah-'dohr*
letter	la carta	*lah 'kahr-tah*
letter of credit	la carta de crédito	*lah 'kahr-tah deh 'kreh-dee-toh*
letter of guaranty	la carta de garantía	*lah 'kahr-tah deh gah-rahn-'tee-ah*
letter of indemnity	la garantía de indemnización	*lah gah-rahn-'tee-ah deh een-dehm-nee-sah-see-'ohn*
letter of introduction	la carta de presentación	*lah 'kahr-tah deh preh-sehn-tah-see-'ohn*
letterpress	el texto impreso, la impresión tipográfica	*ehl 'tehks-toh eem-'preh-soh, lah eem-preh-see-'ohn tee-poh-'grah-fee-kah*
level out (v)	nivelar	*nee-beh-'lahr*
leverage	el impulso debido a la emisión de deuda	*ehl eem-'pool-soh deh-'bee-doh ah la eh-mee-see-'ohn deh deh-'oo-dah*
leveraged equity	acciones con aplancamiento	*ahk-see-'oh-nehs kohn ah-plahn-kah-mee-'eh-toh*
levy taxes (v)	imponer contribuciones	*eem-poh-'nehr kohn-tree-boo-see-'oh-nehs*
liability	el pasivo	*ehl pah-'see-boh*

liability for tax	sujeto a impuesto	*soo-'heh-toh ah eem-'pweh-stoh*
liability insurance	los seguros de responsabilidad civil	*lohs seh-'goo-rohs deh reh-spohn-sah-bee-lee-'dahd*
liaison	el enlace	*ehl ehn-'lah-seh*
libel	la calumnia	*lah kah-'loom-nee-ah*
license	la licencia	*lah lee-'sehn-see-ah*
license fees	los derechos de la licencia	*lohs deh-'reh-chohs deh lah lee-'sehn-see-ah*
licensed warehouse	el almacén autorizado	*ehl ahl-mah-'sehn ow-toh-ree-'sah-doh*
lien	el gravamen, la hipoteca	*ehl grah-'bah-mehn, lah ee-poh-'teh-kah*
life cycle (of a product)	el ciclo de duración (de un producto)	*ehl 'see-kloh deh doo-rah-see-'ohn (deh oon proh-'dook-toh)*
life insurance policy	la póliza de seguro de vida	*lah 'poh-lee-sah deh seh-'goo-roh deh 'bee-dah*
life member	el miembro de por vida	*ehl mee-'ehm-broh deh pohr 'bee-dah*
life of a patent	la vida de una patente	*lah 'bee-dah deh 'oo-nah pah-'tehn-teh*
lifeboat	le bote salvavidas (m)	*ehl 'boh-teh sahl-bah-'bee-dahs*
lighterage	los gastos de lanchaje	*lohs 'gah-stohs deh lahn-'chah-heh*
limestone	la piedra caliza	*lah pee'eh-drah kah-'lee-sah*
limit order (stock market)	la orden con precio prefijado	*lah 'ohr-dehn kohn 'preh-see-oh preh-fee-'hah-doh*
limited liability	la responsabilidad limitada	*lah reh-spohn-sah-bee-lee-'dahd lee-mee-'tah-dah*
limited partnership	la sociedad limitada	*lah soh-see-eh-dahd lee-mee-'tah-dah*
line	la línea, el renglón	*la 'lee-neh-ah, ehl rehn-'glohn*
line drawing	el dibujo lineal	*ehl dee-'boo-hoh lee-neh-'ahl*
line executive	el ejecutivo de la organización	*ehl eh-heh-koo-'tee-boh deh lah ohr-gah-nee-sah-see-'ohn*

line of business	la línea de negocios	*lah 'lee-neh-ah deh neh-'goh-see-ohs*
linear	lineal	*lee-neh-'ahl*
linear programming	la programación lineal	*lah proh-grah-mah-see-'ohn lee-neh-'ahl*
linear terms	los términos lineales	*lohs 'tehr-mee-nohs lee-neh-'ah-les*
linen	la mantelería	*lah mahn-teh-leh-'ree-ah*
lingerie	la ropa interior	*lah 'roh-pah een-teh-ree-'ohr*
lining	el forro	*ehl 'foh-rroh*
link	el vínculo, la unión	*ehl 'been-koo-loh, lah oo-nee-'ohn*
liquid assets	los activos líquidos, los activos de fácil realización	*lohs ahk-'tee-bohs 'lee-kee-dohs, lohs ahk-'tee-bohs deh 'fah-seel reh-ah-lee-sah-see-'ohn*
liquidating dividend	el dividendo de capital	*ehl dee-bee-'dehn-doh deh kah-pee-'tahl*
liquidation	la liquidación	*lah lee-kee-dah-see-'ohn*
liquidation value	el valor de liquidación	*ehl bah-'lohr deh lee-kee-dah-see-'ohn*
liquidity	la liquidez	*lah lee-kee-'dehs*
liquidity preference	la preferencia por la liquidez	*lah preh-feh-'rehn-see-ah pohr lah lee-kee-'dehs*
liquidity ratio	el índice de liquidez	*ehl 'eeh-dee-seh deh lee-kee-'dehs*
list	la lista	*lah 'lees-tah*
list (v)	listar	*lees-'tahr*
list price	el precio de catálogo	*ehl 'preh-see-oh deh kah-'tah-loh-goh*
listed securities	los valores bursátiles (escritos en la bolsa)	*lohs bah-'loh-rehs boor-'sah-tee-lehs (ehs-'kree-tohs ehn lah 'bohl-sah)*
listing	el listado	*ehl lee-'stah-doh*
liter	el litro	*ehl 'lee-troh*
litigation	la litigación	*lah lee-tee-gah-see-'ohn*
living beings	los seres vivos	*lohs 'seh-rehs 'bee-bohs*
living trust	el fideicomiso inter vivos	*ehl fee-deh-ee-koh-'mee-soh 'een-tehr 'bee-bohs*

lizard skin	la piel de lagarto	*lah pee-'ehl deh lah-'gahr-toh*
load (sales charge)	los cargos (sobre ventas)	*lohs 'kahr-gohs ('soh-breh 'behn-tahs)*
load factor	el coeficiente de cargamento	*ehl koh-eh-fee-see-'ehn-teh deh kahr-gah-'mehn-toh*
loan	el préstamo	*ehl 'preh-stah-moh*
loan stocks	las acciones prestadas	*lahs ahk-see-'oh-nehs preh-'stah-dahs*
lobbying	el cabildeo	*ehl kah-beel-'deh-oh*
local customs	las costumbres locales	*lahs koh-'stoom-brehs loh-'kah-lehs*
local taxes	los impuestos locales	*lohs eem-'pweh-stohs loh-'kah-lehs*
locate	localizar, descubrir	*loh-kah-lee-'sahr, dehs-koo-'breer*
lock in (rate of interest) (v)	aprovechar el tipo de interés vigente, fijar el tipo de interés	*ah-proh-beh-'chahr ehl 'tee-poh deh een-teh-'rehs bee-'hehn-teh, fee-'hahr ehl 'tee-poh deh een-teh-'rehs*
lock out	el cierre, el paro forzoso	*ehl see-'eh-rreh, ehl 'pah-roh fohr-'soh-soh*
log off (v)	poner fin a una sesión	*poh-'nehr feen ah 'oo-nah seh-see-'ohn*
log on (v)	iniciar una sesión	*ee-nee-see-'ahr 'oo-nah seh-see-'ohn*
log	el registro cronológico	*ehl reh-'hees-troh kroh-noh-'loh-hee-koh*
logistics	la logística	*lah loh-'heehs-tee-kah*
logo	el logotipo	*ehl loh-goh-'tee-poh*
long hedge	la compra compensadora, la protección al que ha comprado algo	*lah 'kohm-prah kohm-pehn-sah-'doh-rah, lah proh-tehk-see-'ohn ahl keh ah kohm-'prah-doh 'ahl-goh*
long product	las planchas rectangulares usadas para la manufactura	*lahs 'plahn-chahs rehk-tahn-goo-'lah-rehs oo-'sah-dahs 'pah-rah lah mah-noo-fahk-'too-rah*
long sleeves	las mangas largas	*lahs 'mahn-gahs 'lahr-gahs*
long ton	la tonelada de 2240 libras	*lah toh-neh-'lah-dah deh 2240 'lee-brahs*

long-range plan	la planificación de largo plazo	*lah plah-nee-fee-kah-see-'ohn deh 'lahr-goh 'plah-soh*
long-term capital account	la cuenta de capital a largo plazo	*lah 'kwehn-tah deh kah-pee-'tahl ah 'lahr-goh 'plah-soh*
long-term debt	la deuda a largo plazo	*lah deh-'oo-dah ah 'lahr-goh 'plah-soh*
long-term interest	el interés a largo plazo	*ehl een-teh-'rehs ah 'lahr-goh 'plah-soh*
loop	el bucle	*ehl 'boo-kleh*
loss	la pérdida	*lah 'pehr-dee-dah*
loss leader	el artículo barato para atraer clientes	*ehl ahr-'tee-koo-loh bah-'rah-toh 'pah-rah ah-trah-'ehr klee-'ehn-tehs*
loss-loss ratio	la relación entre prima y pérdidas	*lah reh-lah-see-'ohn 'ehn-treh 'pree-mah ee 'pehr-dee-dahs*
lot	el lote, la cuota, la partida	*ehl 'loh-teh, lah 'kwoh-tah, lah pahr-'tee-dah*
low-income	de ingresos bajos	*deh een-'greh-sohs 'bah-hohs*
low-interest loans	los préstamos a bajo interés	*lohs 'preh-stah-mohs ah 'bah-hoh een-teh-'rehs*
low-yield bonds	los bonos de rendimiento bajo	*lohs 'boh-nohs deh rehn-dee-mee-'ehn-toh 'bah-hoh*
lower case	la minúscula, la caja baja	*lah mee-'noos-koo-lah, lah 'kah-hah 'bah-hah*
lump sum	la suma global	*lah 'soo-mah gloh-'bahl*
luxury goods	los bienes de lujo	*lohs bee-'eh-nehs deh 'loo-hoh*
luxury tax	el impuesto sobre lujos	*ehl eem-pweh-stoh 'soh-breh 'loo-hohs*

M

machine language	el lenguaje máquina	*ehl lehn-'gwah-heh 'mah-kee-nah*
machinery	la maquinaria	*lah mah-kee-'nah-ree-ah*

macro	macro, macro instrucción	*mah-kroh, 'mah-kroh een-strook-see-'ohn*
macroeconomics	la macroeconomía	*lah mah-kroh-eh-koh-noh-'mee-ah*
magnetic memory	la memoria en cinta magnética	*lah meh-'moh-ree-ah ehn 'seen-tah mahg-'neh-tee-kah*
magnetic tape	la cinta magnética	*lah 'seen-tah mahg-'neh-tee-kah*
magnum (2 bottles in one)	la botella de dos litros	*lah boh-'teh-yah deh dohs 'lee-trohs*
mail order	el pedido hecho por correo	*ehl peh-'dee-doh 'eh-choh pohr koh-'rreh-oh*
mailing list	la planilla de direcciones	*lah plah-'nee-yah deh dee-rehk-see-'oh-nehs*
mainframe	la unidad principal	*lah oo-nee-'dahd preen-see-'pahl*
mainframe computer	la computadora principal	*lah kohm-poo-tah-'doh-rah preen-see-'pahl*
maintenance	el mantenimiento	*ehl mahn-teh-nee-mee-'ehn-toh*
maintenance contract	el contrato de mantenimiento	*ehl kohn-'trah-toh deh mahn-teh-nee-mee-'ehn-toh*
maintenance margin	el margen de mantenimiento	*ehl 'mahr-hehn deh mahn-teh-nee-mee-'ehn-toh*
maize	el maíz	*ehl mah-'ees*
majority interest	el interés mayoritario	*ehl een-teh-'rehs mah-yoh-ree-'tah-ree-oh*
make available (v)	hacer disponible	*ah-'sehr dees-poh-'nee-bleh*
make ready (v)	preparar	*preh-pah-'rahr*
make-or-buy decision	la decisión de hacer o comprar	*lah deh-see-see-'ohn deh ah-'sehr oh kohm-'prahr*
maker (of a check, draft)	el girador	*ehl hee-rah-'dohr*
makeshift	provisional	*proh-bee-see-oh-'nahl*
makeup case	el estuche de maquillaje, la maleta de maquillaje	*ehl ehs-'too-cheh deh mah-kee-'yah-heh, lah mah-'leh-tah deh mah-kee-'yah-heh*
malolactic fermentation	la fermentación maloláctica	*lah fehr-mehn-tah-see-'ohn mah-loh-'lahk-tee-kah*

mammal	el mamífero	*ehl mah-'mee-feh-roh*
man hour	la hora-hombre	*lah 'oh-rah 'ohm-breh*
manage (v)	dirigir, gerenciar	*dee-ree-'heer, heh-rehn-see-'ahr*
managed costs	los costos controlados	*lohs 'koh-stohs kohn-troh-'lah-dohs*
managed economy	la economía controlada	*lah eh-koh-noh-'mee-ah*
management	la gerencia, la administración	*lah heh-'rehn-see-ah, lah ahd-mee-nee-strah-see-'ohn*
management accounting	la contabilidad administrativa	*lah kohn-tah-bee-lee-'dahd ahd-mee-nee-strah-'tee-bah*
management by objectives	la administración por medio de objetivos	*lah ahd-mee-nee-strah-see-'ohn pohr 'meh-dee-oh deh ohb-heh-'tee-bohs*
management chart	el organigrama gerencial	*ehl ohr-gah-nee-'grah-mah heh-rehn-see-'ahl*
management consultant	el consultor gerencial	*ehl kohn-sool-'tohr heh-rehn-see-'ahl*
management fee	el honorario de administración	*ehl oh-noh-'rah-ree-oh deh ahd-mee-nee-strah-see-'ohn*
management group	el grupo administrativo, el grupo gerencial	*ehl 'groo-poh ahd-mee-nee-strah-'tee-boh, ehl 'groo-poh heh-rehn-see-'ahl*
management team	el equipo administrativo, el equipo gerencial	*ehl eh-'kee-poh ahd-mee-nee-strah-'tee-boh, ehl eh-'kee-poh heh-rehn-see-'ahl*
manager	el gerente	*ehl heh-'rehn-teh*
mandate	el mandato	*ehl mahn-'dah-toh*
mandatory redemption	la amortización obligatoria	*lah ah-mohr-tee-sah-see-'ohn oh-blee-gah-'toh-ree-ah*
manganese ore	el mineral de manganeso	*ehl mee-neh-'rahl deh mahn-gah-'neh-soh*
manicuring kit	el estuche de manicura, el estuche de arreglarse las uñas	*ehl ehs-'too-cheh deh mah-nee-'koo-rah, ehl ehs-'too-cheh deh ah-rreh-'glahr-seh lahs 'oo-nyahs*
manifest	el manifiesto	*ehl mah-nee-fee-'eh-stoh*

mankind	la humanidad	*lah oo-mah-nee-'dad*
manmade fibers	las fibras artificiales	*lahs 'fee-brahs ahr-tee-fee-see-'ah-lehs*
manpower	la fuerza de trabajo	*lah 'fwehr-sah deh trah-'bah-hoh*
manual operation	la operación manual	*lah oh-peh-rah-see-'ohn mah-noo-'ahl*
manual workers	los obreros manuales	*lohs oh-'breh-rohs mah-noo-'ah-lehs*
manufacturer	el fabricante	*ehl fah-bree-'kahn-teh*
manufacturer's agent	el agente del fabricante	*ehl ah-'hehn-teh dehl fah-bree-'kahn-teh*
manufacturer's representative	el representante del fabricante	*ehl reh-preh-sehn-'tahn-teh dehl fah-bree-'kahn-teh*
manufacturing capacity	la capacidad de manufacturación	*lah kah-pah-see-'dahd deh mah-noo-fahk-too-rah-see-'ohn*
manufacturing control	el control de fabricación, el control de manufactura	*ehl kohn-'trohl deh fah-bree-kah-see-'ohn, ehl kohn-'trohl deh mah-noo-fahk-'too-rah*
margin call	la demanda para margen adicional	*lah deh-'mahn-dah 'pah-rah 'mahr-hehn ah-dee-see-oh-'nahl*
margin of safety	el margen de seguridad	*ehl 'mahr-hehn deh seh-goo-ree-'dahd*
margin requirements	las estipulaciones del margen	*lahs eh-stee-poo-lah-see-'oh-nehs dehl 'mahr-hehn*
marginal account	la cuenta marginal	*lah 'kwehn-tah mahr-hee-'nahl*
marginal cost	el costo marginal	*ehl 'koh-stoh mahr-hee-'nahl*
marginal pricing	la valoración marginal	*lah bah-loh-rah-see-'ohn mahr-hee-'nahl*
marginal productivity	la productividad marginal	*lah proh-dook-tee-bee-'dahd mahr-hee-'nahl*
marginal revenue	los ingresos marginales	*lohs een-'greh-sohs mahr-hee-'nah-lehs*
marine or maritime cargo insurance	los seguros de cargo marítimo	*lohs seh-'goo-rohs deh 'kahr-goh mah-'ree-tee-moh*

marine underwriter	el suscritor de seguro marítimo	*ehl soo-skree-'tohr deh seh-'goo-roh mah-'ree-tee-moh*
maritime contract	el contrato marítimo	*ehl kohn-'trah-toh mah-'ree-tee-moh*
markdown	la reducción de precio	*lah reh-dook-see-'ohn deh 'preh-see-oh*
market	el mercado	*ehl mehr-'kah-doh*
market (v)	mercadear, comerciar	*mehr-kah-deh-'ahr, koh-mehr-'see-ahr*
market access	el acceso al mercado	*ehl ak-seh-soh ahl mehr-'kah-doh*
market appraisal	el avalúo de mercado	*ehl ah-bah-loo-oh deh mehr-'kah-doh*
market concentration	la concentración en el mercado	*lah kohn-sehn-trah-see-'ohn ehn ehl mehr-'kah-doh*
market dynamics	la dinámica del mercado	*lah dee-'nah-mee-kah dehl mehr-'kah-doh*
market forces	los factores del mercado	*lohs fahk-'toh-rehs dehl mehr-'kah-doh*
market forecast	la predicción del mercado	*lah preh-deek-see-'ohn dehl mehr-'kah-doh*
market index	el índice del mercado	*ehl 'een-dee-seh dehl mehr-'kah-doh*
market management	la administración del mercado	*lah ahd-mee-nee-strah-see-'ohn dehl mehr-'kah-doh*
market penetration	la penetración al mercado	*lah peh-neh-trah-see-'ohn ahl mehr-'kah-doh*
market plan	el plan del mercado	*ehl plahn dehl mehr-'kah-doh*
market position	el estado del mercado	*ehl eh-'stah-doh dehl mehr-'kah-doh*
market potential	el potencial en el mercado	*ehl poh-tehn-see-'ahl ehn ehl mehr-'kah-doh*
market price	el precio del mercado	*ehl 'preh-see-oh dehl mehr-'kah-doh*
market rating	la clasificación de un mercado, la clasificación del mercado	*lah klah-see-fee-kah-see-'ohn deh oon mehr-'kah-doh, lah klah-see-fee-kah-see-'ohn dehl mehr-'kah-doh*

market report	el informe del mercado	*ehl een-'fohr-me dehl mehr-'kah-doh*
market research	las investigaciones del mercado	*lahs een-beh-stee-gah-see-'oh-nehs dehl mehr-kah-doh*
market saturation	la saturación del mercado	*lah sah-too-rah-see-'ohn dehl mehr-'kah-doh*
market share	la participación en el mercado	*lah pahr-tee-see-pah-see-'ohn ehn ehl mehr-kah-doh*
market survey	el estudio del mercado	*ehl eh-'stoo-dee-oh dehl mehr-'kah-doh*
market trends	las tendencias del mercado	*lahs tehn-'dehn-see-'ahs dehl mehr-'kah-doh*
market value	el valor del mercado	*ehl bah-'lohr dehl mehr-'kah-doh*
market-maker (securities)	el comprador de valores para su propia cuenta y de su cuenta	*ehl kohm-prah-'dohr deh bah-'loh-rehs pah-rah soo 'proh-pee-ah 'kwehn-tah ee deh-soo-'kwehn-tah*
marketable securities	los valores comerciables	*lohs bah-'loh-rehs koh-mehr-see-'ah-lehs*
marketing	el márketing, el mercadeo	*ehl mahr-keht-teeng, ehl mehr-kah-'deh-oh*
marketing budget	el presupuesto de mercadeo	*ehl preh-soo-'pweh-stoh deh mehr-kah-'deh-oh*
marketing concept	el concepto de mercadeo	*ehl kohn-'sehp-toh deh mehr-kah-'deh-oh*
marketing plan	el plan del mercado	*ehl plahn dehl mehr-'kah-doh*
marketplace	el mercado	*ehl mehr-'kah-doh*
markup	el margen de ganancias, el aumento de precio	*ehl 'mahr-hehn deh gah-'nahn-see-'ahs, ehl ow-'mehn-toh deh 'preh-see-oh*
marsh	el pantano	*ehl pahn-'tah-noh*
mass communications	la comunicación de masas	*lah koh-moo-nee-kah-see-'ohn deh 'mah-sahs*
mass media	los medios públicos de comunicación	*lohs 'meh-dee-ohs 'poo-blee-kohs deh koh-moo-nee-kah-see-'ohn*
mass production	la fabricación en serie	*lah fah-bree-kah-see-'ohn ehn 'seh-ree-eh*

matched samples	las muestras que hacen juego	*lahs 'mweh-strahs keh 'ah-sehn hoo-'eh-goh*
materials	los materiales	*lohs mah-teh-ree-'ah-lehs*
maternity leave	la ausencia por permiso de maternidad	*lah ow-'sehn-see-ah pohr pehr-'mee-soh deh mah-tehr-nee-'dahd*
mathematical model	el modelo matemático	*ehl moh-'deh-loh mah-teh-'mah-teh-koh*
matrix management	la gerencia matricial	*lah heh-'rehn-see-ah mah-tree-see-ahl*
maturity	el vencimiento	*ehl behn-see-mee-'ehn-toh*
maturity date	la fecha de vencimiento	*lah 'feh-chah deh behn-see-mee-'ehn-toh*
maximize (v)	llevar al máximo	*yeh-'bahr ahl 'mahk-see-moh*
mean	el promedio	*ehl proh-'meh-dee-oh*
means	los medios	*lohs 'meh-dee-ohs*
measure (v)	medir	*meh-'deer*
mechanic's lien	el promedio, el gravamen de constructor	*ehl proh-'meh-dee-oh, ehl grah-'bah-mehn deh kohn-strook-'tohr*
mechanical engineer	el ingeniero mecánico	*ehl een-heh-nee-'eh-roh meh-'kah-nee-koh*
mechanical engineering	la ingeniería mecánica	*lah een-heh-nee-eh-'ree-ah meh-'kah-nee-koh*
median	la mediana	*lah meh-dee-'ah-nah*
mediation	la mediación	*lah meh-dee-ah-see-'ohn*
medicine	la medicina	*lah meh-dee-'see-nah*
medium (term)	el plazo intermedio	*ehl 'plah-soh een-tehr-'meh-dee-oh*
medium of exchange	el medio de cambio	*ehl 'meh-dee-oh deh 'kahm-bee-oh*
meet the price	pagar el precio	*pah-'gahr ehl 'preh-see-oh*
meeting	la reunión	*lah reh-oo-nee-'ohn*
member firm	la empresa asociada	*lah ehm-'preh-sah ah-soh-see-'ah-dah*
member of firm	el socio de la empresa	*ehl 'soh-syoh deh lah ehm-'preh-sah*
memorandum	el memorándum, la nota	*ehl meh-moh-'rahn-doom, lah 'noh-tah*

memory	la memoria	*lah meh-'moh-ree-ah*
mercantile	mercantil	*mehr-kahn-'teel*
mercantile agency	la agencia mercantil	*lah ah-'hehn-see-ah mehr-kahn-'teel*
mercantile law	el derecho mercantil	*ehl deh-'reh-choh mehr-kahn-'teel*
merchandise	las mercancías	*lahs mehr-kahn-'see-ahs*
merchant	el comerciante	*ehl koh-mehr-see-'ahn-teh*
merchant bank	el banco mercantil, la casa de aceptaciones	*ehl 'bahn-koh mehr-kahn-'teel, lah 'kah-sah deh ah-sehp-tah-see-'oh-nehs*
merchant guild	el gremio mercantil	*ehl 'greh-mee-oh mehr-kahn-'teel*
merge (v)	intercalar, fusionar archivos	*een-tehr-kah-'lahr, foo-see-oh-'nahr ahr-'chee-bohs*
merger	la fusión de empresas	*lah foo-see-'ohn deh ehm-'preh-sahs*
message	el mensaje	*ehl mehn-'sah-heh*
metals	los metales	*lohs meh-'tah-lehs*
methane	el metano	*ehl meh-'tah-noh*
method	el método	*ehl 'meh-toh-doh*
metrification	la adopción del sistema métrico	*lah ah-dohp-see-'ohn dehl sees-'teh-mah 'meh-tree-koh*
microchip	la microficha	*lah mee-kroh-'fee-chah*
microcomputer	la microcomputadora	*lah mee-kroh-kohm-poo-tah-'doh-rah*
microfiche	el microfichero	*ehl mee-kroh-fee-'cheh-roh*
microfilm	la micropelícula	*lah mee-kroh-peh-'lee-koo-lah*
microphone	el micrófono	*ehl mee-'kroh-foh-noh*
microorganism	el micro-organismo	*ehl mee-kroh-ohr-gah-'nees-moh*
microprocessor	el microprocesador	*ehl mee-kroh-proh-seh-sah-'dohr*
microwave	el microonda	*ehl mee-kroh-'ohn-dah*
middle man	el intermediario	*ehl een-tehr-meh-dee-'ah-ree-oh*

M

middle management	la gerencia intermediaria	*lah heh-'rehn-see-ah een-tehr-meh-dee-'ah-ree-ah*
migration	la migración	*lah mee-grah-see-'ohn*
mileage	el millaje, el kilometraje	*ehl mee-'yah-heh, ehl kee-loh-meh-'trah-hey*
milling (grain)	la molienda	*lah moh-lee-'ehn-dah*
milling (wood)	el fresado	*ehl freh-'sah-doh*
minicomputer	la minicomputadora	*lah mee-nee-kohm-poo-tah-'doh-rah*
minimum reserves	las reservas mínimas	*lahs reh-'sehr-bahs 'mee-nee-mahs*
minimum wage	el salario mínimo	*ehl sah-'lah-ree-oh 'mee-nee-moh*
mink	el visón	*ehl bee-'sohn*
minority interests	los intereses minoritarios	*lohs een-teh-'reh-sehs mee-noh-ree-'tah-ree-ohs*
mint	la casa de moneda, la emisión de moneda	*lah 'kah-sah deh moh-'neh-dah, lah eh-mee-see-'ohn deh moh-'neh-dah*
mint (v)	acuñar, imprimir	*ah-koo-'nyahr, eem-pree-'meer*
miscalculation	el cálculo erróneo, el mal cálculo	*ehl 'kahl-koo-loh eh-'rroh-neh-oh, ehl mahl 'kahl-koo-loh*
miscellaneous	misceláneo	*mee-seh-'lah-neh-oh*
misleading	engañoso	*ehn-gah-'nyoh-soh*
misunderstanding	la mala interpretación, el malentendido	*lah 'mah-lah een-tehr-preh-tah-see-'ohn, ehl mahl-ehn-tehn-'dee-doh*
mix	la mezcla	*lah 'mehs-klah*
mixed cost	el costo mixto	*ehl 'koh-stoh 'meeks-toh*
mixed sampling	el muestreo mixto	*ehl mweh-'streh-oh 'meeks-toh*
mixer	el mezclador	*ehl mehs-klah-'dohr*
mobility of labor	la movilidad laboral	*lah moh-bee-lee-'dahd lah-boh-'rahl*
mock-up	la maqueta	*lah mah-'keh-tah*
mode	la moda	*lah 'moh-dah*

model	el modelo (ropa-cloth), el/la modelo (persona-person)	*ehl moh-'deh-loh ('roh-pah), ehl/lah moh-'deh-loh (pehr-'soh-nah)*
modem	el móden, el modulador-demodulador	*ehl moh-'dehn, ehl moh-doo-lah-dohr deh-moh-doo-lah-'dohr*
modern	moderno	*moh-'dehr-noh*
modular production	la producción modular	*lah proh-dook-see-'ohn moh-doo-'lahr*
mole	el mol	*ehl mohl*
molecule	la molécula	*lah moh-'leh-koo-lah*
monetary base	la base monetaria	*lah 'bah-seh moh-neh-'tah-ree-ah*
monetary credits	los créditos monetarios	*lohs 'kreh-dee-tohs moh-neh-'tah-ree-ohs*
monetary policy	la política monetaria	*lah poh-'lee-tee-kah moh-neh-'tah-ree-ah*
money	el dinero, la moneda	*ehl dee-'neh-roh, lah moh-'neh-dah*
money broker	el corredor de dinero	*ehl koh-rreh-'dohr deh dee-'neh-roh*
money exchange	la tienda de moneda	*lah tee-'ehn-dah deh moh-'neh-dah*
money manager	el gerente monetario	*ehl heh-'rehn-teh moh-neh-'tah-ree-oh*
money market	el mercado monetario	*ehl mehr-'kah-doh moh-neh-'tah-ree-oh*
money market account	cuenta de mercado monetario	*'kwehn-tah deh mehr-'kah-doh moh-neh-'tah-ree-oh*
money order	el giro postal	*ehl 'hee-roh poh-'stahl*
money supply	la oferta de dinero	*lah oh-'fehr-tah deh dee-'neh-roh*
monitor	el monitor	*ehl moh-nee-'tohr*
monopoly	el monopolio	*ehl moh-noh-'poh-lee-oh*
monopsony	el monopsonio	*ehl moh-nohp-'soh-nee-oh*
Monte Carlo techniques	las técnicas de Monte Carlo	*lahs 'tehk-nee-kahs deh 'mohn-teh 'kahr-loh*
moonlighting	el pluriempleo	*ehl ploo-ree-ehm-'pleh-oh*
morale	la moral	*lah moh-'rahl*
moratorium	la moratoria	*lah moh-rah-'toh-ree-ah*

Moroccan leather	la piel marroquí	*lah pee-'ehl mah-rroh-'kee*
morphine	la morfina	*lah mohr-'fee-nah*
mortgage	la hipoteca	*lah ee-poh-'teh-kah*
mortgage bank	el banco hipotecario	*ehl 'bahn-koh ee-poh-teh-'kah-ree-oh*
mortgage bond	el bono hipotecario	*ehl 'boh-noh ee-poh-teh-'kah-ree-oh*
mortgage certificate	el título de hipoteca	*ehl 'tee-too-loh deh ee-poh-'teh-kah*
mortgage debenture	la obligación hipotecaria	*lah oh-blee-gah-see-'ohn ee-poh-teh-'kah-ree-ah*
most-favored nation	el país más favorecido	*ehl pah-'ees mahs fah-boh-reh-'see-doh*
motion	la moción	*lah moh-see-'ohn*
motivation study	el estudio de la motivación	*ehl eh-'stoo-dee-oh deh lah moh-tee-bah-see-'ohn*
move block	mover el bloque	*moh-'behr ehl 'bloh-keh*
movement of goods	el transporte de mercancías	*ehl trahns-'pohr-teh deh mehr-kahn-'see-ahs*
moving average	el promedio móvil	*ehl proh-'meh-dee-oh 'moh-beel*
moving expenses	los gastos de mudanzas	*lohs 'gah-stohs deh moo-'dahn-sahs*
moving parity	la paridad móvil	*lah pah-ree-'dahd 'moh-beel*
multicurrency	la multiplicidad de monedas	*lah mool-tee-plee-see-'dahd deh moh-'neh-dahs*
multilateral agreement	el acuerdo multilateral	*ehl ah-'kwehr-doh mool-tee-lah-teh-'rahl*
multilateral trade	el comercio multilateral	*ehl koh-'mehr-see-oh mool-tee-lah-teh-'rahl*
multinational corporation	la empresa multinacional	*lah ehm-'preh-sah mool-tee-nah-see-oh-'nahl*
multinational oil company (MNOC)	compañía petrolera multinacional	*kohm-pah-'nyee-ah peh-troh-'leh-rah mool-tee-nah-see-oh-'nahl*
multiple exchange rate	el tipo de cambio múltiple	*ehl 'tee-poh deh 'kahm-bee-oh 'mool-tee-pleh*
multiple taxation	la imposición múltiple de impuestos	*lah eem-poh-see-see-'ohn 'mool-tee-pleh deh eem-'pweh-stohs*

multiples	los múltiplos	*lohs 'mool-tee-plohs*
multiplier	el multiplicador	*ehl mool-tee-plee-kah-'dohr*
multiprogramming	la programación múltiiple	*lah proh-grah-mah-see-'ohn 'mool-tee-pleh*
municipal bond	el título municipal	*ehl 'tee-too-loh moo-nee-see-'pahl*
mutual fund	el fondo mutualista	*ehl 'fohn-doh 'moo-too-ah-'lees-tah*
mutual savings bank	el banco de ahorro mutuo	*ehl 'bahn-koh deh ah-'oh-rroh 'moo-too-oh*
mutually exclusive classes	las clases mutuamente excluyentes	*lahs 'klah-sehs moo-too-ah-'mehn-teh eks-cloo-'yehn-teh*

N

named inland point of importation	el punto interior designado de importación	*ehl 'poon-toh een-teh-ree-'ohr deh-seeg-'nah-doh deh eem-pohr-tah-see-'ohn*
named point of destination	el punto de destino designado	*ehl 'poon-toh deh deh-'stee-noh deh-seeg-'nah-doh*
named point of exportation	el punto de exportación designado	*ehl 'poon-toh deh ehks-pohr-tah-see-'ohn deh-seeg-'nah-doh*
named point of origin	el punto de origen designado	*ehl 'poon-toh deh oh-'ree-hehn deh-seeg-'nah-doh*
named port of importation	el puerto de importación designado	*ehl 'pwehr-toh deh eem-pohr-tah-see-'ohn deh-seeg-'nah-doh*
named port of shipment	el puerto de embarque designado	*ehl 'pwehr-toh deh ehm-'bahr-keh deh-seeg-'nah-doh*
napkin	la servilleta	*lah sehr-bee-'yeh-tah*
napkin ring	el servilletero, el aro de servilleta	*ehl sehr-bee-yeh-'teh-roh, ehl 'ah-roh deh sehr-bee-'yeh-tah*
narcotic	el narcótico	*ehl nahr-'koh-tee-koh*
national bank	el banco nacional	*ehl 'bahn-koh nah-see-oh-'nahl*

M

national debt	la deuda nacional	*lah deh-'oo-dah nah-see-oh-'nahl*
nationalism	el nacionalismo	*ehl nah-see-oh-nah-'lees-moh*
nationalization	la nacionalización	*lah nah-see-oh-nah-lee-sah-see-'ohn*
native produce	los productos agrícolas naturales	*lohs proh-'dook-tohs ah-'gree-koh-lahs nah-too-'rah-lehs*
natural beauty	la belleza natural	*lah bee-'yeh-sah nah-too-'rahl*
natural gas	el gas natural	*ehl gahs nah-too-'rahl*
natural resources	los recursos naturales	*lohs reh-'koor-sohs nah-too-'rah-lehs*
natural science	la ciencia natural	*lah see-'ehn-see-ah nah-too-'rahl*
near money	el cuasi-dinero	*ehl koo-'ah-see-dee-'neh-roh*
neck (of bottle)	el cuello, el gollete	*ehl 'kweh-yoh, ehl goh-'yeh-teh*
needle	la aguja	*lah ah-'goo-hah*
needs analysis	el análisis de las necesidades	*ehl ah-'nah-lee-sees deh lahs neh-seh-see-'dah-dehs*
negative cash flow	el flujo de caja negativo	*ehl 'floo-hoh deh 'kah-hah neh-gah-'tee-boh*
negative pledge	la pignoración	*lah peeg-noh-rah-see-'ohn*
negligent	negligente	*nehg-lee-'hehn-teh*
negotiable	negociable, transmisible	*neh-goh-see-'ah-bleh, trahns-mee-'see-bleh*
negotiable securities	los valores negociables	*lohs bah-'loh-rehs neh-goh-see-'ah-blehs*
negotiate (v)	gestionar, negociar	*hehs-tee-oh-'nahr, neh-goh-see-'ahr*
negotiated sale	la venta negociada, la venta otorgada sin competencia	*lah 'behn-tah neh-goh-see-'ah-dah, lah 'behn-tah oh-tohr-'gah-dah seen kohm-peh-'tehn-see-ah*
negotiation	la negociación	*lah neh-goh-see-ah-see-'ohn*
net	neto	*'neh-toh*
net asset	el activo neto	*ehl ahk-'tee-boh 'neh-toh*

net asset value	el valor del activo neto	*ehl bah-'lohr dehl ahk-'tee-boh 'neh-toh*
net borrowed assets	los activos prestados netos	*lohs ahk-'tee-bohs preh-'stah-dohs 'neh-tohs*
net borrowed reserves	las reservas prestadas netas	*lahs reh-'sehr-bahs preh-'stah-dahs 'neh-tahs*
net cash flow	el flujo de caja neto	*ehl 'floo-hoh deh 'kah-hah 'neh-toh*
net change	el cambio neto	*ehl 'kahm-bee-oh 'neh-toh*
net equity asset	el activo de propiedad neto	*ehl ahk-'tee-boh deh proh-pee-eh-'dahd 'neh-toh*
net income	el ingreso neto	*ehl een-'greh-soh neh-toh*
net investment	la inversión neta	*lah een-behr-see-'ohn 'neh-tah*
net loss	la pérdida neta	*lah 'pehr-dee-dah 'neh-tah*
net margin	el beneficio neto, el margen neto	*ehl beh-neh-'fee-see-oh 'neh-toh*
net position (of a trader)	la posición neta	*lah poh-see-see-'ohn 'neh-tah*
net present value (NPV)	el valor actual neto, el valor presente neto	*ehl bah-'lohr ahk-too-'ahl 'neh-toh, ehl bah-'lohr preh-'sehn-teh 'neh-toh*
net profit	el beneficio neto, la utilidad neta	*ehl beh-neh-'fee-see-oh 'neh-toh, lah oo-tee-lee-'dahd 'neh-tah*
net sales	las ventas netas	*lahs 'behn-tahs 'neh-tahs*
net working capital	el capital de trabajo neto	*ehl kah-pee-'tahl deh trah-'bah-hoh 'neh-toh*
net worth	el capital neto	*ehl kah-pee-'tahl 'neh-toh*
network	la red	*lah rehd*
network (v)	desarrollar relaciones comerciales	*dehs-ah-rroh-'yahr reh-lah-see-'oh-nehs koh-mehr-see-'ah-lehs*
new issue	la nueva emisión	*lah noo-'eh-bah eh-mee-see-'ohn*
new money	el dinero nuevo	*ehl dee-'enh-roh noo-'eh-boh*
new product development	el desarrollo de un nuevo producto	*ehl dehs-ah-'rroh-yoh deh oon noo-'eh-boh proh-'dook-toh*

newsprint	el papel de periódico	*ehl pah-'pehl deh peh-ree-'oh-dee-koh*
night depository	el depósito nocturno	*ehl deh-'poh-see-toh nohk-'toor-noh*
nitrate	el nitrato	*ehl nee-'trah-toh*
nitric acid	el ácido nítrico	*ehl 'ah-see-doh 'nee-tree-koh*
nitrite	el nitrito	*ehl nee-'tree-toh*
nitrogen	el nitrógeno	*ehl nee-'troh-heh-noh*
nitrogen dioxide	el dióxido de nitrógeno	*ehl dee-'ohk-see-doh deh nee-'troh-heh-noh*
no par value	sin valor nominal	*seen bah-'lohr noh-mee-'nahl*
no problem	no hay problema	*`noh ah-ee proh-'bleh-mah*
nominal price	el precio nominal	*ehl 'preh-see-oh noh-mee-'nahl*
nominal yield	el rendimiento nominal	*ehl rehn-dee-mee-'ehn-toh noh-mee-'nahl*
noncumulative preferred stocks	las acciones preferentes no acumulativas	*lahs ahk-see-see-'oh-nehs preh-feh-'rehn-tehs noh ah-koo-moo-lah-'tee-bahs*
noncurrent asset	el activo no circulante	*ehl ahk-'tee-boh noh seer-koo-'lahn-teh*
nondurable goods	los bienes no duraderos	*lohs bee-'eh-nehs noh doo-rah-'deh-rohs*
nonfeasance	la falta de cumplimiento	*lah 'fahl-tah deh koom-plee-mee-'ehn-toh*
nonmember	no es miembro de	*noh ehs mee-'ehm-broh deh*
nonprofit	con fines no lucrativos, no lucrativo	*kohn 'fee-nehs noh loo-krah-'tee-bohs, noh loo-krah-'tee-boh*
nonresident	no residente	*noh reh-see-'dehn-teh*
nonvoting stocks	las acciones sin derechos de votar	*lahs ahk-see-'oh-nehs seen deh-'reh-chohs deh boh-'tahr*
norm	la norma	*lah 'nohr-mah*
not otherwise indexed by name	no archivado por nombre en cualquier otra forma	*noh ahr-chee-'bah-doh pohr 'nohm-breh ehn kwahl-kee-'eh-rah 'oh-trah 'fohr-mah*

N

notary	el notario público	*ehl noh-'tah-ree-oh 'poo-blee-koh*
note	el bono simple	*'ehl boh-noh 'seem-pleh*
notes payable	las cuentas por pagar	*lahs 'kwehn-tahs pohr pah-'gahr*
notes receivable	las cuentas por cobrar	*lahs 'kwehn-tahs pohr koh-'brahr*
novation	la novación	*lah noh-bah-see-'ohn*
null and void	nulo y sin valor	*'noo-loh ee seen bah-'lohr*
nullify (v)	anular, invalidar	*ah-noo-'lahr, een-bah-lee-'dahr*
numerical control	el control numérico	*ehl kohn-'trohl noo-'meh-ree-koh*

O

obligation	la obligación	*lah ohb-lee-gah-see-'ohn*
obsolence	la antigüedad, la obsolescencia	*lah ahn-tee-gweh-'dahd, lah ohb-soh-'lehn-see-ah*
occupation	la ocupación, la profesión	*lah oh-koo-pah-see-'ohn, lah proh-feh-see-'ohn*
occupational hazard	el riesgo ocupacional	*ehl ree-'ehs-goh oh-koo-pah-see-oh-'nahl*
odd lot broker	el corredor de menos de cien acciones	*ehl koh-rreh-'dohr deh 'meh-nohs deh see-'ehn ahk-see-'oh-nehs*
odd lots	las acciones de menos de centenas	*lahs ahk-see-'oh-nehs de sehn-'teh-nahs*
odometer	el odómetro	*ehl oh-'doh-meh-troh*
off board (stock market)	fuera de la bolsa	*'fweh-rah deh lah 'bohl-sah*
off line	desalineado, fuera de línea	*dehs-ah-lee-neh-'ah-doh, 'fweh-rah deh 'lee-neh-ah*
off the books	fuera de los libros, cancelado en los libros	*'fweh-rah deh lohs 'lee-brohs, kahn-seh-'lah-doh ehn lohs 'lee-brohs*
offer (v)	ofrecer	*oh-freh-'sehr*
offer for sale (v)	ofrecer en venta	*oh-freh-'sehr ehn 'behn-tah*

offered price	el precio de oferta, el precio de venta	*ehl 'preh-see-oh deh oh-'fehr-tah, ehl 'preh-see-oh deh 'behn-tah*
offered rate	el tipo de oferta, el tipo ofrecido	*ehl 'tee-poh deh oh-'fehr-tah, ehl 'tee-poh oh-freh-'see-doh*
office	la oficina	*lah oh-fee-'see-nah*
office management	la administración de la oficina	*lah ahd-mee-nee-strah-see-'ohn deh lah oh-fee-'see-nah*
official paper	el documento	*ehl doh-koo-'mehn-toh*
offset printing	la imprenta por offset	*lah eem-'prehn-tah pohr ohf-'seht*
offshore company	la sucursal situada fuera del país donde reside la casa matriz	*lah soo-koor-'sahl see-too-'ah-dah 'fweh-rah dehl pah-'ees 'dohn-deh reh-'see-deh lah 'kah-sah mah-'trees*
offshore drilling	la perforación a poca distancia de la costa	*lah pehr-foh-rah-see-'ohn ah 'poh-kah dees-'tahn-see-ah deh lah 'koh-stah*
oil	el petróleo	*ehl peh-'troh-leh-oh*
oil (crude)	el crudo, el petróleo, el aceite petróleo	*el 'kroo-doh, ehl peh-'troh-leh-oh, ehl ah-'seh-ee-teh peh-'troh-leh-oh,*
oil (diesel)	el carburante diesel	*ehl kahr-boo-'rahn-teh dee-eh-'sehl*
oil (heavy fuel)	el fuel-oil pesado	*ehl foo-'ehl oh-'yool peh-'sah-doh*
oil (light fuel)	el fuel-oil (aceite combustible) ligero	*ehl foo-'ehl oh-'yeel (ah-'see-ee-teh kohm-boo-'stee-bleh) lee-'heh-roh*
oil (lubricating)	el lubricante para cilindros	*ehl loo-bree-'kahn-teh 'pah-rah see-'leen-drohs*
oil company	la compañía petrolera	*lah kohm-pah-'nee-ah peh-troh-'leh-rah*
oil exporting country	los países exportadores de petróleo	*lohs pah'ee-sehs ehks-pohr-tah-'doh-rehs deh peh-'troh-leh-oh*
oil field	el yacimiento petrolífero	*ehl yah-see-mee-'ehn-toh peh-troh-'lee-feh-roh*
oil filter	el filtro de aceite	*ehl 'feel-troh deh ah-'seh-ee-teh*

0

oil importing countries	los países importadores de petróleo	*lohs pah'ee-sehs eem-pohr-tah-'doh-rehs deh peh-'troh-leh-oh*
oil industry	la industria petrolera	*lah een-'doos-tree-ah peh-troh-'leh-rah*
oil industry (indigenous)	la industria petrolera indígena	*lah een-'doos-tree-ah peh-troh-'leh-rah een-'dee-heh-nah*
oil industry (integrated)	la industria petrolera integrada	*lah een-'doos-tree-ah peh-troh-'leh-rah een-teh-'grah-dah*
oil pump	la bomba de aceite	*lah 'bohm-bah deh ah-'seh-ee-teh*
oil spill	el derrame de petróleo (m)	*ehl deh-'rrah-meh deh peh-'troh-leh-oh*
oilcloth	el hule	*ehl 'oo-leh*
oil-importing developing company (IODC)	los países importadores de petróleo en vías de desarrollo	*lohs pah'ee-sehs ehks-pohr-tah-'doh-rehs deh peh-'troh-leh-oh ehn 'bee-ahs deh dehs-ah-'rroh-yoh*
ointment	el ungüento	*ehl oon-'gwehn-toh*
oligopoly	el oligopolio	*ehl oh-lee-goh-'poh-lee-oh*
oligopsony	el oligopsonio	*ehl oh-lee-gohp-'soh-nee-oh*
omit (v)	excluir, suprimir	*ehks-kloo-'eer, soo-pree-'meer*
on account of	a cuenta de el embarcado	*ah 'kwehn-tah deh*
on consignment	en consignación	*ehn kohn-seeg-nah-see-'ohn*
on demand	a presentación	*ah preh-sehn-tah-see-'ohn*
on the back	en el reverso, al dorso	*ehl ehl reh-'behr-soh, ahl 'dohr-soh*
on-line	conectado, directo, en línea	*koh-nehk-'tah-doh, dee-'rehk-toh, ehn 'lee-neh-ah*
on-the-job training	el aprendizaje por rutina	*ehl ah-prehn-dee-'sah-heh pohr roo-'tee-nah*
open account	la cuenta abierta	*lah 'kwehn-tah ah-bee-'ehr-tah*
open cover	el efectivo para cubrir letras en blanco	*ehl eh-fehk-'tee-boh 'pah-rah koo-'breer 'leh-trahs ehn 'blahn-koh*

open door policy	la política de puerta abierta	*lah poh-'lee-tee-kah deh 'pwehr-tah ah-bee-'ehr-tah*
open market	el mercado abierto	*ehl mehr-'kah-doh ah-bee-'ehr-toh*
open market operations (money policy)	las operaciones del mercado abierto	*lahs oh-peh-rah-see-'oh-nehs dehl mehr-'kah-doh ah-bee-'ehr-toh*
open order	el pedido abierto, la orden abierta	*ehl peh-'dee-doh ah-bee-'ehr-toh, lah 'orh-dehn ah-bee-'ehr-tah*
open shop	el gremio abierto, el taller franco	*ehl 'greh-mee-oh ah-bee-'ehr-toh, ehl tah-'yehr 'frahn-koh*
opening balance	el saldo inicial	*ehl 'sahl-doh ee-nee-see-'ahl*
opening price	el precio de apertura	*ehl 'preh-see-oh deh ah-pehr-'too-rah*
operating budget	el presupuesto funcional de operaciones	*ehl preh-soo-'pweh-stoh foonk-see-oh-'nahl*
operating expenses	los gastos de operación	*lohs 'gah-stohs deh oh-peh-rah-see-'ohn*
operating income	las ganancias de operación	*lahs gah-'nahn-see-ahs deh oh-peh-rah-see-'ohn*
operating profit	la utilidad operacional, el beneficio de operación	*lah oo-tee-lee-'dahd oh-peh-rah-see-oh-'nahl, ehl beh-neh-'fee-see-oh deh oh-peh-rah-see-'ohn*
operating statement	el estado de operación, el financiero operacional	*ehl eh-'stah-doh deh oh-peh-rah-see-'ohn, ehl fee-nahn-see-'eh-roh oh-peh-rah-see-oh-'nahl*
operations audit	la auditoría de operaciones	*lah ow-dee-toh-'ree-ah deh oh-peh-rah-see-'oh-nehs*
operations headquarters	la oficina principal de operaciones	*lah oh-fee-'see-nah preen-see-'pahl deh oh-peh-rah-see-'oh-nehs*
operations management	la administración	*lah ahd-mee-nees-trah-'see-ohn*
operator (machine)	el maquinista	*ehl mah-kee-'nee-stah*
opium	el opio	*ehl 'oh-pee-oh*
opportunity costs	los costos de oportunidad	*lohs 'koh-stohs deh oh-pohr-too-nee-'dahd*

optic (adj)	óptico	*'ohp-tee-koh*
option	la opción	*lah ohp-see-'ohn*
optional	discrecional	*dees-kreh-see-oh-'nahl*
oral bid (stock exchange)	la oferta verbal	*lah oh-'fehr-tah behr-'bahl*
order	el pedido	*ehl peh-'dee-doh*
order (v)	pedir	*peh-'deer*
order form	la planilla de pedido	*lah plah-'nee-yah deh peh-'dee-doh*
order number	el número del pedido	*ehl 'noo-meh-roh dehl peh-'dee-doh*
order of the day	el orden del día	*ehl 'ohr-dehn dehl 'dee-ah*
order, place an (v)	ordenar	*ohr-deh-'nahr*
ordinary capital	el capital ordinario	*ehl kah-pee-'tahl ohr-dee-'nah-rre-oh*
ore	el mineral	*ehl mee-neh-'rahl*
organic (adj)	orgánico	*ohr-'gah-nee-koh*
organic chemistry	la química orgánica	*lah 'kee-mee-kah ohr-'gah-nee-kah*
organization	la organización	*lah ohr-gah-nee-sah-see-'ohn*
organization chart	el organigrama	*ehl ohr-gah-nee-'grah-mah*
Organization of Petroleum- Exporting Countries (OPEC)	Organización de Países Exportadores de Petróleo (OPEP)	*ohr-gah-nee-sah-see-'ohn deh pah-'ee-sehs ehks-pohr-tah-'doh-rehs deh peh-'troh-leh-oh*
original cost	el costo original	*ehl 'koh-stoh oh-ree-hee-'nahl*
original entry	el asiento original	*ehl ah-see-'ehn-toh oh-ree-hee-'nahl*
original maturity	el vencimiento original	*ehl behn-see-mee-'ehn-toh oh-ree-hee-'nahl*
oscillator	el oscilador	*ehl oh-see-lah-'dohr*
ostrich skin	la piel de avestruz	*lah pee-'ehl deh ah-beh-'stroos*
other assets	los otros activos	*lohs 'oh-trohs ahk-'tee-bohs*
otter	la nutria	*lah 'noo-tree-ah*

out of style	fuera de moda, pasado de moda	*'fweh-rah deh 'moh-dah, pah-'sah-doh deh 'moh-dah*
outbid (v)	ofrecer la postura mayor	*oh-freh-'sehr lah poh-'stoo-rah mah-'yohr*
outlay	el desembolso, el gasto	*ehl dehs-ehm-'bohl-soh, ehl 'gah-stoh*
outlet	el mercado	*ehl mehr-'kah-doh*
outlook	la perspectiva	*lah pehr-spehk-'tee-bah*
out-of-pocket expenses	los gastos efectivos	*lohs 'gah-stohs eh-fehk-'tee-bohs*
output	la producción, la salida	*lah proh-dook-see-'ohn lah sah-'lee-dah*
outsized articles	los artículos de tamaño especial (mayor que el común)	*lohs ahr-'tee-koo-lohs deh tah-'mah-nyoh eh-speh-see-'ahl (mah-'yohr keh ehl koh-'moon)*
outstanding contract	el contracto pendiente	*ehl kohn-'trah-toh pehn-dee-'ehn-teh*
outstanding debt	la deuda no cobrada	*lah deh-'oo-dah noh koh-'brah-dah*
outstanding stocks	las acciones en circulación	*lahs ahk-see-'ohnehs ehn seer-koo-lah-see-'ohn*
outturn	la producción total	*lah proh-dook-see-'ohn toh-'tahl*
over-the-counter quotation	la cotización en ventanilla	*lah koh-tee-sah-see-'ohn ehn behn-tah-'nee-yah*
overage	el sobrante	*ehl soh-'brahn-teh*
overbought	sobrecomprado	*soh-breh-kohm-'prah-doh*
overcapitalized	capitalizado en exceso	*kah-pee-tah-lee-'sah-doh ehn ehk-'seh-soh*
overcharge (v)	poner una carga excesiva	*poh-'nehr 'oo-nah 'kahr-gah exk-seh-'see-bah*
overdraft	el sobregiro, la cuenta en descubierto	*ehl soh-breh-'hee-roh, lah 'kwehn-tah ehn dehs-koo-bee-'ehr-toh*
overdraw (v)	sobregirar	*soh-breh-hee-'rahr*
overdrawn account	la cuenta en descubierto	*lah 'kwehn-tah ehn dehs-koo-bee-'ehr-toh*
overdue	vencido	*behn-'see-doh*
overhang	la proyección	*lah proh-yehk-see-'ohn*

overhead	los gastos generales fijos	*lohs 'gah-stohs heh-neh-'rah-lehs 'fee-hohs*
overhead costs	los gastos generales	*lohs 'gah-stohs heh-neh-'rah-lehs*
overlap	la duplicación	*lah doo-plee-kah-see-'ohn*
overnight	de un día para otro	*deh oon 'dee-ah 'pah-rah 'oh-troh*
overpaid	sobrepagado	*soh-breh-pah-'gah-doh*
overseas common point	el punto en común de ultramar	*ehl 'poon-toh ehn koh-'moon deh ool-trah-'mahr*
oversold	sobrevendido (vendido en exceso)	*soh-breh-behn-'dee-doh (behn-'dee-doh ehn ehk-'seh-soh)*
overstock	el abarrotar	*ehl ah-bah-rroh-'tahr*
oversubscribed	sobresuscrito	*soh-breh-soos-'kree-toh*
oversupply	la sobreoferta	*lah soh-breh-oh-'fehr-tah*
overtime	el tiempo extra	*ehl tee-'ehm-poh 'ehks-trah*
overvalued	sobrevaluado	*soh-breh-bah-loo-'ah-doh*
owner	el propietario	*ehl proh-pee-eh-'tah-ree-oh*
owner's equity	los recursos propios de los propietarios	*lohs reh-'koor-sohs 'proh-pee-ohs deh lohs proh-pee-eh-'tah-ree-ohs*
ownership	la propiedad	*lah proh-pee-eh-'dahd*
oxidation	la oxidación	*lah ohk-see-dah-see-'ohn*
oxides	los óxidos	*lohs 'ohk-see-dohs*
ozone layer	la capa de ozono	*lah 'kah-pah de oh-'soh-noh*
ozone	el ozono	*ehl oh-'soh-noh*

P

p/e ratio	la razón precio-ganancia por acciones	*lah rah-'sohn 'preh-see-oh-gah-'nahn-see-ah pohr akh-see-'oh-nehs*
package deal	el convenio de conjunto, el negocio en paquete, la transacción de conjunto	*ehl kohn-'beh-nee-oh deh kohn-'hoon-toh, ehl neh-'goh-see-oh ehn pah-'keh-teh, lah trahn-sahk-see-'ohn deh kohn-'hooon-toh*

packaging	el embalaje	*ehl ehm-bah-'lah-heh*
packing	el relleno	*ehl reh-'yeh-noh*
packing case	el embalaje de cajas	*ehl ehm-bah-'lah-heh deh 'kah-hahs*
packing list	las especificaciones de embalaje	*lahs eh-speh-see-fee-kah-see-'oh-nehs deh ehm-bah-'lah-heh*
pact	el pacto	*ehl 'pahk-toh*
page	la página	*lah 'pah-hee-nah*
page makeup	la compaginación	*lah kohm-pah-hee-nah-see-'ohn*
paid holiday	el día feriado pagado, las vacaciones pagadas	*ehl 'dee-ah feh-ree-'ah-doh pah-'gah-doh, lahs bah-kah-see-'ohnehs pah'gah-dahs*
paid in full	pagado en su totalidad	*pah-'gah-doh ehn soo toh-tah-lee-'dahd*
paid up capital	el capital desembolsado	*ehl kah-pee-'tahl dehs-ehm-bohl-'sah-doh*
paid up shares	las acciones pagadas	*lahs ahk-see-'oh-nehs pah-'gah-dahs*
paid-in surplus	el superávit pagado	*ehl soo-peh-'rah-beet pah-'gah-doh*
paint	la pintura	*lah peen-'too-rah*
pallet	la paleta	*lah pah-'leh-tah*
palletized freight	la carga en paleta	*lah 'kahr-gah ehn pah-'leh-tah*
pamphlet	el panfleto	*ehl pahn-'fleh-toh*
paper	el papel	*ehl pah-'pehl*
paper holder	la carpeta	*lah kahr-'peh-tah*
paper profits	los beneficios por realizar	*lohs beh-neh-'fee-see-ohs pohr reh-ah-lee-'sahr*
paperback	el libro en rústica	*ehl 'lee-broh ehn 'roos-tee-kah*
par	par	*pahr*
par value	el valor par	*ehl bah-'lohr pahr*
parallel circuit	el circuito paralelo	*ehl seer-koo-'ee-toh pah-rah-'leh-loh*
parcel post	el envío de paquetes por correo	*ehl ehn-'bee-oh deh pah-'keh-tehs pohr koh-'rreh-oh*

P

parent company	la compañía matriz	*lah kohm-pah-'nyee-ah mah-'trees*
parity	la paridad	*lah pah-ree-'dahd*
parity income ratio	la razón de paridad de ingresos	*lah rah-'sohn deh pah-ree-'dahd deh een-'greh-sohs*
parity price	el precio de paridad	*ehl 'preh-see-oh deh pah-ree-'dahd*
park	el parque	*ehl 'pahr-keh*
park (national)	el parque nacional	*ehl 'pahr-keh nah-see-oh-'nahl*
park (protected)	el parque protegido	*'ehl pahr-keh proh-teh-'hee-doh*
partial cargo	el cargamento parcial	*ehl 'kahr-gah-'mehn-toh pahr-see-'ahl*
partial payment	el pago parcial	*ehl 'pah-goh pahr-see-'ahl*
participating preferred stocks	las acciones preferidas participantes	*lahs ahk-see-'oh-nehs preh-feh-'ree-dahs pahr-tee-see-'pahn-tehs*
participation fee	la cuota de participación	*lah 'kwoh-tah deh pahr-tee-see-pah-see-'ohn*
participation loan	el préstamo en participación	*ehl 'preh-stah-moh ehn pahr-tee-see-pah-see-'ohn*
particle	la partícula	*lah pahr-'tee-koo-lah*
particular average loss	la pérdida por avería simple	*lah 'pehr-dee-dah pohr ah-beh-'ree-ah 'seem-pleh*
partner	el socio	*ehl 'soh-see-oh*
partnership	la sociedad	*lah soh-see-eh-'dahd*
parts	las partes	*lahs 'pahr-tehs*
passbook	la libreta bancaria	*lah lee-'breh-tah bahn-'kah-ree-ah*
passed dividends	los dividendos omitidos	*lohs dee-bee-'dehn-dohs oh-mee-tee-dohs*
passport case	la cartera del pasaporte	*lah kahr-'teh-rah dehl pah-sah-'pohr-teh*
past due	vencido	*behn-'see-doh*
pastry server	la paleta de servir tortas (bizcocho)	*lah pah-'leh-tah deh sehr-'beer 'tohr-tahs (bees-'koh-choh)*
patent	la patente	*lah pah-'tehn-teh*

patent application	la solicitud de patente	*lah soh-lee-see-'tood deh pah-'tehn-teh*
patent law	el derecho de patente	*ehl deh-'reh-choh deh pah-'tehn-teh*
patent pending	la patente pendiente	*lah pah-'tehn-teh pehn-dee-'ehn-teh*
patent royalty	la regalía por uso de patente	*lah reh-gah-'lee-ah pohr 'oo-soh deh pah-'tehn-teh*
patented process	el proceso patentado	*ehl proh-'seh-soh pah-tehn-'tah-doh*
path	el camino	*ehl kah-'mee-noh*
pattern	el diseño, el patrón	*ehl dee-'seh-nyoh, ehl pah-'trohn*
pay (v)	pagar	*pah-'gahr*
pay as you go	el pago de impuesto a medida que el contribuyente recibe sus ingresos	*ehl 'pah-goh deh eem-'pweh-stoh ah meh-'dee-dah keh ehl kohn-tree-boo-'yehn-teh reh-'see-beh soos een-'greh-sohs*
pay off (v)	cancelar	*kahn-seh-'lahr*
payable on demand	pagadero a la vista	*pah-gah-'deh-roh ah lah 'bee-stah*
payable to bearer	pagadero al portador	*pah-gah-'deh-roh ahl pohr-tah-'dohr*
payable to order	pagadero a la orden	*pah-gah-'deh-roh ah lah 'ohr-dehn*
payback period	el plazo de reembolso	*ehl 'plah-soh deh reh-ehm-'bohl-soh*
payee	el perceptor	*ehl pehr-sehp-'tohr*
payload	la carga útil	*lah 'kahr-gah 'oo-teel*
paymaster	el pagador	*ehl pah-gah-'dohr*
payment	el pago	*ehl 'pah-goh*
payment in full	el pago total	*ehl 'pah-goh toh-'tahl*
payment in kind	el pago en especie	*ehl 'pah-goh ehn eh-'speh-see-eh*
payment period	el período de pago	*ehl peh-'ree-oh-doh deh 'pah-goh*
payment refused	el pago negado	*ehl 'pah-goh neh-'gah-doh*
payroll	la nómina	*lah 'noh-mee-nah*

payroll tax	el impuesto sobre la nómina	*ehl eem-'pweh-stoh 'soh-breh lah 'noh-mee-nah*
peak load	la carga máxima, la máxima carga	*lah 'kahr-gah 'mahk-see-mah, lah 'mahk-see-mah 'kahr-gah*
pegged price	el precio fijo	*ehl 'preh-see-oh 'fee-hoh*
pegging	la estabilización de precios	*lah eh-stah-bee-lee-sah-see-'ohn deh 'preh-see-ohs*
pellet	la píldora	*lah 'peel-doh-rah*
penalty	la multa	*lah 'mool-tah*
penalty clause	la cláusula penal	*lah 'klow-soo-lah peh-'nahl*
penalty-fraud action	la penalidad por fraude	*lah peh-nah-lee-'dahd pohr 'frow-deh*
penguin	el pingüino	*ehl peen-'gwee-noh*
penny stocks	las acciones cotizadas a menos de un dólar	*lahs ahk-see-'ohnsee-'ohn-nehs koh-tee-'sah-dahs ah 'meh-nohs deh oon 'doh-lahr*
pension fund	el fondo de jubilación	*ehl 'foh-doh deh hoo-bee-lah-see-'ohn*
pensioner	el pensionista	*ehl pen-see-oh-'nees-tah*
pepper mill	el molinillo de pimienta	*ehl moh-lee-'nee-yoh deh pee-mee'ehn-tah*
pepper shaker	el pimentero	*ehl pee-mehn-'teh-roh*
per capita	por habitante	*pohr ah-bee-'tahn-teh*
per diem	por día, el viático	*pohr 'dee-ah, ehl bee-'ah-tee-koh*
per share	por acción	*pohr ahk-see-'ohn*
percentage earnings	el porcentaje de las ganancias	*ehl pohr-sehn-'tah-heh deh lahs gah-'nahn-see-ahs*
percentage of profit	el porcentaje de la utilidad	*ehl pohr-sehn-'tah-heh deh lah oo-tee-lee-'dahd*
perfect binding	la encuadernación perfecta	*lah ehn-kwah-dehr-nah-see-'ohn pehr-'fehk-tah*
performance bond	la fianza de cumplimento	*lah fee-'ahn-sah deh koom-plee-mee-'ehn-toh*
periodic inventory	el inventario periódico	*ehl een-behn-'tah-ree-oh peh-ree-'oh-dee-koh*
peripheral	periférico	*peh-ree-'feh-ree-koh*
perish (v)	perecer	*peh-reh-'sehr*

perks	los beneficios personales que resultan del consumo de bienes de la empresa	*lohs beh-neh-'fee-see-ohs pehr-soh-'nah-lehs keh reh-'sool-tahn dehl kohn-'soo-moh deh bee-'eh-nehs deh lah ehm-'preh-sah*
permit	el permiso	*ehl pehr-'mee-soh*
perpetual inventory	el inventario permanente	*ehl een-behn-'tah-ree-oh pehr-mah-'nehn-teh*
personal computer	la computadora personal, la microcomputadora	*lah kohm-poo-tah-'doh-rah pehr-soh-'nahl, lah mee-kroh-kohm-poo-tah-'doh-rah*
personal consumer benefits resulting from	beneficios personales que resultan del consumo de	*lohs beh-neh-'fee-see-ohs pehr-soh-'nah-lehs keh reh-'sool-tahn dehl kohn-'soo-moh deh*
personal deduction	el desgravamen personal	*ehl dehs-grah-'bah-mehn pehr-soh-'nahl*
personal exemption	la exención personal	*lah ehk-sehn-see-'ohn pehr-soh-'nahl*
personal income tax	el impuesto sobre el ingreso personal	*ehl eem-'pweh-stoh 'soh-breh ehl een-'greh-soh pehr-soh-'nahl*
personal liability	la responsabilidad personal, el riesgo personal	*lah reh-spohn-sah-bee-lee-'dahd pehr-soh-'nahl, ehl ree-'ehs-goh pehr-soh-'nahl*
personal property	la propiedad personal	*lah proh-pee-eh-'dahd pehr-soh-'nahl*
personality test	la prueba de personalidad	*lah proo-'eh-bah deh pehr-soh-nah-lee-'dahd*
personnel	el personal	*ehl pehr-soh-'nahl*
personnel administration	la administración de personal	*lah ahd-mee-nee-stra-see-'ohn deh pehr-soh-'nahl*
personnel department	el departamento de personal	*ehl deh-pahr-tah-'mehn-toh deh pehr-soh-'nahl*
personnel management	la administración de personal	*lah ahd-mee-nee-strah-see-'ohn deh pehr-soh-'nahl*
personnel placement	la ubicación	*lah oo-bee-kah-see-'ohn*
petrochemical	petroquímico	*peh-troh-'kee-mee-koh*
petrodollars	los petrodólares	*lohs peh-troh-'doh-lah-rehs*

petroleum	el petróleo	*ehl peh-'troh-leh-oh*
pharmaceutical (adj)	farmacéutico (adj)	*fahr-mah-'seh-oo-tee-koh*
pharmacist	el farmacéutico	*ehl fahr-mah-'seh-oo-tee-koh*
phase in (v)	incorporar gradualmente	*een-kohr-poh-'rahr grah-doo-ahl-'mehn-teh*
phase out	eliminar gradualmente	*eh-lee-mee-'nahr grah-doo-ahl-'mehn-teh*
phenol	el fenol	*ehl feh-'nohl*
phosphate	el fosfato	*ehl fohs-'fah-toh*
physical characteristics	las características físicas	*lahs kah-rehk-teh-'reès-tee-kahs 'fee-see-kahs*
Physical Quality of Life Index (PQLI)	Indice General de la Calidad de Vida	*'een-dee-seh heh-neh-'rahl deh lah kah-lee-'dahd deh 'bee-dah*
physical inventory	el inventario físico	*ehl een-behn-'tah-ree-oh 'fee-see-koh*
physician	el médico	*ehl 'meh-dee-koh*
phytosanitary regulations	las regulaciones fitosanitanas	*lahs reh-goo-lah-see-'oh-nehs fee-toh-sah-nee-tah-nahs*
pica	el cícero	*ehl 'see-seh-roh*
pick up and deliver (v)	recoger y entregar	*reh-koh-'hehr ee ehn-'trahr*
picket line	el piquete de huelga, la línea de huelga	*ehl pee-'keh-teh deh 'wehl-gah, lah 'lee-neh-ah deh 'wehl-gah*
pickling	la limpieza con baño químico	*lah leem-pee-'eh-sah kohn 'bah-nyoh 'kee-mee-koh*
pie chart	el diagrama de sectores	*ehl dee-ah-'grah-mah deh sehk-'toh-rehs*
piecework	el trabajo a destajo	*ehl trah-'bah-hoh ah dehs-'tah-hoh*
pig iron	el lingote de hierro	*ehl leen-'goh-teh deh 'yeh-roh*
pigskin	la piel de cerdo	*lah pee-'ehl deh 'sehr-doh*
pilfer (v)	hurtar	*oor-'tahr*
pilferage	el hurto	*ehl 'oor-toh*
pill	la píldora	*lah 'peel-doh-rah*

pilotage	los derechos de cabotage	*lohs deh-'reh-chohs deh kah-boh-'tah-heh*
pinion	el piñón	*ehl pee-'nyohn*
pipeline	el oleoducto	*ehl oh-leh-oh-'dook-toh*
pipes and tubes	los tubos y las cañerías	*lohs 'too-bohs ee lahs kah-'nyeh-'ree-ahs*
pitcher	la jarra	*lah 'hah-rrah*
place an order (v)	hacer un pedido	*ah-'sehr oon peh-'dee-doh*
place of business	el domicilio de la empresa	*ehl doh-mee-'see-lee-oh deh lah ehm-'preh-sah*
place setting	el cubierto, el servicio de mesa individual	*ehl koo-bee'ehr-toh, ehl sehr-'bee-see-oh*
placement (personnel)	la contratación de personal	*lah kohn-trah-tah-see-'ohn deh pehr-soh-'nahl*
plague	la plaga	*lah 'plah-gah*
plan	el plan	*ehl plahn*
plankton	el planctón (m)	*ehl plahnk-'tohn*
plankton (sea)	el planctón marino	*ehl plahnk-'tohn mah-'ree-noh*
planet	el planeta (m)	*ehl plah-'neh-tah*
planned obsolescence	la obsolescencia planificada	*lah ohb-soh-leh-'sehn-see-ah plah-nee-fee-'kah-dah*
plant capacity	la capacidad de la planta, la capacidad productiva de la planta	*lah kah-pah-see-'dahd deh lah 'plahn-tah, lah kah-pah-see-'dahd proh-dook-'tee-bah deh lah 'plahn-tah*
plant location	la ubicación de la planta	*lah oo-bee-kah-see-'ohn deh lah 'plahn-tah*
plant manager	el gerente de planta	*ehl heh-'rehn-teh deh 'plahn-tah*
plate (printing)	el estereotipo, la lámina, el grabado	*ehl eh-steh-reh-oh-'tee-poh, lah 'lah-mee-nah, ehl grah-'bah-doh*
plate (dish)	el plato	*ehl 'plah-toh*
plate (of metal)	la plancha, la lámina	*lah 'plahn-chah, lah 'lah-mee-nah*
pleat	el pliegue, el plisado	*ehl plee-'eh-geh, ehl plee-sah-doh*
pleated (adj)	plegado, plisado	*pleh-'gah-doh, plee-'sah-doh*

pledge	la garantía, la prenda	*lah gah-rahn-'tee-ah, lah 'prehn-dah*
plenary meeting	la reunión plenaria	*lah reh-oo-see-'ohn pleh-'nah-ree-ah*
plot (v)	trazar	*trah-'sahr*
plow back (earnings) (v)	reinvertir	*reh-een-behr-'teer*
plug-in (adj)	enchufable	*ehn-choo-'fah-bleh*
plus accrued interest	más interés acumulado	*mahs een-teh-'rehs ah-koo-moo-'lah-doh*
point	el punto	*ehl 'poon-toh*
point (percentage) (mortgage term)	el punto	*ehl 'poon-toh*
point (tip)	la punta	*lah 'poon-tah*
point of order	el punto de orden	*ehl 'poon-toh deh 'ohr-dehn*
point of sale	el punto de venta	*ehl 'poon-toh deh 'behn-tah*
poison (v)	envenenar	*ehn-beh-neh-'nahr*
policy (performance standard)	la política	*lah poh-'lee-tee-kah*
policy holder	el tenedor de póliza	*ehl teh-neh-'dohr deh 'poh-lee-sah*
polymer	el polímero	*ehl poh-'lee-meh-roh*
pool (funds) (v)	mancomunar fondos	*man-koh-moo-'nahr 'fohn-dohs*
pool (v)	combinar	*kohm-bee-'nahr*
pooling of interests	mancomunar intereses	*mahn-koh-moo-'nahr een-teh-'reh-sehs*
poplin	el poplin	*ehl 'pohp-leen*
port	puerto de entrada o salida	*'pwehr-tah deh ehn-'trah-dah oh sah-'lee-dah*
port facilities	las facilidades portuarias	*lahs fah-see-lee-'dah-dehs pohr-too-'ah-ree-ahs*
portfolio	la cartera	*lah kahr-'teh-rah*
portfolio management	la administración de cartera	*lah ahd-mee-nee-strah-see-'ohn deh kahr-'teh-rah*
position limit	la posición límite	*lah poh-see-see-'ohn 'lee-mee-teh*

positive cash flow	el flujo de caja positivo	*ehl 'floo-hoh deh 'kah-hah poh-see-'tee-boh*
post (v) (bookkeeping)	pasar del diario al mayor, asentar	*pah-'sahr dehl dee-'ah-ree-oh ahl mah-'yohr, ah-sehn-'tahr*
post-edit (v)	post-editar	*pohst-eh-dee-'tahr*
postdate	postdatar	*pohs-dah-tahr*
postdated	fechado (con fecha adelantada)	*feh-'chah-doh (kohn 'feh-chah ah-deh-lahn-'tah-dah)*
postpone (v)	posponer, postergar	*pohs-poh-'nehr, poh-stehr-'gahr*
potential buyer	el comprador potencial	*ehl kohm-prah-'dohr poh-tehn-see-'ahl*
potential sales	las ventas potenciales	*lahs 'behn-tahs poh-tehn-see-'ah-lehs*
pottery	la alfarería, la cerámica	*lah ahl-fah-reh-'ree-ah, lah seh-'rah-mee-kah*
powder	la pólvora	*lah 'pohl-boh-rah*
power	la potencia, la energía	*lah poh-'tehn-see-ah, lah eh-nehr-'hee-ah*
power of attorney	el mandato, el poder, la carta poder	*ehl mahn-'dah-toh, ehl poh-'dehr, lah 'kahr-tah poh-'dehr*
power steering	la dirección neumática	*lah dee-rehk-see-'ohn neh-oo-'mah-tee-kah*
power supply	la fuente de energía, suministro de energía	*lah 'fwehn-teh deh eh-nehr-'hee-ah, soo-mee-'nees-troh deh eh-nehr-'hee-ah*
power switch off	el interruptor parado	*ehl een-teh-rroop-'tohr pah-'rah-doh*
power switch on	el interruptor en marcha	*ehl een-teh-rroop-'tohr ehn 'mahr-chah*
practical	práctico	*'prahk-tee-koh*
pre-emptive right	el derecho de prioridad, el derecho preferencial	*ehl deh-'reh-choh deh pree-oh-ree-'dahd, ehl deh-'reh-choh preh-feh-rehn-see-'ahl*
prefabrication	la prefabricación	*lah preh-fah-breek-kah-see-'ohn*
preface	el prólogo	*ehl 'proh-loh-goh*

preferential debts	las deudas preferenciales	*lahs deh-'oo-dahs preh-feh-rehn-see-'ah-lehs*
preferred stock	las acciones preferidas, acciones preferentes	*lahs ahk-see-'oh-nehs preh-feh-'ree-dahs, ahk-see-'oh-nehs preh-feh-'rehn-tehs*
preferred tariff	la tarifa preferencial	*lah tah-'ree-fah preh-feh-rehn-see-'ahl*
preliminary prospectus	el prospecto preliminar	*ehl proh-'spehk-toh preh-lee-mee-'nahr*
premises	los establecimientos, el local	*lohs eh-stah-bleh-see-mee-'ehn-tohs, ehl loh-'kahl*
premium offer	la oferta de prima	*lah oh-'fehr-tah deh 'pree-mah*
prepaid expenses (balance sheet)	los cargos diferidos	*lohs 'kahr-gohs dee-feh-'ree-dohs*
prepare (v)	preparar	*preh-pah-'rahr*
prepay (v)	prepagar	*preh-pah-'gahr*
prescription	la receta	*lah reh-'seh-tah*
president	el presidente	*ehl preh-see-'dehn-teh*
press book	el libro impreso	*ehl 'lee-broh eem-'preh-soh*
pressure	la presión	*lah preh-see-'ohn*
preventive maintenance	el mantenimiento preventivo	*ehl mahn-tehe-nee-mee-'ehn-toh preh-behn-'tee-boh*
preview	la vista anticipada	*'lah bees-tah ahn-tee-see-'pah-dah*
price	el precio	*ehl 'preh-see-oh*
price (v)	valorar	*bah-loh-'rahr*
price cutting	la reducción de precios	*lah reh-dook-see-'ohn deh 'preh-see-ohs*
price differential	la diferencia de precios	*lah dee-feh-'rehn-see-ah deh 'preh-see-ohs*
price elasticity	la elasticidad de precio	*lah eh-lahs-tee-see-'dahd deh 'preh-see-oh*
price fixing	la fijación de precios	*lah fee-hah-see-'ohn deh 'preh-see-ohs*
price index	el índice de precio	*ehl 'een-dee-seh deh 'preh-see-oh*

price limit	el precio límite	*ehl 'preh-see-oh 'lee-mee-teh*
price list	la lista de precios	*lah 'lees-tah deh 'preh-see-ohs*
price range	la variación de precio	*lah bah-ree-ah-see-'ohn deh 'preh-see-oh*
price support	el precio de sostenimiento	*ehl 'preh-see-oh deh sohs-teh-nee-mee-'ehn-toh*
price tick	el cambio pequeño de precio, el precio del fiado	*ehl 'kahm-bee-oh peh-'keh-nyoh deh 'preh-see-oh, ehl 'preh-see-oh dehl fee-'ah-doh*
price war	la competencia de precios, la guerra de precios	*lah kohm-peh-'tehn-see-ah deh 'preh-see-ohs, lah 'geh-rrah deh 'preh-see-ohs*
price-earnings ratio	la relación precio-utilidad por acción	*la reh-lah-see-'ohn 'preh-see-oh-oo-tee-lee-dahd pohr ahk-see-ohn*
primary market	el mercado primario	*ehl mehr-'kah-doh pree-'mah-ree-oh*
primary reserves	las reservas primarias	*lahs reh-'sehr-bahs pree-'mah-ree-ahs*
prime cost	el costo primo	*ehl 'koh-stoh 'pree-moh*
prime rate	la tasa preferencial, tipo preferencial	*lah 'tah-sah preh-feh-rehn-see-'ahl, 'tee-poh preh-feh-rehn-see-'ahl*
prime time	el tiempo preferencial	*ehl tee-'ehm-poh preh-feh-rehn-see-'ahl*
principal	el principal	*ehl preen-see-'pahl*
print	la impresión	*lah eem-preh-see-'ohn*
print (fabric)	el estampado	*ehl eh-stahm-'pah-doh*
print run	la tirada	*lah tee-'rah-dah*
printed circuit	el circuito impreso	*ehl seer-koo-'ee-toh eem-'preh-soh*
printed matter	los impresos	*lohs eem-'preh-sohs*
printer	la impresora	*lah eem-preh-'soh-rah*
printing	la impresión	*lah eem-preh-see-'ohn*
printout	la hoja impresa, salida impresa	*lah 'oh-hah eem-'preh-sah, sah-'lee-dah eem-'preh-sah*

P

priority	la prioridad	*lah pree-oh-ree'dahd*
private fleet	la flota privada	*lah 'floh-tah preh-'bah-dah*
private label (or brand)	la marca privada	*lah 'mahr-kah preh-'bah-dah*
private placement (finance)	la colocación privada	*lah koh-loh-kah-see-'ohn preh-'bah-dah*
pro forma invoice	la factura pro-forma	*lah fahk-'too-rah proh-'fohr-mah*
pro forma statement	el balance pro-forma, el estado financiero simulado	*ehl bah-'lahn-seh proh-'fohr-mah, ehl eh-'stah-doh fee-nahn-see-'eh-roh see-moo-'lah-doh*
probate	la verificación testamentaria	*lah beh-ree-fee-kah-see-'ohn tehs-tah-mehn-'tah-ree-ah*
problem	el problema	*ehl proh-'bleh-mah*
problem analysis	el análisis del problema	*ehl ah-'nah-lee-sees dehl proh-'bleh-mah*
problem solving	la solución de problemas	*lah soh-loo-see-'ohn deh proh-'bleh-mahs*
proceeds	el producto	*ehl proh-'dook-toh*
process	el proceso	*ehl proh-'seh-soh*
process (v)	procesar	*proh-seh-'sahr*
processing error	el error de procesamiento	*ehl eh-'rrohr deh proh-seh-sah-mee-'ehn-toh*
processor	el procesador	*ehl proh-seh-sah-'dohr*
procurement	la obtención	*lah ohb-tehn-see-'ohn*
product	el producto	*ehl proh-'dook-toh*
product analysis	el análisis del producto	*ehl ah-'nah-lee-sees dehl proh-'dook-toh*
product design	el diseño del producto	*ehl dee-'seh-nyoh dehl proh-'dook-toh*
product development	el desarrollo del producto	*ehl deh-sah-'rroh-yoh dehl proh-'dook-toh*
product dynamics	la dinámica del producto	*lah dee-'nah-mee-kah dehl proh-'dook-toh*
product group	el grupo de productos	*ehl 'groo-poh deh ehl proh-'dook-tohs*
product life	la vida del producto	*lah 'bee-dah dehl proh-'dook-toh*

product line	la línea de productos	*lah· 'lee-neh-ah deh proh-'dook-toh*
product management	la gerencia de producción	*lah heh-'rehn-see-ah deh proh-dook-see-'ohn*
product profitability	la rentabilidad del producto	*lah rehn-tah-bee-lee-'dahd dehl proh-'dook-toh*
production	la producción	*lah proh-dook-see-'ohn*
production costs	los costos de producción	*lohs 'koh-stohs deh proh-dook-see-'ohn*
production line	la línea de montaje	*lah 'lee-neh-ah deh mohn-'tah-heh*
production process	el processo de producción, el proceso productivo	*ehl proh-'seh-soh deh proh-dook-see-'ohn, ehl proh-'seh-soh proh-dook-'tee-boh*
production schedule	el programa de producción	*ehl proh-'grah-mah deh proh-dook-see-'ohn*
productivity	la productividad	*lah proh-dook-tee-bee-'dahd*
productivity campaign	la campaña de productividad	*lah kahm-'pah-nyah deh proh-dook-tee-bee-'dahd*
profession	la profesión	*lah proh-feh-see-'ohn*
profit	la utilidad	*lah oo-tee-lee-'dahd*
profit factor	el factor de beneficio, el factor de la utilidad	*ehl fahk-'tohr deh beh-neh-'fee-see-oh*
profit impact	el impacto del beneficio	*ehl eem-'ahk-toh dehl beh-neh-'fee-see-oh*
profit margin	el margen de beneficio, el margen del beneficio	*ehl 'mahr-hehn deh beh-neh-'fee-see-oh, ehl 'mahr-hehn dehl beh-neh-'fee-see-oh*
profit projection	la estimación de beneficio	*lah eh-stee-mah-see-'ohn deh beh-neh-'fee-see-oh*
profit sharing	las participaciones en los beneficicios	*lahs pahr-tee-see-pah-see-'oh-nehs ehn lohs beh-neh-'fee-see-ohs*
profit-and-loss statement	el estado de ganancias y pérdidas	*ehl eh-'stah-doh deh gah-'nahn-see-ahs ee 'pehr-dee-dahs*
profit-taking	la realización de beneficio	*lah reh-ah-lee-sah-see-'ohn deh beh-neh-'fee-see-oh*
profitability	la rentabilidad	*lah rehn-tah-bee-lee-'dahd*

P

profitability analysis	el análisis de la rentabilidad	*ehl ah-'nah-lee-sees lah rehn-tah-bee-lee-'dahd*
program	el programa	*ehl proh-'grah-mah*
program (v)	programar	*proh-grah-'mahr*
progress	el progreso	*ehl proh-'greh-soh*
prohibited goods	los bienes prohibidos	*lohs bee-'eh-nehs proh-ee-'bee-dohs*
project	el proyecto	*ehl proh-'yehk-toh*
project (v)	proyectar	*proh-yehk-'tahr*
project planning	la planificación de proyecto	*lah plah-nee-fee-kah-see-'ohn deh proh-'yehk-toh*
promissory note	el pagaré	*ehl pah-gah-'reh*
promotion	la promoción	*lah proh-moh-see-'ohn*
prompt	pronto	*'prohn-toh*
proof of loss	la prueba de pérdida	*lah proo-'eh-bah deh 'pehr-dee-dah*
proofreading	la corrección de prueba	*lah koh-rehk-see-'ohn deh proo-'eh-bah*
property	la propiedad	*lah proh-pee-eh-'dahd*
proprietor	el dueño, el propietario	*ehl 'dweh-nyoh, ehl proh-pee-eeh-'tah-ree-oh*
propulsion	la propulsión	*lah proh-pool-see-'ohn*
prospectus	el prospecto	*ehl proh-'spehk-toh*
protectionism	el proteccionismo	*ehl proh-tehk-see-oh-'nees-moh*
protest (banking, law)	el protesto	*ehl proh-'tehs-toh*
protocol	el protocolo	*ehl proh-toh-'koh-loh*
prototype	el prototipo	*ehl proh-toh-'tee-poh*
proxy	el poder	*ehl poh-'dehr*
proxy statement	la carta poder	*lah 'kahr-tah poh-'dehr*
prudent man rule	la norma del hombre prudente	*lah 'nohr-mah dehl 'ohm-breh proo-'dehn-teh*
public auction	la subasta pública	*lah soo-'bahs-tah 'poo-blee-kah*
public company	la compañía pública	*lah kohm-pah-'nyee-ah 'poo-blee-kah*

public domain	el dominio público	*ehl doh-'mee-nee-oh 'poo-blee-koh*
public funds	los fondos públicos	*lohs 'fohn-dohs 'poo-blee-kohs*
public offering	la oferta pública	*lah oh-'fehr-tah 'poo-blee-kah*
public opinion poll	el sondeo de opinión publica	*ehl sohn-'deh-oh deh oh-pee-nee-'ohn*
public property	la propiedad pública	*lah proh-pee-eh-'dahd 'poo-blee-kah*
public relations	las relaciones públicas	*lahs reh-lah-see-'oh-nehs 'poo-blee-kahs*
public sale	la subasta con aviso anticipado	*lah soo-bahs-ta kohn-nah-bee-soh-ahn-tee-see-pah-doh*
public sector	el sector público	*ehl sehk-'tohr 'poo-blee-koh*
public utility	los servicios públicos	*lohs sehr-'bee-see-ohs 'poo-blee-kohs*
public works	los trabajos públicos	*lohs trah-'bah-hohs 'poo-blee-kohs*
publicity	la publicidad	*lah poo-blee-see-'dahd*
publisher	el publicador	*ehl poo-blee-kah-'dohr*
pumping station	la estación de bombeo	*lah ehs-tah-see-'ohn deh bohm-'beh-oh*
punch card	la tarjeta para perforar	*lah tahr-'heh-tah 'pah-rah pehr-foh-'rahr*
purchase (v)	comprar	*kohm-'prahr*
purchase order	la orden de compra	*lah 'ohr-dehn deh 'kohm-prah*
purchase price	el precio de compra	*ehl 'preh-see-oh deh 'kohm-prah*
purchasing agent	el agente comprador	*ehl ah-'hehn-teh kohm-prah-'dohr*
purchasing manager	el gerente comprador	*ehl heh-'rehn-teh kohm-prah-'dohr*
purchasing power	el poder adquisitivo	*ehl poh-'dehr ahd-kee-see-'tee-boh*
pure risk	el riesgo puro	*ehl ree-'ehs-goh 'poo-roh*
purgative	el purgante	*ehl poor-'gahn-teh*
purification	la purificación	*lah poo-ree-fee-kah-see-'ohn*

P

purse	el monedero, el bolso	*ehl moh-neh-'deh-roh, ehl 'bohl-soh*
put and call	la venta y compra (opción)	*lah 'behn-tah ee 'kohm-prah (ohp-see-'ohn)*
put in a bid (v)	licitar	*lee-see-'tahr*
put option	la opción de venta	*lah ohp-see-'ohn deh 'behn-tah*
pyramid selling	la venta piramidal	*lah 'behn-tah pee-rah-mee-'dahl*
pyramiding	la piramidación	*lah pee-rah-mee-dah-see-'ohn*

Q

qualifications	los requisitos	*lohs reh-kee-'see-tohs*
qualified acceptance endorsement	el endoso limitado	*ehl ehn-'doh-soh lee-mee-'tah-doh*
quality control	el control de calidad	*ehl kohn-'trohl deh kah-lee-'dahd*
quality goods	los bienes de calidad	*lohs bee-'eh-nehs deh kah-lee-'dahd*
quantity	la cantidad	*lah kahn-tee-'dahd*
quantity discount	el descuento por cantidad	*ehl dehs-'kooh-ehn-toh pohr kahn-tee-'dahd*
quasi-public company	la compañía cuasi-pública	*lah kohm-pah-'nyee-ah koo-'ah-see-'poo-blee-kah*
quench (v)	templar	*tehm-'plahr*
quick access storage	la memoria de acceso rápido	*lah meh-'moh-ree-ah deh ahk-'seh-soh 'rah-pee-doh*
quick assets	los activos disponibles	*lohs ahk-'tee-bohs dees-poh-'nee-blehs*
quit claim deed	el instrumento de renuncia	*ehl een-stroo-'mehn-toh deh reh-'noon-see-ah*
quorum	el quórum	*ehl koo-'oh-room*
quota	la cuota	*lah 'kwoh-tah*
quota system	el sistema de cuotas	*ehl sees-'teh-mah deh 'kwoh-tahs*
quotation	la cotización	*lah koh-tee-sah-see-'ohn*

R

rabbit	el conejo	*ehl koh-'neh-hoh*
raccoon	el mapache	*ehl mah-'pah-cheh*
rack jobber	el mayorista de estantes	*ehl mah-yoh-'rees-tah deh ehs-tahn-tehs*
radial tire	el neumático radial	*ehl neh-oo-'mah-tee-koh rah-dee-'ahl*
radiation	la radiación	*lah rah-dee-ah-see-'ohn*
radioactive (adj)	radiactivo	*rah-dee-oh-ahk-'tee-boh*
rail shipment	el embarque ferroviario	*ehl ehm-'bahr-keh feh-rroh-bee-'ah-ree-oh*
railway transportation	el transporte por ferrocarriles	*ehl trahns-'pohr-teh pohr feh-rroh-kah-'rree-lehs*
rain check	el boleto válido para la próxima sessión	*ehl boh-'leh-toh 'bah-lee-doh 'pah-rah lah 'prohk-see-mah seh-see-'ohn*
rain forest	la pluvisilva	*lah ploo-bee-'seel-bah*
raincoat	el impermeable	*ehl eem-pehr-meh-'ah-bleh*
rains	las lluvias	*lahs 'yoo-bee-ahs*
raising capital	conseguir capital	*kohn-seh-'geer kah-pee-'tahl*
rally	la recuperación	*lah reh-koo-peh-rah-see-'ohn*
random access memory (RAM)	el acceso al azar a la memoria, memoria de acceso directo	*ehl ahk-'seh-soh ahl ah-'sahr ah lah meh-'moh-ree-ah, meh-'moh-ree-ah deh ahk-'seh-soh dee-'rehk-toh*
random sample	la muestra al azar	*lah 'mweh-strah ahl ah-'sahr*
range	la escala	*lah eh-'skah-lah*
rate	la tasa	*lah 'tah-sah*
rate of growth	la tasa de crecimiento	*lah 'tah-sah deh kreh-see-mee-'ehn-toh*
rate of increase	la tasa de incremento	*lah 'tah-sah deh een-kreh-'mehn-toh*
rate of interest	el tipo de interés	*ehl 'tee-poh deh een-teh-'rehs*

rate of return	la tasa de rendimiento	*lah 'tah-sah deh rehn-dee-mee-'ehn-toh*
ratio	la proporción, la relación	*lah proh-pohr-see-'ohn, lah reh-lah-see-'ohn*
ration (v)	racionar	*rah-see-oh-'nahr*
raw materials	las materias primas	*lahs mah-'teh-ree-ahs 'pree-'mahs*
rayon	el rayón	*ehl rah-'yohn*
reach (v)	alcanzar	*ahl-kahn-'sahr*
reactant	el reactante	*ehl reh-ahk-'tahn-teh*
ready cash	el efectivo disponible	*ehl eh-fehk-'tee-boh dees-poh-'nee-bleh*
ready-to-wear	la ropa hecha, confeccionado	*lah 'roh-pah 'eh-chah, kohn-fehk-see-oh-'nah-doh*
reagent	el reactivo	*ehl reh-ahk-'tee-boh*
real assets	los activos reales	*lohs ahk-'tee-bohs reh-'ah-lehs*
real estate	los bienes raíces	*lohs bee-'eh-nehs rah-'ee-sehs*
real investment	la inversión real	*lah een-behr-see-'ohn reh-'ahl*
real price	el precio real	*ehl 'preh-see-oh reh-'ahl*
real time	el tiempo real	*ehl tee'ehm-poh reh-'ahl*
real value	el valor real	*ehl bah-'lohr reh-'ahl*
real wages	los salarios reales	*lohs sah-'lah-ree-ohs reh-'ah-lehs*
ream	la resma	*lah 'rehs-mah*
rear axle	el eje trasero	*ehl 'eh-heh trah-'seh-roh*
reasonable care	el cuidado razonable	*ehl kwee-'dah-doh rah-soh-'nah-bleh*
rebars	los refuerzos de acero	*lohs reh-'fwehr-sohs deh ah-'seh-roh*
rebate	la rebaja	*lah reh-'bah-hah*
reboot (v)	arrancar	*ah-rrahn-'kahr*
recapitalization	la recapitalización	*lah reh-kah-pee-tah-lee-sah-see-'ohn*
receipt	el recibo	*ehl reh-'see-boh*

receiver	el receptor, el radio	*ehl reh-sehp-'tohr, ehl 'rah-dee-oh*
recession	la recesión	*lah reh-seh-see-'ohn*
reciprocal training	el entrenamiento recíproco	*ehl ehn-treh-nah-mee-'ehn-toh reh-'see-proh-koh*
record	el disco	*ehl 'dees-koh*
record (v)	grabar, registrar	*grah-'bahr, reh-hees-'trahr*
record date	la fecha del cierre del registro	*lah 'feh-chah dehl see-'eh-rreh dehl reh-'hee-stroh*
record player	el tocadiscos	*ehl toh-kah-'dees-kohs*
recourse	el recurso	*ehl reh-'koor-soh*
recovery (accounts receivable)	la recuperación (cuentas por cobrar)	*lah reh-koo-peh-rah-see-'ohn ('kwehn-tahs pohr koh-'brahr)*
recovery of expenses	la recuperación de gastos	*lah reh-koo-peh-rah-see-'ohn deh 'gah-stohs*
recycle	reciclar	*reh-see-'klahr*
recycling	el reciclaje (m)	*ehl reh-see-'klah-heh*
Red List of Threatened Animals	lista roja de animales amenazados	*'lees-tah 'roh-hah deh ah-nee-'mah-lehs ah-meh-nah-'sah-dohs*
red tape	los trámites burocráticos	*lohs 'trah-mee-tehs boo-roh-'krah-tee-kohs*
redeemable bond	el bono redimible	*ehl 'boh-noh reh-dee-'mee-bleh*
redemption allowance	la asignación por la amortización	*lah ah-seeg-nah-see-'ohn pohr lah ah-mohr-tee-sah-see-'ohn*
redemption fund	el fondo de amortización	*ehl 'fohn-doh deh ah-mohr-tee-sah-see-'ohn*
redemption premium	la prima de rescate	*lah 'pree-mah deh rehs-'kah-teh*
rediscount rate	la tasa de redescuento	*lah 'tah-sah deh reh-dehs-'kwehn-toh*
reduction	la reducción	*lah reh-dook-see-'ohn*
re-export (v)	reexportar	*reh-ehks-pohr-'tahr*
reference number	el número de referencia	*ehl 'noo-meh-roh deh reh-feh-'rehn-see-ah*
refill	relleno	*reh-'yeh-noh*

R

refinancing	el refinanciamiento	*ehl reh-fee-nahn-see-ah-mee-'ehn-toh*
refine (v)	refinar	*reh-fee-'nahr*
refinery	la refinería	*lah reh-fee-neh-'ree'ah*
refinery (home-based)	la refinería doméstica	*lah reh-fee-neh-'ree-ah doh-mehs-tee-kah*
refinery (market based)	la refinería localizada en el país del consumidor	*lah reh-fee-neh-'ree-ah loh-kah-lee-'sah-dah ehn ehl pah-'ees dehl kohm-soo-mee-'dohr*
reflation	la reflación	*lah reh-flah-see-'ohn*
refund	el reembolso	*ehl reh-ehm-'bohl-soh*
refuse payment	el pago rehusado	*ehl 'pah-goh reh-oo-'sah-doh*
regarding	referente a	*reh-feh-'rehn-teh ah*
register marks	las marcas registradas	*lahs 'mahr-kahs reh-hees-'trah-dahs*
registered check	el cheque registrado	*ehl 'cheh-keh reh-hee-'strah-doh*
registered mail	el correo certificado	*ehl koh-'rreh-oh sehr-tee-fee-'kah-doh*
registered representative	el representante registrado	*ehl reh-preh-sehn-'tahn-teh reh-hee-'strah-doh*
registered security	el título valor registrado	*ehl 'tee-too-loh bah-'lohr reh-hee-'strah-doh*
registered trademark	la marca registrada	*lah 'mahr-kah reh-hee-'strah-dah*
regression analysis	el análisis de regresión	*ehl ah-'nah-lee-sees deh reh-greh-see-'ohn*
regressive tax	el impuesto regresivo	*ehl eem-'pweh-stoh reh-greh-'see-boh*
regular warehouse	el almacén ordinario	*ehl ahl-mah-'sehn ohr-dee-'nah-ree-oh*
regulation	la regulación	*lah reh-goo-lah-see-'ohn*
reimburse (v)	reembolsar	*reh-ehm-bohl-'sahr*
reinsurer	el reasegurador	*ehl reh-ah-seh-goo-rah-'dohr*
reliable source	la fuente segura	*lah 'fwehn-teh seh-'goo-rah*
remainder	el residuo	*ehl reh-'see-doo-oh*
remedies	los remedios	*lohs reh-'meh-dee-ohs*

R

remedy (law)	el recurso	*ehl reh-'koor-soh*
remission duty	la remisión de impuestos	*lah reh-mee-see-'ohn deh eem-'pweh-stohs*
remission of a tax	la disminuición de un impuesto	*lah dees-mee-noo-ee-see-'ohn deh oon eem-'pweh-stoh*
remuneration	la remuneración	*lah reh-moo-neh-rah-see-'ohn*
renegotiate (v)	renegociar	*reh-neh-goh-see-'ahr*
renew (v)	renovar	*reh-noh-'bahr*
rent (v)	alquilar	*ahl-kee-'lahr*
reorder (v)	reordenar	*reh-ohr-deh-'nahr*
reorganization	la reorganización	*lah reh-ohr-gah-nee-sah-see-'ohn*
repay (v)	reembolsar, repago	*reh-ehm-bohl-'sahr, reh-'pah-goh*
repayment provision	la claúsula de reembolso	*lah 'klow-soo-lah deh reh-ehm-'bohl-soh*
repeat keys	las teclas repetidoras	*lahs 'teh-klahs reh-peh-tee-'doh-rahs*
repeat order	el pedido suplementario	*ehl peh-'dee-doh soo-pleh-mehn-'tah-ree-oh*
replacement cost	el costo de reemplazo, el costo de sustitución	*ehl 'koh-stoh deh reh-ehm-'plah-soh, ehl 'koh-stoh de soo-stee-too-see-'ohn*
replacement parts	los repuestos	*lohs reh-'pweh-stohs*
reply (v)	responder	*reh-spohn-'dehr*
report	el informe	*ehl een-'fohr-meh*
repossession	la reposesión	*lah reh-poh-seh-see-'ohn*
representative	el representante	*ehl reh-preh-sehn-'tahn-teh*
reproduction costs	los costos de reproducción	*lohs 'koh-stohs deh reh-proh-dook-see-'ohn*
reptiles	los reptiles	*lohs rehp-'tee-lehs*
request for bid	la solicitud de ofertas	*lah soh-lee-see-'tood deh oh-'fehr-tahs*
requirements	las necesidades, los requerimientos	*lahs neh-seh-see-'dah-dehs, lohs reh-keh-ree-mee-'ehn-tohs*
resale	la reventa	*lah reh-'behn-tah*

R

research	la investigación	*lah een-behe-stee-gah-see-'ohn*
research and development	la investigación y el desarrollo	*lah een-beh-stee-gah-see-'ohn ee ehl deh-sah-'rroh-yoh*
reserve	la reserva	*lah reh-'sehr-bah*
reset (v)	restaurar	*rehs-tah-oo-'rahr*
resident buyer	el comprador residente	*ehl kohm-prah-'dohr reh-see-'dehn-teh*
resolution	el convenio	*ehl kohn-'beh-nee-oh*
resolution (legal document)	la resolución, el acuerdo	*lah reh-soh-loo-see-'ohn, ehl ah-'kwehr-doh*
resonance	la resonancia	*lah reh-soh-'nahn-see-ah*
resource allocation	la aplicación de los recursos, la asignación de recursos	*lah ah-plee-kah-see-'ohn deh lohs reh-koor-sohs*
resources	los recursos	*lohs reh-'koor-sohs*
response time	tiempo de respuesta	*tee-'ehm-poh deh reh-'spweh-stah*
responsibility	la responsabilidad	*lah reh-spohn-sah-bee-lee-'dahd*
restart (v)	arrancar	*ah-rrahn-'kahr*
restrictions on export	las restricciones sobre las exportaciones	*lahs reh-strick-see-'oh-nehs 'soh-breh lahs exks-pohr-'tah-see-'oh-nehs*
restrictive labor practices	las prácticas laborales restrictivas	*lahs 'prahk-tee-kahs lah-boh-'rah-lehs reh-streek-'tee-bahs*
restructure (v)	reestructurar	*reh-ehs-trook-too-'rahr*
resume (v)	reanudar	*reh-an-noo-'dahr*
retail	al por menor	*ahl pohr meh-'nohr*
retail merchandise	la mercancía al por menor	*lah mehr-kahn-'see-ah pohr meh-'nohr*
retail outlet	el mercado de ventas al por menor	*ehl mehr-'kah-doh deh 'behn-tahs pohr meh-'nohr*
retail price	el precio al detalle, el precio al por menor	*ehl 'preh-see-oh ahl deh-'tah-yeh, ehl 'preh-see-oh pohr meh-'nohr*

retail sales tax	el impuesto sobre ventas al detalle, el impuesto sobre rentas al por menor	*ehl eem-pweh-stoh 'soh-breh 'behn-tahs ahl deh-'tah-yeh, ehl eem-'pweh-stoh 'soh-breh 'rehn-tahs pohr meh-'nohr*
retail trade	el comercio al detalle, el comercio al por menor, las utilidades acumuladas	*ehl koh-'mehr-see-oh, ehl koh-'mehr-see-oh pohr meh-'nohr, lahs oo-tee-lee-'dah-dehs*
retained earnings	los ingresos retenidos	*lohs een-'greh-sohs reh-teh-'nee-dohs*
retained profits	las ganancias retenidas	*lahs gah-'nahn-see-ahs reh-teh-'nee-dahs*
retirement	el retiro, la jubilación	*ehl reh-'tee-roh, lah hoo-bee-lah-see-'ohn*
retrieval	la recuperación	*lah reh-koo-peh-rah-see-'ohn*
retroactive	retroactivo	*reh-troh-ahk-'tee-boh*
return on assets managed	el retorno sobre activos administrados	*ehl reh-'tohr-noh 'soh-breh ahk-'tee-bohs ahd-mee-nee-'strah-dohs*
return on capital	el rendimiento sobre capital, el retorno sobre capital	*ehl rehn-dee-mee-'ehn-toh 'soh-bre kah-pee-'tahl, ehl reh-'tohr-noh 'soh-breh kah-pee-'tahl*
return on equity	el rendimiento sobre recursos propios	*ehl rehn-dee-mee-'ehn-toh 'soh-breh reh-'koor-sohs 'proh-pee-ohs*
return on investment	el rendimiento de las inversiones, el rendimiento sobre inversión	*ehl rehn-dee-mee-'ehn-toh deh lahs een-behr-see-'oh-nehs, ehl rehn-dee-mee-'ehn-toh 'soh-breh een-behr-see-'ohn*
return on sales	el rendimiento sobre ventas	*ehl rehn-dee-mee-'ehn-toh 'soh-breh 'behn-tahs*
revaluation	la revaluación	*lah reh-eh-bah-loo-ah-see-'ohn*
revenue	los ingresos	*lohs een-'greh-sohs*
revenue bond	el bono de ingreso	*ehl 'boh-noh deh een-'greh-soh*
reverse stock split	el retiro proporcional de acciones	*ehl reh-'tee-roh proh-pohr-see-oh'nahl deh ahk-see-'oh-nehs*
revocable trust	el fideicomiso revocable	*ehl fee-deh-ee-koh-'mee-soh reh-boh-'kah-bleh*

R

revolving credit	el crédito rotativo	*ehl 'kreh-dee-toh roh-tah-'tee-boh*
revolving fund	el fondo rotativo	*ehl 'fohn-doh roh-tah-'tee-boh*
revolving letter of credit	la carta de crédito renovable	*lah 'kahr-tah deh 'kreh-dee-toh reh-noh-'bah-bleh*
reward	la recompensa	*lah reh-kohm-'pehn-sah*
rhinoceros	el rinoceronte	*ehl ree-noh-seh-'rohn-teh*
ribbon	cinta de impresor	*'seen-tah deh eem-preh-'sohr*
rider (contracts)	el anexo	*ehl ah-'nehk-soh*
right of recourse	el derecho de recurso	*ehl deh-'reh-choh deh reh-'koor-soh*
right of way	el servidumbre de paso, el servidumbre de vía	*ehl sehr-bee-'doom-breh deh 'pah-soh, ehl sehr-bee-'doom-breh deh 'bee-ah*
rights	los derechos	*lohs deh-'reh-chohs*
ring	el aro	*ehl 'ah-roh*
ripe (adj)	maduro	*mah-'doo-roh*
risk	el riesgo	*ehl ree-'ehs-goh*
risk analysis	el análisis de riesgo	*ehl ah-'nah-lee-sees deh ree-'ehs-goh*
risk assessments	la evaluación de riesgos	*lah eh-bah-loo-ah-see-'ohn deh ree-'ehs-gohs*
risk capital	el capital de especulación, el riesgo de capital	*ehl kah-pee-'tahl deh ehs-peh-koo-lah-see-'ohn, ehl ree-'ehs-goh deh kah-pee-'tahl*
risk of default	el riesgo de incumplimiento	*ehl ree-'ehs-goh deh een-koom-plee-mee-'ehn-toh*
risky (adj)	arriesgado	*ah-rree-ehs-'gah-doh*
river	el río	*ehl ree-oh*
robot	el robot, el autómata	*ehl roh-'boht, ehl ow-'toh-mah-tah*
rod	la varilla	*lah bah-'ree-yah*
roll back	la reducción a precio anterior	*lah reh-dook-see-'ohn ah 'preh-see-oh ahn-teh-ree-'ohr*
rolling mill	el taller de laminación	*ehl tah-'yehr deh lah-mee-nah-see-'ohn*

rolling stock	el material rodante	*ehl mah-teh-ree-'ahl roh-'dahn-teh*
rollover	la renovación	*lah reh-noh-bah-see-'ohn*
rough draft	el borrador	*ehl boh-rrah-'dohr*
rough estimate	la estimación aproximada	*lah ehs-tee-mah-see-'ohn ah-prohk-see-'mah-dah*
round lot	el número de acciones de ciento o múltiples de ciento	*ehl 'noo-meh-roh deh ahk-see-'oh-nehs deh see-'ehn-toh o 'mool-tee-plehs deh see-'ehn-toh*
routine	la rutina	*lah roo-'tee-nah*
royalty (payment)	el pago de regalía	*ehl 'pah-goh deh reh-gah-'lee-ah*
run time	el tiempo de ejecución	*ehl tee-'ehm-poh deh eh-heh-koo-see-'ohn*
running expenses	los gastos corrientes	*lohs 'gah-stohs koh-rree-'ehn-tehs*
rush order	el pedido urgente	*ehl peh-'dee-doh oor-'hehn-teh*

S

S

sable	la marta	*lah 'mahr-tah*
saccharin	la sacarina	*lah sah-kah-'ree-nah*
saddle	la silla de montar	*lah 'see-yah deh mohn-'tahr*
safe deposit box	la caja de seguridad de depósitos	*lah 'kah-hah deh seh-goo-ree-'dahd deh deh-'poh-see-tohs*
safeguard	el resguardo, la garantía	*ehl rehs-'gwahr-doh, lah gah-rahn-'tee-ah*
salad plate	el plato de ensalada	*ehl 'plah-toh deh ehn-sah-'lah-dah*
salary	el sueldo	*ehl 'swehl-doh*
sale through mail order	la venta por correo	*lah 'behn-tah pohr koh-'rreh-oh*
sales	las ventas	*lahs 'behn-tahs*
sales analysis	el análisis de ventas	*ehl ah-'nah-lee-sees deh 'behn-tahs*
sales budget	el presupuesto de ventas	*ehl preh-soo-'pweh-stoh deh 'behn-tahs*

sales estimate	la estimación de ventas, las ventas estimadas	*lah ehs-tee-mah-see-'ohn deh 'behn-tahs, lahs 'behn-tahs ehs-tee-'mah-dahs*
sales force	el personal de ventas	*ehl pehr-soh-'nahl deh 'behn-tahs*
sales forecast	el pronóstico de ventas, la predicción de ventas	*ehl proh-'noh-stee-koh deh 'behn-tahs, lah pre-deek-see-'ohn deh 'behn-tahs*
sales management	la gerencia de ventas	*lah heh-'rehn-see-ah deh 'behn-tahs*
sales promotion	la promoción de ventas	*lah proh-moh-see-'ohn deh 'behn-tahs*
sales quota	la cuota de ventas	*lah 'kwoh-tah deh 'behn-tahs*
sales tax	el impuesto sobre las ventas	*ehl eem-'pweh-stoh 'soh-breh lahs 'behn-tahs*
sales territory	el territorio de ventas	*ehl teh-rree-'toh-ree-oh deh 'behn-tahs*
sales turnover	la rotación de ventas	*lah roh-tah-see,'ohn deh 'behn-tahs*
sales volume	el volumen de ventas	*ehl boh-'loo-mehn deh 'behn-tahs*
salt	la sal	*lah sahl*
salt shaker	el salero	*ehl sah-'leh-roh*
salvage (v)	rescatar	*rehs-kah-'tahr*
salvage charges	los cargos de rescate	*lohs 'kahr-gohs deh rehs-'kah-teh*
salvage value	el valor de rescate	*ehl bah-'lohr deh rehs-'kah-teh*
salve	el ungüento, la pomada	*ehl oon-'gwehn-toh, lah poh-'mah-dah*
sample (v)	muestrear	*moo-'eh-streh-ahr*
sample line	la línea de muestreo	*lah 'lee-neh-ah deh 'moo-eh-'streh-oh*
sample size	el tamaño de muestra	*ehl tah-'mah-nyoh deh moo-'eh-strah*
satellite dish	la parabólica	*lah pah-rah-'boh-lee-kah*
saucer	el platillo, la salsera	*ehl plah-'tee-yoh, lah sahl-'seh-rah*
savings	los ahorros	*lohs ah-'oh-rrohs*

savings account	la cuenta de ahorro	*lah 'kwehn-tah deh ah-'oh-roh*
savings bank	el banco de ahorro	*ehl 'bahn-koh deh ah-'oh-roh*
savings bond	el bono de ahorro	*ehl 'boh-noh deh ah-'oh-roh*
scale	la báscula	*lah 'bahs-koo-lah*
scalper	el especulador en bolsa	*ehl eh-speh-koo-lah-'dohr ehn 'bohl-sah*
scan (v)	examinar, explorar	*ehk-sah-mee-'nahr, ehk-sploh-'rahr*
scanner	el dispositivo de exploración	*ehl dees-poh-see-'tee-boh deh ehk-sploh-rah-see-'ohn*
scanning	la exploración	*lah ehks-ploh-rah-see-'ohn*
scarf	la bufanda	*lah boo-'fahn-dah*
schedule	el horario, el itinerario	*ehl oh-'rah-ree-oh, ehl ee-tee-neh-'tah-ree-oh*
scissor case	el estuche de tijeras	*ehl ehs-'too-cheh deh tee-'heh-rahs*
scoring	el rayado	*ehl rah-'yah-doh*
scrap	el deshecho	*ehl deehs-'eh-choh*
screen	la pantalla	*lah pahn-'tah-yah*
screen (printing term)	la trama	*lah 'trah-mah*
screening	la selección	*lah seh-lehk-see-'ohn*
script	la escritura	*lah eh-'skree-'too-rah*
sea level	el nivel del mar (m)	*ehl nee-'behl dehl mahr*
sealed bid	la propuesta sellada, la oferta cerrada	*lah proh-'pweh-stah seh-'yah-dah, lah oh-'fehr-tah seh-'rrah-dah*
sealskin	la piel de foca	*lah pee'ehl deh 'foh-kah*
search	la búsqueda	*lah 'boos-keh-dah*
search (v)	buscar	*boos-'kahr*
seasonal	estacional	*eh-stah-see-oh-'nahl*
seat	el asiento	*ehl ah-see'ehn-toh*
seawater	el agua del mar (f)	*ehl 'ah-gwah dehl mahr*
seawater desalination plant	la instalación de climatización	*lah een-stah-lah-see-'ohn deh klee-mah-tee-sah-see-'ohn*

seaweed	las algas (f)	*lahs 'ahl-gahs*
second mortgage	la segunda hipoteca	*lah seh-'goon-dah ee-poh-'teh-kah*
second position	la segunda posición	*lah seh-'goon-dah poh-see-see-'ohn*
secondary market (securities)	el mercado secundario de valores	*ehl mehr-'kah-doh seh-koon-'dah-ree-oh deh bah-'loh-rehs*
secondary offering (securities)	la venta secundaria	*lah 'behn-tah seh-koon-'dah-ree-ah*
secretary	la secretaria, el secretario	*lah seh-kreh-'tah-ree-ah, ehl seh-kreh-'tah-ree-oh*
secured accounts	las cuentas aseguradas	*lahs 'kwehn-tahs ah-seh-goo-'rah-dahs*
secured liability	el pasivo garantizado	*ehl pah-'see-boh gah-rahn-tee-'sah-doh*
securities	los títulos, los valores	*lohs 'tee-too-lohs, lohs bah-'loh-rehs*
security	la garantía	*lah gah-rahn-'tee-ah*
sedan	el sedán	*ehl seh-'dahn*
sedative	el sedante, el calmante	*ehl seh-'dahn-teh, ehl kahl-'mahn-teh*
sediment	el sedimento	*ehl seh-dee-'mehn-toh*
self-appraisal	el auto-evalúo	*ehl 'ow-toh-eh-bah-'loo-oh*
self-employed man	el trabajador por su cuenta	*ehl trah-bah-hah-'dohr pohr soo 'kwehn-tah*
self-management	la auto-administración	*lah 'ow-toh-ahd-mee-nee-strah-see-'ohn*
self-service	el servicio personal, el auto-servicio	*ehl sehr-'bee-see-oh pehr-soh-'nahl, ehl 'ow-toh sehr-'bee-see-oh*
self-sufficient	autosuficiente	*ow-toh-soo-fee-see-'ehn-teh*
sell (v)	vender	*behn-'dehr*
sell and leaseback	la venta e inmediato arrendamiento de lo vendido	*lah 'behn-tah eh een-meh-dee-'ah-toh ah-rrehn-dah-mee-'ehn-toh deh loh behn-'dee-doh*
semi-arid	semiárido	*seh-mee-'ah-ree-doh*
semi-variable costs	los costos semi-variables	*lohs 'koh-stohs 'seh-mee-bah-ree-'ah-blehs*

semis	los productos semiterminados de acero o hierro	*lohs proh-'dook-tohs seh-mee-tehr-mee-'nah-dohs deh ah-'seh-roh oh 'yeh-roh*
senior issue	la emisión prioritaria	*lah eh-mee-see-'ohn pree-oh-ree-'tah-ree-ah*
seniority	la prelación, la prioridad	*lah preh-lah-see-'ohn, lah pree-oh-ree-'dahd*
separation	la separación	*lah seh-pah-rah-see-'ohn*
serial bonds	las obligaciones con vencimiento escalonado	*lahs oh-blee-gah-see,'oh-nehs kohn behn-see-mee-'ehn-toh ehs-kah-loh-'nah-doh*
serial storage	el almacenaje de serie	*ehl ahl-mah-seh-'nah-heh deh 'seh-ree'eh*
serum	el suero	*ehl 'sweh-roh*
service (v)	mantener, servir	*mahn-teh-'nehr, sehr-'beer*
service contract	el contrato de servicio	*ehl kohn-'trah-toh deh sehr-'bee-see-oh*
service station	la gasolinera	*lah gah-soh-lee-'neh-rah*
set-up costs	los costos de instalación	*lohs 'koh-stohs deh een-stah-lah-see-'ohn*
settlement	el arreglo	*ehl ah-'rreh-gloh*
severance pay	la indemnización par despido	*lah een-dehm-nee-sah-see-'ohn pohr dehs-'pee-doh*
sew (v)	coser	*koh-'sehr*
sewing kit	el estuche de costura	*ehl ehs-'too-cheh deh kohs-'too-rah*
sewing machine	la máquina de coser	*lah 'mah-kee-nah deh koh-'sehr*
sewn (adj)	cosido	*koh-'see-doh*
shareholder	el accionista	*ehl ahk-see-oh-'nees-tah*
shareholder's equity	el capital de accionistas	*ehl kah-pee-'tahl deh ahk-see-oh-'nees-tahs*
shareholders' meeting	la reunión de accionistas	*lah reh-oo-nee-'ohn deh ahk-see-oh-'nees-tahs*
shares	las participaciones	*lahs pahr-tee-see-pah-see-'oh-nehs*
sheet (paper)	la hoja de papel	*lah 'oh-hah deh pah-'pehl*
sheets	las hojas	*lahs 'oh-hahs*

S

shift	el cambio	*ehl 'kahm-bee-oh*
shift (labor)	el turno de trabajo	*ehl 'toor-noh deh trah-'bah-hoh*
ship (m)	el buque	*ehl 'boo-keh*
shipment	el despacho, el envío	*ehl dehs-'pah-choh, ehl ehn-'bee-oh*
shipper	el fletador, el remitente	*ehl fleh-tah-'dohr, ehl reh-mee-'tehn-teh*
shipping agent	el consignatario de transporte	*ehl kohn-seeg-nah-'toh-ree-oh deh trahns-'pohr-teh*
shipping charges	los cargos de transporte	*lohs 'kahr-gohs deh trahns-'pohr-teh*
shipping expenses	los gastos de embarque, los gastos de transporte	*lohs 'gah-stohs deh ehm-'bahr-keh, lohs 'gah-stohs deh trahns-'pohr-teh*
shipping instructions	las instrucciones de embarque	*lahs een-strook-see-'oh-nehs deh ehm-'bahr-keh*
shirt	la camisa	*lah kah-'mee-sah*
shock absorber	el amortiguador	*ehl ah-mohr-tee-gwah-'dohr*
shoe	el zapato	*ehl sah-'pah-toh*
shopping center	el centro comercial	*ehl 'sehn-troh koh-mehr-see-'ahl*
short delivery	la entrega en descubierto	*lah ehn-'treh-gah ehn dehs-koo-bee-'ehr-toh*
(to be) short of (v)	faltar	*fahl-'tahr*
short position	la posición en descubierto	*lah poh-see-see-'ohn ehn dehs-koo-bee-'ehr-toh*
short sales	las ventas al descubierto	*lahs 'behn-tahs ahl dehs-koo-bee-'ehr-toh*
short shipment	el envío incompleto	*ehl ehn-'bee-oh een kohm-'pleh-toh*
short sleeves	las mangas cortas	*lahs 'mahn-gahs 'kohr-tahs*
short supply	la escasez	*lah ehs-kah-'sehs*
short wave	la onda corta	*lah 'ohn-dah 'kohr-tah*
short-term capital account	la cuenta de capital de corto plazo	*lah 'kwehn-tah deh kah-pee-'tahl deh 'kohr-toh 'plah-soh*
short-term debt	la deuda a corto plazo	*lah deh-'oo-dah 'kohr-toh 'plah-soh*

short-term financing	el financiamiento a corto plazo	*ehl fee-nahn-see-ah-mee-'ehn-toh 'kohr-toh 'plah-soh*
shortage	la escasez	*lah ehs-kah-'sehs*
shoulder pad	la hombrera	*lah ohm-'breh-rah*
sick leave	el permiso por enfermedad	*ehl pehr-'mee-soh pohr ehn-fehr-meh-'dahd*
sight draft	el pagaré a la vista	*ehl pah-gah-'reh ah lah 'bees-tah*
signature	la firma	*lah 'feer-mah*
silent partner	el socio comanditario	*ehl 'soh-see-oh*
silicon	el silicio	*ehl see-'lee-see-oh*
silk	la seda	*lah 'seh-dah*
silk factory	la fábrica de seda	*lah 'fah-bree-kah deh 'seh-dah*
silk goods	los artículos de seda	*lohs ahr-'tee-koo-lohs deh 'seh-dah*
silk manufacturers	los fabricantes de seda	*lohs fah-bree-'kahn-tehs deh 'seh-dah*
silkworm	el gusano de seda	*ehl goo-'sah-noh deh 'seh-dah*
silverware	los cubiertos	*lohs koo-bee-'ehr-tohs*
simulate (v)	simular	*see-moo-'lahr*
sinking fund	la amortización de obligaciones, el fondo de amortización	*lah ah-mohr-tee-sah-see-'ohn deh ohb-lee-gah-see-'oh-nehs, ehl 'fohn-doh deh ah-mohr-tee-sah-see-'ohn*
sinus	el seno	*ehl 'seh-noh*
six-cylinder engine	el motor de seis cilindros	*ehl moh-'tohr deh 'seh-ees see-'leen-drohs*
size	la talla, el tamaño	*lah 'tah-yah, ehl tah-'mah-nyoh*
skilled labor	la mano de obra especializada	*lah 'mah-noh deh 'oh-brah eh-speh-see-ah-lee-'sah-dah*
skin	la piel	*lah pee-'ehl*
skin (grape)	el hollejo	*ehl oh-'yeh-hoh*
skirt	la falda, la saya	*lah 'fahl-dah, lah 'sah-yah*
slabs	las lozas	*lahs 'loh-sahs*

S

slacks	los pantalones	*lohs pahn-tah-'loh-nehs*
sleeping pill	la píldora para dormir	*lah 'peel-doh-rah 'pah-rah dohr-'meer*
sliding parity	la paridad móvil	*lah pah-'ree-dahd 'moh-beel*
sliding scale	la escala móvil	*lah eh-'skah-lah 'moh-beel*
slippers	las zapatillas	*lahs sah-pah-'tee-yahs*
slump	el descenso brusco de precios	*ehl deh-'sehn-soh 'broos-koh deh 'preh-see-ohs*
small business	el negocio pequeño	*ehl neh-'goh-see-oh peh-'keh-nyoh*
smog	el smog (m)	*ehl ehs-'mohg*
smog (urban)	el smog urbano	*ehl ehs-'mohg oor-'bah-noh*
snakeskin	la piel de culebra, la piel de serpiente	*lah pee-'ehl deh koo-'leh-brah, ehl lah pee-'ehl deh sehr-pee-'ehn-teh*
sneeze (v)	estornudar	*ehs-tohr-noo-'dahr*
socialism	el socialismo	*ehl soh-see-ah-'lees-moh*
socks	los calcetines	*lohs kahl-seh-'tee-nehs*
soft currency	la moneda débil (blando)	*lah moh-'neh-dah 'deh-beel ('blahn-doh)*
soft goods	los paños, los géneros	*lohs 'pah-nee-ohs, lohs 'heh-neh-rohs*
soft loan	el préstamo débil, el préstamo repagable en moneda inestable	*ehl 'preh-stah-moh 'deh-beel, ehl 'preh-stah-moh reh-pah-'gah-bleh ehn moh-'neh-dah een-eh-'stah-bleh*
soft sell	la venta débil	*lah 'behn-tah 'deh-beel*
softcover	la cubierta rústica	*lah koo-bee-'ehr-tah*
software	el programa de computación, los programas y sistemas de programación, el software	*ehl proh-'grah-mah deh kohm-poo-tah-see-'ohn, lohs proh-'grah-mahs ee sees-'teh-mahs de proh-grah-mah-see-'ohn, ehl sohft-'wehr*
software broker	el intermediario en programa de computación, el agente de software	*ehl een-tehr-meh-dee-'ah-ree-oh ehn proh-'grah-mah deh kohm-poo-tah-see-'ohn, ehl ah-'hehn-teh deh sohft-'wehr*

solar (adj)	solar	*soh-'lahr*
sole agent	el agente único	*ehl ah-'hehn-teh 'oo-nee-koh*
sole proprietorship	el propietario único	*ehl proh-pee-eh-'tah-ree-oh 'oo-nee-koh*
sole rights	los derechos únicos	*lohs deh-'reh-chohs 'oo-nee-kohs*
solid state	semiconductor	*seh-mee-kohn-dook-'tohr*
solubility	la solubilidad	*lah soh-loo-bee-lee-'dahd*
solute	el soluto	*ehl soh-'loo-toh*
solution	la solución	*lah soh-loo-see-'ohn*
solvency	la solvencia	*lah sohl-'behn-see-ah*
solvent	el solvente	*ehl soh-'behn-teh*
sound	el sonido	*ehl soh-'nee-doh*
soup dish	el plato de sopa	*ehl 'plah-toh deh 'soh-pah*
sour (adj)	agrio	*'ah-gree-oh*
source	la fuente, el origen	*lah 'fwehn-teh, ehl oh-'ree-hehn*
spare tire	la rueda de repuesta	*lah roo-'eh-dah deh reh-'pweh-stah*
spark plug	la bujía	*lah boo-'hee-ah*
sparkling wine	el vino espumoso	*ehl 'bee-noh ehs-poo-'moh-soh*
speaker	el altavoz, el altoparlante	*ehl ahl-tah-'bos, ehl ahl-toh-pahr-'lahn-teh*
specialist	el/la especialista (m/f)	*ehl/lah eh-speh-see-ah-'lees-tah*
specialist (oil industry)	el especialista en la industria petrolera	*ehl eh-speh-see-ah-'lees-tah ehn lah een-'doos-tree-ah peh-troh-'leh-rah*
specialist (stock exchange)	el especialista (el miembro de la bolsa de valores responsable de mantener un mercado ordenado y justo en las acciones registradas)	*ehl eh-speh-see-ah-'lees-tah (ehl mee-'ehm-broh deh lah 'bohl-sah deh bah-'loh-rehs reh-spohn-'sah-bleh deh mahn-teh-'nehr oon mehr-'kah-doh ohr-deh-'nah-doh ee 'hoos-toh ehn lahs ak-see-'oh-nehs reh-hee'-strah-dahs)*

S

specialty goods	los productos de especiali- dad, los bienes especiales	*lohs proh-'dook-tohs deh eh-speh-see-ah-lee-'dahd, lohs bee-'eh-nehs eh- speh-see-'ah-lehs*
specialty steels	los aceros especializados	*lohs ah-'seh-rohs eh-speh- see-ah-lee-'sah-dohs*
specific duty	el impuesto específico, el arancel aduanero específico	*ehl eem-'pweh-stoh eh-speh- 'see-fee-koh, ehl ah-rahn- 'sehl ah-dwah-'neh-roh eh-speh-'see-fee-koh*
spectrophotometry	la espectometría	*lah ehs-pehk-toh-meh- 'tree'ah*
spectrum	el espectro	*ehl ehs-'pehk-troh*
speculator	el especulador	*ehl eh-speh-koo-lah-'dohr*
speed up (v)	acelerar	*ah-seh-leh-'rahr*
speedometer	el velocímetro	*ehl beh-loh-'see-meh-troh*
spin off	la transferencia de activo a otra compañía sin cambio de accionistas	*lah trahns-feh-'rehn-see-ah deh ahk-'tee-boh ah 'oh- trah 'kahm-bee-oh de ahk-see-oh-'nees-tahs*
spine	el lomo	*ehl 'loh-moh*
spoilage	el desperdicio, el deterioro	*ehl dehs-pehr-'dee-see-oh, ehl deh-teh-ree-'oh-roh*
sponsor (of fund, of partnership)	el promotor (de fondos en una sociedad)	*ehl proh-moh-'tohr (deh 'fohn-dohs deh 'oo-nah soh-see-eh-'dahd)*
spoon	la cuchara	*lah koo-'chah-rrah*
spot delivery	la entrega inmediata	*lah ehn-'treh-gah een-meh- dee-'ah-tah*
spot market	el mercado al contado	*ehl mehr-'kah-doh ahl kohn- 'tah-doh*
spread	la diferencia	*lah dee-feh-'rehn-see-ah*
spreadsheet	la hoja electrónica	*lah 'oh-hah eh-lehk-'troh- nee-kah*
spring	el muelle	*ehl 'mweh-yeh*
stabilize (v)	estabilizar	*eh-stah-bee-lee-'sahr*
staff	el personal, los funcionarios	*ehl pehr-soh-'nahl, lohs foonk-see-oh-'nah-ree- ohs*

S

staff and line	la combinación de los órganos asesores con los de ejecución	*lah kohm-bee-nah-see-'ohn deh lohs 'ohr-gah-nohs ah-seh-'soh-rehs kohn lohs deh eh-heh-koo-see-'ohn*
staff assistant	el asistente de personal	*ehl ah-sees-'tehn-teh deh pehr-soh-'nahl*
staff organization	la organización del personal	*lah ohr-gah-nee-sah-see-'ohn dehl pehr-soh-'nahl*
stagflation	la estagflación, la recesión con inflación	*lah eh-stahg-flah-see-'ohn, lah reh-seh-see-'ohn kohn een-flah-see-'ohn*
stainless steel	el acero inoxidable	*ehl ah-'seh-roh een-ohk-see-'dah-bleh*
stale check	el cheque vencido	*ehl 'cheh-keh behn-'see-doh*
stalking (v)	encañar	*ehn-kah-'nyahr*
stand in line (v)	estar parado en la cola	*eh-'stahr pah-'rah-doh ehn lah 'koh-lah*
stand-alone text processor	el procesador de palabras solitario	*ehl proh-seh-sah-'dohr deh pah-'lah-brahs soh-lee-'tah-ree-oh*
stand-alone workstation	la estación de trabajo solitario	*lah eh-stah-see-'ohn deh trah-'bah-hoh soh-lee-'tah-ree-oh*
standard costs	los costos estándar, los costos normales	*lohs 'koh-stohs eh-'stahn-dahr, lohs 'koh-stohs nohr-'mah-lehs*
standard deviation	la desviación estándar	*lah dehs-bee-ah-see-'ohn eh-'stahn-dahr*
standard of living	el estándar de vida, el nivel de vida	*ehl eh-'stahn-dahr deh 'bee-dah, ehl nee-'behl deh 'bee-dah*
standard practice	la práctica normal	*lah 'prahk-tee-kah nohr-'mahl*
standard time	la hora estándar	*lah 'oh-rah eh-'stahn-dahr*
standardization	la estandardización, la regulación, la uniformación	*lah eh-stahn-dahr-dee-sah-see-'ohn, lah reh-goo-lah-see-'ohn, lah oo-nee-fohr-mah-see-'ohn*
standby fee	la comisión de garantía	*lah koh-mee-see-'ohn deh gah-rahn-'tee-ah*
standing charges	los cargos establecidos	*lohs 'kahr-gohs eh-stah-bleh-'see-dohs*

S

standing costs	los costos establecidos	*lohs 'koh-stohs eh-stah-bleh-'see-dohs*
standing order	la instrucción permanente, la orden permanente	*lah een-strook-see-'ohn pehr-mah-'nehn-teh, lah 'ohr-dehn pehr-mah-'nehn-teh*
starch	el almidón, la fécula	*ehl ahl-mee-'dohn, lah 'feh-koo-lah*
start-up cost	el costo de arranque, el costo de establecerse	*ehl 'koh-stoh deh ah-'rrahn-keh, ehl 'koh-stoh deh eh-stah-bleh-'sehr-seh*
starter	el arranque	*ehl ah-'rrahn-keh*
statement	el estado	*ehl eh-'stah-doh*
statement of account	el estado de cuenta	*ehl eh-'stah-doh deh 'kwehn-tah*
statistics	la estadística	*lah eh-stah-'dees-tee-kah*
statute	el estatuto	*ehl eh-stah-'too-toh*
statute of limitations	el estatuto de limitaciones	*ehl eh-stah-'too-toh deh lee-mee-tah-see-'oh-nehs*
steel mill	el taller siderúrgico	*ehl tah-'yehr see-deh-'roor-hee-koh*
steering	la conducción, el manejo	*lah kohn-dook-see-'ohn, ehl mah-'neh-hoh*
steering wheel	el volante	*ehl boh-'lahn-teh*
stereophonic (adj)	estereofónico	*eh-steh-reh-oh-'foh-nee-koh*
stimulant	el estimulante	*ehl ehs-tee-moo-'lahn-teh*
stitch	la puntada	*lah poon-'tah-dah*
stock	la acción	*lah ahk-see-'ohn*
stock certificate	el certificado de acciones	*ehl sehr-tee-fee-'kah-doh deh ahk-see-'oh-nehs*
stock control	el control de existencias, el control del inventario	*ehl kohn-'trohl deh ehk-ees-'tehn-see-ahs, ehl kohn-'trohl dehl een-behn-'tah-ree-oh*
stock dividend	dividendos en acciones	*dee-bee-'dehn-dohs ehn ahk-see-'oh-nehs*
stock exchange	la bolsa de valores	*lah 'bohl-sah deh bah-'loh-rrehs*
stock index	el índice de acciones	*ehl 'een-dee-seh deh ahk-see-'oh-nehs*

S

stock market	el mercado de acciones	*ehl mehr-'kah-doh deh ahk-see-'oh-nehs*
stock option	la opción de acciones	*lah ohp-see-'ohn deh ahk-see-'oh-nehs*
stock portfolio	la cartera de acciones	*lah kahr-'teh-rah deh ahk-see-'oh-nehs*
stock power	el poder accionario	*ehl poh-'dehr ahk-see-oh-'nah-ree-oh*
stock profit	el beneficio en acciones	*ehl beh-neh-'fee-see-oh ehn ahk-see-'oh-nehs*
stock purchase	la compra de acciones	*lah 'kohm-prah deh ahk-see-'oh-nehs*
stock split	el aumento gratuito de las acciones para reducir su precio, la división de acciones	*ehl ow-'mehn-toh grah-too-ee-toh deh lahs ahk-see-'oh-nehs 'pah-rah reh-doo-'seer soo 'preh-see-oh, lah dee-bee-see-'ohn deh ahk-see-'oh-nehs*
stock takeover	la adquisición mayoritaria de acciones	*lah ahd-kee-see-see-'ohn mah-yoh-ree-'tah-ree-ah deh ahk-see-'oh-nehs*
stock turnover	la rotación del inventario	*lah roh-tah-see-'ohn dehl een-behn-'tah-ree-oh*
stock-in-trade	el intercambio en acciones	*ehl een-tehr-'cam-bee-oh ehn ahk-see-'oh-nehs*
stockbroker	el corredor de bolsa	*ehl koh-rreh-'dohr deh 'bohl-sah*
stockholder	el accionista	*ehl ahk-see-oh-'nees-tah*
stockholder's equity	los recursos propios de los accionistas	*lohs reh-'koor-sohs 'proh-pee-ohs deh lohs ahk-see-oh-'nees-tahs*
stockings	las medias de mujer	*lahs 'meh-dee-ahs deh moo-'hehr*
stoneware	el gres	*ehl grehs*
stop-loss order	la orden de pérdida limitada	*lah 'ohr-dehn deh 'pehr-dee-dah lee-mee-'tah-dah*
storage	el almacenaje	*ehl ahl-mah-seh-'nah-heh*
storage facility	la facilidad de almacenamiento	*lah fah-see-lee-'dahd deh ahl-mah-seh-nah-mee-'ehn-toh*
store	la tienda	*lah tee-'ehn-dah*
store (v)	almacenar	*ahl-mah-seh-'nahr*

S

stowage	el arrumaje, la estiba	*ehl ah-rroo-'mah-heh, lah eh-'stee-bah*
stowage charges	los cargos de estiba	*lohs 'kahr-gohs deh eh-'stee-bah*
straddle	la operación de bolsa con opción de compra o venta	*lah oh-peh-rah-see-'ohn deh 'bohl-sah kohn ohp-see-'ohn deh 'kohm-prah oh 'behn-tah*
strapping tape	la cinta de encajonar	*lah 'seen-tah deh ehn-kah-noh-'nahr*
strategic articles	los artículos estratégicos	*lohs ahr-'tee-koo-lohs eh-strah-'teh-hee-kohs*
stratosphere	la estratosfera	*lah ehs-trah-tohs-'feh-rah*
streamline (v)	simplificar	*seem-plee-fee-'kahr*
stress	tensión nerviosa	*tehn-see-'ohn nehr-bee-'oh-sah*
stress management	la administración de tensión, el control de tensión	*lah ahd-mee-nee-strah-see-'ohn deh tehn-see-'ohn, ehl kohn-'trohl deh tehn-see-'ohn*
strike (v)	parar (el trabajo)	*pah-'rahr (ehl trah-'bah-hoh)*
strikebreaker	el obrero que reemplaza al huelguista	*ehl oh-'breh-roh keh reh-ehm-'plah-sah ahl wehl-'gees-tah*
stripping (v)	desmontar	*dehs-mohn-'tahr*
structural shapes	el hierro perfilado	*ehl 'yeh-roh pehr-fee-'lahpdoh*
stuffing	el relleno	*ehl reh-'yeh-noh*
style	el estilo	*ehl eh-'stee-loh*
stylist	el estilista	*ehl eh-stee-'lees-tah*
subcontract	el subcontrato	*ehl soob-kohn-'trah-toh*
subcontractor	el subcontratista	*ehl soob-kohn-trah-'tees-tah*
subject to availability	sujeto a disponibilidad	*soo-'heh-toh ah dees-poh-nee-bee-lee-'dahd*
sublet (v)	subarrendar	*soob-ah-rrehn-'dahr*
submit to	someterse a	*soh-meh-'tehr-seh ah*
subroutine	subrutina	*soob-roo-'tee-nah*
subscription price	el precio de subscripción	*ehl 'preh-see-oh deh soob-skree-see-'ohn*

subsidiary	el subsidiario	*ehl soob-see-dee-ah-ree-oh*
subsidy	el subsidio	*ehl soob-'see-dee-oh*
substandard	inferior al nivel normal	*een-feh-ree-'ohr ahl nee-'behl nohr-'mahl*
suede	la cabritilla, el ante, la gamuza	*lah kah-bree-'tee-yah, ehl 'ahn-teh, lah gah-'moo-sah*
suede jacket	la chaqueta de cabritilla, la chaqueta de ante	*lah chah-'keh-tah deh kah-bree-'tee-yah, lah chah-'keh-tah deh 'ahn-teh*
sugar bowl	la azucarera	*lah ah-soo-kah-'reh-rah*
sugar content	el contenido de azúcar	*ehl kohn-teh-'nee-doh deh ah-'soo-kahr*
suit	el traje	*ehl 'trah-heh*
suitcase	la maleta	*lah mah-'leh-tah*
sulfate	el sulfato	*ehl sool-'fah-toh*
sulfuric acid	el ácido sulfúrico	*ehl 'ah-see-doh sool-'foo-ree-koh*
sulphamide	la sulfamide	*lah sool-fah-'mee-deh*
super alloys	las superaleaciones	*lahs soo-pehr-ah-leh-ah-see-'oh-nehs*
superconductor	el superconductor	*ehl soo-pehr-kohn-dook-'tohr*
supersede (v)	invalidar, reemplazar	*een-bah-lee-'dahr, reh-ehm-plah-'sahr*
supervisor	el supervisor	*ehl soo-pehr-bee-'sohr*
supplier	el abastecedor, el oferente, el suministrador	*ehl ah-bah-steh-seh-'dohr, ehl oh-feh-'rehn-teh, ehl soo-mee-nee-strah-'dohr*
supply	abastecer	*ah-bah-steh-'sehr*
supply (v)	oferta, abastecimiento	*oh-'fehr-tah, ah-bah-steh-see-mee-'ehn-toh*
supply and demand	la oferta y demanda	*lah oh-'fehr-tah ee deh-'mahn-dah*
support activities	las actividades de apoyo, las actividades de sostenimentio	*lahs ahk-tee-bee-'dah-dehs deh ah-'poh-yoh, lahs ahk-tee-bee-'dah-dehs deh sohs-teh-nee-mee-'ehn-toh*
suppression	la eliminación	*lah eh-lee-mee-nah-see-'ohn*

S

surcharge	el recargo	*ehl reh-'kahr-goh*
surety company	la compañía garante	*lah kohm-pah-'nyee-ah gah-'rahn-teh*
surface	la superficie (f)	*lah soo-pehr-'fee-see-eh*
surface areas (land)	los suelos	*lohs 'sweh-lohs*
surplus capital	el superávit de capital	*ehl soo-peh-'rah-beet deh kah-pee-'tahl*
surplus goods	el exceso de productos, el superávit de bienes	*ehl ehk-'seh-soh deh proh-'dook-tohs, ehl soo-peh-'rah-beet deh bee-'eh-nehs*
surtax	el impuesto adicional	*ehl eem-'pweh-stoh ah-dee-see-oh-'nahl*
suspend payment	suspender el pago	*soos-pehn-'dehr ehl 'pah-goh*
suspension	la suspensión	*lah soos-pehn-see-'ohn*
sustain	sostener	*sohs-teh-'nehr*
sustenance	sustento	*soos-'tehn-toh*
swamp	el pantano	*ehl pahn-'tah-noh*
swamp (mangrove)	el pantano manglar	*ehl pahn-'tah-noh mahn-'glahr*
switch	el interruptor	*ehl een-teh-rroop-'tohr*
switching charges	los cargos de cambio de títulos	*lohs 'kahr-gohs deh 'kahm-bee-oh deh 'tee-too-lohs*
sworn	jurado	*hoo-'rah-doh*
symbol	el símbolo	*ehl 'seem-boh-loh*
syndicate	el sindicato	*ehl seen-deeh-'kah-toh*
synthesis	la síntesis	*lah 'seen-teh-sees*
syringe	la jeringuilla, la jeringa	*lah heh-reen-'gee-yah, lah heh-'reen-gah*
systems analysis	el análisis de sistema	*ehl ah-'nah-lee-sees deh sees-'teh-mah*
systems design	el diseño de sistemas	*ehl dee-'seh-nyoh deh sees-'teh-mahs*
systems engineering	la ingeniería de sistemas	*lah een-geh-nee-eh-'ree-ah deh sees-'teh-mahs*
systems management	la administración de sistemas	*lah ahd-mee-nees-trah-'syon deh sees-'teh-mahs*

T

table of contents	el índice	*ehl 'een-dee-seh*
tablecloth	el mantel	*ehl mahn-'tehl*
tablespoon	la cuchara	*lah koo-'chah-rah*
tablet	la tableta, la pastilla	*lah tah-'bleh-tah, lah pah-'stee-yah*
tabulate (v)	tabular	*tah-boo-'lahr*
tackle (fishing)	los avíos de pescar	*lohs ah-'bee-ohs deh pehs-'kahr*
taffeta	el tafetán	*ehl tah-feh-'tahn*
tailor	el sastre	*ehl 'sah-streh*
take down (v)	tomar nota	*toh-'mahr 'noh-tah*
take off (v)	rebajar	*reh-bah-'hahr*
take out (v)	extraer, sacar	*ehks-trah-'ehr, sah-'kahr*
take-home pay	la paga líquida	*lah 'pah-gah 'lee-kee-dah*
takeover	la adquisición mayoritaria	*lah ahd-kee-see-see-'ohn mah-yoh-ree-'tah-ree-ah*
takeover bid	la oferta para la adquisición	*lah oh-'fehr-tah 'pah-rah lah ahd-kee-see-see-'ohn*
tan (v)	curtir, broncear	*koor-'teer, brohn-seh-'ahr*
tangible asset	el activo tangible	*ehl ahk-'tee-boh tahn-'hee-bleh*
tank	tanque	*'tahn-keh*
tank (cement storage)	tanque para el almacenamiento de cemento	*'tahn-keh 'pah-rah ehl ahl-mah-seh-nah-mee-'ehn-toh deh seh-'mehn-toh*
tank (drinking water)	tanque para el agua potable	*'tahn-keh 'pah-rah ehl 'ah-gwah poh-'tah-bleh*
tank (jet fuel)	tanque de carburante para helicópteros	*'tahn-keh deh kahr-boo-'rahn-teh 'pah-rah eh-lee-'kohp-teh-rohs*
tank (salt water)	tanque de reserva para agua salada	*'tahn-keh deh reh-'sehr-bah 'pah-rah 'ah-gwah sah-'lah-dah*
tanker	el barcotanque, el tanquero	*ehl bahr-koh-'tahn-keh, ehl tahn-'keh-roh*
tanner	el curtidor	*ehl koor-tee-'dohr*

tannery	la curtiduría, la tenería	*lah koor-tee-doo-'ree-ah, lah teh-neh-'ree-ah*
tape recorder	la grabadora, el magnetófono	*lah grah-bah-'doh-rah, ehl mahg-neh-'toh-foh-noh*
target price	el precio objetivo	*ehl 'preh-see-oh ohb-heh-'tee-boh*
tariff	la tarifa, el arancel	*lah tah-'ree-fah, ehl ah-rahn-'sehl*
tariff barriers	las barreras arancelarias	*lahs bah-'rreh-rahs ah-rahn-seh-'lah-ree-ahs*
tariff charge	el cargo arancelario	*ehl 'kahr-goh ah-rahn-seh-'lah-ree-oh*
tariff classification	la clasificación arancelaria	*lah klah-see-fee-kah-see-'ohn ah-rahn-seh-'lah-ree-ah*
tariff commodity	los aranceles sobre bienes	*lohs ah-rahn-'seh-lehs 'soh-breh bee-'eh-nehs*
tariff differential	la diferencia de tarifas	*lah dee-feh-'rehn-see-ah deh tah-'ree-fahs*
tariff war	la guerra arancelaria	*lah 'geh-rrah ah-rahn-seh-'lah-ree-ah*
task force	la fuerza de trabajo	*lah 'fwewhr-sah deh trah-'bah-hoh*
tasting (wine tasting)	la degustación de vino	*lah deh-goos-tah-see-'ohn deh 'bee-noh*
tax	el impuesto	*ehl eem-'pweh-stoh*
tax allowance	la concesión tributaria	*lah kohn-seh-see-'ohn tree-boo-'tah-ree-ah*
tax base	la base imponible	*lah 'bah-seh eem-poh-'nee-bleh*
tax burden	la carga impositiva	*lah 'kahr-gah eem-poh-see-'tee-bah*
tax collector	el recaudador de impuesto	*ehl reh-kow-dah-'dohr deh eem-'pweh-stoh*
tax deduction	el desgravamen impositivo	*ehl dehs-grah-'bah-mehn ehm-poh-see-'tee-boh*
tax evasion	la evasión de impuestos	*lah eh-bah-see-'ohn deh eem-'pweh-stohs*
tax haven	el sitio donde no se paga impuesto o se paga muy poco	*ehl 'see-tee-oh 'dohn-deh noh seh 'pah-gah eem-'pweh-stoh oh seh 'pah-gah moo-ee 'poh-koh*

tax relief	el desgravamen	*ehl dehs-grah-'bah-mehn*
tax shelter	la protección contra los impuestos	*lah proh-tehk-see-'ohn 'kohn-trah lohs eem-'pweh-stohs*
tax shield	ahorro fiscal contra impuestos	*lah ah-'oh-roh fee-skahl 'kohn-trah eem-pweh-stohs*
taxation	la tributación	*lah tree-boo-tah-see-'ohn*
tax-free income	los ingresos libre de impuestos	*lohs een-'greh-sohs 'lee-breh deh eem-'pweh-stohs*
team management	la gerencia por equipo	*lah heh-'rehn-see-ah pohr eh-'kee-poh*
teapot	la tetera	*lah teh-'teh-rah*
teaspoon	la cucharita	*lah lah koo-chah-'ree-tah*
technology	la tecnología	*lah tehk-noh-loh-'hee-ah*
telecommuni-cations	las telecomunicaciones	*lahs teh-leh-koh-moo-nee-kah-see-'oh-nehs*
telemarketing	el telemercadeo	*ehl teh-leh-mehr-kah-'deh-oh*
teleprocessing	el teleproceso, el teleprocesamiento	*ehl teh-leh-proh-'seh-soh, ehl teh-leh-proh-seh-sah-mee-'ehn-toh*
teller	el cajero	*ehl kah-'heh-roh*
temperature	la temperatura	*lah tehm-peh-rah-'too-rah*
tender (v)	ofrecer	*oh-freh-'sehr*
tender offer	la oferta de compra	*lah oh-'fehr-tah deh 'kohm-prah*
term bond	el bono a plazo de una emisión en que tienen el mismo vencimiento	*ehl 'boh-noh ah 'plah-soh deh 'oo-nah eh-mee-see-'ohn ehn keh tee-'eh-nehn ehl 'mees-moh behn-see-mee-'ehn-toh*
term insurance	los seguros a plazo	*lohs seh-'goh-rohs ah 'plah-soh*
term loan	préstamo a más de un año, el préstamo a plazo	*'preh-stah-moh ah mahs deh oon 'ah-nyoh, ehl 'preh-stah-moh ah 'plah-soh*
terminal	el terminal	*ehl tehr-mee-'nahl*
terminate (v)	terminar	*tehr-mee-'nahr*
terms of sale	los términos de la venta	*lohs 'tehr-mee-nohs deh lah 'behn-tah*

T

terms of trade	los términos de intercambio	*lohs 'tehr-mee-nohs deh deh een-tehr-'kahm-bee-oh*
territorial waters	las aguas territoriales	*lahs 'ah-gwahs teh-rree-toh-ree-'ah-lehs*
territory	el territorio	*ehl teh-rree-'toh-ree-oh*
test tube	el tubo de ensayo	*ehl 'too-boh deh ehn-'sah-yoh*
thermometer	el termómetro	*ehl tehr-'moh-meh-troh*
thin market	el mercado con poca actividad	*ehl mehr-'kah-doh kohn 'poh-kah ahk-tee-bee-'dahd*
thread	el hilo, la hebra	*ehl 'ee-loh, lah 'eh-brah*
threat	la amenaza	*lah ah-meh-'nah-sah*
threatened (adj)	amenazado	*ah-meh-nah-'sah-doh*
throughput	la producción fijada	*lah proh-dook-see-'ohn fee-'hah-dah*
ticker tape	la cinta del indicador automático	*lah 'seen-tah dehl een-dee-kah-'dohr ow-toh-'mah-tee-koh*
tie	la corbata	*lah kohr-'bah-tah*
tied aid	la ayuda condicionada	*lah ah-'yoo-dah kohn-dee-see-oh-'nah-dah*
tied loan	el préstamo condicionado	*ehl 'preh-stah-moh kohn-dee-see-oh-'nah-doh*
tight market	el mercado ajustado	*ehl mehr-'kah-doh ah-hoo-'stah-doh*
time and motion	el tiempo y movimiento	*ehl tee-'ehm-poh ee moh-bee-mee-'ehn-toh*
time bill (of exchange)	la letra a plazo	*lah 'leh-trah ah 'plah-soh*
time deposit	el depósito a plazo	*ehl deh-'poh-see-toh ah 'plah-soh*
time lag	atraso de tiempo	*ah-'trah-soh deh tee-'ehm-poh*
time zone	el huso horario	*ehl oo-soh oh-'rah-ree-oh*
timetable	el horario, el itinerario	*ehl oh-'rah-ree-oh, ehl ee-tee-neh-'rah-ree-oh*
tip (inside information)	el dato confidencial	*ehl 'dah-toh kohn-fee-sehn-see-'ahl*
tire	el neumático	*ehl neh-oo-'mah-tee-koh*

title	el título	*ehl 'tee-too-loh*
title insurance	los seguros de título	*lohs seh-'goo-rohs deh 'tee-too-loh*
titration	la titulación	*lah tee-too-lah-see-'ohn*
to have authority (v)	tener autoridad	*teh-'nehr ow-toh-ree-'dahd*
to the bearer	al portador	*ahl pohr-tah-'dohr*
toiletry kit	el estuche de artículos de tocador	*ehl ehs-'too-cheh deh ahr-'tee-koo-lohs deh toh-kah-'dohr*
tombstone	el documento público donde se enumeran a los aseguradores de una emisión de valores	*ehl doh-koo-'mehn-toh 'poo-blee-koh 'dohn-deh seh eh-noo-'meh-rahn ah lohs ah-seh-goo-rah-'doh-rehs deh 'oo-nah eh-mee-see-'ohn deh bah-'loh-rehs*
tonnage	el tonelaje	*ehl toh-neh-'lah-heh*
tools (hardware)	las herramientas	*lahs eh-rrah-mee-'ehn-tahs*
tools	los instrumentos	*lohs een-stroo-'mehn-tohs*
top management	la alta gerencia	*lah 'ahl-tah heh-'rehn-see-ah*
top price	el precio máximo	*ehl 'preh-see-oh 'mahk-see-moh*
top quality	la calidad máxima	*lah kah-lee-'dahd 'mahk-see-mah*
torque	el momento de torsión	*ehl moh-'mehn-toh deh tohr-see-'ohn*
tort	el agravio indemnizable	*ehl ah-'grah-bee-oh een-dehm-nee-'sah-bleh*
tote bag	la mochila	*lah moh-'cheh-yah*
toughness	la tenacidad	*lah teh-nah-see-'dahd*
tourist area	la zona turística	*lah 'soh-nah too-'rees-tee-kah*
toxicology	la toxicología	*lah tok-see-koh-loh-'hee-ah*
toxin	la toxina	*lah tok-'see-nah*
track	pista (disco), canal (cinta)	*'pees-tah ('dees-koh), kah-'nahl ('seen-tah)*
trade	el comercio, el intercambio, el intercambio compensatorio	*ehl koh-'mehr-see-oh, ehl een-tehr-'kahm-bee-oh kohm-pehn-sah-'toh-ree-oh*

T

trade (v)	intercambiar	*een-tehr-kahm-bee-'ahr*
trade acceptance	la aceptación comercial	*lah ah-sehp-tah-see-'ohn koh-mehr-see-'ahl*
trade agreement	el acuerdo comercial	*ehl ah-'kwehr-doh koh-mehr-see-'ahl*
trade association	la asociación comercial	*lah ah-soh-see-ah-see-'ohn koh-mehr-see-'ahl*
trade barrier	la barrera al intercambio comercial	*lah bah-'rreh-rrah ahl een-tehr-'kahm-bee-oh koh-mehr-see-'ahl*
trade commission	la comisión comercial	*lah koh-mee-see-'ohn koh-mehr-see-'ahl*
trade credit	el crédito comercial	*ehl 'kreh-dee-toh koh-mehr-see-'ahl*
trade date	la fecha del intercambio	*lah 'feh-chah dehl een-tehr-'kahm-bee-oh*
trade discount	el descuento comercial	*ehl dehs-'kwehn-toh koh-mehr-see-'ahl*
trade fair	la feria comercial	*lah 'feh-ree-ah koh-mehr-see-'ahl*
trade house	la casa de comercio	*lah 'kah-sah deh koh-'mehr-see-oh*
trade union	el gremio de obreros	*ehl 'greh-mee-oh deh oh-'breh-rohs*
trademark	la marca de fábrica	*lah 'mahr-kah deh 'fah-bree-kah*
trader	el comerciante	*ehl koh-mehr-see-'ahn-teh*
trading company	la compañía de intercambio comercial	*lah kohm-pah-'nyee-ah deh een-tehr-'kahm-bee-oh koh-mehr-see-'ahl*
trading floor	el parquet	*ehl pahr-'keht*
trading limit	el límite de intercambio	*ehl 'lee-mee-teh deh een-tehr-'kahm-bee-oh*
trainee	el aprendiz, el personal de adiestramiento	*ehl ah-prehn-'dees, ehl pehr-soh-'nahl deh ah-dee-eh-strah-mee-'ehn-toh*
training group	el grupo de entrenamiento	*ehl 'groo-poh deh ehn-treh-nah-mee-'ehn-toh*
tranche	el tramo	*ehl 'trah-moh*
tranquilizer	el tranquilizante	*ehl trahn-kee-lee-'sahn-teh*
transaction	la transacción	*lah trahn-sahk-see-'ohn*

transceiver	receptor/emisor	*reh-sehp-'tohr/eh-mee-'sohr*
transfer	la transferencia	*lah trahns-feh-'rehn-see-ah*
transfer agent	el agente de transferencia	*ehl ah-'hehn-teh deh trahns-feh-'rehn-see-ah*
transferred	transferido	*trahns-feh-'ree-doh*
transformer	el transformador	*ehl trahns-fohr-mah-'dohr*
translate (v)	traducir	*trah-doo-'seer*
translator	el traductor	*ehl trah-dook-'tohr*
transliterate (v)	convertir carácteres	*kohn-behr-'teer kah-'rahk-teh-rehs*
transmitter (v)	transmitir	*trahns-mee-'teer*
transportation	el transporte	*ehl trahns-'pohr-teh*
traveler's check	el cheque de viajero	*ehl 'cheh-keh deh bee-ah-'heh-roh*
treasurer	el tesorero	*ehl teh-soh-'reh-roh*
treasury bills	las letras del Tesoro	*lahs 'leh-trahs dehl teh-'soh-roh*
treasury bonds	los bonos del Tesoro	*lohs 'boh-nohs dehl teh-'soh-roh*
treasury notes	las billetes del Tesoro	*lahs bee-'yeh-tehs dehl teh-'soh-roh*
treasury stock	las acciones de tesorerías	*lahs ahk-see-'oh-nehs deh teh-soh-reh-'ree-ahs*
treaty	el convenio	*ehl kohn-'beh-nee-oh*
tree	el árbol	*ehl 'ahr-bohl*
trend	la tendencia	*lah tehn-'dehn-see-ah*
trial balance	el balance de comprobación	*ehl bah-'lahn-seh deh kohm-proh-bah-see-'ohn*
tropics	los trópicos	*lohs 'troh-pee-kohs*
troubleshoot (v)	investigar y resolver un problema, mediar en una desavenencia	*een-beh-stee'gahr ee reh-sohl-'behr oon proh-'bleh-mah, meh-dee-'ahr ehn 'oo-nah dehs-ah-beh-'nehn-see-ah*
truck load	la camionada	*lah kah-mee-oh-'nah-dah*
trunk	el baúl	*ehl bah-'ool*
trust	el fideicomiso	*ehl fee-deh-ee-koh-'mee-soh*
trust company	la compañía fiduciaria	*lah kohm-pah-'nyee-ah fee-doo-see-'ah-ree-ah*

T

trust fund	el fondo de fideicomiso	*ehl 'fohn-doh deh fee-deh-ee-koh-'mee-soh*
trustee	el fideicomisario	*ehl fee-deh-ee-koh-mee-'sah-ree-oh*
turbine	la turbina	*lah toor-'bee-nah*
tureen	la sopera	*lah 'soh-pah*
turnkey company	la sociedad creada con un fin específico	*lah soh-see-eh-'dahd kreh-'ah-dah kohn oon feen ehs-peh-'see-fee-koh*
tuxedo	el "smoking," el esmoquin	*ehl 'smoh-keen, ehl eh-'smoh-keen*
two-tiered market	el mercado de dos niveles	*ehl mehr-'kah-doh deh dohs nee-'beh-lehs*
type of vine	el tipo de vid, el tipo de parra	*ehl 'tee-poh deh beed, ehl 'tee-poh deh 'pah-rrah*

U

unaccompanied goods	los bienes no acompañados	*lohs bee-'eh-nehs noh ah-kohm-pah-'nyah-dohs*
unbleached linen	el hilo crudo	*ehl 'ee-loh 'kroo-doh*
uncollectable accounts	las cuentas incobrables	*lahs 'kwehn-tahs een-koh-'brah-blehs*
undercapitalization	la insuficiencia de capital	*lah een-soo-fee-see-'ehn-see-ah deh kah-pee-'tahl*
undercut (v)	socavar, vender por debajo del precio de un competidor	*soh-kah-'bahr, behn-'dehr pohr deh-'bah-hoh dehl 'preh-see-oh deh oon kohm-'peh-teep'dohr*
underdeveloped	subdesarrollado	*soob-dehs-ah-rroh-'yah-doh*
underdeveloped nations	las naciones subdesarrolladas	*lahs nah-see-'oh-nehs soob-dehs-ah-rroh-'yah-dahs*
underestimate (v)	subestimar	*soob-eh-stee-'mahr*
underpaid	el sueldo insuficiente, subpagado	*ehl 'swehl-doh een-soo-fee-see-'ehn-teh, soob-pah-'gah-doh*
undersigned	el suscrito	*ehl soos-kree-toh*
understanding (agreement)	el acuerdo	*ehl ah-'kwehr-doh*

undertake (v)	emprender, acometer	*ehm-prehn-'dehr, ah-koh-meh-'tehr*
undervalue (v)	tasar en menos del valor real	*tah-'sahr ehn 'meh-nohs dehl bah-'lohr reh-'ahl*
underwriter	el asegurador	*ehl ah-seh-goo-rah-'dohr*
unearned increment	la plusvalía	*lah ploos-bah-'lee-ah*
unearned revenue	los ingresos no merecidos	*lohs een-'greh-sohs noh meh-reh-'see-dohs*
unemployment	el desempleo	*ehl dehs-ehm-'pleh-oh*
unemployment compensation	la compensación por desempleo	*lah kohm-pehn-sah-see-'ohn pohr dehs-ehm-'pleh-oh*
unfair	injusto	*een-'hoos-toh*
unfavorable	desfavorable	*dehs-fah-boh-'rah-bleh*
unfeasible	impracticable, poco probable	*eem-prahk-tee-'kah-bleh, 'poh-koh proh-'bah-bleh*
unfermented grape juice	el zumo de uva no fermentado	*ehl 'soo-moh deh 'oo-bah noh fehr-mehn-'tah-doh*
unformatted (adj)	no ajustado a formato	*noh ah-hoos-'tah-doh ah fohr-'mah-toh*
unfunded debt	la deuda flotante	*lah deh-'oo-dah floh-'tahn-teh*
union contract	el contrato sindical	*ehl kohn-'trah-toh seen-dee-'kahl*
Union for the Conservation of Nature and Natural Resources	Unión para la Conservación de la ñaturaleza y los Recursos Naturales	*oo-nee-'ohn 'pah-rah lah kohn-sehr-bah-see-'ohn deh lah nah-too-rah-'leh-sah ee lohs reh-'koor-sohs nah-too-'rah-lehs*
union label	la marca sindical	*lah 'mahr-kah seen-dee-'kahl*
unit cost	el costo unitario	*ehl 'koh-stoh oo-nee-'tah-ree-oh*
unit load discount	el descuento unitario por carga	*ehl dehs-'kwehn-toh oo-nee-'tah-ree-oh pohr 'kahr-gah*
unit price	el precio unitario	*ehl 'preh-see-oh oo-nee-'tah-ree-oh*
unlisted	no registrado	*noh reh-hee-'strah-doh*
unload (v)	descargar	*dehs-kahr-'gahr*
unloading	el descargue, la descarga	*ehl dehs 'kahr-geh, lah dehs kahr-gah*

U

unsecured liability	el pasivo no garantizado	*ehl pah-'see-boh noh gah-rahn-tee-'sah-doh*
unsecured loan	el préstamo no garantizado	*ehl 'preh-stah-moh noh gah-rahn-tee-'sah-doh*
unskilled labor	el trabajo no calificado	*ehl trah-'bah-hoh noh kah-lee-fee-'kah-doh*
up to our expectations	hasta nuestras expectivas, las expectativas realizadas	*'ah-stah 'nweh-strahs ehk-spehk-'tee-bahs, lahs ehk-spehk-'tee-bahs reh-ah-lee-'sah-dahs*
update (v)	actualizar	*ahk-too-ah-lee-'sahr*
uploading	conversión ascendente	*kohn-behr-see-'ohn ah-sehn-'dehn-teh*
upmarket	el mercado alcista	*ehl mehr-'kah-doh ahl-'sees-tah*
upturn	la tendencia alcista	*lah tehn-'dehn-see-ah ahl-'sees-tah*
urban renewal	la renovación urbana	*lah reh-noh-bah-see-'ohn oor-'bah-nah*
urban sprawl	el desarrollo urbano	*ehl dehs-ah-'rroh-yoh oor-'bah-noh*
use tax	el impuesto de uso	*ehl eem-'pwehs-toh deh 'oo-soh*
useful life	la vida útil	*lah 'bee-dah 'oo-teel*
user	el usuario	*ehl oo-soo-'ah-ree-oh*
user-friendly	concebido para el usuario, fácil para el usuario	*kohn-seh-'bee-doh 'pah-rah ehl oo-soo-'ah-ree-oh, 'fah-seel 'pah-rah ehl oo-soo-'ah-ree-oh*
usury	la usura	*lah oo-'soo-rah*
utility	la utilidad	*lah oo-tee-lee-'dahd*
utilization capacity	la capacidad de utilización	*lah kah-pah-see-'dahd deh oo-tee-lee-sah-see-'ohn*

V

V8 engine	el motor V8	*ehl moh-'tohr V8*
vaccine	la vacuna	*lah bah-'koo-nah*
vacuum	el vacío	*ehl bah-'see-oh*

vacuum melting furnace	el horno de fusión al vacío	*ehl 'ohr-noh deh foo-see-'ohn ahl bah-'see-oh*
valid	válido	*'bah-lee-doh*
validate (v)	validar	*bah-'lee-'dahr*
valuation	la valuación	*lah bah-loo-ah-see-'ohn*
value	el valor	*ehl bah-'lohr*
value of firm	valor de la empresa	*bah-'lohr deh lah ehm-'preh-sah*
value-added tax (V.A.T.)	el impuesto sobre el valor añadido (I.V.A.)	*ehl eem-'pwehs-toh 'soh-breh ehl bah-'lohr ah-nyah-'dee-doh*
valve	la válvula	*lah 'bahl-boo-lah*
valve engineering	el estudio de los componentes de un artículo	*ehl eh-'stoo-dee-oh deh lohs kohm-poh-'nehn-tehs deh oon ahr-'tee-koo-loh*
variable annuity	la anualidad variable	*lah ah-noo-ah-lee-'dahd bah-ree-'ah-bleh*
variable costs	los costos variables	*lohs 'koh-stohs bah-ree-'ah-blehs*
variable import levy	la imposición variable sobre importaciones	*lah eem-poh-see-see-'ohn bah-ree-'ah-bleh 'soh-breh eem-pohr-tah-see-'oh-nehs*
variable margin	el margen variable	*ehl 'mahr-hehn bah-ree-'ah-bleh*
variable rate	la tasa variable	*lah 'tah-sah bah-ree-'ah-bleh*
variable rate mortgage	la hipoteca con intereses variables	*lah ee-poh-'teh-kah kohn een-'teh-'reh-sehs bah-ree-'ah-blehs*
variance	la varianza	*lah bah-ree-'ahn-sah*
vat	la cuba, la tina	*lah 'koo-bah, lah 'tee-nah*
vector	el vector	*ehl behk-'tohr*
vegetation	el vegetal (m)	*ehl beh-heh-'tahl*
vegetation (aquatic)	el vegetal acuático	*ehl beh-heh-'tahl ah-'kwah-tee-koh*
vehicle	el vehículo	*ehl beh-'ee-koo-loh*
vehicle (motorized)	motorizado vehículo	*moh-toh-ree-'sah-doh beh-'ee-koo-loh*
veil	el velo	*ehl 'beh-loh*

V

velocity of money	la velocidad de la moneda	*lah beh-loh-see-'dahd deh lah moh-'neh-dah*
vendor	el vendedor	*ehl behn-deh-'dohr*
vendor's lien	el gravamen del vendedor	*ehl grah-'bah-mehn dehl behn-deh-'dohr*
venture capital	capital de especulación, el capital especulativo, la empresa nueva en la que se arriesga capital	*kah-pee-'tahl deh eh-speh-koo-lah-see-'ohn, ehl kah-pee-'tahl ehs-peh-koo-lah-'tee-boh, lah ehm-'preh-sah 'nwweh-bah ehn lah keh seh ah-rree-'ehs-gah kah-pee-'tahl*
verify (v)	verificar, controlar	*beh-ree-fee-'kahr, kohn-troh-'lahr*
vertical integration	la integración vertical, organización vertical	*lah een-teh-grah-see-'ohn behr-tee-'kahl, ohr-gah-nee-sah-see-'ohn behr-tee-'kahl*
vessel (sea)	el buque	*ehl 'boo-keh*
vest	el chaleco	*ehl chah-'leh-koh*
vested interests	los intereses creados	*lohs een-teh-'reh-sehs creh-'ah-dohs*
vested rights	los derechos adquiridos	*lohs deh-'reh-chohs ahd-kee-'ree-dohs*
veto	el veto	*ehl 'beh-toh*
vice-president	el vice-presidente	*ehl bee-seh-preh-see-'dehn-teh*
videocassette player	el tocador de videocassette	*ehl toh-kah-'dohr deh bee-deh-oh-kah-'seh-teh*
vine	la vid	*lah beed*
vineyard	la viña, el viñedo	*lah 'bee-nyah, ehl bee-'nyeh-doh*
vintage	la vendimia, la cosecha	*lah behn-'dee-mee-ah*
vintage year	el año de cosecha, el año clásico	*ehl 'ah-nyoh deh koh-'seh-chah, ehl 'ah-nyoh 'klah-see-koh*
vintner	el vinatero	*ehl bee-nah-'teh-roh*
vintry	la vinatería	*lah-bee-nah-teh-'ree-ah*
visible balance of trade	la balanza comercial visible	*lah bah-'lahn-sah koh-mehr-see-'ahl bee-'see-bleh*

vitamin	la vitamina	*lah bee-tah-'mee-nah*
voice-activated	la voz activada	*lah bohs ahk-tee-'bah-dah*
void	inválido, nulo	*een-'bah-lee-doh, 'noo-loh*
voided check	el cheque anulado	*ehl 'cheh-kee ah-noo-'lah-doh*
volatile market	el mercado inestable	*ehl mehr-'kah-doh een-eh-'stah-bleh*
volt	el voltio	*ehl 'bohl-tee-oh*
voltage	el voltaje	*ehl bohl-'tah-heh*
volume	el volumen	*ehl boh-'loo-mehn*
volume discount	el descuento sobre el volumen	*ehl dehs-'kwehn-toh 'soh-breh ehl boh-'loo-mehn*
voting right	el derecho al voto	*ehl deh-'reh-choh ahl 'boh-toh*
voucher	el comprobante	*ehl kohm-proh-'bahn-teh*

W

wage	el salario	*ehl sah-'lah-ree-oh*
wage dispute	la disputa salarial	*lah dees-'poo-tah sah-lah-ree-'ahl*
wage earner	el trabajador	*ehl trah-bah-hah-'dohr*
wage freeze	el congelamiento de salarios	*ehl kohn-heh-lah-mee-'ehn-toh deh sah-'lah-ree-ohs*
wage level	el nivel salarial	*ehl nee-'behl sah-lah-ree-'ahl*
wage scale	la escala salarial	*lah ehs-'kah-lah sah-lah-ree-'ahl*
wage structure	la estructura salarial	*lah ehs-trook-'too-rah*
wage-price spiral	el espiral de precios y salarios	*ehl ehs-pee-'rahl deh 'preh-see-ohs ee sah-'lah-ree-ohs*
waiver clause	la cláusula de exención	*lah 'klow-soo-lah deh ehks-ehn-see-'ohn*
walk out (v)	declararse en huelga	*deh-klah-'rahr-seh ehn 'wehl-gah*
want-ad	el anuncio clasificado	*ehl ah-'noon-see-oh klah-see-fee-'kah-doh*

warehouse	el almacén, el depósito	*ehl ahl-mah-'sehn, ehl deh-'poh-see-toh*
warehouseman	el almacenador	*ehl ahl-mah-seh-nah-'dohr*
warm (adj)	cálido	*'kah-lee-doh*
warming effect	el efecto invernadero	*ehl eh-'fehk-toh een-behr-nah-'deh-roh*
warning	el aviso	*ehl ah-'bee-soh*
warrant	el certificado de opción	*ehl sehr-tee-fee-'kah-doh deh ohp-see-'ohn*
warrant (v)	el garantizar	*ehl gah-rahn-tee-'sahr*
warranty	la garantía	*lah gah-rahn-'tee-ah*
waste	el desgaste	*ehl dehs-'gah-steh*
wasting asset	el activo desperdiciado	*ehl ahk-'tee-boh dehs-pehr-dee-see-'ah-doh*
watch strap	la correa de reloj	*lah koh-'rreh-ah deh reh-'loh*
water pump	la bomba de agua	*lah 'bohm-bah deh 'ah-gwah*
waters	aguas	*'ah-gwahs*
watt	el vatio	*ehl 'bah-tee-oh*
wave	la onda	*lah 'ohn-dah*
waves (of sea)	las olas del mar	*lahs 'oh-lahs dehl mahr*
waybill	el manifiesto de carga	*ehl mah-nee-fee-'ehs-toh deh 'kahr-gah*
wealth	la fortuna, la riqueza	*lah fohr-'too-nah, lah ree-'keh-sah*
weapons	las armas	*lahs 'ahr-mahs*
weapons (atomic)	las armas atómicas	*lahs 'ahr-mahs ah-'toh-mee-kahs*
wear and tear	el deterioro natural debido al uso	*ehl deh-teh-ree-'oh-roh nah-too-'rahl deh-'bee-doh ahl 'oo-soh*
weaver	el tejedor	*ehl teh-heh-'dohr*
web offset	el cilindro de offset	*ehl see-'leen-droh deh ohf-'seht*
weekly return	el retorno semanal	*ehl reh-'tohr-noh seh-mah-'nahl*
weight	el peso	*ehl 'peh-soh*
weighted average	la media ponderada	*lah 'meh-dee-ah pohn-deh-'rah-dah*

W

well (drilled)	el pozo	*ehl 'poh-soh*
well-being	bienestar	*bee-ehn-eh-'stahr*
well-being (economic)	el bienestar económico	*ehl bee-ehn-eh-'stahr eh-koh-'noh-mee-koh*
well-being (social)	el bienestar social	*ehl bee-ehn-eh-'stahr soh-see-'ahl*
wharfage charge	el cargo por muelle	*ehl 'kahr-goh pohr 'mweh-yeh*
wheel	la rueda	*lah roo-'eh-dah*
when issued	las operaciones con acciones antes de su emisión	*lahs oh-peh-rah-see-'oh-nehs kohn ahk-see-'oh-nehs 'ahn-tehs deh soo eh-mee-see-'ohn*
whip	el látigo, la fusta	*ehl 'lah-tee-goh, lah 'foos-tah*
white-collar worker	el/la oficinista	*ehl/lah oh-fee-see-'nees-tah*
wholesale market	el mercado al por mayor	*ehl mehr-'kah-doh ahl pohr mah-'yohr*
wholesale price	el precio al por mayor	*ehl 'preh-see-oh ahl pohr mah-'yohr*
wholesale trade	el intercambio a nivel de mayorista	*ehl een-tehr-'kahn-bee-oh ah nee-'behl deh mah-yohr-'rees-tah*
wholesaler	el mayorista	*ehl mah-yohr-'rees-tah*
wildcat strike	la huelga no sancionada por el sindicato	*lah 'wehl-gah noh sahnk-see-oh-'nah-dah pohr ehl seen-dee-'kah-toh*
will	el testamento	*ehl tehs-tah-'mehn-toh*
windfall profit	el beneficio imprevisto	*ehl beh-neh-'fee-see-oh eem-preh-'bees-toh*
window	la ventana	*lah behn-'tah-nah*
window dresser	el escaparatista, el decorador de escaparates	*ehl ehs-kah-pah-'rah-'tees-tah, ehl deh-koh-rah-'dohr deh ehs-kah-pah-'rah-tehs*
window dressing	la modificación para mantener una apariencia	*lah moh-dee-fee-kah-see-'ohn 'pah-rah mahn-teh-nehr 'oo-nah ah-pah-ree-'ehn-see-ah*
winds	el viento	*ehl bee-'ehn-toh*
windshield	el parabrisas	*ehl pah-rah-'bree-sahs*

W

wine	el vino	*ehl 'bee-noh*
wine cellar	la bodega	*lah boh-'deh-gah*
wine cooperative	la cooperativa de vino	*lah koh-oh-peh-rah-'tee-bah deh 'bee-noh*
wine steward	el sumiller	*ehl soo-mee-'yehr*
winegrower	el viticultor	*ehl bee-tee-kool-'tohr*
winemaker	el vinicultor	*ehl bee-nee-kool-'tohr*
winepress	el lagar	*ehl lah-'gahr*
wire	el alambre, el cable	*ehl ah-'lahm-breh, ehl 'kah-bleh*
wire transfer	la transferencia cablegráfica	*lah trahns-feh-'rehn-see-ah*
with average	con avería	*kohn ah-beh-'ree-ah*
with regard to	referente a	*reh-feh-'rehn-teh ah*
withholding tax	la retención de impuesto	*lah reh-tehn-see-'ohn deh eem-'pweh-stoh*
witness	el testigo	*ehl tehs-'tee-goh*
wool	la lana	*lah 'lah-nah*
word	la palabra	*lah pah-'lah-brah*
word processing	el procesamiento de palabra, el tratamiento de palabra	*ehl proh-seh-sah-mee-'ehn-toh deh pah-'lah-brah, ehl trah-tah-mee-'ehn-toh deh pah-'lah-brah*
word processor	el procesador de palabras, la computadora	*ehl proh-seh-sah-'dohr deh pah-'lah-brahs, lah kohm-poo-tah-'doh-rah*
work (v)	trabajar	*trah-bah-'hahr*
work aesthetic (environment)	la estética laboral	*lah ehs-'teh-tee-kah lah-boh-'rahl*
work area	el área de trabajo	*ehl 'ah-reh-ah deh trah-'bah-hoh*
work by contract	el trabajo por contrato	*ehl trah-'bah-hoh pohr kohn-'trah-toh*
work committee	el comité de trabajo	*ehl koh-mee-'teh deh trah-'bah-hoh*
work council	el concejo de trabajo	*ehl kohn-'seh-hoh deh trah-'bah-hoh*
work cycle	el ciclo de trabajo	*ehl 'see-kloh deh trah-'bah-hoh*
work ethic	la ética laboral	*lah 'eh-tee-kah lah-boh-'rahl*

work file	el archivo de trabajo	*ehl ahr-'chee-boh deh trah-'bah-hoh*
work force	la fuerza laboral	*lah 'fwehr-sah lah-boh-'rahl*
work in progress	el trabajo en progreso	*ehl trah-'bah-hoh ehn proh-'greh-soh*
work load	la carga de trabajo	*lah 'kahr-gah deh trah-'bah-hoh*
work order	la orden de trabajo	*lah 'ohr-dehn deh trah-'bah-hoh*
workday	el día de trabajo, la jornada	*ehl 'dee-ah deh trah-'bah-hoh, lah hor-'nah-dah*
working assets	los activos de trabajo	*lohs ahk-'tee-bohs deh trah-'bah-hoh*
working balance	el saldo de operación, los fondos de operación	*ehl 'sahl-doh deh oh-peh-rah-see-'ohn, lohs 'fohn-dohs deh oh-peh-rah-see-'ohn*
working capital	el capital de trabajo	*ehl kah-pee-'tahl deh trah-'bah-hoh*
working class	la clase trabajadora	*lah 'klah-seh trah-bah-hah-'doh-rah*
working contract	el contrato vigente	*ehl kohn-'trah-toh bee-'hehn-teh*
working funds	los fondos de operación	*lohs 'foh-dohs deh oh-peh-rah-see-'ohn*
working hours	las horas de trabajo	*lahs 'oh-rahs deh trah-'bah-hoh*
working papers	los documentos de trabajo	*laohs doh-koo-'mehn-tohs deh trah-'bah-hoh*
working tools	los instrumentos de trabajo	*lohs een-stroo-'mehn-tohs deh trah-'bah-hoh*
workplace	el sitio de trabajo	*ehl 'see-tee-oh deh trah-'bah-hoh*
workshop	el taller, los ejercicios prácticos	*ehl tah-'yehr, lohs eh-hehr-'see-see-ohs 'prahk-tee-kohs*
workstation	la estación de trabajo	*lah ehs-tah-see-'ohn deh trah-'bah-hoh*
World Bank	el Banco Mundial	*lah ehl 'bahn-koh moon-dee-'ahl*
worry	la preocupación	*lah preh-oh-koo-pah-see-'ohn*

worthless	sin valor	*seen bah-'lohr*
writ	el mandamiento, la escritura	*ehl mahn-dah-mee-'ehn-toh, lah ehs-kree-'too-rah*
write down (v)	poner por escrito	*poh'nehr pohr ehs-'kree-toh*
write off (v)	cancelar una partida doble	*kahn-seh-'lahr 'oo-nah pahr-'tee-dah 'doh-bleh*
written agreement	el acuerdo escrito	*ehl ah-'kwehr-doh ehs-'kree-toh*
written bid (stock exchange)	la oferta por escrito	*lah oh-'fehr-tah pohr ehs-'kree-toh*

Y

yardstick	el patrón, la medida de yardas	*ehl pah-'trohn, lah meh-'dee-dah deh 'yahr-dahs*
yarn	el hilo	*ehl 'ee-loh*
year	el año	*ehl 'ah-nyoh*
year-end	el cierre de ejercicio	*ehl see-'eh-rreh deh eh-hehr-'see-see-oh*
yeast	la levadura	*lah leh-bah-'doo-rah*
yield	la producción, el rendimiento (financial)	*lah proh-dook-see-'ohn, ehl rehn-dee-mee-'ehn-toh*
yield to maturity	el rendimiento hasta el vencimiento, rentabilidad al vencimiento	*ehl rehn-dee-mee-'ehn-toh 'ahs-tah ehl behn-see-mee-'ehn-toh, rehn-tah-bee-lee-'dahd ahl behn-see-mee-'ehn-toh*

Z

zero coupon	el cupón cero	*ehl koo-'pohn 'seh-roh*
zinc	el zinc, el cinc	*ehl seenk, ehl seenk*
zip code	el código postal	*ehl 'koh-dee-goh pohs-'tahl*
zipper	la cremallera	*lah kreh-mah-'yeh-rah*
zone	la zona	*lah 'soh-nah*
zoning law	la ordenanza municipal sobre construcción	*lah ohr-deh-'nahn-sah moo-nee-see-'pahl 'soh-breh kohn-strook-see-'ohn*

A

a cuenta de	*ah 'kwehn-tah deh*	on account of
a flote	*ah 'floh-teh*	afloat
a igual trabajo, igual salario	*ah ee-'gwahl trah-'bah-hoh, ee-'gwahl sah-'lah-ree-oh*	equal pay for equal work
a la apertura	*ah lah ah-pehr-'too-rah*	at the opening
a la par	*ah lah pahr*	at par
a la vista	*ah lah 'bees-tah*	at sight, at call
a presentación	*ah preh-sehn-tah-see-'ohn*	on demand
a todo riesgo	*ah 'toh-doh ree-'ehs-goh*	against all risks
abandonar	*ah-bahn-doh-'nahr*	abandon (v)
abandono (m)	*ehl ah-bahn-'doh-noh*	abandonment
abarrotar	*ah-bah-rroh-t'ahr*	overstock (v)
abarrote (m)	*ehl ah-bah-'rroh-teh*	dunnage, broken stowage
abastecedor (m)	*ehl ah-bah-steh-seh-'dohr*	supplier
abastecimiento (m)	*ehl ah-bah-steh-see-mee-'ehn-toh*	supply
abastecer	*ah-bah-steh-'sehr*	supply (v)
abogado (m)	*ehl ah-boh-'gah-doh*	attorney, lawyer
abrigo (m)	*ehl ah-bree-goh*	coat
abrir la compañía	*ah-'breer lah kohm-pah-'nyee-ah*	go public (v)
absoluto	*ahb-soh-'loo-toh*	absolute (adj)
absorber	*ahb-sohr-'behr*	absorb (v)
absorber la pérdida	*ahb-sohr-'behr lah 'pehr-dee-dah*	absorb the loss (v)
absorción de costos (f)	*lah ahb-sohr-see-'ohn deh 'kohs-tohs*	absorption costing
abundante	*ah-boon-'dahn-teh*	abundant (adj)
acanaladura (f)	*lah ah-kah-nah-lah-doo-rah*	flute, groove
acarreo (m)	*ehl ah-kah-'rreh-oh*	drayage, back haul
acceso (m)	*ehl ahk-'seh-soh*	access
acceso al azar a la memoria	*ehl ahk-s'eh-soh ahl ah-'sahr ah lah meh-'moh-ree-ah*	random access memory

A

acceso al mercado	*ehl ak-'seh-soh ahl mehr-'kah-doh*	market access
accidente industrial (m)	*ehl ahk-see-'dehn-teh een-doo-stree-'ahl*	industrial accident
acción (f)	*lah ahk-see-'ohn*	stock
acción civil	*lah ahk-see-'ohn see-'beel*	civil action
acciones autorizadas (fpl)	*lahs ahk-see-'oh-nehs ow-toh-ree-'sah-dahs*	authorized shares
acciones comunes	*lahs ahk-see-'oh-nehs koh-'moo-nehs*	common stocks
acciones con aplancamiento	*lahs ahk-see-'oh-nehs kohn ah-plahn-kah-mee-'ehn-toh*	leveraged equity
acciones cotizadas a menos de un dólar	*lahs ahk-see-'ohn-nehs koh-tee-'sah-dahs ah 'meh-nohs deh oon 'doh-lahr*	penny stocks
acciones de crecimiento	*lahs ahk-see-'oh-nehs deh kreh-see-mee-ehn-toh*	growth stocks
acciones de menos de centenas	*lahs ahk-see-'oh-nehs de sehn-teh-nahs*	odd lots
acciones de tesorerías	*lahs ahk-see-'oh-nehs deh teh-soh-reh-'ree-ahs*	treasury stock
acciones emitidas	*lahs ahk-see-'oh-nehs eh-mee-'tee-dahs*	issued shares
acciones en circulación	*lahs ahk-see-'oh-nehs ehn seer-koo-lah-see-'ohn*	outstanding stocks
acciones ordinarias	*ehl ahk-see-'oh-nehs ohr-dee-'nah-ree-ahs*	common stock
acciones pagadas	*lahs ahk-see-'oh-nehs pah-'gah-dahs*	paid up shares
acciones preferentes	*lahs ahk-see-'oh-nehs preh-feh-'rehn-tehs*	preferred stock
acciones preferentes acumulativas	*lahs ahk-see-'oh-nehs preh-feh-'rehn-tehs ah-koo-moo-lah-'tee-bahs*	cumulative preferred stocks
acciones preferentes no acumulativas	*lahs ahk-see-'oh-nehs preh-feh-rehn-tehs noh ah-koo-moo-lah-'tee-bahs*	noncumulative preferred stocks
acciones preferidas	*lahs ahk-see-'oh-nehs preh-feh-'ree-dahs*	preferred stock

A

acciones preferidas convertibles	*lahs ahk-see-'oh-nehs preh-feh-'ree-dahs kohn-behr-'tee-blehs*	convertible preferred stocks
acciones preferidas de primera	*lahs ahk-see-'oh-nehs preh-feh-'ree-dahs deh pree-'meh-rah*	first preferred stocks
acciones preferidas participantes	*lahs ahk-see-'oh-nehs preh-feh-ree-dahs pahr-tee-see-'pahn-tehs*	participating preferred stocks
acciones prestadas	*lahs ahk-see-'oh-nehs preh-'stah-dahs*	loan stocks
acciones sin derechos a voto	*lahs ahk-see-'oh-nehs seen deh-'reh-chohs ah boh-toh*	nonvoting stocks
accionista (m)	*ehl ahk-see-oh-'nees-tah*	shareholder, stockholder
aceite (m)	*ehl ah-'seh-ee-teh*	oil (crude)
aceite bruto	*ehl ah'see-ee-teh 'broo-toh*	crude oil
acelerador (m)	*ehl ah-seh-leh-rah-dohr*	gas pedal
acelerar	*ah-seh-leh-'rahr*	speed up (v)
aceptación (f)	*lah ah-sehp-tah-see-'ohn*	acceptance
aceptación bancaria	*lah ah-sehp-tah-see-'ohn bahn-'kah-ree-ah*	bank acceptance
aceptación comercial	*lah ah-sehp-tah-see-'ohn koh-mehr-see-'ahl*	trade acceptance
aceptación condicional	*lah ah-sehp-tah-see-'ohn kohn-dee-see-oh-'nahl*	conditional acceptance
aceptación de marca	*lah ah-sehp-tah-see-'ohn deh 'mahr-kah*	brand acceptance
aceptación general	*lah ah-sehp-tah-see-'ohn heh-neh-'rahl*	general acceptance
aceptación por parte de los consumidores	*lah ah-sehp-tah-see-'ohn pohr 'pahr-teh deh lohs kohn-soo-mee-'doh-rehs*	consumer acceptance
aceptante (m)	*ehl ah-sehp-'tahn-teh*	acceptor
aceptar	*ah-sehp-'tahr*	accept (v)
acero (m) al carbono	*ehl ah-seh-roh ahl kahr-boh-noh*	carbon steel
acero inoxidable	*ehl ah-seh-roh-een-ohk-see-dah-bleh*	stainless steel
aceros (mpl) especializados	*lohs ah-seh-rohs-eh-speh-see-ah-lee-sah-dohs*	specialty steels

A

acetato (m)	*ehl ah-seh-tah-toh*	acetate
acetona (f)	*lah ah-seh-toh-nah*	acetone
ácido (m)	*ehl ah-see-doh*	acid
ácido acético	*ehl ah-see-doh-ah-seh-tee-koh*	acetic acid
ácido clorhídrico	*ehl 'ah-see-doh kloh-'ree-dree-koh*	hydrochloric acid
ácido nítrico	*ehl ah-see-doh nee-tree-koh*	nitric acid
ácido sulfúrico	*ehl ah-see-doh sool-foo-ree-koh*	sulfuric acid
acometer	*ah-koh-meh-'tehr*	undertake (v)
aconsejar	*ah-kohn-seh-'hahr*	advise (v)
acoplador acústico (m)	*ehl ah-koh-plah-'dohr ah-'koos-tee-koh*	acoustic coupler
acoplamiento mutuo (m)	*ehl ah-koh-plah-mee-'ehn-toh 'moo-too-oh*	interface
acordado y satisfecho	*ah-kohr-'dah-doh ee sah-tees-'feh-choh*	agreed and satisfied
acre (0.4047 hectareas) (m)	*ehl ah-kreh (0.4047 ehk-tah-reh-ahs)*	acre
acreditar	*ah-kreh-dee-'tahr*	credit (v)
acreedor (m)	*ehl ah-kreh-ee-'dohr*	creditor
acreedor inoportuno	*ah-kreh-ee-'dohr een-oh-pohr-'too-noh*	dunner
acrónimo (m)	*ehl ah-'kroh-nee-moh*	acronym
actividad comercial (f)	*lah ahk-tee-bee-'dahd koh-mehr-see-'ahl*	business activity
activada por la voz	*ahk-tee-bah-dah pohr lah bohs*	voice activated
actividades de apoyo (fpl)	*lahs ahk-tee-bee-'dah-dehs deh ah-'poh-yoh*	support activities
actividades de sostenimiento	*lahs ahk-tee-bee-'dah-dehs deh sohs-teh-nee-mee-'ehn-toh*	support activities
activo (m)	*ehl ahk-'tee-boh*	asset
activo circulante	*ehl ahk-'tee-boh seer-koo-'lahn-teh*	current asset
activo de propiedad neto	*ehl ahk-'tee-boh deh proh-pee-eh-'dahd 'neh-toh*	net equity asset

A

activo desperdiciado	*ehl ahk-'tee-boh dehs-pehr-dee-see-'ah-doh*	wasting asset
activo fijo	*ehl ahk-'tee-boh 'fee-hoh*	capital asset, fixed asset
activo flotante	*ehl ahk-'tee-boh floh-'tahn-teh*	floating asset
activo intangible	*ehl ahk-'tee-boh een-tahn-'hee-bleh*	intangible asset
activo neto	*ehl ahk-'tee-boh 'neh-toh*	net asset
activo no circulante	*ehl ahk-'tee-boh noh seer-koo-'lahn-teh*	noncurrent asset
activo tangible	*ehl ahk-tee-boh tahn-hee-bleh*	tangible asset
activos acumulados (mpl)	*lohs ahk-'tee-bohs ah-koo-moo-'lah-dohs*	accrued assets
activos congelados	*lohs ahk-tee-bohs kohn-heh-'lah-dohs*	frozen assets
activos de facil realización	*lohs ahk-'tee-bohs deh 'fah-seel reh-ah-lee-sah-see-'ohn*	liquid assets
activos de trabajo	*lohs ahk-tee-bohs deh trah-bah-hoh*	working assets
activos diferidos	*lohs ahk-tee-bohs dee-feh-'ree-dohs*	deferred assets
activos disponibles	*lohs ahk-tee-bohs dees-poh-'nee-blehs*	quick assets
activos escondidos	*lohs ahk-tee-bohs ehs-kohn-'dee-dohs*	hidden assets
activos fijos	*lohs ahk-tee-bohs 'fee-hohs*	fixed assets
activos líquidos	*lohs ahk-tee-bohs 'lee-kee-dohs*	liquid assets
activos prestados netos	*lohs akh-tee-bohs preh-'stah-dohs neh-tohs*	net borrowed assets
activos productivos	*lohs ahk-'tee-bohs proh-dook-'tee-bohs*	active assets
activos reales	*lohs ahk-'tee-bohs reh-'ah-lehs*	real assets
actual	*ahk-too-'ahl*	up to date, current
actualizar	*ahk-too-ah-lee-'sahr*	update (v)
actuario (m)	*ehl ahk-too-'ah-ree-oh*	actuary

A

acuerdo (m)	*ehl ah-'kwehr-doh*	resolution (legal document), understanding (agreement), agreement, covenant (promises)
acuerdo comercial	*ehl ah-kwehr-doh koh-mehr-see-'ahl*	trade agreement
acuerdo de caballeros	*ehl ah-'kwehr-doh deh kah-bah-'yeh-rohs*	gentleman's agreement (verbal)
acuerdo de cooperación	*ehl ah-kwehr-doh deh koh-oh-peh-rah-see-'ohn*	cooperation agreement
acuerdo escrito	*ehl ah-'kwehr-doh ehs-'kree-toh*	written agreement
acuerdo implícito	*ehl ah-kwehr-doh eem-'plee-see-toh*	implied agreement
acuerdo integral	*ehl ah-'kwehr-doh een-teh-'grahl*	across-the-board settlement
acuerdo multilateral	*ehl ah-kwehr-doh mool-tee-lah-teh-'rahl*	multilateral agreement
acumulación (f)	*lah ah-koo-moo-lah-see-ohn*	accrual
acumular	*ah-koo-moo-'lahr*	accrue, lay up (v)
acumulativo	*ah-koo-moo-lah-'tee-boh*	cumulative
acuñar	*ah-koo-'nyahr*	mint (v)
acusar	*ah-koo-'sahr*	acknowledge (v)
acusar recibo de	*ah-koo-'sahr reh-'see-boh deh*	acknowledge receipt of (v)
adelantar	*ah-deh-lahn-'tahr*	advance (v)
adelantos y retrasos (m)	*ah-deh-'lahn-tohs ee reh-'trah-sohs*	leads and lags
adjudicación (f)	*lah ahd-hoo-dee-kah-see-'ohn*	adjudication
adjudicar	*ahd-hoo-dee-'kahr*	adjudge (v)
adjuntar	*ahd-hoon-'tahr*	attach (v)
administración (f)	*lah ahd-mee-nees-trah-see-'ohn*	management, operations management
administración de cartera	*lah ahd-mee-nees-trah-see-'ohn deh kahr-'teh-rah*	portfolio management
administración de la oficina	*lah ahd-mee-nees-trah-see-'ohn deh lah oh-fee-'see-nah*	office management
administración de personal	*lah ahd-mee-nee-strah-see-'ohn deh pehr-soh-'nahl*	personnel management, personnel administration

administración de sistemas	*lah ahd-mee-nee-strah-see-'ohn deh sees-teh-mas*	systems management
administración del mercado	*lah ahd-mee-nee-strah-see-'ohn deh mehr-'kah-doh*	market management
administración por medio de objetivos	*lah ahd-mee-nee-strah-see-'ohn pohr 'meh-dee-oh deh ohb-heh-'tee-bohs*	management by objectives
administrador (m)	*ehl ahd-mee-nee-strah-'dohr*	administrator
administrador de aduanas	*ehl ahd-mee-nee-strah-'dohr deh ah-'dwah-nahs*	collector of customs
administradora (f)	*lah ahd-mee-nee-strah-'doh-rah*	administratrix
administrar	*ahd-mee-nee-'strahr*	manage (v)
adopción del sistema métrico (f)	*lah ah-dohp-see-'ohn dehl sees-'teh-mah 'meh-tree-koh*	metrification
adquirir	*ahd-kee-'reer*	acquire (v)
adquisición (f)	*lah ahd-kee-see-see-'ohn*	acquisition
adquisición de datos	*lah ahd-kee-see-see-'ohn deh 'dah-tohs*	data acquisition
adquisición mayoritaria de acciones	*lah ahd-kee-see-see-'ohn mah-yoh-ree-'tah-ree-ah deh ahk-see-'oh-nehs*	stock takeover
adquisición mayoritaria	*lah ahd-kee-see-see-'ohn mah-yoh-ree-'tah-ree-ah*	takeover
aduana (f)	*lah ah-'dwah-nah*	customs
afidávit (m)	*ehl ah-fee-'dah-beet*	affidavit
afiliado (m)	*ehl ah-fee-lee-'ah-doh*	affiliate
afiliado internacional	*ehl ah-fee-lee-'ah-doh een-tehr-nah-see-oh-'nahl*	affiliate (international)
afiliado local	*ehl ah-fee-lee-'ah-doh loh-'kahl*	affiliate (local)
afiliar	*ah-fee-lee-'ahr*	affiliate (v)
agencia (f)	*lah ah-'hehn-see-ah*	agency
agencia bancaria	*lah ah-'hehn-see-ah bahn-'kah-ree-ah*	agency bank
agencia de colocaciones	*lah ah-'hehn-see-ah deh koh-loh-kah-see-'oh-nehs*	employment agency
agencia de publicidad	*lah ah-'hehn-see-ah deh poo-blee-see-'dahd*	advertising agency

agencia gubernamental	*lah ah-'hehn-see-ah goo-behr-mehn-'tahl*	government agency
agencia mercantil	*lah ah-'hehn-see-ah mehr-kahn-'teel*	mercantile agency
agenda (f)	*lah ah-'hehn-dah*	agenda
agente (m)	*ehl ah-'hehn-teh*	agent
agente comprador	*ehl ah-'hehn-teh kohm-prah-'dohr*	purchasing agent
agente de aduana	*ehl ah-'hehn-teh deh ah-'dwah-nah*	customs broker
agente de exportaciones	*ehl ah-'hehn-teh deh ehks-pohr-'tah-see-'oh-nehs*	export agent
agente de póliza de fletes	*ehl ah-'hehn-teh deh 'poh-lee-sah deh 'fleh-tehs*	charterparty agent
agente de software	*ehl ah-'hehn-teh deh 'sohf-wehr*	software broker
agente de transferencia	*ehl ah-'hehn-teh deh trahns-feh-'rehn-see-ah*	transfer agent
agente del fabricante	*ah-'hehn-teh dehl fah-bree-'kahn-teh*	manufacturer's agent
agente desfoliante (m)	*ehl ah-'hehn-teh dehs-foh-lee-'ahn-teh*	defoliating agent
agente expedidor	*ah-'hehn-teh ehks-peh-dee-'dohr*	forwarding agent
agente fiscal	*ah-'hehn-teh fees-'kahl*	fiscal agent
agente único	*ehl ah-'hehn-teh 'oo-nee-koh*	sole agent
agotado	*ah-goh-'tah-doh*	exhausted (adj)
agotamiento (m)	*ehl ah-goh-tah-mee-'ehn-toh*	attrition
agotar	*ah-goh-'tahr*	exhaust (v)
agradecimiento (m)	*ehl reh-koh-noh-see-mee-ehn-toh*	acknowledgment
agravio indemnizable (m)	*ehl ah-'grah-bee-oh een-dehm-nee-'sah-bleh*	tort
agricultura (f)	*lah ah-gree-kool-'too-rah*	agriculture
agrio	*ah-gree-oh*	sour (adj)
agua del mar (m)	*ehl 'ah-gwah dehl mahr*	seawater
aguas (fpl)	*lahs 'ah-gwahs*	waters

aguas territoriales	*lahs 'ah-gwahs teh-rree-toh-ree-'ah-lehs*	territorial waters
aguja (f)	*lah ah-goo-hah*	needle
agujero (m)	*ehl ah-goo-'heh-roh*	hole
ahorro fiscal contra impuestos (f)	*lah ah-'oh-roh fee-skahl 'kohn-trah eem-pweh-stohs*	tax shield
ahorros (m)	*lohs ah-'oh-rrohs*	savings
aislador (m)	*ehl ah-see-slah-dohr*	insulator
ajustar	*ah-hoo-'stahr*	adjust (v)
ajuste de los impuestos fronterizos (m)	*ehl ah-'hoo-steh deh lohs eem-'pweh-stohs frohn-teh-'ree-sohs*	border tax adjustment
ajuste lineal	*ehl ah-'hoos-teh lee-neh-'ahl*	across-the-board settlement
al cierre	*ahl see-'eh-reh*	at the close
al dorso	*ahl dohr-soh*	on the back
al portador	*ahl pohr-tah-'dohr*	to the bearer
al precio (del mercado) o mejor	*ahl 'preh-see-oh (dehl mehr-'kah-doh) oh meh-'hohr*	at or better than (market price)
alambre (m)	*ehl ah-lahm-breh*	wire
alcanzar	*ahl-kahn-'sahr*	reach (v)
alcista (m)	*ehl ahl-'sees-tah*	bull
aleación (f) de acero	*lah ah-leh-ah-see-ohn deh ah-seh-roh*	alloy steel
alfarería (f)	*lah ahl-fah-reh-ree-ah*	earthenware, pottery
algas (fpl)	*lahs 'ahl-gahs*	algae, seaweed
algodón (m)	*ehl ahl-goh-'dohn*	cotton
algoritmo (m)	*ehl ehl-goh-'reet-moh*	algorithm
alimentar	*ah-lee-mehn-'tahr*	feed (v)
alineación (f)	*lah ah-lee-neh-ah-see-'ohn*	justification (margin)
almacén (m)	*ehl ahl-mah-'sehn*	warehouse
almacén afianzado	*ehl ahl-mah-'sehn ah-fee-ahn-'sah-doh*	licensed warehouse
almacén autorizado	*ehl ahl-mah-'sehn ow-toh-ree-'sah-doh*	licensed warehouse

almacén ordinario	*ehl ahl-mah-'sehn ohr-dee-'nah-ree-oh*	regular warehouse
almacenador (m)	*ehl ahl-mah-seh-nah-'dohr*	warehouseman
almacenaje (m)	*ehl ahl-mah-seh-'nah-heh*	storage
almacenaje de la computadora	*ehl ahl-mah-seh-'nah-heh deh lah kohm-poo-tah-'doh-rah*	computer storage
almacenaje de serie	*ehl ahl-mah-seh-'nah-heh deh 'seh-ree-eh*	serial storage
almacenaje por acceso directo	*ehl ahl-mah-seh-'nah-heh pohr ahk-'seh-soh dee-'rehk-toh*	direct access storage
almacenaje provisorio	*ehl ahl-mah-seh-'nah-heh proh-bee-'soh-ree-oh*	field warehousing
almacenamiento de datos (m)	*ehl alh-mah-seh-nah-mee-'ehn-toh deh 'dah-tohs*	data storage
almacenar	*ahl-mah-seh-'nahr*	store (v)
almidón (m)	*ehl ahl-mee-dohn*	starch
alquilar	*ahl-kee-'lahr*	rent (v)
alquiler (m)	*ehl ahl-kee-'lehr*	lease
alquiler de equipo	*ehl ahl-kee-'lehr deh eh-'kee-poh*	equipment leasing
alta fidelidad (f)	*lah ahl-tah fee-deh-lee-dahd*	high fidelity
alta gerencia (f)	*lah 'ahl-tah heh-'rehn-see-ah*	top management
altavoz (m)	*ehl ahl-tah-bos*	speaker
alteración (f)	*lah ahl-teh-rah-see-'ohn*	alteration
alto horno (m)	*ehl ahl-toh ohr-noh*	blast furnace
altoparlante (m)	*ehl ahl-toh-pahr-lahn-teh*	speaker
alza (m)	*ehl 'ahl-sah*	appreciation
amenaza (f)	*lah ah-meh-'nah-sah*	threat
amenazado	*ah-meh-nah-'sah-doh*	threatened (adj)
amina (f)	*lah ah-'mee-nah*	amine
amoníaco (m)	*ehl ah-moh-'nee-ah-koh*	ammonia
amortiguador (m)	*ehl ah-mohr-tee-gwah-'dohr*	shock absorber
amortización (f)	*lah ah-mohr-tee-sah-see-'ohn*	amortization

amortización de obligaciones	*lah ah-mohr-tee-sah-see-'ohn deh ohb-lee-gah-see-'oh-nehs*	sinking fund
amortización obligatoria	*lah ah-mohr-tee-sah-see-'ohn oh-blee-gah-'toh-ree-ah*	mandatory redemption
amperaje (m)	*ehl ahm-peh-rah-heh*	ampere
ampliar	*ahm-plee-'ahr*	enlarge (v), blowup (v)
amplificador (m)	*ehl ahm-plee-fee-kah-dohr*	amplifier
amplitud modulada (f)	*lah ahm-plee-tood moh-doo-lah-dah*	amplitude modulation (AM)
añadido (m)	*ehl ah-nyah-'dee-doh*	allonge
analgésico (m)	*ehl ah-nahl-'heh-see-koh*	analgesic
análisis (m)	*ehl ah-'nah-lee-sees*	analysis
análisis de costos	*ehl ah-'nah-lee-sees deh 'koh-stohs*	cost analysis
análisis de costos y beneficios	*ehl ah-'nah-lee-sees deh 'koh-stohs ee beh-neh-'fee-see-ohs*	cost-benefit analysis
análisis de entradas y salidas	*ehl ah-'nah-lee-sees deh ehn-'trah-dahs ee sah-'lee-dahs*	input-output analysis
análisis de factores	*ehl ah-'nah-lee-sees deh fahk-'toh-rehs*	factor analysis
análisis de inversiones	*ehl ah-'nah-lee-sees deh een-behr-see-'oh-nehs*	investment analysis
análisis de la competencia	*ehl ah-'nah-lee-sees deh lah kohm-peh-'tehn-see-ah*	competitor analysis
análisis de la rentabilidad	*ehl ah-'nah-lee-sees deh lah rehn-tah-bee-lee-'dahd*	profitability analysis
análisis de las necesidades	*ehl ah-'nah-lee-sees deh lahs neh-seh-see-'dah-dehs*	needs analysis
análisis de regresión	*ehl ah-'nah-lee-sees deh reh-greh-see-'ohn*	regression analysis
análisis de riesgo	*ehl ah-'nah-lee-sees deh ree-'ehs-goh*	risk analysis
análisis de sistema	*ehl ah-'nah-lee-sees deh sees-'teh-mah*	systems analysis
análisis de ventas	*ehl ah-'nah-lee-sees deh 'behn-tahs*	sales analysis

A

análisis del camino crítico	*ehl ah-'nah-lee-sees dehl kah-'mee-noh 'kree-tee-koh*	critical path analysis
análisis del problema	*ehl ah-'nah-lee-sees dehl proh-'bleh-mah*	problem analysis
análisis del producto	*ehl ah-'nah-lee-sees dehl proh-'dook-toh*	product analysis
análisis del puntal de arqueo	*ehl ah-'nah-lee-sees dehl poon-'tahl deh ahr-'keh-oh*	depth analysis
análisis del punto donde los ingresos son iguales a los egresos	*ehl ah-'nah-lee-sees dehl 'poon-toh 'dohn-deh lohs een-'greh-sohs sohn ee-'gwah-lehs ah lohs eh-'greh-sohs*	breakeven analysis
análisis del trabajo	*ehl ah-'nah-lee-sees dehl trah-'bah-hoh*	job analysis
análisis financiero	*ehl ah-'nah-lee-sees fee-nahn-see-'eh-roh*	financial analysis
análisis funcional	*ehl ah-'nah-lee-sees foon-see-oh-'nahl*	functional analysis
analista (m)	*ehl ah-nah-'lees-tah*	analyst
anestésico (m)	*ehl ah-neh-steh-tee-koh*	anesthetic
anexo (m)	*ehl ah-'nehk-soh*	addendum, rider (contracts)
anfibios (mpl)	*lohs ahn-'fee-bee-ohs*	amphibians
ángulo de incidencia (m)	*ehl 'ahn-goo-loh deh een-see-'dehn-see-ah*	angle of incidence
año (m)	*ehl 'ah-nyoh*	year
año base	*ehl 'ah-nyoh 'bah-seh*	base year
año de cosecha	*ehl ah-nyoh deh koh-seh-chah*	vintage year
año fiscal	*ehl 'ah-nyoh fees-'kahl*	fiscal year
ante (m)	*ehl ahn-teh*	suede
antedicho	*ahn-teh-'dee-choh*	above-mentioned
anticipar	*ahn-tee-see-'pahr*	advance (v)
anticoagulante (m)	*ehl ahn-tee-koh-ah-goo-lahn-teh*	anticoagulant
anticolinérgico (m)	*ehl ahn-tee-koh-lee-nehr-hee-koh*	anticholinergic
antigüedad (f)	*lah ahn-tee-gweh-'dahd*	obsolescence

A

antiinflamatorio (m)	*ehl ahn-tee-een-flah-mah-toh-ree-oh*	anti-inflammatory
anual	*ah-noo-'ahl*	annual
anualidad (f)	*lah ah-noo-ah-lee-'dahd*	annuity
anualidad variable	*lah ah-noo-ah-lee-'dahd bah-ree-'ah-bleh*	variable annuity
anualidades diferidas (fpl)	*lahs ah-noo-ah-lee-'dah-dehs dee-feh-'ree-dahs*	deferred annuities
anular	*ah-noo-'lahr*	nullify (v)
anuncio clasificado (m)	*ehl ah-'noon-see-oh klah-see-fee-'kah-doh*	want-ad
anuncio publicitario	*ehl ah-'noon-see-oh poo-blee-see-'tah-ree-oh*	commercial ad
aplancamiento financiero (m)	*ehl ah-plahn-kah-mee-'ehn-toh fee-nahn-see-'eh-roh*	financial leverage
aplicación de los recursos (f)	*lah ah-plee-kah-see-'ohn deh lohs reh-'koor-sohs*	resource allocation
apoyo recíproco del producto aplicado (m)	*ehl ah-'poh-yoh reh-'see-proh-koh dehl proh-'dook-toh ah-plee-'kah-doh*	applied proceeds swap
aprendiz (m)	*ehl ah-prehn-'dees*	apprentice, trainee
aprendizaje por rutina (m)	*ehl ah-prehn-dee-'sah-heh pohr roo-'tee-nah*	on-the-job training
aprobación (f)	*lah ah-proh-bah-see-'ohn*	approval
aprobar	*ah-proh-'bahr*	approve (v)
aprovechar el tipo de interés vigente	*ah-proh-beh-'chahr ehl 'tee-poh deh een-teh-'rehs bee-'hehn-teh*	lock in (rate of interest) (v)
arancel (m)	*ehl ah-rahn-'sehl*	tariff, duty
arancel aduanero específico	*ehl ah-rahn-'sehl ah-dwah-'neh-roh ehs-peh-'see-fee-koh*	specific duty
arancel combinado	*ehl ah-rahn-'sehl kohm-bee-'nah-doh*	combination duty
arancel compensatorio	*ehl ah-rahn-'sehl kohm-pehn-sah-'toh-ree-oh*	countervailing duty
arancel de importación	*ehl ah-rahn-'sehl deh eem-pohr-tah-see-'ohn*	import tariff, import duty
aranceles sobre bienes (m)	*lohs ah-rahn-'seh-lehs 'soh-breh bee-'eh-nehs*	tariff commodity

arbitraje (m)	*ehl ahr-bee-'trah-heh*	arbitrage, arbitration
arbitraje de interés	*ehl ahr-bee-'trah-heh deh een-teh-'rehs*	interest arbitrage
arbitraje industrial	*ehl ahr-bee-'trah-heh een-doos-tree-'ahl*	industrial arbitration
árbitro (m)	*ehl 'ahr-bee-troh*	arbitrator
árbol (m)	*ehl 'ahr-bohl*	tree
archivo (m)	*ehl ahr-'chee-boh*	file
archivo de trabajo	*ehl ahr-'chee-boh deh trah-'bah-hoh*	work file
área de trabajo (m)	*ehl 'ah-reh-ah deh trah-'bah-hoh*	work area
áreas de obligación (fpl)	*lahs 'ah-reeh-ahs deh oh-blee-gah-see-'ohn*	bond areas
armamentos (m)	*lohs ahr-mah-'mehn-tohs*	armaments
armas (fpl)	*lahs 'ahr-mahs*	arms, weapons
armas atómicas	*lahs 'ahr-mahs ah-'toh-mee-kahs*	weapons (atomic)
aro (m)	*ehl ah-roh*	ring
aro de servilleta	*ehl ah-roh deh sehr-bee-yeh-tah*	napkin ring
arrancar	*ah-rrahn-'kahr*	reboot (v), restart (v)
arranque (m)	*ehl ah-rrahn-keh*	starter
arrastrar un saldo al siguiente período	*ah-rrahs-'trahr oon 'sahl-doh ahl see-gee-'ehn-teh peh-'ree-oh-doh carryover (v)*	carryover (v)
arrecife de coral (m)	*ehl ah-rreh-'see-feh deh koh-rahl*	coral reef
arreglo (m)	*ehl ah-'rreh-gloh*	settlement
arreglo total	*ehl ah-'rreh-gloh toh-'tahl*	full settlement
arrendador (m)	*ehl ah-rrehn-dah-'dohr*	lessor
arrendamiento (m)	*ehl ah-rrehn-dah-mee-'ehn-toh*	lease
arrendamiento financiero	*ehl ah-rrehn-dah-mee-'ehn-toh fee-nahn-see-'eh-roh*	financial lease
arrendatario (m)	*ehl ah-rrehn-dah-'tah-ree-oh*	lessee
arriesgado	*ah-rree-ehs-'gah-doh*	risky (adj)

arrumaje (m)	*ehl ah-rroo-'mah-heh*	stowage
artesano (m)	*ehl ahr-teh-'sah-noh*	journeyman
artículo barato para atraer clientes (m)	*ehl ahr-'tee-koo-loh bah-'rah-toh 'pah-rah ah-trah-'ehr klee-'ehn-tehs*	loss leader
artículos (mpl) de seda	*lohs ahr-tee-koo-lohs deh seh-dah*	silk goods
artículos de cuero	*lohs ahr-tee-koo-lohs deh 'kweh-roh*	leather goods
artículos de tamaño especial (mayor que el común)	*lohs ahr-'tee-koo-lohs deh tah-'mah-nyoh ehs-peh-see-'ahl ('mah-yohr keh ehl koh-'moon)*	outsized articles
artículos estratégicos	*lohs ahr-'tee-koo-lohs ehs-trah-'teh-hee-kohs*	strategic articles
asamblea (f)	*lah ah-sahm-'bleh-ah*	assembly
asegurador (m)	*ehl ah-seh-goo-rah-'dohr*	insurance underwriter, underwriter
asentar	*ah-sehn-'tahr*	post (bookkeeping) (v)
asesoría de empleados (f)	*lah ah-seh-soh-'ree-ah deh ehm-pleh-'ah-dos*	employee counseling
asiento (m)	*ehl ah-see-ehn-toh*	seat
asiento de ajuste	*ehl ah-see-'ehn-toh deh ah-'hoo-steh*	adjusting entry
asiento de caja	*ehl ah-see-'ehn-toh deh deh 'kah-hah*	cash entry
asiento de cierre	*ehl ah-see-'ehn-toh deh see-'eh-reh*	closing entry (accounting)
asiento de importación	*ehl ah-see-'ehn-toh deh eem-pohr-tah-see-'ohn*	import entry
asiento del mayor	*ehl ah-see-'ehn-toh deh dehl mah-'yohr*	ledger entry
asiento en el debe	*ehl ah-see-'ehn-toh ehn ehl 'deh-beh*	debit entry
asiento original	*ehl ah-see-'ehn-toh oh-ree-hee-'nahl*	original entry
asignación (f)	*lah ah-seeg-nah-see-'ohn*	appropriation, allowance
asignación de costos	*lah ah-seeg-nah-see-'ohn deh 'koh-stohs*	allocation of costs
asignación de recursos	*lah ah-seeg-nah-see-'ohn deh reh-'koor-sohs*	resource allocation

asignación de responsabilidades	*lah ah-seeg-nah-see-'ohn deh reh-spohn-sah-bee-lee-'dah-dehs*	allocation of responsibilities
asignación de terreno	*lah ah-seeg-nah-see-'ohn deh teh-'rreh-noh*	acreage allotment
asignación por depreciaciones de capital	*lah ah-seeg-nah-see-'ohn pohr deh-preh-see-ah-see-'ohnehs deh kah-pee-'tahl*	capital allowance
asignación por la amortización	*lah ah-seeg-nah-see-'ohn pohr lah ah-mohr-tee-sah-see-'ohn*	redemption allowance
asignación presupuestaria	*lah ah-seeg-nah-see-'ohn preh-soo-pwehs-'tah-ree-ah*	budget appropriation
asignador (m)	*ehl ah-seeg-nah-'dohr*	assigner
asignar	*ah-seeg-'nahr*	allot (v), assign (v)
asignatario (m)	*ehl ah-seeg-nah-'tah-ree-oh*	asignee
asistente (m)	*ehl ah-sees-'tehn-teh*	assistant
asistente al gerente	*ehl ah-sees-'tehn-teh ahl heh-'rehn-teh*	deputy manager
asistente de personal	*ehl ah-sees-'tehn-teh deh pehr-soh-'nahl*	staff assistant
asociación comercial (f)	*lah ah-soh-see-ah-see-'ohn koh-mehr-see-'ahl*	trade association
asociado (m)	*ehl ah-soh-see-'ah-doh*	affiliate
aspirina (f)	*lah ahs-pee-ree-nah*	aspirin
atesorar	*ah-teh-soh-'rahr*	hoard (v)
atestación (f)	*la ah-tehs-tah-see-'ohn*	attestation
atmósfera (f)	*lah aht-'mohs-feh-rah*	atmosphere
atómico	*ah-toh-mee-koh*	atomic (adj)
átomo (m)	*ehl 'ah-toh-moh*	atom
atrasar la fecha	*ah-trah-'sahr lah 'feh-chah*	back date (v)
atraso de tiempo (m)	*ehl ah-'trah-soh deh tee-'ehm-poh*	time lag
atrasos (m)	*lohs ah-'trah-sohs*	arrears
auditor (m)	*ehl ow-dee-'tohr*	auditor
auditorear	*ow-dee-toh-reh-'ahr*	audit (v)

auditoría anual (f)	*lah ow-dee-toh-'ree-ah ah-noo-'ahl*	annual audit
auditoría de operaciones	*lah ow-dee-toh-'ree-ah deh oh-peh-rah-see-'oh-nehs*	operations audit
auditoría del balance general	*lah ow-dee-toh-'ree-ah dehl bah-'lahn-seh heh-neh-'rahl*	auditing balance sheet
auditoría interna	*lah ow-dee-toh-'ree-ah een-'tehr-nah*	internal audit
aumento (m)	*ehl ow-'mehn-toh*	accretion, increase
aumento de capital	*ehl ow-'mehn-toh deh kah-pee-'tahl*	capital increase
aumento de precio	*ehl ow-'mehn-toh deh 'preh-see-oh*	markup
aumento gratuito de las acciones para reducir su precio	*ehl ow-'mehn-toh grah-too-'ee-toh deh lahs ahk-see-'oh-nehs 'pah-rah reh-doo-'seer soo 'preh-see-oh*	stock split
ausencia de los propietarios (f)	*lah ow-'sehn-see-ah deh lohs proh-pee-eh-'tah-ree-ohs*	absentee ownership
ausencia por permiso de maternidad	*lah ow-'sehn-see-ah pohr pehr-'mee-soh deh mah-tehr-nee-'dahd*	maternity leave
ausencia por permiso	*lah ow-'sehn-see-ah pohr pehr-'mee-soh*	leave of absence
ausentismo (m)	*ehl ow-sehn-'tees-moh*	absenteeism
autarquía (f)	*lah ow-tahr-'kee-ah*	autarchy
autenticidad (de oro) (f)	*lah ow-tehn-tee-see-'dahd (deh 'oh-roh)*	authenticity (gold)
auto-administra-ción (f)	*lah ow-toh-ahd-mee-nee-strah-see-'ohn*	self-management
auto-evalúo (m)	*ehl ow-toh-eh-bah-'loo-oh*	self-appraisal
auto-servicio (m)	*ehl ow-toh-sehr-'bee-see-oh*	self-service
autómata (m)	*ehl ow-'toh-mah-tah*	robot
automático	*ow-toh-'mah-tee-koh*	automatic
automatización (m)	*lah ow-toh-mah-tee-sah-see-'ohn*	automation
autónomo	*ow-'toh-noh-moh*	autonomous

A

autoridad de vivienda (f)	*lah ow-toh-ree-'dahd deh bee-bee-'ehn-dah*	housing authority
autorizar	*ow-toh-ree-'sahr*	authorize (v)
autosuficiente	*ow-toh-soo-fee-see-'ehn-teh*	self-sufficient
auxiliar (m)	*ehl owk-see-lee-'ahr*	ancillary
avaluar	*ah-bah-loo-'ahr*	assess (v)
avalúo de gastos de capital (m)	*ehl ah-bah-'loo-oh deh 'gahs-tohs deh kah-pee-'tahl*	capital expenditure appraisal
avalúo de inversiones	*ehl ah-bah-'loo-oh deh een-behr-see-'oh-nehs*	investment appraisal
avalúo de mercado	*ehl ah-bah-'loo-oh deh mehr-'kah-doh*	market appraisal
avalúo financiero	*ehl ah-bah-'loo-oh fee-nahn-see-'eh-roh*	financial appraisal
avería (f)	*lah ah-beh-'ree-ah*	breakdown
aves (fpl)	*lahs 'ah-behs*	birds
avíos de pescar (mpl)	*lohs ah-'bee-ohs deh pehs-'kahr*	tackle (fishing)
aviso	*ah-'bee-soh*	warning
aviso anticipado (m)	*ehl ah-'bee-soh ahn-tee-see-'pah-doh*	advance notice
aviso clasificado	*ehl ah-'bee-soh klah-see-fee-'kah-doh*	classified ad
aviso de entrega	*ehl ah-'bee-soh deh ehn-'treh-gah*	delivery notice
aviso de expedición	*ehl ah-'bee-soh deh ehks-peh-dee-see-'ohn*	advice notice
ayuda condicionada (f)	*lah ah-'yoo-dah kohn-dee-see-oh-'nah-dah*	tied aid
azucarera (f)	*lah ah-soo-kah-reh-rah*	sugar bowl

B

bajista (m)	*ehl bah-'hees-tah*	bear
bajo-par	*'bah-hoh pahr*	below par
balance (m)	*ehl bah-'lahn-seh*	balance sheet
balance de comprobación	*ehl bah-'lahn-seh deh kohm-proh-bah-see-'ohn*	trial balance

balance desfavorable	*ehl bah-lahn-seh dehs-fah-boh-'rah-bleh*	adverse balance
balance general	*ehl bah-'lahn-seh heh-neh-'rahl*	balance sheet
balance pro-forma	*ehl bah-'lahn-seh proh 'fohr-mah*	pro forma statement
balanza comercial (f)	*lah bah-'lahn-sah koh-mehr-see-'ahl*	balance of trade
balanza comercial visible	*lah bah-'lahn-sah koh-mehr-see-'ahl bee-'see-bleh*	visible balance of trade
balanza de pagos	*lah bah-'lahn-sah deh 'pah-gohs*	balance of payments
bancarrota (f)	*lah bahn-kah-'rroh-tah*	bankruptcy, business failure
banco (m)	*ehl 'bahn-koh*	bank
banco al por menor	*ehl 'bahn-koh ahl pohr meh-'nohr*	retail bank
banco central	*ehl 'bahn-koh sehn-'trahl*	central bank
banco comercial	*ehl 'bahn-koh koh-mehr-see-'ahl*	commercial bank
banco corresponsal	*ehl 'bahn-koh koh-rreh-spohn-'sahl*	correspondent bank
banco de ahorro	*ehl 'bahn-koh deh ah-'oh-rroh*	savings bank
banco de ahorro mutuo	*ehl 'bahn-koh deh ah-'oh-rroh 'moo-too-oh*	mutual savings bank
banco de centralización (m)	*ehl 'bahn-koh deh sehn-trah-lee-sah-see-'ohn*	concentration bank
banco de datos (m)	*ehl 'bahn-koh deh 'dah-tohs*	computer bank, data bank
banco de exportaciones-importaciones	*ehl 'bahn-koh deh ehks-pohr-tah-see-'oh-nehs eem-pohr-tah-see-'oh-nehs*	export-import bank
banco gubernamental	*ehl 'bahn-koh goo-behr-nah-mehn-'tahl*	government bank
banco hipotecario	*ehl 'bahn-koh ee-poh-teh-'kah-ree-oh*	mortgage bank
banco inversionista	*ehl 'bahn-koh een-behr-see-oh-'nees-tah*	investment bank
banco mercantil	*ehl 'bahn-koh mehr-kahn-'teel*	merchant bank

Banco Mundial	*ehl 'bahn-koh moon-dee-'ahl*	World Bank
banco nacional	*ehl 'bahn-koh nah-see-oh-'nahl*	national bank
banco representante	*ehl 'bahn-koh reh-preh-sehn-'tahn-teh*	agent bank
bandeja (f) para queso	*lah bahn-deh-hah pah-rah keh-soh*	cheese tray
baratería (f)	*lah bah-rah-teh-'ree-ah*	barratry
barato	*bah-'rah-toh*	cheap (adj)
barbitúricos (mpl)	*lohs bahr-bee-too-ree-kohs*	barbiturates
barcotanque (m)	*ehl bahr-koh-'tahn-keh*	tanker
barras (fpl)	*lahs bah-rrahs*	bars
barrera (f)	*lah bah-'rreh-rah*	barrier
barrera al intercambio comercial	*lah bah-'rreh-rah ahl een-tehr-'kahm-bee-oh koh-mehr-see-'ahl*	trade barrier
barreras arancelarias (fpl)	*lahs bah-'rreh-rahs ah-rahn-seh-'lah-ree-ahs*	tariff barriers
barril (m)	*ehl bah-rreel*	cask, barrel
báscula (f)	*lah bahs-koo-tah*	scale
base (f)	*lah bah-seh*	base
base de contado	*lah 'bah-seh deh kohn-'tah-doh*	cash basis
base de datos	*lah 'bah-seh deh 'dah-tohs*	data base
base imponible	*lah 'bah-seh eem-poh-'nee-bleh*	tax base
base monetaria	*lah 'bah-seh moh-neh-'tah-ree-ah*	base currency, monetary base
bastidor (m)	*ehl bah-stee-dohr*	chassis
basura (f)	*lah bah-'soo-rrah*	garbage
baudio (m)	*ehl 'baw-dee-oh*	baud
baúl (m)	*ehl bah-ool*	trunk
beber	*beh-behr*	drink (v)
belleza natural (f)	*lah bee-'yeh-sah nah-too-'rahl*	natural beauty
benceno (m)	*ehl behn-seh-noh*	benzene

beneficiario (m)	*ehl beh-neh-fee-see-'ah-ree-oh*	beneficiary
beneficio (m)	*ehl beh-neh-'fee-see-oh*	profit
beneficio bruto	*ehl beh-neh-'fee-see-oh 'broo-toh*	gross margin, gross profit
beneficio de operación	*ehl beh-neh-'fee-see-oh deh oh-peh-rah-see-'ohn*	operating profit
beneficio en acciones	*ehl beh-neh-'fee-see-oh ehn ahk-see-'oh-nehs*	stock profit
beneficio imprevisto	*ehl beh-neh-'fee-see-oh eem-preh-'bees-toh*	windfall profit
beneficio neto	*ehl beh-neh-'fee-see-oh 'neh-toh*	net margin, net profit
beneficios adicionales al sueldo (mpl)	*lohs beh-neh-'fee-see-ohs ah-dee-see-oh-'nah-lehs ahl 'swehl-doh*	fringe benefits
beneficios personales que resultan del consumo de	*lohs beh-neh-'fee-see-ohs pehr-soh-'nah-lehs keh reh-'sool-tahn dehl kohn-'soo-moh deh*	personal consumer benefits resulting from
beneficios por realizar	*lohs beh-neh-'fee-see-ohs pohr reh-ah-lee-'sahr*	paper profits
biela (f)	*lah bee-eh-lah*	connecting rod
bienes (mpl)	*lohs bee-'eh-nehs*	goods
bienes acompañados	*lohs bee-'eh-nehs ah-kohm-pah-'nyah-dohs*	accompanied goods
bienes afianzados	*lohs bee-'eh-nehs ah-fee-ahn-'sah-dohs*	bonded goods
bienes así como así	*lohs bee-'eh-nehs ah-'see 'koh-moh ah-'see*	as-is goods
bienes de calidad	*lohs bee-'eh-nehs deh kah-lee-'dahd*	quality goods
bienes de capital	*lohs bee-'eh-nehs deh kah-pee-'tahl*	capital goods
bienes de consumo	*lohs bee-'eh-nehs deh kohm-'soo-moh*	consumer goods
bienes de la empresa	*bee-'eh-nehs deh lah ehm-'preh-sah*	perks
bienes de lujo	*lohs bee-'eh-nehs deh 'loo-hoh*	luxury goods
bienes durables	*lohs bee-'eh-nehs doo-'rah-blehs*	durable goods

bienes especiales	*lohs bee-'eh-nehs eh-speh-see-'ah-lehs*	specialty goods
bienes fungibles	*lohs bee-'eh-nehs foon-'hee-blehs*	fungible goods
bienes industriales	*lohs bee-'eh-nehs een-doo-stree-'ah-lehs*	industrial goods
bienes intermedios	*lohs bee-'eh-nehs een-tehr-'meh-dee-ohs*	intermediary goods
bienes muebles	*lohs bee-'eh-nehs 'mweh-blehs*	chattels
bienes no acompañados	*lohs bee-'eh-nehs noh ah-kohm-pah-'nyah-dohs*	unaccompanied goods
bienes no duraderos	*lohs bee-'eh-nehs noh doo-rah-'deh-rohs*	nondurable goods
bienes prohibidos	*lohs bee-'eh-nehs proh-ee-'bee-dohs*	prohibited goods
bienes raíces	*lohs bee-'eh-nehs rah-'ee-sehs*	real estate
bienes raíces comuneros	*lohs bee-'eh-nehs rah-'ee-sehs koh-moo-'neh-rohs*	joint estate
bienes tangibles	*lohs bee-'eh-nehs tahn-'hee-blehs*	corpus
bienestar (m)	*ehl bee-ehn-eh-'stahr*	well-being
bienestar económico	*ehl bee-ehn-eh-'stahr eh-koh-'noh-mee-koh*	well-being (economic)
bienestar social	*ehl bee-ehn-eh-'stahr soh-see-'ahl*	well-being (social)
bifurcacion (f)	*lah bee-foor-kah-see-'oh*	branching
billete de moneda de curso legal (m)	*ehl bee-'yeh-teh deh moh-'neh-dah deh 'koor-soh leh-'gahl*	legal tender
billetero (m)	*ehl bee-yeh-teh-roh*	billfold
binario	*bee-'nah-ree-oh*	binary (adj)
biodiversidad (f)	*lah bee-oh-dee-behr-see-'dahd*	biodiversity
biología (f)	*lah bee-oh-loh-hee-ah*	biology
biólogo (m)	*ehl bee-oh-loh-goh*	biologist
bioquímica (f)	*lah bee-oh-kee-mee-kah*	biochemistry
bit (m)	*ehl beet*	bit

blanco y negro	*blahn-koh ee neh-groh*	black and white (adj)
bloque (m)	*ehl 'bloh-keh*	block
bloqueo (m)	*ehl bloh-'keh-oh*	blockage
bloqueo de fondos	*ehl bloh-'keh-oh deh 'fohn-dohs*	blockage of funds
blusa (f)	*lah bloo-sah*	blouse
bodega (f)	*lah boh-'deh-gah*	wine cellar
boicot (m)	*ehl boh-ee-'koht*	boycott
boleto válido para la próxima sesión	*ehl boh-'leh-toh 'bah-lee-doh 'pah-rah lah 'prohk-see-mah seh-see-'ohn*	rain check
bolsa (f)	*lah 'boh-sah*	exchange (stock, commodity)
bolsa para ropa	*lah bohl-sah pah-rah roh-pah*	garment bag
bolsa de valores	*lah 'bohl-sah deh bah-'loh-rehs*	stock exchange
bolso (m)	*ehl bohl-soh*	purse
bolso de mano	*ehl bohl-soh deh mah-noh*	handbag
bomba (f) de aceite	*lah bohm-bahdeh ah-seh-ee-teh*	oil pump
bomba de agua	*lah bohm-bah deh ah-gwah*	water pump
bonanza (f)	*lah boh-'nahn-sah*	boom
bono (m)	*ehl 'boh-noh*	bond
bono a plazo de una emisión en que tienen el mismo vencimiento	*ehl 'boh-noh ah 'plah-soh deh 'oo-nah eh-mee-see-'ohn ehn keh tee-'eh-nehn ehl 'mees-moh behn-see-mee-'ehn-toh*	term bond
bono al portador	*ehl 'boh-noh ahl pohr-tah-'dohr*	bearer bond
bono de ahorro	*ehl 'boh-noh deh ah-'oh-rroh*	savings bond
bono de ingreso	*ehl 'boh-noh deh een-'greh-soh*	revenue bond
bono de lastre	*ehl 'boh-noh deh 'lahs-treh*	ballast bonus
bono hipotecario	*ehl 'boh-noh ee-poh-teh-'kah-ree-oh*	mortgage bond
bono pagadero en moneda nacional	*ehl 'boh-noh pah-gah-'deh-roh ehn moh-'neh-dah nah-see-oh-'nahl*	currency bond

B

bono redimible	ehl 'boh-noh reh-dee-'mee-bleh	redeemable bond
bono simple	ehl 'boh-noh 'seem-pleh	note
bono sin intereses	ehl 'boh-noh seen een-teh-'reh-sehs	flat bond
bonos de ganancias (mpl)	los 'boh-nohs deh gah-'nahn-see-ahs	income bonds
bonos de rendimiento bajo	los 'boh-nohs deh rehn-dee-mee-'ehn-toh 'bah-hoh	low-yield bonds
bonos de respaldo	los 'boh-nohs deh reh-'spahl-doh	back-up bonds
bonos de Tesorería Británica	los 'boh-nohs deh teh-soh-reh-'ree-ah bree-'tah-nee-kah	gilt (British govt. securities)
bonos del gobierno	los 'boh-nohs deh goh-bee-'ehr-noh	government bonds
bonos del Tesoro	lohs 'boh-nohs dehl teh-'soh-roh	treasury bonds
borrador (m)	ehl boh-rrah-'dohr	rough draft
borrar	boh-'rrahr	clear (v)
botánica (f)	lah boh-tah-nee-kah	botany
botas (fpl)	lahs boh-tahs	boots
bote salvavidas (m)	ehl 'boh-teh sahl-bah-'bee-dahs	lifeboat
botella (f)	lah boh-teh-yah	bottle
botella de dos litros	lah boh-teh-yah deh dohs lee-trohs	magnum (2 bottles in one)
botón (m)	ehl bah-tohn	button
broncear	brohn-seh-ahr	tan (v)
bruto (m)	ehl 'broo-toh	crude oil
bucle (m)	ehl 'boo-kleh	loop
buena entrega (de valores) (f)	lah 'bweh-nah ehn-'treh-gahdeh bah-'loh-rehs	good delivery (securities)
bufanda (f)	lah boo-fahn-dah	scarf
bujía (f)	lah boo-hee-ah	spark plug
buque (m)	ehl 'boo-keh	ship, vessel (sea)
bureta (f)	lah boo-reh-tah	buret
burócrata (m)	ehl boo-'roh-krah-tah	bureaucrat

buscar	*boos-'kahr*	search (v)
buscar trabajo	*boo-'skahr-trah-'bah-hoh*	job search (v)
búsqueda (f)	*lah 'boos-keh-dah*	search
búsqueda de ejecutivos	*lah 'boos-keh-dah deh eh-heh-koo-'tee-bohs*	executive search
byte (m)	*ehl 'bah-eet*	byte

C

caballos de fuerza (mpl)	*lohs kah-bah-yohs deh fwehr-sah*	horsepower
cabildeo (m)	*ehl kah-beek-'deh-oh*	lobbying
cable (m)	*ehl 'kah-bleh*	cable, wire
cable coaxial (m)	*ehl kah-bleh koh-ahks-ee-'ahl*	coaxial cable
cabritilla (f)	*lah kah-bree-'tee-yah*	kidskin, suede
cachemira (f)	*lah kah-cheh-'mee-rah*	cashmere
cadena de mando (la jerarquía) (f)	*lah kah-'deh-nah deh 'mahn-doh*	chain of command
cadena de tiendas	*lah kad-'deh-nah deh tee-'ehn-dahs*	chain store
cafetera (f)	*lah kah-feh-teh-rah*	coffeepot
caja (f)	*lah kah-hah*	case
caja (f) baja	*lah kah-hah bah-hah*	lower case
caja de seguridad de depósitos	*lah 'kah-hah deh seh-goo-ree-'dahd deh deh-'poh-see-tohs*	safe deposit box
caja del ascensor	*lah 'kah-hah dehl ah-sehn-'sohr*	elevator shaft
cajero (m)	*ehl kah-'heh-roh*	teller
calcetines (mpl)	*lohs kahl-seh-'tee-nehs*	socks
calcio (m)	*ehl 'kahl-see-oh*	calcium
calculadora (f)	*lah kahl-koo-lah-'doh-rah*	calculator
cálculo erróneo	*'kahl-koo-loh eh-'rroh-neh-oh*	miscalculation
calefacción casera (f)	*lah kah-leh-fahk-see-'ohn kah-'seh-rah*	home heating

calentamiento global (m)	*ehl kah-lehn-tah-mee-'ehn-toh gloh-'bahl*	global warming
calidad comercial (f)	*lah kah-lee-'dahd koh-mehr-see-'ahl*	commercial grade
calidad máxima	*lah kah-lee-'dahd 'mahk-see-mah*	top quality
cálido	*'kah-lee-doh*	warm (adj)
calmante (m)	*ehl kahl-'mahn-teh*	sedative
calor (m)	*ehl kah-'lohr*	heat
calumnia (f)	*lah kah-'loom-nee-ah*	libel
cámara de comercio (f)	*lah 'kah-mah-rah deh koh-'mehr-see-oh*	chamber of commerce
cámara de compensación	*lah 'kah-mah-rah deh kohm-pehn-sah-see-'ohn*	clearinghouse
cambiar	*kahm-bee-'ahr*	to change (v)
cambio (m)	*ehl 'kahm-bee-oh*	change, shift
cambio (m) automático de velocidades	*ehl 'kahm-bee-oh ow-toh-mah-tee-koh deh beh-loh-see-dah-dehs*	automatic gearshift
cambio de velocidades	*ehl 'kahm-bee-oh deh beh-loh-see-dah-dehs*	gearshift
cambio exterior	*ehl 'kahm-bee-oh ehks-teh-ree-'ohr*	foreign exchange
cambio neto	*ehl 'kahm-bee-oh 'neh-toh*	net change
cambio pequeño de precio	*ehl 'kahm-bee-oh peh-'keh-nyoh deh 'preh-see-oh*	price trick
cambios inminentes	*ehl 'kahm-bee-ohs eem-mee-'nehn-tehs*	impending changes
camino (m)	*ehl kah-'mee-noh*	path
camionada (f)	*lah kah-mee-oh-'nah-dah*	truck load
camisa (f)	*lah kah-'mee-sah*	shirt
campaña de publicidad (f)	*lah kahm-'pah-nyah deh poo-blee-see-'dahd*	advertising campaign
campaña para conseguir anunciadores	*lah kahm-'pah-nyah 'pah-'rah kohn-seh-'geer ah-noon-see-ah-'doh-rehs*	advertising drive
campo (m)	*ehl 'kahm-poh*	field
canal (m)	*ehl kah-nahl*	channel
canal (cinta)	*ehl kah-'nahl ('seen-tah)*	track

canal de distribución	*ehl kah-'nahl deh dees-tree-boo-see-'ohn*	channel of distribution
cancelado en los libros	*kahn-seh-'lah-doh ehn lohs 'lee-brohs*	off the books
cancelar	*kahn-seh-'lahr*	cancel, pay off (v)
cancelar una partida doble	*kahn-seh-'lahr 'oo-nah pahr-'tee-dah 'doh-bleh*	write off (v)
cansancio debido al vuelo	*kahn-'sahn-see-oh deh-'bee-doh ahl 'bweh-loh*	jet lag
cantidad	*lah kahn-tee-'dahd*	quantity
capa de ozono (f)	*lah 'kah-pah de oh-'soh-noh*	ozone layer
capacidad (f)	*lah kah-pah-see-'dahd*	capacity
capacidad de empaquetar	*lah kah-pah-see-'dahd deh ehm-pah-keh-'tahr*	bale capacity
capacidad de la planta	*lah kah-pah-see-'dahd deh lah 'plahn-tah*	plant capacity
capacidad de manufactura-ción	*lah kah-pah-see-'dahd deh mah-noo-fahk-too-rah-see-'ohn*	manufacturing capacity
capacidad de refinación	*lah kah-pah-see-'dahd deh reh-fee-nah-see-'ohn*	refining capacity
capacidad de utilización	*lah kah-pah-see-'dahd deh oo-tee-lee-sah-see-'ohn*	utilization capacity
capacidad ociosa	*lah kah-pah-see-'dahd oh-see-'oh-sah*	idle capacity
capacidad (f) productiva de la planta	*lah kah-pah-see-'dahd proh-dook-'tee-bah deh lah 'plahn-tah*	plant capacity
capataz (m)	*ehl kah-pah-'tahs*	foreman
capital (m)	*ehl kah-pee-'tahl*	capital
capital de accionistas	*ehl kah-pee-'tahl deh ahk-see-oh-'nees-tahs*	shareholder's equity
capital de especulación	*ehl kah-pee-'tahl deh ehs-peh-koo-lah-see-'ohn*	risk capital, venture capital
capital de trabajo	*ehl kah-pee-'tahl deh trah-'bah-hoh*	working capital
capital de trabajo neto	*ehl kah-pee-'tahl deh trah-'bah-hoh 'neh-toh*	net working capital
capital desembolsado	*ehl kah-pee-'tahl dehs-ehm-bohl-'sah-doh*	paid up capital

C

capital especulativo	*ehl kah-pee-'tahl ehs-peh-koo-lah-'tee-boh*	venture capital
capital fijo	*ehl kah-pee-'tahl 'fee-hoh*	fixed capital
capital invertido	*ehl kah-pee-'tahl een-behr-'tee-doh*	invested capital
capital legal	*ehl kah-pee-'tahl leh-'gahl*	legal capital
capital neto	*ehl kah-pee-'tahl 'neh-toh*	net worth
capital ordinario	*ehl kah-pee-'tahl ohr-dee-'nah-ree-oh*	ordinary capital
capital propio	*ehl kah-pee-'tahl 'proh-pee-oh*	equity
capital social	*ehl kah-pee-'tahl soh-see-'ahl*	capital stock
capitalismo (m)	*ehl kah-pee-tah-'lees-moh*	capitalism
capitalización (f)	*lah kah-pee-tah-lee-sah-see-'ohn*	capitalization
capitalización continua	*lah kah-pee-tah-lee-sah-see-'ohn kohn-'tee-noo-ah*	continuous compounding
capitalizado en exceso	*kah-pee-tah-lee-'sah-doh ehn ehk-'seh-soh*	overcapitalized
capítulo (m)	*ehl kah-'pee-too-loh*	chapter
capucha (f)	*lah kah-'pooh-chah*	hood
carácter de memoria (m)	*ehl kah-'rahk-tehr deh meh-'moh-ree-ah*	byte
características físicas (fpl)	*lahs kah-rehk-teh-'rees-tee-kahs 'fee-see-kahs*	physical characteristics
carbón (m)	*ehl kahr-'bohn*	coal
carburante diesel (m)	*ehl kahr-boo-'rahn-teh dee-eh-'sehl*	oil (diesel)
carga (f)	*lah 'kahr-gah*	cargo
carga de cromo	*lah kahr-gah deh kroh-moh*	charge chrome
carga de fardos	*lah 'kahr-gah deh 'fahr-dohs*	bale cargo
carga de trabajo	*lah 'kahr-gah deh trah-'bah-hoh*	work load
carga delantera	*lah 'kahr-gah deh-lahn-'teh-rah*	headload
carga impositiva	*lah 'kahr-gah eem-poh-see-'tee-bah*	tax burden

carga máxima	*lah 'kahr-gah 'mahk-see-mah*	peak load
carga promedia	*lah 'kahr-gah proh-'meh-dee-ah*	burden rate
carga seca	*lah 'kahr-gah 'seh-kah*	dry cargo
carga útil	*lah 'kahr-gah 'oo-teel*	payload
cargamento parcial	*ehl 'kahr-gah-'mehn-toh pahr-see-'ahl*	partial load
cargamento por la puerta delantera	*ehl kahr-gah-'mehn-toh pohr lah 'pwehr-tah deh-lahn-'teh-rah*	front-end loading
cargo (m)	*ehl 'kahr-goh*	debit
cargo arancelario	*ehl 'kahr-goh ah-rahn-seh-'lah-ree-oh*	tariff charge
cargo de admisión	*ehl 'kahr-goh deh ahd-mee-see-'ohn*	cover charge
cargo de muelle por desembarco	*ehl 'kahr-goh deh 'mweh-yeh pohr dehs-ehm-'bahr-koh*	dock handling charge
cargo por muelle	*ehl 'kahr-goh pohr 'mweh-yeh*	wharfage charge
cargo variable	*ehl 'kahr-goh bah-ree-'ah-bleh*	floating charge
cargos (m)	*lohs 'kahr-gohs*	charges
cargos (sobre ventas)	*lohs 'kahr-gohs ('soh-breh 'behn-tahs)*	aload (sales charge)
cargos bancarios	*lohs 'kahr-gohs bahn-'kah-ree-ohs*	bank charges
cargos de cambio de títulos	*lohs 'kahr-gohs deh 'kahm-bee-oh deh 'tee-too-lohs*	switching charges
cargos de desembarco	*lohs 'kahr-gohs deh dehs-ehm-'bahr-koh*	dock handling charge
cargos de estiba	*lohs 'kahr-gohs deh eh-'stee-bah*	stowage charges
cargos de rescate	*lohs 'kahr-gohs deh rehs-'kah-teh*	salvage charges
cargos de transporte	*lohs 'kahr-gohs deh trahns-'pohr-teh*	shipping charges
cargos diferidos	*lohs 'kahr-gohs dee-feh-'ree-dohs*	deferred assets, deferred charges, prepaid expenses (balance sheet)

cargos establecidos	*lohs 'kahr-gohs eh-stah-bleh-'see-dohs*	standing charges
cargos fijos	*lohs 'kahr-gohs 'fee-hohs*	fixed charges
carnet (m)	*ehl kahr-'neht*	carnet
carpeta (f)	*lah kahr-peh-tah*	paper holder
carpeta (f) dura	*lah kahr-'peh-tah 'doo-rah*	hardcover
carretaje (m)	*ehl kah-rreh-'tah-heh*	drayage
carro (m)	*ehl kah-rroh*	car
carrocería (f)	*lah kah-rro-seh-ree-ah*	bodywork
carta (f)	*lah 'kahr-tah*	letter
carta con anexos	*lah 'kahr-tah kohn ah-'nehk-sohs*	cover letter
carta de consignación	*lah 'kahr-tah deh kohn-seeg-nah-see-'ohn*	consignment note
carta de crédito	*lah 'kahr-tah deh 'kreh-dee-toh*	letter of credit
carta de crédito bancaria	*lah 'kahr-tah deh 'kreh-dee-toh bahn-'kah-ree-ah*	bank letter of credit
carta de crédito renovable	*lah 'kahr-tah deh 'kreh-dee-toh reh-noh-'bah-bleh*	revolving letter of credit
carta de fletamiento sin tripulación ni combustible	*lah 'kahr-tah deh fleh-tah-mee-'ehn-toh seen tree-poo-lah-see-'ohn nee kohm-boos-'tee-bleh*	bareboat charter
carta de garantía	*lah 'kahr-tah deh gah-rahn-'tee-ah*	letter of guaranty
carta de inversión	*lah 'kahr-tah deh een-behr-see-'ohn*	investment letter
carta de presentación	*lah 'kahr-tah deh preh-sehn-tah-see-'ohn*	letter of introduction
carta de transmisión	*lah 'kahr-tah deh trans-mee-see-'ohn*	cover letter
carta modelo	*lah 'kahr-tah moh-'deh-loh*	form letter
carta poder	*lah 'kahr-tah poh-'dehr*	proxy statement, power of attorney
cartel (m)	*ehl kahr-'tehl*	cartel
cartelera (f)	*lah kahr-teh-'leh-rah*	billboard
cartera (f)	*lah kahr-'teh-rah*	billfold, briefcase, portfolio

cartera de acciones	*lah kahr-'teh-rah deh ahk-see-'oh-nehs*	stock portfolio
cartera de mano	*lah kahr-teh-rah deh mah-noh*	handbag
cartera de papeles	*lah kahr-teh-rah deh pah-'pehl-ehs*	attaché case
cartera del pasaporte	*lah kahr-teh-rah dehl pah-sah-'pohr-teh*	passport case
casa de aceptaciones (f)	*lah 'kah-sah deh ah-sehp-tah-see-'oh-nehs*	acceptance house, merchant bank
casa de comercio	*lah 'kah-sah deh koh-'mehr-see-oh*	trade house
casa de moneda	*lah 'kah-sah deh moh-'neh-dah*	mint
casa exportadora	*lah 'kah-sah ehks-pohr-tah-'doh-rah*	export house
casa matriz	*lah 'kah-sah mah-'trees*	head office, headquarters
casette (m)	*ehl kah-'seh-teh*	cassette
castor (m)	*ehl kahs-tohr*	beaver
catalizador (m)	*ehl kah-tah-lee-sah-dohr*	catalyst
catálogo (m)	*ehl kah-'tah-loh-goh*	catalogue
cátodo (m)	*ehl 'kah-toh-doh*	cathode
caza (f)	*lah 'kah-sah*	hunting
caza excesiva	*lah 'kah-hah ehk-seh-'see-bah*	hunting (excessive)
cedente (m)	*ehl seh-'dehn-teh*	assigner
censo (m)	*ehl 'sehn-soh*	census
centralización (f)	*lah sehn-trah-lee-sah-see-'ohn*	centralization
centro comercial (m)	*ehl 'sehn-troh koh-mehr-see-'ahl*	shopping center
centro de computación	*ehl 'sehn-troh de kohm-poo-tah-see-'ohn*	computer center
centro de consumo	*ehl 'sehn-troh deh kohn-'soo-moh*	consuming center
certificado (m)	*ehl sehr-tee-fee-'kah-doh*	certificate
certificado de acciones	*ehl sehr-tee-fee-'kah-doh deh ahk-see-'oh-nehs*	stock certificate

C

certificado de antigüedad auténtica	*ehl sehr-tee-fee-'kah-doh deh ahn-tee-gweh-'dahd ow-'tehn-tee-kah*	antique authenticity certificate
certificado de depósito	*ehl sehr-tee-fee-'kah-doh deh deh-'poh-see-toh*	certificate of deposit
certificado de desembarque	*ehl sehr-tee-fee-'kah-doh deh dehs-ehm-'bahr-keh*	landing certificate
certificado de opción	*ehl sehr-tee-fee-'kah-doh deh ohp-see-'ohn*	warrant
certificado de origen	*ehl sehr-tee-fee-'kah-doh deh oh-'ree-hehn*	certificate of origin
certificado de uso	*ehl sehr-tee-fee-'kah-doh deh 'oo-soh*	final end-use certificate
cesionario (m)	*ehl seh-see-oh-'nah-ree-oh*	assignee
chip (m)	*ehl cheep*	chip
cicero (m)	*ehl see-'seh-roh*	pica
ciclo (m)	*ehl 'see-kloh*	cycle
ciclo biológico	*ehl 'see-kloh bee-oh-'loh-hee-koh*	cycle (biological)
ciclo de duración (de un producto)	*ehl 'see-koh deh doo-rah-see-'ohn (deh oon proh-'dook-toh)*	life cycle (of a product)
ciclo de trabajo	*ehl 'see-kloh deh trah-'bah-hoh*	work cycle
ciclo económico	*ehl 'see-kloh eh-koh-'noh-mee-koh*	business cycle
ciencia natural (f)	*lah see-'ehn-see-ah nah-too-'rahl*	natural science
cierre (m)	*ehl see-'eh-rreh*	lock out
cierre de ejercicio	*ehl see-'eh-rreh deh eh-hehr-'see-see-oh*	year-end
cigüeñal (m)	*ehl see-gweh-'nyahl*	crankshaft
cilindro (m) de offset	*ehl see-'leen-droh deh ohf-seht*	web offset
cinc (m)	*ehl seenk*	zinc
cinta de encajonar (f)	*lah seen-tah deh ehn-kah-hoh-'nahr*	strapping tape
cinta de impresor	*lah 'seen-tah deh eem-preh-'sohr*	ribbon

cinta del indicador automático	*lah 'seen-tah dehl een-dee-kah-'dohr ow-toh-'mah-tee-koh*	ticker tape
cinta magnética	*lah 'seen-tah mahg-'neh-tee-kah*	magnetic tape
cinta magnetofónica	*lah seen-tah mahg-neh-toh-'foh-nee-kah*	cassette
cinto (m)	*ehl seen-toh*	belt (prize: cinto negro is black belt)
circuitería física (f)	*lah seer-koo-ee-teh-'ree-ah 'fee-see-kah*	hardware
circuito (m)	*ehl seer-koo-'ee-too*	circuit
circuito impreso	*ehl seer-koo-'ee-toh eem-preh-soh*	printed circuit
circuito integrado	*ehl seer-koo-'ee-toh een-teh-grah-doh*	integrated circuit, chip
circuito paralelo	*ehl seer-koo-'ee-toh pah-rah-leh-loh*	parallel circuit
circulación de cheques en descubierto (f)	*lah seer-koo-lah-see-'ohn deh 'cheh-kehs ehn dehs-koo-bee-'ehr-toh*	kiting checks (banking)
cita (engagement) (f)	*lah 'see-tah*	appointment
clarificación (f)	*lah klah-ree-fee-kah-see-'ohn*	clearing
clase trabajadora (f)	*lah 'klah-seh trah-bah-hah-'doh-rah*	working class
clases mutuamente excluyentes (fpl)	*lahs 'klah-sehs moo-too-ah-'mehn-teh ehks-kloo-'yehn-tehs*	mutually exclusive classes
clasificación arancelaria (f)	*lah klah-see-fee-kah-see-'ohn ah-rahn-seh-'lah-ree-ah*	tariff classification
clasificación de bonos	*lah klah-see-fee-kah-see-'ohn deh 'boh-nohs*	bond rating
clasificación de créditos	*lah klah-see-fee-kah-see-'ohn deh 'kreh-dee-tohs*	credit rating
clasificación del mercado	*lah klah-see-fee-kah-see-'ohn dehl mehr-'kah-doh*	market rating
clasificación según factores	*lah klah-see-fee-kah-see-'ohn seh-'goon fahk-'toh-rehs*	factor rating

C

cláusula de escape (f)	*lah 'klow-soo-lah deh ehs-'kah-peh*	escape clause
cláusula de exención	*lah 'klow-soo-lah deh ehks-ehn-see-'ohn*	waiver clause
cláusula monetaria	*lah 'klow-soo-lah moh-neh-'tah-ree-ah*	currency clause
cláusula oro	*lah 'klow-soo-lah 'oh-roh*	gold clause
cláusula para el vencimiento anticipado de una deuda	*lah 'klow-soo-lah 'pah-rah ehl vehn-see-mee-'ehn-toh ahn-tee-see-'pah-doh deh 'oo-nah deh-'oo-dah*	acceleration clause
cláusula penal	*lah 'klow-soo-lah peh-'nahl*	penalty clause
cláusula que cubre las pérdidas por defectos propios del buque o mercancías	*lah 'klow-soo-lah keh 'koo-breh lahs 'pehr-dee-dahs dehl 'boo-keh oh mehr-kahn-'see-ahs*	Jason Clause
cláusula sobre el tipo móvil de salario, alquiler, etc.	*lah 'klow-soo-lah 'soh-breh ehl 'tee-poh 'moh-beel deh sah-'lah-ree-oh, ahl-kee-'lehr*	escalator clause
claúsula de reembolso	*lahs 'klow-soo-lah deh reh-ehm-'bohl-soh*	repayment provision
cliente (m)	*ehl klee-'ehn-teh*	customer
clima (m)	*ehl klee-mah*	climate
cloroformo (m)	*ehl kloh-roh-fohr-moh*	chloroform
cloruro (m)	*ehl kloh-roo-roh*	chloride
coaseguro (m)	*ehl koh-ah-seh-'goo-roh*	co-insurance
cobertura (f)	*lah koh-behr-'too-rah*	coverage
cobertura a futuro	*lah koh-behr-'too-rah ah foo-'too-roh*	forward cover
cobrar a la entrega	*koh-'brahr ah lah ehn-'treh-gah*	collect on delivery
cobre (m)	*ehl koh-breh*	cooper
cobro adelantado	*ehl 'koh-broh ah-deh-lahn-'tah-doh*	front-end fee
codicilo (m)	*ehl koh-dee-'see-loh*	codicil
codificar	*koh-dee-fee-'kahr*	encode (v)
código (m) binario	*ehl koh-dee-goh bee-nah-ree-oh*	binary code

código de trabajo	*ehl 'koh-dee-goh deh trah-'bah-hoh*	labor code
código postal	*ehl 'koh-dee-goh pohs-'tahl*	zip code
código utilizado como estándard en los EE.UU. para el intercambio de información entre sistemas de procesamiento de datos	*'koh-dee-goh oo-tee-lee-'sah-doh 'koh-moh ehs-'tahn-dahrd ehn lohs eh-'stah-dohs oo-'nee-dohs 'pah-rah ehl een-tehr-'kahm-bee-oh deh een-fohr-mah-see-'ohn 'ehn-treh sees-'teh-mahs deh proh-seh-sah-mee-'ehn-toh deh 'dah-tohs*	ASCII
coeficiente de cargamento (m)	*ehl koh-eh-fee-see-'ehn-teh deh kahr-gah-'mehn-toh*	load factor
coeficiente de solvencia	*ehl koh-eh-fee-see-'ehn-teh deh-sohl-'behn-see-ah*	current ratio
colateral (m)	*ehl koh-lah-teh-'rahl*	collateral
colección de caracteres de un tipo particular (f)	*lah koh-lehk-see-'ohn deh kah-rahk-'teh-rehs deh oon 'tee-poh pahr-tee-koo-'lahr*	font
colega (m)	*ehl koh-'leh-gah*	colleague
colocación privada (f)	*lah koh-loh-kah-see-'ohn pree-'bah-dah*	private placement (finance)
coloquio (m)	*ehl koh-'loh-kee-oh*	colloquium
columna (f)	*lah koh-'loom-nah*	column
combinación (f)	*lah kohm-nee-nah-see-'ohn*	combination
combinación de los órganos asesores con los de ejecución	*lah kohm-bee-nah-see-'ohn deh lohs 'ohr-gah-nohs ah-seh-'soh-rehs kohn lohs de eh-heh-koo-see-'ohn*	staff and line
combinar	*kohm-bee-'nahr*	pool (v)
combustible (m)	*ehl kohm-boo-'stee-bleh*	fuel
combustible para motores	*ehl kohm-boo-'stee-bleh 'pah-rah moh-'toh-rehs*	fuel (motor)
comerciante (m)	*ehl koh-mehr-see-'ahn-teh*	merchant, trader, jobber, dealer
comerciar	*koh-mehr-see-'ahr*	to trade, to deal, to market (v)
comercio (m)	*ehl koh-'mehr-see-oh*	commerce, dealership, trade

C

comercio al detalle	*ehl koh-mehr-see-oh ahl deh-'tah-yeh*	retail trade
comercio al por mayor	*ehl koh-'mehr-see-oh ahl pohr mah-'yohr*	retail trade
comercio exterior	*ehl koh-'mehr-see-oh ehks-teh-ree-'ohr*	foreign trade
comercio interestatal	*ehl koh-'mehr-see-oh een-teh-rehs-tah-'tahl*	interstate commerce
comercio mercantil	*ehl ehl koh-'mehr-see-oh mehr-kahn-'teel*	commodity exchange
comercio multilateral	*koh-'mehr-see-oh mool-tee-lah-teh-'rahl*	multilateral trade
comisión (f)	*lah koh-mee-see-'ohn*	commission fee
comisión comercial	*lah koh-mee-see-'ohn koh-mehr-see-'ahl*	trade commission
comisión de garantía	*lah koh-mee-see-'ohn deh gah-rahn-'tee-ah*	standby fee
comité de trabajo (m)	*ehl koh-mee-'teh deh trah-'bah-hoh*	work committee
comité ejecutivo	*ehl koh-mee-'teh eh-heh-koo-'tee-boh*	executive committee
compaginación (f)	*lah kohm-pah-hee-nah-see-ohn*	page makeup
compañía (f)	*lah kohm-pah-'nyee-ah*	company
compañía aseguradora	*lah kohm-pah-'nyee-ah ah-seh-goo-rah-'doh-rah*	insurance company
compañía asociada	*lah kohm-pah-'nyee-ah ah-soh-see-'ah-dah*	associate company
compañía cerrada	*lah kohm-pah-'nyee-ah seh-'rrah-dah*	closely held corporation
compañía cuasi-pública	*lah kohm-pah-'nyee-ah kwah-see-'poo-blee-kah*	quasi-public company
compañía de fianzas	*lah kohm-pah-'nyee-ah deh fee-'ahn-sahs*	guaranty company
compañía de intercambio comercial	*lah kohm-pah-'nyee-ah deh een-tehr-'kahm-bee-oh koh-mehr-see-'ahl*	trading company
compañía de inversiones	*lah kohm-pah-'nee-ah deh een-behr-see-'oh-nehs*	investment trust
compañía doméstica	*lah kohm-pah-'nyee-ah doh-'mehs-tee-kah*	domestic corporation

compañía estatal	*lah kohm-pah-'nyee-ah eh-stah-'tahl*	company (state-owned)
compañía extranjera	*lah kohm-pah-'nyee-ah ehk-strahn-'heh-rah*	alien corporation, foreign corporation (to country)
compañía fiduciaria	*lah kohm-pah-'nyee-ah fee-doo-see-'ah-ree-ah*	trust company
compañía financiera	*lah kohm-pah-'nyee-ah fee-nahn-see-'eh-rah*	finance company
compañía foránea	*lah kohm-pah-'nyee-ah foh-'rah-neh-ah*	foreign corporation (to region)
compañía garante	*lah kohm-pah-'nyee-ah gah-'rahn-teh*	surety company
compañía inversionista	*lah kohm-pah-'nyee-ah een-behr-see-oh-'nees-tah*	investment company
compañía matriz	*lah kohm-pah-'nyee-ah mah-'trees*	holding company, parent company
compañía nacionalizada	*lah kohm-pah-'nyee-ah nah-see-oh-nah-lee-'sah-dah*	company (nationalized)
compañía petrolera	*lah kohm-pah-'nee-ah peh-troh-'leh-rah*	oil company
compañía petrolera multinacional	*lah kohm-pah-'nyee-ah peh-troh-'leh-rah mool-tee-nah-see-oh-'nahl*	multinational oil company (MNOC)
compañía privada	*lah kohm-pah-'nyee-ah pree-'bah-dah*	company (privately-owned)
compañía privatizada	*lah kohm-pah-'nyee-ah pree-'bah-tee-'sah-dah*	company (privatized)
compañía pública	*lah kohm-pah-'nyee-ah 'poo-blee-kah*	public company
comparar y escoger el puesto por el salario	*kohm-pah-'rahr ee ehs-koh-'hehr ehl 'pwehs-toh pohr ehl sah-'lah-ree-oh*	job shop
compensación del ejecutivo (f)	*lah kohm-pehn-sah-see-'ohn dehl eh-heh-koo-'tee-boh*	executive compensation
compensación por desempleo	*lah kohm-pehn-sah-see-'ohn pohr dehs-ehm-'pleh-oh*	unemployment compensation
competencia (f)	*lah kohm-peh-'tehn-see-ah*	competition
competencia de precios	*lah kohm-peh-'tehn-see-ah deh 'preh-see-ohs*	price war
competidor (m)	*ehl kohm-peh-tee-'dohr*	competitor
componente (m)	*ehl kohm-poh-'nehn-teh*	component

comportamiento de las ganancias (m)	*ehl kohm-pohr-tah-mee-'ehn-toh deh lahs gah-'nahn-see-ahs*	earnings performance
composición (f)	*lah kohm-poh-see-see-ohn*	composition, layout
compra a futuro (f)	*lah 'kohm-prah ah foo-'too-roh*	forward purchase
compra al mejor	*lah 'kohm-prah ahl meh-'hohr*	buy at best
compra compensadora	*lah 'kohm-prah kohm-pehn-sah-'doh-rah*	long hedge
compra de acciones	*lah 'kohm-prah deh ahk-see-'oh-nehs*	stock purchase
compra impulsiva	*lah 'kohm-prah eem-pool-'see-bah*	impulse buying
comprador (m)	*ehl kohm-prah-'dohr*	buyer
comprador de valores para su propia cuenta	*ehl kohm-prah-'dohr deh bah-'loh-rehs 'pah-rah soo 'proh-pee-ah 'kwehn-tah*	market-maker (securities)
comprador potencial	*ehl kohm-prah-dohr poh-tehn-see-ahl*	potential buyer
comprador residente	*ehl kohm-prah-'dohr reh-see-'dehn-teh*	resident buyer
comprar	*kohm-'prahr*	purchase (v)
comprar a la apertura	*kohm-'prahr ah lah ah-pehr-'too-rah*	buy on opening
comprar al cierre	*kohm-'prahr ahl see-'eh-rreh*	buy on close
comprar la parte de	*kohm-'prahr lah 'pahr-teh deh*	buy out (v)
compresor del aire (m)	*ehl kohm-preh-'sohr dehl 'ah-ee-reh*	air compressor
comprobante (m)	*ehl kohm-proh-'bahn-teh*	voucher
comprobante de venta	*ehl kohm-proh-'bahn-teh deh 'behn-tah*	bill of sale
compromiso (m)	*ehl kohm-proh-'mee-soh*	commitment
compuesto (m)	*ehl kohm-'pweh-stoh*	compound
compuesto químico	*ehl kohm-'pweh-stoh 'kee-mee-koh*	compound (chemical)
compuestos (mpl)	*lohs kohm-'pwehs-tohs*	compounds

compulsión (f)	*lah kohm-pool-see-'ohn*	duress
computadora (f)	*lah kohm-poo-tah-'doh-rah*	computer
computadora análoga	*lah kohm-poo-tah-'doh-rah ah-'nah-loh-gah*	analogue computer
computadora digital	*lah kohm-poo-tah-'doh-rah dee-hee-'tahl*	digital computer
computadora híbrida	*lah kohm-poo-tah-'doh-rah 'ee-bree-dah*	hybrid computer
computadora personal	*lah kohm-poo-tah-'doh-rah pehr-soh-'nahl*	personal computer
computadora principal	*lah kohm-poo-tah-'doh-rah preen-see-'pahl*	mainframe computer
comunicación en masa (f)	*lah koh-moo-nee-kah-see-'ohn ehn 'mah-sah*	mass communications
comunicar	*koh-moo-nee-'kahr*	interface (v)
comunismo	*ehl koh-moo-'nees-moh*	communism
con avería	*kohn ah-beh-'ree-ah*	with average
con fines no lucrativos	*kohn 'fee-nehs noh loo-krah-'tee-bohs*	nonprofit
concebido para el usuario	*kohn-seh-'bee-doh 'pah-rah ehl oo-soo-'ah-ree-oh*	user-friendly
conceder un sobregiro	*kohn-seh-'dehr oon soh-breh-'hee-roh*	grant an overdraft (v)
concentración (f)	*lah kohn-sehn-trah-see-'ohn*	concentration
concentración en el mercado	*lah kohn-sehn-trah-see-'ohn ehn ehl mehr-'kah-doh*	market concentration
concentraciones (fpl)	*lahs kohn-sehn-trah-see-'oh-nehs*	concentrations
concepto de la capacidad de pago (m)	*ehl kohn-'sehp-toh deh lah kah-pah-see-'dahd deh 'pah-goh*	ability-to-pay concept
concepto del mercadeo	*ehl kohn-'sehp-toh dehl mehr-kah-'deh-oh*	marketing concept
concesión (f)	*lah kohn-seh-see-'ohn*	allowance
concesión de tierras	*lah kohn-seh-see-'ohn deh tee-'eh-rrahs*	land grant
concesión recíproca de licencias	*lah kohn-seh-see-'ohn reh-'see-proh-kah deh lee-'sehn-see-ahs*	cross-licensing
concesión tributaria	*lah kohn-seh-see-'ohn tree-boo-'tah-ree-ah*	tax allowance

concesionario autorizado (m)	*ehl kohn-seh-see-oh-'nah-ree-oh ow-toh-ree-'sah-doh*	authorized dealer
condensador (m)	*ehl kohn dehn-sah-'dohr*	condensor
condición (f)	*lah kohn-dee-see-'ohn*	character
condiciones de atraque y muellaje (fpl)	*lahs kohn-dee-see-'oh-nehs deh ah-'trah-keh ee mweh-'yah-heh*	berth terms
condiciones de crédito	*lahs kohn-dee-see-'oh-nehs deh 'kreh-dee-toh*	credit terms
conducción (f)	*lah kohn-dook-see-'ohn*	steering
conductor (m)	*ehl kohn-dook-tohr*	conductor, driver
conectado	*koh-nehk-'tah-doh*	on-line
conejo (m)	*ehl koh-neh-hoh*	rabbit
confeccionado	*kohn-fehk-see-oh-'nah-doh*	ready to wear
confidencial	*kohn-fee-dehn-see-'ahl*	confidential
confiscación (f)	*lah kohn-fees-kah-see-'ohn*	escheat
confiscación de pedido	*lah kohn-fees-kah-see-'ohn deh peh-'dee-doh*	confirmation of order
conflicto de intereses (m)	*ehl kohn-'fleek-toh deh een-teh-'reh-sehs*	conflict of interests
conflicto laboral	*ehl kohn-'fleek-toh lah-boh-'rahl*	labor freeze
congelamiento de salarios (m)	*ehl kohn-heh-lah-mee-'ehn-toh deh sah-'lah-ree-ohs*	wage freeze
conglomerado (m)	*ehl kohn-gloh-meh-'rah-doh*	conglomerate
conocimiento (m)	*ehl koh-noh-see-mee-'ehn-toh*	knowledge
conocimiento de embarque con reservas	*ehl koh-noh-see-mee-'ehn-toh deh ehm-'bahr-keh kohn reh-'sehr-bahs*	foul bill of lading
conocimiento de embarque	*ehl koh-noh-see-mee-'ehn-toh deh ehm-'bahr-keh*	bill of lading
conocimiento de transporte interior	*ehl koh-noh-see-mee-'ehn-toh deh trahns-'pohr-teh een-teh-ree-'ohr*	inland bill of lading
conocimientos técnicos especializados	*ehl koh-noh-see-mee-'ehn-tohs 'tehk-nee-kohs ehs-peh-see-ah-lee-'sah-dohs*	know-how
consecuencias de una ocurrencia (f)	*lahs kohn-seh-'kwehn-see-ahs deh 'oo-nah oh-koo-'rehn-see-ah*	backwash effect

conseguir capital	*kohn-seh-'geer kah-pee-'tahl*	raising capital
consejero sobre inversiones (m)	*ehl kohn-seh-'heh-roh 'soh-breh een-behr-see-'oh-nehs*	investment adviser
consejo asesor (m)	*ehl kohn-'seh-hoh ah-seh-'sohr*	advisory council
consejo de trabajo (m)	*ehl kohn-'seh-hoh deh trah-'bah-hoh*	work council
conservación (f)	*lah kohn-sehr-bah-see-'ohn*	conservation
consignación (f)	*lah kohn-seeg-nah-see-'ohn*	consignment, appropriation
consignatario (m)	*ehl kohn-seeg-nah-'tah-ree-oh*	consignee
consignatario de transporte	*ehl kohn-seeg-nah-'tah-ree-oh deh trahs-'pohr-teh*	shipping agent
consolidación (f)	*lah kohn-soh-lee-dah-see-'ohn*	consolidation
consorcio (m)	*ehl kohn-'sohr-see-oh*	consortium
constituir	*kohn-stee-too-'eer*	incorporate (v)
consultor (m)	*ehl kohn-sool-'tohr*	consultant
consultor generencial	*ehl kohn-sool-'tohr heh-rehn-see-'ahl*	management consultant
consumidor (m)	*ehl kohn-soo-mee-'dohr*	consumer
consumo (m)	*ehl kohn-'soo-moh*	consumption (of provisions)
consumo animal	*ehl kohn-'soo-moh ah-nee-'mahl*	consumption (animal)
consumo de gasolina	*ehl kohn-see-moh deh gah-soh-lee-nah*	gas consumption
consumo humano	*ehl kohn-'soo-moh oo-'mah-noh*	consumption (human)
contabilidad (f)	*lah kohn-tah-bee-lee-'dahd*	bookkeeping
contabilidad administrativa	*lah kohn-tah-bee-lee-'dahd deh ahd-mee-nee-strah-'tee-bah*	management accounting
contabilidad de agotamiento	*lah kohn-tah-bee-lee-'dahd deh ah-goh-tah-mee-'ehn-toh*	depletion accounting
contabilidad de costos	*lah kohn-tah-bee-lee-'dahd deh 'koh-stohs*	cost accounting
contado	*ahl kohn-'tah-doh*	cash basis

contador (m)	*ehl kohn-tah-'dohr*	accountant
contador público	*ehl kohn-tah-'dohr 'pool-blee-koh*	certified public accountant (C.P.A.), chartered accountant
contaminar	*kohn-tah-mee-'nahr*	contaminate (v)
contenido (m)	*ehl kohn-teh-nee-doh*	content
contenido acídico	*ehl kohn-teh-nee-doh ah-'see-dee-koh*	acid content
contenido alcohólico	*ehl kohn-teh-nee-doh ahl-koh-oh-lee-koh*	alcoholic content
contenido de azúcar	*ehl kohn-teh-nee-doh deh ah-soo-kahr*	sugar content
contingencias (f)	*lahs kohn-teen-'hehn-see-ahs*	contingencies
continuación del pedido (f)	*lah kohn-tee-noo-ah-see-'ohn dehl peh-'dee-doh*	follow-up order
contralor (m)	*ehl kohn-trah-'lohr*	comptroller, controller
contralorar	*kohn-trah-loh-'rahr*	audit (v)
contratación de personal (f)	*lah kohn-trah-tah-see-'ohn deh pehr-soh-'nahl*	placement (personnel)
contratar	*kohn-trah-'tahr*	hire (v)
contrato (m)	*ehl kohn-'trah-toh*	contract
contrato a futuro	*ehl kohn-'trah-toh ah foo-'too-roh*	forward contract
contrato colectivo	*ehl kohn-'trah-toh koh-lehk-'tee-boh*	collective bargaining
contrato de costo más tanto fijo	*ehl kohn-'trah-toh deh 'kohs-toh mahs 'tahn-toh 'fee-hoh*	cost-plus contract
contrato de mantenimiento	*ehl kohn-'trah-toh deh mahn-teh-nee-mee-'ehn-toh*	maintenance contract
contrato de servicio	*ehl kohn-'trah-toh deh sehr-'bee-see-oh*	service contract
contrato de traspaso	*ehl kohn-'trah-toh deh trahs-'pah-soh*	deed of transfer
contrato de venta de las exportaciones	*ehl kohn-'trah-toh deh lahs ehks-pohr-tah-see-'oh-nehs*	export sales contract

contrato de venta	*ehl kohn-'trah-toh deh 'behn-tah*	deed of sale
contrato de ventas condicional	*ehl kohn-'trah-toh deh 'behn-tahs kohn-dee-see-oh-'nahl*	conditional sales contract
contrato marítimo	*ehl kohn-'trah-toh mah-'ree-tee-moh*	maritime contract
contrato pendiente	*ehl kohn-'trah-toh pehn-dee-'ehn-teh*	outstanding contract
contrato sindical	*ehl kohn-'trah-toh seen-dee-'kahl*	union contract
contrato vigente	*ehl kohn-'trah-toh bee-'hehn-teh*	working contract
control (m)	*ehl kohn-'trohl*	control
control cruzado	*ehl kohn-'trohl kroo-'sah-doh*	crosscheck
control de agotamiento	*ehl kohn-'trohl deh ah-goh-tah-mee-'ehn-toh*	depletion control
control de calidad	*ehl kohn-'trohl deh kah-lee-'dahd*	quality control
control de cambio	*ehl kohn-'trohl deh 'kahm-bee-oh*	exchange control
control de costos	*ehl kohn-'trohl deh 'koh-stohs*	cost control
control de crédito	*ehl kohn-'trohl deh 'kreh-dee-toh*	credit control
control de existencias	*ehl kohn-'trohl deh ehk-ees-'tehn-see-ahs*	stock control
control de fabricación	*ehl kohn-'trohl deh fah-bree-kah-see-'ohn*	manufacturing control
control de manufactura	*ehl kohn-'trohl deh mah-noo-fahk-'too-rah*	manufacturing control
control de tensión	*ehl kohn-'trohl deh tehn-see-'ohn*	stress management
control del inventario	*ehl kohn-'trohl dehl een-behn-'tah-ree-oh*	inventory control, stock control
control financiero	*ehl kohn-'trohl fee-nahn-see-'eh-roh*	financial control
control numérico	*ehl kohn-'trohl noo-'meh-ree-koh*	numerical control
controlar	*kohn-troh-'lahr*	verify (v)

C

conveniencia paritaria (f)	*lah kohn-beh-nee-'ehn-see-ah pah-ree-'tah-ree-ah*	accommodation parity
convenio (m)	*ehl kohn-'beh-nee-oh*	bargain, agreement, treaty, resolution
convenio colectivo	*ehl kohn-'beh-ne-oh koh-lehk-'tee-boh*	collective bargaining
convenio de aceptación	*ehl kohn-'beh-ne-oh deh ah-seh-tah-see-'ohn*	acceptance agreement
convenio de arbitraje	*ehl kohn-'beh-ne-oh deh ahr-bee-'trah-heh*	arbitration agreement
convenio de conjunto	*ehl kohn-'beh-ne-oh deh kohn-'hoon-toh*	package deal
convenio de trabajo colectivo	*ehl kohn-'beh-ne-oh deh trah-'bah-hoh koh-lehk-'tee-boh*	collective agreement
convenio escrito en el que intervienen tres personas: el otorgante, el cesionario, y el depositario	*ehl kohn-'beh-nee-oh ehs-'kree-toh ehl ehl keh een-tehr-bee-'eh-nehn trehs pehr-'soh-nahs: ehl oh-tohr-'gahn-teh, ehl seh-see-oh-'nah-ree-oh, ee ehl deh-poh-see-'tah-ree-oh*	escrow
conversión ascendente (f)	*lah kohn-behr-see-'ohn ah-sehn-'dehn-teh*	uploading
conversión descendente	*lah kohn-behr-see-'ohn deh-sehn-'dehn-teh*	downloading
conversión monetaria	*lah kohn-behr-see-'ohn moh-neh-'tah-ree-ah*	currency
convertir caracteres (f)	*lah kohn-behr-'teer kah-'rahk-teh-rehs*	transliterate (v)
convocar junta	*kohn-boh-'kahr 'hoon-tah*	call (v) a meeting
cooperativa (f)	*lah koh-oh-peh-rah-'tee-bah*	cooperative
cooperativa vinícola	*lah koh-oh-peh-rah-'tee-bah bee-'nee-koh-lah*	wine cooperative
copa (f)	*lah koh-pah*	glass
copa de champaña	*lah koh-pah deh chahm-pah-nyah*	champagne glass
copia dura (f)	*lah 'koh-pee-ah 'doo-rah*	hard copy
copia física que se hace del contenido de un disco o una cinta	*lah 'koh-pee-ah 'fee-see-kah keh seh 'ah-seh dehl kohn-teh-'nee-doh deh oon 'dees-koh oh 'oo-nah 'seen-tah*	backup

copia impresa	lah 'koh-pee-ah eem-preh-sah	hard copy
copia literal de contratos legales pasados	lah 'koh-pee-ah lee-teh-'rahl deh kohn-'trah-tohs leh-'gah-lehs pah-'sah-dohs	boiler plate (contract)
copiar	koh-pee-ahr	copy (v)
copropietario (m)	ehl koh-proh-pee-eh-'tah-ree-oh	joint owner
corbata (f)	lah kohr-bah-tah	tie
corbata de lazo	lah kohr-bah-tah deh lah-soh	bow tie
corcho (m)	ehl kohr-choh	cork
cordero (m)	ehl kohr-deh-roh	lamb
corporación (f)	lah kohr-poh-rah-see-'ohn	corporation
correa (f)	lah koh-'rreh-ah	belt (automobile)
correa de reloj	lah koh-'rreh-ah deh reh-'loh	watch strap
correa transportadora	lah koh-rreh-ah trans-pohr-tah-doh-rah	conveyor belt
corrección (f) de prueba	lah koh-rehk-see-ohn deh proo-eh-bah	proofreading
corredor (m)	ehl koh-rreh-'dohr	broker
corredor de bienes raíces	ehl koh-rreh-dohr deh bee-'eh-nehs rah-'ee-sehs	real estate agent
corredor de bolsa	ehl koh-rreh-'dohr deh 'bohl-sah	stockbroker
corredor de dinero	ehl koh-rreh-'dohr deh dee-'neh-roh	money broker
corredor de menos de cien acciones	ehl koh-rreh-'dohr deh 'meh-nohs deh 'see-ehn ahk-see-'oh-nehs	odd lot broker
corredor de seguros	ehl koh-rreh-'dohr deh seh-'goo-rohs	insurance broker
corredor de valores	ehl koh-rreh-'dohr deh bah-'loh-rehs	bill broker
corregir	koh-rreh-'heer	debug (v)
correo aéreo (m)	ehl koh-'rreh-oh ah-'eh-reh-oh	air express

correo certificado	*ehl koh-'rreh-oh sehr-tee-fee-'kah-doh*	registered mail
correo directo	*ehl koh-'rreh-oh dee-'rehk-toh*	direct mail
correo electrónico	*ehl koh-'rreh-oh eh-lehk-'troh-nee-koh*	electronic mail
correspondencia (f)	*lah koh-rreh-spohn-'dehn-see-ah*	correspondence
corriente (f)	*lah koh-rree-'ehn-teh*	current
corriente alterna	*lah koh-rree-'ehn-teh ahl-tehr-nah*	alternating current
corriente directa	*lah koh-rree-'ehn-teh dee-rehk-tah*	direct current
cortar	*kohr-tahr*	cut (v)
cortisona (f)	*lah kohr-tee-soh-nah*	cortisone
cosecha (f)	*lah koh-'seh-chah*	crop
cosecha de uva	*lah koh-seh-chah deh oo-bahs*	grape harvest
coser	*koh-'sehr*	sew (v)
cosido	*koh-'see-doh*	sewn (adj)
costo descargado (m)	*ehl 'koh-stoh dehs-kahr-'gah-doh*	landed costs
costa (f)	*lah 'koh-stah*	coast
costado de	*ahl koh-'stah-doh deh*	alongside
coste (m)	*ehl 'koh-steh*	cost
costear	*kohs-teh-'ahr*	cost (v)
costeño	*koh-'steh-nyoh*	coastal (adj)
costo (m)	*ehl 'koh-stoh*	cost
costo colectivo	*ehl 'koh-stoh koh-lehk-'tee-boh*	joint cost
costo de arranque	*ehl 'koh-stoh deh ah-'rrahn-keh*	start-up cost
costo de capital	*ehl 'koh-stoh deh kah-ee-'tahl*	cost of capital
costo de establecerse	*ehl 'koh-stoh deh ehs-tah-bleh-'sehr-seh*	start-up cost
costo de factura	*ehl 'koh-stoh deh fahk-'too-rah*	invoice cost

costo de reemplazo	*ehl 'koh-stoh deh reh-ehm-'plah-soh*	replacement cost
costo de ventas	*ehl 'koh-stoh deh 'behn-tahs*	cost of goods sold
costo de vida	*ehl 'koh-stoh deh 'bee-dah*	cost of living
costo directo	*ehl 'koh-stoh dee-'rehk-toh*	direct cost
costo efectivo	*ehl 'koh-stoh eh-fehk-'tee-boh*	cost-effective (adj)
costo indirecto	*ehl 'koh-stoh een-dee-'rehk-toh*	indirect cost
costo marginal	*ehl 'koh-stoh mahr-hee-'nahl*	marginal cost
costo mixto	*ehl 'koh-stoh 'meek-stoh*	mixed cost
costo original	*ehl 'koh-stoh oh-ree-hee-'nahl*	original cost
costo primo	*ehl 'koh-stoh 'pree-moh*	prime cost
costo promedio	*ehl 'koh-stoh proh-'meh-dee-oh*	average cost
costo real	*ehl 'koh-stoh reh-'ahl*	actual cost
costo según factores	*ehl 'koh-stoh sey-goon fahk-'toh-rehs*	factor cost
costo total	*ehl 'koh-stoh toh-'tahl*	all-in-all cost
costo unitario	*ehl 'koh-stoh oo-nee-'tah-ree-oh*	unit cost
costo unitario promedio	*ehl 'koh-stoh oo-nee-'tah-ree-oh proh-'meh-dee-oh*	average unit cost
costo verdadero	*ehl 'koh-stoh oo-nee-'tah-ree-behr-dah-'deh-roh*	actual cost
costo y flete	*ehl 'koh-stoh ee 'fleh-teh*	cost and freight
costos controlados (mpl)	*lohs 'koh-stohs kohn-troh-'lah-dohs*	managed costs
costos de desembarco	*lohs 'koh-stohs deh dehs-ehm-'bahr-koh*	landing costs
costos de distribución	*lohs 'koh-stohs deh dees-tree-boo-see-'ohn*	distribution costs
costos de instalación	*lohs 'koh-stohs deh een-stah-lah-see-'ohn*	set-up costs
costos de oportunidad	*lohs 'koh-stohs deh oh-pohr-too-nee-'dahd*	opportunity costs
costos de producción	*lohs 'koh-stohs deh proh-dook-see-'ohn*	production costs

C

costos de reproducción	*lohs 'koh-stohs deh reh-proh-dook-see-'ohn*	reproduction costs
costos de sustitución	*lohs 'koh-stohs deh sos-tee-too-see-'ohn*	replacement costs
costos establecidos	*lohs 'koh-stohs eh-stah-bleh-'see-dohs*	standing costs
costos estándar	*lohs 'koh-stohs eh-'stahn-dahr*	standard costs
costos evitables	*lohs 'koh-stohs eh-bee-'tah-blehs*	avoidable costs
costos fijos	*lohs 'koh-stohs 'fee-hohs*	fixed costs
costos incrementados	*lohs 'koh-stohs een-kreh-mehn-'tah-dohs*	increased costs
costos normales	*lohs 'koh-stohs nohr-'mah-lehs*	standard costs
costos semi-variables	*lohs 'koh-stohs seh-mee-bah-ree-'ah-blehs*	semi-variable costs
costos variables	*lohs 'koh-stohs bah-ree-'ah-blehs*	variable costs
costumbres locales (f)	*lahs ehl kohs-'toom-brehs loh-'kah-lehs*	local customs
cotización (f)	*lah koh-tee-sah-see-'ohn*	quotation
cotización directa	*lah koh-tee-sah-see-'ohn dee-'rehk-tah*	direct quotation
cotización en ventanilla	*lah koh-tee-sah-see-'ohn ehn behn-tah-'nee-yah*	over-the-counter quotation
creciente	*kreh-see-'ehn-teh*	growing (adj)
crecimiento (m)	*ehl kreh-see-mee-'ehn-toh*	growth, increase
crecimiento corporativo	*ehl kreh-see-mee-'ehn-toh kohr-poh-rah-'tee-boh*	corporate growth
crecimiento demográfico	*ehl kreh-see-mee-'ehn-toh deh-moh-'grah-fee-koh*	increase (demographic)
crecimiento económico	*ehl kreh-see-mee-'ehn-toh eh-koh-'noh-mee-koh*	increase (economic)
crédito (m)	*ehl 'kreh-dee-toh*	credit
crédito a plazos	*ehl 'kreh-dee-toh ah 'plah-sohs*	installment credit
crédito al consumidor	*ehl 'kreh-dee-toh ahl kohn-soo-mee-'dohr*	consumer credit

crédito al fabricante con respaldo de un crédito exterior	*ehl 'kreh-dee-toh ahl fah-bree-'kahn-teh kohn rehs-'pahl-doh deh oon 'kreh-dee-toh ehks-teh-ree-'ohr*	back-to-back credit
crédito bancario	*ehl 'kreh-dee-toh bahn-'kah-ree-oh*	bank credit
crédito comercial	*ehl 'kreh-dee-toh koh-mehr-see-'ahl*	trade credit
crédito de aceptación	*ehl 'kreh-dee-toh deh ah-sehp-tah-see-'ohn*	acceptance credit
crédito de exportación	*ehl 'kreh-dee-toh deh ehks-pohr-tah-see-'ohn*	export credit
crédito de firma por aval	*ehl 'kreh-dee-toh pohr ah-'bahl*	accommodation credit
crédito del comprador	*ehl 'kreh-dee-toh dehl kohm-prah-'dohr*	buyer credit
crédito mercantil	*ehl 'kreh-dee-toh mehr-kahn-'teel*	good will
crédito para gastos de capital	*ehl 'kreh-dee-toh 'pah-rah 'gahs-tohs deh kah-pee-'tahl*	investment credit
crédito rotativo	*ehl 'kreh-dee-toh roh-tah-'tee-boh*	revolving credit
créditos monetarios (mpl)	*lohs 'kreh-dee-tohs moh-neh-'tah-ree-ohs*	monetary credits
cremallera (f)	*lah kreh-mah-yeh-rah*	zipper
crisol (m)	*ehl kree-sohl*	crucible
cristal (m) soplado	*ehl kree-stahl soh-'plah-doh*	hand-blown glass
cristalización (f)	*lah krees-tah-lee-sah-see-ohn*	crystallization
criterio para invertir (m)	*ehl kree-'teh-ree-oh 'pah-rah een-behr-'teer*	investment criteria
cromo (m)	*ehl kroh-moh*	chromium
crudo (m)	*ehl 'kroo-doh*	crude oil
crudo	*kroo-doh*	crude (adj)
crudo en exceso	*ehl 'kroo-doh ehn ehk-'seh-soh*	crude oil (excess)
cuadrícula (f)	*lah kwah-dree-koo-lah*	grid
cuadro de actividades (m)	*ehl 'kwah-droh deh ahk-tee-bee-'dah-dehs*	activity chart

cualidad (f)	*lah kwah-lee-dahd*	character
cuanto antes	*'kwahn-toh 'ahn-tehs*	as soon as possible
cuasi-dinero (m)	*'kwah-see dee-'neh-roh*	near money
cuatro colores (mpl)	*lohs kwah-trohs koh-loh-rehs*	four-color
cuba (f)	*lah koo-bah*	vat
cubierta (f)	*lah koo-bee-ehr-tah*	cover, deck
cubierta inferior	*lah koo-bee-'ehr-tah een-feh-ree-'ohr*	deck (lower)
cubierta intermedia	*lah koo-bee-'ehr-tah een-tehr-'meh-dee-ah*	deck (middle)
cubierta rústica	*lah koo-bee-ehr-tah*	softcover
cubierta superior	*lah koo-bee-'ehr-tah soo-peh-ree-'ohr*	deck (top, main)
cubierto (m)	*ehl koo-bee-ehr-toh*	place setting
cubiertos (mpl)	*lohs koo-bee-ehr-tohs*	cutlery, silverware
cubrir con colgaduras	*koo-breer kohn kohl-gah-doo-rahs*	drape (v)
cuchara (f)	*lah koo-chah-rah*	tablespoon
cucharita (f)	*lah koo-chah-ree-tah*	teaspoon
cuchillo (m)	*ehl koo-'chee-yoh*	knife
cuchillo de trinchar	*ehl koo-'chee-yoh deh treen-chah*	carving knife
cuello (m)	*ehl kweh-yoh*	collar, neck (of bottle)
cuenca (f)	*lah 'kwehn-kah*	basin
cuenca marina	*lah 'kwehn-kah mah-'ree-nah*	basin (marine)
cuenta (f)	*lah 'kwehn-tah*	account
cuenta abierta (f)	*lah 'kwehn-tah ah-bee-'ehr-tah*	open account
cuenta activa	*lah 'kwehn-tah ahk-'tee-bah*	active account
cuenta atrasada	*lah 'kwehn-tah ah-trah-'sah-dah*	delinquent account
cuenta bancaria	*lah 'kwehn-tah bahn-'kah-ree-ah*	bank account
cuenta colectiva	*lah 'kwehn-tah koh-lehk-'tee-bah*	group account

cuenta corriente	*lah 'kwehn-tah koh-rree-'ehn-tah*	current account, checking account
cuenta de ahorro	*lah 'kwehn-tah deh ah-'oh-rroh*	savings account
cuenta de capital a corto plazo	*lah 'kwehn-tah deh kah-pee-'tahl ah 'kohr-toh 'plah-soh*	short-term capital account
cuenta de capital a largo plazo	*lah 'kwehn-tah deh kah-pee-'tah ah 'lahr-goh 'plah-soh*	long-term capital account
cuenta de capital	*lah 'kwehn-tah deh kah-pee-'tahl*	capital account
cuenta de crédito	*lah 'kwehn-tah deh 'kreh-dee-toh*	charge account
cuenta de depósito	*lah 'kwehn-tah deh deh-'poh-see-toh*	deposit account
cuenta de gastos	*lah 'kwehn-tah deh 'gahs-tohs*	expense account
cuenta de ingreso	*lah 'kwehn-tah deh een-'greh-soh*	income account
cuenta de mercado monetario	*lah 'kwehn-tah deh mehr-'kah-doh moh-neh-'tah-ree-oh*	money market account
cuenta de plica	*lah 'kwehn-tah deh 'plee-kah*	escrow account
cuenta del mayor	*lah 'kwehn-tah dehl mah-'yohr*	ledger account
cuenta detallada	*lah 'kwehn-tah deh-tah-'yah-dah*	itemized account
cuenta discrecionaria	*lah 'kwehn-tah dees-kreh-see-oh-'nah-ree-ah*	discretionary account
cuenta en descubierto	*lah 'kwehn-tah dehs-koo-bee-'ehr-toh*	overdraft, overdrawn account
cuenta mancomunada (en participación)	*lah 'kwehn-tah mahn-koh-moo-'nah-dah (ehn pahr-tee-see-pah-see-'ohn)*	joint account
cuenta marginal	*lah 'kwehn-tah mahr-hee-'nahl*	marginal account
cuenta saldada	*lah 'kwehn-tah sahl-'dah-dah*	closed account (accounting)
cuentas anuales (fpl)	*lahs 'kwehn-tahs ah-noo-'ah-lehs*	annual accounts

C

cuentas aseguradas	*lahs 'kwehn-tahs ah-seh-goo-'rah-dahs*	secured accounts
cuentas incobrables	*lahs 'kwehn-tahs een-koh-'brah-blehs*	uncollectable accounts
cuentas mancomunadas	*lahs 'kwehn-tahs mahn-koh-moo-'nah-dahs*	group account
cuentas por cobrar	*lahs 'kwehn-tahs pohr koh-'brahr*	accounts receivable, notes receivable
cuentas por pagar	*lahs 'kwehn-tahs pohr pah-'gahr*	accounts payable, notes payable
cuero (m)	*ehl 'kweh-roh*	cowhide, leather, skin
cuero de becerro	*ehl 'kweh-roh deh beh-seh-rroh*	calfskin
cuero de vaca	*ehl 'kweh-roh deh bah-kah*	cowhide
cuerpo (m)	*ehl kwehr-poh*	body
cuidado razonable (m)	*ehl kwee-'dah-doh rah-soh-'nah-bleh*	reasonable care
cultivo (m)	*ehl kool-'tee-boh*	farming
cuota (f)	*lah 'kwoh-tah*	quota, allotment, lot
cuota de exportación	*lah 'kwoh-tah deh ehks-pohr-tah-see-'ohn*	export quota
cuota de importación	*lah 'kwoh-tah deh eem-pohr-tah-see-'ohn*	import quota
cuota de participación	*lah 'kwoh-tah deh pahr-tee-see-pah-see-'ohn*	participation fee
cuota de ventas	*lah 'kwoh-tah deh 'behn-tahs*	sales quota
cupón (m)	*ehl koo-'pohn*	coupon (bond interest)
cupón cero	*ehl koo-'pohn 'seh-roh*	zero coupon
cursiva	*koor-see-bah*	italic (adj)
curso del comerciante (m)	*ehl 'koor-soh dehl koh-mehr-see-'ahn-teh*	jobber's turn
cursor (m)	*ehl koor-'sohr*	cursor
curtidor (m)	*ehl koor-tee-dohr*	tanner
curtiduría (f)	*lah koor-tee-doo-'ree-ah*	tannery
curtir	*koor-'teer*	tan (v)
curva de campana (f)	*lah 'koor-bah deh kahm-'pah-nah*	bell-shaped curve

curva de frecuencia	*lah 'koor-bah deh freh-'kwehn-see-ah*	frequency curve
curva del aprendizaje	*lah 'koor-bah dehl ah-preh-dee-'sah-heh*	learning curve

CH

chaleco (m)	*ehl chah-leh-koh*	vest
chaqueta (f)	*lah chah-keh-tah*	coat
chaqueta (f) de ante	*lah chah-keh-tah deh ahn-teh*	suede jacket
chaqueta (f) deportiva	*lah chah-keh-tah deh pohr-tee-bah*	blazer
chaqueta de cabritilla	*lah chah-keh-tah deh kah-bree-tee-yah*	suede jacket
chaqueta de cuero	*lah chah-keh-tah deh 'kweh-roh*	leather jacket
cheque (m)	*ehl 'cheh-keh*	check
cheque anulado	*ehl 'cheh-kee ah-noo-'lah-doh*	voided check
cheque bancario	*ehl 'cheh-keh bahn-'kah-ree-oh*	bank check
cheque cancelado	*ehl 'cheh-keh kahn-seh-'lah-doh*	cancelled check
cheque certificado	*ehl 'cheh-keh sehr-tee-fee-'kah-doh*	certified check
cheque de gerencia	*ehl 'cheh-keh deh heh-'rehn-see-ah*	cashier's check
cheque de viajero	*ehl 'cheh-keh deh bee-ah-'heh-roh*	traveler's check
cheque registrado	*ehl 'cheh-keh reh-hee-'strah-doh*	registered check
cheque vencido	*ehl c'heh-keh behn-'see-doh*	stale check
cheques cobrados y no abonados (m)	*'cheh-kehs koh-'brah-dohs ee noh ah-boh-'nah-dohs*	float (outstanding checks)
chip (m)	*ehl cheep*	chip
chófer (m)	*ehl 'choh-fehr*	driver

D

daño (m)	*ehl 'dah-nyoh*	damage (environmental)
daño accidental	*ehl 'dah-nyoh ahk-see-dehn-'tahl*	accidental damage
daños y perjuicios (m)	*lohs 'dah-nyohs ee pehr-'hoo-ee-see-ohs*	damage
dar entrada	*dahr ehn-'trah-dah*	enter (v)
dar formato	*dahr fohr-'mah-toh*	format (v)
dar la vuelta	*'dahr lah 'bwehl-tah*	go around (v)
dato confidencial (m)	*ehl 'dah-toh kohn-fee-sehn-see-'ahl*	tip (inside information)
datos (m)	*lohs 'dah-tohs*	data
datos-entrada a la computadora	*lohs 'dah-tohs ehn-'trah-dah ah lah kohm-poo-tah-'doh-rah*	computer input
de puerta en puerta (ventas)	*deh 'pwehr-tah ehn 'pwehr-tah (behn-tahs)*	door-to-door (sales)
de un día para otro	*deh oon 'dee-ah 'pah-rah 'oh-troh*	overnight
de uso general	*deh oo-soh geh-neh-'rahl*	large-scale
debate (m)	*ehl deh-'bah-teh*	dispute
debatir	*deh-bah-'teer*	dispute (v)
débito (m)	*ehl 'deh-bee-toh*	debit, debit entry
decantador (m)	*ehl deh-kahn-tah-'dohr*	decanter
decisión de hacer o comprar (f)	*lah deh-see-see-'ohn deh ah-'sehr oh kohm-'prahr*	make-or-buy decision
declaración provisional	*lah deh-klah-rah-see-'ohn proh-bee-see-oh-'nahl*	bill of sight
declarar una huelga	*deh-klah-'rahr 'oo-nah 'wehl-gah*	call (v) (a strike)
declararse en huelga	*deh-klah-'rahr-seh ehn 'wehl-gah*	walk out (v)
decorador de escaparates (m)	*ehl deh-koh-rah-dohr deh ehs-kah-pah-rah-tehs*	window dresser
deducción (f)	*lah deh-kook-see-'ohn*	deduction
deducción por impuestos pagados en el exterior	*lah deh-kook-see-'ohn pohr eem-'pweh-stohs pah-'gah-dohs ehn ehl ehks-teh-ree-'ohr*	foreign tax credit

deducible	*deh-doo-'see-bleh*	deductible
defecto (programa) (m)	*ehl deh-'fehk-toh (proh-'grah-mah)*	bug
defecto en el programa de computación	*ehl deh-'fehk-toh ehn ehl proh-'grah-mah deh kohm-poo-tah-see-'ohn*	bug (defect in computer program)
defectuoso	*deh-fehk-too-'oh-soh*	defective
déficit (m)	*ehl 'deh-fee-seet*	deficit
deflación (f)	*lah deh-flah-see-'ohn*	deflation
deforestación (f)	*lah deh-foh-reh-stah-see-'ohn*	deforestation
degrado (m)	*ehl deh-'grah-doh*	demotion
degustación (f) de vino	*lah deh-goos-tah-see-'ohn deh bee-noh*	tasting (wine tasting)
dejar hacer	*deh-'hahr ah-'sehr*	laissez-faire
delfín (m)	*ehl dehl-'feen*	dolphin
deliberación (f)	*lah deh-lee-beh-rah-see-'ohn*	consideration (bus. law)
demanda (f)	*lah deh-'mahn-dah*	demand
demanda agregada	*lah deh-'mahn-dah ah-greh-'gah-dah*	aggregate demand
demanda o oferta inelástica	*lah deh-'mahn-dah oh oh-'fehr-tah een-eh-'lahs-tee-kah*	inelastic demand or supply
demanda para margen adicional	*lah deh-'mahn-dah 'pah-rah 'mahr-hehn ah-dee-see-oh-'nahl*	margin call
demandar	*deh-mahn-'dahr*	demand (v)
demográfico	*deh-moh-'grah-fee-koh*	demographic
demora (f)	*lah deh-'moh-rah*	demurrage, delay
densidad (f)	*lah dehn-see-'dahd*	density
departamento (m)	*ehl deh-pahr-tah-'mehn-toh*	department
departamento arrendado	*ehl deh-pahr-tah-'mehn-toh ah-rrehn-'dah-doh*	leased department
departamento de contabilidad	*ehl deh-pahr-tah-'mehn-toh deh kohn-tah-bee-lee-'dahd*	accounting department
departamento de ingeniería y diseño	*ehl deh-pahr-tah-'mehn-toh deh een-heh-nee-eh-'ree-ah ee dee-'seh-nyoh*	engineering and design department

D

departamento de personal	*ehl deh-pahr-tah-'mehn-toh deh pehr-soh-'nahl*	personnel department
depositaria (f)	*lah deh-poh-see-'tah-ree-ah*	depository
depósito (m)	*ehl deh-'poh-see-toh*	deposit, warehouse
depósito a la vista	*ehl deh-'poh-see-toh ah lah 'bees-tah*	demand deposit
depósito a plazo	*ehl deh-'poh-see-toh ah 'plah-soh*	time deposit
depósito bancario	*ehl deh-'poh-see-toh bahn-'kah-ree-oh*	bank deposit
depósito nocturno	*ehl deh-'poh-see-toh nohk-'toor-noh*	night depository
depósitos de importación (mpl)	*ehl deh-'poh-see-toh deh eem-pohr-tah-see-'ohn*	import deposits
depreciación (f)	*lah deh-preh-see-ah-see-'ohn*	depreciation
depreciación acelerada	*lah deh-preh-see-ah-see-'ohn ah-seh-leh-'rah-dah*	accelerated depreciation
depreciación acumulada	*lah deh-preh-see-ah-see-'ohn ah-koo-moo-'lah-dah*	accrued depreciation, accumulated depreciation
depreciación de la moneda	*lah deh-preh-see-ah-see-'ohn deh lah moh-'neh-dah*	depreciation of currency
depresión (f)	*depresión (f)*	depression
derecho (m) de autor	*ehl deh-reh-choh deh ow-tohr*	copyright
derecho al voto	*ehl deh-'reh-choh ahl 'boh-toh*	voting right
derecho de aduana	*ehl deh-'reh-choh deh ah-'dwah-nah*	customs duty
derecho de patente	*ehl deh-'reh-choh deh pah-'tehn-teh*	patent law
derecho de prioridad	*ehl deh-'reh-choh deh pree-oh-ree-'dahd*	pre-emptive right
derecho de recurso	*ehl deh-'reh-choh deh reh-'koor-soh*	right of recourse
derecho mercantil	*ehl deh-'reh-choh mehr-kahn-'teel*	mercantile law
derecho preferencial	*ehl deh-'reh-choh preh-feh-rehn-see-'ahl*	pre-emptive right

derecho protector contra importación a precios arbitrarios	*ehl deh-'reh-choh proh-tehk-'tohr 'kohn-trah eem-pohr-tah-see-'ohn ah 'preh-see-ohs ahr-bee-'trah-ree-ohs*	anti-dumping duty
derechos (mpl)	*lohs deh-'reh-chos*	duties, rights
derechos adquiridos	*lohs deh-'reh-chohs ahd-kee-'ree-dohs*	acquired rights, vested rights
derechos de anclaje	*lohs deh-'reh-chohs deh ahn-'klah-heh*	anchorange (dues)
derechos de autor	*lohs deh-'reh-chohs deh ow-'tohr*	copyright
derechos de cabotaje	*lohs deh-reh-choz deh kah-boh-tah-heh*	pilotage
derechos de exportación	*lohs deh-'reh-chohs deh ehks-pohr-tah-see-'ohn*	export duty
derechos de la licencia	*lohs deh-'reh-chohs deh lah lee-'sehn-see-ah*	license fees
derechos de practicaje	*lohs deh-'reh-chohs deh prahk-tee-'kah-heh*	pilotage
derechos económicos	*lohs deh-'reh-chohs eh-koh-'noh-mee-kohs*	entitlements
derechos portuarios	*lohs deh-'reh-chohs pohr-too-'ah-ree-ohs*	harbor dues
derechos únicos	*lohs deh-'reh-chohs 'oo-nee-kohs*	sole rights
derrame de petróleo (m)	*ehl deh-'rrah-meh deh peh-'troh-leh-oh*	oil spill
desalineado	*dehs-ah-lee-neh-'ah-doh*	off line
desaparición (f)	*lah dehs-ah-pah-ree-see-'ohn*	disappearance
desarrollado	*dehs-ah-rroh-'yah-doh*	developed (adj)
desarrollar	*dehs-ah-rroh-'yahr*	develop (v)
desarrollar relaciones comerciales	*dehs-ah-roh-'yahr reh-lah-see-'oh-nehs koh-mehr-see-'ah-lehs*	network (v)
desarrollo (m)	*ehl deh-sah-'rroh-yoh*	development
desarrollo de un nuevo producto	*ehl dehs-ah-'rroh-yoh deh oon noo-'eh-boh proh-'dook-toh*	new product development
desarrollo del producto	*ehl dehs-ah-'rroh-yoh dehl proh-'dook-toh*	product development

D

D

desarrollo económico	*ehl deh-sah-'rroh-yoh eh-koh-'noh-mee-koh*	development (economic)
desarrollo urbano	*ehl deh-sah-'rroh-yoh oor-'bah-noh*	development (urban)
descarga (f)	*lah dehs-'kahr-gah*	unloading, exhaust
descargar	*dehs-kahr-'gahr*	discharge, unload (v)
descargo (m)	*ehl dehs-'kahr-goh*	charge-off
descenso (m)	*ehl deh-'sehn-soh*	demotion
descenso brusco de precios	*ehl deh-'sehn-soh 'broos-koh deh 'preh-see-ohs*	slump
descongelador (m)	*ehl dehs-kohn-heh-lah-dohr*	defroster
descripción del trabajo (f)	*lah dehs-kreep-see-'ohn dehl trah-'bah-hoh*	job description
descubrimiento de (aceite) (m)	*ehl dehs-koo-bree-mee-'ehn-toh deh ah-'seh-ee-teh*	find (oil)
descubrir	*dehs-koo-'breer*	locate (v)
descuento (m)	*ehl dehs-'kwehn-toh*	discount, drawback
descuento cambiario	*ehl dehs-'kwehn-toh kahm-bee-'ah-ree-oh*	exchange discount
descuento comercial	*ehl dehs-'kwehn-toh koh-mehr-see-'ahl*	trade discount
descuento en efectivo	*ehl dehs-'kwehn-toh ehn eh-fehk-'tee-boh*	cash discount
descuento por cantidad	*ehl dehs-kwehn-toh pohr kahn-tee-dahd*	quantity discount
descuento por pronto pago	*ehl dehs-'kwehn-toh pohr 'prohn-toh 'pah-goh*	cash discount
descuento sobre el volumen	*ehl dehs-'kwehn-toh 'soh-breh ehl boh-'loo-mehn*	volume discount
descuento unitario por carga	*ehl dehs-'kwehn-toh oo-nee-'tah-ree-oh pohr 'kahr-gah*	unit load discount
desembolso (m)	*ehl dehs-ehm-'bohl-soh*	outlay, disbursement
desempleo (m)	*ehl dehs-ehm-'pleh-oh*	unemployment
desequilibrio (m)	*ehl dehs-eh-kee-'lee-bree-oh*	imbalance
desertificación (f)	*lah deh-sehr-tee-fee-kah-see-'ohn*	desertification
desfalco (m)	*ehl dehs-'fahl-koh*	embezzlement
desfavorable	*dehs-fah-boh-'rah-bleh*	unfavorable

desgaste (m)	*ehl dehs-'gah-steh*	waste
desgravamen (m)	*ehl dehs-grah-'bah-mehn*	tax relief
desgravamen impositivo	*ehl dehs-grah-'bah-mehn eem-poh-see-'tee-boh*	tax deduction
desgravamen personal	*ehl dehs-grah-'bah-mehn pehr-soh-'nahl*	personal deduction
deshecho (m)	*ehl dehs-'eh-choh*	scrap
desierto (m)	*ehl deh-see-'ehr-toh*	desert
desincentivo (m)	*ehl dehs-een-sehn-'tee-boh*	disincentive
desmontar	*dehs-mohn-'tahr*	stripping (v)
despacho (m)	*ehl dehs-'pah-choh*	shipment
despacho directo del fabricante al detallista	*ehl dehs-'pah-choh dee-'rehk-toh dehl fah-bree-'kahn-teh ahl deh-tah-'yees-tah*	drop shipment
despedir	*dehs-peh-'deer*	discharge, fire (v)
desperdicio (m)	*ehl dehs-pehr-'dee-see-oh*	spoilage
despido (m)	*ehl dehs-'pee-doh*	lay-off
despoblación forestal (f)	*lah dehs-poh-blah-see-'ohn foh-reh-'stahl*	deforestation
despojamiento (m)	*ehl dehs-poh-hah-mee-'ehn-toh*	divestment
después del día de vencimiento	*dehs-'pwehs dehl 'dee-ah deh behn-see-mee-'ehn-toh*	afterdate
desteñir	*dehs-teh-'nyeer*	bleed (v) (in printing)
destilación (f)	*lah dehs-tee-lah-see-ohn*	distillation
destrucción (f)	*lah deh-strook-see-'ohn*	destruction
desventaja (f)	*lah dehs-behn-'tah-hah*	handicap, disadvantage
desviación estándar (f)	*lah dehs-bee-ah-see-'ohn eh-'stahn-dahr*	standard deviation
desvío (m)	*ehl dehs-'bee-oh*	diversion
detallar	*deh-tah-'yahr*	itemize (v)
detallista (m)	*ehl deh-tah-'yees-tah*	dealer
detector (m)	*ehl deh-tehk-'tohr*	detector
deterioro (m)	*ehl deh-teh-ree-'oh-roh*	spoilage, deterioration
deterioro natural debido al uso	*ehl deh-teh-ree-'oh-roh deh-'bee-doh ahl 'oo-soh*	wear and tear

D

deuda (f)	*lah deh-'oo-dah*	debt
deuda a corto plazo	*lah deh-'oo-dah ah 'kohr-toh 'plah-soh*	short-term debt
deuda a largo plazo	*lah deh-'oo-dah ah 'lahr-goh 'plah-soh*	long-term debt
deuda con vencimiento de más de un año	*lah deh-'oo-dah kohn behn-see-mee-'ehn-toh deh mahs deh oon 'ah-nyoh*	funded debt
deuda consolidada	*lah deh-'oo-dah kohn-soh-lee-'dah-dah*	funded debt
deuda extranjera	*lah deh-'oo-dah ehks-trahn-'heh-rah*	foreign debt
deuda flotante	*lah deh-'oo-dah floh-'tahn-teh*	floating debt, unfunded debt
deuda incobrable	*lah deh-'oo-dah een-koh-'brah-bleh*	bad debt
deuda nacional	*lah deh-'oo-dah nah-see-oh-'nahl*	national debt
deuda no cobrada	*lah deh-'oo-dah noh koh-'brah-dah*	outstanding debt
deudas activas (fpl)	*lahs deh-'oo-dahs ahk-'tee-bahs*	active debts
deudas preferenciales	*lahs deh-'oo-dah preh-feh-rehn-see-'ah-lehs*	preferential debts
devaluación (f)	*lah deh-bah-loo-ah-see-'ohn*	devaluation
devoluciones por adelantado (fpl)	*lahs deh-boh-loo-see-'oh-nehs pohr ah-deh-lahn-'tah-doh*	advance refunding
día de liquidación en bolsa (m)	*ehl 'dee-ah deh lee-kee-dah-see-'ohn ehm 'bohl-sah*	account day
día feriado bancario	*ehl 'dee-ah feh-ree-'ah-doh*	bank holiday
día feriado pagado	*ehl 'dee-ah feh-ree-'ah-doh pah-'gah-doh*	paid holiday
día festivo legal	*ehl 'dee-ah fehs-tee-boh leh-'gahl*	legal holiday
diabetis (f)	*lah dee-ah-beh-tees*	diabetes
diacidificación biológica (f)	*lah dee-ah-see-dee-fee-kah-see-ohn bee-oh-loh-hee-kah*	biological diacidizing
diagrama (m)	*ehl dee-ah-'grah-mah*	graph

diagrama de flujo	*ehl dee-ah-'grah-mah deh 'floo-hoh*	flow chart
diagrama de sectores	*ehl dee-ah-'grah-mah deh sehk-'toh-rehs*	pie chart
diario (m)	*ehl dee-'ah-ree-oh*	daily, journal
diás de estadía (mpl)	*lohs 'dee-ahs deh ehs-tah-'dee-ah*	lay time, lay days
dibujo (m) lineal	*ehl dee-boo-hoh lee-neh-'ahl*	line drawing
diccionario (m)	*ehl deek-see-oh-'nah-ree-oh*	dictionary
diferencia (f)	*lah dee-feh-'rehn-see-ah*	spread
diferencia bruta	*lah dee-feh-'rehn-see-ah 'broo-tah*	gross spread
diferencia de precios	*lah dee-feh-'rehn-see-ah deh 'preh-see-ohs*	price differential
diferencia de tarifas	*lah dee-feh-'rehn-see-ah deh tah-'ree-fahs*	tariff differential
diferencia entre precio y costo tan pequeña que puede originar la quiebra	*lah dee-feh-'rehn-see-ah 'ehn-treh 'preh-see-oh ee 'koh-stoh tahn peh-'keh-nyah keh 'pweh-deh oh-ree-hee-'nahr lah kee-'eh-brah*	cost-price squeeze
diferencia entre precios de entrega inmediata y futura	*lah dee-feh-'rehn-see-ah 'ehn-treh 'preh-see-ohs deh ehn-'treh-gah een-meh-dee-'ah-tah ee foo-'too-rah*	backwardation
digital	*dee-hee-'tahl*	digital (adj)
digital (f)	*lah dee-hee-'tahl*	digitalis
dígito binario (m)	*ehl 'dee-hee-toh bee-'nah-ree-oh*	bit
dilución (f)	*lah dee-loo-see-'ohn*	dilution
dinámica de grupo (f)	*lah dee-'nah-mee-kah deh 'groo-poh*	group dynamics
dinámica del mercado	*lah dee-'nah-mee-kah dehl mehr-'kah-doh*	market dynamics
dinámica del producto	*lah dee-'nah-mee-kah dehl proh-'dook-toh*	product dynamics
dinero (m)	*ehl dee-'neh-roh*	money
dinero a la vista	*ehl dee-'neh-roh ah lah 'bees-tah*	call money

D

dinero en circulación	*ehl dee-'neh-roh ehn seer-koo-lah-see-'ohn*	currency
dinero nuevo	*ehl dee-'neh-roh noo-'eh-boh*	new money
diodo (m)	*ehl dee-'oh-doh*	diode
dióxido de nitrógeno (m)	*ehl dee-'ohk-see-doh deh nee-'troh-heh-noh*	nitrogen dioxide
dirección neumática (f)	*lah dee-rehk-see-'ohn neh-oo-'mah-tee-kah*	power steering
direcciones (fpl)	*lahs dee-rehk-see-'oh-nehs*	guidelines
directo	*dee-'rehk-toh*	on-line
director (m)	*ehl dee-rehk-'tohr*	director
director ejecutivo	*ehl dee-rehk-'tohr eh-heh-koo-'tee-boh*	executive director, chief executive
director financiero	*ehl dee-rehk-'tohr fee-nahn-see-'eh-roh*	financial director
directorio (m)	*ehl dee-rehk-'toh-ree-oh*	directory
directorio entrelazado	*ehl dee-rehk-'toh-ree-oh ehn-treh-lah-'sah-doh*	interlocking directorate
dirigir	*dee-ree-'heer*	manage (v)
disco (m)	*ehl 'dees-koh*	disk, record
disco compacto	*ehl 'dees-koh kohm-'pahk-toh*	compact disk
disco flexible	*ehl 'dees-koh flehk-'see-bleh*	floppy disk
disco flexible de capacidad pequeña	*ehl 'dees-koh flehk-'see-bleh deh kah-pah-see-'dahd peh-'keh-nyah*	diskette
disco láser	*ehl 'dees-koh 'lah-sehr*	laser disk
discrecional	*dees-kreh-see-oh-'nahl*	optional
discusión (f)	*lah dees-koo-see-'ohn*	dispute
discusión laboral	*lah dees-koo-see-'ohn lah-boh-'rahl*	labor dispute
discutir	*dees-koo-'teer*	dispute (v)
diseñador (m)	*ehl dee-seh-nyah-dohr*	designer
diseñador de alta costura	*ehl dee-seh-nyah-dohr deh ahl-tah-koh-stoo-rah*	high fashion designer
diseñar	*dee-seh-nyahr*	design (v)
diseño (m)	*ehl dee-'seh-nyoh*	pattern, layout

diseño de sistemas	*ehl dee-'seh-nyoh deh sees-'teh-mahs*	systems design
diseño del producto	*ehl dee-'seh-nyoh dehl proh-'dook-toh*	product design
disminución (f)	*lah dees-mee-noo-see-'ohn*	abatement
disminución de la producción para el interior en favor de la exportación en naciones subdesarrolladas	*lah dees-mee-noo-see-'ohn deh lah proh-dook-see-'ohn 'pah-rah ehl een-teh-ree-'ohr ehn fah-'bohr deh lah ehks-pohr-tah-see-'ohn ehn nah-see-'oh-nehs soob-dehs-ah-rroh-'yah-dahs*	backwash effect
disminución de un impuesto	*lah dees-mee-noo-see-'ohn deh oon eem-'pwehs-toh*	remission of a tax
disponbilidades (f)	*lahs dees-poh-nee-bee-lee-'dah-dehs*	actuals
disponible	*dees-poh-'nee-bleh*	at call, available
dispositivo (m)	*ehl dees-poh-see-'tee-boh*	device
dispositivo de disco	*ehl dees-poh-see-'tee-boh deh 'dees-koh*	disk drive
dispositivo de exploración	*ehl dees-poh-see-'tee-boh deh ehk-sploh-rah-see-'ohn*	scanner
disputa salarial (f)	*lah dees-'poo-tah sah-lah-ree-'ahl*	wage dispute
disputar	*dees-poo-'tahr*	dispute (v)
distribución (f)	*lah dees-tree-boo-see-'ohn*	distribution
distribuidor (m)	*ehl dees-tree-boo-ee-'dohr*	distributor
distribuir	*dees-tree-boo-'eer*	distribute (v)
diurético (m)	*ehl dee-oo-'reh-tee-koh*	diuretic
diversificación (f)	*lah dee-behr-see-fee-kah-see-'ohn*	diversification
dividendo (m)	*ehl dee-bee-'dehn-doh*	dividend
dividendo de capital	*ehl dee-bee-'dehn-doh deh kah-pee-'tahl*	liquidating dividend
dividendo en efectivo	*ehl dee-bee-'dehn-doh ehn eh-fehk-'tee-boh*	cash dividend
dividendo incluso	*ehl dee-bee-'dehn-doh een-'kloo-soh*	cum dividend

dividendos en acciones (mpl)	*lohs dee-bee-'dehn-dohs ehn ahk-see-'oh-nehs*	stock dividend
dividendos extras	*lohs dee-bee-'dehn-dohs 'ehks-trahs*	extra dividends
dividendos omitidos	*lohs dee-bee-'dehn-dohs oh-mee-'tee-dohs*	passed dividends
divisas (f)	*lahs dee-'bee-sahs*	foreign exchange (hard currencies)
división de acciones (f)	*lah dee-bee-see-'ohn deh ahk-see-'oh-nehs*	stock split
división del trabajo	*lah dee-bee-see-'ohn dehl trah-'bah-hoh*	division of labor
dobladillo (m)	*ehl doh-blah-'dee-yoh*	hem
documentación (f)	*lah doh-koo-mehn-tah-see-'ohn*	documentation
documento (m)	*ehl doh-koo-'mehn-toh*	document, indenture, official paper, instrument
documento avalado	*ehl doh-koo-'mehn-toh ah-bah-'lah-doh*	accommodation paper
documento director	*ehl doh-koo-'mehn-toh dee-rehk-'tohr*	direct paper
documento limpio	*ehl doh-koo-'mehn-toh 'leem-pee-oh*	clean document
documento público donde se enumeran a los aseguradores de una emisión de valores	*ehl doh-koo-'mehn-toh 'poo-blee-koh 'dohn-deh seh eh-noo-'meh-rahn ah lohs ah-seh-goo-rah-'doh-rehs deh 'oo-nah eh-mee-see-'ohn deh bah-'loh-rehs*	tombstone
documentos de trabajo (mpl)	*lohs doh-koo-'mehn-tohs deh trah-'bah-hoh*	working papers
domicilio de la empresa (m)	*ehl doh-mee-'see-lee-oh deh lah ehm-'preh-sah*	place of business
dominio público (m)	*ehl doh-'mee-nee-oh 'poo-blee-koh*	public domain
donación (f)	*lah doh-nah-see-'ohn*	bequest
dosis (f)	*lah 'doh-sees*	dosage, dose
dotación (f)	*lah doh-tah-see-'ohn*	endowment
droga (f)	*lah 'droh-gah*	drug
dueño (m)	*ehl 'dweh-nyoh*	proprietor
dueño ausente	*ehl 'dweh-nyoh ow-'sehn-teh*	absentee ownership

D

duopolio (m)	*ehl doo-oh-'poh-lee-oh*	duopoly
duplicación (f)	*lah doo-plee-kah-see-'ohn*	overlap
dureza (f)	*lah do-'reh-sah*	hardness

E

econometría (f)	*lah eh-koh-noh-meh-'tree-ah*	econometrics
economía (f)	*lah eh-koh-noh-'mee-ah*	economics
economía controlada	*lah eh-koh-noh-'mee-ah kohn-troh-'lah-dah*	managed economy
economía de aficionados	*lah eh-koh-noh-'mee-ah deh ah-fee-see-oh-'nah-dohs*	jawbone (economics)
economía de escala	*lah eh-koh-noh-'mee-ah deh ehs-'kah-lah*	economy of scale
economía keynesiana	*lah eh-koh-noh-'mee-ah keh-neh-see-'ah-nah*	Keynesian economics
económico	*eh-koh-'noh-mee-koh*	economic
ecosistema (m)	*ehl eh-koh-sees-'teh-mah*	ecosystem
editar	*eh-dee-'tahr*	edit (v)
editorial de despacho (f)	*lah eh-dee-toh-ree-'ahl deh dehs-'pah-choh*	desktop publishing
editorial de sobremesa	*lah eh-dee-toh-ree-'ahl deh soh-breh-'meh-sah*	desktop publishing
efectivo (m)	*ehl eh-fehk-'tee-boh*	cash
efectivo disponible	*ehl eh-fehk-'tee-boh dees-poh-'nee-bleh*	ready cash
efectivo pagado por adelantado	*ehl eh-fehk-'tee-boh pah-'gah-doh pohr ah-deh-lahn-'tah-doh*	cash in advance
efectivo para cubrir letras en blanco	*ehl eh-fehk-'tee-boh 'pah-rah koo-'breer 'leh-trahs ehn 'blahn-koh*	open cover
efecto contra dos personas (m)	*ehl eh-'fehk-toh 'kohn-trah dohs pehr-'soh-nahs*	two-name paper
efecto invernadero	*ehl eh-'fehk-toh een-behr-nah-'deh-roh*	warming effect
efectos agrícolas (mpl)	*lohs eh-'fehk-tohs ah-'gree-koh-lahs*	agricultural paper
eficiencia (f)	*lah eh-fee-see-'ehn-see-ah*	efficiency

egreso (m)	*ehl eh-'greh-soh*	disbursement
eje (m) de leva	*ehl eh-heh deh 'leh-bah*	camshaft
eje trasero	*ehl eh-heh trah-'seh-roh*	rear axle
ejecutivo (m)	*ehl eh-heh-koo-'tee-boh*	executive
ejecutivo de cuentas	*ehl eh-heh-koo-'tee-boh deh 'kwehn-tahs*	account executive
ejecutivo de la organización	*ehl eh-heh-koo-'tee-boh deh lah ohr-gah-nee-sah-see-'ohn*	line executive
ejecutor testamentario (m)	*ehl eh-heh-koo-'tohr tehs-tah-mehn-'tah-ree-oh*	executor
ejemplar (m)	*ehl eh-hehm-'plahr*	copy (text)
ejemplar gratuito	*ehl eh-hehm-'plahr grah-too-'ee-toh*	complimentary copy
ejercicio (período) financiero (m)	*ehl eh-hehr-'see-see-oh (peh-'ree-oh-doh) fee-nahn-see-'eh-roh*	financial period
ejercicio financiero	*ehl eh-hehr-'see-see-oh fee-nahn-see-'eh-roh*	financial year
ejercicio período contable	*ehl eh-hehr-'see-see-oh peh-'ree-oh-doh kohn-'tah-bleh*	accounting period
ejercicios prácticos (mpl)	*lohs eh-hehr-'see-see-ohs 'prahk-tee-kohs*	workshop
elaboración de los datos (f)	*lah eh-lah-boh-rah-see-'ohn deh lohs 'dah-tohs*	data processing
elasticidad de precio (f)	*lah eh-lahs-tee-see-'dahd deh 'preh-see-oh*	price elasticity
electricidad (f)	*lah eh-lehk-tree-see-'dahd*	electricity
electrodo (m)	*ehl eh-lehk-'troh-doh*	electrode
electroestática (f)	*lah eh-lehk-troh-eh-'stah-tee-kah*	electrostatic
electrólisis (f)	*lah eh-lehk-'troh-lee-sees*	electrolysis
electromecánica (f)	*lah eh-lehk-troh-meh-'kah-nee-kah*	electromagnetics
electrón (m)	*ehl eh-lehk-'trohn*	electron
electrónico	*eh-lehk-'troh-nee-koh*	electronic (adj)
elefante (m)	*ehl eh-leh-'fahn-teh*	elephant
elemento (m)	*ehl eh-leh-'mehn-toh*	element

elementos sobresalientes financieros (mpl)	*lohs eh-leh-'mehn-tohs soh-breh-sah-lee-'ehn-tehs fee-nahn-see-'eh-rohs*	financial highlights
eliminación (f)	*lah eh-lee-mee-nah-see-'ohn*	dropout, suppression
eliminar	*eh-lee-mee-'nahr*	delete (v)
eliminar gradualmente	*eh-lee-mee-'nahr grah-doo-ahl-'mehn-teh*	phase out
embalaje (m)	*ehl ehm-bah-'lah-heh*	packaging
embalaje de cajas	*ehl ehm-bah-'lah-heh deh 'kah-hahs*	packing case
embargo (m)	*ehl ehm-'bahr-goh*	embargo
embargue ferroviario (m)	*ehl ehm-'bahr-geh feh-rroh-bee-'ah-ree-oh*	rail shipment
embarque futuro	*ehl ehm-'bahr-keh foo-'too-roh*	forward shipment
embarques aéreos (mpl)	*lohs ehm-'bahr-kehs ah-'eh-reh-ohs*	air shipments
embarques ilegales	*lohs ehm-'bahr-kehs ee-leh-'gah-lehs*	illegal shipments
embrague (m)	*ehl ehm-'brah-gee*	clutch
emisión (f)	*lah eh-mee-see-'ohn*	issue (stock)
emisión de bonos	*lah eh-mee-see-'ohn deh 'boh-nohs*	bond issue
emisión de moneda	*lah eh-mee-see-'ohn deh moh-'neh-dah*	mint
emisión fiduciaria	*lah eh-mee-see-'ohn deh fee-doo-see-'ah-ree-ah*	fiduciary issue
emisión prioritaria	*lah eh-mee-see-'ohn pree-oh-ree-'tah-ree-ah*	senior issue
emisiones (fpl)	*lahs eh-mee-see-'oh-nehs*	emissions
emisiones tóxicas	*lahs eh-mee-see'oh-nehs 'tohk-see-kahs*	emissions (toxic)
emitir	*eh-mee-'teer*	issue (v)
emitir	*eh-mee-'teer*	broadcast (v) (radio)
emitir valores	*eh-mee-'teer bah-'loh-rehs*	float (v) (issue stock)
emplazamiento (m)	*ehl ehm-plah-sah-mee-'ehn-toh*	garnishment
empleado (m)	*ehl ehm-pleh-'ah-doh*	employee

E

emprender	*ehm-prehn-'dehr*	undertake (v)
empresa (f)	*lah ehm-'preh-sah*	firm, enterprise
empresa asociada	*lah ehm-'preh-sah ah-soh-see-'ah-dah*	member firm
empresa de alta tecnología	*lah ehm-'preh-sah deh 'ahl-tah tehk-noh-loh-'hee-ah*	high technology firm
empresa de crédito	*lah ehm-'preh-sah deh 'kreh-dee-toh*	lending firm
empresa de transporte	*lah ehm-'preh-sah deh trahns-'pohr-teh*	freight forwarder, common carrier
empresa de transporte por contrato	*lah ehm-'preh-sah deh trahns-'pohr-teh pohr kohn-'trah-toh*	contract carrier
empresa multinacional	*lah ehm-'preh-sah mool-tee-nah-see-oh-'nahl*	multinational corporation
empresa nueva en la que se arriesga capital	*lah ehm-'preh-sah noo-'eh-bah ehn lah keh seh ah-rree-'ehs-gah kah-pee-'tahl*	venture capital
empresario (m)	*ehl eem-'preh-'sah-ree-oh*	entrepreneur
empresas vinculadas a otras que operan como si no lo fueran (fpl)	*lahs ehm-'preh-sahs been-koo-'lah-dahs ah 'oh-trahs keh oh-'peh-rahn 'koh-moh see noh loh 'fweh-rahn*	arm's length
en consignación	*ehn kohn-seeg-nah-see-ohn*	on consignment
en el futuro	*ehn ehl foo-'too-roh*	down the line
en el mejor de los casos	*ehn ehl meh-'hohr deh lohs 'kah-sohs*	at best
en el mercado	*ehn ehl mehr-'kah-doh*	at the market
en el reverso	*ehn ehl reh-'behr-soh*	on the back
en fábrica	*ehn 'fah-bree-kah*	ex mill
en la mina	*ehn lah 'mee-nah*	ex mine
en línea	*ehn 'lee-neh-ah*	on line
en mora	*ehn 'moh-rah*	overdue
en respuesta a	*ehn rehs-'pwehs-tah ah*	in reply to
en tránsito	*ehn 'trahn-see-toh*	in transit
en vías de desarrollo	*ehn 'bee-ahs deh dehs-ah-'rroh-yoh*	developing (adj)
en y desde	*ehn ee 'dehs-deh*	at and from

encaje (m)	*ehl ehn-kah-heh*	lace
encañar	*ehn-kah-nyahr*	stalking (v)
encarte (m)	*ehl ehn-kahr-teh*	insert
encendido (f)	*ehl ehn-sehn-dee-doh*	ignition
enchufable	*ehn-choo-'fah-bleh*	plug-in (adj)
encuadernación (f) perfecta	*lah ehn-kwah-dehr-nah-see-ohn pehr-fehk-tah*	perfect binding
endeudado	*ehn-dee-oo-'dah-doh*	in the red
endeudamiento (m)	*ehl ehn-deh-oo-dah-mee-'ehn-toh*	indebtedness
endosatorio (m)	*ehl ehn-doh-sah-'toh-ree-oh*	endorsee
endoso (m)	*ehl ehn-'doh-soh*	endorsement
endoso de favor	*ehl ehn-'doh-soh deh fah-'bohr*	accommodation endorsement
endoso limitado	*ehl ehn-'doh-soh lee-mee-'tah-doh*	qualified acceptance endorsement
energía (f)	*lah eh-nehr-'hee-ah*	power, energy
enfermedad (f)	*lah ehn-fehr-meh-'dahd*	disease
enfermedad contagiosa	*lah ehn-fehr-meh-'dahd kohn-tah-hee-'oh-sah*	disease (contagious)
enfermedad mortal	*lah ehn-fehr-meh-'dahd mohr-'tahl*	disease (deadly)
enfermedad respiratoria	*lah ehn-fehr-meh-'dahd reh-spee-rah-'toh-ree-ah*	disease (respiratory)
engaño (m)	*ehl ehn-'gah-nyoh*	double dealing, fraud, deceit
engañoso	*ehn-gah-'nyoh-soh*	misleading
enlace (m)	*ehl ehn-'lah-seh*	liaison
enlace de comunicación	*ehl ehn-'lah-seh deh koh-moo-nee-kah-see-'ohn*	communication link
enmendar	*ehn-mehn-'dahr*	amend (v)
enmienda (f)	*lah ehn-mee-'ehn-dah*	amendment
ensamblar	*ehn-sahm-'blahr*	assemble (v)
ensayo (m)	*ehl ehn-'sah-yoh*	assay
entrada (f)	*lah ehn-'trah-dah*	input, entry
entrada de aduana	*lah ehn-'trah-dah deh ah-'dwah-nah*	customs entry
entrada de datos	*lah ehn-'trah-dah deh 'dah-tohs*	data entry

E

entrada de efectivo	*lah ehn-'trah-dah deh eh-fehk-'tee-boh*	cash entry
entrada en el libro mayor	*lah ehn-'trah-dah ehn ehl 'lee-broh mah-'yohr*	ledger entry
entrar	*ehn-'trahr*	enter (v)
entre bancos 'ehn-treh 'bahn-kohs	*'ehn-treh 'bahn-kohs*	interbank
entredós (m)	*ehl ehn-treh-dohs*	insert
entrega (f)	*lah ehn-'treh-gah*	delivery
la entrega al momento y pago en efectivo	*lah ehn-'tren-gah ahl moh-mehn-toh ee 'pah-goh ehn eh-fehk-'tee-boh*	cash delivery
entrega en descubierto	*lah ehn-'treh-gah ehn dehs-koo-bee-'ehr-toh*	short delivery
entrega inmediata	*lah ehn-'treh-gah een-meh-dee-'ah-tah*	spot delivery
entregas diferidas (fpl)	*lahs ehn-'treh-gahs dee-feh-'ree-dahs*	deferred deliveries
entrenamiento recíproco (m)	*ehl ehn-treh-nah-mee-'ehn-toh reh-'see-proh-koh*	reciprocal training
entrevista (f)	*lah ehn-treh-'bees-tah*	interview
envasado en la viña	*ehn-bah-sah-doh ehn lah bee-nyah*	estate bottled
envase (m)	*ehl ehn-'bah-seh*	container
envejecimiento (m)	*ehl ehn-beh-heh-see-mee-ehn-toh*	aging
envenenar	*ehn-beh-neh-'nahr*	poison (v)
envío (m)	*ehl ehn-'bee-oh*	shipment, dispatch
envío de paquetes por correo	*ehl ehn-'bee-oh deh pah-'keh-tehs pohr koh-'rreh-oh*	parcel post
envío incompleto	*ehl ehn-'bee-oh een-kohm-'pleh-toh*	short shipment
enzima (f)	*lah ehn-'see-mah*	enzyme
equilibrio (m)	*ehl eh-kee-'lee-bree-oh*	balance (economic)
equipo (m)	*ehl eh-'kee-poh*	rolling stock, equipment
equipo administrativo	*ehl eh-'kee-poh ahd-mee-nee-strah-'tee-boh*	management team

E

equipo auxiliar	*ehl eh-'kee-poh owk-see-lee-ahr*	ancillary
equipo gerencial	*ehl eh-'kee-poh heh-rehn-'see-'ahl*	management team
equipos (mpl)	*lohs eh-'kee-pohs*	hardware
ergonomía (f)	*lah ehr-goh-noh-'mee-ah*	ergonomics
erogación (f)	*lah eh-roh-gah-see-'ohn*	expenditure
erosión	*eh-roh-see-'ohn*	erosion
error (m)	*ehl eh-'rrohr*	error
error de procesamiento	*ehl eh-'rrohr deh proh-seh-sah-mee-'ehn-toh*	processing error
escala (f)	*lah eh-'skah-lah*	range
escala móvil	*lah eh-'skah-lah 'moh-beel*	sliding scale
escala salarial	*lah eh-'skah-lah sah-lah-ree-'ahl*	wage scale
escaparatista (m)	*ehl ehs-kah-pah-rah-'tees*	window dresser
escape (m)	*ehl ehs-'kah-peh*	exhaust
escasez (f)	*lah ehs-kah-'sehs*	shortage, short supply
escritura (f)	*lah ehs-kree-'too-rah*	deed, script, writ
escritura de constitución (de una sociedad anónima)	*lah ehs-kree-'too-rah deh kohn-stee-too-see-'ohn (deh oo-nah soh-see-eh-dahd ah-'noh-nee-mah)*	certificate of incorporation
escritura de fideicomiso	*lah ehs-kree-'too-rah deh fee-deh-ee-koh-'mee-soh*	deed of trust
escudilla (f)	*lah ehs-koo-'dee-yah*	bowl
esmerilaje (m)	*ehl ehs-mehs-ree-lah-heh*	grinding
esmoquin (m)	*ehl ehs-'moh-keen*	tuxedo
especialista (m/f)	*eh-speh-see-ah-'lees-tah*	specialist
especialista (el miembro de la bolsa de valores responsable de mantener un mercado ordenado y justo en las acciones registradas) (m/f)	*ehs-peh-see-ah-'lees-tah (ehl mee-'ehm-broh deh lah 'bohl-sah deh bah-loh-rehs rehs-pohn-'sah-bleh deh mahn-teh-'nehr oon mehr-'kah-doh ohr-deh-'nah-doh ee 'hoos-toh ehn lahs ahk-see-'oh-nehs reh-hees-'trah-dahs)*	specialist (stock exchange)

E

especialista en la industria petrolera (m/f)	*eh-speh-see-ah-'lees-tah ehn lah een-'doos-tree-ah peh-troh-'leh-rah*	specialist (oil industry)
especificaciones de embalaje (f)	*lahs ehs-peh-see-fee-kah-see-'ohn-nehs deh ehm-bah-'lah-heh*	packing list
espectro (m)	*ehl ehs-pehk-troh*	spectrum
espectrometría (f)	*lah ehs-pehk-troh-meh-tree-ah*	spectrophotometry
especulador (m)	*ehl ehs-peh-koo-lah-'dohr*	speculator
especulador en bolsa	*ehl ehs-peh-koo-lah-'dohr ehn 'bohl-sah*	scalper
especulador sobre la baja del mercado	*ehl ehs-peh-koo-lah-'dohr 'soh-breh lah 'bah-hah dehl mehr-'kah-doh*	bear
espiral de precios y salarios (m)	*ehl ehs-pee-'rahl deh preh-see-'ohs ee sah-'lahr-ee-ohs*	wage-price spiral
estabilización de precios (m)	*lah ehs-tah-bee-lee-sah-see-'ohn deh 'preh-see-ohs*	pegging
estabilizar	*eh-stah-bee-lee-'sahr*	stabilize (v)
establecimientos (m)	*lohs ehs-tah-bleh-see-mee-'ehn-tohs*	premises
estación de bombeo (f)	*lah ehs-tah-see-'ohn deh bohm-'beh-oh*	pumping station
estación de trabajo	*lah ehs-tah-see-'ohn deh trah-'bah-hoh*	workstation
estación de trabajo solitario	*lah ehs-tah-see-'ohn deh trah-'bah-hoh soh-lee-'tah-ree-oh*	stand-alone workstation
estacional	*ehs-tah-see-oh-'nahl*	seasonal
estadística (f)	*lah ehs-tah-'dees-tee-kah*	statistics
estado (m)	*ehl ehs-'tah-doh*	statement
estado de cuenta bancaria	*ehl eh-'stah-doh deh 'kwehn-tah bahn-'kah-ree-ah*	bank statement
estado de cuenta	*ehl ehs-'tah-doh deh 'kwehn-tah*	statement of account
estado de flujo de caja	*ehl eh-'stah-doh deh 'floo-hoh deh 'kah-hah*	cash flow statement

estado de ganancias y pérdidas	*ehl eh-'stah-doh deh gah-'nahn-see-ahs ee 'pehr-dee-dahs*	income statement, profit-and-loss statement
estado de operación	*ehl eh-'stah-doh deh oh-peh-rah-see-'ohn*	operating statement
estado del mercado	*ehl eh-'stah-doh dehl mehr-'kah-doh*	market position
estado financiero	*ehl eh-'stah-doh fee-nahn-see-'eh-roh*	financial statement, balance sheet
estado financiero consolidado	*ehl eh-'stah-doh fee-nahn-see-'eh-roh kohn-soh-lee-'dah-doh*	consolidated financial statement
estado financiero simulado	*ehl eh-'stah-doh fee-nahn-see-'eh-roh see-moo-'lah-doh*	pro form statement
estado intermedio	*ehl eh-'stah-doh een-tehr-'meh-dee-oh*	interim statement
estagflación (f)	*lah ehs-tahg-flah-see-'ohn*	stagflation
estampado (m)	*ehl eh-stahm-'pah-doh*	print
estancamiento (m)	*ehl ehs-tahn-kah-mee-'ehn-toh*	deadlock
estancia (f)	*lah ehs-'tahn-see-ah*	estate (or chateau)
estándar de vida (m)	*ehl eh-'stahn-dahr deh 'bee-dah*	standard of living
estandardización (f)	*lah eh-stahn-dahr-dee-sah-see-'ohn*	standardization
estar parado en la cola	*eh-'stahr pah-'rah-doh ehn lah 'koh-lah*	stand in line (v)
estatuto (m)	*ehl eh-stah-'too-toh*	statute
estatuto de limitaciones (m)	*ehl eh-stah-'too-toh deh lee-mee-tah-see-'oh-nehs*	statute of limitations
estatutos (mpl)	*lohs ehs-tah-'too-tohs*	by-laws
estereofónico	*eh steh-reh-oh-'foh-nee-koh*	stereophonic (adj)
estereoptipo (m)	*ehl eh-steh-reh-oh-'tee-poh*	stereotype
estética laboral (f)	*lah ehs-'teh-tee-kah lah-boh-'rahl*	work aesthetic (environment)
estilista (m)	*ehl eh-stee-lees-tah*	stylist
estilo (m)	*ehl eh-stee-loh*	style
estimación (f)	*lah ehs-tee-mah-see-'ohn*	estimate, forecast

E

estimación aproximada	*lah ehs-tee-mah-see-'ohn ah-prohk-see-'mah-dah*	guessmate, rough estimate
estimación de beneficio	*lah ehs-tee-mah-see-'ohn deh beh-neh-'fee-see-oh*	profit projection
estimación de ventas	*lah ehs-tee-mah-see-'ohn deh 'behn-tahs*	sales estimate
estimar	*ehs-tee-'mahr*	estimate, forecast (v)
estimulante (m)	*ehl ehs-tee-moo-'lahn-teh*	stimulant
estipulaciones del margen (f)	*lahs ehs-tee-poo-lah-see-'oh-nehs dehl 'mahr-hehn*	margin requirements
estornudar	*ehs-tohr-noo-dahr*	sneeze (v)
estrategia comercial (f)	*lah ehs-trah-'teh-hee-ah koh-mehr-see-'ahl*	business strategy
estrategia competitiva	*lah ehs-trah-'teh-hee-ah kohm-peh-tee-'tee-bah*	competitive strategy
estrategia inversionista	*lah ehs-trah-'teh-hee-ah een-behr-see-oh-'nees-tah*	investment strategy
estratósfera (f)	*lah ehs-trah-'tohs-feh-rah*	stratosphere
estructura de capital (f)	*lah ehs-trook-'too-ah deh kah-pee-'tahl*	capital
estría (f)	*lah ehs-'tree-ah*	flute (arquit.)
estructura corporativa (f)	*lah ehs-trook-'too-rah kohr-poh-rah-'tee-bah*	corporate structure
estructura salarial	*lah ehs-trook-'too-rah sah-lah-ree-'ahl*	wage structure
estuche de arreglarse las uñas (m)	*ehl ehs-'too-cheh deh ah-rreh-'glahr-seh lahs 'oo-nyahs*	manicuring kit
estuche (m) de artículos de tocador	*ehl ehs-'too-cheh deh ahr-'tee-koo-lohs deh toh-kah-'dohr*	toiletry kit
estuche de costura	*ehl ehs-'too-cheh deh kohs-'too-rah*	sewing kit
estuche de gafas	*ehl ehs-'too-cheh deh 'gah-fas*	eyeglass case
estuche de manicura	*ehl ehs-'too-cheh deh mah-nee-'koo-rah*	manicuring kit
estuche de tijeras	*ehl ehs-'too-cheh deh tee-'heh-rahs*	scissor case
estudio de la motivación (m)	*ehl eh-'stoo-dee-oh deh lah moh-tee-vah-see-'ohn*	motivation study

E

estudio de los componentes de un artículo	*ehl eh-'stoo-dee-oh deh lohs kohm-poh-'nehn-tehs deh oon ahr-'tee-koo-loh*	valve engineering
estudio del mercado	*ehl eh-'stoo-dee-oh dehl mehr-'kah-doh*	market survey
étano (m)	*ehl 'eh-tah-noh*	ethane
etanol (m)	*ehl eh-tah-'nohl*	ethanol
éter (m)	*ehl 'eh-tehr*	ether
ética laboral (f)	*lah 'eh-tee-kah lah-boh-'rahl*	work ethic
etiqueta (f)	*lah eh-tee-keh-tah*	label
eurobono (m)	*ehl eh-oo-roh-'boh-noh*	Eurobond
eurodólar (m)	*ehl ee-oo-roh-'doh-lahr*	Eurodollar
euromoneda (f)	*lah eh-oo-roh-moh-'neh-dah*	Eurocurrency
evaluación (f)	*lah eh-bah-loo-ah-see-'ohn*	evaluation
evaluación de riesgos	*lah eh-bah-loo-ah-see-'ohn deh ree-'ehs-gohs*	risk assessments
evaluación del trabajo	*lah eh-bah-loo-ah-see-'ohn dehl trah-'bah-hoh*	job evaluation
evasión de impuestos (f)	*lah eh-bah-see-'ohn deh eem-'pwehs-tohs*	tax evasion
evitar las pérdidas ocasionadas por las fluctuaciones de precios	*eh-bee-'tahr lahs 'pehr-dee-dahs oh-kah-see-oh-'nah-dahs pohr lahs flook-too-ah-see-'oh-nehs deh 'preh-see-ohs*	hedge (v)
ex buque	*ehks 'boo-keh*	ex ship
examinar	*ehk-sah-mee-'nahr*	scan (v)
excedente de capital (m)	*ehk-seh-'dehn-teh deh kah-pee-'tahl*	capital surplus
exceso de población (m)	*ehl ehk-'seh-soh deh poh-blah-see-'ohn*	excess population
exceso de productos (m)	*ehl ehk-'seh-soh deh proh-'dook-tohs*	surplus goods
excluir	*ehks-kloo-'eer*	omit (v)
excursión de placer (f)	*lah ehks-koor-see-'ohn deh plah-'sehr*	joy ride
exención (f)	*lah ehks-ehn-see-'ohn*	exemption
exención personal	*lah ehks-ehn-see-'ohn pehr-soh-'nahl*	personal exemption

E

éxito comercial (m)	*ehl 'ehk-see-toh koh-mehr-see-'ahl*	business success
exoneración bancaria (f)	*lah ehks-oh-neh-rah-see-'ohn bahn-'kah-ree-ah*	bank release
expectativas realizadas (f)	*lahs ehk-spehk-tah-'tee-bahs reh-ah-lee-'sah-dahs*	up to our expectations
expedidor de fletes (m)	*ehl ehks-peh-dee-'dohr deh 'fleh-tehs*	freight forwarder
experimento (m)	*ehl ehks-peh-ree-'mehn-toh*	experiment
exploración (f)	*lah ehks-ploh-rah-see-'ohn*	exploration, scanning
exploración doméstica	*lah ehks-ploh-rah-see-'ohn doh-'mehs-tee-kah*	exploration (local)
explorar	*ehks-ploh-'rahr*	explore (v), scan (v)
exportación, para la	*lah ehks-pohr-tah-see-'ohn, 'pah-rah lah*	export, for
exportaciones de capital (fpl)	*lahs ehks-pohr-tah-see-'oh-nehs deh kah-pee-'tahl*	capital exports
exportaciones esenciales	*lahs ehks-pohr-tah-see-'oh-nehs eh-sehn-see-'ah-lehs*	key exports
exportar	*ehks-pohr-'tahr*	export (v)
expropriación (f)	*lah ehks-proh-pree-ah-see-'ohn*	expropriation
expulsar	*ehs-pool-'sahr*	eject (v)
extinción (f)	*lah ehk-steenk-see-'ohn*	extinction
extraer	*ehks-trah-'ehr*	take out (v)

F

fábrica (f)	*lah fah-bree-kah*	factory
fábrica (f) de terminación	*lah fah-bree-kah deh tehr-mee-nah-see-ohn*	finishing mill
fábrica (m) de seda	*lah fah-bree-kah deh seh-dah*	silk factory
fabricación (f) de vasos de cristal	*lah fah-bree-kah-see-'ohn deh bah-sohs deh kree-stahl*	crystal glass manufacturing
fabricación en serie	*lah fah-bree-kah-see-'ohn ehn 'seh-ree-eh*	mass production
fabricante (m)	*ehl fah-bree-'kahn-teh*	manufacturer

fabricantes (mpl) de seda	*lohs fah-bree-kahn-tehs deh seh-dah*	silk manufacturers
fácil para el usuario	*'fah-seel 'pah-rah ehl oo-soo-'ah-ree-oh*	user-friendly
facilidad de almacenamiento (f)	*lah fah-see-lee-'dahd deh ahl-mah-seh-nah-mee-'ehn-toh*	storage facility
facilidades portuarias (fpl)	*lahs fah-see-lee-'dah-dehs pohr-too-'ah-ree-ahs*	port facilities
facsímil (m)	*ehl fahk-'see-meel*	fax
factor (m)	*ehl fahk-'tohr*	factor
factor de beneficio	*ehl fahk-'tohr deh beh-neh-'fee-see-oh*	profit factor
factor de carga	*ehl fahk-'tohr deh 'kahr-gah*	factor, load
factor de costo	*ehl fahk-'tohr deh 'kohs-toh*	cost factor
factor de la utilidad	*ehl fahk-'tohr deh lah oo-tee-lee-'dahd*	profit factor
factores del mercado (mpl)	*lohs fahk-'toh-rehs dehl mehr-'kah-doh*	market
factorización (f)	*lah fahk-toh-ree-sah-see-'ohn*	factoring
factura (f)	*lah fahk-'too-rah*	invoice, bill
factura comercial	*lah fahk-'too-rah koh-mehr-see-'ahl*	commercial invoice
factura consular	*lah fahk-'too-rah kohn-soo-'lahr*	consular invoice
factura de venta	*lah kohm-proh-'bahn-teh deh 'behn-tah*	bill of sale
factura pro-form	*lah fahk-'too-rah proh-'fohr-mah*	pro forma invoice
facturación cíclica (f)	*lah fahk-'too-rah-see-'ohn 'see-klee-kah*	cycle billing
falda (f)	*lah fahl-dah*	skirt
falsificación (f)	*lah ahl-see-fee-kah-see-'ohn*	forgery, counterfeit
falso flete (m)	*ehl 'fahl-soh 'fleh-teh*	dead freight
falta de cumplimiento (f)	*lah 'fahl-tah deh koom-lee-mee-'ehn-toh*	nonfeasance
falta de incentivo	*lah 'fahl-tah deh een-sehn-'tee-boh*	disincentive

F

faltar	*fahl-'tahr*	default, be short of (v)
farmacéutico (m)	*ehl fahr-mah-seh-'oo-tee-koh*	pharmacist
farmacéutico	*fahr-mah-seh-'oo-tee-koh*	pharmaceutical (adj)
farmacia (f)	*lah fahr-'mah-see-ah*	drugstore
fase descendente (f)	*lah 'fah-seh dehs-sehn-'dehn-teh*	down swing
fauna y flora (f)	*lah 'fah-oo-nah ee 'floh-rah*	fauna and flora
fax (m)	*ehl fahks*	fax
fecha de entrega (f)	*lah 'feh-chah deh ehn-'treh-gah*	date of delivery, delivery date
fecha de vencimiento	*lah 'feh-chah deh behn-see-mee-'ehn-toh*	expiry date, maturity date
fecha del cierre del registro	*lah 'feh-chah dehl see-'eh-rreh dehl reh-'hees-troh*	record date
fecha del intercambio	*lah 'feh-chah dehl een-tehr-'kahm-bee-oh*	trade date
fecha previa	*lah 'feh-chah 'preh-bee-ah*	back date
fechado (con fecha adelantada)	*feh-'chah-doh (kohn 'feh-chah ah-deh-lahn-'tah-dah)*	postdated
fécula (f)	*lah 'feh-koo-lah*	starch
fenol (m)	*ehl feh-'nohl*	phenol
feria comercial (f)	*lah 'feh-ree-ah koh-mehr-see-'ahl*	trade fair
fermentación maloláctica (f)	*lah fehr-mehn-tah-see-ohn mah-loh-lahk-tee-kah*	malolactic fermentation
ferroaleaciones (fpl)	*lahs feh-rroh-ah-leh-ah-see-oh-nehs*	ferroalloys
fertilizante (m)	*ehl fehr-tee-lee-'sahn-teh*	fertilizer
fianza (f)	*lah fee-'ahn-sah*	guaranty bond
fianza de cumplimento	*lah fee-'ahn-sah deh koom-plee-'mehn-toh*	performance bond
fianza de fidelidad	*lah fee-'ahn-sah deh fee-deh-lee-'dahd*	fidelity bond
fianza general	*lah fee-'ahn-sah heh-neh-'rahl*	blanket bond
fibras artificiales (f)	*lahs 'fee-brahs ahr-tee-fee-see-'ah-lehs*	man-made fibers
fichero (m)	*ehl fee-'cheh-roh*	file

F

fideicomisario (m)	*ehl fee-deh-ee-koh-mee-'sah-ree-oh*	trustee
fideicomiso (m)	*ehl fee-deh-ee-koh-'mee-soh*	trust
fideicomiso activo	*ehl fee-deh-ee-koh-'mee-soh ahk-'tee-boh*	active trust
fideicomiso inter vivos	*ehl fee-deh-ee-koh-'mee-soh 'een-tehr 'bee-bohs*	living trust
fideicomiso revocable	*ehl fee-deh-ee-koh-'mee-soh reh-boh-'kah-bleh*	revocable trust
fiduciario (m)	*ehl fee-doo-see-ah-ree-oh*	fiduciary
fijación de precios (f)	*lah fee-hah-see-'ohn deh 'preh-see-ohs*	price fixing
fijar el tipo de interés	*fee-'hahr ehl 'tee-poh deh een-teh-'rehs*	lock in (rate of interest) (v)
filtración (f)	*lah feel-trah-see-'ohn*	leakage
filtro (m)	*ehl 'feel-troh*	filter
filtro de aceite	*ehl feel-troh deh ah-seh-ee-teh*	oil filter
filtro de aire	*ehl feel-troh deh ah-ee-reh*	air filter
fin (m)	*ehl feen*	end
fin de bloque	*ehl feen deh 'bloh-keh*	end of block
fin de datos	*ehl feen deh 'dah-tohs*	end of data
fin de ingresos bajos	*ehl feen deh een-'greh-sohs 'bah-hohs*	low-income
fin de moda	*ehl feen deh moh-dah*	fashionable
fin de trabajo	*ehl feen deh trah-'bah-hoh*	end of job
final del período (m)	*ehl fee-'nahl dehl peh-'ree-oh-doh*	end of periods
finalizar	*fee-nah-lee-'sahr*	finalize (v)
financiación interna (f)	*lah fee-nahn-see-ah-see-'ohn een-'tehr-nah*	internal funding
financiamiento a corto plazo (m)	*ehl fee-nahn-see-ah-mee-'ehn-toh ah 'kohr-toh 'plah-soh*	short-term financing
financiamiento adelantado	*ehl fee-nahn-see-ah-mee-'ehn-toh ah-deh-lahn-'tah-doh*	front-end financing
financiamiento mediante déficit	*ehl fee-nahn-see-ah-mee-'ehn-toh meh-dee-'ahn-teh 'deh-fee-seet*	deficit financing

F

financiar	*fee-nahn-see-'ahr*	finance (v)
firma (f)	*lah 'feer-mah*	signature, firm
firma autorizada	*lah 'feer-mah ow-toh-ree-'sah-dah*	authorized signature
firmeza (f)	*lah feer-'meh-sah*	firmness
fletador (m)	*ehl fleh-tah-'dohr*	shipper
fletamento (m)	*ehl fleh-tah-'mehn-toh*	affreightment
fletar todas las especies	*fleh-'tahr 'toh-dahs lahs eh-'speh-see-ahs*	freight all kinds (v)
flete (m)	*ehl 'fleh-teh*	freight
flete aéreo	*ehl 'fleh-teh ah-'eh-reh-oh*	air freight
flete incluído	*ehl 'fleh-teh een-kloo-'ee-doh*	freight included
flete pagado	*ehl 'fleh-teh pah-'gah-doh*	advance freight
flete pagado por adelantado	*ehl 'fleh-teh pah-'gah-doh pohr ah-deh-lahn-'tah-doh*	freight prepaid
flete por cobrar	*ehl 'fleh-teh pohr koh-'brahr*	freight collect
flota privada (f)	*lah 'floh-tah pree-'bah-dah*	private fleet
flujo de caja (m)	*ehl 'floo-hoh deh 'kah-hah*	cash flow
fondo (m)	*ehl 'fohn-doh*	fund
fondo de amortización	*ehl 'fohn-doh deh ah-mohr-tee-sah-see-'ohn*	sinking fund
fondo de contingencia	*ehl 'fohn-doh deh kohn-teen-'hehn-see-ah*	contingency fund
fondo de fideicomiso	*ehl 'fohn-doh deh fee-deh-ee-koh-'mee-soh*	trust fund
fondo de jubilación	*ehl 'fohn-doh deh hoo-bee-lah-see-'ohn*	pension fund
fondo de rescate	*ehl fohn-doh deh rehs-kah-teh*	redemption fund
fondo de seguros	*ehl 'fohn-doh deh seh-'goo-rohs*	insurance fund
fondo mutualista	*ehl 'fohn-doh 'moo-twah-'lees-tah*	mutual fund
fondo rotativo	*ehl 'fohn-doh roh-tah-'tee-boh*	revolving fund
fondos de asesora-miento (mpl)	*lohs 'fohn-dohs deh ah-seh-soh-rah-mee-'ehn-toh*	advisory funds

F

fondos de operación	*lohs 'fohn-dohs deh oh-peh-rah-see-'ohn*	working funds, working balance
fondos públicos	*lohs 'fohn-dohs 'poo-blee-kohs*	public funds
formato (m)	*ehl fohr-'mah-toh*	format
formulario de solicitud (m)	*ehl fohr-moo-'lah-ree-oh deh soh-lee-see-'tood*	application form
forro (m)	*ehl foh-rroh*	lining
fortuna (f)	*lah fohr-'too-nah*	estate, wealth, fortune
fosfato (m)	*ehl fohs-fah-toh*	phosphate
foso de abastecimiento de combustibles (m)	*ehl 'foh-soh deh ah-bah-steh-see-mee-'ehn-toh deh kohm-boo-'stee-blehs*	fueling pit
fracasar	*frah-kah-'sahr*	fail
fracaso (m)	*ehl frah-'kah-soh*	failure (project)
franco a bordo	*'frahn-koh ah 'bohr-doh*	free on board
franco en el almacén	*'frahn-koh ehn ehl ahl-mah-'sehn*	ex warehouse
franco en el muelle	*'frahn-koh ehn ehl 'mweh-yeh*	ex dock
franco en fábrica	*'frahn-koh ehn 'fah-bree-kah*	ex factory
franquicia (f)	*lah frahn-'kee-see-ah*	franchise
fraude (m)	*ehl 'frow-deh*	fraud
freno (m)	*ehl 'freh-noh*	brake
fresado (m)	*ehl freh-'sah-doh*	milling (wood)
frontera (f)	*lah frohn-'teh-rah*	border
fuel-oil (aceite combustible) ligero (m)	*ehl foo-'ehl oh-'yeel (ah-'see-ee-teh kohm-boo-'stee-bleh) lee-'heh-roh*	oil (light fuel)
fuel-oil pesado	*ehl foo-'ehl oh-'yeel peh-'sah-doh*	oil (heavy fuel)
fuente (f)	*lah 'fwehn-teh*	source
fuente de energía	*lah 'fwehn-teh deh eh-nehr-'hee-ah*	power supply
fuente segura	*lah 'fwehn-teh seh-'goo-rah*	reliable source
fuentes (fpl) de energía	*lahs 'fwehn-tehs deh eh-nehr-'hee-ah*	energy sources

F

fuera de la bolsa	*'fweh-rah deh lah 'bohl-sah*	off board (stock market)
fuera de línea	*'fweh-rah deh 'lee-neh-ah*	off line
fuera de los libros	*'fweh-rah deh lohs 'lee-brohs*	off the books
fuera de moda	*fweh-rah deh 'moh-dah*	out of style
fuerza de trabajo	*'fwehr-sah deh trah-'bah-hoh*	manpower, task force
fuerza laboral	*'fwehr-sah lah-boh-'rahl*	labor force, work force
fuerza mayor	*'fwehr-sah mah-'yohr*	act of God, force majeure
función biológica (f)	*lah foonk-see-'ohn bee-oh-'loh-hee-kah*	biological function
funcionarios (mpl)	*lohs foonk-see-oh-'nah-ree-ohs*	staff
funda (f) de las llaves	*lah foon-dah deh lahs yah-behs*	key case
funda de pistola	*lah foon-dah deh pees-toh-lah*	gun holster
fundición (f)	*lah foon-dee-see-ohn*	foundry, font
fusión (f)	*lah foo-see-'ohn*	amalgamation
fusión de empresas	*lah foo-see-'ohn deh ehm-'preh-sahs*	merger
fusionar archivos	*foo-see-oh-'nahr ahr-'chee-bohs*	merge (v)
fusta (f)	*lah foos-tah*	whip
futuros (m)	*lohs foo-'too-rohs*	futures

G

galerada (f)	*lah gah-leh-rah-dah*	galley proof
galvanizado (m)	*ehl gahl-bah-nee-sah-doh*	galvanizing
gamuza (f)	*lah gah-'moo-sah*	suede
ganancias (fpl)	*lahs gah-'nahn-see-ahs*	earnings
ganancias (las pérdidas) de capital	*lahs gah-'nahn-see-ahs (lahs 'pehr-dee-dahs) deh kah-pee-'tahl*	capital gains (losses)
ganancias de operación	*lahs gah-'nahn-see-ahs deh oh-peh-rah-see-'ohn*	operating income

ganancias retenidas	*lahs gah-'nahn-see-ahs reh-teh-'nee-dahs*	retained profits
ganancias sobre los activos	*lahs gah-'nahn-see-ahs 'soh-breh lohs ahk-'tee-bohs*	earnings on assets
ganga (f)	*lah 'gahn-gah*	bargain (sale)
garantía (f)	*lah gah-rahn-'tee-ah*	guarantee, pledge, safe-guard, warranty, security
garantía de indemnización	*lah gah-rahn-'tee-ah deh een-dehm-nee-sah-see-'ohn*	letter of indemnity
garantizar	*gah-rahn-tee-'sahr*	warrant (v), guarantee (v)
gas (m)	*ehl gahs*	gas
gas líquido	*ehl gahs 'lee-kee-doh*	gas (liquid petroleum)
gas natural	*ehl gahs nah-too-'rahl*	natural gas
gasolina (f)	*lah gah-soh-'lee-nah*	fuel
gasolina de aviación	*lah gah-soh-'lee-nah deh ah-bee-ah-see-'ohn*	fuel (aviation)
gasolina normal	*lah gah-soh-'lee-nah nohr-'mahl*	gasoline (regular)
gasolina super	*lah gah-soh-'lee-nah soo-'pehr*	gasoline (super grade)
gasolinera (f)	*lah gah-soh-lee-'neh-rah*	service station
gasto (m)	*ehl 'gah-stoh*	outlay
gastos (mpl)	*lohs 'gah-stohs*	expenses
gastos acumulados por pagar	*lohs 'gah-stohs ah-koo-moo-'lah-dohs pohr pah-'gahr*	accrued expenses
gastos administrativos	*lohs 'gah-stohs ahd-mee-nee-strah-'tee-bohs*	administrative expenses
gastos controlables	*lohs 'gah-stohs kohn-troh-'lah-blehs*	controllable costs
gastos corrientes	*lohs 'gah-stohs koh-rree-'ehn-tehs*	running expenses
gastos de capital	*lohs 'gah-stohs deh kah-pee-'tahl*	capital expenditurer, capital spending
gastos de embarque	*gastos de embarque*	shipping expenses
gastos de estadía	*lohs 'gah-stohs deh ehs-'tah-dee-ah*	demurrage

G

gastos de interés	*lohs 'gah-stohs deh een-teh-'rehs*	interest expenses
gastos de lanchaje	*lohs 'gah-stohs deh lahn-'chah-heh*	lighterage
gastos de mudanzas	*lohs 'gah-stohs deh moo-'dahn-sahs*	moving expenses
gastos de operación	*lohs 'gah-stohs deh oh-peh-rah-see-'ohn*	operating expenses
gastos de publicidad	*lohs 'gah-stohs deh poo-blee-see-'dahd*	advertising expenses
gastos de transporte	*lohs 'gah-stohs deh trahns-'pohr-teh*	shipping expenses
gastos deficitarios	*lohs 'gah-stohs deh-fee-see-'tah-ree-ohs*	deficit spending
gastos directos	*lohs 'gah-stohs dee-'rehk-tohs*	direct expenses
gastos efectivos	*lohs 'gah-stohs eh-fehk-'tee-bohs*	out-of-pocket expenses
gastos fijos	*lohs 'gah-stohs 'fee-hohs*	fixed expenses
gastos generales	*lohs 'gah-stohs heh-neh-'rah-lehs*	overhead costs
gastos generales de fabricación	*lohs 'gah-stohs heh-neh-'rah-lehs deh fah-bree-kah-see-'ohn*	factory overhead
gastos generales fijos	*lohs 'gah-stohs heh-neh-'rah-lehs 'fee-hohs*	overhead
gastos indirectos	*lohs 'gah-stohs een-dee-'rehk-tohs*	indirect expenses
gastos menudos	*lohs 'gah-stohs meh-'noo-dohs*	incidental expenses
gemelos (mpl)	*lohs heh-'meh-lohs*	cuff link
generaciones futuras (fpl)	*lahs heh-neh-rah-see-'oh-nehs foo-'too-rahs*	future generations
generador (m)	*ehl heh-neh-rah-'dohr*	generator
géneros (mpl)	*lohs 'hey-ney-rohs*	soft goods
gerencia (f)	*lah heh-'rehn-see-ah*	administration, management
gerencia de crédito	*lah heh-'rehn-see-ah deh 'kreh-dee-toh*	credit management
gerencia de negocios	*lah heh-'rehn-see-ah deh neh-'goh-see-ohs*	business management

G

gerencia de producción	*lah heh-'rehn-see-ah deh proh-dook-see-'ohn*	production management
gerencia de ventas	*lah heh-'rehn-see-ah deh 'behn-tahs*	sales management
gerencia intermediaria	*lah heh-'rehn-see-ah een-tehr-meh-dee-'ah-ree-ah*	middle management
gerencia matricial	*lah heh-'rehn-see-ah mah-tree-see-'ahl*	matrix management
gerencia por equipo	*lah heh-'rehn-see-ah pohr eh-'kee-poh*	team management
gerente (m)	*ehl heh-'rehn-teh*	manager
gerente asistente	*ehl heh-'rehn-teh ah-sees-'tehn-teh*	assistant manager
gerente comprador	*ehl heh-'rehn-teh kohm-prah-'dohr*	purchasing manager
gerente de exportaciones	*ehl heh-'rehn-teh deh ehks-pohr-tah-see-'oh-nehs*	export manager
gerente de marca	*ehl heh-rehn-teh deh 'mahr-kah*	brand manager
gerente de planta	*ehl heh-'rehn-teh deh 'plahn-tah*	plant manager
gerente de publicidad	*ehl heh-'rehn-teh deh poo-blee-see-'dahd*	advertising manager
gerente de zona	*ehl heh-'rehn-teh deh 'soh-nah*	area manager
gerente general asistente	*ehl heh-'rehn-teh heh-neh-'rahl ah-sees-'tehn-teh*	assistant general manager
gerente general	*ehl heh-'rehn-teh heh-neh-'rahl*	general manager
gerente monetario	*ehl heh-'rehn-teh moh-neh-'tah-ree-oh*	money manager
gestión financiera (f)	*lah hehs-tee-ohn fee-nahn-'see-eh-rah*	financial management
gestionar	*hehs-tee-oh-'nahr*	negotiate (v)
girado (m)	*ehl hee-'rah-doh*	drawee
girador (m)	*ehl hee-rah-'dohr*	drawer (of a check), maker (of a check, draft)
giro (m)	*ehl 'hee-roh*	bill
giro bancario	*ehl 'hee-roh bahn-'kah-ree-oh*	bank draft, bank money order

G

giro postal	*ehl 'hee-roh pohs-'tahl*	money order
glaseado	*glah-see-'ah-'doh*	glossy (adj)
gobierno (m)	*ehl goh-bee-'ehr-noh*	government
gollete (m)	*ehl goh-'yeh-teh*	neck
gota (f) para los ojos	*lah goh-tah pah-rah lohs oh-hohs*	eyedrop
grabadora (f)	*lah grah-bah-'doh-rah*	tape recorder
grabar	*grah-'bahr*	record (v)
grado (m)	*ehl 'grah-doh*	degree
gráfica (f)	*lah 'grah-fee-kah*	graph
gramo (m)	*ehl 'grah-moh*	gram
gran almacén (m)	*ehl grahn ahl-mah-'sehn*	department store
grano (m)	*ehl 'grah-noh*	grain
gravamen (m)	*ehl grah-'bah-mehn*	encumbrance, lien
gravamen combinado	*ehl grah-'bah-mehn kohm-bee-'nah-doh*	combination duty
gravamen de constructor	*ehl grah-'bah-mehn deh kohn-strook-'tohr*	mechanic's lien
gravamen del vendedor	*ehl grah-'bah-mehn dehl behn-deh-'dohr*	vendor's lien
gravitación terrestre (f)	*lah grah-bee-tah-see-'ohn teh-'rreh-streh*	gravitation of earth
gremio abierto (m)	*ehl 'greh-mee-oh ah-bee-'ehr-toh*	open shop
gremio de obreros	*ehl 'greh-mee-oh deh oh-'breh-rohs*	trade union
gremio mercantil	*ehl 'greh-mee-oh mehr-kahn-'teel*	merchant guilt
gres (m)	*ehl grehs*	stoneware
grúa (f)	*lah 'groo-ah*	crane
grúa giratoria	*lah 'groo-ah hee-rah-'toh-ree-ah*	crane (revolving)
grupo (m)	*ehl 'groo-poh*	batch
grupo administrativo	*ehl 'groo-poh ahd-mee-nee-strah-'tee-boh*	management group
grupo de entrenamiento	*ehl 'groo-poh deh ehn-treh-nah-mee-'ehn-toh*	training group

grupo de productos	*ehl 'groo-poh deh proh-'dook-tohs*	product group
grupo gerencial	*ehl 'groo-poh heh-rehn-see-'ahl*	management group
guanaco (m)	*ehl gwah-'nah-koh*	guanaco
guantes (mpl)	*lohs gwahn-tehs*	gloves
guerra arancelaria (f)	*lah 'geh-rrah ah-rahn-seh-'lah-ree-ah*	tariff war
guerra de precios	*lah 'geh-rrah deh 'preh-see-ohs*	price war
guía para fabricar piezas idénticas (m)	*ehl 'gee-ah 'pah-rah fah-bree-'kahr pee-'eh-sahs ee-'dehn-tee-kahs*	jig (production)
gusano de seda (m)	*ehl goo-sah-noh deh seh-dah*	silkworm

H

hábitat (m)	*ehl 'ah-bee-taht*	environment
hacer disponible	*ah-'sehr dees-poh-'nee-bleh*	make available (v)
hacer efectivo	*ah-'sehr eh-fehk-'tee-boh*	cash (v)
hacer un pedido	*ah-'sehr oon peh-'dee-doh*	place an order (v)
hasta nuestras expectativas	*'ahs-tah noo-'eh-strahs ehk-spehk-tah-'tee-bahs*	up to our expectations
hebra (f)	*lah eh-brah*	thread
heces (fpl)	*lahs eh-sehs*	dregs
hectárea (2.47 acres) (f)	*lah ehk-tah-reh-ah*	hectare
heladas (fpl)	*lahs eh-'lah-dahs*	frosts
heliografía (f)	*lah eh-lee-oh-grah-'fee-ah*	blueprint
herencia	*lah eh-'rehn-see-ah*	estate
herramientas (fpl)	*lahs eh-rrah-mee-'ehn-tahs*	tools (hardware)
hexaclorofeno (m)	*ehl ehk-sah-kloh-roh-feh-noh*	hexachlorophene
hidrocarburo (m)	*ehl ee-droh-kahr-'boo-roh*	hydrocarbon
hidrocarburos (mpl)	*lohs ee-droh-kahr-'boo-rohs*	hydrocarbons
hidrólisis (f)	*lah ee-'droh-lee-sees*	hydrolysis

hidrosulfato (m)	*ehl ee-droh-sool-fah-toh*	hydrosulfate
hierro (m)	*ehl 'yeh-roh*	iron
hierro fundido	*ehl 'yeh-rroh foon-dee-doh*	cast iron
hierro perfilado	*ehl 'yeh-roh pehr-fee-lahpdoh*	structural shapes
hilo (m)	*ehl 'ee-loh*	thread, yarn
hilo crudo	*ehl 'ee-loh 'kroo-doh*	unbleached linen
hipertensión (f)	*lah 'ee-pehr-tehn-see-'ohn*	hypertension
hipoteca (f)	*lah ee-poh-'teh-kah*	lien, mortage, hypothecation
hipoteca con intereses variables	*lah ee-poh-'teh-kah kohn een-teh-'reh-sehs bah-ree-'ah-blehs*	variable rate mortage
hipoteca sobre bienes muebles	*lah ee-poh-'teh-kah 'soh-breh bee-'eh-nehs 'mweh-blehs*	chattel mortgage
hoja (f)	*lah 'oh-hah*	leaf
hoja de papel	*lah oh-hah deh pah-pehl*	sheet
hoja de acontecimientos	*lah 'oh-hah deh ah-kohn-teh-see-mee-'ehn-tohs*	fact sheet
hoja electrónica	*lah 'oh-hah eh-lehk-'troh-nee-kah*	spreadsheet
hoja impresa	*lah 'oh-hah eem-'preh-sah*	printout
hojal (m)	*ehl oh-'hahl*	buttonhole
hojas (fpl)	*lahs oh-hahs*	sheets
hombre (m)	*ehl 'ohm-breh*	man
hombre independiente	*ehl 'ohm-breh een-deh-pehn-dee-'ehn-teh*	freelancer
hombrera (f)	*lah ohm-breh-rah*	shoulder pad
homogeneidad (f)	*lah oh-moh-heh-neh-ee-dahd*	homogeneity
honorario de administración (m)	*ehl oh-noh-'rah-ree-oh deh ahd-mee-nee-strah-see-'ohn*	management fee
honorarios de agencia (mpl)	*lohs oh-noh-'rah-ree-ohs deh ah-'hehn-see-ah*	agency fee
hora estándar (f)	*lah 'oh-rah ehs-'tahn-dahr*	standard time
hora-hombre	*lah 'oh-rah-'ohm-breh*	man hour
horario (m)	*ehl oh-'rah-ree-oh*	schedule, timetable

horas de trabajo (fpl)	*lahs 'oh-rahs deh trah-'bah-hoh*	working hours
hormona (f)	*lah ohr-moh-nah*	hormone
horno (m)	*ehl ohr-noh*	furnace
horno de arco voltaico	*ehl ohr-noh deh ahr-koh bohl-'tah-ee-koh*	electric arc furnace
horno de fusión al vacío	*ehl 'ohr-noh deh foo-see-'ohn ahl bah-'see-oh*	vacuum melting furnace
horno de inducción	*ehl ohr-noh deh een-dook-see-'ohn*	induction furnace
horno de ladrillo	*ehl ohr-noh deh lah-'dree-yoh*	cupola
huelga general (f)	*lah 'wehl-gah heh-neh-'rahl*	general strike
huelga no sancionada por el sindicato	*lah 'wehl-gah noh sahnk-see-oh-'nah-dah pohr ehl seen-dee-'kah-toh*	wildcat strike
hule (m)	*ehl 'oo-leh*	oilcloth
humanidad	*lah oo-mah-nee-'dahd*	mankind
hurtar	*oor-'tahr*	pilfer (v)
hurto (m)	*ehl 'oor-toh*	pilferage
huso horario (m)	*ehl 'oo-soh oh-'rah-ree-oh*	time zone

I

icono (m)	*ehl ee-'koh-noh*	icon
identificación bancaria (f)	*lah ee-dehn-tee-fee-kah-see-'ohn bahn-'kah-ree-ah*	bank carnet
ignición (f)	*lah eeg-nee-see-'ohn*	ignition
ilegal	*ee-leh-'gahl*	illegal
imagen corporativa (f)	*lah ee-'mah-hehn kohr-poh-rah-'tee-bah*	corporate image
imagen de la marca	*lah ee-'mah-hehn deh lah 'mahr-kah*	brand image
imitación (f)	*lah ee-mee-tah-see-'ohn*	imitation
impactar	*eem-pahk-'tahr*	impact on (v)
impacto del beneficio (m)	*ehl eem-'pahk-toh dehl beh-neh-'fee-see-oh*	profit impact
impase (m)	*ehl eem-'pah-seh*	deadlock

impermeable (m)	*ehl eem-pehr-meh-ah-bleh*	raincoat
implicación (f)	*lah eem-plee-kah-see-'ohn*	implication
imponer contribuciones	*eem-poh-'nehr kohn-tree-boo-see-'oh-nehs*	levy taxes (v)
importación (f)	*lah eem-pohr-tah-see-'ohn*	import
importador vigente (m)	*ehl eem-pohr-tah-'dohr bee-'hehn-teh*	importer of record
importar	*eem-pohr-'tahr*	import (v)
importe debido (m)	*ehl eem-'pohr-teh deh-'bee-doh*	amount due
importe vencido	*ehl eem-'pohr-teh behn-'see-doh*	amount due
imposición múltiple de impuestos (f)	*lah eem-poh-see-'ohn 'mool-tee-pleh deh eem-'pwehs-tohs*	multiple taxation
imposición variable sobre importaciones	*lah eem-poh-see-'ohn bah-ree-'ah-bleh 'soh-breh eem-pohr-tah-see-'oh-nehs*	variable import levy
impracticable	*eem-prahk-tee-'kah-bleh*	unfeasible
imprenta por offset (f)	*lah eem-'prehn-tah pohr ohf-'seht*	offset printing
impresión (f)	*lah eem-preh-see-'ohn*	print, printing
impresión tipográfica	*lah eem-preh-see-'ohn tee-poh-'grah-fee-kah*	letterpress
impresora (f)	*lah eem-preh-'soh-rah*	printer
impresora láser	*lah eem-preh-'soh-rah 'lah-sehr*	laser printer
impresora por matriz de puntos	*lah eem-preh-'soh-rah pohr mah-'trees deh 'poon-tohs*	dot matrix printer
impresos (mpl)	*lohs eem-'preh-sohs*	printed matter
imprimir	*eem-pree-'meer*	mint (v)
impuesto (m)	*ehl eem-'pweh-stoh*	tax
impuesto a la corporación	*ehl eem-'pweh-stoh ah lah kohr-poh-rah-see-'ohn*	corporation tax
impuesto a las exportaciones	*ehl eem-'pweh-stoh ah lahs ehks-pohr-tah-see-'oh-nehs*	export tax

impuesto adicional	*ehl eem-'pweh-stoh ah-dee-see-oh-'nahl*	surtax
impuesto al consumo	*ehl eem-'pweh-stoh ahl kohn-'soo-moh*	excise tax
impuesto anti-dumping	*ehl eem-'pweh-stoh ahn-tee-'doom-peeng*	anti-dumping duty
impuesto de exportación	*ehl eem-'pweh-stoh deh ehks-pohr-tah-see-'ohn*	export duty
impuesto de importación	*ehl eem-'pweh-stoh deh eem-pohr-tah-see-'ohn*	import tax
impuesto de uso	*ehl eem-'pwehs-toh deh 'oo-soh*	use tax
impuesto específico	*ehl eem-'pweh-stoh ehs-peh-'see-fee-koh*	specific duty
impuesto indirecto	*ehl eem-'pweh-stoh een-dee-'rehk-toh*	indirect tax
impuesto regresivo	*ehl eem-'pweh-stoh reh-greh-'see-boh*	regressive tax
impuesto sobre el ingreso personal	*ehl eem-'pweh-stoh 'soh-breh ehl een-'greh-soh pehr-soh-'nahl*	personal income tax
impuesto sobre el valor añadido (I.V.A.)	*ehl eem-'pweh-stoh 'soh-breh ehl bah-'lohr ah-nyah-'dee-doh*	value-added tax (V.A.T.)
impuesto sobre la nómina	*ehl eem-'pweh-stoh 'soh-breh lah 'noh-mee-nah*	payroll tax
impuesto sobre la renta	*ehl eem-'pweh-stoh 'soh-breh lah 'rehn-tah*	income tax
impuesto sobre las ventas	*ehl eem-'pweh-stoh 'soh breh lahs 'behn-tahs*	sales tax
impuesto sobre lujos	*ehl eem-'pweh-stoh 'soh-breh 'loo-hohs*	luxury tax
impuesto sobre rentas al por menor	*ehl eem-'pweh-stoh 'soh-breh 'rehn-tahs ahl pohr meh-'nohr*	retail sales tax
impuesto sucesorio	*ehl eem-'pweh-stoh soo-seh-'soh-ree-oh*	estate tax, inheritance tax
impuestos (mpl)	*lohs eem-'pweh-stohs*	duties
impuestos acumulados	*lohs eem-'pweh-stohs ah-koo-moo-'lah-dohs*	accrued taxes
impuestos ad valorem	*lohs eem-'pweh-stohs ahd bah-'loh-rehm*	duty ad valorem

impuestos atrasados	*lohs eem-'pweh-stohs ah-trah-'sah-dohs*	back taxes
impuestos de exportación	*lohs eem-'pweh-stohs deh ehks-pohr-tah-see-'ohn*	export taxes
impuestos diferidos	*lohs eem-'pweh-stohs dee-feh-'ree-dohs*	deferred taxes
impuestos indirectos	*lohs eem-'pweh-stohs een-dee-'rehk-tohs*	excise duties
impuestos locales	*lohs eem-'pweh-stohs loh-'kah-lehs*	local taxes
impuestos sobre tierras	*lohs eem-'pweh-stohs 'soh-breh tee-'eh-rrahs*	land taxes
impulso debido a la emisión de deuda (m)	*ehl eem-'pool-soh deh-'bee-doh ah lah eh-mee-see-'ohn deh deh-'oo-dah*	leverage
impulsor de discos (m)	*ehl eem-pool-'sohr deh 'dees-kohs*	disk drive
impureza (f)	*lah eem-poo-reh-sah*	impurity
imputado	*eem-poo-'tah-doh*	imputed
incautar	*een-kow-'tahr*	impound (v)
incentivo (m)	*ehl een-sehn-'tee-boh*	incentive
incentivo financiero	*ehl een-sehn-'tee-boh fee-nahn-see-'eh-roh*	financial incentive
incertidumbre sobre la tendencia salarial (f)	*lah een-sehr-tee-'doom-breh 'soh-breh lah tehn-'dehn-see-ah sah-lah-ree-'ahl*	wage drift
incineración (f)	*lah een-see-neh-rah-see-'ohn*	burning
incinerador (m)	*ehl een-see-neh-rah-'dohr*	incinerator
incorporar	*een-kohr-poh-'rahr*	incorporate (v)
incorporar gradualmente	*een-kohr-poh-'rahr grah-doo-ahl-'mehn-teh*	phase in (v)
incrementar	*een-kreh-mehn-tahr*	increase (v)
incumplir	*een-koom-'pleer*	default (v)
indemnización (f)	*lah een-dehm-nee-sah-see-'ohn*	indemnity, compensation
indemnización par despido	*lah een-dehm-nee-sah-see-'ohn pahr dehs-'pee-doh*	severance pay
indexación (f)	*lah een-dehk-sah-see-'ohn*	indexing

indicaciones (f)	*lahs een-dee-kah-see-'oh-nehs*	guidelines
indicador anticipado (m)	*ehl een-dee-kah-'dohr ahn-tee-see-'pah-doh*	leading indicator
indicador de rezago	*ehl een-dee-kah-'dohr deh reh-'sah-goh*	lagging indicator
indicadores económicos (mpl)	*lohs een-dee-kah-'doh-rehs eh-koh-'noh-mee-kohs*	economic indicators
índice (m)	*ehl 'een-dee-seh*	index (indicator), table of contents
índice compuesto	*ehl 'een-dee-seh kohm-'pweh-stoh*	composite index
índice contable	*ehl 'een-dee-seh kohn-'tah-bleh*	accounting ratio
índice de acciones	*ehl 'een-dee-seh deh ahk-see-'oh-nehs*	stock index
índice de crecimiento	*ehl 'een-dee-seh deh kreh-see-mee-'ehn-toh*	growth index
Indice General de la Calidad de Vida	*ehl 'een-dee-seh heh-neh-'rahl deh lah kah-lee-'dahd deh 'bee-dah*	Physical Quality of Life Index (PQLI)
índice de liquidez	*ehl 'een-dee-seh deh lee-kee-'dehs*	liquidity ratio
índice de precio	*ehl 'een-dee-seh deh 'preh-see-oh*	price index
índice de precios al consumidor	*ehl 'een-dee-seh deh 'preh-see-ohs ahl kohn-soo-mee-dor*	consumer price index
índice del mercado	*ehl 'een-dee-seh dehl mehr-'kah-doh*	market index
índices del balance (mpl)	*lohs 'een-dee-sehs dehl bah-'lahn-seh*	balance ratios
indumentaria (f)	*lah een-doo-mehn-'tah-ree-ah*	apparel
industria (f)	*lah een-'doos-tree-ah*	industry
industria bancaria	*lah een-'doos-tree-ah bahn-'kah-ree-ah*	banking industry
industria creciente	*lah een-'doos-tree-ah kreh-see-'ehn-teh*	growth industry
industria del mercado libre	*lah een-'doos-tree-ah dehl mehr-'kah-doh 'lee-breh*	free market industry

I

industria naciente	*lah een-'doos-tree-ah nah-see-'ehn-teh*	infant industry
industria pesada	*lah een-'doos-tree-ah peh-'sah-dah*	heavy industry
industria petrolera	*lah een-'doos-tree-ah peh-troh-'leh-rah*	oil industry
industria petrolera indígena	*lah een-'doos-tree-ah peh-troh-'leh-rah een-'dee-heh-nah*	oil industry (indigenous)
industria petrolera integrada	*lah een-'doos-tree-ah peh-troh-'leh-rah een-teh-'grah-dah*	oil industry (integrated)
ineficiente	*een-eh-fee-see-'ehn-teh*	inefficient
inestabilidad (f)	*lah een-ehs-tah-bee-lee-'dahd*	instability
inferior al nivel	*een-feh-ree-'ohr ahl nee-'behl*	normal substandard
inflación (f)	*lah een-flah-see-'ohn*	inflation
inflacionista	*een-flah-see-oh-'nees-tah*	inflationary
información (f)	*lah een-fohr-mah-see-'ohn*	information
información particular a computadoras	*lah een-fohr-mah-see-'ohn pahr-tee-koo-'lahr ah kohm-poo-tah-'doh-rahs*	data
informe (m)	*ehl een-'fohr-meh*	report
informe anual	*ehl een-'fohr-meh ah-noo-'ahl*	annual report
informe de ganancias	*ehl een-'fohr-meh deh gah-'nahn-see-ahs*	earnings report
informe del mercado	*ehl een-'fohr-meh dehl mehr-'kah-doh*	market report
infraestructura (f)	*lah een-frah-ehs-trook-'too-rah*	infrastructure
ingeniería (f)	*lah een-heh-nee-eh-'ree-ah*	engineering
ingeniería civil	*lah een-heh-nee-eh-'ree-ah see-'beel*	civil engineering
ingeniería de diseño	*lah een-heh-nee-eh-'ree-ah deh dee-'seh-nyoh*	design engineering
ingeniería de sistemas	*lah een-heh-nee-eh-'ree-ah deh sees-'teh-mahs*	systems engineering
ingeniería eléctrica	*lah een-heh-nee-eh-'ree-ah eh-'lehk-tree-kah*	electrical engineering

ingeniería industrial	*lah een-heh-nee-eh-'ree-ah een-doo-stree-'ahl*	industrial engineering
ingeniería mecánica	*lah een-heh-nee-eh-'ree-ah meh-'kah-nee-kah*	mechanical engineering
ingeniero (m)	*ehl een-heh-nee-'eh-roh*	engineer
ingeniero mecánico	*ehl een-heh-nee-eh-roh meh-'kah-nee-koh*	mechanical engineer
ingreso neto (m)	*ehl een-'greh-soh 'neh-toh*	net income
ingresos (mpl)	*lohs een-'greh-sohs*	income
ingresos acumulados	*lohs een-'greh-sohs ah-koo-moo-'lah-dohs*	accrued revenue
ingresos ajustados	*lohs een-'greh-sohs ah-hoos-'tah-dohs*	adjusted earned income
ingresos brutos	*lohs een-'greh-sohs 'broo-tohs*	gross income
ingresos diferidos	*lohs een-'greh-sohs dee-feh-'ree-dohs*	deferred income
ingresos disponibles	*lohs een-'greh-sohs dees-poh-'nee-blehs*	disposable income
ingresos libre de impuestos	*lohs een-'greh-sohs 'lee-breh-deh eem-'pweh-stohs*	tax-free income
ingresos marginales	*lohs een-'greh-sohs mahr-hee-'nah-lehs*	marginal revenue
ingresos no merecidos	*lohs een-'greh-sohs noh meh-reh-'see-dohs*	unearned revenue
ingresos por hora	*lohs een-'greh-sohs pohr 'oh-rah*	hourly earnings
ingresos por intereses	*lohs een-'greh-sohs pohr een-teh-'reh-sehs*	interest income
ingresos retenidos	*lohs een-'greh-sohs reh-teh-'nee-dohs*	retained earnings
ingresos verdaderos	*lohs een-'greh-sohs behr-dah-'deh-rohs*	actual income
iniciador de ajustes (m)	*ehl ee-nee-see-ah-'dohr deh ah-'hoos-tehs*	adjustment trigger
iniciar una sesión	*ee-nee-see-'ahr 'oo-nah seh-see-'ohn*	log on (v)
injusto	*een-'hoos-toh*	unfair
innovación (f)	*lah een-noh-bah-see-'ohn*	innovation
insolvente	*eeh-sohl-'behn-teh*	insolvent

inspección (f)	*lah een-spehk-see-'ohn*	inspection
inspeccionar	*een-spehk-see-oh-'nahr*	audit (v)
inspector (m)	*ehl een-spehk-'tohr*	inspector
inspector bancario	*ehl een-spehk-'tohr bahn-'kah-ree-oh*	bank examiner
inspiración	*lah een-spee-rah-see-'ohn*	brainstorming
instalación de climatización (f)	*lah een-stah-lah-see-'ohn deh klee-mah-tee-sah-see-'ohn*	seawater desalination plant
instalación de destilación	*lah een-stah-lah-see-'ohn de deh-stee-lah-see-'ohn*	distillation plant
instalaciones (fpl)	*lahs een-stah-lah-see-'oh-nehs*	facilities
instrucción permanente (f)	*lah een-strook-see-'ohn pehr-mah-'nehn-teh*	standing order
instrucciones de embarque (fpl)	*lahs een-strook-see-'oh-nehs deh ehm-'bahr-keh*	shipping instructions
instruir	*eens-troo-'eer*	instruct
instrumento (m)	*ehl doh-koo-'mehn-toh*	instrument
instrumento de renuncia	*ehl een-stroo-'mehn-toh deh reh-'noon-see-ah*	quit claim deed
instrumentos (mpl)	*lohs een-stroo-'mehn-tohs*	tools
instrumentos de trabajo	*lohs een-stroo-'mehn-tohs deh trah-'bah-hoh*	working tools
insuficiencia de capital (f)	*lah een-soo-fee-see-'ehn-see-ah*	undercapitalization
insuficiente	*een-soo-fee-see-'ehn-teh*	inadequate
insulina (f)	*lah een-soo-'lee-nah*	insulin
insumo (m)	*ehl een-'soo-moh*	input
integración vertical (f)	*lah een-teh-grah-see-'ohn behr-tee-'kahl*	vertical integration
interactivo	*een-tehr-ahk-'tee-boh*	interactive (adj)
intercalar	*een-tehr-kah-'lahr*	merge (v)
intercambiar	*een-tehr-kahm-bee-'ahr*	exchange, trade (v)
intercambio (m)	*ehl een-tehr-'kahm-bee-oh*	trade
intercambio a nivel de mayorista	*ehl een-tehr-'kahm-bee-oh ah-nee-'behl deh mah-yohr-'rees-tah*	wholesale trade

intercambio bancario	*ehl een-tehr-'kahm-bee-oh bahn-'kah-ree-oh*	bank exchange
intercambio compensatorio	*ehl een-tehr-'kahm-bee-oh kohm-pehn-sah-'toh-ree-oh*	trade
intercambio después de las horas regulares	*ehl een-tehr-'kahm-bee-oh dehs-'pwehs deh lahs 'oh-rahs reh-goo-'lah-rehs*	after-hours trading
intercambio en acciones	*ehl een-tehr-'kahm-bee-oh ehn ahk-see-'ohn-nehs*	stock-in-trade
intercambio monetario	*ehl een-tehr-'kahm-bee-oh moh-neh-'tah-ree-oh*	currency exchange
interés (m)	*ehl een-teh-'rehs*	interest
interés a largo plazo	*ehl een-teh-'rehs ah 'lahr-goh 'plah-soh*	long-term interest
interés acumulado	*ehl een-teh-'rehs ah-koo-moo-'lah-doh*	accrued interest
interés compuesto	*ehl een-teh-'rehs kohm-'pweh-stoh*	compound interest
interés incoado	*ehl een-teh-'rehs een-koh-'ah-doh*	inchoate interest
interés mayoritario	*ehl een-teh-'rehs mah-yoh-ree-'tah-ree-oh*	majority interest
interés predominante	*ehl een-teh-'rehs preh-doh-mee-'nahn-teh*	controlling interest
intereses creados (mpl)	*lohs een-teh-'reh-sehs creh-'ah-dohs*	vested interests
intereses minoritarios	*lohs een-teh-'reh-sehs mee-noh-ree-'tah-ree-ohs*	minority interests
interestatal	*een-tehr-'ehs-tah-tahl*	interstate
interfaz	*ehl een-tehr-'fahs*	interface
interino (m)	*ehl een-teh-'ree-noh*	interim
interior	*een-teh-ree-'ohr*	internal
intermediario (m)	*ehl een-tehr-meh-dee-'ah-ree-oh*	intermediary, middle man, broker
intermediario de exportaciones	*ehl een-tehr-meh-dee-'ah-ree-oh deh ehks-pohr-tah-see-'oh-nehs*	export middleman
intermediario en programa de computación	*ehl een-tehr-meh-dee-'ah-ree-oh ehn proh-'grah-mah deh kohm-poo-tah-see-'ohn*	software broker

I

interno	*een-'tehr-noh*	internal (adj)
intérprete (m/f)	*een-'tehr-preh-teh*	interpreter
interruptor (m)	*ehl een-teh-rroop-tohr*	switch
interruptor en marcha	*ehl een-teh-rroop-'tohr ehn 'mahr-chah*	power switch on
interruptor parado	*ehl een-teh-rroop-'tohr pah-'rah-doh*	power switch off
intervenir	*een-tehr-beh-'neer*	intervene (v)
interventor (m)	*ehl een-tehr-behn-'tohr*	auditor
inundación	*lah een-oon-'dah-see-'ohn*	glut
inundación del mercado con precios por debajo del costo	*lah een-oon-dah-see-'ohn dehl mehr-'kah-doh kohn 'preh-see-ohs pohr deh-'bah-hoh dehl 'koh-stoh*	dumping goods in foreign markets
invalidar	*een-bah-lee-'dahr*	invalidate, nullify, supersede (v)
inválido	*een-'bah-lee-doh*	void
inventario (m)	*ehl een-behn-'tah-ree-oh*	inventory
inventario a costos más viejos	*ehl een-behn-'tah-ree-oh ah 'koh-stohs mahs bee-'eh-hohs*	last in-first out
inventario de bienes terminados	*ehl een-behn-'tah-ree-oh deh bee-'eh-nehs tehr-mee-'nah-dohs*	finished goods inventory
inventario físico	*ehl een-behn-'tah-ree-oh 'fee-see-koh*	physical inventory
inventario periódico	*ehl een-behn-'tah-ree-oh peh-ree-'oh-dee-koh*	periodic inventory
inventario permanente	*ehl een-behn-'tah-ree-oh pehr-mah-'nehn-teh*	perpetual inventory
inventario según libros	*ehl een-behn-'tah-ree-oh seh-'goon 'lee-brohs*	book inventory
inversión (f)	*lah een-behr-see-'ohn*	investment
inversión bruta	*lah een-behr-see-'ohn 'broo-tah*	gross investment
inversión cualificada	*lah een-behr-see-'ohn kwah-lee-fee-'kah-dah*	investment grade
inversión en acciones	*lah een-behr-see-'ohn ehn ahk-see-'oh-nehs*	equity investment
inversión fija	*lah een-behr-see-'ohn 'fee-hah*	fixed investment

inversión legal	*lah een-behr-see-'ohn leh-'gahl*	legal investment
inversión neta	*lah een-behr-see-'ohn 'neh-tah*	net investment
inversión real	*lah een-behr-see-'ohn reh-'ahl*	real investment
inversiones directas (fpl)	*lahs een-behr-see-'oh-nehs dee-'rehk-tahs*	direct investments
inversionista institutional (m)	*ehl een-behr-see-oh-nees-tah een-stee-too-see-oh-'nahl*	institutional investor
inversores (mpl)	*lohs een-behr-'soh-rehs*	investors
invertebrado (m)	*ehl een-behr-teh-'brah-doh*	invertebrate
invertir	*een-behr-'teer*	invest (v)
investigación (f)	*lah een-behs-tee-gah-see-'ohn*	research
investigación acerca de los hábitos de consumo	*lah een-behs-tee-gah-see-'ohn ah-'sehr-kah deh lohs 'ah-bee-tohs deh kohn-'soo-moh*	consumer research
investigación aplicada	*lah een-behs-tee-gah-see-'ohn ah-plee-'kah-dah*	action research
investigación publicitaria	*lah een-behs-tee-gah-see-'ohn poo-blee-see-'tah-ree-ah*	advertising research
investigación y desarrollo	*lah een-behs-tee-gah-see-'ohn ee dehs-ah-'rroh-yoh*	research and development
investigaciones del mercado (fpl)	*lahs een-behs-tee-gah-see-'oh-nehs dehl mehr-'kah-doh*	market research
investigar y resolver un problema	*een-beh-steego-gahr ee reh-sohl-behr oon-proh-bleh-mah*	troubleshoot (v)
invisible	*een-bee-'see-bleh*	invisible
invitación a concurso (f)	*lah een-bee-tah-see-'ohn ah kohn-'koor-soh*	invitation to bid
inyección (f)	*lah een-yehk-see-'ohn*	injection
isótopo (m)	*ehl ee-'soh-toh-poh*	isotope
itinerario	*ee-tee-neh-'rah-ree-oh*	schedule, timetable

I

J

jarabe (m) para la tos	*ehl hah-rah-beh pah-rah lah tohs*	cough syrup
jarra (f)	*lah hah-rrah*	pitcher
jefe (m)	*ehl 'heh-feh*	leader
jefe contador	*ehl 'heh-feh kohn-tah-'dohr*	chief accountant
jefe de compras	*ehl 'heh-feh deh 'kohm-prahs*	chief buyer
jeringa (f)	*lah heh-'reen-gah*	syringe
jornada (f)	*lah hohr-'nah-dah*	workday
jornalero (m)	*ehl hohr-nah-'leh-roh*	journeyman
jubilación (f)	*lah hoo-bee-lah-see-'ohn*	retirement
juicio (m)	*ehl hoo-'ee-see-oh*	lawsuit, adjudication
junción (f)	*lah hoon-see-'ohn*	interface
junta (f)	*lah 'hoon-tah*	commission (agencies)
junta directiva	*lah 'hoon-tah dee-rehk-'tee-bah*	board of directors
junta ejecutiva	*lah 'hoon-tah eh-heh-koo-'tee-bah*	executive board
juntas de inspectores (fpl)	*lahs 'hoon-tahs deh een-spehk-'toh-rehs*	boards of supervisors
jurado (m)	*ehl hoo-'rah-doh*	sworn
jurisdicción (f)	*lah hoo-rees-deek-see-'ohn*	jurisdiction
justificar	*hoos-tee-fee-'kahr*	justify (v)
justo valor de mercado (m)	*ehl 'hoo-stoh bah-'lohr deh mehr-'kah-doh*	fair market value

K

kilometraje	*kee-loh-meh-trah-hey*	distance, mileage (in kilometers)

L

labor (m)	*ehl lah-'bohr*	labor
laboratorio (m)	*ehl lah-boh-rah-'toh-ree-oh*	laboratory

lagar (m)	*ehl lah-'gahr*	winepress
lago (m)	*ehl 'lah-goh*	lake
laguna (f)	*lah lah-'goo-nah*	lagoon
lámina (f)	*lah lah-mee-nah*	plate
laminado (m) en caliente	*ehl lah-mee-nah-doh ehn kah-lee-ehn-teh*	hot rolling
laminado en frío	*ehl lah-mee-nah-doh ehn free-oh*	cold rolling
laminador (m) continuo	*ehl lah-mee-nah-dohr kohn-tee-noo-oh*	continuous caster
lana (f)	*lah lah-nah*	wool
latigazo (m)	*ehl lah-tee-'gah-soh*	lash
látigo (m)	*ehl 'lah-tee-goh*	whip
laxante (m)	*ehl lahk-'sahn-teh*	laxative
lealtad a la marca (f)	*lah leh-ahl-'tahd ah lah 'mahr-kah*	brand loyalty
legado (m)	*ehl leh-'gah-doh*	legacy, bequest
legislación del trabajo (f)	*lah leh-hee-slah-see-'ohn dehl trah-'bah-hoh*	labor code
lengua	*lah lehn-'gwah*	language (national)
lenguaje (m)	*ehl lehn-'gwah-heh*	language (mode of speech)
lenguaje algorítmico	*ehl lehn-'gwah-heh ahl-goh-'reet-mee-koh*	algorithmic language
lenguaje de computación	*ehl lehn-'gwah-heh deh kohm-poo-tah-see-'ohn*	computer language
lenguaje máquina	*ehl lehn-'gwah-heh 'mah-kee-nah*	machine language
letra a plazo (f)	*lah 'leh-trah ah 'plah-soh*	time bill (of exchange)
letra aceptada	*lah 'leh-trah ah-sehp-'tah-dah*	acceptance bill
letra de cambio	*lah 'leh-trah deh 'kahm-bee-oh*	bill of exchange, draft, bill
letra sobre el interior	*lah 'leh-trah 'soh-breh ehl een-teh-ree-'ohr*	domestic bill
letras de cambio comerciales (fpl)	*lahs 'leh-trahs deh 'kahm-bee-oh koh-mehr-see-'ah-lehs*	commercial draft
letras de cambio extranjeras	*lahs 'leh-trahs deh 'kahm-bee-oh ehks-trahn-'heh-rahs*	foreign bill of exchange

letras del Tesoro	*lahs leh-trahs dehl teh-'soh-roh*	treasury bills
levadura (f)	*lah leh-bah-doo-rah*	yeast
levantar el censo	*leh-bahn-'tahr ehl 'sehn-soh*	census (to take the) (v)
ley (f)	*lah leh*	law
ley de rendimientos decrecientes	*lah leh deh rehn-dee-mee-'ehn-tohs deh kreh-see-'ehn-tehs*	law of diminishing returns
ley del trabajo	*lah leh dehl trah-'bah-hoh*	labor law
leyes antimono-polio (fpl)	*lahs 'leh-yehs ahn-tee-moh-noh-'poh-lee-oh*	antitrust laws
librado (m)	*ehl lee-'brah-doh*	drawee
librador (m)	*ehl lee-brah-'dohr*	drawer (of a check)
libre al costado del vapor	*'lee-breh ahl koh-'stah-doh dehl bah-'pohr*	free alongside ship
libre comercio (m)	*ehl 'lee-breh koh-'mehr-see-oh*	free trade
libre de avería particular	*'lee-breh deh ah-beh-'ree-ah pahr-tee-koo-'lahr*	free of particular average
libre de gravamen	*'lee-breh deh grah-'bah-mehn*	free and clear
libre de impuestos	*'lee-breh deh eem-'pweh-stohs*	duty free
libre empresa	*'lee-breh ehm-'preh-sah*	free enterprise
libre sobre carril	*'lee-breh 'soh-breh kah-'rreel*	free on rail
libreta bancaria (f)	*lah lee-'breh-tah bahn-'kah-ree-ah*	passbook
libro (m)	*ehl lee-broh*	book
libro de caja	*ehl 'lee-broh deh 'kah-hah*	cash book
libro de tapa dura	*ehl 'lee-broh deh tah-pah 'doo-rah*	hard cover
libro en rústica	*ehl lee-broh ehn 'roos-tee-kah*	paperback
libro impreso	*ehl lee-broh eem-preh-soh*	press book
libro mayor	*ehl 'lee-broh mah-'yohr*	ledger
licencia (f)	*lah lee-'sehn-see-ah*	license, franchise
licencia de importación	*lah lee-'sehn-see-ah deh eem-pohr-tah-see-'ohn*	import license

licitar	*lee-see-'tahr*	put in a bid (v)
líder (m)	*ehl 'lee-dehr*	leader
líder laboral	*ehl 'lee-dehr lah-boh-'rahl*	labor leader
límite de intercambio (m)	*ehl 'lee-mee-teh deh een-tehr-'kahm-bee-oh*	trading limit
limpieza (f) con baño químico	*lah leem-pee-eh-sahkohn bah-nyoh kee-mee-koh*	pickling
línea (f)	*'lee-neh-ah*	line
línea de crédito	*lah 'lee-neh-ah deh 'kreh-dee-toh*	credit line
línea de crédito a la vista	*lah 'lee-neh-ah deh 'kreh-dee-toh ah lah 'bees-tah*	demand line of credit
línea de ensamblaje	*lah lee-neh-ah deh ehn-sahm-blah-heh*	assembly line
Línea de Fecha Internacional	*lah 'lee-neh-ah deh 'feh-chah een-tehr-nah-see-oh-'nahl*	International Date Line
línea de huelga	*lah 'lee-neh-ah deh 'wehl-gah*	picket line
línea de montaje	*lah 'lee-neh-ah deh mohn-'tah-heh*	assembly line, production line
línea de muestreo	*lah 'lee-neh-ah deh mwehs-'treh-oh*	sample line
línea de negocios	*lah 'lee-neh-ah deh neh-'goh-see-ohs*	line of business
línea de productos	*lah 'lee-neh-ah deh proh-'dook-tohs*	product line
lineal	*lee-neh-'ahl*	linear
lingote de hierro (m)	*ehl leen-goh-teh deh 'yeh-roh*	pig iron
lingotera (f)	*lah leen-goh-'teh-rah*	ingot mold
lingotes (mpl)	*lohs leen-'goh-tehs*	billets, ingots
liquidación (f)	*lah lee-kee-dah-see-'ohn*	liquidation
liquidez (f)	*lah lee-kee-'dehs*	liquidity
lista (f)	*lah 'lees-tah*	list
lista de artículos exentos de derechos	*lah 'lees-tah deh ahr-'tee-koo-lohs ehk-'sehn-tohs deh deh-'reh-chohs*	free list (commodities without duty)
lista de precios	*lah 'lees-tah deh 'preh-see-ohs*	price list

lista de verificación	*lah 'lees-tah deh beh-ree-fee-kah-see-'ohn*	checklist
lista roja de animales amenazados	*lah 'lees-tah 'roh-hah deh ah-nee-'mah-lehs ah-meh-nah-'sah-dohs*	Red List of Threatened Animals
listado (m)	*ehl lee-'stah-doh*	listing
listar	*lees-'tahr*	list (v)
litigación (f)	*lah lee-tee-gah-see-'ohn*	litigation
litro (m)	*ehl lee-troh*	liter
lo más pronto posible (mpl)	*loh mahs 'prohn-toh poh-'see-bleh*	as soon as possible
local (m)	*ehl loh-'kahl*	premises
localidad de reparto aprobada (f)	*lah loh-kah-lee-'dahd deh reh-'pahr-toh ah-proh-'bah-dah*	approved delivery facility
localizar	*loh-kah-lee-'sahr*	locate (v)
logística (f)	*lah loh-'heeh-stee-kah*	logistics
logotipo (m)	*ehl loh-goh-'tee-poh*	logo
lomo (m)	*ehl loh-moh*	spine
longitud (f)	*lah lohn-hee-tood*	footage
lote (m)	*ehl 'loh-teh*	lot, batch
lote ordenado económico	*ehl 'loh-teh ohr-deh-'nah-doh eh-koh-'noh-mee-koh*	economic order quantity
loza (f)	*la 'loh-sah*	china
lozas (fpl)	*lahs loh-sahs*	slabs
lubricante para cilindros (m)	*ehl loo-bree-'kahn-teh 'pah-rah see-'leen-drohs*	oil (lubricating)
lucro (m)	*ehl 'loo-kroh*	profit
lustroso	*loos-troh-soh*	glossy (adj)

LL

llevar al máximo	*yeh-'bahr ahl 'mahk-see-moh*	maximize (v)
lluvia ácida (f)	*lah 'yoo-bee-ah 'ah-see-dah*	acid rain
lluvias (fpl)	*lahs 'yoo-bee-ahs*	rains

M

macro (f)	*lah 'mah-kroh*	macro
macro instrucción	*lah 'mah-kroh een-strook-see-'ohn*	macro
macroeconomía (f)	*lah mah-kroh-eh-koh-noh-'mee-ah*	macroeconomics
maduro	*mah-doo-roh*	ripe (adj)
magnetófono (f)	*ehl mahg-neh-toh-'foh-noh*	tape recorder
maíz (m)	*ehl mah-'ees*	maize
mal cálculo (m)	*ehl 'kahl-koo-loh*	miscalculation
mala interpreta-ción (f)	*lah 'mah-lah een-tehr-preh-tah-see-'ohn*	misunderstanding
malentendido	*mahl-ehn-tehn-'dee-doh*	misunderstanding
maleta (f)	*lah mah-leh-tah*	suitcase
maleta de maquillaje	*lah mah-leh-tah deh mah-kee-tah-heh*	makeup case
maleta para ropa	*lah mah-leh-tah pah-rah roh-pah*	garment bag
maletín (m)	*ehl mah-leh-'teen*	briefcase
maletín ejecutivo	*ehl mah-leh-'teen eh-heh-koo-'tee-boh*	attache case
mamífero (m)	*ehl mah-'mee-feh-roh*	mammal
mancomunar fondos	*mahn-koh-moo-'nahr 'fohn-dohs*	pool (funds) (v)
mancomunar intereses	*mahn-koh-moo-'nahr een-teh-'reh-sehs*	pooling of interests
mandamiento (m)	*ehl mahn-dah-mee-'ehn-toh*	writ
mandato (m)	*ehl mahn-'dah-toh*	mandate, power of attorney
mando (m)	*ehl 'mahn-doh*	command
manejador (m)	*ehl mah-neh-hah-'dohr*	handler
manejo (m)	*ehl mah-'neh-hoh*	administration (handling of), steering
manejo de caja	*ehl mah-'neh-hoh deh 'kah-hah*	cash management
manejo de quejas	*ehl mah-'neh-hoh deh 'keh-hahs*	grievance procedure
mangas (fpl) cortas	*lahs mahn-gahs 'kohr-tahs*	short sleeves

mangas largas	*lahs mahn-gahs lahr-gahs*	long sleeves
manglar (m)	*ehl mahn-'glahr*	swamp (mangrove)
manifiesto (m)	*ehl mah-nee-fee-'eh-stoh*	manifest
manifiesto de carga	*ehl mah-nee-fee-'eh-stoh deh 'kahr-gah*	waybill
mano de obra directa (f)	*lah 'mah-noh deh 'oh-brah dee-'rehk-tah*	direct labor (accounting)
mano de obra especializada	*lah 'mah-noh deh 'oh-brah ehs-peh-see-ah-lee-'sah-dah*	skilled labor
mano de obra indirecta	*lah 'mah-noh deh 'oh-brah een-dee-'rehk-tah*	indirect labor
mantel (m)	*ehl mahn-tehl*	tablecloth
mantelería (f)	*lah mahn-teh-leh-ree-ah*	linen
mantener	*mahn-teh-'nehr*	service (v)
mantener al corriente	*mahn-teh-'nehr ahl koh-rree-'ehn-teh*	keep posted (v)
mantenimiento (m)	*ehl mahn-teh-nee-mee-'ehn-toh*	maintenance
mantenimiento de libros por partida doble	*ehl mahn-teh-nee-mee-'ehn-toh deh 'lee-brohs pohr pahr-'tee-dah 'doh-bleh*	double-entry bookkeeping
mantenimiento preventivo	*ehl mahn-teh-nee-mee-'ehn-toh preh-behn-'tee-boh*	preventative maintenance
mantequillera (f)	*lah mahn-teh-kee-'yeh-rah*	butter dish
manufactura (f) de vasos de cristal	*lah mah-noo-fahk-too-rah deh bah-sohs deh kree-stahl*	crystal glass manufacturing
mapache (m)	*ehl mah-pah-cheh*	raccoon
maqueta (f)	*lah mah-'keh-tah*	mock-up, dummy
máquina (f) de coser	*lah mah-kee-nah deh koh-sehr*	sewing machine
maquinaria (f)	*lah mah-kee-'nah-ree-ah*	machinery
máquinas (fpl)	*lahs 'mah-kee-nahs*	hardware
maquinista (m)	*ehl mah-kee-'nees-tah*	operator (machine)
marca de fábrica (f)	*lah 'mahr-kah deh 'fah-bree-kah*	brand, trademark
marca privada	*lah 'mahr-kah pree-'bah-dah*	private label (or brand)

M

marca registrada	*lah 'mahr-kah reh-hee-'strah-dah*	registered trademark
marca sindical	*lah 'mahr-kah seen-dee-'kahl*	union label
marcas (fpl) registradas	*lahs mahr-kahs reh-hees-'trah-dahs*	register marks
margen al futuro (m)	*ehl 'mahr-hehn ahl foo-'too-roh*	forward margin
margen bruto	*ehl 'mahr-hehn 'broo-toh*	gross margin
margen de beneficio	*ehl 'mahr-hehn deh beh-neh-'fee-see-oh*	profit margin
margen de ganancias	*ehl 'mahr-hehn deh gah-'nahn-see-ahs*	markup
margen de mantenimiento	*ehl 'mahr-hehn deh mahn-teh-nee-mee-'ehn-toh*	maintenance
margen de prestación	*ehl 'mahr-hehn deh prehs-tah-see-'ohn*	lending margin
margen de seguridad	*ehl 'mahr-hehn deh seh-goo-ree-'dahd*	margin of safety
margen del beneficio	*ehl 'mahr-hehn dehl beh-neh-'fee-see-oh*	profit margin
margen variable	*ehl 'mahr-hehn bah-ree-'ah-bleh*	variable margin
márketing (m)	*ehl 'mahr-keht-teeng*	marketing
marta (f)	*lah mahr-tah*	sable
más interés acumulado	*mahs een-teh-'rehs ah-koo-moo-'lah-doh*	plus accrued interest
material rodante (m)	*ehl mah-teh-ree-'ahl roh-'dahn-teh*	rolling stock
materiales (mpl)	*lohs mah-teh-ree-'ah-lehs*	materials
materiales primas	*lohs mah-teh-ree-'ah-lehs 'pree-mahs*	raw materials
mayorista (m)	*ehl mah-yoh-'rees-tah*	jobber, wholesaler
mayorista de estantes	*ehl mah-yoh-'rees-tah deh ehs-'tahn-tehs*	rack jobber
mayúscula (m)	*lah mah yoos-koo-lah*	capital
media aritmética (f)	*lah 'meh-dee-ah ah-reet-'meh-tee-kah*	arithmetic mean
media ponderada	*lah 'meh-dee-ah pohn-deh-'rah-dah*	weighted average

mediación (f)	*lah meh-dee-ah-see-'ohn*	mediation
mediar en una desavenencia	*meh-dee-'ahr ehn 'oo-nah dehs-ah-beh-'nehn-see-ah*	troubleshoot (v)
medias (fpl) de mujer	*lahs 'meh-dee-ahs deh moo-'hehr*	stockings
medicina (f)	*lah meh-dee-'see-nah*	medicine
médico (m)	*ehl meh-dee-koh*	physician
medida de yardas (f)	*lah meh-'dee-dah deh 'yahr-dahs*	yardstick
medidas para la protección de los derechos personales (fpl)	*lahs meh-'dee-dahs 'pah-rah lah -proh-tehk-see-'ohn deh lohs deh-'reh-chohs pehr-soh-'nah-lehs*	affirmative action
medio (m)	*ehl 'meh-dee-oh*	mean
medio ambiente	*ehl 'meh-dee-oh ahm-bee-'ehn-teh*	environment
medio de cambio	*ehl 'meh-dee-oh deh 'kahm-bee-oh*	medium of exchange
medios (mpl)	*lohs 'meh-dee-ohs*	means
medios de publicidad	*lohs 'meh-dee-ohs deh poo-blee-see-'dahd*	advertising media
medios públicos de comunicación	*lohs 'meh-dee-ohs 'poo-blee-kohs deh koh-moo-nee-kah-see-'ohn*	mass media
medir	*meh-'deer*	measure (v)
mejor postor (m)	*ehl meh-'hohr poh-'stohr*	highest bidder
mejorar	*meh-hoh-'rahr*	improve upon (v)
mejoras (fpl)	*lahs meh-'hoh-rahs*	improvements
memorándum (m)	*ehl meh-moh-'rahn-doom*	memorandum
memoria (f)	*lah meh-'moh-ree-ah*	memory
memoria de acceso directo	*lah meh-'moh-ree-ah deh ahk-'seh-soh dee-'rehk-toh*	random access memory (RAM)
memoria de acceso rápido	*lah meh-'moh-ree-ah deh ahk-'seh-soh 'rah-pee-doh*	quick access storage
memoria de la computadora	*lah meh-'moh-ree-ah deh lah kohm-poo-tah-'doh-rah*	computer memory

memoria en cinta magnética	*lah meh-'moh-ree-ah ehn 'seen-tah mahg-'neh-tee-kah*	magnetic memory
menos de cien acciones	*'meh-nohs deh 'see-ehn ahk-see-'oh-nehs*	broken lot
menos de un camión completo	*'meh-nohs deh oon kah-mee-'ohn kohm-'pleh-toh*	less-than-a-truckload
menos de un vagón completo	*'meh-nohs deh oon bah-'gohn kohm-'pleh-toh*	less-than-a-carload
mensaje (m)	*ehl mehn-'sah-heh*	dispatch, message
mercadear	*mehr-kah-deh-ahr*	market (v)
mercadeo (m)	*ehl mehr-kah-'deh-oh*	marketing
mercadería acompañada (f)	*lah mehr-kah-deh-'ree-ah ah-kohm-pah-'nyah-dah*	accompanied goods
mercado (m)	*ehl mehr-'kah-doh*	outlet, market, marketplace
mercado abierto	*ehl mehr-'kah-doh ah-bee-'ehr-toh*	open market
mercado actual	*ehl mehr-'kah-doh ahk-tooh-'ahl*	spot market
mercado ajustado	*ehl mehr-'kah-doh ah-hoo-'stah-doh*	tight market
mercado al por mayor	*ehl mehr-'kah-doh ahl pohr mah-'yohr*	wholesale market
mercado alcista	*ehl mehr-'kah-doh ahl-'sees-tah*	upmarket
mercado bajista	*ehl mehr-'kah-doh bah-'hees-tah*	bear market
Mercado Común	*ehl mehr-'kah-doh koh-'moon*	Common Market
mercado con poca actividad	*ehl mehr-'kah-doh kohn 'poh-kah ahk-tee-bee-'dahd*	thin market
mercado de acciones	*ehl mehr-'kah-doh deh ahk-see-'oh-nehs*	stock market
mercado de alcistas	*ehl mehr-'kah-doh deh ahl-'sees-tahs*	bull market
mercado de capital	*ehl mehr-'kah-doh deh kah-pee-'tahl*	capital market
mercado de compradores	*ehl mehr-'kah-doh deh kohm-prah-'doh-rehs*	buyers' market

M

mercado de divisas	*ehl mehr-'kah-doh deh dee-'bee-sahs*	foreign exchange market
mercado de dos niveles	*ehl mehr-'kah-doh deh dohs nee-'beh-lehs*	two-tiered market
mercado de ventas al por menor	*ehl mehr-'kah-doh deh 'behn-tahs ahl pohr meh-'nohr*	retail outlet
mercado doméstico	*ehl mehr-'kah-doh doh-'mehs-tee-koh*	home market
mercado futuro	*ehl mehr-'kah-doh foo-'too-roh*	forward market
mercado gris	*ehl mehr-'kah-doh grees*	gray market
mercado inestable	*ehl mehr-'kah-doh een-eh-'stah-bleh*	volatile market
mercado invertido (inverso)	*ehl mehr-'kah-doh een-behr-'tee-doh (een-'behr-soh)*	inverted market
mercado laboral	*ehl mehr-'kah-doh lah-boh-'rahl*	labor market
mercado libre	*ehl mehr-'kah-doh 'lee-breh*	free market
mercado marginal	*ehl mehr-'kah-doh mahr-hee-'nahl*	fringe market
mercado monetario	*ehl mehr-'kah-doh moh-neh-'tah-ree-oh*	money market
mercado negro	*ehl mehr-'kah-doh 'neh-groh*	black market
mercado primario	*ehl mehr-'kah-doh pree-'mah-ree-oh*	primary market
mercado secundario de valores	*ehl mehr-'kah-doh seh-koon-'dah-ree-oh deh bah-'loh-rehs*	secondary market (securities)
mercancía (f)	*lah mehr-kahn-'see-ah*	commodity
mercancía al por menor	*lah mehr-kahn-'see-ah ahl pohr meh-'nohr*	retail merchandise
mercancías (fpl)	*lahs mehr-kahn-'see-ahs*	goods, merchandise
mercancías secas o finas	*lahs mehr-kahn-'see-ahs 'seh-kahs oh 'fee-nahs*	dry goods
mercantil	*mehr-kahn-'teel*	mercantile
mes de la entrega (m)	*ehl mehs deh lah ehn-'treh-gah*	contract month
metales (mpl)	*lohs meh-'tah-lehs*	metals

metano (m)	*ehl meh-'tah-noh*	methane
meter guión para separar sílabas	*meh-'tehr gee-'ohn 'pah-rah seh-pah-'rahr 'see-lah-bahs*	hyphenate (v)
método (m)	*ehl 'meh-toh-doh*	method
método de acumulación	*ehl 'meh-toh-doh deh ah-koo-moo-lah-see-'ohn*	accrued method
método de contabilidad	*ehl 'meh-toh-doh deh kohn-tah-bee-lee-'dahd*	accounting method
mezcla (f)	*lah 'mehs-klah*	mix
mezcla de recursos de energía	*lah 'mehs-klah deh reh-'koor-sohs deh eh-nehr-'hee-ah*	energy (mix)
mezclador (m)	*ehl mehs-klah-'dohr*	mixer
mezclar	*mehs-'klahr*	blend (v)
micro-organismo (m)	*ehl mee-kroh-ohr-gah-'nees-moh*	microorganism
microcomputadora (f)	*lah mee-kroh-kohm-poo-tah-'doh-rah*	microcomputer, personal computer
microficha (f)	*lah mee-kroh-'fee-chah*	microchip
microfichero (m)	*ehl mee-kroh-fee-'cheh-roh*	microfiche
micrófono (m)	*ehl mee-'kroh-foh-noh*	microphone
micrológico (m)	*ehl mee-kroh-'loh-hee-koh*	chip
microonda (m)	*ehl mee-kroh-'ohn-dah*	microwave
micropelícula (f)	*lah mee-kroh-peh-'lee-koo-lah*	microfilm
microprocesador (m)	*ehl mee-kroh-proh-seh-sah-'dohr*	microprocessor
miembro de por vida (m)	*ehl mee-'ehm-broh deh pohr 'bee-dah*	life member
migración (f)	*lah mee-grah-see-'ohn*	migration
millaje (m)	*ehl mee-'yah-heh*	mileage
mineral (m)	*ehl mee-neh-rahl*	ore
mineral de hierro	*ehl mee-neh-'rahl deh 'yeh-roh*	iron ore
mineral de manganeso	*ehl mee-neh-'rahl deh mahn-gah-'neh-soh*	manganese ore
minicomputadora (f)	*lah mee-nee-kohm-poo-tah-'doh-rah*	minicomputer

minúscula (f)	*lah mee-'noos-koo-lah*	lower case
misceláneo	*mee-seh-'lah-neh-oh*	miscellaneous
mochila (f)	*lah moh-'cheh-lah*	tote bag
moción (f)	*lah moh-see-'ohn*	motion
moda (f)	*lah 'moh-dah*	mode, fashion
modelo (m)	*ehl moh-'deh-loh*	model
modelo de equilibrio	*ehl moh-'deh-loh deh eh-kee-'lee-bree-oh*	covariance
modelo matemático	*ehl moh-'deh-loh mah-teh-'mah-tee-koh*	mathematical model
modem (m)	*ehl 'moh-dehm*	modem
moderno	*moderno*	modern
modificación para mantener una apariencia (f)	*lah moh-dee-fee-kah-see-'ohn 'pah-rah mahn-teh-'nehr 'oo-nah ah-pah-ree-'ehn-see-ah*	window dressing
modificación por índice	*lah moh-dee-fee-kah-see-'ohn pohr 'een-dee-seh*	indexing
modulación de frecuencia (f)	*lah moh-doo-lah-see-'ohn deh freh-'kwehn-see-ah*	frequency modulation (FM)
modulador-demodulador (m)	*ehl moh-doo-lah-'dohr deh-moh-doo-lah-'dohr*	modem
mol (m)	*ehl mohl*	mole
molécula (f)	*lah moh-'leh-koo-lah*	molecule
molido	*moh-lee-doh*	ground (adj)
molienda (f)	*lah moh-lee-'ehn-dah*	milling (grain)
molinillo (m) de pimienta	*ehl moh-lee-'nee-yoh deh pee-mee 'ehn-tah*	pepper mill
momento (m) de torsión	*ehl moh-'mehn-toh deh tohr-see-ohn*	torque
moneda (f)	*lah moh-'neh-dah*	money
moneda bloqueada	*lah moh-'neh-dah bloh-keh-'ah-dah*	blocked currency
moneda de curso legal	*lah moh-'neh-dah deh 'koor-soh leh-'gahl*	legal tender
moneda débil (blanda)	*lah moh-'neh-dah 'deh-beel ('blahn-dah)*	soft currency

moneda estable	*lah moh-'neh-dah ehs-'tah-bleh*	hard currency
moneda extranjera	*lah moh-'neh-dah ehs-trahn-'heh-rah*	foreign currency, foreign exchange
moneda fraccionaria	*lah moh-'neh-dah frahk-see-oh-'nah-ree-ah*	hard currency
monedero (m)	*ehl moh-neh-'deh-roh*	purse
monitor (m)	*ehl moh-nee-'tohr*	monitor
monopolio legal (m)	*ehl moh-noh-'poh-lee-oh leh-'gahl*	legal monopoly
monopsonio (m)	*ehl moh-nohp-'soh-nee-oh*	monopsony
monóxido de carbono (m)	*ehl moh-'nohk-see-doh deh kahr-'boh-noh*	carbon monoxide
montacargas (m)	*ehl mohn-tah-'kahr-gahs*	elevator
montaje (m)	*ehl mohn-'tah-heh*	device
montar	*mohn-'tahr*	assemble (v)
moral (f)	*lah moh-'rahl*	morale
moratoria (f)	*lah moh-rah-'toh-ree-ah*	moratorium
morfina (f)	*lah mohr-'fee-nah*	morphine
mortalidad (f)	*lah mohr-tah-lee-'dahd*	death rate
mortalidad infantil	*lah mohr-tah-lee-'dahd een-fahn-'teel*	death rate (infant)
motor (m)	*ehl moh-'tohr*	engine
motor de cuatro cilindros	*ehl moh-'tohr deh kwah-troh see-'leen-dros*	four-cylinder engine
motor de seis cilindros	*ehl moh-tohr deh seh-ees see-'leen-drohs*	six-cylinder engine
motor V8	*ehl moh-'tohr V8*	V8 engine
mover el bloque	*moh-'behr ehl 'bloh-keh*	to move the block (v)
movilidad laboral (f)	*lah moh-bee-lee-'dahd lah-boh-'rahl*	mobility of labor
muelle (m)	*ehl mweh-yeh*	spring
muelle el recibo de muelle	*ehl 'mweh-yeh, ehl reh-'see-boh deh 'mweh-yeh*	dock (ship's receipt)
muestra al azar (f)	*lah 'mweh-strah ahl ah-'sahr*	random sample
muestra de aceptación	*lah 'mweh-strah deh ah-sehp-tah-see-'ohn*	acceptance sampling

muestras que hacen juego (fpl)	*lahs 'mweh-strahs keh 'ah-sehn hoo-'eh-goh*	matched samples
muestrear	*mweeh-streh-'ahr*	sample (v)
muestreo mixto (m)	*ehl moo-ehs-'treh-oh 'meeks-toh*	mixed sampling
multa (f)	*lah 'mool-tah*	fine, quality
multiplicador (m)	*ehl mool-tee-plee-kah-'dohr*	multiplier
multiplicidad de monedas (f)	*lah mool-tee-plee-see-'dahd deh moh-'neh-dahs*	multicurrency
múltiplos (mpl)	*lohs 'mool-tee-plohs*	multiples

N

nacionalismo (m)	*ehl nah-see-oh-nah-'lees-moh*	nationalism
nacionalización (f)	*lah nah-see-oh-nah-lee-sah-see-'ohn*	nationalization
naciones subdesarrolladas (f)	*lahs nah-see-'oh-nehs soob-dehs-ah-rroh-'yah-dahs*	underdeveloped nations
narcótico (m)	*ehl nahr-koh-tee-koh*	narcotic
necesidades (f)	*lahs neh-seh-see-'dah-dehs*	requirements
negligente	*nehg-lee-'hehn-teh*	negligent
negociable	*neh-goh-see-'ah-bleh*	negotiable
negociación (f)	*lah neh-goh-see-ah-see-'ohn*	negotiation
negociaciones arancelarias lineales (fpl)	*lahs neh-goh-see-ah-see-'oh-nehs ah-rahn-seh-'lah-ree-ahs lee-neh-'ah-lehs*	across-the-board tariff negotiation
negociante (m)	*ehl neh-goh-see-'ahn-teh*	dealer
negociar	*neh-goh-see-'ahr*	negotiate (v)
negocio (m)	*ehl neh-'goh-see-oh*	deal, dealership
negocio en paquete	*ehl neh-'goh-see-oh ehn pah-'keh-teh*	package deal
negocio en participación	*ehl neh-'goh-see-oh ehn pahr-tee-see-pah-see-'ohn*	joint venture
negocio pequeño	*ehl neh-'goh-see-oh peh-'keh-nyoh*	small business

N

negrita (f)	*lah-neh-gree-tah*	boldface
neto	*'neh-toh*	net
neumático (m)	*ehl neh-oo-'mah-tee-koh*	tire (Spain and South America)
neumático radial	*ehl neh-oo-'mah-tee-koh rah-dee-'ahl*	radial tire (Spain and South America)
nitrato (m)	*ehl nee-'trah-toh*	nitrate
nitrito (m)	*ehl nee-'tree-toh*	nitrite
nitrógeno	*ehl nee-'troh-heh-noh*	nitrogen
nivel de calidad (m)	*ehl nee-'behl deh kah-lee-'dahd*	acceptable level
nivel de vida	*ehl nee-'behl deh 'bee-dah*	standard of living
nivel del mar	*ehl nee-'behl dehl mahr*	sea level
nivel salarial	*ehl nee-'behl sah-lah-ree-'ahl*	wage level
nivelar	*nee-beh-'lahr*	level out (v)
no aceptar	*noh ah-sehp-'tahr*	dishonor (as a check) (v)
no ajustado a formato	*noh ah-hoos-'tah-doh ah fohr-'mah-toh*	unformatted (adj)
no archivado por nombre en cualquier otra forma	*noh ahr-chee-'bah-doh pohr 'nohm-breh ehn kwahl-kee-'eh-rah 'oh-trah 'fohr-mah*	not otherwise indexed by name
no es miembro de	*noh ehs mee-'ehm-broh deh*	nonmember
no hay problema	*noh ah-ee proh-'bleh-mah*	no problem
no lucrativo	*noh loo-krah-'tee-boh*	nonprofit
no registrado	*noh reh-hee-'strah-doh*	unlisted
no residente	*noh reh-see-'dehn-teh*	nonresident
nombramiento (m)	*ehl nohm-brah-mee-'ehn-toh*	appointment
nómina (f)	*lah 'noh-mee-nah*	payroll
norma (f)	*lah 'nohr-mah*	norm
norma del hombre prudente	*lah 'nohr-mah dehl 'ohm-breh proo-'dehn-teh*	prudent man rule
norma para poder ejercer la exigibilidad a la vista	*lah 'nohr-mah 'pah-rah poh-'dehr eh-hehr-'sehr lah ehk-see-bee-lee-'dahd ah lah 'bees-tah*	call rule
nota bancaria (f)	*lah 'noh-tah bahn-'kah-ree-ah*	bank note

nota de crédito	*lah 'noh-tah deh 'kreh-dee-toh*	credit note
nota de débito	*lah 'noh-tah deh 'deh-bee-toh*	debit
nota de pago grande generalmente al final	*lah 'noh-tah deh 'pah-goh 'grahn-deh heh-neh-rahl-'mehn-teh ahl fee-'nahl*	balloon note
notación binaria (f)	*lah noh-tah-see-'ohn bee-'nah-ree-ah*	binary notation
notario público (m)	*ehl noh-'tah-ree-oh 'poo-blee-koh*	notary
notificación de reparto (m)	*lah noh-tee-fee-kah-see-'ohn deh reh-'pahr-toh*	allotment letter
novación (f)	*lah noh-bah-see-'ohn*	novation
nubes (fpl)	*lahs 'noo-behs*	clouds
nudo (m)	*ehl 'noo-doh*	knot (nautical)
nueva emisión (f)	*lah noo-'eh-bah eh-mee-see-'ohn*	new issue
nulo y sin valor	*'noo-loh ee seen bah-'lohr*	null and void
número de acciones de ciento o múltiples de ciento (m)	*ehl 'noo-meh-roh deh ahk-see-'oh-nehs deh see-'ehn-toh oh 'mool-tee-plehs deh see-'ehn-toh*	round lot
número de cuenta	*ehl 'noo-meh-roh deh 'kwehn-tah*	account number
número de referencia	*ehl 'noo-meh-roh deh referencia*	reference number
número del pedido	*ehl 'noo-meh-roh deh peh-'dee-doh*	order number

O

objetivo de la compañía (m)	*ehl ohb-heh-'tee-boh deh lah kohm-pah-'nyee-ah*	company goal
objetos (mpl) de barro	*lohs ohn-heh-tohs deh bah-rroh*	earthenware
obligación (f)	*lah ohb-lee-gah-see-'ohn*	obligation, bond
obligación hipotecaria	*lah ohb-lee-gah-see-'ohn ee-poh-teh-'kah-ree-ah*	bond, mortgage debenture

obligaciones (sinónimo genérico de deuda) (fpl)	*lahs obh-lee-gah-see-'ohn-ehs (see-'noh-nee-moh heh-'neh-ree-koh deh deh-'oo-dah)*	debentures
obligaciones agrícolas	*lahs ohb-lee-gah-see-'ohn-ehs ah-'gree-koh-lahs*	agricultural paper
obligaciones con vencimiento escalonado	*lahs ohb-lee-gah-see-'ohn-ehs kohn behn-see-mee-'ehn-toh ehs-kah-loh-'nah-doh*	serial bonds
obligaciones convertibles	*lahs ohb-lee-gah-see-'ohn-ehs kohn-behr-'tee-blehs*	convertible debentures
obligado a	*oh-blee-'gah-doh ah*	liable to
obra muerta (f)	*lah 'oh-brah 'mwehr-tah*	freeboard
obrar recíprocamente	*oh-'brahr reh-'see-proh-kah-'mehn-teh*	interact (v)
obrero (m)	*ehl oh-'breh-roh*	blue collar worker, laborer
obrero (m) automotriz	*ehl oh-breh-roh ow-toh-moh-trees*	automotive worker
obrero que reemplaza al huelguista	*ehl oh-'breh-roh keh reh-ehm-'plah-sah ahl wehl-'gees-tah*	strikebreaker
obreros manuales (mpl)	*lohs oh-'breh-rohs mah-noo-'ah-lehs*	manual workers
obsolescencia (f)	*lah ohb-soh-leh-'sehn-see-ah*	obsolescence
obsolescencia planificada	*lah ohb-soh-leh-'sehn-see-ah plah-nee-fee-'kah-dah*	planned obsolescence
obstáculo	*ehl ohb-'stah-koo-loh*	handicap
obtención (f)	*lah ohb-tehn-see-'ohn*	procurement
ocupación (f)	*lah oh-koo-pah-see-'ohn*	occupation
odómetro (m)	*ehl oh-'doh-meh-troh*	odometer
oferente (m)	*ehl oh-feh-'rehn-teh*	supplier
oferta (f)	*lah oh-'fehr-tah*	supply
oferta agregada	*lah oh-'fehr-tah ah-greh-'gah-dah*	aggregate supply
oferta de compra	*lah oh-'fehr-tah deh 'kohm-prah*	tender offer
oferta de dinero	*lah oh-'fehr-tah deh dee-'neh-roh*	money supply

oferta de prima	*lah oh-'fehr-tah deh 'pree-mah*	premium offer
oferta para la adquisición	*lah oh-'fehr-tah 'pah-rah lah ahd-kee-see-see-'ohn*	takeover bid
oferta por escrito	*lah oh-'fehr-tah pohr ehs-'kree-toh*	written bid (stock exchange)
oferta pública	*lah oh-'fehr-tah 'poo-blee-kah*	public offering
oferta verbal	*lah oh-'fehr-tah behr-'bahl*	oral bid (stock exchange)
oferta y demanda	*lah oh-'fehr-tah ee deh-'mahn-dah*	supply and demand
oficina (f)	*lah oh-fee-'see-nah*	office
oficina de crédito	*lah oh-fee-'see-nah deh 'kreh-dee-toh*	credit bureau
oficina principal de operaciones	*lah oh-fee-'see-nah preen-see-'pahl deh oh-peh-rah-see-'oh-nehs*	operations headquarters
oficina principal	*lah oh-fee-'see-nah preen-see-'pahl*	headquarters
oficinista (m/f)	*ehl/lah oh-fee-see-'nees-tah*	white-collar worker
ofrecer en venta	*oh-freh-'sehr ehn 'behn-tah*	offer for sale (v)
ofrecer la postura mayor	*oh-freh-'sehr lah poh-'stoo-rah mah-'yohr*	outbid (v)
ofrecer	*oh-freh-'sehr*	offer (v), tender (v)
olas del mar (fpl)	*lahs 'oh-lahs dehl mahr*	waves (of sea)
oleoducto (m)	*ehl oh-leh-oh-'dook-toh*	pipeline
oligopolio (m)	*ehl oh-lee-goh-'poh-lee-oh*	oligopoly
oligopsonio (m)	*ehloh-lee-gohp-'soh-nee-oh*	oligopsony
omisión (f)	*lah oh-mee-see-'ohn*	dropout
onda (f)	*lah 'ohn-dah*	wave
onda corta	*lah 'ohn-dah 'kohr-tah*	short wave
opción (f)	*lah ohp-see-'ohn*	option
opción a futuro	*lah ohp-see-'ohn ah foo-'too-roh*	futures option
opción de adquerir acciones a precio fijo	*lah ohp-see-'ohn deh ahd-keh-reer ak-see-'oh-nehs ah 'preh-see-oh fee-ho*	stock option

opción de bolsa con opción de compra o venta	*lah ohp-see-'ohn deh 'bohl-sah kohn ohp-see-'ohn deh 'kohm-prah oh 'behn-tah*	straddle
opción de retiro (bono) anticipadamente	*lah ohp-see-'ohn deh reh-'tee-roh ('boh-noh) ahn-tee-see-pah-dah-'mehn-teh*	call option
opción de venta	*lah ohp-see-'ohn deh 'behn-tah*	put option
opción del comprador	*lah ohp-see-'ohn dehl kohm-prah-'dohr*	buyers' option
operación manual (f)	*lah oh-peh-rah-see-'ohn mah-noo-'ahl*	manual operation
operaciones auxiliares (fpl)	*lahs oh-peh-rah-see-'oh-nehs owx-see-lee-'ah-rehs*	ancillary operations
operaciones con acciones antes de su emisión	*lahs oh-peh-rah-see-'oh-nehs 'ahn-tehs deh soo eh-mee-see-'ohn*	when issued
operaciones del mercado abierto	*lahs oh-peh-rah-see-'oh-nehs dehl mehr-'kah-doh ah-bee-'ehr-toh*	open market operations (money policy)
opio (m)	*ehl 'oh-pee-oh*	opium
óptico	*ohp-tee-koh*	optic (adj)
orden abierta (f)	*lah 'ohr-dehn ah-bee-'ehr-toh*	open order
orden alternativa	*lah 'ohr-dehn ahl-tehr-nah-'tee-bah*	alternative order
orden con precio prefijado	*lah 'ohr-dehn kohn 'prehe-see-oh preh-fee-'hah-doh*	limit order (stock market)
orden de compra	*lah 'ohr-dehn deh 'kohm-prah*	purchase order
orden de pérdida limitada	*lah 'ohr-dehn deh 'pehr-dee-dah lee-mee-'tah-dah*	stop-loss order
orden de trabajo	*lah 'ohr-dehn deh trah-'bah-hoh*	work order
orden del día	*ehl 'ohr-dehn dehl 'dee-ah*	order of the day, agenda
orden discrecionaria	*lah 'ohr-dehn dees-kreh-see-oh-'nah-ree-ah*	discretionary order
orden general	*lah 'ohr-dehn heh-neh-'rahl*	blanket order

O

orden permanente	*lah 'ohr-dehn pehr-mah-'nehn-teh*	standing order
orden que caduca después de un día	*lah 'ohr-dehn keh kah-'doo-kah dehs-'pwehs deh oon 'dee-ah*	day order (stockmarket)
ordenador (m)	*ehl ohr-deh-nah-dohr*	computer (Spain)
ordenanza municipal sobre construcción (f)	*lah ohr-deh-'nahn-sah moo-nee-see-'pahl 'soh-breh kohn-strook-see-'ohn*	zoning law
ordenar	*ohr-deh-'nahr*	order, place an (v)
orgánico	*ohr-'gah-nee-koh*	organic (adj)
organigrama (m)	*ehl ohr-hag-nee-'grah-mah*	organization chart
organigrama gerencial	*ehl ohr-gah-nee-'grah-mah heh-rehn-see-'ahl*	management chart
organismo (m)	*ehl ohr-gah-'nees-moh*	commission (agency)
organización (f)	*lah ohr-gah-nee-sah-see-'ohn*	layout, organization
Organización de Países Exportadores de Petróleo (OPEP)	*lah ohr-gah-nee-sah-see-'ohn deh pah-'ee-sehs ehks-pohr-tah-'doh-rehs deh peh-'troh-leh-oh*	Organization of Petroleum-Exporting Countries (OPEC)
organización del personal	*lah ohr-gah-nee-sah-see-'ohn dehl pehr-soh-'nahl*	staff organization
organización vertical	*lah ohr-gah-nee-sah-see-'ohn behr-tee-'kahl*	vertical integration
origen (m)	*ehl oh-'ree-hehn*	source
oscilador (m)	*ehl oh-see-lah-dohr*	oscillator
otros activos (mpl)	*lohs 'oh-trohs ahk-'tee-bohs*	other assets
oxidación (f)	*lah ohk-see-dah-see-'ohn*	oxidation
óxidos (mpl)	*lohs 'ohk-see-dohs*	oxides
ozono (m)	*ehl oh-'soh-noh*	ozone

P

(al) por menor	*ahl pohr meh-'nohr*	retail
pacto (m)	*ehl 'pahk-toh*	bargain, pact, agreement
pagadero a la orden	*pah-gah-'deh-roh ah lah 'ohr-dehn*	payable to order

pagadero a la vista	*pah-gah-'deh-roh ah lah 'bee-stah*	payable on demand
pagadero al portador	*pah-gah-'deh-roh ahl pohr-tah-'dohr*	payable to bearer
pagado en su totalidad	*pah-'gah-doh ehn soo toh-tah-lee-'dahd*	paid in full
pagador (m)	*ehl pah-gah-'dohr*	paymaster
pagar	*pah-'gahr*	pay (v)
pagar el precio del comprador	*pah-'gahr ehl 'preh-see-oh dehl kohm-prah-'dohr*	meet the price
pagaré (m)	*ehl pah-gah-'reh*	promissory note
pagaré a la vista	*ehl pah-gah-'reh ah lah 'bees-tah*	sight draft
pagaré a respaldo	*ehl pah-gah-'reh a reh-'spahl-doh*	backed note
pagaré financiero	*ehl pah-gah-'reh fee-nahn-see-'eh-roh*	commercial paper
página (f)	*lah pah-hee-nah*	page
pago (m)	*ehl 'pah-goh*	payment
pago de efectivo contra entrega	*ehl 'pah-goh deh eh-fehk-'tee-boh 'kohn-trah ehn-'treh-gah*	cash on delivery
pago de impuesto a medida que el contribuyente recibe sus ingresos	*ehl 'pah-goh deh eem-'pweh-stoh ah meh-'dee-dah keh ehl kohn-tree-boo-'yehn-teh reh-'see-beh soos een-'greh-sohs*	pay as you go
pago en efectivo antes de la entrega	*ehl 'pah-goh deh eh-fehk-'tee-boh 'ahn-tehs deh lah ehn-'treh-gah*	cash before delivery
pago en especie	*ehl 'pah-goh ehn eh-'speh-see-eh*	payment in kind
pago global	*ehl 'pah-goh gloh-'bahl*	balloon payment
pago grande generalmente al final	*ehl 'pah-goh 'grahn-deh heh-neh-rahl-'mehn-teh ahl fee-'nahl*	balloon payment
pago ilegal para incumplir algunas condiciones de un contrato	*ehl 'pah-goh ee-leh-'gahl 'pah-rah een-koom-'pleer ahl-'goo-nahs kohn-dee-see-'oh-nehs deh oon kohn-'trah-toh*	kickback

P

pago incial	*ehl 'pah-goh ee-nee-see-'ahl*	down payment
pago negado	*ehl 'pah-goh neh-'gah-doh*	payment refused
pago parcial	*ehl 'pah-goh pahr-see-'ahl*	partial payment
pago por adelantado	*ehl 'pah-goh pohr ah-deh-lahn-'tah-doh*	advance payment
pago por derechos de patente	*ehl 'pah-goh pohr deh-'reh-chos deh pah-'tehn-teh*	royalty (payment)
pago rehusado	*ehl 'pah-goh reh-oo-'sah-doh*	refuse payment
pago total	*ehl 'pah-goh toh-'tahl*	payment in full, full settlement
país (m)	*ehl pah-ees*	country
país de origen	*ehl pah-'ees deh oh-'ree-hehn*	country of origin
país de riesgo	*ehl pah-'ees deh ree-'ehs-goh*	country of risk
país más favorecido	*ehl pah-'ees mahs fah-boh-reh-'see-doh*	most-favored nation
países exportadores de petróleo (mpl)	*lahs pah'ee-sehs ehks-pohr-tah-'doh-rehs deh peh-'troh-leh-oh*	oil exporting countries
países importadores de petróleo en vías de desarrollo	*lahs pah'ee-sehs ehks-pohr-tah-'doh-rehs deh peh-'troh-leh-oh ehn 'bee-ahs deh dehs-ah-'rroh-yoh*	oil-importing developing countries (IODC)
países importadores de petróleo	*lahs pah'ee-sehs eem-pohr-tah-'doh-rehs deh peh-'troh-leh-oh*	oil importing countries
pájaros (mpl)	*lohs 'pah-hah-rohs*	birds
palabra (f)	*lah pah-'lah-brah*	word
palanca de juegos (f)	*lah pah-'lahn-kah deh 'hweh-gohs*	joystick
paleta (f)	*lah pah-'leh-tah*	pallet
paleta de servir tortas (bizcocho)	*lah pah-'leh-tah deh sehr-beer 'tohr-tahs (bees-koh-choh)*	pastry server
panera (f)	*lah pah-'neh-rah*	breadbasket
panfleto (m)	*ehl pahn-'fleh-toh*	pamphlet
paños	*pah-'nyos*	soft goods
pantalla (f)	*lah pahn-'tah-yah*	screen

pantalones (mpl)	*lohs pahn-tah-'loh-nehs*	slacks
pantano (m)	*ehl pahn-'tah-noh*	marsh, swamp
pañuelo (m)	*ehl pah-nyoo-eh-loh*	handkerchief
papel (m)	*ehl pah-'pehl*	paper
papel cuché	*ehl pah-'pehl koo-'cheh*	coated paper
papel revestido	*ehl pah-ehl reh-vehs-'tee-doh*	coated paper
par	*pahr*	par
para exportar	*'pah-rah ehks-pohr-'tahr*	for export
para la entrega futura	*'pah-rah lah ehn-'treh-gah foo-'too-rah*	for forwarding
parabólica (f)	*lah pah-rah-'boh-lee-kah*	satellite dish
parabrisas (m)	*ehl pah-rah-'bree-sahs*	windshield
parachoques (m)	*ehl pah-rah-choh-kehs*	bumper
parar (el trabajo)	*pah-'rahr (ehl trah-'bah-hoh)*	strike (v)
paridad (f)	*lah pah-ree-'dahd*	parity
paridad de interés	*lah pah-ree-'dahd deh een-teh-'rehs*	interest parity
paridad móvil	*lah pah-ree-'dahd 'moh-beel*	crrawling peg, moving parity, sliding parity
paro forzoso (m)	*ehl 'pah-roh fohr-'soh-soh*	lockout
parque (m)	*ehl 'pahr-keh*	park
parque nacional	*ehl pahr-keh nah-see-oh-'nahl*	park (national)
parque protegido	*ehl pahr-keh proh-teh-'hee-doh*	park (protected)
parquet (m)	*ehl pahr-'keht*	trading floor
parte de renta reservada para uso futuro (f)	*lah 'pahr-teh deh 'rehn-tah reh-sehr-'bah-dah 'pah-rah 'oo-soh foo-'too-roh*	dead rent
partes (fpl)	*lahs 'pahr-tehs*	parts
participación accionaria (f)	*lah pahr-tee-see-pah-see-'ohn ahk-see-oh-'nah-ree-ah*	equity share
participación en el mercado	*lah pahr-tee-see-pah-see-'ohn ehn ehl mehr-'kah-doh*	market share

participaciones (fpl)	*lahs pahr-tee-see-pah-see-'oh-nehs*	shares
participaciones en los beneficios	*lahs pahr-tee-see-pah-see-'oh-nehs ehn lohs beh-neh-'fee-see-ohs*	profit sharing
partícula (f)	*lah pahr-'tee-koo-lah*	particle
partida (f)	*lah pahr-'tee-dah*	item, lot
partida a precio global	*lah pahr-'tee-dah ah 'preh-see-oh gloh-'bahl*	job lot
partida incompleta	*lah pahr-'tee-dah een-kohm-'pleh-tah*	broken lot
pasado de moda	*pah-'sah-doh deh 'moh-dah*	out of style
pasar del diario al mayor	*pah-'sahr dehl dee-'ah-ree-oh ahl mah-'yohr*	post (v) (bookkeeping)
pasivo (m)	*ehl pah-'see-boh*	liability
pasivo asumido	*ehl pah-'see-boh ah-soo-'mee-doh*	assumed liability
pasivo contingente	*ehl pah-'see-boh kohn-teen-'hehn-ten*	contingent liability
pasivo garantizado	*ehl pah-'see-boh gah-rahn-tee-'sah-doh*	secured liability
pasivo no garantizado	*ehl pah-'see-boh noh gah-rahn-tee-'sah-doh*	unsecured liability
pasivo verdadero	*ehl pah-'see-boh behr-dah-'deh-roh*	actual liability
pasivos a largo plazo (mpl)	*lohs pah-'see-bohs ah 'lahr-goh 'plah-soh*	fixed liabilities
pasivos circulantes	*lohs pah-'see-bohs seer-koo-'lahn-tehs*	current liabilities
pasivos diferidos	*lohs pah-'see-bohs dee-feh-'ree-dohs*	deferred liabilities
pastilla (f)	*lah pahs-'tee-yah*	tablet
pastilla para la tos	*lah pahs-'tee-yah pah-rah lah tohs*	cough drop
patente (f)	*lah pah-'tehn-teh*	patent
patente pendiente	*lah pah-'tehn-teh pehn-dee-'ehn-teh*	patent pending
patrimonio (m)	*ehl pah-tree-'moh-nee-oh*	estate
patrón (m)	*ehl pah-'trohn*	pattern, yardstick
patrón oro	*ehl pah-'trohn 'oh-roh*	gold standard

peces (mpl)	*lohs 'peh-sehs*	fish
pedal (m) de embrague	*ehl peh-dahl deh ehm-'brah-gue*	clutch pedal
pedal de freno	*ehl peh-dahl deh freh-noh*	brake pedal
pedal de gasolina	*ehl peh-dahl deh gah-soh-lee-nah*	gas pedal
pedido (m)	*ehl peh-'dee-doh*	order
pedido abierto	*ehl peh-'dee-doh ah-bee-'ehr-toh*	open order
pedido hecho por correo	*ehl peh-'dee-doh 'eh-choh pohr koh-'rreh-oh*	mail order
pedido previo pendiente de entrega	*ehl peh-'dee-doh 'preh-bee-oh pehn-dee-'ehn-teh deh ehn-'treh-gah*	back order
pedido suplementario	*ehl peh-'dee-doh soo-pleh-mehn-'tah-ree-oh*	repeat order
pedido urgente	*ehl peh-'dee-doh oor-'hehn-teh*	rush order
pedidos pendientes (mpl)	*lohs peh-'dee-dohs pehn-dee-'ehn-tehs*	backlog
pedir	*peh-'deer*	order (v), to place an order (v)
pedir la devolución de dinero	*peh-'deer lah deh-boh-loo-see-'ohn deh dee-'neh-roh*	call (v) in money
pedir prestado	*peh-'deer preh-'stah-doh*	borrow (v)
peligro (m)	*ehl peh-'lee-groh*	danger
pelo (m) de camello	*ehl peh-loh deh kah-meh-yoh*	camel's hair
penalidad por fraude (f)	*lah peh-nah-lee-'dahd pohr 'frow-deh*	penalty-fraud action
penetración al mercado (f)	*lah peh-neh-trah-see-'ohn ahl mehr-'kah-doh*	market penetration
pensionista (m)	*ehl pen-see-oh-'nees-tah*	pensioner
perceptor (m)	*ehl pehr-sehp-'tohr*	payee
pérdida (f)	*lah 'pehr-dee-dah*	loss
pérdida bruta	*lah 'pehr-dee-dah 'broo-tah*	gross loss
pérdida general promedio	*lah 'pehr-dee-dah heh-neh-'rahl proh-'meh-dee-oh*	general average loss

P

pérdida neta	*lah 'pehr-dee-dah 'neh-tah*	net loss
pérdida por avería simple	*lah 'pehr-dee-dah pohr ah-beh-'ree-ah*	particular average loss
pérdida por conversión de moneda	*lah 'pehr-dee-dah pohr kohn-behr-see-'ohn deh moh-'neh-dah*	exchange loss
pérdida total efectiva	*lah 'pehr-dee-dah toh-'tahl eh-fehk-'tee-bah*	actual total loss
perecer	*peh-reh-'sehr*	perish (v)
pérfil de aquisición (m)	*ehl 'pehr-feel deh ah-kee-see-see-'ohn*	acquisition profile
perforación a poca distancia de la costa (f)	*lah pehr-foh-rah-see-'ohn ah 'poh-kah dees-'tahn-see-ah deh lah 'koh-stah*	offshore drilling
periférico	*peh-ree-'feh-ree-koh*	peripheral
periódico (m)	*ehl peh-ree-'oh-dee-koh*	daily newspaper
período contable (m)	*ehl peh-'ree-oh doh kohn-'tah-bleh*	account period
período de baja	*ehl peh-'ree-oh-doh deh 'bah-hah*	down period
período de capitalización	*ehl peh-'ree-oh-doh deh kah-pee-tah-lee-sah-see-'ohn*	compounding intervals
período de cobro	*ehl peh-'ree-oh-doh deh 'koh-broh*	collection period
período de gracia	*ehl peh-'ree-oh-doh deh 'grah-see-ah*	grace period
período de interés	*ehl peh-'ree-oh-doh deh een-teh-'rehs*	interest period
período de pago	*ehl peh-'ree-oh-doh deh 'pah-goh*	payment period
período de paralización	*ehl peh-'ree-oh-doh deh pah-rah-lee-sah-see-'ohn*	downtime
período de posesión	*ehl peh-'ree-oh-doh deh poh-seh-see-'ohn*	holding period
período medio	*ehl peh-'ree-oh-doh 'meh-dee-oh*	half-life (bonds)
permiso (m)	*ehl pehr-'mee-soh*	permit
permiso de declaración	*ehl pehr-'mee-soh deh deh-klah-rah-see-'ohn*	entry permit

permiso de entrada	*ehl pehr-'mee-soh deh ehn-'trah-dah*	entry permit
permiso de exportación cultural	*ehl pehr-'mee-soh deh ehks-pohr-tah-see-'ohn kool-too-'rahl*	cultural export permit
permiso de exportación	*ehl pehr-'mee-soh deh ehks-pohr-tah-see-'ohn*	export permit
permiso impositivo	*ehl pehr-'mee-soh eem-poh-see-'tee-boh*	excise license
permiso legal para constituir una compañía	*ehl pehr-'mee-soh leh-'gahl 'pah-rah kohn-stee-too-'eer 'oo-nah kohm-pah-'nyee-ah*	charter
permiso por enfermedad	*ehl pehr-'mee-soh pohr ehn-fehr-meh-dahd*	sick leave
permitir	*pehr-mee-'teer*	allow (v)
permuta (f)	*lah pehr-moo-tah*	bartering
permutar	*pehr-moo-'tahr*	barter (v)
persona jurídica (f)	*lah pehr-'soh-nah hoo-'ree-dee-kah*	legal entity
personal (m)	*ehl pehr-soh-'nahl*	staff, human resources, personnel
personal de adiestramiento	*ehl pehr-soh-'nahl deh ah-dee-eh-strah-mee-'ehn-toh*	trainee
personal de ventas	*ehl pehr-soh-'nahl deh behn-tahs*	sales force
perspectiva (f)	*lah pehr-spehk-'tee-bah*	outlook
peso (m)	*ehl 'peh-soh*	weight
peso bruto	*ehl 'peh-soh 'broo-toh*	gross weight
petrodólares (m)	*lohs peh-troh-'doh-lah-rehs*	petrodollars
petróleo (m)	*ehl peh-'troh-leh-oh*	petroleum, oil
petróleo crudo	*ehl peh-'troh-leh-oh 'kroo-doh*	crude oil
petroquímico	*peh-troh-'kee-mee-koh*	petrochemical
pez (m. sing.)	*ehl pehs*	fish
piedra (f) caliza	*lah pee-'eh-drah kah-'lee-sah*	limestone
piel de avestruz (f)	*lah pee-'ehl deh ah-beh-stroos*	ostrich skin
piel de cerdo	*lah pee-'ehl deh 'sehr-doh*	pigskin

piel de culebra	*lah pee-'ehl deh koo-leh-brah*	snakeskin
piel de foca	*lah pee-'ehl deh foh-kah*	sealskin
piel de lagarto	*lah pee-'ehl deh lah-gahr-toh*	lizard skin
piel marroquí	*lah pee-'ehl mah-rroh-kee*	Moroccan leather
piel de serpiente	*lah pee-'ehl deh sehr-pee-ehn-teh*	snakeskin
pignoración (f)	*lah peeg-noh-rah-see-'ohn*	negative pledge
píldora (f)	*lah 'peel-doh-rah*	pellet, pill
píldora para dormir	*lah 'peel-doh-rah pah-rah dohr-'meer*	sleeping pill
pimentero (m)	*ehl pee-mehn-'teh-roh*	pepper shaker
pingüino (m)	*ehl peen-'gwee-noh*	penguin
piñón (m)	*ehl pee-'nyohn*	pinion
pintado a mano	*peen-tah-doh ah 'mah-noh*	hand-painted
pintura (f)	*lah peen-'too-rah*	paint
piquete de huelga (m)	*ehl pee-'keh-teh deh 'wehl-gah*	picket line
piramidación (f)	*lah pee-rah-mee-dah-see-'ohn*	pyramiding
pista (disco) (f)	*lah 'pees-tah ('dees-koh)*	track
pista de auditoría	*lah 'peehs-tah deh ow-dee-toh-'ree-ah*	audit trail
pistolera (f)	*lah pees-toh-'leh-rah*	holster
pitillera (f)	*lah pee-tee-'yeh-rah*	cigarette case
pizarrón electrónico (m)	*ehl pee-sah-'rrohn eh-lehk-'troh-nee-koh*	electronic whiteboard
placas (fpl)	*lahs 'plah-kahs*	license plates
plaga (f)	*lah 'plah-gah*	plague
plan (m)	*ehl plahn*	plan, layout
plan comercial	*ehl plahn koh-mehr-see-'ahl*	business plan
plan de venta a plazos	*ehl plahn deh 'behn-tah ah 'plah-sohs*	installment plan
plan del mercado	*ehl plahn dehl mehr-'kah-doh*	market plan, marketing plan
plancha (f)	*lah 'plahn-chah*	plate

planchas (fpl) rectangulares usadas para la manufactura	*lahs 'plahn-chahs rehk-tahn-goo-'lah-rehs oo-'sah-dahs pah-rah- lah mah-noo-fahk-'too-rah*	long product
planchuelas (fpl) rectangulares de hierro o acero	*lahs plah-choo-'eh-lah rehk-tahn-goo-'lah-rehs deh 'yeh-roh o ah-'seh-roh*	flat products
planctón (m)	*ehl plahnk-'tohn*	plankton
planctón marino	*ehl plahnk-'tohn mah-'ree-noh*	plankton (sea)
planeta (m)	*ehl plah-'neh-tah*	planet
planificación corporativa (f)	*lah plah-nee-fee-kah-see-'ohn kohr-poh-rah-'tee-bah*	corporate planning
planificación de largo plazo	*lah plah-nee-fee-kah-see-'ohn deh 'lahr-goh 'plah-soh*	long-range plan
planificación de proyecto	*lah plah-nee-fee-kah-see-'ohn deh proh-'yehk-toh*	project planning
planificación financiera	*lah plah-nee-fee-kah-see-'ohn fee-nahn-see-'eh-rah*	financial planning
planificación industrial	*lah plah-nee-fee-kah-see-'ohn een-doos-tree-'ahl*	industrial planning
planilla de direcciones (f)	*lah plah-'nee-yah deh dee-rehk-see-'oh-nehs*	mailing list
planilla de pedido	*lah plah-'nee-yah deh peh-'dee-doh*	order form
plano (m)	*ehl 'plah-noh*	blueprint
plataforma de perforación (f)	*lah plah-tah-'fohr-mah deh pehr-foh-rah-see-'ohn*	drilling rig
platillo (m)	*ehl plah-'tee-yoh*	saucer
plato (m)	*ehl 'plah-toh*	dish, plate
plato de ensalada	*ehl 'plah-toh deh ehn-sah-'lah-dah*	salad plate
plato de postre	*ehl plah-toh deh 'poh-streh*	dessert plate
plato de sopa	*ehl plah-toh deh 'soh-pah*	soup dish
playa (f)	*lah 'plah-yah*	beach
plazo (m)	*ehl 'plah-soh*	deadline
plazo de reembolso (m)	*ehl 'plah-soh deh reh-ehm-'bohl-soh*	payback period
plazo fijo	*ehl 'plah-soh 'fee-hoh*	fixed term

P

plazo intermedio	*ehl 'plah-soh een-tehr-'meh-dee-oh*	medium (term)
plegado	*pleh-'gah-doh*	pleated (adj)
pleito (m)	*ehl pleh-'ee-toh*	dispute
pleito legal	*ehl pleh-'ee-toh leh-'gahl*	lawsuit
plisado (m)	*ehl plee-'sah-doh*	pleat
plomo (m)	*ehl 'ploh-moh*	lead (metal)
pluriempleo (m)	*ehl ploo-ree-ehm-'pleh-oh*	moonlighting
plusvalía (f)	*lah ploos-bah-'lee-ah*	unearned increment
pluvisilva	*ploo-bee-'seel-bah*	rain forest
pocillo (m)	*ehl poh-see-yoh*	espresso cup
poco probable	*'poh-koh proh-'bah-bleh*	unfeasible
poder (m)	*ehl poh-'dehr*	proxy, power of attorney
poder accionario	*ehl poh-'dehr ahk-see-oh-'nah-ree-oh*	stock power
poder adquisitivo	*ehl poh-'dehr ahd-kee-see-'tee-boh*	purchasing power
poder para negociar	*ehl poh-'dehr 'pah-rah neh-goh-see-'ahr*	bargaining power
polímero (m)	*ehl poh-'lee-meh-roh*	polymer
política (f)	*lah poh-'lee-tee-kah*	policy (performance standard)
política comercial	*lah poh-'lee-tee-kah koh-mehr-see-'ahl*	business policy
política de distribución	*lah poh-'lee-tee-kah deh dees-tree-boo-see-'ohn*	distribution policy
política de inversión	*lah poh-'lee-tee-kah deh een-behr-see-'ohn*	investment policy
política de la compañía	*lah poh-'lee-tee-kah deh lah kohm-pah-'nyee-ah*	company policy
política de puerta abierta	*lah poh-'lee-tee-kah deh 'pwehr-tah ah-bee-'ehr-tah*	open door policy
política monetaria	*lah poh-'lee-tee-kah mon-neh-'tah-ree-ah*	monetary policy
póliza de flotilla (f)	*lah 'poh-lee-sah deh floh-'tee-yah*	fleet policy
póliza de seguro de vida	*lah 'poh-lee-sah deh seh-'goo-roh deh 'bee-dah*	life insurance policy

póliza de seguros	*lah 'poh-lee-sah deh seh-'goo-rohs*	insurance policy
póliza que protege contra pérdidas	*lah 'poh-lee-sah keh proh-'teh-heh 'kohn-trah 'pehr-dee-dahs*	floater
pólvora (f)	*lah pohl-boh-rah*	powder
pomada (f)	*lah poh-'mah-dah*	salve
poner fin a una sesión	*poh-'nehr feen ah 'oo-nah seh-see-'ohn*	log off (v)
poner por escrito	*poh-'nehr pohr ehs-'kree-toh*	write down (v)
poner una carga excesiva	*poh-'nehr 'oo-nah 'kahr-gah ehk-seh-'see-bah*	overcharge (v)
poplín (m)	*ehl poh-'pleen*	poplin
por acción	*pohr ahk-see-'ohn*	per share
por debajo de la línea	*pohr deh-'bah-hoh deh lah 'lee-neh-ah*	below the line
por debajo de la par	*pohr de-'bah-hoh deh lah pahr*	below par
por día	*pohr 'dee-ah*	per diem
por encima de la par	*pohr ehn-'see-mah deh lah pahr*	above par
por habitante	*pohr ah-bee-'tahn-teh*	per capita
por toda la industria	*pohr 'toh-dah lah een-'doos-tree-ah*	industry-wide
porcelana (f)	*lah pohr-seh-'lah-nah*	china
porcelana traslúcida	*lah pohr-seh-'lah-nah trahs-'loo-see-dah*	bone china
porcentaje de cobertura (m)	*ehl pohr-sehn-'tah-heh deh koh-behr-'too-rah*	cover ratio
porcentaje de la utilidad	*ehl pohr-sehn-'tah-heh deh lah oo-tee-lee-'dahd*	percentage of profit
porcentaje de las ganancias	*ehl pohr-sehn-'tah-heh deh lahs gah-'nahn-see-ahs*	percentage earnings
pormenorizar	*pohr-meh-noh-ree-'sahr*	itemize (v)
portador (m)	*ehl pohr-tah-'dohr*	bearer, holder of negotiable instruments
portafolio (m)	*ehl pohr-tah-'foh-lee-oh*	briefcase
porte a...incluso	*'pohr-teh ah...een-'kloo-soh*	freight allowed to...

P

posición en descubierto (f)	*lah poh-see-see-'ohn ehn dehs-koo-bee-'ehr-toh*	short position
posición límite	*lah poh-see-see-'ohn 'lee-mee-teh*	position limit
posición neto	*lah poh-see-see-'ohn 'neh-toh*	net position (of a trader)
posponer	*pohs-poh-'nehr*	postpone (v)
post-editar	*pohst-eh-dee-'tahr*	post-edit (v)
postdatar	*pohs-dah-'tahr*	postdate
postergar	*pohs-tehr-'gahr*	postpone (v)
posterior a la fecha de presentación	*pohs-teh-ree-'ohr ah lah 'feh-cha deh preh-sehn-tah-see-'ohn*	after-sight
potencia (f)	*lah poh-tehn-see-ah*	power
potencial en el mercado (m)	*ehl poh-tehn-see-'ahl ehn ehl mehr-'kah-doh*	market potential
potencial para crecimiento	*ehl poh-tehn-see-'ahl 'pah-rah kreh-see-mee-'ehn-toh*	growth potential
pozo (m)	*ehl 'poh-soh*	well (drilled)
práctica normal (f)	*lah 'prahk-tee-kah nohr-'mahl*	standard practice
prácticas comerciales justas (fpl)	*lahs 'prahk-tee-kahs koh-mehr-see-'ah-lehs 'hoos-tahs*	fair trade
prácticas laborales restrictivos	*lahs 'prahk-tee-kahs lah-boh-'rah-lehs reh-streek-'tee-bohs*	restrictive labor practices
práctico	*'prahk-tee-koh*	practical
precio (m)	*ehl 'preh-see-oh*	price
precio ajustado de costo, seguro y flete	*ehl 'preh-see-oh ah-hoos-'tah-doh deh 'koh-stoh, seh-'goo-roh ee 'fleh-teh*	adjusted CIF price
precio al detalle	*ehl 'preh-see-oh ahl deh-'tah-yeh*	retail price
precio al por mayor	*ehl 'preh-see-oh ahl pohr mah-'yohr*	wholesale price
precio al por menor	*ehl 'preh-see-oh ahl pohr meh-'nohr*	retail price
precio base	*ehl 'pree-see-oh 'bah-seh*	base price
precio bruto	*ehl 'preh-see-oh 'broo-toh*	gross price

precio competitivo	*ehl 'preh-see-oh kohm-peh-tee-'tee-boh*	competitive price
precio de amortización de valores (los bonos antes de vencimiento)	*ehl 'preh-see-oh deh ah-mohr-tee-sah-see-'ohn deh bah-'loh-rehs (lohs 'boh-nohs 'ahn-tehs deh behn-see-mee-'ehn-toh)*	call price
precio de apertura	*ehl 'preh-see-oh deh ah-pehr-'too-rah*	opening price
precio de catálogo	*ehl 'preh-see-oh deh kah-'tah-loh-goh*	list price
precio de cierre	*ehl 'preh-see-oh deh see-'eh-rreh*	closing price
precio de compra	*ehl 'preh-see-oh deh 'kohm-prah*	purchase price
precio de compra y venta	*ehl 'preh-see-oh deh 'kohm-prah ee 'behn-tah*	bid and asked price
precio de emisión	*ehl 'preh-see-oh deh eh-mee-see-'ohn*	issue price
precio de entrega	*ehl 'preh-see-oh deh ehn-'treh-gah*	delivery price
precio de oferta	*ehl 'preh-see-oh deh oh-'fehr-tah*	offered price
precio de paridad	*ehl 'preh-see-oh deh pah-ree-'dahd*	parity price
precio de subscripción	*ehl 'preh-see-oh deh soob-skreep-see-'ohn*	subscription price
precio de venta	*ehl 'preh-see-oh deh 'behn-tah*	asking price, offered price
precio del fiado	*ehl 'preh-see-oh dehl fee-'ah-doh*	price tick
precio del mercado	*ehl 'preh-see-oh dehl mehr-'kah-doh*	market price
precio del oro	*ehl 'preh-see-oh dehl 'oh-roh*	gold price
precio doble	*ehl 'preh-see-oh 'doh-bleh*	double-pricing
precio estimado	*ehl 'preh-see-oh eh-stee-'mah-doh*	estimated price
precio fijo	*ehl 'preh-see-oh 'fee-hoh*	pegged price
precio límite	*ehl preh-see-oh 'lee-mee-teh*	price limit
precio máximo	*ehl 'preh-see-oh 'mahk-see-moh*	top price

P

precio nominal	*ehl 'preh-see-oh noh-mee-'nahl*	nominal price
precio objetivo	*ehl 'preh-see-oh ohb-heh-'tee-boh*	target price
precio promedio	*ehl 'preh-see-oh proh-'meh-dee-oh*	average price
precio real	*ehl 'preh-see-oh reh-'ahl*	real price
precio unitario	*ehl 'preh-see-oh oo-nee-'tah-ree-oh*	unit price
predicción de ventas (f)	*lah preh-deek-see-'ohn deh 'behn-tahs*	sales forecast
predicción del mercado	*lah preh-deek-see-'ohn dehl mehr-'kah-doh*	market forecast
prefabricación (f)	*lah preh-fah-breek-kah-see-'ohn*	prefabrication
preferencia por la liquidez (f)	*lah preh-feh-'rehn-see-ah pohr lah lee-kee-'dehs*	liquidity preference
prelación (f)	*lah preh-lah-see-'ohn*	seniority
prenda (f)	*lah 'prehn-dah*	pledge
preocupación (f)	*lah preh-oh-koo-pah-see-'ohn*	worry
prepagar	*preh-pah-'gahr*	prepay (v)
preparar	*preh-pah-'rahr*	make ready, prepare (v)
presidente (f)	*ehl preh-see-'dehn-teh*	president
presidente de la junta directiva	*ehl preh-see-'dehn-teh deh lah 'hoon-tah dee-rehk-'tee-bah*	chairman of the board
presidente delegado	*ehl preh-see-'dehn-teh deh-leh-'gah-doh*	deputy chairman
presidente ejecutivo	*ehl preh-see-'dehn-teh eh-heh-koo-'tee-boh*	chief executive
presión (f)	*lah preh-see-ohn*	pressure
prestaciones adicionales al sueldo (fpl)	*lahs prehs-tah-see-'oh-nehs ah-dee-see-oh-'nah-lehs ahl 'swehl-doh*	fringe benefits
préstamo (m)	*ehl 'preh-stah-moh*	loan
préstamo a más de un año	*ehl 'preh-stah-moh ah mahs deh oon 'ah-nyoh*	term loan
préstamo a plazo fijo	*ehl 'preh-stah-moh ah 'plah-soh 'fee-hoh*	term loan

préstamo bancario	*ehl 'preh-stah-moh bahn-'kah-ree-oh*	bank loan
préstamo condicionado	*ehl 'preh-stah-moh kohn-dee-see-oh-'nah-doh*	tied loan
préstamo débil	*ehl 'preh-stah-moh 'deh-beel*	soft loan
préstamo diario	*ehl 'preh-stah-moh dee-'ah-ree-oh*	day loan
préstamo en participación	*ehl 'preh-stah-moh ehn pahr-tee-see-pah-see-'ohn*	participation loan
préstamo fiduciario	*ehl 'preh-stah-moh fee-doo-see-'ah-ree-oh*	fiduciary loan
préstamo no garantizado	*ehl 'preh-stah-moh noh gah-rahn-tee-'sah-doh*	unsecured loan
préstamo reembolsable a la vista	*ehl 'preh-stah-moh reh-ehm-bohl-'sah-bleh ah lah 'bees-tah*	call loan
préstamo repagable en moneda inestable	*ehl 'preh-stah-moh reh-pah-'gah-bleh ehn moh-'neh-dah een-eh-'stah-bleh*	soft loan
préstamo subsidiario	*ehl 'preh-stah-moh soob-see-dee-'ah-ree-oh*	back-to-back loan
préstamos a bajo interés (mpl)	*lohs 'preh-stah-mohs ah 'bah-hoh een-teh-'rehs*	low-interest loans
presupuesto (m)	*ehl preh-soo-'pwehs-toh*	budget
presupuesto de caja	*ehl preh-soo-'pweh-stoh deh 'kah-hah*	cash budget
presupuesto de gastos de capital	*ehl preh-soo-'pweh-stoh deh 'gah-stohs deh kah-pee-'tahl*	capital budget
presupuesto de inversión	*ehl preh-soo-'pweh-stoh deh een-behr-'see-'ohn*	investment budget
presupuesto de mercadeo	*ehl preh-soo-'pweh-stoh deh mehr-kah-'deh-oh*	marketing budget
presupuesto de publicidad	*ehl preh-soo-'pwehs-toh deh poo-blee-see-'dahd*	advertising budget
presupuesto de ventas	*ehl preh-soo-'pweh-stoh deh 'behn-tahs*	sales budget
presupuesto estimado	*ehl preh-soo-'pwehs-toh ehs-tee-'mah-doh*	budget forecast

presupuesto funcional de operaciones	*ehl preh-soo-'pweh-stoh foonk-see-oh-'nahl deh oh-peh-rah-see-'oh-nehs*	operating budget
presupuesto inversionista	*ehl preh-soo-'pweh-stoh een-behr-see-oh-'nees-tah*	investment budget
presupuesto provisional	*ehl preh-soo-'pweh-stoh proh-bee-see-oh-'nahl*	interim budget
prima (f)	*lah 'pree-mah*	bonus (premium)
prima de rescate	*lah 'pree-mah deh rehs-'kah-teh*	redemption premium
prima de seguros	*lah 'pree-mah deh seh-'goo-rohs*	insurance premium
prima del comprador	*lah 'pree-mah dehl kohm-prah-'dohr*	buyer's premium
prima escalonada	*lah 'pree-mah ehs-kah-loh-'nah-dah*	acceleration premium
primero que entra-el primero que sale (m)	*ehl pree-'meh-roh keh 'ehn-trah-ehl pree-'meh-roh keh 'sah-leh*	first in-first out
principal (m)	*ehl preen-see-'pahl*	principal
prioridad (f)	*lah pree-oh-ree-'dahd*	priority, seniority
problema (m)	*ehl proh-'bleh-mah*	problem
procesador (m)	*ehl proh-seh-sah-'dohr*	processor
procesador de palabras	*ehl proh-seh-sah-'dohr deh pah-'lah-brahs*	word processor
procesador de palabras solitario	*ehl proh-seh-sah-'dohr deh pah-'lah-brahs soh-lee-'tah-ree-oh*	stand-alone text processor
procesamiento de datos (m)	*ehl proh-seh-sah-mee-'ehn-toh deh 'dah-tohs*	data processing
procesamiento de palabra	*ehl proh-seh-sah-mee-'ehn-toh deh pah-'lah-brah*	word processing
procesamiento en función al orden de llegada	*ehl proh-seh-sah-mee-'ehn-toh ehn foonk-see-'ohn ahl 'ohr-dehn deh yeh-'gah-dah*	batch processing
procesar	*proh-seh-'sahr*	process (v)
proceso (m)	*ehl proh-'seh-soh*	process
proceso de ajuste	*ehl proh-'seh-soh deh ah-'hoo-steh*	adjustment process

proceso de producción	*ehl proh-'seh-soh deh proh-dook-see-'ohn*	production process
proceso de promediar	*ehl proh-'seh-soh deh proh-meh-dee-'ahr*	averaging
proceso electrolítico	*ehl proh-'seh-soh eh-lehk-troh-'lee-tee-koh*	electrolytic process
proceso patentado	*ehl proh-'seh-soh pah-tehn-'tah-doh*	patented process
proceso productivo	*ehl proh-'seh-soh proh-dook-'tee-boh*	production process
producción (f)	*lah proh-dook-see-'ohn*	production, output, yield
producción en cadena	*lah proh-dook-see-'ohn ehn kah-'deh-nah*	assembly line
producción en lote	*lah proh-dook-see-'ohn ehn 'loh-teh*	batch production
producción fijada	*lah proh-dook-see-'ohn fee-'hah-dah*	throughput
producción modular	*lah proh-dook-see-'ohn moh-doo-'lahr*	modular production
producción total	*lah proh-dook-see-'ohn toh-'tahl*	outturn
productividad (f)	*lah proh-dook-tee-bee-'dahd*	productivity
producto (m)	*ehl proh-'dook-toh*	product, proceeds
producto final	*ehl proh-'dook-toh fee-'nahl*	end product
producto nacional bruto	*ehl proh-'dook-toh nah-see-oh-'nahl 'broo-toh*	gross national product
producto territorial bruto	*ehl proh-'dook-toh teh-rree-toh-ree-'ahl 'broo-toh*	gross domestic product
productos (mpl) semiterminados de acero o hierro	*lohs proh-'dook-tohs seh-mee-tehr-mee-'nah-dohs deh ah-'seh-roh oh 'yeh-roh*	semis
productos agrícolas	*lohs proh-'dook-tohs ah-'gree-koh-lahs*	agricultural products
productos agrícolas naturales	*lohs proh-'dook-tohs ah-'gree-koh-lahs nah-too-'rah-lehs*	native produce
productos alimenticios	*lohs proh-'dook-tohs ah-lee-meh-'tee-see-ohs*	foodstuffs
productos de especialidad	*lohs proh-'dook-tohs deh eh-speh-see-ah-lee-'dahd*	specialty goods

P

P

productos terminados	*lohs proh-dook-tohs tehr-mee-nah-dohs*	finished products
profesión (f)	*lah proh-feh-see-'ohn*	occupation, career, profession
programa (m)	*ehl proh-'grah-mah*	program
programa de computación	*ehl proh-'grah-mah deh kohm-poo-tah-see-'ohn*	software
programa de inversión	*ehl proh-'grah-mah deh een-behr-see-'ohn*	investment program
programa de producción	*ehl proh-'grah-mah- deh proh-dook-see-'ohn*	production schedule
programación de computadora (f)	*lah proh-grah-mah-see-'ohn deh kohm-poo-tah-'doh-rah*	computer program
programación lineal	*lah proh-grah-mah-see-'ohn lee-neh-'ahl*	linear programming
programación múltiple	*lah proh-grah-mah-see-'ohn 'mool-tee-pleh*	multiprogramming
programar	*proh-grah-'mahr*	program (v)
programas y sistemas de programación (mpl)	*lohs proh-'grah-mahs ee sees-'teh-mahs de proh-grah-mah-see-'ohn*	software
progreso (m)	*ehl proh-'greh-soh*	progress
prohibición judicial (f)	*lah proh-ee-bee-see-'ohn hoo-dee-see-'ahl*	injunction
prójimos (mpl)	*lohs 'proh-hee-mohs*	fellow man, fellow creature
prólogo (m)	*ehl proh-loh-goh*	preface
promedio (m)	*ehl proh-'meh-dee-oh'*	average, mean
promedio de costo en dólares	*ehl proh-'meh-dee-oh deh 'koh-stoh ehn 'doh-lah-rehs*	dollar cost averaging
promedio móvil	*ehl proh-'meh-dee-oh 'moh-beel*	moving average
promoción (f)	*lah proh-moh-see-'ohn*	promotion
promoción de ventas	*lah proh-moh-see-'ohn deh 'behn-tahs*	sales promotion
promotor (de fondos en una sociedad) (m)	*ehl proh-moh-'tohr (deh 'fohn-dohs deh 'oo-nah soh-see-eh-'dahd)*	sponsor (of fund, of partnership)
pronosticar	*proh-noh-stee-'kahr*	forecast (v)

pronóstico (m)	*ehl proh-'noh-stee-koh*	forecast
pronóstico de ventas	*ehl proh-'noh-stee-koh deh 'behn-tahs*	sales forecast
pronto	*'prohn-toh*	prompt
propiedad (f)	*lah proh-pee-eh-'dahd*	ownership, property
propiedad conjunta	*lah proh-pee-eh-'dahd kohn-'hoon-tah*	joint ownership
propiedad personal	*lah proh-pee-eh-'dahd pehr-soh-'nahl*	personal property
propiedad pública	*lah proh-pee-eh-'dahd 'poo-blee-kah*	public property
propiedades culturales (f)	*lah proh-pee-eh-'dah-dehs kool-too-'rah-lehs*	cultural property
propietario único	*ehl proh-pee-eh-'tah-ree-oh 'oo-nee-koh*	sole proprietorship
propina (f)	*lah proh-'pee-nah*	gratuity
proporción (f)	*lah proh-pohr-see-'ohn*	ratio
propuesta sellada (f)	*lah proh-'pweh-stah seh-'yah-dah*	sealed bid
propulsión (f)	*lah proh-pool-see-'ohn*	propulsion
prospecto (m)	*ehl proh-'spehk-toh*	prospectus
prospecto preliminar	*ehl proh-'spehk-toh preh-lee-mee-'nahr*	preliminary
prospectus prosperidad repentina (f)	*ehl proh-'spehk-toos proh-speh-ree-'dahd reh-pehn-'tee-nah*	boom
protección al que ha comprado algo (f)	*lah proh-tehk-see-'ohn ahl keh ah kohm-'prah-doh 'ahl-goh*	long hedge
protección contra la exigibilidad a la vista	*lah proh-tehk-see-'ohn 'kohn-trah lah ehk-see-hee-bee-lee-'dahd ah lah 'bees-tah*	call protection
protección contra los impuestos	*lah proh-tehk-see-'ohn 'kohn-trah lohs eem-'pweh-stohs*	tax shelter
protección de un fichero	*lah proh-tehk-see-'ohn deh oon fee-'cheh-roh*	file protection
proteccionismo (m)	*ehl proh-tehk-see-oh-'nees-moh*	protectionism
protesto (m)	*ehl proh-'tehs-toh*	protest (banking, law)

protocolo (m)	*ehl proh-toh-'koh-loh*	protocol
prototipo (m)	*ehl proh-toh-tee-poh*	prototype
provisión (f)	*lah proh-bee-see-'ohn*	supply, provision
provisión para depreciación	*lah proh-bee-see-'ohn 'pah-rah deh-preh-see-ah-see-'ohn*	depreciation allowance
provisional	*proh-bee-see-oh-'nahl*	interim, makeshift
proyección (f)	*lah proh-yehk-see-'ohn*	overhang
proyectar	*proh-yehk-'tahr*	project (v)
proyecto (m)	*ehl proh-'yehk-toh*	project
proyecto de presupuesto	*ehl proh-'yehk-toh deh preh-soo-'pweh-stoh*	budget forecast
prueba (f)	*lah proo-'eh-bah*	assay
prueba de aceptación	*lah proo-'eh-bah deh ah-sehp-tah-see-'ohn*	acceptance test
prueba de copia	*lah proo-'eh-bah deh 'koh-pee-ah*	copy testing
prueba de fuego	*lah proo-'eh-bah deh 'fweh-goh*	acid test
prueba de perdida	*lah proo-'eh-bah deh 'pehr-dee-dah*	proof of loss
prueba de personalidad	*lah proo-'eh-bah deh pehr-soh-nah-lee-'dahd*	personality test
publicador (m)	*ehl poo-blee-kah-'dohr*	publisher
publicidad (f)	*lah poo-blee-see-'dahd*	advertising, publicity
publicidad cooperativa	*lah poo-blee-see-'dahd koo-oh-peh-rah-'tee-bah*	cooperative advertising
publicidad institucional	*lah poo-blee-see-'dahd eens-tee-too-see-oh-'nahl*	institutional advertising
puerto de embarque designado (m)	*ehl 'pwehr-toh deh ehm-'bahr-keh deh-seeg-'nah-doh*	named port of shipment
puerto de entrada o salida	*ehl 'pwehr-tah deh ehn-'trah-dah oh sah-'lee-dah*	port of entry or origin (comp. or coastal)
puerto de importación designado	*ehl 'pwehr-toh deh eem-pohr-tah-see-'ohn deh-seeg-'nah-doh*	named port of importation
puerto libre	*ehl 'pwehr-toh 'lee-breh*	free port
puesto en buque	*'pwehs-toh ehn 'boo-keh*	ex ship

puesto en el muelle	*pweh-stoh ehn ehl 'mweh-yeh*	ex dock
puja (f)	*lah 'poo-hah*	auction market
pulgada (f)	*lah pool-gah-dah*	inch
puño (m) francés	*ehl poo-nyoh frahn-sehs*	French cuff
punta	*lah 'poon-tah*	point (tip)
puntada (f)	*lah poon-'tah-dah*	stitch
punto (m)	*ehl 'poon-toh*	point (percentage) (mortgage term)
punto de base	*ehl 'poon-toh deh 'bah-seh*	basis point (1/100%)
punto de destino designado	*ehl 'poon-toh deh dehs-'tee-noh deh-seeg-'nah-doh*	named point of destination
punto de exportación designado	*ehl 'poon-toh deh ehks-pohr-tah-see-'ohn deh-seeg-'nah-doh*	named point of exportation
punto de interrupción	*ehl 'poon-toh deh een-teh-roop-see-'ohn*	breakpoint
punto de orden	*ehl 'poon-toh deh 'ohr-dehn*	point of order
punto de origen designado	*ehl 'poon-toh deh oh-'ree-hehn deh-seeg-'nah-doh*	named point of origin
punto de venta	*ehl 'poon-toh deh 'behn-tah*	point of sale
punto donde los ingresos son iguales a los egresos	*ehl 'poon-toh 'dohn-deh lohs een-'greh-sohs sohn ee-'gwah-lehs ah lohs eh-'greh-sohs*	break-even point
punto en común de ultramar	*ehl 'poon-toh ehn koh-'moon deh ool-trah-'mahr*	overseas common point
punto interior designado del país de importación	*ehl 'poon-toh een-teh-ree-'ohr deh-seeg-'nah-doh dehl 'pah-'ees deh een-pohr-tah-see-'ohn*	named inland point in country of importation
puntos de entrega (mpl)	*lohs 'poon-tohs deh ehn-'treh-gah*	delivery points
purgante (m)	*ehl poor-gahn-teh*	purgative
purificación (f)	*lah poo-ree-fee-kah-see-'ohn*	purification

P

Q

que ahorra trabajo	*keh ah-'oh-rrah trah-'bah-hoh*	labor-saving
quiebra (f)	*lah kee-'eh-brah*	bankruptcy
química (f)	*lah 'kee-mee-kah*	chemistry
química	*'kee-mee-kah*	chemical (adj)
química analítica	*lah 'kee-mee-kah ah-nah-'lee-tee-kah*	analytic chemistry
química inorgánica	*lah 'kee-mee-kah een-ohr-'gah-nee-kah*	inorganic chemistry
química orgánica	*lah 'kee-mee-kah ohr-gah-nee-kah*	organic chemistry
químico	*'kee-mee-koh*	chemical (adj)
quorum (m)	*ehl koo-'oh-room*	quorum

R

racimo (m) de uvas	*ehl rah-'see-moh-deh oo-bahs*	grape bunch
racionar	*rah-see-oh-'nahr*	ration (v)
radiación (f)	*lah rah-dee-ah-see-'ohn*	radiation
radiactivo	*rah-dee-oh-ahk-'tee-boh*	radioactive (adj)
radio (m)	*ehl rah-dee-oh*	receiver
rata de retorno real después de impuestos (f)	*lah 'rah-tah deh reh-'tohr-noh reh-'ahl des-'pwehs deh eem-'pweh-stohs*	after-tax real rate of return
ratio de deuda con interés fijo a intereses mas la deuda (m)	*ehl 'rah-see-oh deh deh-'oo-dah kohn een-teh-'rehs 'fee-hoh ah een-teh-'reh-ses mahs lah deh-'oo-dah*	after-tax real rate of return
rayado (m)	*ehl rah-'yah-doh*	scoring
rayo (m)	*ehl 'rah-yoh*	beam
rayón (m)	*ehl 'rah-yohn*	rayon
razón de paridad de ingresos (f)	*lah rah-'sohn deh pah-ree-'dahd deh een-'greh-sohs*	parity income ratio
razón precio-ganancia por acciones	*lah rah-'sohn 'preh-see-oh gah-'nahn-see-ah pohr ahk-see-'oh-nehs*	p/e ratio

reactivo (m)	*ehl reh-ahk-'tee-boh*	reagent
realce acentuado (m)	*ehl reh-'ahl-seh ah-sehn-too-'ah-doh*	highlight
realimentación (f)	*lah reh-ah-lee-mehn-tah-see-'ohn*	feedback
realización de beneficio (f)	*lah reh-ah-lee-sah-see-'ohn deh beh-neh-'fee-see-oh*	profit-taking
reanudar	*reh-an-noo-'dahr*	resume (v)
reasegurador (m)	*ehl reh-ah-seh-goo-rah-'dohr*	reinsurer
rebaja (f)	*lah reh-'bah-hah*	allowance, rebate, drawback, abatement
rebajar	*reh-bah-'hahr*	take off (v)
recapitalización (f)	*lah reh-kah-pee-tah-lee-sah-see-'ohn*	recapitalization
recargo (m)	*ehl reh-'kahr-goh*	surcharge
recargos por bultos pesados (mpl)	*reh-'kahr-gohs pohr 'bool-tohs peh-'sah-dohs*	heavy lift charges
recaudador de impuesto (m)	*ehl reh-kow-dah-'dohr deh eem-'pweh-stoh*	tax collector
receptor (m)	*ehl reh-sehp-'tohr*	receiver
receptor/emisor (m)	*ehl reh-sehp-'tohr/eh-mee-'sohr*	transceiver
recesión (f)	*lah reh-seh-see-'ohn*	recession
recesión con inflación	*lah reh-seh-see-'ohn kohn een-flah-see-'ohn*	stagflation
receso económico (m)	*ehl reh-'seh-soh eh-koh-'noh-mee-koh*	downturn
receta (f)	*lah reh-'seh-tah*	prescription
recibo (m)	*ehl reh-'see-boh*	receipt
recibo de muelle	*ehl reh-'see-boh deh 'mweh-yeh*	dock (ship's receipt)
recibo para pago preliminar	*ehl reh-'see-boh 'pah-rah' pah-goh preh-lee-mee-'nahr*	binder
reciclaje (m)	*ehl reh-see-'klah-heh*	recycling
reciclar	*reh-see-'klahr*	recycle (v)
reclamación (f)	*lah reh-klah-mah-see-'ohn*	claim

reclamo indirecto (m)	*ehl reh-'klah-moh een-dee-'rehk-toh*	indirect claim
reclutador de ejecutivo (m)	*ehl reh-kloo-tah-'dohr de eh-heh-koo-'tee-boh*	headhunter
recocido (m)	*ehl reh-koh-'hee-doh*	annealing
recoger y entregar	*reh-koh-'hehr ee ehn-treh-'gahr*	pick up and deliver (v)
recompensa (f)	*lah reh-kohm-'pehn-sah*	reward
recompra (f)	*lah reh-'kohm-prah*	buy back
reconocer	*reh-koh-noh-'sehr*	acknowledge (v)
reconocimiento de marca (m)	*ehl reh-koh-noh-see-mee-'ehn-toh deh 'mahr-kah*	brand recognition
recorrido (m)	*ehl rreh-koh-'rree-doh*	routing
recorte (m)	*ehl reh-'kohr-teh*	cutback
recuperación (f)	*lah reh-koo-peh-rah-see-'ohn*	rally, retrieval
recuperación (cuentas por cobrar)	*lah reh-koo-peh-rah-see-'ohn ('kwehn-tahs pohr koh-'brahr)*	recovery (accounts receivable)
recuperación de gastos	*lah reh-koo-peh-rah-see-'ohn deh 'gah-stohs*	recovery of expenses
recurso (m)	*ehl reh-'koor-soh*	recourse, remedy (law)
recursos (mpl)	*lohs reh-'koor-sohs*	resources
recursos humanos	*lohs reh-'koor-sohs oo-'mah-nohs*	human resources
recursos naturales	*lohs reh-'koor-sohs nah-too-'rah-lehs*	natural resources
recursos propios	*lohs reh-'koor-sohs 'proh-pee-ohs*	equity
recursos propios de los accionistas	*lohs reh-'koor-sohs 'proh-pee-ohs deh lohs ahk-see-oh-'nees-tahs*	stockholder's equity
recursos propios de los propietarios	*lohs reh-'koor-sohs 'proh-pee-ohs deh lohs proh-pee-eh-'tah-ree-ohs*	owner's equity
red (f)	*lah rehd*	network
red de distribución	*lah rehd de dees-tree-boo-see-'ohn*	distribution network
redacción de los datos de entrada (f)	*lah reh-dahk-see-'ohn deh lohs 'dah-tohs deh ehn-'trah-dah*	editing of input

reducción (f)	*lah reh-dook-see-'ohn*	reduction
reducción a precio anterior	*lah reh-dook-see-'ohn ah 'preh-see-oh ahn-teh-ree-'ohr*	roll back
reducción de costos	*lah reh-dook-see-'ohn deh 'koh-stohs*	cost reduction
reducción de gastos	*lah reh-dook-see-'ohn deh 'gah-stohs*	cutback
reducción de precio	*lah reh-dook-see-'ohn deh 'preh-see-oh*	markdown
reducción de precios	*lah reh-dook-see-'ohn deh deh 'preh-see-ohs*	price cutting
reducción en el consumo	*lah reh-dook-see-'ohn ehn ehl kohn-'soo-moh*	consumption reduction
reducido	*reh-doo-'see-doh*	downgraded (adj)
reembolsar	*reh-ehm-bohl-'sahr*	reimburse, repay (v)
reembolso (m)	*ehl reh-ehm-'bohl-soh*	refund
reembolso a la vista	*ehl reh-ehm-'bohl-soh ah lah 'bees-tah*	call feature
reemplazar	*reh-ehm-plah-'sahr*	supersede (v)
reestructurar	*reh-ehs-trook-too-'rahr*	restructure (v)
reexportar	*reh-ehks-pohr-'tahr*	re-export (v)
referencia de crédito (f)	*lah reh-feh-'rehn-see-ah deh 'kreh-dee-toh*	credit reference
referente a	*reh-feh-'rehn-teh ah*	regarding, with regard to
refinanciamiento (m)	*ehl reh-fee-nahn-see-ah-mee-'ehn-toh*	refinancing
refinar	*reh-fee-nahr*	refine (v)
refinería (f)	*lah reh-fee-neh-ree-ah*	refinery
refinería doméstica	*lah reh-fee-neh-'ree-ah doh-'mehs-tee-kah*	refinery (home-based)
refinería localizada en el país del consumidor	*lah reh-fee-neh-'ree-ah loh-kah-lee-'sah-dah ehn ehl pah-'ees dehl kohm-soo-mee-'dohr*	refinery (market based)
reflación (f)	*lah reh-flah-see-'ohn*	reflation
reforma agraria (f)	*lah reh-'fohr-mah ah-'grah-ree-ah*	land reform
reformar	*reh-fohr-'mahr*	amend (v)

R

refuerzos (mpl) de acero	*lohs reh-fwehr-sohs deh ah-'seh-roh*	rebars
regalía por uso de patente (f)	*lah reh-gah-'lee-ah pohr 'oo-soh deh pah-'tehn-teh*	patent royalty
registrar	*reh-hees-'trahr*	record (v)
registro cronológico (m)	*ehl reh-'hees-troh kroh-noh-'loh-hee-koh*	log
regulación (f)	*lah reh-goo-lah-see-'ohn*	regulation, standardization
regulaciones de exportación (fpl)	*lahs reh-goo-lah-see-'oh-nehs deh ehks-pohr-tah-see-'ohn*	export regulations
regulaciones de importación	*lahs reh-goo-lah-see-'oh-nehs deh eem-pohr-tah-see-'ohn*	import regulations
regulaciones fitosanitarias	*lahs reh-goo-lah-see-'oh-nehs fee-toh-sah-nee-'tah-ree-ahs*	phytosanitary regulations
reino animal (m)	*ehl 'reh-ee-noh ah-nee-'mahl*	animal kingdom
reinvertir	*reh-een-behr-'teer*	plow back (earnings) (v)
rejilla (f) del radiador	*lah reh-hee-yah dehl rah-dee-ah-'dohr*	grille
relación (f)	*lah reh-lah-see-'ohn*	ratio
relacion de alimentación	*lah reh-lah-see-'ohn deh ah-lee-mehn-tah-see-'ohn*	feed ratio
relación capital-producto	*lah reh-lah-see-'ohn kah-pee-'tahl proh-'dook-toh*	capital-output ratio
relación entre prima y pérdidas	*lah reh-lah-see-'ohn 'ehn-treh 'pree-mah ee 'pehr-dee-dahs*	loss-loss ratio
relación precio-utilidad por acción	*la reh-lah-see-'ohn 'preh-see-oh-oo-tee-lee-'dahd pohr ahk-see-'ohn*	price-earnings ratio
relaciones con inversionistas (fpl)	*lahs reh-lah-see-'oh-nehs kohn een-behr-see-oh-'nees-tahs*	investor relations
relaciones entre empleados	*lahs reh-lah-see-'oh-nehs 'ehn-treh ehm-pleh-'ah-dohs*	employee relations
relaciones industriales	*lahs reh-lah-see-'oh-nehs een-doos-tree-'ah-lehs*	industrial relations

relaciones laborales	*lahs reh-lah-see-'oh-nehs lah-boh-'rah-lehs*	labor relations
relaciones públicas	*lahs reh-lah-see-'oh-nehs 'poo-blee-kahs*	public relations
relleno (m)	*ehl reh-'yeh-noh*	packing, stuffing, refill
remedios (mpl)	*lohs reh-'meh-dee-ohs*	remedies
remisión de impuestos (f)	*lah reh-mee-see-'ohn deh eem-'pweh-stohs*	remission duty
remitente (m)	*ehl reh-mee-'tehn-teh*	shipper
remuneración (f)	*lah reh-moo-neh-rah-see-'ohn*	remuneration
rendimiento (m)	*ehl rehn-dee-mee-'ehn-toh*	yield
rendimiento bruto	*ehl rehn-dee-mee-'ehn-toh 'broo-toh*	gross yield
rendimiento corriente	*ehl rehn-dee-mee-'ehn-toh koh-rree-'ehn-teh*	current yield
rendimiento de las ganancias	*ehl rehn-dee-mee-'ehn-toh deh lahs gah-'nahn-see-ahs*	earnings yield, income yield
rendimiento de las inversiones	*ehl rehn-dee-mee-'ehn-toh deh lahs een-behr-see-'oh-nehs*	return on investment
rendimiento del dividendo	*ehl rehn-dee-mee-'ehn-toh dehl dee-bee-'dehn-doh*	dividend yield
rendimiento efectivo	*ehl rehn-dee-mee-'ehn-toh eh-fehk-'tee-boh*	effective yield
rendimiento en el trabajo	*ehl rehn-dee-mee-'ehn-toh ehn ehl trah-'bah-hoh*	job performance
rendimiento fijo (uniforme)	*ehl rehn-dee-mee-'ehn-toh 'fee-hoh (oo-nee-'fohr-meh)*	flat yield
rendimiento hasta el vencimiento	*ehl rehn-dee-mee-'ehn-toh 'ahs-tah ehl behn-see-mee-'ehn-toh*	yield to maturity
rendimiento nominal	*ehl rehn-dee-mee-'ehn-toh noh-mee-'nahl*	nominal yield
rendimiento sobre capital	*ehl rehn-dee-mee-'ehn-toh 'soh-bre kah-pee-'tahl*	return on capital
rendimiento sobre inversión	*ehl rehn-dee-mee-'ehn-toh 'soh-bre een-behr-see-'ohn*	return on investment

R

rendimiento sobre recursos propios	*ehl rehn-dee-mee-'ehn-toh 'soh-breh reh-'koor-sohs 'proh-pee-ohs*	return on equity
rendimiento sobre ventas	*ehl rehn-dee-mee-'ehn-toh 'soh-breh 'behn-tahs*	return on sales
renegociar	*reh-neh-goh-see-'ahr*	renegotiate (v)
renglón (m)	*ehl rehn-'glohn*	line
renovación (f)	*lah reh-noh-bah-see-'ohn*	rollover
renovación urbana	*lah reh-noh-bah-see-'ohn oor-'bah-nah*	urban renewal
renovar	*reh-noh-'bahr*	renew (v)
renta	*'rehn-tah*	income
renta fija	*rehn-tah fee-hah*	fixed income
rentabilidad (f)	*lah rehn-tah-bee-lee-'dahd*	profitability
rentabilidad al vencimiento	*lah rehn-tah-bee-lee-'dahd ahl behn-see-mee-'ehn-toh*	yield to maturity
rentabilidad del producto	*lah rehn-tah-bee-lee-'dahd dehl proh-'dook-toh*	product profitability
rentabilidad por dividendos	*lah rehn-tah-bee-lee-'dahd pohr dee-bee-'dehn-dohs*	dividend yield
reordenar	*reh-ohr-deh-'nahr*	reorder (v)
reorganización (f)	*lah reh-ohr-gah-nee-sah-see-'ohn*	reorganization
repagar	*reh-pah-'gahr*	repay (v)
repartición grupal de sugerencias para crear ideas generales	*lah re-pahr-tee-see-'ohn groo-pahl deh soo-gehr-'ehn-see-ahs pah-rah kreh-ahr ee-'deh-ahs heh-nehr-'ahl-lehs*	brainstorming
reposesión (f)	*lah reh-poh-seh-see-'ohn*	repossession
represa (f)	*lah reh-'preh-sah*	dam
representante (m)	*ehl reh-preh-sehn-'tahn-teh*	representative
representante del fabricante	*ehl reh-preh-sehn-'tahn-teh dehl fah-bree-'kahn-teh*	manufacturer's representative
representante registrado	*ehl reh-preh-sehn-'tahn-teh reh-hee-'strah-doh*	registered representative
reproducir datos	*reh-proh-doo-'seer 'dah-tohs*	copy (v)
reptiles (mpl)	*lohs rehp-'tee-lehs*	reptiles

R

repuestos (mpl)	*lohs reh-'pweh-stohs*	replacement parts
requerimientos (m)	*lohs reh-keh-ree-mee-'ehn-tohs*	requirements
requisitos (mpl)	*lohs reh-kee-'see-tohs*	requirements
rescatar	*rehs-kah-'tahr*	salvage, buy back (v)
rescatar anticipadamente	*reh-skah-'tahr ahn-tee-see-pah-dah-'mehn-teh*	call (v) (the debt)
reserva (f)	*lah reh-'sehr-bah*	reserve
reservas de oro (fpl)	*lahs reh-'sehr-bahs deh 'oh-roh*	gold reserves
reservas mínimas	*lahs reh-'sehr-bahs 'mee-nee-mahs*	minimum reserves
reservas prestadas netas	*lahs reh-'sehr-bahs preh-'stah-dahs 'neh-tahs*	net borrowed reserves
reservas primarias	*lahs reh-'sehr-bahs pree-'mah-ree-ahs*	primary reserves
resguardo (m)	*ehl rehs-'gwahr-doh*	safeguard
residuo (m)	*ehl reh-'see-doo-oh*	remainder
resma (f)	*lah rehs-mah*	ream
resolución (f)	*lah reh-soh-loo-see-'ohn*	resolution (legal document)
respaldo y la satisfacción (m)	*ehl reh-'spahl-doh ee lah sah-tees-fahk-see-'ohn*	backing and filling
respaldo y soporte	*ehl reh-'spahl-doh ee-soh-'pohr-teh*	backing support
responder	*reh-spohn-'dehr*	reply (v)
responsabilidad (f)	*lah reh-spohn-sah-bee-lee-'dahd*	accountability, responsibility
responsabilidad del comprador	*lah reh-spohn-sah-bee-lee-'dahd dehl kohm-prah-'dohr*	buyer's responsibility
responsabilidad limitada	*lah reh-spohn-sah-bee-lee-'dahd lee-mee-'tah-dah*	limited liability
responsabilidad mancomunada	*lah reh-spohn-sah-bee-lee-'dahd mahn-koh-moo-'nah-dah*	joint liability
responsabilidad personal	*lah reh-spohn-sah-bee-lee-'dahd pehr-soh-'nahl*	personal liability
responsabilidad solidaria	*lah reh-spohn-sah-bee-lee-'dahd soh-lee-'dah-ree-ah*	joint liability
restaurar	*rehs-tah-oo-'rahr*	reset (v)

R

restricciones sobre las exporta- ciones (fpl)	*lahs reh-streek-see-'oh-nehs 'soh-breh lahs ehks-pohr- tah-see-'oh-nehs*	restrictions on export
resultados esperados (mpl)	*lohs reh-sool-'tah-dohs ehs- peh-'rah-dohs*	expected results
resumen del título (m)	*ehl reh-'soo-mehn dehl 'tee- too-lah*	abstract of title
retardo (m)	*ehl reh-'tahr-doh*	delay
retención de impuesto (f)	*lah reh-tehn-see-'ohn deh eem-'pweh-stoh*	withholding tax
retirar	*reh-tee-'rahr*	call back (v)
retiro (m)	*ehl reh-'tee-roh*	retirement
retiro proporcional de acciones	*ehl reh-'tee-roh proh-pohr- see-oh-'nahl deh ahk-see- 'oh-nehs*	reverse stock split
retorno razonable (m)	*ehl reh-'tohr-noh rah-soh- 'nah-bleh*	fair return
retorno semanal	*ehl reh-'tohr-noh seh-mah- 'nahl*	weekly return
retroactivo	*reh-troh-ahk-'tee-boh*	retroactive
retroalimentación (f)	*lah reh-troh-ah-lee-mehn- tah-see-'ohn*	feedback
retroceder en una unidad	*reh-troh-seh-'dehr ehn 'oo- nah oo-nee-'dahd*	backspace (v)
reunión (f)	*lah reh-oo-nee-'ohn*	meeting
reunión de accionistas	*lah reh-oo-nee-'ohn deh ahk-see-oh-'nees-tahs*	shareholders' meeting
reunión de la junta	*lah reh-oo-nee-'ohn deh lah 'hoon-tah*	board meeting
reunión general	*lah reh-oo-nee-'ohn heh- neh-'rahl*	general meeting
reunión plenaria	*lah reh-oo-nee-'ohn pleh- 'nah-ree-ah*	plenary meeting
revalorización (f)	*lah reh-bah-loh-ree-sah-see- 'ohn*	appreciation
revaluación (f)	*lah reh-eh-bah-loo-ah-see- 'ohn*	revaluation
reventa (f)	*lah reh-'behn-tah*	resale
revolución verde (f)	*lah reh-boh-loo-see-'ohn 'behr-deh*	green revolution
riego (m)	*ehl ree-'eh-goh*	irrigation

riesgo (m)	*ehl ree-'ehs-goh*	risk
riesgo agregado	*ehl ree-'ehs-goh ah-greh-'gah-doh*	aggregate risk
riesgo de cambio	*ehl ree-'ehs-goh deh 'kahm-bee-oh*	exchange risk
riesgo de capital	*ehl ree-'ehs-goh deh kah-pee-'tahl*	risk capital
riesgo de incumplimiento	*ehl ree-'ehs-goh deh een-koom-plee-mee-'ehn-toh*	risk of default
riesgo del transportador	*ehl ree-'ehs-goh dehl trahns-pohr-tah-'dohr*	carrier's risk
riesgo económico	*ehl ree-'ehs-goh eh-koh-'noh-mee-koh*	business risk
riesgo ocupacional	*ehl ree-'ehs-goh oh-koo-pah-see-oh-'nahl*	occupational hazard
riesgo personal	*ehl ree-'ehs-goh pehr-soh-'nahl*	personal liability
riesgo puro	*ehl ree-'ehs-goh 'poo-roh*	pure risk
rinoceronte (m)	*ehl ree-noh-seh-'rohn-teh*	rhinoceros
río (m)	*ehl 'ree-oh*	river
riqueza (f)	*lah ree-'keh-sah*	wealth
ropa (f) hecha	*lah roh-pah 'eh-chah*	ready-to-wear
ropa interior	*lah roh-pah een-teh-ree-'ohr*	lingerie
rotación de las cosechas (f)	*lah roh-tah-see-'ohn deh lahs koh-'seh-chahs*	crop rotation
rotación de personal	*lah roh-tah-see-'ohn deh pehr-soh-'nahl*	labor turnover
rotación de ventas	*lah roh-tah-see-'ohn deh 'behn-tahs*	sales turnover
rotación del activo	*lah roh-tah-see-'ohn dehl ahk-'tee-boh*	asset turnover
rotación del inventario	*lah roh-tah-see-'ohn dehl een-behn-'tah-ree-oh*	inventory turnover, stock turnover
rotación impropia de las cosechas	*lah roh-tah-see-'ohn eem-'proh-pee-ah deh lahs koh-'seh-chahs*	crop rotation (improper)
rueda (f)	*lah roo-eh-dah*	wheel
rueda de repuesto	*lah roo-'eh-dah deh reh-'pweh-stoh*	spare tire
rutina (f)	*lah roo-'tee-nah*	routine

R

S

sabor	*ehl sah-bohr*	body (in winemaking)
sabor a frutas (m)	*ehl sah-bohr ah-froo-tahs*	fruity
sacacorcho (m)	*ehl sah-kah-kohr-chohs*	corkscrew
sacar	*sah-'kahr*	take out (v), draw off (v)
sacarina (f)	*lah sah-kah-'ree-nah*	saccharin
saco (m)	*ehl 'sah-koh*	coat
sal (f)	*lah 'sahl*	salt
sala de conferencias (f)	*lah 'sah-lah deh kohn-feh-'rehn-see-ahs*	board room, conference room
sala de operaciones de bolsa	*lah 'sah-lah deh oh-peh-rah-see-'oh-nehs deh 'bohl-sah*	floor (of exchange)
salario (m)	*ehl sah-'lah-ree-oh*	wage
salario mínimo	*ehl sah-'lah-ree-oh 'mee-nee-moh*	minimum wage
salario mínimo garantizado por indexación	*ehl sah-'lah-ree-oh 'mee-nee-moh gah-rahn-tee-'sah-doh pohr een-dehk-sah-see-'ohn*	index-linked guaranteed minimum wage
salarios reales (mpl)	*lohs sah-'lah-ree-ohs reh-'ah-lehs*	real wages
saldo (m)	*ehl 'sahl-doh*	balance (of an account)
saldo bancario	*ehl 'sahl-doh bahn-'kah-ree-oh*	bank balance
saldo compensatorio	*ehl 'sahl-doh kohm-pehn-sah-'toh-ree-oh*	compensating balance
saldo crediticio	*ehl 'sahl-doh kreh-dee-'tee-see-oh*	credit balance
saldo de caja	*ehl 'sahl-doh deh 'kah-hah*	cash balance
saldo de la cuenta	*ehl 'sahl-doh deh la 'kwehn-tah*	account balance
saldo de operación	*ehl 'sahl-doh deh oh-peh-rah-see-'ohn*	working balance
saldo inicial	*ehl 'sahl-doh ee-nee-'see-ahl*	opening balance
salero (m)	*ehl sah-'leh-roh*	salt shaker
sales (fpl)	*lahs 'sah-lehs*	salts

salida (f)	*lah sah-'lee-dah*	output
salida de información de la computadora	*lah sah-'lee-dah deh een-fohr-mah-see-'ohn deh lah kohm-poo-tah-'doh-rah*	computer output
salida impresa	*lah sah-'lee-dah eem-'preh-sah*	printout, hard copy
salir	*sah-'leer*	exit (v)
salir sin ganar ni perder	*sah-'leer seen gah-'nahr nee pehr-'dehr*	break even (v)
salsera (f)	*lah sahl-'seh-rah*	gravy boat
sangrar	*sahn-'grahr*	bleed (v)
sangre (f)	*lah 'sahn-greh*	blood
sastre (m)	*ehl 'sah-streh*	tailor
satisfacción del consumidor (f)	*lah sah-tees-fahk-see-'ohn dehl kohn-soo-mee-'dohr*	consumer satisfaction
saturación (f)	*lah sah-too-rah-see-'ohn*	glut
saturación del mercado	*lah sah-too-rah-see-'ohn dehl mehr-'kah-doh*	market saturation
saya (f)	*lah 'sah-yah*	skirt
secante (m)	*ehl seh-'kahn-teh*	blotter
seco	*'seh-koh*	dry (adj)
secretaria (f), secretario (m)	*lah seh-kreh-'tah-ree-ah ehl seh-kreh-'tah-ree-oh*	secretary
secretario ejecutivo	*ehl seh-kreh-'tah-ree-oh eh-heh-koo-'tee-boh*	executive secretary
sector público (m)	*ehl sehk-'tohr 'poo-blee-koh*	public sector
seda (f)	*lah 'seh-dah*	silk
sedán (m)	*ehl seh-'dahn*	sedan
sedante (m)	*ehl seh-'dahn-teh*	sedative
sedimento (m)	*ehl seh-dee-'mehn-toh*	sediment
seguir	*seh-'geer*	follow up (v)
según aviso	*seh-'goon ah-'bee-soh*	as per advice
según los libros	*seh-'goon lohs 'lee-brohs*	asset value
segunda hipoteca (f)	*lah seh-'goon-dah ee-poh-'teh-kah*	second mortgage
segunda posición	*lah seh-'goon-dah poh-see-see-'ohn*	second position

S

seguro industrial (m)	*ehl seh-'goo-roh een-doos-tree-'ahl*	industrial insurance
seguro que cubre los riesgos de un directivo	*seh-'goo-roh keh 'koo-breh lohs ree-'ehs-gohs deh oon dee-rehk-'tee-boh*	key-man insurance
seguros (mpl)	*lohs seh-'goo-rohs*	insurance
seguros a plazo	*lohs seh-'goo-rohs ah 'plah-soh*	term insurance
seguros colectivos	*lohs seh-'goo-rohs koh-lehk-'tee-bohs*	group insurance
seguros contra accidentes	*lohs seh-'goo-rohs 'kohn-trah ahk-see-'dehn-tehs*	casualty insurance
seguros de cargo marítimo	*lohs seh-'goo-rohs deh 'kahr-goh mah-'ree-tee-moh*	marine or maritime cargo insurance
seguros de créditos	*lohs seh-'goo-rohs deh 'kreh-dee-tohs*	credit insurance
seguros de responsabilidad civil	*lohs seh-'goo-rohs deh reh-spohn-sah-bee-lee-'dahd see-'beel*	liability insurance
seguros de título	*lohs seh-'goo-rohs deh 'tee-too-lah*	title insurance
selección (f)	*lah seh-lehk-see-'ohn*	screening
selección de directivos de otras empresas	*lah seh-lehk-see-'ohn deh dee-rehk-'tee-bohs deh 'oh-trahs ehm-'preh-sahs*	headhunter
semiárido	*seh-mee-'ah-ree-doh*	semi-arid (adj)
semiconductor (m)	*ehl seh-mee-kohn-dook-'tohr*	solid state
seno (m)	*ehl 'seh-noh*	sinus
sequía (f)	*lah seh-'kee-ah*	drought
seres vivos (mpl)	*lohs 'seh-rehs 'bee-bohs*	living beings
serie (f)	*lah 'seh-ree-eh*	batch
serpentín (m)	*ehl sehr-pehn-'teen*	coil
servicio al cliente (m)	*ehl sehr-'bee-see-oh ahl klee-'ehn-teh*	customer service
servicio consultivo	*ehl sehr-'bee-see-oh kohn sool-'tee-boh*	advisory service
servicio de correo	*ehl sehr-'bee-see-oh deh koh-'rreh-oh*	courier service
servicio de mensajero	*ehl sehr-'bee-see-oh deh mehn-sah-'heh-roh*	courier service

servicio de post-venta	*ehl sehr-'bee-see-oh deh pohst-'behn-tah*	after-sales-service
servicio personal	*ehl sehr-'bee-see-oh pehr-soh-'nahl*	self-service
servicios finan-cieros (mpl)	*lohs sehr-'bee-see-ohs fee-nahn-see-'eh-rohs*	financial service
servicios públicos	*lohs sehr-'bee-see-ohs 'poo-blee-kohs*	public utility
servidumbre de paso (m)	*ehl sehr-bee-'doom-breh deh 'pah-soh*	right of way
servidumbre de vía	*ehl sehr-bee-'doom-breh deh 'bee-ah*	right of way
servilleta (f)	*lah sehr-bee-'yeh-tah*	napkin
servilletero (m)	*ehl sehr-bee-yeh-'teh-roh*	napkin ring
servir	*sehr-'beer*	service (v)
siempre y cuando	*see-'ehm-preh ee 'kwahn-doh*	as if and when
silicio (m)	*ehl see-'lee-see-oh*	silicon
silla (m) de montar	*lah see-yah deh mohn-'tahr*	saddle
símbolo (m)	*ehl 'seem-boh-loh*	symbol
simplificar	*seem-plee-fee-'kahr*	streamline (v)
simular	*see-moo-'lahr*	simulate (v)
sin cambios	*seen 'kahm-bee-ohs*	gearless
sin derechos	*seen deh-'reh-chohs*	ex rights
sin dividendo	*seen dee-bee-'dehn-doh*	ex dividend
sin testar	*seen tehs-'tahr*	intestate
sin valor	*seen bah-'lohr*	worthless
sin valor nominal	*seen bah-'lohr noh-mee-'nahl*	no par value
sindicato industrial (m)	*ehl seen-dee-'kah-toh een-doos-'tree-'ahl*	industrial union
sindicato laboral	*ehl seen-dee-'kah-toh lah-boh-'rahl*	labor union
síntesis (f)	*lah 'seen-teh-sees*	synthesis
sistema de cuotas (m)	*ehl sees-'teh-mah deh 'kwoh-tahs*	quota system

S

sistema de pago al contado con el transporte pagado por el comprador	*ehl sees-'teh-mah deh 'pah-goh ahl kohn-'tah-doh kohn ehl trahs-'pohr-teh pah-'gah-doh pohr ehl kohm-prah-'dohr*	cash-and-carry
sistema gerencial integrado	*ehl sees-'teh-mah heh-rehn-see-'ahl een-teh-'grah-doh*	integrated management system
sitio de exploración (m)	*ehl 'see-tee-oh deh ehks-ploh-rah-see-'ohn*	exploration site
sitio de trabajo	*ehl 'see-tee-oh deh trah-'bah-hoh*	workplace
sitio donde no se paga impuesto o se paga muy poco	*ehl 'see-tee-oh 'dohn-deh noh seh 'pah-gah eem-'pweh-stoh oh seh 'pah-gah 'moo-ee 'poh-koh*	tax haven
smog (m)	*ehl ehs-'mohg*	smog
smog urbano	*ehl ehs-'mohg oor-'bah-noh*	smog (urban)
smoking (m)	*ehl ehs-'moh-keen*	tuxedo
soborno (m)	*ehl soh-'bohr-noh*	graft
sobrante (m)	*ehl soh-'brahn-teh*	overage
sobre la línea	*'soh-breh lah 'lee-neh-ah*	above-the-line
sobre la par	*'soh-breh lah 'pahr*	above par
sobrecomprado	*'soh-breh-kohm-'prah-doh*	overbought
sobrecubierta (f)	*lah soh-breh-koo-bee-'ehr-tah*	jacket (book)
sobregirar	*soh-breh-hee-'rahr*	overdraw (v)
sobregiro (m)	*ehl soh-breh-'hee-roh*	overdraft
sobreoferta (f)	*lah soh-breh-oh-'fehr-tah*	oversupply
sobrepagado	*soh-breh-pah-'gah-doh*	overpaid
sobresuscrito	*soh-breh-soo-'skree-toh*	oversubscribed
sobrevaluado	*soh-breh-bah-loo-'ah-doh*	overvalued
sobrevencido	*soh-bree-behn-'see-doh*	overdue
sobrevendido (vendido en exceso)	*soh-breh-behn-'dee-doh (behn-'dee-doh ehn ehk-'seh-soh)*	oversold
socavar	*soh-kah-'bahr*	undercut (v)
socialismo (m)	*ehl soh-see-ah-'lees-moh*	socialism
sociedad (f)	*lah soh-see-eh-'dahd*	partnership

sociedad anónima	*lah soh-see-eh-'dahd ah-'noh-nee-mah*	corporation
sociedad colectiva (en nombre colectivo)	*lah soh-see-eh-'dahd koh-lehk-'tee-bah (ehn 'nohm-breh koh-lehk-'tee-boh)*	general partnership
sociedad creada con un fin específico	*lah soh-see-eh-'dahd kreh-'ah-dah kohn oon feen ehs-peh-'see-fee-koh*	turnkey company
sociedad en comandita por acciones	*lah soh-see-eh-'dad ehn koh-mahn-'dee-tah pohr ahk-see-'oh-nehs*	joint stock company
sociedad inversionista controladora	*lah soh-see-eh-'dahd een-behr-see-oh-'nees-tah kohn-troh-lah-'doh-rah*	holding company
sociedad limitada	*lah soh-see-eh-'dahd lee-mee-'tah-dah*	limited partnership
socio (m)	*ehl 'soh-see-oh*	partner
socio comanditario	*ehl 'soh-see-oh kloh-mahn-dee-'tah-ree-oh*	silent partner
socio de la empresa	*ehl 'soh-see-oh deh lah ehm-'preh-sah*	member of firm
socio menor	*ehl 'soh-see-oh meh-'nohr*	junior partner
software (m)	*ehl sohft-'wehr*	software
solar	*soh-'lahr*	solar (adj)
solicitud (f)	*lah soh-lee-see-'tood*	application form
solicitud de ofertas	*lah soh-lee-see-'tood deh oh-'fehr-tahs*	request for bid
solicitud de patente	*lah soh-lee-see-'tood deh pah-'tehn-teh*	patent application
solubilidad (f)	*lah soh-loo-bee-lee-'dahd*	solubility
solución (f)	*lah soh-loo-see-'ohn*	solution
solución de problemas	*lah soh-lee-see-'ohn deh proh-'bleh-mahs*	problem solving
soluto (m)	*ehl soh-'loo-toh*	solute
solvente (m)	*ehl soh-'behn-teh*	solvent
someterse a	*soh-meh-'tehr-seh ah*	submit to (v)
sonido (m)	*ehl soh-'nee-doh*	sound
sopera (f)	*lah soh-'peh-rah*	tureen

S

sostenamiento artificial de precios (m)	*ehl soh-steh-nee-'mee-ehn-toh ahr-tee-fee-see-'ahl deh-'preh-see-ohs*	price support
sostener	*sohs-teh-'nehr*	sustain (v)
subarrendar	*soob-ah-rrehn-'dahr*	sublet (v)
subasta (f)	*lah soo-'bah-stah*	auction market
subasta con aviso anticipado	*lah soo-'bahs-tah 'kohn ah-'bee-soh ahn-tee-see-'pah-doh*	public auction
subastador (m)	*ehl soo-bah-stah-'dohr*	bidder
subcontratar	*soob-kohn-trah-'tahr*	farm out (v)
subcontratista (m)	*ehl soob-kohn-trah-'tees-tah*	subcontractor
subcontrato (m)	*ehl soob-kohn-'trah-toh*	subcontract
subdesarrollado	*soob-dehs-ah-rroh-'yah-doh*	underdeveloped
subestimar	*soob-eh-stee-'mahr*	underestimate (v)
subpagado	*soob-pah-'gah-doh*	underpaid
subproducto (m)	*ehl soob-proh-'dook-toh*	by-product
subrutina (f)	*lah soob-roo-'tee-nah*	subroutine
subsidiario (m)	*ehl soob-see-dee-'ah-ree-oh*	subsidiary
sucursal (f)	*lah soo-koor-'sahl*	branch office
sucursal situada fuera del país donde reside la casa matriz	*lah soo-koor-'sahl see-too-'ah-dah 'fweh-rah dehl pah-'ees 'dohn-deh reh-'see-deh lah 'kah-sah mah-'trees*	offshore company
sueldo (m)	*ehl 'swehl-doh*	salary
sueldo después de deducciones	*ehl-'swehl-doh dehs-pwehs deh deh-dook-'syoh-nehs*	take home pay
sueldo insuficiente	*ehl 'swehl-doh een-soo-fee-see-'ehn-teh*	underpaid
suelos (mpl)	*lohs 'sweh-lohs*	surface areas (land)
suero (m)	*ehl 'sweh-roh*	serum
sujeto a	*soo-'heh-toh ah*	liable to
sujeto a disponibilidad	*soo-'heh-toh ah dees-poh-nee-bee-lee-'dahd*	subject to availability
sujeto a impuesto	*soo-'heh-toh ah eem-'pweh-stoh*	liability for tax
sulfamide (f)	*lah sool-fah-'mee-dah*	sulphamide

S

sulfato (m)	*ehl sool-fah-toh*	sulfate
suma (f)	*lah 'soo-mah*	amount
suma global	*lah 'soo-mah gloh-'bahl*	lump sum
suma pasada al frente	*lah 'soo-mah pah-'sah-dah ahl 'frehn-teh*	carryover
sumiller (m)	*ehl soo-mee-'yehr*	wine steward
suministrador (m)	*ehl soo-mee-nees-trah-'dohr*	supplier
suministro de energía (m)	*ehl soo-mee-'nees-troh deh eh-nehr-'hee-ah*	power supply
superaleaciones (fpl)	*lahs soo-pehr-ah-leh-ah-see-'oh-nehs*	super alloys
superávit de bienes (m)	*ehl soo-peh-'rah-beet deh 'bee-eh-nehs*	surplus goods
superávit de capital	*ehl soo-peh-'rah-beet deh kah-pee-'tahl*	surplus capital
superávit pagado	*ehl soo-peh-'rah-beet pah-'gah-doh*	paid-in surplus
superconductor (m)	*ehl soo-pehr-kohn-dook-'tohr*	superconductor
superficie (f)	*lah soo-pehr-'fee-see-eh*	surface
suprimir	*soo-pree-'meer*	omit (v)
suscrito (m)	*ehl soos-'kree-toh*	undersigned
suscrito de seguro marítimo	*ehl soos-'kree-toh deh seh-'goo-roh mah-'ree-tee-moh*	marine underwriter
suspender el pago	*soos-pehn-'dehr ehl 'pah-goh*	suspend payment
suspensión (f)	*lah soos-pehn-see-'ohn*	suspension
sustento (m)	*ehl soos-'tehn-toh*	sustenance

T

tabular	*tah-boo-'lahr*	tabulate (v)
tafetán (m)	*ehl tah-feh-'tahn*	taffeta
tala (f)	*lah 'tah-lah*	felling (of a tree)
talla (f)	*lah 'tah-yah*	size
taller (m)	*ehl tah-'yehr*	workshop

taller de laminación	*ehl tah-'yehr deh lah-mee-nah-see-'ohn*	rolling mill
taller franco	*ehl tah-'yehr 'frahn-koh*	open shop
taller siderúrgico	*ehl tah-'yehr see-deh-'roor-hee-koh*	steel mill
talón bancario (m)	*ehl tah-'lohn bahn-'kah-ree-oh*	counter check
tamaño (m)	*ehl tah-'mah-nyoh*	size
tamaño de muestra	*ehl tah-'mah-nyoh deh moo-'eh-strah*	sample size
tanque (m)	*ehl 'tahn-keh*	tank
tanque de gasolina	*ehl 'tahn-keh deh gah-soh-'lee-nah*	gasoline tank
tanque de carburante para helicópteros	*ehl 'tahn-keh deh kahr-boo-'rahn-teh 'pah-rah eh-lee-'kohp-teh-rohs*	tank (jet fuel)
tanque de reserva para agua salada	*ehl 'tahn-keh deh reh-'sehr-bah 'pah-rah 'ah-gwah sah-'lah-dah*	tank (salt water)
tanque para el agua potable	*ehl 'tahn-keh 'pah-rah ehl 'ah-gwah poh-'tah-bleh*	tank (drinking water)
tanque para el almacenamiento de cemento	*ehl 'tahn-keh 'pah-rah ehl ahl-mah-seh-nah-mee-'ehn-toh deh seh-'mehn-toh*	tank (cement storage)
tanquero (m)	*ehl tahn-'keh-roh*	tanker
tarifa flexible (f)	*lah tah-'ree-fah flek-'see-bleh*	flexible tariff
tarifa preferencial	*lah tah-'ree-fah preh-feh-rehn-see-'ahl*	preferred tariff
tarifas diferenciales (fpl)	*lahs tah-'ree-fahs dee-feh-rehn-see-'ah-lehs*	differential tariffs
tarjeta comercial (f)	*lah tahr-'heh-tah koh-mehr-see-'ahl*	business card
tarjeta de crédito	*lah tahr-'heh-tah deh 'kreh-dee-toh*	credit card
tarjeta para perforar	*lah tahr-'heh-tah 'pah-rah pehr-foh-'rahr*	punch card
tarjetero (m)	*ehl tahr-heh-'teh-roh*	card case
tasa (f)	*lah 'tah-sah*	rate

T

tasa ajustada	*lah 'tah-sah ah-hoo-'stah-dah*	adjusted rate
tasa central	*lah 'tah-sah sehn-'trahl*	central rate
tasa de aumento	*lah 'tah-sah deh ow-'mehn-toh*	accession rate
tasa de crecimiento	*lah 'tah-sah deh kreh-see-mee-'ehn-toh*	rate of growth
tasa de incremento	*lah 'tah-sah deh een-kreh-'mehn-toh*	rate of increase
tasa de inflación	*lah 'tah-sah deh een-flah-see-'ohn*	inflation rate
tasa de rendimiento	*lah 'tah-sah deh rehn-dee-mee-'ehn-toh*	rate of return
tasa flotante	*lah 'tah-sah floh-'tahn-teh*	floating rate
tasa interna de rentabilidad	*lah 'tah-sah een-'tehr-nah deh rehn-tah-bee-lee-'dahd*	internal rate of return (IRR)
tasa interna de retorno	*lah 'tah-sah een-'tehr-nah deh reh-'tohr-noh*	internal rate of return
tasa preferencial	*lah 'tah-sah preh-feh-rehn-see-'ahl*	prime rate
tasa redescuento	*lah 'tah-sah deh reh-dehs-'kwehn-toh*	rediscount rate
tasa uniformal	*lah 'tah-sah oo-nee-fohr-'mahl*	flat rate
tasa variable	*lah 'tah-sah bah-ree-'ah-bleh*	variable rate
tasación (f)	*lah tah-sah-see-'ohn*	assessment, appraisal
tasador (m)	*ehl tah-sah-'dohr*	appraiser
tasar	*tah-'sahr*	assess (v)
tasar en menos del valor real	*tah-'sahr ehn 'meh-nohs dehl bah-'lohr reh-'ahl*	undervalue (v)
taza (f)	*lah 'tah-sah*	cup
taza de café expreso	*lah tah-sah deh kah-feh ehk-spreh-soh*	espresso cup
techo (m)	*ehl 'teh-choh*	ceiling
teclado (m)	*ehl teh-'klah-doh*	keyboard
teclar (la computadora)	*teh-'klahr (lah kohm-poo-tah-'doh-rah)*	keypunch (v)

T

teclas repetidoras (fpl)	*lahs 'teh-klahs reh-peh-tee-'doh-rahs*	repeat keys
técnicas de Monte Carlo (f)	*lahs 'tehk-nee-kahs deh 'mohn-teh 'kahr-loh*	Monte Carlo techniques
técnico (m) de laboratorio	*ehl 'tehk-nee-koh deh lah-boh-rah-'toh-ree-oh*	laboratory technician
tecnología (f)	*lah tehk-noh-loh-'hee-ah*	technology
tejedor (m)	*ehl teh-heh-'dohr*	weaver
tela (f)	*lah 'teh-lah*	fabric
telecomunicaciones (fpl)	*lahs teh-leh-koh-moo-nee-kah-see-'oh-nehs*	telecommunications
teléfono celular (m)	*ehl teh-'leh-foh-noh seh-loo-'lahr*	cellular phone
telemercadeo (m)	*ehl teh-leh-mehr-kah-'deh-oh*	telemarketing
teleprocesamiento (m)	*ehl teh-leh-proh-seh-sah-mee-'ehn-toh*	teleprocessing
teleproceso (m)	*ehl teh-leh-proh-'seh-soh*	teleprocessing
televisión (f) por cable	*lah teh-leh-bee-see-'ohn pohr 'kah-bleh*	cable television
temblor (m)	*ehl tehm-'blohr*	earthquake
temperatura (f)	*lah tehm-peh-rah-'too-rah*	temperature
templar	*tehm-'plahr*	quench (v)
tenacidad (f)	*lah teh-nah-see-'dahd*	toughness
tendencia (f)	*lah tehn-'dehn-see-ah*	trend
tendencia alcista	*lah tehn-'dehn-see-ah ahl-'sees-tah*	upturn
tendencias del mercado (fpl)	*lahs tehn-'dehn-see-ahs dehl mehr-'kah-doh*	market trends
tenedor (m)	*ehl teh-neh-'dohr*	bearer, fork
tenedor de póliza	*ehl teh-neh-'dohr deh 'poh-lee-sah*	policy holder
tenedor legítimo	*ehl teh-neh-'dohr leh-'hee-tee-moh*	holder in due course
tener autoridad	*teh-'nehr ow-toh-ree-'dahd*	to have authority (v)
tenería (f)	*lah teh-neh-'ree-ah*	tannery
teñir	*teh-'nyeer*	dye (v)
tensión nerviosa (f)	*lah tehn-see-'ohn nehr-bee-'oh-sah*	stress

terminal de computadora (m)	*ehl tehr-mee-'nahl de kohm-poo-tah-'doh-rah*	computer terminal
terminar	*tehr-mee-'nahr*	terminate (v)
término (m)	*ehl 'tehr-mee-noh*	deadline
términos de intercambio (mpl)	*lohs 'tehr-mee-nohs deh een-tehr-'kahm-bee-oh*	terms of trade
términos de la venta	*lohs 'tehr-mee-nohs deh lah 'behn-tah*	terms of sale
términos lineales	*lohs 'tehr-mee-nohs lee-neh-'ah-lehs*	linear terms
termómetro (m)	*ehl tehr-'moh-meh-troh*	thermometer
terrateniente (m)	*ehl teh-rrah-teh-nee-'ehn-teh*	landowner
terreno (m)	*ehl teh-'rreh-noh*	land
territorio (m)	*ehl teh-rree-'toh-ree-oh*	territory
territorio de ventas	*ehl teh-rree-'toh-ree-oh deh 'behn-tahs*	sales territory
tesorero (m)	*ehl teh-soh-'reh-roh*	treasurer
testamento (m)	*ehl tehs-tah-'mehn-toh*	will
testigo (m)	*ehl tehs-'tee-goh*	witness
tetera (f)	*lah teh-'teh-rah*	teapot
texto impreso (m)	*ehl tehks-toh eem-preh-soh*	letterpress
tiempo concurrido (m)	*ehl tee-'ehm-poh kohn-koo-'ree-doh*	attended time
tiempo cortado a la mitad	*ehl tee-'ehm-poh kohr-'tah-doh ah lah mee-'tahd*	double time
tiempo de anticipación	*ehl tee-'ehm-poh deh ahn-tee-see-pah-see-'ohn*	lead time
tiempo de ejecución	*ehl tee-'ehm-poh deh eh-heh-koo-see-'ohn*	run time
tiempo de respuesta	*ehl tee-'ehm-poh deh reh-'spweh-stah*	response time
tiempo estimado (la hora estimada) de llegada	*ehl tee-'ehm-poh ehs-tee-'mah-doh (lah oh-rah ehs-tee-'mah-dah) deh yeh-'gah-dah*	estimated time of arrival
tiempo estimado (la hora estimada) de salida	*ehl tee-'ehm-poh ehs-tee-'mah-doh (lah 'oh-rah ehs-tee-'mah-dah) deh sah-'lee-dah*	estimated time of departure

T

tiempo extra	*ehl tee-'ehm-poh 'ehk-strah*	overtime
tiempo improductivo	*ehl tee-'ehm-poh eem-proh-dook-'tee-boh*	downtime
tiempo libre	*ehl tee-'ehm-poh 'lee-breh*	free time
tiempo muerto	*ehl tee-'ehm-poh 'mwehr-toh*	down time
tiempo preferencial	*ehl tee-'ehm-poh preh-feh-rehn-see-'ahl*	prime time
tiempo real	*ehl tee-'ehm-poh reh-'ahl*	real time
tiempo y movimiento	*ehl tee-'ehm-poh ee moh-bee-mee-'ehn-toh*	time and motion
tienda (f)	*lah tee-'ehn-dah*	store
tienda de moneda	*lah tee-'ehn-dah deh moh-'neh-dah*	coin store
tienda por departamentos	*lah tee-'ehn-dah pohr deh-pahr-tah-'mehn-tohs*	department store
Tierra (f)	*lah tee-'eh-rrah*	Earth
tierra (f)	*lah tee-'eh-rrah*	land
tina (f)	*lah tee-nah*	vat
tinta (f)	*lah teen-tah*	ink
tipo base (m)	*ehl 'tee-poh 'bah-seh*	base rate
tipo de cambio	*ehl 'tee-poh deh 'kahm-bee-oh*	exchange, forward exchange rate
tipo de cambio fijo ajustable	*ehl 'tee-poh deh 'kahm-bee-oh ah-hoos-'tah-bleh*	adjustable peg
tipo de cambio fijo	*ehl 'tee-poh deh 'kahm-bee-oh 'fee-hoh*	fixed rate of exchange
tipo de cambio flotante	*ehl 'tee-poh deh 'kahm-bee-oh floh-'tahn-teh*	floating exchange rate
tipo de cambio múltiple	*ehl 'tee-poh deh 'kahm-bee-oh 'mool-tee-pleh*	multiple exchange rate
tipo de descuento	*ehl 'tee-poh deh dehs-'kwehn-toh*	discount rate
tipo de interés bancario	*ehl 'tee-poh deh een-teh-'rehs bahn-'kah-ree-oh*	bank rate
tipo de interés	*ehl 'tee-poh deh een-teh-'rehs*	rate of interest
tipo de interés para préstamos diarios	*ehl 'tee-poh deh een-teh-'rehs 'pah-rah 'prehs-tah-mohs dee-'ah-ree-ohs*	call rate

tipo de letra	*ehl tee-poh deh leh-trah*	font
tipo de oferta	*ehl 'tee-poh deh oh-'fehr-tah*	offered rate
tipo de vid	*ehl tee-poh deh beed*	type of vine
tipo ofrecido	*ehl 'tee-poh oh-freh-'see-doh*	offered rate
tipo preferencial	*ehl 'tee-poh preh-feh-rehn-see-'ahl*	prime rate
tipos variables (mpl)	*lohs 'tee-pohs bah-ree-'ah-bleh*	floating rates
tirada (f)	*lah tee-rah-dah*	print run
titulación (f)	*lah tee-too-lah-see-'ohn*	titration
titular (m)	*ehl tee-too-lahr*	headline
título (m)	*ehl 'tee-too-loh*	title
títutlo municipal	*ehl 'tee-too-loh moo-nee-see-'pahl*	municipal bond
título al portador	*ehl 'tee-too-loh ahl pohr-tah-'dohr*	bearer bond
título de hipoteca	*ehl 'tee-poh deh ee-poh-'teh-kah*	mortgage certificate
título poder	*ehl 'tee-too-loh poh-'dehr*	bond power
título valor registrado	*ehl 'tee-too-loh reh-hees-'trah-doh*	registered security
títulos (mpl)	*lohs 'tee-too-lohs*	securities
tocadiscos (m)	*ehl toh-kah-'dees-kohs*	record player
tocador (m) de videocassette	*ehl toh-kah-dohr deh bee-deh-oh-kah-seh-teh*	videocassette player
todo o nada	*'toh-doh oh 'nah-dah*	all or none
tomar nota	*toh-'mahr 'noh-tah*	take down (v)
tonel (m)	*ehl 'toh-nehl*	cask (225 litres)
tonelada de 2240 libras (f)	*lah toh-neh-'lah-dah deh dohs meel dohs-see-'ehn-tahs kwah-'rehn-tah 'lee-brahs*	long ton
tonelaje (m)	*ehl toh-neh-'lah-heh*	tonnage
torre de perforación (f)	*lah 'toh-rreh deh pehr-foh-rah-see-'ohn*	derrick
toser	*toh-'sehr*	cough (v)
total de una columna (m)	*ehl toh-'tahl deh 'oo-nah koh-'loom-nah*	footing (accounting)

T

toxicología (f)	*lah tok-see-koh-loh-'hee-ah*	toxicology
toxina (f)	*lah tok-'see-nah*	toxin
trabajador (m)	*ehl trah-bah-hah-'dohr*	laborer, wage earner
trabajador por su cuenta	*ehl trah-bah-hah-'dohr pohr soo kwehn-tah*	self-employed man
trabajador que cambia de un puesto a otro	*ehl trah-bah-hah-'dohr keh 'kahm-bee-ah deh oon 'pweh-stoh ah 'oh-troh*	job hopper
trabajar	*trah-bah-'hahr*	work (v)
trabajar independientenente	*trah-bah-'hahr een-deh-pen-dee-ehn-teh-'mehn-teh*	freelance
trabajo (m)	*ehl trah-'bah-hoh*	job, labor
trabajo a destajo	*ehl trah-'bah-hoh ah dehs-'tah-hoh*	piecework
trabajo en progreso	*ehl trah-'bah-hoh ehn proh-'greh-soh*	work in progress
trabajo no calificado	*ehl trah-'bah-hoh non kah-lee-fee-'kah-doh*	unskilled labor
trabajo por contrato	*ehl trah-'bah-hoh pohr kohn-'trah-toh*	work by contract
trabajo-intensivo	*ehl trah-'bah-hoh-een-tehn-'see-boh*	labor-intensive
trabajos públicos (mpl)	*lohs trah-'bah-hohs 'poo-blee-kohs*	public works
tracción (f) delantera	*lah trahk-see-'ohn deh-lahn-'teh-rah*	front-wheel drive
traducir	*trah-doo-'seer*	translate (v)
traductor (m)	*ehl trah-dook-'tohr*	translator
traje (m)	*ehl 'trah-heh*	suit
trámites burocráticos (m)	*lohs 'trah-mee-tehs boo-roh-'krah-tee-kohs*	red tape
trama (f)	*lah 'trah-mah*	screen (printing term)
tramo (m)	*ehl 'trah-moh*	tranche
tramo de ingresos	*ehl 'trah-moh deh een-'greh-sohs*	income bracket
tranquilizante (m)	*ehl trahn-kee-lee-'sahn-teh*	tranquilizer
transacción de conjunto (f)	*lah trahn-sahk-see-'ohn deh kohn-'hoon-toh*	package deal

transferencia cablegráfica (f)	*lah trahns-feh-'rehn-see-ah kah-bleh-'grah-fee-kah*	cable transfer, wire transfer
transferencia de activo a otra compañía sin cambio de accionistas	*lah trahns-feh-'rehn-see-ah deh ahk-'tee-boh ah 'oh-trah kohm-pah-'nyee-ah seen 'kahm-bee-oh deh ahk-see-oh-'nees-tahs*	spin off
transferido	*trahns-feh-'ree-doh*	transferred
transferir al pasado	*trahns-feh-'reer ahl pah-'sah-doh*	carry back (v)
transformador (m)	*ehl trahns-fohr-mah-'dohr*	transformer
transformar	*trans-fohr-'mahr*	convert (v)
transmisible	*trahns-mee-'see-bleh*	negotiable
transmitir (TV)	*trahns-mee-'teer*	broadcast (v)
transmitir	*trahns-mee-'teer*	transmit (v)
transportador (m)	*ehl trahns-pohr-tah-'dohr*	carrier, conveyor
transporte (m)	*ehl trahns-'pohr-teh*	transportation
transporte de mercancías	*ehl trahns-'pohr-teh deh mehr-kahn-'see-ahs*	movement of goods
transporte por ferrocarriles (m)	*ehl trahns-'pohr-teh pohr feh-rroh-kah-'ree-lehs*	railways transportation
transportista asegurado (m)	*ehl trahns-pohr-'tees-tah ah-seh-goo-'rah-doh*	bonded carrier
transportista de futuros	*ehl trahns-pohr-'tees-tah deh foo-'too-rohs*	contract carrier
tratamiento de palabra (m)	*ehl trah-tah-mee-'ehn-toh deh pah-'lah-brah*	word processing
trazado (m)	*ehl trah-'sah-doh*	layout
trazar	*trah-'sahr*	plot (v)
tributación (f)	*lah tree-boo-tah-see-'ohn*	taxation
tributación doble	*lah tree-boo-tah-see-'ohn 'doh-bleh*	double taxation
trópicos (m)	*lohs 'troh-pee-kohs*	tropics
trueque	*ehl-'troo-'eh-keh*	barter
tubo (m) de ensayo	*ehl too-boh deh ehn-sah-yoh*	test tube
tubos (mpl) y cañerías (fpl)	*lohs 'too-bohs ee lahs kah-nyeh-'ree-ahs*	pipes and tubes

T

turbina (f)	*lah toor-'bee-nah*	turbine
turno de trabajo (m)	*ehl 'toor-noh deh trah-'bah-hoh*	shift (labor)

U

---

ubicación (f)	*lah oo-bee-kah-see-'ohn*	personnel placement
ubicación de la planta	*lah oo-bee-kah-see-'ohn deh lah 'plahn-tah*	plant location
últimas entradas-primeras salidas	*'ool-tee-mahs ehn-'trah-dahs-pree-'meh-rahs sah-'lee-dahs*	last in-first out
ungüento (m)	*ehl oon-'gwehn-toh*	ointment, salve
unidad de velocidad de transmisión de información (f)	*lah oo-nee 'dahd deh beh-loh-see-'dahd deh trans-mee-see-'ohn deh een-fohr-mah-see-'ohn*	baud
unidad principal	*lah oo-nee-'dahd preen-see-'pahl*	mainframe
unidad elemental de información del sistema binario	*lah oo-nee-'dahd eh-leh-mehn-'tahl de een-fohr-mah-see-'ohn dehl sees-'teh-mah bee-'nah-ree-oh*	bit
unidad procesadora central	*lah oo-nee-'dahd proh-seh-sah-'doh-rah sehn-'trahl*	central processing unit (computers)
unidad que gobierna el soporte	*lah oo-nee-'dahd keh goh-bee-'ehr-nah ehl soh-'pohr-teh*	drive
uniformación (f)	*lah oo-nee-fohr-mah-see-'ohn*	standardization
unión (f)	*lah oo-nee-'ohn*	link
unión aduanera	*lah oo-nee-'ohn ah-dwah-'neh-rah*	customs union
unión crediticia	*lah oo-nee-'ohn kreh-dee-'tee-see-ah*	credit union
Unión para la Conservación de la Naturaleza y los Recursos Naturales	*lah oo-nee-'ohn 'pah-rah lah kohn-sehr-bah-see-'ohn deh lah nah-too-rah-'leh-sah ee lohs reh-'koor-sohs nah-too-'rah-lehs*	Union for the Conservation of Nature and Natural Resources

usuario (m)	*ehl oo-soo-'ah-ree-oh*	user
usura (f)	*lah oo-'soo-rah*	usury
utilidad (f)	*lah oo-tee-lee-'dahd*	utility, profit
utilidad bruta	*lah oo-tee-lee-'dahd 'broo-tah*	gross profit
utilidad neta	*lah oo-tee-lee-'dahd 'neh-toh*	net profit
utilidad operacional	*lah oo-tee-lee-'dahd oh-peh-rah-see-oh-'nahl*	operating profit
utilidad por acción	*lah oo-tee-lee-'dahd pohr ahk-see-'ohn*	earnings per share
utilidades (fpl)	*lahs oo-tee-lee-'dah-dehs*	earnings
utilidades acumuladas	*lahs oo-tee-lee-'dah-dehs ah-koo-moo-'lah-dahs*	retail trade
uva (f)	*lah 'oo-bah*	grape

V

vacaciones pagadas (fpl)	*lahs bah-kah-see-'oh-nehs pah-'gah-dahs*	paid holidays
vacío (m)	*ehl bah-'see-oh*	vacuum
vacuna (f)	*lah bah-'koo-nah*	vaccine
vagón batea (m)	*ehl bah-'gohn bah-'teh-ah*	flat car
vagonada (f)	*lah bah-goh-'nah-dah*	carload
validar	*bah-lee-'dahr*	validate (v)
valor (m)	*ehl bah-'lohr*	value
valor actual neto	*ehl bah-'lohr ahk-too-'ahl 'neh-toh*	net present value (NPV)
valor al portador	*ehl bah-'lohr ahl pohr-tah-'dohr*	bearer security
valor de acarreo	*ehl bah-'lohr deh ah-kah-'rreh-oh*	carrying value
valor de cambio	*ehl bah-'lohr deh 'kahm-bee-oh*	exchange value
valor de conversión	*ehl bah-'lohr deh kohn-behr-see-'ohn*	conversion price
valor de la empresa	*ehl bah-'lohr deh lah ehm-'preh-sah*	value of firm

valor de la más alta categoría	*ehl bah-'lohr deh lah mahs 'ahl-tah kah-teh-goh-'ree-ah*	blue chip stock
valor de la obligación	*ehl bah-'lohr deh lah oh-blee-gah-see-'ohn*	bond value
valor de liquidación	*ehl bah-'lohr deh lee-kee-dah-see-'ohn*	liquidation value
valor de rescate	*ehl bah-'lohr deh rehs-'kah-teh*	salvage value
valor de rescate (póliza de seguros)	*ehl bah-'lohr deh rehs-'kah-teh ('poh-lee-sah deh seh-'goo-rohs)*	cash surrender value
valor del activo	*ehl bah-'lohr dehl ahk-'tee-boh*	asset value
valor del activo neto	*ehl bah-'lohr dehl ahk-'tee-boh 'neh-toh*	net asset value
valor del mercado	*ehl bah-'lohr dehl mehr-'kah-doh*	market value
valor imponible	*ehl bah-'lohr eem-poh-'nee-bleh*	assessed valuation
valor intrínsico	*ehl bah-'lohr een-'treen-see-koh*	instrinsic value
valor líquido	*ehl bah-'lohr 'lee-kee-doh*	equity
valor neto actual	*ehl bah-'lohr 'neh-toh ahk-too-ahl*	net present value
valor nominal	*ehl bah-'lohr noh-mee-'nahl*	face value
valor par	*ehl bah-'lohr pahr*	par value
valor real	*ehl bah-'lohr reh-'ahl*	real value
valor secundario	*ehl bah-'lohr seh-koon-'dah-ree-oh*	junior security
valor según libros	*ehl bah-'lohr seh-'goon 'lee-brohs*	book value
valor según libros por acción	*ehl bah-'lohr seh-'goon 'lee-brohs pohr ahk-see-'ohn*	book value per share
valoración (f)	*lah bah-loh-rah-see-'ohn*	job analysis
valoración marginal	*lah bah-loh-rah-see-'ohn mahr-hee-'nahl*	marginal pricing
valorar	*bah-loh-'rahr*	price (v)
valores (fpl)	*lahs bah-'loh-rehs*	securities

Spanish	Pronunciation	English
valores aprobados	*lahs bah-'loh-rehs ah-proh-'bah-doh*	approved securities
valores bursátiles (escritos en la bolsa)	*lahs bah-'loh-rehs boor-'sah-tee-lehs (ehs-'kree-tohs ehn lah 'bohl-sah)*	listed securities
valores comerciables	*lahs bah-'loh-rehs koh-mehr-see-'ah-blehs*	marketable securities
valores descontados	*lahs bah-'loh-rehs dehs-kohn-'tah-dohs*	discount securities
valores extranjeros	*lahs bah-'loh-rehs ehks-trahn-'heh-rohs*	foreign securities
valores negociables	*lahs bah-'loh-rehs neh-goh-see-'ah-blehs*	negotiable securities
valuador (m)	*ehl bah-loo-ah-'dohr*	appraiser
válvula (f)	*lah bahl-hoo-lah*	valve
variación de precio (f)	*lah bah-ree-ah-see-'ohn deh 'preh-see-oh*	price range
variar	*bah-ree-'ahr*	float (rates) (v)
varilla (f)	*lah bah-'ree-yah*	rod
vaso (m)	*ehl 'bah-soh*	glass
vaso de champaña	*ehl 'bah-soh deh chahm-'pah-nyah*	champagne glass
vatio (m)	*ehl bah-'tee-oh*	watt
vector (m)	*ehl behk-'tohr*	vector
vegetal (m)	*ehl beh-heh-'tahl*	vegetation
vegetal acuático	*ehl beh-heh-'tahl ah-'kwah-tee-koh*	vegetation (aquatic)
vehículo (m)	*ehl beh-'ee-koo-loh*	vehicle
vehículo motorizado	*ehl beh-'ee-koo-loh moh-toh-ree-'sah-doh*	vehicle (motorized)
vela (f)	*lah 'beh-lah*	candlestick
velo (m)	*ehl 'beh-loh*	veil
velocidad (f)	*lah beh-loh-see-'dahd*	velocity (car)
velocímetro (m)	*ehl beh-loh-'see-meh-troh*	speedometer
vencimiento (m)	*ehl behn-see-mee-'ehn-toh*	maturity
vencimiento original	*ehl behn-see-mee-'ehn-toh oh-ree-hee-'nahl*	original maturity
vendaje (m)	*ehl behn-'dah-heh*	dressing

V

vendedor (m)	*ehl behn-deh-'dohr*	vendor
vender	*behn-'dehr*	sell (v)
vender nueva-mente a quienes compramos	*behn-'dehr noo-eh-bah-'mehn-teh ah kee-'eh-nehs kohm-'prah-mohs*	back selling (v)
vender por debajo del precio de un competidor	*behn-'dehr pohr deh-'bah-hoh dehl 'preh-see-oh deh oon kohm-peh-tee-'dohr*	undercut (v)
vendimia (f)	*lah behn-'dee-mee-ah*	grape harvest, vintage
venta atosigante (f)	*lah 'behn-tah ah-toh-see-'gahn-teh*	hard sell
venta débil	*lah 'behn-tah 'deh-beel*	soft sell
venta directa	*lah 'behn-tah dee-'rehk-tah*	direct selling
venta e inmediato arrendamiento de lo vendido	*lah 'behn-tah eh een-meh-dee-'ah-toh ah-rrehn-dah-mee-'ehn -toh deh loh behn-'dee-doh*	sell and leaseback
venta negociada	*lah 'behn-tah neh-goh-see-'ah-dah*	negotiated sale
venta otorgada sin competencia	*lah 'behn-tah oh-tohr-'gah-dah seen kohm-peh-'tehn-see-ah*	negotiated sale
venta piramidal	*lah 'behn-tah pee-rah-mee-'dahl*	pyramid selling
venta por correo	*lah 'behn-tah pohr koh-'rreh-oh*	sale through mail order
venta secundaria	*lah 'behn-tah seh-koon-'dah-ree-ah*	secondary offering (securities)
venta y compra (opción)	*lah 'behn-tah ee 'kohm-prah (ohp-see-'ohn)*	put and call
ventaja competitiva (f)	*lah 'behn-tah kohm-peh-tee-'tee-bah*	competitive advantage, competitive edge
ventana (f)	*lah behn-'tah-nah*	window
ventas (f)	*lahs behn-tahs*	sales
ventas adicionales	*lahs 'behn-tahs ah-dee-see-oh-'nah-lehs*	add-on-sales
ventas al descubierto	*lahs 'behn-tahs ahl dehs-koo-bee-'ehr-toh*	short sales
ventas brutas	*lahs 'behn-tahs 'broo-tahs*	gross sales
ventas estimadas	*lahs 'behn-tahs ehs-tee-'mah-dahs*	sales estimate

ventas netas	*lahs 'behn-tahs 'neh-tahs*	net sales
ventas potenciales	*lahs 'behn-tahs poh-tehn-see-'ah-lehs*	potential sales
verificación de errores (f)	*lah beh-ree-fee-kah-see-'ohn deh eh-'rroh-rehs*	error checking
verificación testamentaria	*lah beh-ree-fee-kah-see-'ohn tehs-tah-mehn-'tah-ree-ah*	probate
verificar	*beh-ree-fee-'kahr*	check (v)
vestido (m)	*ehl behs-'tee-doh*	apparel, clothing, dress
viático	*ehl bee-'ah-tee-koh*	per diem
vid (f)	*lah beed*	vine
vida de una patente (f)	*lah 'bee-dah deh 'oo-nah pah-'tehn-teh*	life of a patent
vida del producto (f)	*lah 'bee-dah dehl proh-'dook-toh*	product life
vida económica	*lah 'bee-dah eh-koh-'noh-mee-kah*	economic life
vida promedio	*lah 'bee-dah proh-'meh-dee-oh*	average life
vida útil	*lah 'bee-dah 'oo-teel*	useful life
vidrio soplado (m)	*ehl bee-dree-oh soh-'plah-doh*	hand-blown glass
viento (m)	*ehl bee-'ehn-toh*	winds
vinatero (m)	*ehl bee-nah-'teh-roh*	vintner
vínculo (m)	*ehl 'been-koo-loh*	link
vínculo de comunicación	*ehl 'been-koo-loh deh koh-moo-nee-kah-see-'ohn*	communication link
viñedo (m)	*ehl bee-nyeh-doh*	vineyard
vinicultor (m)	*ehl bee-nee-kool-'tohr*	winemaker
vino (m)	*ehl 'bee-noh*	wine
vino espumoso	*ehl 'bee-noh ehs-poo-'moh-soh*	sparkling wine
vino espumoso clasificado	*ehl bee-noh ehs-poo-moh-soh klah-see-fee-'kah-doh*	classified sparkling wine
vino seco	*ehl 'bee-noh 'seh-koh*	dry wine
vista anticipada (f)	*lah 'bees-tah ahn-tee-see-'pah-dah*	preview
vitamina (f)	*lah bee-tah-'mee-nah*	vitamin

viticultor (m)	*ehl bee-tee-kool-'tohr*	winegrower
volante (m)	*ehl boh-'lahn-teh*	steering wheel
voltaje (m)	*ehl bohl-'tah-heh*	voltage
voltio (m)	*ehl 'bohl-tee-oh*	volt
volumen (m)	*ehl boh-'loo-mehn*	volume
volumen de ventas	*ehl boh-'loo-mehn deh 'behn-tahs*	sales volume
volumen verdadero del mercado	*ehl boh-'loo-mehn behr-dah-'deh-roh dehl mehr-'kah-doh*	actual market volume

Y

yacimiento petrolífero (m)	*ehl yah-see-mee-'ehn-toh peh-troh-'lee-feh-roh*	oil field
yodo (m)	*ehl 'yoh-doh*	iodine
yugos (mpl)	*lohs 'yoo-gohs*	cuff link

Z

zapatería (f)	*lah sah-pah-teh-'ree-ah*	boot shop
zapatero	*sa-pah-'teh-roh*	shoemaker
zapatillas (fpl)	*lahs sah-pah-'tee-yahs*	slippers
zapato (m)	*ehl sah-'pah-toh*	shoe
zinc (m)	*ehl 'seenk*	zinc
zona (f)	*lah 'soh-nah*	zone
zona de libre cambio	*lah 'soh-nah deh 'lee-breh 'kahm-bee-oh*	free trade zone
zona turística	*lah 'soh-nah too-'rees-tee-kah*	tourist area
zorra (f)	*lah 'soh-rrah*	fox
zumo (m) de uva no fermentado	*ehl 'soo-moh deh 'oo-bah noh fehr-mehn-'tah-doh*	unfermented grape juice

KEY WORDS FOR KEY INDUSTRIES

The dictionary that forms the centerpiece of *Spanish for the Business Traveler* is a compendium of some 3,000 words that you are likely to use or encounter as you do business abroad. It will greatly facilitate fact-finding about the business possibilities that interest you, and will help guide you through negotiations as well as reading documents. To supplement the dictionary, we have added a special feature—groupings of key terms about fourteen industries. As you explore any of these industries, you'll want to have this book at your fingertips to help make sure you don't misunderstand or overlook an aspect that could have a material effect on the outcome of your business decision. The industries covered in the vocabulary lists are the following:

- *chemicals*
- *chinaware and tableware*
- *computers, data processing*
- *electronics*
- *fashion*
- *international finance*
- *iron and steel*
- *leather goods*
- *motor vehicles*
- *petroleum*
- *pharmaceuticals*
- *printing and publishing*
- *winemaking*
- *world environment*

CHEMICALS

English to Spanish

acetate	el acetato	*ehl ah-seh-'tah-toh*
acetic acid	el ácido acético	*ehl 'ah-see-doh ah-'seh-tee-koh*
acetone	la acetona	*lah ah-seh-'toh-nah*
acid	el ácido	*ehl 'ah-see-doh*
amine	la amina	*lah ah-mee-nah*
ammonia	el amoníaco	*ehl ah-moh-'nee-ah-koh*
analysis	el análisis	*ehl ah-'nah-lee-sees*
analytic chemistry	la química analítica	*lah 'kee-mee-kah ah-nah-'lee-tee-kah*
atom	el átomo	*ehl 'ah-toh-moh*
atomic (adj)	atómico	*ah-'toh-mee-koh*
base	la base	*lah 'bah-seh*
benzene	el benceno	*ehl behn-'seh-noh*
biochemistry	la bioquímica	*lah bee-oh-'kee-mee-kah*
biologist	el biólogo	*ehl bee-'oh-loh-goh*
biology	la biología	*lah bee-oh-loh-'hee-ah*
buret	la bureta	*lah boo-'reh-tah*
carbon	el carbón	*ehl kahr-'bohn*
catalyst	el catalizador	*ehl kah-tah-lee-sah-'dohr*
chemical (adj)	químico	*'kee-mee-koh*
chemistry	la química	*lah 'kee-mee-kah*
chloride	el cloruro	*ehl kloh-'roo-roh*
chloroform	el cloroformo	*ehl kloh-roh-'fohr-moh*
component	el componente	*ehl kohm-poh-'nehn-teh*
composition	la composición	*lah kohm-poh-see-see-'ohn*
compound	el compuesto	*ehl kohm-'pweh-stoh*
concentration	la concentración	*lah kohn-sehn-trah-see-'ohn*
cracking	el craqueo	*ehl krah-'keh-oh*
crystallization	la cristalización	*lah krees-tah-lee-sah-see-'ohn*
degree	el grado	*ehl 'grah-doh*

density	la densidad	*lah dehn-see-'dahd*
distillation	la destilación	*lah dehs-tee-lah-see-'ohn*
dosage	la dosis	*lah 'doh-sees*
electrolysis	la electrólisis	*lah eh-lehk-'troh-lee-sees*
electron	el electrón	*ehl eh-lehk-'trohn*
element	el elemento	*ehl eh-leh-'mehn-toh*
engineer	el ingeniero	*ehl een-heh-nee-'eh-roh*
enzyme	la enzima	*lah ehn-'see-mah*
ethane	el étano	*ehl 'eh-tah-noh*
ether	el éter	*ehl 'eh-tehr*
gram	el gramo	*ehl 'grah-moh*
homogeneity	la homogeneidad	*lah oh-moh-heh-neh-ee-'dahd*
hydrocarbon	el hidrocarburo	*ehl ee-droh-kahr-'boo-roh*
hydrochloric acid	el ácido hidroclorídrico	*ehl 'ah-see-doh ee-droh-kloh-'ree-dree-koh*
hydrolysis	la hidrólisis	*lah ee-'droh-lee-sees*
hydrosulfate	el hidrosulfato	*ehl ee-droh-sool-'fah-toh*
impurity	la impureza	*lah eem-poo-'reh-sah*
inorganic chemistry	la quimica inorgánica	*lah 'kee-mee-kah een-ohr-'gah-nee-kah*
isotope	el isótopo	*ehl ee-'soh-toh-poh*
laboratory	el laboratorio	*ehl lah-boh-rah-'toh-ree-oh*
methane	el metano	*ehl meh-'tah-noh*
mole	el mol	*ehl mohl*
molecule	la molécula	*lah moh-'leh-koo-lah*
natural gas	el gas natural	*ehl gahs nah-too-'rahl*
nitrate	el nitrato	*ehl nee-'trah-toh*
nitric acid	el ácido nítrico	*ehl 'ah-see-doh 'nee-tree-koh*
nitrite	el nitrito	*ehl nee-'tree-toh*
organic chemistry	la química orgánica	*lah 'kee-mee-kah ohr-'gah-nee-kah*
oxidation	la oxidación	*lah ohk-see-dah-see-'ohn*
petroleum	el petróleo	*ehl peh-'troh-leh-oh*
phosphate	el fosfato	*ehl fohs-'fah-toh*

polymer	el polímero	*ehl poh-'lee-meh-roh*
product	el producto	*ehl proh-'dook-toh*
purification	la purificación	*lah poo-ree-fee-kah-see-'ohn*
reactant	el reactante	*ehl reh-ahk-'tahn-teh*
reagent	el reactivo	*ehl reh-ahk-'tee-boh*
reduction	la reducción	*lah reh-dook-see-'ohn*
refine (v)	refinar	*reh-fee-'nahr*
refinery	la refinería	*lah reh-fee-neh-'ree-ah*
research	la investigación	*lah een-behe-stee-gah-see-'ohn*
salt	la sal	*lah sahl*
solubility	la solubilidad	*lah soh-loo-bee-lee-'dahd*
solute	el soluto	*ehl soh-'loo-toh*
solution	la solución	*lah soh-loo-see-'ohn*
solvent	el solvente	*ehl soh-'behn-teh*
spectrophotometry	la espectrometría	*lah ehs-pehk-troh-meh-'tree'ah*
spectrum	el espectro	*ehl ehs-'pehk-troh*
sulfate	el sulfato	*ehl sool-'fah-toh*
sulfuric acid	el ácido sulfúrico	*ehl 'ah-see-doh sool-'foo-ree-koh*
test tube	el tubo de ensayo	*ehl 'too-boh deh ehn-'sah-yoh*
titration	la titulación	*lah tee-too-lah-see-'ohn*
yield	la producción, el rendimiento	*lah proh-dook-see-'ohn, ehl rehn-dee-mee-'ehn-toh*

Spanish to English

ácido (m)	*ehl 'ah-see-doh*	acid
ácido acético	*ehl 'ah-see-doh ah-'seh-tee-koh*	acetic acid
ácido clorhídrico	*ehl 'ah-see-doh kloh-'ree-dree-koh*	hydrochloric acid
ácido nítrico	*ehl 'ah-see-doh 'nee-tree-koh*	nitric acid
ácido sulfúrico	*ehl 'ah-see-doh sool-'foo-ree-koh*	sulfuric acid

acetato (m)	*ehl ah-seh-'tah-toh*	acetate
acetona (f)	*lah ah-seh-'toh-nah*	acetone
amina (f)	*lah ah-mee-nah*	amine
amoníaco (m)	*ehl ah-moh-'nee-ah-koh*	ammonia
análisis (m)	*ehl ah-'nah-lee-sees*	analysis
atómico	*ah-'toh-mee-koh*	atomic (adj)
átomo (m)	*ehl 'ah-toh-moh*	atom
base (f)	*lah 'bah-seh*	base
benceno (m)	*ehl behn-'seh-noh*	benzene
biología (f)	*lah bee-oh-loh-'hee-ah*	biology
biólogo (m)	*ehl bee-'oh-loh-goh*	biologist
bioquímica (f)	*lah bee-oh-'kee-mee-kah*	biochemistry
bureta (f)	*lah boo-'reh-tah*	buret
carbón (m)	*ehl kahr-'bohn*	carbon
catalizador (m)	*ehl kah-tah-lee-sah-'dohr*	catalyst
cloroformo (m)	*ehl kloh-roh-'fohr-moh*	chloroform
cloruro (m)	*ehl kloh-'roo-roh*	chloride
componente (m)	*ehl kohm-poh-'nehn-teh*	component
composición (f)	*lah kohm-poh-see-see-'ohn*	composition
compuesto (m)	*ehl kohm-'pweh-stoh*	compound
concentración (f)	*lah kohn-sehn-trah-see-'ohn*	concentration
craqueo (m)	*ehl krah-'keh-oh*	cracking
cristalización (f)	*lah krees-tah-lee-sah-see-'ohn*	crystallization
densidad (f)	*lah dehn-see-'dahd*	density
destilación (f)	*lah dehs-tee-lah-see-'ohn*	distillation
dosis (f)	*lah 'doh-sees*	dosage
étano (m)	*ehl 'eh-tah-noh*	ethane
éter (m)	*ehl 'eh-tehr*	ether
electrón (m)	*ehl eh-'lehk-'trohn*	electron
electrólisis (f)	*lah eh-lehk-'troh-lee-sees*	electrolysis
elemento (m)	*ehl eh-leh-'mehn-toh*	element
enzina (f)	*lah ehn-'see-mah*	enzyme
espectro (m)	*ehl ehs-'pehk-troh*	spectrum

espectrometría (f)	*lah ehs-pehk-troh-meh-'tree-'ah*	spectrophotometry
fosfato (m)	*ehl fohs-'fah-toh*	phosphate
gas (m) natural	*ehl gahs nah-too-'rahl*	natural gas
grado (m)	*ehl 'grah-doh*	degree
gramo (m)	*ehl 'grah-moh*	gram
hidrocarburo (m)	*ehl ee-droh-kahr-'boo-roh*	hydrocarbon
hidrólisis (f)	*lah ee-'droh-lee-sees*	hydrolysis
hidrosulfato (m)	*ehl ee-droh-sool-'fah-toh*	hydrosulfate
homogeneidad (f)	*lah oh-moh-heh-neh-ee-'dahd*	homogeneity
impureza (f)	*lah eem-poo-'reh-sah*	impurity
ingeniero (m)	*ehl een-heh-nee-'eh-roh*	engineer
investigación (f)	*lah een-behe-stee-gah-see-'ohn*	research
isótopo (m)	*ehl ee-'soh-toh-poh*	isotope
laboratorio (m)	*ehl lah-boh-rah-'toh-ree-oh*	laboratory
metano (m)	*ehl meh-'tah-noh*	methane
mol (m)	*ehl mohl*	mole
molécula (f)	*lah moh-'leh-koo-lah*	molecule
nitrato (m)	*ehl nee-'trah-toh*	nitrate
nitrito (m)	*ehl nee-'tree-toh*	nitrite
oxidación (f)	*lah ohk-see-dah-see-'ohn*	oxidation
petróleo (m)	*ehl peh-'troh-leh-oh*	petroleum
polímero (m)	*ehl poh-'lee-meh-roh*	polymer
producción (f)	*lah proh-dook-see-'ohn*	yield
producto (m)	*ehl proh-'dook-toh*	product
purificación (f)	*lah poo-ree-fee-kah-see-'ohn*	purification
químico	*'kee-mee-koh*	chemical (adj)
química (f)	*lah 'kee-mee-kah*	chemistry
química analítica	*lah 'kee-mee-kah ah-nah-'lee-tee-kah*	analytic chemistry
química inorgánica	*lah 'kee-mee-kah een-ohr-'gah-nee-kah*	inorganic chemistry
química orgánica	*lah 'kee-mee-kah ohr-'gah-nee-kah*	organic chemistry

reactivo (m)	*ehl reh-ahk-'tee-boh*	reagent
reducción (f)	*lah reh-dook-see-'ohn*	reduction
refinar	*reh-fee-'nahr*	refine (v)
refinería (f)	*lah reh-fee-neh-'ree-ah*	refinery
rendimiento (m)	*ehl rehn-dee-mee-'ehn-toh*	yield
sal (f)	*lah sahl*	salt
solubilidad (f)	*lah soh-loo-bee-lee-'dahd*	solubility
solución (f)	*lah soh-loo-see-'ohn*	solution
soluto (m)	*ehl soh-'loo-toh*	solute
solvente (m)	*ehl soh-'behn-teh*	solvent
sulfato (m)	*ehl sool-'fah-toh*	sulfate
titulación (f)	*lah tee-too-lah-see-'ohn*	titration
tubo (m) de ensayo	*ehl 'too-boh deh ehn-'sah-yoh*	test tube

CHINAWARE AND TABLEWARE		

English to Spanish

bone china	la porcelana traslúcida	*lah pohr-'seh-'lah-nah trahs-loo-'see-dah*
bowl	el plato hondo, el cuenco, la escudilla	*ehl 'plah-toh 'hon-doh, ehl 'kwehn-koh, lah ehs-koo-'dee'yah*
breadbasket	la panera	*lah pah-'neh-rah*
butter dish	la mantequillera	*lah mahn-teh-kee-'yeh-rah*
candlestick	la vela	*lah 'beh-lah*
carving knife	el trinchador, el cuchillo de trinchar	*ehl treen-chah-'dohr, ehl koo-'chee-yoh deh treen-'chahr*
champagne glass	el vaso de champaña, la copa de champaña	*ehl 'bah-soh deh chahm-'pah-nyah, lah 'koh-pah deh chahm-'pah-nyah*
cheese tray	la bandeja para queso	*lah bahn-'deh-hah 'pah-rah 'keh-soh*
china	la porcelana, la loza	*lah pohr-seh-'lah-nah, la 'loh-sah*
coffeepot	la cafetera	*lah kah-feh-'teh-rah*
crystal glass manufacturing	la manufactura de vasos de cristal, la fabricación de vasos de cristal	*lah mah-noo-fahk-'too-rah deh 'bah-sohs deh kree-'stahl, lah fah-bree-kah-see-'ohn deh 'bah-sohs deh kree-'stahl*
cup	la taza	*lah 'tah-sah*
cutlery	los cubiertos, la cuchillería	*lohs koo-bee-'ehr-tohs, lah koo-chee-yeh-'ree-ah*
decanter	el decantador	*ehl deh-kahn-tah-'dohr*
dessert plate	el plato de postre	*ehl 'plah-toh deh 'poh-streh*
dinner plate	el plato	*ehl 'plah-toh*
dish	el plato	*ehl 'plah-toh*
earthenware	la alfarería, los objetos de barro	*lah ahl-fah-reh-'ree-ah, lohs ohb-'heh-tohs deh 'bah-rroh*
espresso cup	la taza de café expreso, el pocillo	*lah 'tah-sah deh kah-'feh ehk-'spreh-soh, ehl poh-'see-yoh*

flute	la acanaladura, la estría	*lah ah-kah-nah-lah-'doo-rah, lah ehs-'tree-ah*
fork	el tenedor	*ehl teh-neh-'dohr*
glass	el vaso, la copa	*ehl 'bah-soh, lah 'koh-pah*
gravy boat	la salsera	*lah sahl-'seh-rah*
hand-blown glass	el vidrio soplado, el cristal soplado	*ehl 'bee-dree-oh soh-'plah-doh, ehl kree-'stahl soh-'plah-doh*
hand-painted	pintado a mano	*peen-'tah-doh ah 'mah-noh*
knife	el cuchillo	*ehl koo-'chee-yoh*
lace	el encaje	*ehl ehn-'kah-heh*
linen	la mantelería	*lah mahn-teh-leh-'ree-ah*
napkin	la servilleta	*lah sehr-bee-'yeh-tah*
napkin ring	el servilletero, el aro de servilleta	*ehl sehr-bee-yeh-'teh-roh, ehl 'ah-roh deh sehr-bee-'yeh-tah*
oilcloth	el hule	*ehl 'oo-leh*
pastry server	la paleta de servir tortas (bizcocho)	*lah pah-'leh-tah deh sehr-'beer 'tohr-tahs (bees-'koh-choh)*
pepper mill	el molinillo de pimienta	*ehl moh-lee-'nee-yoh deh pee-mee-'ehn-tah*
pepper shaker	el pimentero	*ehl pee-mehn-'teh-roh*
pitcher	la jarra	*lah 'hah-rrah*
place setting	el cubierto, el servicio de mesa individual	*ehl koo-bee-'ehr-toh, ehl sehr-'bee-see-oh een-dee-bee-doo-'ahl*
plate	el plato	*ehl 'plah-toh*
pottery	la alfarería, la cerámica	*lah ahl-fah-reh-'ree-ah, lah seh-'rah-mee-kah*
salad plate	el plato de ensalada	*ehl 'plah-toh deh ehn-sah-'lah-dah*
salt shaker	el salero	*ehl sah-'leh-roh*
saucer	el platillo, la salsera	*ehl plah-'tee-yoh, lah sahl-'seh-rah*
silverware	los cubiertos	*lohs koo-bee-'ehr-tohs*
soup dish	el plato de sopa	*ehl 'plah-toh deh 'soh-pah*
spoon	la cuchara	*lah koo-'chah-rrah*

stainless steel	el acero inoxidable	*ehl ah-'seh-roh een-ohk-see-'dah-bleh*
stoneware	el gres	*ehl grehs*
sugar bowl	la azucarera	*lah ah-soo-kah-'reh-rah*
tablecloth	el mantel	*ehl mahn-'tehl*
tablespoon	la cuchara	*lah koo-'chah-rah*
teapot	la tetera	*lah teh-'teh-rah*
teaspoon	la cucharita	*lah koo-chah-'ree-tah*
thread	el hilo	*ehl 'ee-loh*
tureen	la sopera	*lah soh-'peh-rah*

Spanish to English

unbleached linen	el hilo crudo	*ehl 'ee-loh 'kroo-doh*
acanaladura (f)	*lah ah-kah-nah-lah-'doo-rah*	flute, groove
acero (m) inoxidable	*ehl ah-'seh-roh een-ohk-see-'dah-bleh*	stainless steel
alfarería (f)	*lah ahl-fah-reh-'ree-ah*	earthenware, pottery
aro (m) de servilleta	*ehl 'ah-roh deh sehr-bee-'yeh-tah*	napkin ring
azucarera (f)	*lah ah-soo-kah-'reh-rah*	sugar bowl
bandeja (f) para queso	*lah bahn-'deh-hah pah-rah 'keh-soh*	cheese tray
cafetera (f)	*lah kah-feh-'teh-rah*	coffeepot
copa (f)	*lah 'koh-pah*	glass
copa de champaña	*lah 'koh-pah deh chahm-'pah-nyah*	champagne glass
cristal (m) soplado	*ehl kree-'stahl soh-'plah-doh*	hand-blown glass
cubierto (m)	*ehl koo-bee-'ehr-toh*	place setting
cubiertos (mpl)	*lohs koo-bee-'ehr-tohs*	cutlery, silverware
cuchara (f)	*lah koo-'chah-rah*	tablespoon
cucharita (f)	*lah koo-chah-'ree-tah*	teaspoon
cuchillo (m)	*ehl koo-'chee-yoh*	knife
cuchillo de trinchar	*ehl koo-'chee-yoh deh treen-chahr*	carving knife
decantador (m)	*ehl deh-kahn-tah-'dohr*	decanter
escudilla (f)	*lah ehs-koo-'dee-yah*	bowl

estría (f)	*lah ehs-tree-ah*	flute
fabricación (f) de vasos de cristal	*lah fah-bree-kah-see-'ohn deh 'bah-sohs deh kree-'stahl*	crystal glass manufacturing
gres (m)	*ehl grehs*	stoneware
hebra (f)	*lah eh-brah*	thread
hilo (m)	*ehl 'ee-loh*	thread
hilo crudo	*ehl 'ee-loh 'kroo-doh*	unbleached linen
hule (m)	*ehl 'oo-leh*	oilcloth
jarra (f)	*lah 'hah-rrah*	pitcher
loza (f)	*lah 'loh-sah*	china
mantel (m)	*ehl mahn-tehl*	tablecloth
mantelería (f)	*lah mahn-teh-leh-'ree-ah*	linen
mantequillera (f)	*lah mahn-teh-kee-'yeh-rah*	butter dish
manufactura (f) de vasos de cristal	*lah mah-noo-fahk-t'oo-rah deh 'bah-sohs deh kree-'stahl*	crystal glass manufacturing
molinillo (m) de pimienta	*ehl moh-lee-'nee-yoh deh pee-mee-'ehn-tah*	pepper mill
objetos (mpl) de barro	*lohs ohb-'heh-tohs deh 'bah-rroh*	earthenware
paleta (f) de servir tortas (bizcocho)	*lah pah-'leh-tah deh sehr-'beer 'tohr-tahs (bees-'koh-choh)*	pastry server
panera (f)	*lah pah-'neh-rah*	breadbasket
pimentero (m)	*ehl pee-mehn-'teh-roh*	pepper shaker
pintado a mano	*peen-'tah-doh ah 'mah-noh*	hand-painted
platillo (m)	*ehl plah-'tee-yoh*	saucer
plato (m)	*ehl 'plah-toh*	dish, plate
plato de ensalada	*ehl 'plah-toh deh ehn-sah-'lah-dah*	salad plate
plato de postre	*ehl 'plah-toh deh 'poh-streh*	dessert plate
plato de sopa	*ehl 'plah-toh deh 'soh-pah*	soup dish
pocillo (m)	*ehl poh-'see-yoh*	espresso cup
porcelana (f)	*lah pohr-seh-'lah-nah*	china
porcelana traslúcida	*lah pohr-'seh-'lah-nah trahs-loo-'see-dah*	bone china

salero (m)	*ehl sah-'leh-roh*	salt shaker
salsera (f)	*lah sahl-'seh-rah*	gravy boat
servilleta (f)	*lah sehr-bee-'yeh-tah*	napkin
servilletero (m)	*ehl sehr-bee-yeh-'teh-roh*	napkin ring
sopera (f)	*lah soh-'peh-rah*	tureen
taza (f)	*lah 'tah-sah*	cup
taza de café expreso (f)	*lah 'tah-sah deh kah-'feh ehk-'spreh-soh*	espresso cup
tenedor (m)	*ehl teh-neh-'dohr*	fork
tetera (f)	*lah teh-'teh-rah*	teapot
vaso (m)	*ehl 'bah-soh*	glass
vaso de champaña	*ehl 'bah-soh deh chahm-'pah-nyah*	champagne glass
vela (f)	*lah beh-lah*	candlestick
vidrio (m) soplado (m)	*ehl 'bee-dree-oh soh-'plah-doh*	hand-blown glass

COMPUTERS, DATA PROCESSING

English to Spanish

absolute (adj) absoluto *ahb-soh-'loo-toh*

access el acceso *ehl ahk-'seh-soh*

algorithm el algoritmo *ehl ahl-goh-'reet-moh*

ancillary el auxiliar; el equipo auxiliar *ehl owk-see-lee-'ahr, ehl eh-'kee-poh owk-see-lee-'ahr*

ASCII el código utilizado como estándard en los EE.UU. para el intercambio de información entre sistemas de procesamiento de datos *ehl 'koh-dee-goh oo-tee-lee-'sah-doh 'koh-moh ehs-'tahn-dahrd ehn lohs eh-'stah-dohs oo-'nee-dohs 'pah-rah ehl een-tehr-'kahm-bee-oh deh een-fohr-mah-see-'ohn 'ehn-treh sees-'teh-mahs deh proh-seh-sah-mee-'ehn-toh deh 'dah-tohs*

backspace retroceder en una unidad *reh-troh-seh-'dehr ehn 'oo-nah oo-nee-'dahd*

backup la copia física que se hace del contenido de un disco o una cinta *lah 'koh-pee-ah 'fee-see-kah keh seh 'ah-seh dehl kohn-teh-'nee-doh deh oon 'dees-koh oh 'oo-nah 'seen-tah*

batch el grupo, el lote *ehl 'groo-poh, ehl 'loh-teh*

baud el baudio, la unidad de velocidad de transmisión de información *ehl 'bah-oo-dee-oh, lah oo-nee-'dahd deh beh-loh-see-'dahd deh trahns-mee-see-'ohn deh een-fohr-mah-see-'ohn*

binary (adj) binario *bee-'nah-ree-oh*

bit el bit, unidad elemental de información del sistema binario *ehl beet, oo-nee-'dahd eh-leh-mehn-'tahl de een-fohr-mah-see-'ohn dehl sees-'teh-mah bee-'nah-ree-oh*

block el bloque (m) *ehl 'bloh-keh*

branching las bifurcaciones *lahs bee-foor-kah-see-'oh-nehs*

breakdown la avería *lah ah-beh-'ree-ah*

breakpoint	el punto de interrupción	*ehl 'poon-toh deh een-teh-roop-see-'ohn*
bug	el error; defecto (programa), la avería (máquina)	*ehl eh-'rrohr, deh-'fehk-toh (proh-'grah-mah), lah ah-beh-'ree-ah ('mah-kee-nah)*
button	el botón	*ehl boh-'tohn*
byte	el byte	*ehl bah-eet*
capacity	la capacidad	*lah kah-pah-see-'dahd*
cellular phone	el teléfono celular	*ehl teh-'leh-foh-noh seh-loo-'lahr*
chip	el micrológico, el circuito integrado, el chip (m)	*ehl mee-kroh-'loh-hee-koh, ehl seer-koo-'ee-toh een-teh-'grah-doh, ehl cheep*
circuit	el circuito	*ehl seer-koo-'ee-toh*
clear (v)	borrar	*boh-'rrahr*
column	la columna	*lah koh-'loom-nah*
command	el mando	*ehl 'mahn-doh*
communication link	el enlace de comunicación, el vínculo de comunicación	*ehl ehn-'lah-seh deh koh-moo-nee-kah-see-'ohn, ehl 'been-koo-loh deh koh-moo-nee-kah-see-'ohn*
compact disk	el disco compacto	*ehl 'dees-koh kohm-'pahk-toh*
computer	la computadora, el ordenador (Spain)	*lah kohm-poo-tah-'doh-rah, ehl ohr-deh-nah-'dohr*
control	el control	*ehl kohn-'trohl*
convert (v)	transformar	*trans-fohr-'mahr*
copy (v)	reproducir datos	*reh-proh-doo-'seer 'dah-tohs*
crosscheck	el control cruzado	*ehl kohn-'trohl kroo-'sah-doh*
cursor	el cursor	*ehl koor-'sohr*
cycle	el ciclo	*ehl 'see-kloh*
data bank	el banco de datos	*ehl 'bahn-koh deh 'dah-tohs*
data base	la base de datos	*lah 'bah-seh deh 'dah-tohs*
data entry	la entrada de datos	*lah ehn-'trah-dah deh 'dah-tohs*

data processing	el procesamiento de datos	*ehl proh-seh-sah-mee-'ehn-toh deh 'dah-tohs*
data storage	el almacenamiento de datos	*ehl alh-mah-seh-nah-mee-'ehn-toh deh 'dah-tohs*
delete (v)	eliminar	*eh-lee-mee-'nahr*
desktop publishing	la editorial de despacho, la editorial de sobremesa	*lah eh-dee-toh-ree-'ahl deh dehs-'pah-choh, lah eh-dee-toh-ree-'ahl deh soh-breh-'meh-sah*
device	el dispositivo, el montaje	*ehl dees-poh-see-'tee-boh, ehl mohn-'tah-heh*
dictionary	el diccionario	*ehl deek-see-oh-'nah-ree-oh*
directory	el directorio	*ehl dee-rehk-'toh-ree-oh*
disk	el disco	*ehl 'dees-koh*
disk drive	el dispositivo de disco	*ehl dees-poh-see-'tee-boh deh 'dees-koh*
diskette	el disco flexible de capacidad pequeña	*ehl 'dees-koh flehk-'see-bleh deh kah-pah-see-'dahd peh-'keh-nyah*
documentation	la documentación	*lah doh-koo-mehn-tah-see-'ohn*
dot matrix printer	la impresora por matriz de puntos	*lah eem-preh-'soh-rah pohr mah-'trees deh 'poon-tohs*
downgraded (adj)	reducido	*reh-doo-'see-doh*
downloading	la conversión descendente	*lah kohn-behr-see-'ohn deh-sehn-'dehn-teh*
downtime	el tiempo improductivo	*ehl tee-'ehm-poh eem-proh-dook-'tee-boh*
drive	la unidad que gobierna el soporte	*lah oo-nee-'dahd keh goh-bee-'ehr-nah ehl soh-'pohr-teh*
editing of input	la redacción de los datos de entrada	*lah reh-dahk-see-'ohn deh lohs 'dah-tohs deh ehn-'trah-dah*
eject (v)	expulsar	*ehs-pool-'sahr*
electronic mail	el correo electrónico	*ehl koh-'rreh-oh eh-lehk-'troh-nee-koh*
electromagnetics	la electromecánica	*lah eh-lehk-troh-meh-'kah-nee-kah*
encode (v)	codificar	*koh-dee-fee-'kahr*

end	el fin	*ehl feen*
end of block	de bloque	*deh 'bloh-keh*
end of data	de datos	*deh 'dah-tohs*
end of job	de trabajo	*deh trah-'bah-hoh*
enter (v)	dar entrada, entrar	*dahr ehn-'trah-dah, ehn-'trahr*
error checking	la verificación de errores	*lah beh-ree-fee-kah-see-'ohn deh eh-'rroh-rehs*
exit (v)	salir	*sah-'leer*
fax	el facsímil, el fax	*ehl fahk-'see-meel, ehl fahks*
feed (v)	alimentar	*ah-lee-mehn-'tahr*
feedback	la realimentación, la retroalimentación	*lah reh-ah-lee-mehn-tah-see-'ohn,lah reh-troh-ah-lee-mehn-tah-see-'ohn*
field	el campo	*ehl 'kahm-poh*
file	el archivo, el fichero	*ehl ahr-'chee-boh, ehl fee-'cheh-roh*
file protection	la protección de un fichero	*lah proh-tehk-see-'ohn deh oon fee-'cheh-roh*
floppy disk	el disco flexible	*ehl 'dees-koh flehk-'see-bleh*
flowchart	el diagrama de flujo (m)	*ehl dee-ah-'grah-mah deh 'floo-hoh*
font	la colección de caracteres de un tipo particular	*lah koh-lehk-see-'ohn deh kah-rahk-'teh-rehs deh oon 'tee-poh pahr-tee-koo-'lahr*
format	el formato	*ehl fohr-'mah-toh*
format (v)	dar formato	*dahr fohr-'mah-toh*
hard copy	la copia dura, la salida impresa	*lah 'koh-pee-ah 'doo-rah, lah sah-'lee-dah eem-'preh-sah*
hardware	las máquinas, los equipos	*lahs 'mah-kee-nahs, lohs eh-'kee-pohs*
highlight	el realce acentuado	*ehl reh-ahl-'seh ah-sehn-too-'ah-doh*
icon	el icono	*ehl ee-'koh-noh*
indexing	la modificación por índice	*lah moh-dee-fee-kah-see-'ohn pohr 'een-dee-seh*
information	la información	*lah een-fohr-mah-see-'ohn*

input	la entrada	*lah ehn-'trah-dah*
interactive (adj)	interactivo	*een-tehr-ahk-'tee-boh*
interface	el interfaz, acoplamiento mutuo, la junción	*ehl een-tehr-'fahs, ah-koh-plah-mee-'ehn-toh 'moo-too-oh, lah hoonk-see-'ohn*
interface (v)	comunicar	*koh-moo-nee-'kahr*
internal (adj)	interno	*een-'tehr-noh*
interpreter	el intérprete	*ehl een-'tehr-preh-teh*
justification (margin)	la alineación	*lah ah-lee-neh-ah-see-'ohn*
keyboard	el teclado	*ehl teh-'klah-doh*
language	el lenguaje	*ehl lehn-'gwah-heh*
laser disk	el disco láser	*ehl 'dees-koh 'lah-sehr*
laser printer	la impresora láser	*lah em-preh-'soh-rah 'lah-sehr*
layout	el diseño	*ehl dee-'seh-nyoh*
line	la línea, el renglón	*lah'lee-neh-ah, ehl rehn-'glohn*
link	el vínculo, la unión	*ehl 'been-koo-loh, lah oo-nee-'ohn*
list	la lista	*lah 'lees-tah*
list (v)	listar	*lees-'tahr*
lock out	el cierre	*ehl see-'eh-rreh*
log	el registro cronológico	*ehl reh-'hees-troh kroh-noh-'loh-hee-koh*
log off (v)	poner fin a una sesión	*poh-'nehr feen ah 'oo-nah seh-see-'ohn*
log on (v)	iniciar una sesión	*ee-nee-see-'ahr 'oo-nah seh-see-'ohn*
loop	el bucle	*ehl 'boo-kleh*
machine language	el lenguaje máquina	*ehl lehn-'gwah-heh 'mah-kee-nah*
macro	la macro, la macro instrucción	*lah mah-kroh, lah mah-kroh een-strook-see-'ohn*
mainframe	la unidad principal	*lah oo-nee-'dahd preen-see-'pahl*
manual operation	la operación manual	*lah oh-peh-rah-see-'ohn mah-noo-'ahl*

memory	la memoria	*lah meh-'moh-ree-ah*
merge (v)	intercalar, fusionar archivos	*een-tehr-kah-'lahr, foo-see-oh-'nahr ahr-'chee-bohs*
mix	la mezcla	*lah 'mehs-klah*
modem	el modem, el modulador-demodulador	*ehl moh-'dehm,ehl moh-doo-lah-dohr deh-moh-doo-lah-'dohr*
move block	mover el bloque	*moh-'behr ehl 'bloh-keh*
network	la red	*lah rehd*
on-line	conectado, directo, en línea	*koh-nehk-'tah-doh, dee-'rehk-toh, ehn 'lee-neh-ah*
output	la salida	*lah sah-'lee-dah*
path	el camino	*ehl kah-'mee-noh*
personal computer	la computadora personal, la microcomputadora	*lah kohm-poo-tah-'doh-rah pehr-soh-'nahl, lah mee-kroh-kohm-poo-tah-'doh-rah*
plot (v)	trazar	*trah-'sahr*
plug-in (adj)	enchufable	*ehn-choo-'fah-bleh*
port (comp.)	el puerto de entrada o salida (de cables)	*ehl 'pwehr-tah deh ehn-'trah-dah oh sah-'lee-dah deh 'kah-blehs*
post-edit (v)	post-editar	*pohst-eh-dee-'tahr*
power supply	la fuente de energía, el suministro de energía	*lah 'fwehn-teh deh eh-nehr-'hee-ah, ehl soo-mee-'nees-troh deh eh-nehr-'hee-ah*
power switch off	el interruptor parado	*ehl een-teh-rroop-'tohr pah-'rah-doh*
power switch on	el interruptor en marcha	*ehl een-teh-rroop-'tohr ehn 'mahr-chah*
preview	la vista anticipada	*lah 'bees-tah ahn-tee-see-'pah-dah*
print	la impresión	*lah eem-preh-see-'ohn*
printer	la impresora	*lah eem-preh-'soh-rah*
printout	la salida impresa	*lah sah-'lee-dah eem-'preh-sah*
process	el proceso	*ehl proh-'seh-soh*
processor	el procesador	*ehl proh-seh-sah-'dohr*

productivity	la productividad	*lah proh-dook-tee-bee-'dahd*
program	el programa	*ehl proh-'grah-mah*
protocol	el protocolo	*ehl proh-toh-'koh-loh*
quick access storage	la memoria de acceso rápido	*lah meh-'moh-ree-ah deh ahk-'seh-soh 'rah-pee-doh*
random access memory (RAM)	la memoria de acceso directo	*lah meh-'moh-ree-ah deh ahk-'seh-soh dee-'rehk-toh*
range	la escala	*lah eh-'skah-lah*
reboot (v)	arrancar	*ah-rrahn-'kahr*
record (v)	grabar, registrar	*grah-'bahr, reh-hees-'trahr*
repeat keys	las teclas repetidoras	*lahs 'teh-klahs reh-peh-tee-'doh-rahs*
reset (v)	restaurar	*rehs-tah-oo-'rahr*
response time	el tiempo de respuesta	*ehl tee-'ehm-poh deh reh-'spweh-stah*
restart (v)	arrancar	*ah-rrahn-'kahr*
retrieval	la recuperación	*lah reh-koo-peh-rah-see-'ohn*
ribbon	la cinta de impresor	*lah 'seen-tah deh eem-preh-'sohr*
run time	el tiempo de ejecución	*ehl tee-'ehm-poh deh eh-heh-koo-see-'ohn*
satellite dish	la parabólica	*lah pah-rah-'boh-lee-kah*
scan (v)	examinar, explorar	*ehk-sah-mee-'nahr, ehk-sploh-'rahr*
scanner	el dispositivo de exploración	*ehl dees-poh-see-'tee-boh deh ehk-sploh-rah-see-'ohn*
screen	la pantalla	*lah pahn-'tah-yah*
search (v)	buscar	*boos-'kahr*
shift	el cambio	*ehl 'kahm-bee-oh*
software	los programas y sistemas de programación, el software	*lohs proh-'grah-mahs ee sees-'teh-mahs de proh-grah-mah-see-'ohn, ehl sohft-'wehr*
solid state	el semiconductor	*ehl seh-mee-kohn-dook-'tohr*
source	la fuente, el origen	*lah 'fwehn-teh, ehl oh-'ree-hehn*

store (v)	almacenar	*ahl-mah-seh-'nahr*
subroutine	la subrutina	*lah soob-roo-'tee-nah*
superconductor	el superconductor	*ehl soo-pehr-kohn-dook-'tohr*
suppression	la eliminación	*lah eh-lee-mee-nah-see-'ohn*
symbol	el símbolo	*ehl 'seem-boh-loh*
tabulate (v)	tabular	*tah-boo-'lahr*
telecommunications	las telecomunicaciones	*lahs teh-leh-koh-moo-nee-kah-see-'oh-nehs*
teleprocessing	el teleproceso, el teleprocesamiento	*ehl teh-leh-proh-'seh-soh, ehl teh-leh-proh-seh-sah-mee-'ehn-toh*
time lag	el atraso de tiempo	*ehl ah-'trah-soh deh tee-'ehm-poh*
track	la pista (disco), el canal (cinta)	*lah 'pees-tah ('dees-koh), ehl kah-'nahl ('seen-tah)*
transceiver	el receptor/ el emisor	*ehl reh-sehp-'tohr/ehl eh-mee-'sohr*
translate (v)	traducir	*trah-doo-'seer*
translator	el traductor/la traductora	*ehl trah-dook-'tohr, lah trah-dook-'toh-rah*
transliterate (v)	convertir carácteres	*kohn-behr-'teer kah-'rahk-teh-rehs*
unformatted (adj)	no ajustado a formato	*noh ah-hoos-'tah-doh ah fohr-'mah-toh*
update (v)	actualizar	*ahk-too-ah-lee-'sahr*
uploading	la conversión ascendente	*lah kohn-behr-see-'ohn ah-sehn-'dehn-teh*
user	el usuario	*ehl oo-soo-'ah-ree-oh*
user-friendly	concebido para el usuario, fácil para el usuario	*kohn-seh-'bee-doh 'pah-rah ehl oo-soo-'ah-ree-oh, 'fah-seel 'pah-rah ehl oo-soo-'ah-ree-oh*
verify (v)	verificar, controlar	*beh-ree-fee-'kahr, kohn-troh-'lahr*
warning	el aviso	*ehl ah-'bee-soh*
window	la ventana	*lah behn-'tah-nah*
word	la palabra	*lah pah-'lah-brah*

word processing	el procesamiento de palabra, el tratamiento de palabra	*ehl proh-seh-sah-mee-'ehn-toh deh pah-'lah-brah, ehl trah-tah-mee-'ehn-toh deh pah-'lah-brah*
work area	el área de trabajo	*ehl 'ah-reh-ah deh trah-'bah-hoh*
work file	el archivo de trabajo	*ehl ahr-'chee-boh deh trah-'bah-hoh*
workstation	la estación de trabajo	*lah eh-stah-see-'ohn deh trah-'bah-hoh*
zone	la zona	*'soh-nah*

Spanish to English

absoluto	*ahb-soh-'loo-toh*	absolute (adj)
acceso (m)	*ehl ahk-'seh-soh*	access
acoplamiento mutuo (m)	*ehl ah-koh-plah-mee-'ehn-toh 'moo-too-oh*	interface
actualizar	*ahk-too-ah-lee-'sahr*	update (v)
algoritmo (m)	*ehl ahl-goh-'reet-moh*	algorithm
alimentar	*ah-lee-mehn-'tahr*	feed (v)
alineación (f)	*lah ah-lee-neh-ah-see-'ohn*	justification (margin)
almacenamiento de datos (m)	*ehl alh-mah-seh-nah-mee-'ehn-toh deh 'dah-tohs*	data storage
almacenar	*ahl-mah-seh-'nahr*	store (v)
archivo (m)	*ehl ahr-'chee-boh*	file
archivo de trabajo	*ehl ahr-'chee-boh deh trah-'bah-hoh*	work file
área de trabajo (m)	*ehl 'ah-reh-ah deh trah-'bah-hoh*	work area
arrancar	*ah-rrahn-'kahr*	reboot (v), restart (v)
atraso de tiempo (m)	*ehl ah-'trah-soh deh tee-'ehm-poh*	time lag
auxiliar (m)	*ehl owk-see-lee-'ahr*	ancillary
avería (f)	*lah ah-beh-'ree-ah*	breakdown
aviso (m)	*ehl ah-'bee-soh*	warning
banco de datos (m)	*ehl 'bahn-koh deh 'dah-tohs*	data bank
base de datos (f)	*lah 'bah-seh deh 'dah-tohs*	data base

baudio	*ehl 'baw-dee-oh*	baud
bifurcacion (f)	*lah bee-foor-kah-see-'oh*	branching
binario	*bee-'nah-ree-oh*	binary (adj)
bit (m)	*ehl beet*	bit
bloque (m)	*ehl 'bloh-keh*	block
borrar	*boh-'rrahr*	clear (v)
botón (m)	*ehl boh-'tohn*	button
bucle (m)	*ehl 'boo-kleh*	loop
buscar	*boos-'kahr*	search (v)
byte (m)	*ehl bah-eet*	byte
cambio (m)	*ehl 'kahm-bee-oh*	shift
camino (m)	*ehl kah-'mee-noh*	path
campo (m)	*ehl 'kahm-poh*	field
canal (cinta) (m)	*ehl kah-'nahl ('seen-tah)*	track
capacidad (f)	*lah kah-pah-see-'dahd*	capacity
chip (m)	*ehl cheep*	chip
ciclo (m)	*ehl 'see-kloh*	cycle
cierre (m)	*ehl see-'eh-rreh*	lock out
cinta de impresor (f)	*lah 'seen-tah deh eem-preh-'sohr*	ribbon
circuito (m)	*ehl seer-koo-'ee-toh*	circuit
circuito integrado (m)	*ehl seer-koo-'ee-toh een-teh-'grah-doh*	chip
codificar	*koh-dee-fee-'kahr*	encode (v)
código utilizado como estándard en los EE.UU. para el intercambio de información entre sistemas de procesamiento de datos (ASCII) (m)	*ehl 'koh-dee-goh oo-tee-lee-'sah-doh 'koh-moh ehs-'tahn-dahrd ehn lohs eh-'stah-dohs oo-'nee-dohs 'pah-rah ehl een-tehr-'kahm-bee-oh deh een-fohr-mah-see-'ohn 'ehn-treh sees-'teh-mahs deh proh-seh-sah-mee-'ehn-toh deh 'dah-tohs*	ASCII
colección de caracteres de un tipo particular (f)	*lah koh-lehk-see-'ohn deh kah-rahk-'teh-rehs deh oon 'tee-poh pahr-tee-koo-'lahr*	font
columna (f)	*lah koh-'loom-nah*	column

computadora (f)	*lah kohm-poo-tah-'doh-rah*	computer
computadora personal (f)	*lah kohm-poo-tah-'doh-rah pehr-soh-'nahl*	personal computer
comunicar	*koh-moo-nee-'kahr*	interface (v)
concebido para el usuario	*kohn-seh-'bee-doh 'pah-rah ehl oo-soo-'ah-ree-oh*	user-friendly
conectado	*koh-nehk-'tah-doh*	on-line
control (m)	*ehl kohn-'trohl*	control
controlar	*kohn-troh-'lahr*	verify (v)
control cruzado (m)	*ehl kohn-'trohl kroo-'sah-doh*	crosscheck
conversión ascendente (f)	*lah kohn-behr-see-'ohn ah-sehn-'dehn-teh*	uploading
conversión descendente (f)	*lah kohn-behr-see-'ohn deh-sehn-'dehn-teh*	downloading
convertir caracteres	*kohn-behr-'teer kah-rahk-'teh-rehs*	transliterate (v)
copia dura (f)	*lah 'koh-pee-ah 'doo-rah*	hard copy
copia física que se hace del contenido de un disco o una cinta	*lah 'koh-pee-ah 'fee-see-kah keh seh 'ah-seh dehl kohn-teh-'nee-doh deh oon 'dees-koh oh 'oo-nah 'seen-tah*	backup
correo electrónico (m)	*ehl koh-'rreh-oh eh-lehk-'troh-nee-koh*	electronic mail
cursor (m)	*ehl koor-'sohr*	cursor
dar entrada	*dahr ehn-'trah-dah*	enter (v)
dar formato	*dahr fohr-'mah-toh*	format (v)
defecto (programa) (m)	*ehl deh-'fehk-toh (proh-'grah-mah)*	bug
diagrama de flujo (m)	*ehl dee-ah-'grah-mah deh 'floo-hoh*	flowchart
diccionario (m)	*ehl deek-see-oh-'nah-ree-oh*	dictionary
directo	*dee-'rehk-toh*	on-line
directorio (m)	*ehl dee-rehk-'toh-ree-oh*	directory
disco (m)	*ehl 'dees-koh*	disk
disco compacto	*ehl 'dees-koh kohm-'pahk-toh*	compact disk
disco flexible	*ehl 'dees-koh flehk-'see-bleh*	floppy disk

disco flexible de capacidad pequeña	*ehl 'dees-koh flehk-'see-bleh deh kah-pah-see-'dahd peh-'keh-nyah*	diskette
disco láser	*ehl 'dees-koh 'lah-sehr*	laser disk
diseño (m)	*ehl dee-'seh-nyoh*	layout
dispositivo (m)	*ehl dees-poh-see-'tee-boh*	device
dispositivo de disco	*ehl dees-poh-see-'tee-boh deh 'dees-koh*	disk drive
dispositivo de exploración	*ehl dees-poh-see-'tee-boh deh ehk-sploh-rah-see-'ohn*	scanner
documentación (f)	*lah doh-koo-mehn-tah-see-'ohn*	documentation
editorial de despacho (f)	*lah eh-dee-toh-ree-'ahl deh dehs-'pah-choh*	desktop publishing
editorial de sobremesa	*lah eh-dee-toh-ree-'ahl deh soh-breh-'meh-sah*	desktop publishing
electromecánica (f)	*lah eh-lehk-troh-meh-'kah-nee-kah*	electromagnetics
eliminación (f)	*lah eh-lee-mee-nah-see-'ohn*	suppression
eliminar	*eh-lee-mee-'nahr*	delete (v)
en línea	*ehn 'lee-neh-ah*	on-line
enchufable	*ehn-choo-'fah-bleh*	plug-in (adj)
enlace de comunicación (m)	*ehl ehn-'lah-seh deh koh-moo-nee-kah-see-'ohn*	communication link
entrada (f)	*lah ehn-'trah-dah*	input
entrada de datos	*lah ehn-'trah-dah deh 'dah-tohs*	data entry
entrar	*ehn-'trahr*	enter (v)
equipo auxiliar (m)	*ehl eh-'kee-poh owk-see-lee-ahr*	ancillary
equipos (mpl)	*lohs eh-'kee-pohs*	hardware
error (m)	*ehl eh-'rrohr*	bug
escala (f)	*lah eh-'skah-lah*	range
estación de trabajo (f)	*lah eh-stah-see-'ohn deh trah-'bah-hoh*	workstation
examinar	*ehk-sah-mee-'nahr*	scan (v)
explorar	*ehk-sploh-'rahr*	scan (v)

expulsar	*ehs-pool-'sahr*	eject (v)
facíl para el usario	*'fah-seel 'pah-rah ehl oo-soo-'ah-ree-oh*	user-friendly
facsímil (m)	*ehl fahk-'see-meel*	fax
fax (m)	*ehl fahks*	fax
fichero (m)	*ehl fee-cheh-roh*	file
fin (m)	*ehl feen*	end
fin de bloque	*ehl feen deh 'bloh-keh*	end of block
fin de datos	*ehl feen deh 'dah-tohs*	end of data
fin de trabajo	*ehl feen deh trah-'bah-hoh*	end of job
formato (m)	*ehl fohr-'mah-toh*	format
fuente (f)	*lah 'fwehn-teh*	source
fuente de energía	*lah 'fwehn-teh deh eh-nehr-'hee-ah*	power supply
fusionar archivos	*foo-see-oh-'nahr ahr-'chee-bohs*	merge (v)
grabar	*grah-'bahr*	record (v)
grupo (m)	*ehl 'groo-poh*	batch
ícono (m)	*ehl 'ee-koh-noh*	icon
impresión (f)	*lah eem-preh-see-'ohn*	print
impresora (f)	*lah eem-preh-'soh-rah*	printer
impresora láser	*lah eem-preh-'soh-rah 'lah-sehr*	laser printer
impresora por matriz de puntos	*lah eem-preh-'soh-rah pohr mah-'trees deh 'poon-tohs*	dot matrix printer
inferfaz (m)	*ehl een-tehr-'fahs*	interface
información (f)	*lah een-fohr-mah-see-'ohn*	information
iniciar una sesión	*ee-nee-see-'ahr 'oo-nah seh-see-'ohn*	log on (v)
interactivo	*een-tehr-ahk-'tee-boh*	interactive (adj)
intercalar	*een-tehr-kah-'lahr*	merge (v)
interno	*een-'tehr-noh*	internal (adj)
intérprete (m/f)	*een-'tehr-preh-teh*	interpreter
interruptor en marcha (m)	*ehl een-teh-rroop-'tohr ehn 'mahr-chah*	power switch on

interruptor parado	*ehl een-teh-rroop-'tohr pah-'rah-doh*	power switch off
junción (f)	*lah hoonk-see-'ohn*	interface
lenguaje (m)	*ehl lehn-'gwah-heh*	language
lenguaje máquina (m)	*ehl lehn-'gwah-heh 'mah-kee-nah*	machine language
línea (f)	*lah 'lee-neh-ah*	line
lista (f)	*lah 'lees-tah*	list
listar	*lees-'tahr*	list (v)
lote (m)	*ehl 'loh-teh*	batch
macro (f)	*lah 'mah-kroh*	macro
macro instrucción	*lah 'mah-kroh een-strook-see-'ohn*	macro
mando (m)	*ehl 'mahn-doh*	command
máquinas (fpl)	*lahs 'mah-kee-nahs*	hardware
memoria (f)	*lah meh-'moh-ree-ah*	memory
memoria de acceso directo	*lah meh-'moh-ree-ah deh ahk-'seh-soh dee-'rehk-toh*	random access memory (RAM)
memoria de acceso rápido	*lah meh-'moh-ree-ah deh ahk-'seh-soh 'rah-pee-doh*	quick access storage
mezcla (f)	*lah 'mehs-klah*	mix
microcomputadora (f)	*lah mee-kroh-kohm-poo-tah-'doh-rah*	personal computer
micrológico (m)	*ehl mee-kroh-'loh-hee-koh*	chip
móden (m)	*ehl moh-'dehn*	modem
modificación por índice (f)	*lah moh-dee-fee-kah-see-'ohn pohr 'een-dee-seh*	indexing
modulador-demodulador (m)	*ehl moh-doo-lah-dohr deh-moh-doo-lah-dohr*	modem
montaje (m)	*ehl mohn-'tah-heh*	device
mover el bloque	*moh-'behr ehl 'bloh-keh*	to move the block (v)
no ajustado a formato	*noh ah-hoos-'tah-doh ah fohr-'mah-toh*	unformatted (adj)
operación manual (f)	*lah oh-peh-rah-see-'ohn mah-noo-'ahl*	manual operation
ordenador (m)	*ehl ohr-deh-nah-'dohr*	computer (Spain)

origen (m)	*ehl oh-'ree-hehn*	source
palabra (f)	*lah pah-'lah-brah*	word
pantalla (f)	*lah pahn-'tah-yah*	screen
parabólica (f)	*lah pah-rah-'boh-lee-kah*	satellite dish
pista (disco) (f)	*lah 'pees-tah ('dees-koh)*	track
poner fin a una sesión	*poh-'nehr feen ah 'oo-nah seh-see-'ohn*	log off (v)
post-editar	*pohst-eh-dee-'tahr*	post-edit (v)
procesador (m)	*ehl proh-seh-sah-'dohr*	processor
procesamiento de datos (m)	*ehl proh-seh-sah-mee-'ehn-toh deh 'dah-tohs*	data processing
procesamiento de palabra	*ehl proh-seh-sah-mee-'ehn-toh deh pah-'lah-brah*	word processing
proceso (m)	*ehl proh-'seh-soh*	process
productividad (f)	*lah proh-dook-tee-bee-'dahd*	productivity
programa (m)	*ehl proh-'grah-mah*	program
programas y sistemas de programación (mpl)	*lohs proh-'grah-mahs ee sees-'teh-mahs de proh-grah-mah-see-'ohn*	software
protección de un fichero (f)	*lah proh-tehk-see-'ohn deh oon fee-'cheh-roh*	file protection
protocolo (m)	*ehl proh-toh-'koh-loh*	protocol
puerto de entrada o salida de cables (m)	*ehl 'pwehr-tah deh ehn-'trah-dah oh sah-'lee-dah deh 'kah-blehs*	port
punto de interrupción (m)	*ehl 'poon-toh deh een-teh-roop-see-'ohn*	breakpoint
realce acentuado (m)	*ehl reh-ahl-'seh ah-sehn-too-'ah-doh*	highlight
realimentación (f)	*lah reh-ah-lee-mehn-tah-see-'ohn*	feedback
receptor/emisor (m)	*ehl reh-sehp-'tohr/eh-mee-'sohr*	transceiver
recuperación (f)	*lah reh-koo-peh-rah-see-'ohn*	retrieval
red (f)	*lah rehd*	network
redacción de los datos de entrada (f)	*lah reh-dahk-see-'ohn deh lohs 'dah-tohs deh ehn-'trah-dah*	editing of input

reducido	*reh-doo-'see-doh*	downgraded (adj)
registrar	*reh-hees-'trahr*	record (v)
registro cronológico (m)	*ehl reh-'hees-troh kroh-noh-'loh-hee-koh*	log
renglón (m)	*ehl rehn-'glohn*	line
reproducir datos	*reh-proh-doo-'seer 'dah-tohs*	copy (v)
restaurar	*rehs-tah-oo-'rahr*	reset (v)
retroalimentación (f)	*lah reh-troh-ah-lee-mehn-tah-see-'ohn*	feedback
retroceder en una unidad	*reh-troh-seh-'dehr ehn 'oo-nah oo-nee-'dahd*	backspace (v)
salida (f)	*lah sah-'lee-dah*	output
salida impresa	*lah sah-'lee-dah eem-'preh-sah*	printout, hard copy
salir	*sah-'leer*	exit (v)
semiconductor (m)	*ehl seh-mee-kohn-dook-'tohr*	solid state
símbolo (m)	*ehl 'seem-boh-loh*	symbol
software (m)	*ehl sohft-'wehr*	software
subrutina (f)	*lah soob-roo-'tee-nah*	subroutine
suministro de energía (m)	*ehl soo-mee-'nees-troh deh eh-nehr-'hee-ah*	power supply
superconductor (m)	*ehl soo-pehr-kohn-dook-'tohr*	superconductor
tabular	*tah-boo-'lahr*	tabulate (v)
teclado (m)	*ehl teh-'klah-doh*	keyboard
teclas repetidoras (fpl)	*lahs 'teh-klahs reh-peh-tee-'doh-rahs*	repeat keys
telecomunicaciones (fpl)	*lahs teh-leh-koh-moo-nee-kah-see-'oh-nehs*	telecommunications
teléfono celular (m)	*ehl teh-'leh-foh-noh seh-loo-'lahr*	cellular phone
teleprocesamiento (m)	*ehl teh-leh-proh-seh-sah-mee-'ehn-toh*	teleprocessing
teleproceso (m)	*ehl teh-leh-proh-'seh-soh*	teleprocessing
tiempo de ejecución (m)	*ehl tee-'ehm-poh deh eh-heh-koo-see-'ohn*	run time
tiempo de respuesta	*ehl tee-'ehm-poh deh reh-'spweh-stah*	response time

tiempo improductivo	*ehl tee-'ehm-poh eem-proh-dook-'tee-boh*	downtime
traducir	*trah-doo-'seer*	translate (v)
traductor (m)	*ehl trah-dook-'tohr*	translator
transformar	*trans-fohr-'mahr*	convert (v)
tratamiento de palabra (m)	*ehl trah-tah-mee-'ehn-toh deh pah-'lah-brah*	word processing
trazar	*trah-'sahr*	plot (v)
unidad de velocidad de transmisión de información (m)	*lah oo-nee-'dahd deh beh-loh-see-'dahd deh trans-mee-see-'ohn deh enn-fohr-mah-see-'ohn*	baud
unidad elemental de información del sistema binario (f)	*lah oo-nee-'dahd eh-leh-mehn-'tahl de een-fohr-mah-see-'ohn dehl sees-'teh-mah bee-'nah-ree-oh*	bit
unidad principal	*lah oo-nee-'dahd preen-see-'pahl*	mainframe
unidad que gobierna el soporte	*lah oo-nee-'dahd keh goh-bee-'ehr-nah ehl soh-'pohr-teh*	drive
unión (f)	*lah oo-nee-'ohn*	link
usuario (m)	*ehl oo-soo-'ah-ree-oh*	user
ventana (f)	*lah behn-'tah-nah*	window
verificación de errores (f)	*lah beh-ree-fee-kah-see-'ohn deh eh-'rroh-rehs*	error checking
verificar	*beh-ree-fee-'kahr*	verify (v)
vínculo (m)	*ehl 'been-koo-loh*	link
vínculo de comunicación	*ehl 'been-koo-loh deh koh-moo-nee-kah-see-'ohn*	communication link
vista anticipada (f)	*lah 'bees-tah ahn-tee-see-'pah-dah*	preview
zona (f)	*lah 'soh-nah*	zone

	ELECTRONICS	

English to Spanish

alternating current	la corriente alterna	*lah koh-rree-'ehn-teh ahl-tehr-nah*
ampere	el amperaje	*ehl ahm-peh-'rah-heh*
amplifier	el amplificador	*ehl ahm-plee-fee-kah-'dohr*
amplitude modulation (AM)	la amplitud modulada, la modulación de amplitud	*lah ahm-plee-tood moh-doo-'lah-dah, lah moh-doo-lah-see-'ohn*
beam	el rayo	*ehl 'rah-yoh*
binary code	el código binario	*ehl 'koh-dee-goh bee-'nah-ree-oh*
broadcast (v) (radio)	transmitir (TV), emitir	*trahns-mee-teer (TV), eh-mee-'teer*
cable television	la televisión por cable	*lah teh-leh-bee-see-'ohn pohr 'kah-bleh*
cassette	la cinta magnetofónica	*lah 'seen-tah mahg-neh-toh-'foh-nee-kah*
cathode	el cátodo	*ehl 'kah-toh-doh*
channel	el canal	*ehl kah-'nahl*
circuit	el circuito	*ehl seer-koo-'ee-toh*
coaxial cable	el cable coaxial	*ehl 'kah-bleh koh-ahks-ee-'ahl*
computer	la computadora, el ordenador (Spain)	*lah kohm-poo-tah-'doh-rah, ehl ohr-deh-nah-'dohr*
condensor	el condensador	*ehl kohn dehn-sah-'dohr*
conductor	el conductor	*ehl kohn-dook-'tohr*
copper	el cobre	*ehl 'koh-breh*
current	la corriente	*lah koh-rree-'ehn-teh*
detector	el detector	*ehl deh-tehk-'tohr*
digital (adj)	digital	*dee-hee-'tahl*
diode	el diodo	*ehl dee-'oh-doh*
direct current	la corriente directa	*lah koh-rree-'ehn-teh dee-'rehk-tah*
electricity	la electricidad	*lah eh-lehk-tree-see-'dahd*
electrode	el electrodo	*ehl eh-lehk-'troh-doh*
electron	el electrón	*ehl eh-lehk-'trohn*

electronic (adj)	electrónico	*eh-lehk-'troh-nee-koh*
electrostatic	la electroestática	*lah eh-lehk-troh-eh-'stah-tee-kah*
filter	el filtro	*ehl 'feel-troh*
frequency modulation (FM)	la modulación de frecuencia	*lah moh-doo-lah-see-'ohn deh freh-'kwehn-see-ah*
generator	el generador	*ehl heh-neh-rah-'dohr*
high fidelity	la alta fidelidad	*deh 'ahl-tah fee-deh-lee-'dahd*
insulator	el aislador	*ehl ah-ee-slah-'dohr*
integrated circuit	el circuito integrado	*ehl seer-koo-'ee-toh een-teh-'grah-doh*
microphone	el micrófono	*ehl mee-'kroh-foh-noh*
microprocessor	el microprocesador	*ehl mee-kroh-proh-seh-sah-'dohr*
microwave	el microonda	*ehl mee-kroh-'ohn-dah*
mixer	el mezclador	*ehl mehs-klah-'dohr*
optic (adj)	óptico	*'ohp-tee-koh*
oscillator	el oscilador	*ehl oh-see-lah-'dohr*
parallel circuit	el circuito paralelo	*ehl seer-koo-'ee-toh pah-rah-'leh-loh*
power	la potencia, la energía	*lah poh-'tehn-see-ah, lah eh-nehr-'hee-ah*
printed circuit	el circuito impreso	*ehl seer-koo-'ee-toh eem-'preh-soh*
receiver	el receptor, el radio	*ehl reh-sehp-'tohr, ehl 'rah-dee-oh*
record	el disco	*ehl 'dees-koh*
record (v)	grabar	*grah-'bahr*
record player	el tocadiscos	*ehl toh-kah-'dees-kohs*
resonance	la resonancia	*lah reh-soh-'nahn-see-ah*
scanning	la exploración	*lah ehks-ploh-rah-see-'ohn*
screen	la pantalla	*lah pahn-'tah-yah*
short wave	la onda corta	*lah 'ohn-dah 'kohr-tah*
silicon	el silicio	*ehl see-'lee-see-oh*
sound	el sonido	*ehl soh-'nee-doh*
speaker	el altavoz, el altoparlante	*ehl ahl-tah-'bos, ehl ahl-toh-pahr-'lahn-teh*

stereophonic (adj)	estereofónico	*eh-steh-reh-oh-'foh-nee-koh*
switch	el interruptor	*ehl een-teh-rroop-'tohr*
tape recorder	la grabadora, el magnetófono	*lah grah-bah-'doh-rah, ehl mahg-neh-'toh-foh-noh*
transformer	el transformador	*ehl trahns-fohr-mah-'dohr*
transmitter (v)	transmitir	*trahns-mee-'teer*
turbine	la turbina	*lah toor-'bee-nah*
vacuum	el vacío	*ehl bah-'see-oh*
vector	el vector	*ehl behk-'tohr*
videocassette player	el tocador de videocassette	*ehl toh-kah-'dohr deh bee-deh-oh-kah-seh-teh*
volt	el voltio	*ehl 'bohl-tee-oh*
voltage	el voltaje	*ehl bohl-'tah-heh*
watt	el vatio	*ehl 'bah-tee-oh*
wave	la onda	*lah 'ohn-dah*
wire	el cable, el alambre	*ehl 'kah-bleh, ehl ah-'lahm-breh*

Spanish to English

aislador (m)	*ehl ah-see-slah-'dohr*	insulator
alta fidelidad (f)	*lah 'ahl-tah fee-deh-lee-'dahd*	high fidelity
altavoz (m)	*ehl ahl-tah-'bos*	speaker
altoparlante (m)	*ehl ahl-toh-pahr-'lahn-teh*	speaker
amperaje (m)	*ehl ahm-peh-'rah-heh*	ampere
amplificador (m)	*ehl ahm-plee-fee-kah-'dohr*	amplifier
amplitud modulada (f)	*lah ahm-plee-tood moh-doo-'lah-dah*	amplitude modulation (AM)
cable (m)	*ehl 'kah-bleh*	wire
cable coaxial	*ehl 'kah-bleh koh-ahks-ee-'ahl*	coaxial cable
canal (m)	*ehl kah-'nahl*	channel
cátodo (m)	*ehl 'kah-toh-doh*	cathode
cinta (f) magnetofónica	*lah 'seen-tah mahg-neh-toh-'foh-nee-kah*	cassette
circuito (m)	*ehl seer-koo-'ee-too*	circuit

circuito impreso	*ehl seer-koo-'ee-toh eem-'preh-soh*	printed circuit
circuito integrado	*ehl seer-koo-'ee-toh een-teh-'grah-doh*	integrated circuit
circuito paralelo	*ehl seer-koo-'ee-toh pah-rah-'leh-loh*	parallel circuit
código (m) binario	*ehl 'koh-dee-goh bee-'nah-ree-oh*	binary code
computadora (f)	*lah kohm-poo-tah-'doh-rah*	computer
condensador (m)	*ehl kohn dehn-sah-'dohr*	condensor
conductor (m)	*ehl kohn-dook-'tohr*	conductor
corriente (f)	*lah koh-rree-'ehn-teh*	current
corriente alterna	*lah koh-rree-'ehn-teh ahl-tehr-nah*	alternating current
corriente directa	*lah koh-rree-'ehn-teh dee-'rehk-tah*	direct current
detector (m)	*ehl deh-tehk-'tohr*	detector
digital	*dee-hee-'tahl*	digital (adj)
diodo (m)	*ehl dee-'oh-doh*	diode
disco (m)	*ehl 'dees-koh*	record
electricidad (f)	*lah eh-lehk-tree-see-'dahd*	electricity
electrodo (m)	*ehl eh-lehk-'troh-doh*	electrode
electrón (m)	*ehl eh-lehk-'trohn*	electron
electrónico	*eh-lehk-'troh-nee-koh*	electronic (adj)
electroestática (f)	*lah eh-lehk-troh-eh-'stah-tee-kah*	electrostatic
emitir	*eh-mee-'teer*	broadcast (v) (radio)
energía (f)	*lah eh-nehr-'hee-ah*	power
estereofónico	*eh-steh-reh-oh-'foh-nee-koh*	stereophonic (adj)
exploración (f)	*lah ehks-ploh-rah-see-'ohn*	scanning
filtro (m)	*ehl 'feel-troh*	filter
generador (m)	*ehl heh-neh-rah-'dohr*	generator
grabadora (f)	*lah grah-bah-'doh-rah*	tape recorder
interruptor (m)	*ehl een-teh-rroop-'tohr*	switch
magnetófono	*ehl mahg-neh-'toh-foh-noh*	tape recorder
mezclador (m)	*ehl mehs-klah-'dohr*	mixer

micrófono (m)	*ehl mee-'kroh-foh-noh*	microphone
microonda (m)	*ehl mee-kroh-'ohn-dah*	microwave
microprocesador (m)	*ehl mee-kroh-proh-seh-sah-'dohr*	microprocessor
modulación de frecuencia (f)	*lah moh-doo-lah-see-'ohn deh freh-'kwehn-see-ah*	frequency modulation (FM)
onda (f)	*lah 'ohn-dah*	wave
onda corta	*lah 'ohn-dah 'kohr-tah*	short wave
óptico	*'ohp-tee-koh*	optic (adj)
ordenador (m)	*ehl ohr-deh-nah-dohr*	computer (Spain)
oscilador (m)	*ehl oh-see-lah-'dohr*	oscillator
pantalla (f)	*lah pahn-'tah-yah*	screen
potencia (f)	*lah poh-'tehn-see-ah*	power
radio (m)	*ehl 'rah-dee-oh*	receiver
rayo (m)	*ehl 'rah-yoh*	beam
receptor (m)	*ehl reh-sehp-'tohr*	receiver
silicio (m)	*ehl see-'lee-see-oh*	silicon
sonido (m)	*ehl soh-'nee-doh*	sound
televisión (f) por cable	*lah teh-leh-bee-see-'ohn pohr 'kah-bleh*	cable television
tocadiscos (m)	*ehl toh-kah-'dees-kohs*	record player
tocador (m) de videocassette	*ehl toh-kah-'dohr deh bee-deh-oh-kah-seh-teh*	videocassette player
transformador (m)	*ehl trahns-fohr-mah-'dohr*	transformer
transmitir	*trahns-mee-'teer*	transmit (v)
transmitir (TV)	*trahns-mee-'teer*	broadcast (v)
turbina (f)	*lah toor-'bee-nah*	turbine
vacío (m)	*ehl bah-'see-oh*	vacuum
vatio (m)	*ehl 'bah-tee-oh*	watt
vector (m)	*ehl behk-'tohr*	vector
voltaje (m)	*ehl bohl-'tah-heh*	voltage
voltio (m)	*ehl 'bohl-tee-oh*	volt

FASHION

English to Spanish

belt	el cinturón, el cinto	*ehl seen-too-'rohn, ehl 'seen-toh*
blazer	la chaqueta deportiva	*lah chah-'keh-tah deh-pohr-'tee-bah*
blouse	la blusa	*lah 'bloo-sah*
bow tie	la corbata de lazo	*lah kohr-'bah-tah deh 'lah-soh*
button	el botón	*ehl bah-'tohn*
buttonhole	el hojal	*ehl oh-'hahl*
camel's hair	el pelo de camello	*ehl 'peh-loh deh kah-'meh-yoh*
cashmere	la cachemira	*lah kah-cheh-'mee-rah*
coat	el abrigo, el saco	*ehl ah-'bree-goh, ehl 'sah-koh*
collar	el cuello	*ehl 'kweh-yoh*
cuff link	los gemelos, los yugos	*lohs heh-'meh-lohs, lohs 'yoo-gohs*
cut (v)	cortar	*kohr-'tahr*
design (v)	diseñar	*dee-seh-'nyahr*
designer	el diseñador	*ehl dee-'seh-nyah-'dohr*
drape (v)	cubrir con colgaduras	*koo-'breer kohn kohl-gah-'doo-rahs*
dress	el vestido	*ehl beh-'stee-doh*
fabric	la tela	*lah 'teh-lah*
fashion	la moda	*lah 'moh-dah*
fashionable	de moda	*deh 'moh-dah*
footage	la longitud	*lah lohn-hee-'tood*
French cuff	el puño francés	*ehl 'poo-nyoh frahn-'sehs*
handkerchief	el pañuelo	*ehl pah-nyoo-'eh-loh*
hem	el dobladillo	*ehl doh-blah-'dee-yoh*
high fashion designer	el diseñador de alta costura	*ehl dee-seh-nyah-'dohr deh 'ahl-tah koh-'stoo-rah*
hood	la capucha	*lah kah-'pooh-chah*

lingerie	la ropa interior	*lah 'roh-pah een-teh-ree-'ohr*
lining	el forro	*ehl 'foh-rroh*
long sleeves	las mangas largas	*lahs 'mahn-gahs 'lahr-gahs*
model	el modelo (ropa-cloth), el/la modelo (persona-person)	*ehl moh-'deh-loh ('roh-pah), ehl/lah moh-'deh-loh (pehr-'soh-nah)*
needle	la aguja	*lah ah-'goo-hah*
out of style	fuera de moda, pasado de moda	*'fweh-rah deh 'moh-dah, pah-'sah-doh deh 'moh-dah*
pattern	el patrón	*ehl pah-'trohn*
pleat	el pliegue, el plisado	*ehl plee-'eh-geh, ehl plee-sah-doh*
pleated (adj)	plegado, plisado	*pleh-'gah-doh, plee-'sah-doh*
poplin	el poplín	*ehl 'pohp-'leen*
print	el estampado	*ehl eh-stahm-'pah-doh*
raincoat	el impermeable	*ehl eem-pehr-meh-'ah-bleh*
rayon	el rayón	*ehl rah-'yohn*
ready-to-wear	la ropa hecha	*lah 'roh-pah 'eh-chah*
scarf	la bufanda	*lah boo-'fahn-dah*
sew (v)	coser	*koh-'sehr*
sewing machine	la máquina de coser	*lah 'mah-kee-nah deh koh-'sehr*
sewn (adj)	cosido	*koh-'see-doh*
shirt	la camisa	*lah kah-'mee-sah*
shoe	el zapato	*ehl sah-'pah-toh*
short sleeves	las mangas cortas	*lahs 'mahn-gahs 'kohr-tahs*
shoulder pad	la hombrera	*lah ohm-'breh-rah*
silk goods	los artículos de seda	*lohs ahr-'tee-koo-lohs deh 'seh-dah*
silk	la seda	*lah 'seh-dah*
silk factory	la fábrica de seda	*lah 'fah-bree-kah deh 'seh-dah*
silk manufacturers	los fabricantes de seda	*lohs fah-bree-'kahn-tehs deh 'seh-dah*

silkworm	el gusano de seda	*ehl goo-'sah-noh deh 'seh-dah*
size	la talla, el tamaño	*lah 'tah-yah, ehl tah-'mah-nyoh*
skirt	la falda, la saya	*lah 'fahl-dah, lah 'sah-yah*
slacks	los pantalones	*lohs pahn-tah-'loh-nehs*
socks	los calcetines	*lohs kahl-seh-'tee-nehs*
stitch	la puntada	*lah poon-'tah-dah*
stockings	las medias de mujer	*lahs 'meh-dee-ahs deh moo-'hehr*
style	el estilo	*ehl eh-'stee-loh*
stylist	el estilista	*ehl eh-stee-'lees-tah*
suede	la cabritilla, el ante, la gamuza	*lah kah-bree-'tee-yah, ehl 'ahn-teh, lah gah-'moo-sah*
suit	el traje	*ehl 'trah-heh*
taffeta	el tafetán	*ehl tah-feh-'tahn*
tailor	el sastre	*ehl 'sah-streh*
thread	el hilo, la hebra	*ehl 'ee-loh, lah 'eh-brah*
tie	la corbata	*lah kohr-'bah-tah*
tuxedo	el "smoking," el esmoquin	*ehl es-'moh-keen, ehl ehs-'moh-keen*
veil	el velo	*ehl 'beh-loh*
vest	el chaleco	*ehl chah-'leh-koh*
weaver	el tejedor	*ehl teh-heh-'dohr*
window dresser	el escaparatista, el decorador de escaparates	*ehl ehs-kah-pah 'rah-tees-tah, ehl deh-koh-rah-'dohr deh ehs-kah-pah-'rah-tehs*
wool	la lana	*lah 'lah-nah*
yardstick	patrón (m)	*ehl pah-trohn*
yarn	el hilo	*ehl 'ee-loh*
zipper	la cremallera	*lah kreh-mah-'yeh-rah*

Spanish to English

| abrigo (m) | *ehl ah-'bree-goh* | coat |
| aguja (f) | *lah ah-'goo-hah* | needle |

artículos (mpl) de seda	*lohs ahr-'tee-koo-lohs deh 'seh-dah*	silk goods
blusa (f)	*lah 'bloo-sah*	blouse
botón (m)	*ehl bah-'tohn*	button
bufanda (f)	*lah boo-'fahn-dah*	scarf
cachemira (f)	*lah kah-cheh-'mee-rah*	cashmere
calcetines (mpl)	*lohs kahl-seh-'tee-nehs*	socks
camisa (f)	*lah kah-'mee-sah*	shirt
capucha (f)	*lah kah-'pooh-chah*	hood
chaleco (m)	*ehl chah-'leh-koh*	vest
chaqueta (f) deportiva	*lah chah-'keh-tah deh-pohr-'tee-bah*	blazer
cinto (m)	*ehl 'seen-toh*	belt
corbata (f)	*lah kohr-'bah-tah*	tie
corbata de lazo	*lah kohr-'bah-tah deh 'lah-soh*	bow tie
cortar	*kohr-'tahr*	cut (v)
coser	*koh-'sehr*	sew (v)
cremallera (f)	*lah kreh-mah-'yeh-rah*	zipper
cubrir con colgaduras	*koo-'breer kohn kohl-gah-'doo-rahs*	drape (v)
cuello (m)	*ehl 'kweh-yoh*	collar
de moda	*deh 'moh-dah*	fashionable
decorador de escaparates (m)	*ehl deh-koh-rah-'dohr deh ehs-kah-pah-'rah-tehs*	window dresser
diseñador (m)	*ehl dee-'seh-nyah-'dohr*	designer
diseñador de alta costura (m)	*ehl dee-seh-nyah-'dohr deh 'ahl-tah-koh-'stoo-rah*	high fashion designer
diseñar	*dee-seh-'nyahr*	design (v)
dobladillo (m)	*ehl doh-blah-'dee-yoh*	hem
escaparatista (m)	*ehl ehs-kah-pah-'rees-tah*	window dresser
esmoquin (m)	*ehl ehs-'moh-'keen*	tuxedo
estampado (m)	*ehl eh-stahm-'pah-doh*	print
estilista (m)	*ehl eh-stee-'lees-tah*	stylist
estilo (m)	*ehl eh-'stee-loh*	style

fábrica (f) de seda	*lah 'fah-bree-kah deh 'seh-dah*	silk factory
fabricantes (mpl) de seda	*lohs fah-bree-'kahn-tehs deh 'seh-dah*	silk manufacturers
falda (f)	*lah 'fahl-dah*	skirt
forro (m)	*ehl 'foh-rroh*	lining
fuera de moda	*'fweh-rah deh 'moh-dah*	out of style
gamuza (f)	*lah gah-'moo-sah*	suede
gemelos (mpl)	*lohs heh-'meh-lohs*	cuff link
gusano de seda (m)	*ehl goo-'sah-noh deh 'seh-dah*	silkworm
hilo (m)	*ehl ' ee-loh*	thread, yarn
hojal (m)	*ehl oh-'hahl*	buttonhole
hombrera (f)	*lah ohm-'breh-rah*	shoulder pad
impermeable (m)	*ehl ehm eem-pehr-meh-'ah-bleh*	raincoat
lana (f)	*lah 'lah-nah*	wool
longitud (f)	*lah lohn-hee-'tood*	footage
mangas (fpl) cortas	*lahs 'mahn-gahs 'kohr-tahs*	short sleeves
mangas (fpl) largas	*lahs 'mahn-gahs 'lahr-gahs*	long sleeves
máquina (f) de coser	*lah 'mah-kee-nah deh koh-'sehr*	sewing machine
medias (fpl) de mujer	*lahs 'meh-dee-ahs deh moo-'hehr*	stockings
moda (f)	*lah 'moh-dah*	fashion
pañuelo (m)	*ehl pah-nyoo-'eh-loh*	handkerchief
pantalones (mpl)	*lohs pahn-tah-'loh-nehs*	slacks
pasado de moda	*pah-'sah-doh deh 'moh-dah*	out of style
patrón (m)	*ehl páh-trohn*	pattern, yardstick
pelo (m) de camello	*ehl 'peh-loh deh kah-'meh-yoh*	camel's hair
plegado	*pleh-'gah-doh*	pleated (adj)
plisado (m)	*ehl plee-sah-doh*	pleat
poplín (m)	*ehl 'pohp-leen*	poplin
puño (m) francés	*ehl 'poo-nyoh frahn-'sehs*	French cuff
puntada (f)	*lah poon-'tah-dah*	stitch

rayón (m)	*ehl rah-'yohn*	rayon
ropa (f) hecha	*lah 'roh-pah 'eh-chah*	ready-to-wear
ropa interior	*lah 'roh-pah een-teh-ree-'ohr*	lingerie
saco (m)	*ehl 'sah-koh*	coat
sastre (m)	*ehl 'sah-streh*	tailor
saya (f)	*lah 'sah-yah*	skirt
seda (f)	*lah 'seh-dah*	silk
"smoking" (m)	*ehl es-'moh-keen*	tuxedo
tafetán (m)	*ehl tah-feh-'tahn*	taffeta
talla (f)	*lah 'tah-yah*	size
tamaño (m)	*ehl tah-'mah-nyoh*	size
tejedor (m)	*ehl teh-heh-'dohr*	weaver
tela (f)	*lah 'teh-lah*	fabric
traje (m)	*ehl 'trah-heh*	suit
velo (m)	*ehl 'beh-loh*	veil
vestido (m)	*ehl beh-'stee-doh*	dress
yugos (mpl)	*lohs 'yoo-gohs*	cuff link
zapato (m)	*ehl sah-'pah-toh*	shoe

INTERNATIONAL FINANCE

English to Spanish

auction market	la subasta, la puja	*lah soo-'bah-stah, lah 'poo-hah*
balloon payment	el pago global	*ehl 'pah-goh gloh-'bahl*
bidder	el subastador	*ehl soo-bah-stah-'dohr*
bond	la obligación	*lah oh-blee-gah-see-'ohn*
bond value	el valor de la obligación	*ehl bah-'lohr deh lah oh-blee-gah-see-'ohn*
business failure	la quiebra, la bancarrota	*lah kee-'eh-brah, lah bahn-kah-'rroh-tah*
business risk	el riesgo económico	*ehl ree-'ehs-goh eh-koh-'noh-mee-koh*
business success	el éxito comercial	*ehl 'ehk-see-toh koh-mehr-see-'ahl*
call (v) (the debt)	rescatar anticipadamente	*reh-skah-'tahr ahn-tee-see-pah-dah-'mehn-teh*
capital stock	el capital social	*ehl kah-pee-'tahl soh-see-'ahl*
cash discount	el descuento por pronto pago	*ehl dehs-'kwehn-toh pohr 'prohn-toh 'pah-goh*
commercial draft	las letras de cambio comerciales	*lahs 'leh-trahs deh 'kahm-bee-oh koh-mehr-see-'ah-lehs*
commercial paper	el pagaré financiero	*ehl pah-gah-'reh fee-nahn-see-'eh-roh*
common stock	las acciones ordinarias, las acciones comunes	*lahs ahk-see-'ohn-nehs ohr-dee-'nah-ree-ahs, lahs ahk-see-oh-nehs koh-'moo-nehs*
compounding intervals	el período de capitalización	*ehl peh-'ree-oh-doh deh kah-pee-tah-lee-sah-see-'ohn*
concentration bank	el banco de centralización	*ehl 'bahn-koh deh sehn-trah-lee-sah-see-'ohn*
continuous compounding	la capitalización continua gestión	*lah kah-pee-tah-lee-sah-see-'ohn kohn-'tee-noo-ah hehs-tee-'ohn*
conversion price	el valor de conversión	*ehl bah-'lohr deh kohn-behr-see-'ohn*
covariance	el modelo de equilibrio	*ehl moh-'deh-loh deh eh-kee-'lee-bree-oh*

creditor	el acreedor	*ehl ah-kreh-eh-'dohr*
dilution	la dilución	*lah dee-loo-see-'ohn*
dividend yield	la rentabilidad por dividendos	*lah rehn-tah-bee-lee-'dahd pohr dee-bee-'dehn-dohs*
equity	el capital propio	*ehl kah-pee-'tahl 'proh-pee-oh*
factoring	la factorización	*lah fahk-toh-ree-sah-see-'ohn*
failure (project)	el fracaso	*ehl frah-'kah-soh*
financial lease	el arrendamiento financiero	*ehl ah-rrehn-dah-mee-'ehn-toh fee-nahn-see-'eh-roh*
financial leverage	el aplancamiento	*ehl ah-plahn-kah-mee-'ehn-toh*
float (rates)	variar	*bah-ree-'ahr*
floating rates	los tipos variables	*lohs 'tee-pohs bah-ree-'ah-bleh*
foreign exchange market	el mercado de divisas	*ehl mehr-'kah-doh deh dee-'bee-sahs*
forward exchange rate	el tipo de cambio	*ehl 'tee-poh deh 'kahm-bee-oh*
funded debt	la deuda consolidada	*lah deh-'oo-dah kohn-soh-lee-'dah-dah*
inflation rate	la tasa de inflación	*lah 'tah-sah deh een-flah-see-'ohn*
internal rate of return (IRR)	la tasa interna de rentabilidad	*lah 'tah-sah een-'tehr-nah deh rehn-tah-bee-lee-'dahd*
investment grade	la inversión cualificada	*lah een-behr-see-'ohn kwah-lee-fee-'kah-dah*
investors	los inversores	*lohs een-behr-'soh-rehs*
leveraged equity	las acciones con aplancamiento	*lahs ahk-see-'oh-nehs kohn ah-plahn-kah-mee-'ehn-toh*
liquidating dividend	el dividendo de capital	*ehl dee-bee-'dehn-doh deh kah-pee-'tahl*
money market account	la cuenta de mercado monetario	*lah 'kwehn-tah deh mehr-'kah-doh moh-neh-'tah-ree-oh*
net present value (NPV)	el valor actual neto	*ehl bah-'lohr ahk-too-'ahl 'neh-toh*
note	el bono simple	*ehl 'boh-noh 'seem-pleh*

overhead costs	los gastos generales	*los 'gah-stohs heh-neh-'rah-lehs*
preferred stock	las acciones preferentes	*lahs ahk-see-'oh-nehs preh-feh-'rehn-tehs*
prime rate	el tipo preferencial	*ehl 'tee-poh preh-feh-rehn-see-'ahl*
repayment provision	las claúsulas de reembolso	*lahs 'klow-soo-lahs deh reh-ehm-'bohl-soh*
risk of default	el riesgo de incumplimiento	*ehl ree-'ehs-goh deh een-koom-plee-mee-'ehn-toh*
security	la garantía	*lah gah-rahn-'tee-ah*
seniority	la prelación	*lah preh-lah-see-'ohn*
sinking fund	la amortización de obligaciones	*lah ah-mohr-tee-sah-see-'ohn deh ohb-lee-gah-see-'oh-nehs*
standard deviation	la desviación estándar	*lah dehs-bee-ah-see-'ohn eh-'stahn-dahr*
standby fee	la comisión de garantía	*lah koh-mee-see-'ohn deh gah-rahn-'tee-ah*
stock dividend	los dividendos en acciones	*lohs dee-bee-'dehn-dohs ehn ahk-see-'oh-nehs*
stock split	la división de acciones	*lah dee-bee-see-'ohn deh ahk-see-'oh-nehs*
tax shield	el ahorro fiscal contra impuestos	*ehl ah-'oh-rroh fee-'skahl 'kohn-trah eem-pweh-stohs*
term loan	el préstamo a más de un año	*ehl 'preh-stah-moh ah mahs deh oon 'ah-nyoh*
underwriter	el asegurador	*ehl ah-seh-goo-rah-'dohr*
unfunded debt	la deuda flotante	*lah deh-'oo-dah floh-'tahn-teh*
value of firm	el valor de la empresa	*ehl bah-'lohr deh lah ehm-'preh-sah*
venture capital	el capital de especulación	*ehl kah-pee-'tahl deh eh-speh-koo-lah-see-'ohn*
warrant	el certificado de opción	*ehl sehr-tee-fee-'kah-doh deh ohp-see-'ohn*
yield to maturity	la rentabilidad al vencimiento	*lah rehn-tah-bee-lee-'dahd ahl behn-see-mee-'ehn-toh*

Spanish to English

acciones comunes (mpl)	*los ahk-see-'oh-nehs koh-'moo-nehs*	common stocks
acciones con aplancamiento	*lahs ahk-see-'oh-nehs kohn ah-plahn-kah-mee-'ehn-toh*	leveraged equity
acciones ordinarias	*lahs ahk-see-'oh-nehs ohr-dee-'nah-ree-ahs*	common stocks
acciones preferentes	*lahs ahk-see-'oh-nehs preh-feh-'rehn-tehs*	preferred stock
acreedor (m)	*ehl ah-kreh-eh-'dohr*	creditor
ahorro fiscal contra impuestos (f)	*ehl ah-'oh-roh fee-skahl 'kohn-trah eem-pweh-stohs*	tax shield
amortización de obligaciones (f)	*lah ah-mohr-tee-sah-see-'ohn deh ohb-lee-gah-see-'oh-nehs*	sinking fund
aplancamiento (m)	*ehl ah-plahn-kah-mee-'ehn-toh*	financial leverage
arrendamiento financiero (m)	*ehl ah-rrehn-dah-mee-'ehn-toh fee-nahn-see-'eh-roh*	financial lease
aseguador (m)	*ehl ah-seh-goo-rah-'dohr*	underwriter
bancarrota (f)	*lah bahn-kah-'rroh-tah*	business failure
banco de centralización (m)	*ehl 'bahn-koh deh sehn-trah-lee-sah-see-'ohn*	concentration bank
bono simple (m)	*ehl 'boh-noh 'seem-pleh*	note
capital de especulación (m)	*ehl kah-pee-'tahl deh eh-speh-koo-lah-see-'ohn*	venture capital
capital propio (m)	*ehl kah-pee-'tahl 'proh-pee-oh*	equity
capital social (m)	*ehl kah-pee-'tahl soh-see-'ahl*	capital stock
capitalización continua (f)	*lah kah-pee-tah-lee-sah-see-'ohn kohn-'tee-noo-ah*	continuous compounding
certificado de opción (m)	*ehl sehr-tee-fee-'kah-doh deh ohp-see-'ohn*	warrant
claúsulas de reembolso (fpl)	*lahs 'klow-soo-lahs deh reh-ehm-'bohl-soh*	repayment provision
comisión de garantía (f)	*lah koh-mee-see-'ohn deh gah-rahn-'tee-ah*	standby fee

cuenta de mercado monetario (f)	*lah 'kwehn-tah deh mehr-'kah-doh moh-neh-'tah-ree-oh*	money market account
descuento por pronto pago (m)	*ehl dehs-'kwehn-toh pohr 'prohn-toh 'pah-goh*	cash discount
desviación estándar (f)	*lah dehs-bee-ah-see-'ohn eh-'stahn-dahr*	standard deviation
deuda consolidada (f)	*lah deh-'oo-dah kohn-soh-lee-'dah-dah*	funded debt
deuda flotante (f)	*lah deh-'oo-dah floh-'tahn-teh*	unfunded debt
dilución (f)	*lah dee-loo-see-'ohn*	dilution
dividendo de capital (m)	*ehl dee-bee-'dehn-doh deh kah-pee-'tahl*	liquidating dividend
dividendos en acciones (mpl)	*lohs dee-bee-'dehn-dohs ehn ahk-see-'oh-nehs*	stock dividend
división de acciones (f)	*lah dee-bee-see-'ohn deh ahk-see-'oh-nehs*	stock split
éxito comercial (m)	*ehl 'ehk-see-toh koh-mehr-see-'ahl*	business success
factorización (f)	*lah fahk-toh-ree-sah-see-'ohn*	factoring
fracaso (m)	*ehl frah-'kah-soh*	failure (project)
garantía (f)	*lah gah-rahn-'tee-ah*	security
gastos generales (mpl)	*lohs 'gah-stohs heh-neh-'rah-lehs*	overhead costs
inversión cualificada (f)	*lah een-behr-see-'ohn kwah-lee-fee-'kah-dah*	investment grade
inversores (mpl)	*lohs een-behr-'soh-rehs*	investors
letras de cambio comerciales (fpl)	*lahs 'leh-trahs deh 'kahm-bee-oh koh-mehr-see-'ah-lehs*	commercial draft
mercado de divisas (m)	*ehl mehr-'kah-doh deh dee-'bee-sahs*	foreign exchange market
modelo de equilibrio (m)	*ehl moh-'deh-loh deh eh-kee-'lee-bree-oh*	covariance
obligación (f)	*lah oh-blee-gah-see-'ohn*	bond
pagaré financiero (m)	*ehl pah-gah-'reh fee-nahn-see-'eh-roh*	commercial paper
pago global (m)	*ehl 'pah-goh gloh-'bahl*	balloon payment

período de capitalización (m)	*ehl peh-'ree-oh-doh deh kah-pee-tah-lee-sah-see-'ohn*	compounding intervals
prelación (f)	*lah preh-lah-see-'ohn*	seniority
préstamo a más de un año (m)	*ehl 'preh-stah-moh ah mahs deh oon 'ah-nyoh*	term loan
puja (f)	*lah 'poo-hah*	auction market
quiebra (f)	*lah kee-'eh-brah*	business failure
rentabilidad al vencimiento (f)	*lah rehn-tah-bee-lee-'dahd ahl behn-see-mee-'ehn-toh*	yield to maturity
rentabilidad por dividendos	*lah rehn-tah-bee-lee-'dahd pohr dee-bee-'dehn-dohs*	dividend yield
rescatar anticipadamente	*reh-skah-'tahr ahn-tee-see-pah-dah-'mehn-teh*	call (v) (the debt)
riesgo de incumplimiento (m)	*ehl ree-'ehs-goh deh een-koom-plee-mee-'ehn-toh*	risk of default
riesgo económico	*ehl ree-'ehs-goh eh-koh-'noh-mee-koh*	business risk
subasta (f)	*lah soo-'bah-stah*	auction market
subastador (m)	*ehl soo-bah-stah-'dohr*	bidder
tasa de inflación (f)	*lah 'tah-sah deh een-flah-see-'ohn*	inflation rate
tasa interna de rentabilidad	*lah 'tah-sah een-'tehr-nah deh rehn-tah-bee-lee-'dahd*	internal rate of return (IRR)
tipo de cambio (m)	*ehl 'tee-poh deh 'kahm-bee-oh*	forward exchange rate
tipo preferencial	*ehl 'tee-poh preh-feh-rehn-see-'ahl*	prime rate
tipos variables (mpl)	*lohs 'tee-pohs bah-ree-'ah-bleh*	floating rates
valor actual neto (m)	*ehl bah-'lohr ahk-too-'ahl 'neh-toh*	net present value (NPV)
valor de conversión	*ehl bah-'lohr deh kohn-behr-see-'ohn*	conversion price
valor de la empresa	*ehl bah-'lohr deh lah ehm-'preh-sah*	value of firm
valor de la obligación	*ehl bah-'lohr deh lah oh-blee-gah-see-'ohn*	bond value
variar	*bah-ree-'ahr*	float (rates) (v)

IRON AND STEEL

English to Spanish

alloy steel	la aleación de acero	*lah ah-leh-ah-see-'ohn deh ah-'seh-roh*
annealing	el recocido	*ehl reh-koh-'hee-doh*
bars	las barras	*lahs 'bah-rrahs*
billets	los lingotes	*lohs leen-'goh-tehs*
blast furnace	el alto horno	*ehl 'ahl-toh 'ohr-noh*
carbon steel	el acero al carbono	*ehl ah-'seh-roh ahl kahr-'boh-noh*
cast iron	el hierro fundido	*ehl 'yeh-rroh foon-'dee-doh*
charge chrome	la carga de cromo	*lah 'kahr-gah deh 'kroh-moh*
chromium	el cromo	*ehl 'kroh-moh*
coal	el carbón	*ehl kahr-'bohn*
coil	el serpentín	*ehl sehr-pehn-'teen*
cold rolling	el laminado en frío	*ehl lah-mee-'nah-doh ehn 'free-oh*
continuous caster	el laminador continuo	*ehl lah-mee-nah-'dohr kohn-'tee-noo-oh*
conveyor	el transportador	*ehl trahns-pohr-tah-'dohr*
conveyor belt	la correa transportadora	*lah koh-'rreh-ah trans-pohr-tah-'doh-rah*
copper	el cobre	*ehl 'koh-breh*
crucible	el crisol	*ehl kree-'sohl*
cupola	el horno de ladrillo	*ehl 'ohr-noh deh lah-'dree-yoh*
electric arc furnace	el horno de arco voltaíco	*ehl 'ohr-noh deh 'ahr-koh bohl-tah-'ee-koh*
electrolytic process	el proceso electrolítico	*ehl proh-'seh-soh eh-lehk-troh-'lee-tee-koh*
ferroalloys	las ferroaleaciones	*lahs feh-rroh-ah-leh-ah-see-'oh-nehs*
finished products	los productos terminados	*lohs proh-'dook-tohs tehr-mee-'nah-dohs*
finishing mill	la fábrica de terminación	*lah 'fah-bree-kah deh tehr-mee-nah-see-'ohn*

flats products	las planchuelas rectangulares de hierro o acero	*lahs plahn-choo'eh-lahs rehk-tahn-goo-'lah-rehs deh 'yeh-roh o ah-'seh-roh*
foundry	la fundición	*lah foon-dee-see-'ohn*
furnace	el horno	*ehl 'ohr-noh*
galvanizing	el galvanizado	*gahl-bah-nee-'sah-doh*
grinding	el molido, el esmerilaje	*ehl moh-'lee-doh, ehl ehs-meh-ree-'lah-heh*
hardness	la dureza	*lah doo-'reh-sah*
heat	el calor	*ehl kah-'lohr*
hot rolling	el laminado en caliente	*ehl lah-mee-'nah-doh ehn kah-lee-'ehn-teh*
induction furnace	el horno de inducción	*ehl 'ohr-noh deh een-dook-see-'ohn*
ingot mold	la lingotera	*lah leen-goh-'teh-rah*
ingots	los lingotes	*lohs leen-'goh-tehs*
iron ore	el mineral de hierro	*ehl mee-neh-'rahl deh 'yeh-roh*
license plates	las placas	*lahs plah-kahs*
limestone	la piedra caliza	*lah pee-'eh-drah kah-'lee-sah*
long product	las planchas rectangulares usadas para la manufactura	*lahs 'plahn-chahs rehk-tahn-goo-'lah-rehs oo-'sah-dahs 'pah-rah lah mah-noo-fahk-'too-rah*
manganese ore	el mineral de manganeso	*ehl mee-neh-'rahl deh mahn-gah-'neh-soh*
ore	el mineral	*ehl mee-neh-'rahl*
pickling	la limpieza con baño químico	*lah leem-pee-'eh-sah kohn 'bah-nyoh 'kee-mee-koh*
pig iron	el lingote de hierro	*ehl leen-'goh-teh deh 'yeh-roh*
pipes and tubes	los tubos y las cañerías	*lohs 'too-bohs ee lahs kah-'nyeh-'ree-ahs*
plate	la plancha, la lámina	*lah 'plahn-chah, lah 'lah-mee-nah*
powder	la pólvora	*lah 'pohl-boh-rah*
pressure	la presión	*lah preh-see-'ohn*
quench (v)	templar	*tehm-'plahr*

rebars	los refuerzos de acero	*lohs reh-'fwehr-sohs deh ah-'seh-roh*
rod	la varilla	*lah bah-'ree-yah*
rolling mill	el taller de laminación	*ehl tah-'yehr deh lah-mee-nah-see-'ohn*
scale	la báscula	*lah 'bahs-koo-lah*
scrap	el deshecho	*ehl deehs-'eh-choh*
semis	los productos semitermina-dos de acero o hierro	*lohs proh-'dook-tohs seh-mee-tehr-mee-'nah-dohs deh ah-'seh-roh oh 'yeh-roh*
sheets	las hojas	*lahs 'oh-hahs*
slabs	las placas, las lozas	*lahs 'plah-kahs, lahs 'loh-sahs*
specialty steels	los aceros especializados	*lohs ah-'seh-rohs eh-speh-see-ah-lee-'sah-dohs*
stainless steel	el acero inoxidable	*ehl ah-'seh-roh een-ohk-see-'dah-bleh*
steel mill	el taller siderúrgico	*ehl tah-'yehr see-deh-'roor-hee-koh*
structural shapes	el hierro perfilado	*ehl 'yeh-roh pehr-fee-'lah-doh*
super alloys	las superaleaciones	*lahs soo-pehr-ah-leh-ah-see-'oh-nehs*
toughness	la tenacidad	*lah teh-nah-see-'dahd*
vacuum melting furnace	el horno de fusión al vacío	*ehl 'ohr-noh deh foo-see-'ohn ahl bah-'see-oh*
wire	el alambre, el cable	*ehl ah-lamb-breh, ehl 'kah-bleh*

Spanish to English

acero (m) al carbono	*ehl ah-'seh-roh ahl kahr-'boh-noh*	carbon steel
acero inoxidable	*ehl ah-'seh-roh een-ohk-see-'dah-bleh*	stainless steel
aceros (mpl) especializados	*lohs ah-'seh-rohs eh-speh-see-ah-lee-'sah-dohs*	specialty steels
alambre (m)	*ehl ah-lahm-breh*	wire
aleación (f) de acero	*lah ah-leh-ah-see-'ohn deh ah-'seh-roh*	alloy steel

alto horno (m)	ehl 'ahl-toh 'ohr-noh	blast furnace
barras (fpl)	lahs 'bah-rrahs	bars
báscula (f)	lah 'bahs-koo-lah	scale
calor (m)	ehl kah-'lohr	heat
carbón (m)	ehl kahr-'bohn	coal
carga (f) de cromo	lah 'kahr-gah deh 'kroh-moh	charge chrome
cobre (m)	ehl 'koh-breh	copper
correa (f) transportadora	lah koh-'rreh-ah trans-pohr-tah-'doh-rah	conveyor belt
crisol (m)	ehl kree-'sohl	crucible
cromo (m)	ehl 'kroh-moh	chromium
deshecho (m)	ehl deehs-'eh-choh	scrap
dureza (f)	lah do-'reh-sah	hardness
esmerilaje (m)	ehl ehs-meh-ree-'lah-heh	grinding
fábrica (f) de terminación	lah 'fah-bree-kah deh tehr-mee-nah-see-'ohn	finishing mill
ferroaleaciones (fpl)	lahs feh-rroh-ah-leh-ah-see-'oh-nehs	ferroalloys
fundición (f)	lah foon-dee-see-'ohn	foundry
galvanizado (m)	ehl gahl-bah-nee-'sah-doh	galvanizing
hierro (m) fundido	ehl 'yeh-rroh foon-'dee-doh	cast iron
hierro perfilado	ehl 'yeh-roh pehr-fee-'lah-doh	structural shapes
hojas (fpl)	lahs 'oh-hahs	sheets
horno (m)	ehl 'ohr-noh	furnace
horno de arco voltaico	ehl 'ohr-noh deh 'ahr-koh bohl-'tah-ee-koh	electric arc furnace
horno de fusión al vacío	ehl 'ohr-noh deh foo-see-'ohn ahl bah-'see-oh	vacuum melting furnace
horno de inducción	ehl 'ohr-noh deh een-dook-see-'ohn	induction furnace
horno de ladrillo	ehl 'ohr-noh deh lah-'dree-yoh	cupola
lámina (f)	lah 'lah-mee-nah	plate
laminado (m) en caliente	ehl lah-mee-'nah-doh ehn kah-lee-'ehn-teh	hot rolling

laminado en frío	*ehl lah-mee-'nah-doh ehn 'free-oh*	cold rolling
laminador (m) continuo	*ehl lah-mee-nah-'dohr kohn-'tee-noo-oh*	continuous caster
limpieza (f) con baño químico	*lah leem-pee-'eh-sah kohn 'bah-nyoh 'kee-mee-koh*	pickling
lingote de hierro (m)	*ehl leen-'goh-teh deh 'yeh-roh*	pig iron
lingotera (f)	*lah leen-goh-'teh-rah*	ingot mold
lingotes (mpl)	*lohs leen-'goh-tehs*	ingots
lingotes	*lohs leen-'goh-tehs*	billets
lozas (fpl)	*lahs 'loh-sahs*	slabs
mineral (m)	*ehl mee-neh-'rahl*	ore
mineral de hierro	*ehl mee-neh-'rahl deh 'yeh-roh*	iron ore
mineral de manganeso	*ehl mee-neh-'rahl deh mahn-gah-'neh-soh*	manganese ore
piedra (f) caliza	*lah pee-'eh-drah kah-'lee-sah*	limestone
placas (fpl)	*lahs plah-kahs*	license plates
plancha (f)	*lah 'plahn-chah*	plate
planchas (fpl) rectangulares usadas para la manufactura	*lahs 'plahn-chahs rehk-tahn-goo-'lah-rehs oo-'sah-dahs 'pah-rah- lah mah-noo-fahk-'too-rah*	long product
planchuelas (fpl) rectangulares de hierro o acero	*lahs plah-choo-'eh-lahs rehk-tahn-goo-'lah-rehs deh 'yeh-roh o ah-'seh-roh*	flats products
pólvora (f)	*lah 'pohl-boh-rah*	powder
presión (f)	*lah preh-see-'ohn*	pressure
proceso electrolítico (m)	*ehl proh-'seh-soh eh-lehk-troh-'lee-tee-koh*	electrolytic process
productos (mpl) semiterminados de acero o hierro	*lohs proh-'dook-tohs seh-mee-tehr-mee-'nah-dohs deh ah-'seh-roh oh 'yeh-roh*	semis
productos terminados	*lohs proh-'dook-tohs tehr-mee-'nah-dohs*	finished products
recocido (m)	*ehl reh-koh-'hee-doh*	annealing

refuerzos (mpl) de acero	*lohs reh-'fwehr-sohs deh ah-'seh-roh*	rebars
serpentín (m)	*ehl sehr-pehn-'teen*	coil
superaleaciones (fpl)	*lahs soo-pehr-ah-leh-ah-see-'oh-nehs*	super alloys
taller (m) de laminación	*ehl tah-'yehr deh lah-mee-nah-see-'ohn*	rolling mill
taller siderúrgico	*ehl tah-'yehr see-deh-'roor-hee-koh*	steel mill
templar	*tehm-'plahr*	quench (v)
tenacidad (f)	*lah teh-nah-see-'dahd*	toughness
transportador (m)	*ehl trahns-pohr-tah-'dohr*	conveyor
tubos (mpl) y cañerías (fpl)	*lohs 'too-bohs ee lahs kah-'nyeh-'ree-ahs*	pipes and tubes
varilla (f)	*lah bah-'ree-yah*	rod

LEATHER GOODS

English to Spanish

attaché case	el maletín, la cartera de papeles	*ehl mah-leh-'teen, lah kahr-'teh-rah deh pah-'peh-lehs*
beaver	el castor	*ehl kahs-'tohr*
belt	el cinturón, el cinto	*ehl seen-too-'rohn, ehl 'seen-toh*
billfold	el billetero, la cartera	*ehl bee-yeh-'teh-roh, lah kahr-'teh-rah*
blotter	el secante	*ehl seh-'kahn-teh*
boot shop	la zapatería	*lah sah-pah-teh-'ree-ah*
bootmaker	el zapatero	*ehl sah-pah-'teh-roh*
boots	las botas	*lahs 'boh-tahs*
briefcase	la cartera, el portafolio	*lah kahr-'teh-rah, ehl pohr-tah-'foh-lee-oh*
calfskin	el cuero de becerro	*ehl 'kweh-roh deh beh-'seh-rroh*
card case	el tarjetero	*ehl tahr-heh-'teh-roh*
cigarette case	la pitillera	*lah pee-tee-'yeh-rah*
cowhide	el cuero de vaca	*ehl 'kweh-roh deh 'bah-kah*
dye (v)	teñir	*teh-'nyeer*
eyeglass case	el estuche de espejuelos, el estuche de gafas	*ehl eh-'stoo-cheh deh ehs-'pweh-lohs, ehl eh-'stoo-cheh deh gah-fahs*
fox	la zorra	*lah 'soh-rrah*
garment bag	la bolsa para ropa, la maleta para ropa	*lah 'bohl-sah 'pah-rah 'roh-pah, lah mah-'leh-tah 'pah-rah 'roh-pah*
gloves	los guantes	*lohs 'gwahn-tehs*
handbag	el bolso de mano, la cartera de mano	*ehl 'bohl-soh deh 'mah-noh, lah kahr-'teh-rah deh 'mah-noh*
holster (gun)	la pistolera, la funda de pistola	*lah pees-toh-'leh-rah, lah 'foon-dah deh pees-'toh-lah*
key case	la funda de las llaves	*lah 'foon-dah deh lahs 'yah-behs*

kidskin	la cabritilla	*lah kah-bree-'tee-yah*
lamb	el cordero	*ehl kohr-'deh-roh*
leather	la piel, el cuero	*lah pee-'ehl, ehl 'kweh-roh*
leather goods	los artículos de piel, los artículos de cuero	*lohs ahr-'tee-koo-lohs deh pee-'ehl, lohs ahr-'tee-koo-lohs deh 'kweh-roh*
leather jacket	la chaqueta de piel, la chaqueta de cuero	*lah cha-'keh-tah deh pee'ehl, lah chah-'keh-tah deh 'kweh-roh*
lizard skin	la piel de lagarto	*la pee-'ehl deh lah-'gahr-toh*
makeup case	el estuche de maquillaje, la maleta de maquillaje	*ehl ehs-'too-cheh deh mah-kee-'yah-heh, lah mah-'leh-tah deh mah-kee-'yah-heh*
manicuring kit	el estuche de manicura, el estuche de arreglarse las uñas	*ehl ehs-'too-cheh deh mah-nee-'koo-rah, ehl ehs-'too-cheh deh ah-rreh-'glahr-seh lahs 'oo-nyahs*
mink	el visón	*ehl bee-'sohn*
Moroccan leather	la piel marroquí	*lah pee-'ehl mah-rroh-'kee*
ostrich skin	la piel de avestruz	*lah pee'ehl deh ah-beh-'stroos*
otter	la nutria	*lah 'noo-tree-ah*
paper holder	la carpeta	*lah kahr-'peh-tah*
passport case	la cartera del pasaporte	*lah kahr-'teh-rah dehl pah-sah-'pohr-teh*
pigskin	la piel de cerdo	*lak pee-'ehl deh 'sehr-doh*
portfolio	la cartera	*lah kahr-'teh-rah*
purse	el monedero, el bolso	*ehl moh-neh-'deh-roh, ehl 'bohl-soh*
rabbit	el conejo	*ehl koh-'neh-hoh*
raccoon	el mapache	*ehl mah-'pah-cheh*
sable	la marta	*lah 'mahr-tah*
saddle	la silla de montar	*lah 'see-yah deh mohn-'tahr*
scissor case	el estuche de tijeras	*ehl ehs-'too-cheh deh tee-'heh-rahs*
scrap	el deshecho	*ehl deehs-'eh-choh*
sealskin	la piel de foca	*lah pee'ehl deh 'foh-kah*

slippers	las zapatillas	*lahs sah-pah-'tee-yahs*
snakeskin	la piel de culebra, la piel de serpiente	*lah pee-'ehl deh koo-'leh-brah, lah pee-'ehl deh sehr-pee-'ehn-teh*
suede	la cabritilla, el ante, la gamuza	*lah kah-bree-'tee-ya, ehl 'ahn-teh, lah gah-'moo-sah*
suede jacket	la chaqueta de cabritilla, la chaqueta de ante	*lah chah-'keh-tah deh kah-bree-'tee-yah, lah chah-'keh-tah deh 'ahn-teh*
suitcase	la maleta	*lah mah-'leh-tah*
tan (v)	curtir, broncear	*koor-'teer, brohn-seh-'ahr*
tanner	el curtidor	*ehl koor-tee-'dohr*
tannery	la curtiduría, la tenería	*lah koor-tee-doo-'ree-ah, lah teh-neh-'ree-ah*
toiletry kit	el estuche de artículos de tocador	*ehl ehs-'too-cheh deh ahr-'tee-koo-lohs deh toh-kah-'dohr*
tote bag	la mochila	*lah moh-'cheh-yah*
trunk	el baúl	*ehl bah-'ool*
watch strap	la correa de reloj	*lah koh-'rreh-ah deh re-'loh*
whip	el látigo, la fusta	*ehl 'lah-tee-goh, lah 'foos-tah*

Spanish to English

ante (m)	*ehl 'ahn-teh*	suede
artículos de cuero (mpl)	*lohs ahr-'tee-koo-lohs deh 'kweh-roh*	leather goods
baúl (m)	*ehl bah-'ool*	trunk
billetero (m)	*ehl bee-yeh-'teh-roh*	billfold
bolsa (f) para ropa	*lah 'bohl-sah 'pah-rah 'roh-pah*	garment bag
bolso (m)	*ehl 'bohl-soh*	purse
bolso de mano	*ehl 'bohl-soh deh 'mah-noh*	handbag
botas (fpl)	*lahs boh-'tahs*	boots
broncear	*brohn-seh-'ahr*	tan (v)
cabritilla (f)	*lah kah-bree-'tee-yah*	kidskin, suede
carpeta (f)	*lah kahr-'peh-tah*	paper holder

cartera (f)	*lah kahr-'teh-rah*	billfold, briefcase, portfolio
cartera de mano	*lah kahr-'teh-rah deh 'mah-noh*	handbag
cartera de papeles	*lah kahr-'teh-rah deh pah-'pehl-ehs*	attaché case
cartera del pasaporte	*lah kahr-'teh-rah dehl pah-sah-'pohr-teh*	passport case
castor (m)	*ehl kahs-'tohr*	beaver
conejo (m)	*ehl koh-'neh-hoh*	rabbit
cordero (m)	*ehl kohr-'deh-roh*	lamb
correa (f) de reloj	*lah koh-'rreh-ah*	watch strap
cuero (m)	*ehl 'kweh-roh*	cowhide, leather
cuero de becerro	*ehl 'kweh-roh deh beh-seh-rroh*	calfskin
cuero de vaca	*ehl 'kweh-roh deh 'bah-kah*	cowhide
curtidor (m)	*ehl koor-tee-'dohr*	tanner
curtiduría (f)	*lah koor-tee-doo-'ree-ah*	tannery
curtir	*koor-'teer*	tan (v)
chaqueta (f) de ante	*lah chah-'keh-tah deh 'ahn-teh*	suede jacket
chaqueta de cabritilla	*lah chah-'keh-tah deh kah-bree-'ee-yah*	suede jacket
chaqueta de cuero	*lah chah-'keh-tah deh 'kweh-roh*	leather jacket
estuche (m) de artículos de tocador	*ehl ehs-'too-cheh deh ahr-'tee-koo-lohs deh toh-kah-'dohr*	toiletry kit
estuche de espejuelos	*ehl eh-'stoo-cheh deh ehs-peh-'weh-lohs*	eyeglass case
estuche de gafas	*ehl eh-'stoo-cheh deh 'gah-fahs*	eyeglass case
estuche de manicura	*ehl eh-'stoo-cheh deh mah-nee-'koo-rah*	manicuring kit
estuche de tijeras	*ehl ehs-too-cheh deh tee-'heh-rahs*	scissor case
funda (f) de las llaves	*lah 'foon-dah deh lahs 'yah-behs*	bkey case
funda de pistola (f)	*lah 'foon-dah deh pees-'toh-lah*	holster (gun)

fusta (f)	*lah 'foos-tah*	whip
guantes (mpl)	*lohs 'gwahn-tehs*	gloves
látigo (m)	*ehl 'lah-tee-goh*	whip
maleta (f)	*lah mah-'leh-tah*	suitcase
maleta de maquillaje	*lah mah-'leh-tah deh mah-kee-'yah-heh*	makeup case
maleta para ropa	*lah mah-'leh-tah pah-rah 'roh-pah*	garment bag
mapache (m)	*ehl mah-'pah-cheh*	raccoon
marta (f)	*lah 'mahr-tah*	sable
mochila (f)	*lah moh-'cheh-lah*	tote bag
monedero (m)	*ehl moh-neh-'deh-roh*	purse
piel de avestruz (m)	*lah pee'ehl deh ah-beh-stroos*	ostrich skin
piel de cerdo	*lah pee-'ehl deh sehr-doh*	pigskin
piel de culebra	*lah pee-'ehl deh koo-'leh-brah*	snakeskin
piel de foca	*lah pee-'ehl deh 'foh-kah*	sealskin
piel de lagarto	*lah pee-'ehl deh lah-'gahr-toh*	lizard skin
piel de serpiente	*lah pee-'ehl deh sehr-pee-'ehn-teh*	snakeskin
piel marroquí	*lah pee-'ehl mah-rroh-'kee*	Moroccan leather
pistolera (f)	*lah pees-toh-'leh-rah*	holster
pitillera (f)	*lah pee-tee-'yeh-rah*	cigarette case
portafolio (m)	*ehl pohr-tah-'foh-lee-oh*	briefcase
secante (m)	*ehl seh-'kahn-teh*	blotter
silla (m) de montar	*lah 'see-yah deh mohn-'tahr*	saddle
tarjetero (m)	*ehl tahr-heh-'teh-roh*	card case
tenería (f)	*lah teh-neh-'ree-ah*	tannery
teñir	*teh-'nyeer*	dye (v)
zapatería (f)	*lah sah-pah-teh-ree-ah*	boot shop
zapatero	*sah-pah-'teh-ro*	bootmaker
zapatillas (fpl)	*lahs sah-pah-tee-yahs*	slippers
zorra (f)	*lah 'soh-rrah*	fox

MOTOR VEHICLES

English to Spanish

air filter	el filtro de aire	*ehl 'feel-troh deh 'ah-ee-reh*
assembly line	la línea de ensamblaje	*lah 'lee-neh-ah deh ehn-sahm-'blah-heh*
automatic gearshift	el cambio automático de velocidades	*ehl 'kahm-bee-oh ow-toh-'mah-tee-koh deh beh-loh-see-'dah-dehs*
automotive worker	el obrero automotriz	*ehl oh-'breh-roh ow-toh-moh-'trees*
belt	la correa	*lah koh-'rreh-ah*
body (automobile)	el cuerpo	*ehl 'kwehr-poh*
bodywork	la carrocería	*lah kah-rroh-seh-'ree-ah*
brake	los frenos	*lohs 'freh-nohs*
brake pedal	el pedal de freno	*ehl peh-'dahl deh 'freh-noh*
bumper	el parachoque, la defensa	*ehl pah-rah-'choh-keh, lah deh-'fehn-sah*
camshaft	el eje de leva	*ehl 'eh-heh deh 'leh-bah*
car	el carro	*ehl 'kah-rroh*
chassis	el bastidor	*ehl 'bah-stee-dohr*
clutch	el embrague	*ehl ehm-'brah-geh*
clutch pedal	el pedal de embrague	*ehl peh-'dahl deh ehm-'brah-gue*
connecting rod	la biela	*lah bee-'eh-lah*
crankshaft	el cigüeñal	*ehl see-gweh-'nyahl*
defroster	el descongelador	*ehl dehs-kohn-heh-lah-'dohr*
designer	el diseñador	*ehl dee-seh-nyah-'dohr*
distributor	el distribuidor	*ehl dees-tree-boo-ee-'dohr*
driver	el conductor, el chofer	*ehl kohn-dook-'tohr, ehl choh-'fehr*
engine	el motor	*ehl moh-'tohr*
engineer	el ingeniero	*ehl een-hen-nee-'eh-roh*
exhaust	el escape	*ehl ehs-'kah-peh*
fender	el guardabarros, el guardafangos	*ehl gwahr-dah-'bah-rrohs, ehl gwar-dah-'fahn-gohs*

four-cylinder engine	el motor de cuatro cilíndros	*ehl moh-'tohr deh 'kwah-troh see-'leen-drohs*
front-wheel drive	la tracción delantera	*lah trahk-see-'ohn*
gas consumption	el consumo de gasolina	*ehl kohn-'soo-moh deh gah-soh-'lee-nah*
gas pedal	el pedal de gasolina, el acelerador	*ehl peh-'dahl deh gah-soh-'lee-nah, ehl ah-seh-leh-rah-'dohr*
gasoline tank	el tanque de gasolina	*ehl 'tahn-keh deh gah-soh-'lee-nah*
gearshift	el cambio de velocidades	*ehl 'kahm-bee-oh deh beh-loh-see-'dah-dehs*
generator	el generador	*ehl heh-neh-rah-'dohr*
grille	la rejilla del radiador	*lah reh-'hee-yah dehl rah-dee-ah-'dohr*
horsepower	los caballos de fuerza	*lohs kah-'bah-yohs deh 'fwehr-sah*
ignition	la ignición, el encendido	*lah eeg-nee-see-'ohn, ehl ehn-sehn-'dee-doh*
mechanical engineer	el ingeniero mecánico	*ehl een-heh-nee-'eh-roh*
mileage	el millaje, el kilometraje	*ehl mee-'yah-heh, ehl kee-loh-meh-'trah-heh*
odometer	el odómetro	*ehl oh-'doh-meh-troh*
oil filter	el filtro de aceite	*ehl 'feel-troh deh ah-'seh-ee-teh*
oil pump	la bomba de aceite	*lah 'bohm-bah deh ah-'seh-ee-teh*
paint	la pintura	*lah peen-'too-rah*
pinion	el piñón	*ehl pee-'nyohn*
power steering	la dirección neumática	*lah dee-rehk-see-'ohn neh-oo-'mah-tee-kah*
propulsion	la propulsión	*lah proh-pool-see-'ohn*
prototype	el prototipo	*ehl proh-toh-'tee-poh*
radial tire	el neumático radial	*ehl neh-oo-'mah-tee-koh rah-dee-'ahl*
rear axle	el eje trasero	*ehl 'eh-heh trah-'seh-roh*
ring	el aro	*ehl 'ah-roh*
robot	el robot, el autómata	*ehl roh-'boht, ehl ow-'toh-mah-tah*

seat	el asiento	*ehl ah-see-'ehn-toh*
sedan	el sedán	*ehl seh-'dahn*
shock absorber	el amortiguador	*ehl ah-mohr-tee-gwah-'dohr*
six-cylinder engine	el motor de seis cilindros	*ehl moh-'tohr deh 'seh-ees see-'leen-drohs*
spare tire	la rueda de repuesta	*lah roo-'eh-dah deh reh-'pweh-stah*
spark plug	la bujía	*lah boo-'hee-ah*
speedometer	el velocímetro	*ehl beh-loh-'see-meh-troh*
spring	el muelle	*ehl 'mweh-yeh*
starter	el arranque	*ehl ah-'rrahn-keh*
steering	la conducción, el manejo	*lah kohn-dook-see-'ohn, ehl mah-'neh-hoh*
steering wheel	el volante	*ehl boh-'lahn-teh*
suspension	la suspensión	*lah soos-pehn-see-'ohn*
tire	el neumático	*ehl neh-oo-'mah-tee-koh*
torque	el momento de torsión	*ehl moh-'mehn-toh deh tohr-see-'ohn*
V8 engine	el motor V8	*ehl moh-'tohr V8*
valve	la válvula	*lah 'bahl-boo-lah*
water pump	la bomba de agua	*lah 'bohm-bah deh 'ah-gwah*
wheel	la rueda	*lah roo-'eh-dah*
windshield	el parabrisas	*ehl pah-rah-'bree-sahs*

Spanish to English

acelerador (m)	*ehl ah-seh-leh-rah-'dohr*	gas pedal
amortiguador (m)	*ehl ah-mohr-tee-gwah-'dohr*	shock absorber
aro (m)	*ehl 'ah-roh*	ring
arranque (m)	*ehl ah-'rrahn-keh*	starter
asiento (m)	*ehl ah-see-'ehn-toh*	seat
autómata (m)	*ehl ow-'toh-mah-tah*	robot
bastidor (m)	*ehl 'bah-stee-dohr*	chassis
biela (f)	*lah bee-'eh-lah*	connecting rod
bomba (f) de aceite	*lah 'bohm-bah deh ah-'seh-ee-teh*	oil pump

bomba de agua	*lah 'bohm-bah deh 'ah-gwah*	water pump
bujía (f)	*lah boo-'hee-ah*	spark plug
caballos de fuerza (mpl)	*lohs kah-'bah-yohs deh 'fwehr-sah*	horsepower
cambio (m) automático de velocidades	*ehl 'kahm-bee-oh ow-toh-'mah-tee-koh deh beh-loh-see-'dah-dehs*	automatic gearshift
cambio de velocidades	*ehl 'kahm-bee-oh deh beh-loh-see-'dah-dehs*	gearshift
carro (m)	*ehl 'kah-rroh*	car
carrocería (f)	*lah kah-rro-seh-ree-ah*	bodywork
cigüeñal (m)	*ehl see-gweh-'nyahl*	crankshaft
conducción (f)	*lah kohn-dook-see-'ohn*	steering
conductor (m)	*ehl kohn-dook-'tohr*	driver
consumo de gasolina (m)	*ehl kohn-'soo-moh deh gah-soh-l'ee-nah*	gas consumption
correa (f)	*lah koh-'rreh-ah*	belt (automobile)
chófer (m)	*ehl choh-'fehr*	driver
cuerpo (m)	*ehl 'kwehr-poh*	body (automobile)
descongelador (m)	*ehl dehs-kohn-heh-lah-'dohr*	defroster
dirección neumática	*lah dee-rehk-see-ohn neh-oo-mah-tee-kah*	power steering
distribuidor (m)	*ehl dees-tree-boo-ee-'dohr*	distributor
eje (m) de leva	*ehl 'eh-heh deh 'leh-bah*	camshaft
eje trasero	*ehl 'eh-heh trah-'seh-roh*	rear axle
embrague (m)	*ehl ehm-'brah-gee*	clutch
encendido (m)	*ehl ehn-sehn-'dee-doh*	ignition
escape (m)	*ehl ehs-'kah-peh*	exhaust
filtro (m) de aceite	*ehl 'feel-troh deh ah-'seh-ee-teh*	oil filter
filtro de aire	*ehl 'feel-troh deh 'ah-ee-reh*	air filter
frenos (mpl)	*lohs 'freh-nohs*	brake
generador (m)	*ehl heh-neh-rah-'dohr*	generator
ingeniero mecánico	*ehl een-heh-nee-'eh-roh*	mechanical engineer
línea (f) de ensamblaje	*lah 'lee-neh-ah deh ehn-sahm-'blah-heh*	assembly line

manejo (m)	*ehl mah-'neh-hoh*	steering
millaje (m)	*ehl mee-'yah-heh*	mileage
momento (m) de torsión	*ehl moh-'mehn-toh deh tohr-see-'ohn*	torque
motor (m)	*ehl moh-'tohr*	engine
motor de cuatro cilindros	*ehl moh-'tohr deh 'kwah-troh see-'leen-drohs*	four-cylinder engine
motor de seis cilindros	*ehl moh-'tohr deh 'seh-ees see-'leen-drohs*	six-cylinder engine
motor V8	*ehl moh-'tohr beh-'oh-choh*	V8 engine
muelle (m)	*ehl 'mweh-yeh*	spring
neumático (m)	*ehl neh-oo-'mah-tee-koh*	tire (Spain and South America)
neumático radial (m)	*ehl neh-oo-'mah-tee-koh rah-dee-'ahl*	radial tire (Spain and South America)
obrero (m) automotriz	*ehl oh-'breh-roh ow-toh-moh-'trees*	automotive worker
odómetro (m)	*ehl oh-'doh-meh-troh*	odometer
parabrisas (m)	*ehl pah-rah-'bree-sahs*	windshield
parachoques (m)	*ehl pah-rah-'choh-kehs*	bumper
pedal (m) de embrague	*ehl peh-'dahl deh ehm-'brah-gue*	clutch pedal
pedal de freno	*ehl peh-'dahl deh 'freh-noh*	brake pedal
pedal de gasolina	*ehl peh-'dahl deh gah-soh-'lee-nah*	gas pedal
piñón (m)	*ehl pee-'nyohn*	pinion
pintura (f)	*lah peen-'too-rah*	paint
propulsión (f)	*lah proh-pool-see-'ohn*	propulsion
prototipo (m)	*ehl proh-toh-'tee-poh*	prototype
rejilla (f) del radiador	*lah reh-'hee-yah dehl rah-dee-ah-'dohr*	grille
rueda (f)	*lah roo-'eh-dah*	wheel
rueda de repuesto	*lah roo-'eh-dah deh reh-'pweh-stoh*	spare tire
sedán (m)	*ehl seh-'dahn*	sedan
suspensión (f)	*lah soos-pehn-see-'ohn*	suspension
tanque (m) de gasolina	*ehl 'tahn-keh deh gah-soh-'lee-nah*	gasoline tank

tracción (f) delantera	*lah trahk-see-'ohn deh-lahn-'teh-rah*	front-wheel drive
válvula (f)	*lah 'bahl-boo-lah*	valve
velocímetro (m)	*ehl beh-loh-'see-meh-troh*	speedometer
volante (m)	*ehl boh-'lahn-teh*	steering wheel

PETROLEUM

English to Spanish

abundant (adj)	abundante	*ehl ah-boon-'dahn-teh*
access	el acceso	*ehl ahk-'seh-soh*
affiliate	el afiliado	*ehl ah-fee-lee-'ah-doh*
affiliate (local)	el afiliado local	*ehl ah-fee-lee-'ah-doh loh-'kahl*
affiliate (international)	el afiliado internacional	*ehl ah-fee-lee-'ah-doh een-tehr-nah-see-oh-'nahl*
air compressor	el compresor del aire	*ehl kohm-preh-'sohr dehl 'ah-ee-reh*
bank	el banco	*ehl 'bahn-koh*
bank (commercial)	el banco comercial	*ehl 'bahn-koh koh-mehr-see-'ahl*
bank (investment)	el banco inversionista	*ehl 'bahn-koh een-behr-see-oh-'nees-tah*
barrier	la barrera	*lah bah-'rreh-rah*
basin	la cuenca	*lah 'kwehn-kah*
blockage	el bloqueo	*ehl bloh-'keh-oh*
capacity	la capacidad de refinación	*lah kah-pah-see-'dahd deh reh-fee-nah-see-'ohn*
cheap	el barato	*ehl bah-'rah-toh*
company	la compañía	*lah kohm-pah-'nyee-ah*
company (nationalized)	la compañía nacionalizada	*lah kohm-pah-'nyee-ah nah-see-oh-nah-lee-'sah-dah*
company (state-owned)	la compañía estatal	*lah kohm-pah-'nyee-ah eh-stah-'tahl*
company (privately-owned)	la compañía privada	*lah kohm-pah-'nyee-ah pree-'bah-dah*
company (privatized)	la compañía privatizada	*lah kohm-pah-'nyee-ah pree-'bah-tee-'sah-dah*
consuming center	el centro de consumo	*ehl 'sehn-troh deh kohn-'soo-moh*
consumption reduction	la reducción en el consumo	*lah reh-dook-see-'ohn ehn ehl kohn-'soo-moh*
crane	la grúa	*lah 'groo-ah*

crane (revolving)	la grúa giratoria	*lah 'groo-ah hee-rah-'toh-ree-ah*
crude oil	el crudo, el bruto, el aceite bruto, el petróleo crudo	*ehl 'kroo-doh, ehl 'broo-toh, ehl ah-'see-ee-teh 'broo-toh, ehl peh-'troh-leh-oh 'kroo-doh*
crude oil (excess)	el crudo en exceso	*ehl 'kroo-doh ehn ehk-'seh-soh*
deck	la cubierta	*lah koo-bee-'ehr-tah*
deck (lower)	la cubierta inferior	*lah koo-bee-'ehr-tah een-feh-ree-'ohr*
deck (middle)	la cubierta intermedia	*lah koo-bee-'ehr-tah een-tehr-'mee-dee-ah*
deck (top, main)	la cubierta superior	*lah koo-bee-'ehr-tah soo-peh-ree-'ohr*
derrick	la torre de perforación (f)	*lah 'toh-rreh deh pehr-foh-rah-see-'ohn*
develop (v)	desarrollar	*dehs-ah-rroh-'yahr*
developed (adj)	desarrollado	*dehs-ah-rroh-'yah-doh*
developing (adj)	en vías de desarrollo	*ehn 'bee-ahs deh dehs-ah-'rroh-yoh*
distillation plant	la instalación de destilación	*lah een-stah-lah-see-'ohn deh dehs-tee-lah-see-'ohn*
distribution	la distribución	*lah dees-tree-boo-see-'ohn*
drilling rig	la plataforma de perforación	*lah plah-tah-'fohr-mah deh pehr-foh-rah-see-'ohn*
elevator	el montecargas (m)	*ehl mohn-teh-'kahr-gahs*
elevator shaft	la caja del ascensor	*lah 'kah-hah dehl ah-sehn-'sohr*
energy	la energía	*lah eh-nehr-'hee-ah*
energy (mix)	la mezcla de recursos de energía	*lah 'mehs-klah deh reh-'koor-sohs deh eh-nehr-'hee-ah*
energy sources	las fuentes (f) de energía	*lahs 'fwehn-tehs deh eh-nehr-'hee-ah*
entitlements	los derechos económicos	*lohs deh-'reh-chohs eh-koh-'noh-mee-kohs*
exhaust	el escape (m), la descarga	*ehl eh-'skah-peh, lah dehs-'kahr-gah*
exhaust (v)	agotar	*ah-goh-'tahr*
exploration	la exploración	*lah ehks-ploh-rah-see-'ohn*

exploration (local)	la exploración doméstica	*lah ehks-ploh-rah-see-'ohn doh-'mehs-tee-kah*
exploration site	el sitio de exploración	*ehl 'see-tee-oh deh ehks-ploh-rah-see-'ohn*
explore	explorar	*ehks-ploh-'rahr*
find (oil)	el descubrimiento de (aceite)	*ehl dehs-koo-bree-mee-'ehn-toh deh ah-'seh-ee-teh*
fuel	el combustible, la gasolina	*ehl kohm-boo-'stee-bleh, lah gah-soh-'lee-nah*
fuel (aviation)	la gasolina de aviación	*lah gah-soh-'lee-nah deh ah-bee-ah-see-'ohn*
fuel (motor)	el combustible para motores	*ehl kohm-boo-'stee-bleh 'pah-rah moh-'toh-rehs*
fueling pit	el foso de abastecimiento de combustibles	*ehl 'foh-soh deh ah-bah-steh-see-mee-'ehn-toh deh kohm-boo-'stee-blehs*
gas	el gas (m)	*ehl gahs*
gas (liquid petroleum)	el gas líquido	*ehl gahs 'lee-kee-doh*
gas (natural)	el gas natural	*ehl gahs nah-too-'rahl*
gasoline (regular)	la gasolina normal	*lah gah-soh-'lee-nah nohr-'mahl*
gasoline (super grade)	la gasolina super	*lah gah-soh-'lee-nah soo-'pehr*
lifeboat	el bote salvavidas (m)	*ehl 'boh-teh sahl-bah-'bee-dahs*
locate	localizar, descubrir	*loh-kah-lee-'sahr, dehs-koo-'breer*
multinational oil company (MNOC)	la compañía petrolera multi-nacional	*lah kohm-pah-'nyee-ah peh-troh-'leh-rah mool-tee-nah-see-oh-'nahl*
offshore drilling	la perforación a poca distan-cia de la costa	*lah pehr-foh-rah-see-'ohn ah 'poh-kah dees-'tahn-see-ah deh lah 'koh-stah*
oil (diesel)	el carburante diesel	*ehl kahr-boo-'rahn-teh dee-eh-'sehl*
oil (heavy fuel)	el fuel-oil pesado	*ehl foo-'ehl oh-'yool peh-'sah-doh*
oil (light fuel) fuel-oil (aceite combustible) ligero	el fuel-oil (aceite com-bustible) ligero	*ehl foo-'ehl oh-'yeel (ah-'see-ee-teh kohm-boo-'stee-bleh) lee-'heh-roh*

oil (lubricating)	el lubricante para cilindros	*ehl loo-bree-'kahn-teh 'pah-rah see-'leen-drohs*
oil company	la compañía petrolera	*lah kohm-pah-'nee-ah peh-troh-'leh-rah*
oil exporting country	los países exportadores de petróleo	*lohs pah'ee-sehs ehks-pohr-tah-'doh-rehs deh peh-'troh-leh-oh*
oil field	el yacimiento petrolífero	*ehl yah-see-mee-'ehn-toh peh-troh-'lee-feh-roh*
oil importing countries	los países importadores de petróleo	*lohs pah'ee-sehs eem-pohr-tah-'doh-rehs deh peh-'troh-leh-oh*
oil industry	la industria petrolera	*lah een-'doos-tree-ah peh-troh-'leh-rah*
oil industry (indigenous)	la industria petrolera indígena	*lah een-'doos-tree-ah peh-troh-'leh-rah een-'dee-heh-nah*
oil industry (integrated)	la industria petrolera integrada	*lah een-'doos-tree-ah peh-troh-'leh-rah een-teh-'grah-dah*
oil-importing developing company (IODC)	los países importadores de petróleo en vías de desarrollo	*lohs pah'ee-sehs ehks-pohr-tah-'doh-rehs deh peh-'troh-leh-oh ehn 'bee-ahs deh dehs-ah-'rroh-yoh*
Organization of Petroleum-Exporting Countries (OPEC)	la Organización de Países Exportadores de Petróleo (OPEP)	*lah ohr-gah-nee-sah-see-'ohn deh pah-'ee-sehs ehks-pohr-tah-'doh-rehs deh peh-'troh-leh-oh*
output	la producción	*lah proh-dook-see-'ohn*
pipeline	el oleoducto	*ehl oh-leh-oh-'dook-toh*
port facilities	las facilidades portuarias	*lahs fah-see-lee-'dah-dehs pohr-too-'ah-ree-ahs*
pumping station	la estación de bombeo	*lah ehs-tah-see-'ohn deh bohm-'beh-oh*
refinery	la refinería	*lah reh-fee-neh-'ree-ah*
refinery (home-based)	la refinería doméstica	*lah reh-fee-neh-'ree-ah doh-mehs-tee-kah*
refinery (market based)	la refinería localizada en el país del consumidor	*lah reh-fee-neh-'ree-ah loh-kah-lee-'sah-dah ehn ehl pah-'ees dehl kohm-soo-mee-'dohr*

resources	los recursos	*lohs reh-'koor-sohs*
risky (adj)	arriesgado	*ah-rree-ehs-'gah-doh*
sea level	el nivel del mar (m)	*ehl nee-'behl dehl mahr*
seawater	el agua del mar (f)	*ehl 'ah-gwah dehl mahr*
seawater desalination plant	la instalación de climatización	*lah een-stah-lah-see-'ohn deh klee-mah-tee-sah-see-'ohn*
self-sufficient	autosuficiente	*ow-toh-soo-fee-see-'ehn-teh*
service station	la gasolinera	*lah gah-soh-lee-'neh-rah*
size	tamaño	*tah-'mah-nyoh*
source	la fuente (f)	*lah 'fwehn-teh*
specialist	especialista (m/f)	*eh-speh-see-ah-'lees-tah*
specialist (oil industry)	especialista en la industria petrolera	*eh-speh-see-ah-'lees-tah ehn lah een-'doos-tree-ah peh-troh-'leh-rah*
stabilize (v)	estabilizar	*eh-stah-bee-lee-'sahr*
storage facility	la facilidad de almacenamiento	*lah fah-see-lee-'dahd deh ahl-mah-seh-nah-mee-'ehn-toh*
supply	abastecer	*ah-bah-steh-'sehr*
supply (v)	la oferta, el abastecimiento	*lah oh-'fehr-tah, ehl ah-bah-steh-see-mee-'ehn-toh*
tank	el tanque	*ehl 'tahn-keh*
tank (cement storage)	el tanque para el almacenamiento de cemento	*ehl 'tahn-keh 'pah-rah ehl ahl-mah-seh-nah-mee-'ehn-toh deh seh-'mehn-toh*
tank (drinking water)	el tanque para el agua potable	*ehl 'tahn-keh 'pah-rah ehl 'ah-gwah poh-'tah-bleh*
tank (jet fuel)	el tanque de carburante para helicópteros	*ehl 'tahn-keh deh kahr-boo-'rahn-teh 'pah-rah eh-lee-'kohp-teh-rohs*
tank (salt water)	el tanque de reserva para agua salada	*ehl 'tahn-keh deh reh-'sehr-bah 'pah-rah 'ah-gwah sah-'lah-dah*
tanker	el tanquero	*ehl tahn-'keh-roh*
technology	la tecnología	*lah tehk-noh-loh-'hee-ah*
vertical integration	la organización vertical	*lah ohr-gah-nee-sah-see-'ohn behr-tee-'kahl*

Spanish to English

abastecer	*ah-bah-steh-'sehr*	supply (v)
abastecimiento (m)	*ehl ah-bah-steh-see-mee-'ehn-toh*	supply
abundante	*ah-boon-'dahn-teh*	abundant (adj)
acceso (m)	*ehl ahk-'seh-soh*	access
aceite bruto (m)	*ehl ah'see-ee-teh 'broo-toh*	crude oil
afiliado (m)	*ehl ah-fee-lee-'ah-doh*	affiliate
afiliado internacional (m)	*ehl ah-fee-lee-'ah-doh ehl een-tehr-nah-see-oh-'nahl*	affiliate (international)
afiliado local (m)	*ehl ah-fee-lee-'ah-doh ehl loh-'kahl*	affiliate (local)
agotar	*ah-goh-'tahr*	exhaust (v)
agua del mar (m)	*ehl 'ah-gwah dehl mahr*	seawater
arriesgado	*ah-rree-ehs-'gah-doh*	risky (adj)
autosuficiente	*ow-toh-soo-fee-see-'ehn-teh*	self-sufficient
banco (m)	*ehl 'bahn-koh*	bank
banco comercial	*ehl 'bahn-koh koh-mehr-see-'ahl*	bank (commercial)
banco inversionista	*ehl 'bahn-koh een-behr-see-oh-'nees-tah*	bank (investment)
barato	*bah-'rah-toh*	cheap (adj)
barrera (f)	*lah bah-'rreh-rah*	barrier
bloqueo (m)	*ehl bloh-'keh-oh*	blockage
bote salvavidas (m)	*ehl 'boh-teh sahl-bah-'bee-dahs*	lifeboat
bruto (m)	*ehl 'broo-toh*	crude oil
caja del ascensor (f)	*lah 'kah-hah dehl ah-sehn-'sohr*	elevator shaft
capacidad de refinación (f)	*lah kah-pah-see-'dahd deh reh-fee-nah-see-'ohn*	capacity
carburante diesel (m)	*ehl kahr-boo-'rahn-teh dee-'eh-sehl*	oil (diesel)
centro de consumo (m)	*ehl 'sehn-troh deh kohn-'soo-moh*	consuming center
combustible (m)	*ehl kohm-boo-'stee-bleh*	fuel
combustible para motores	*ehl kohm-boo-'stee-bleh 'pah-rah moh-'toh-rehs*	fuel (motor)

compañía (f)	*lah kohm-pah-'nyee-ah*	company
compañía estatal	*lah kohm-pah-'nyee-ah eh-stah-'tahl*	company (state-owned)
compañía nacionalizada	*lah kohm-pah-'nyee-ah nah-see-oh-nah-lee-'sah-dah*	company (nationalized)
compañía petrolera	*lah kohm-pah-'nee-ah peh-troh-'leh-rah*	oil company
compañía petrolera multinacional	*lah kohm-pah-'nyee-ah peh-troh-'leh-rah mool-tee-nah-see-oh-'nahl*	multinational oil company (MNOC)
compañía privada	*lah kohm-pah-'nyee-ah pree-'bah-dah*	company (privately-owned)
compañía privatizada	*lah kohm-pah-'nyee-ah pree-'bah-tee-'sah-dah*	company (privatized)
compresor del aire (m)	*ehl kohm-preh-'sohr dehl 'ah-ee-reh*	air compressor
crudo (m)	*ehl 'kroo-doh*	crude oil
crudo en exceso	*ehl 'kroo-doh ehn ehk-'seh-soh*	crude oil (excess)
cubierta (f)	*lah koo-bee-'ehr-tah*	deck
cubierta inferior	*lah koo-bee-'ehr-tah een-feh-ree-'ohr*	deck (lower)
cubierta intermedia	*lah koo-bee-'ehr-tah een-tehr-'mee-dee-ah*	deck (middle)
cubierta superior	*lah koo-bee-'ehr-tah soo-peh-ree-'ohr*	deck (top, main)
cuenca (f)	*lah 'kwehn-kah*	basin
derechos económicos (mpl)	*lohs deh-'reh-chohs eh-koh-'noh-mee-kohs*	entitlements
desarrollado	*dehs-ah-rroh-'yah-doh*	developed (adj)
desarrollar	*dehs-ah-rroh-'yahr*	develop (v)
descarga (f)	*lah dehs-'kahr-gah*	exhaust
descubrimiento de (aceite) (m)	*ehl dehs-koo-bree-mee-'ehn-toh deh ah-'seh-ee-teh*	find (oil)
descubrir	*dehs-koo-'breer*	locate (v)
distribución (f)	*lah dees-tree-boo-see-'ohn*	distribution
en vías de desarrollo	*ehn 'bee-ahs deh dehs-ah-'rroh-yoh*	developing (adj)
energía (f)	*lah eh-nehr-'hee-ah*	energy

escape (m)	*ehl eh-'skah-peh*	exhaust
especialista (m/f)	*eh-speh-see-ah-'lees-tah*	specialist
especialista en la industria petrolera	*eh-speh-see-ah-'lees-tah ehn lah een-'doos-tree-ah peh-troh-'leh-rah*	specialist (oil industry)
estabilizar	*eh-stah-bee-lee-'sahr*	stabilize (v)
estación de bombeo (f)	*lah ehs-tah-see-'ohn deh bohm-'beh-oh*	pumping station
exploración (f)	*lah ehks-ploh-rah-see-'ohn*	exploration
exploración doméstica (f)	*lah ehks-ploh-rah-see-'ohn doh-'mehs-tee-kah*	exploration (local)
explorar	*ehks-ploh-'rahr*	explore (v)
facilidad de almacenamiento (f)	*lah fah-see-lee-'dahd deh ahl-mah-seh-nah-mee-'ehn-toh*	storage facility
facilidades portuarias (fpl)	*lahs fah-see-lee-'dah-dehs pohr-too-'ah-ree-ahs*	port facilities
foso de abastecimiento de combustibles (m)	*ehl 'foh-soh deh ah-bah-steh-see-mee-'ehn-toh deh kohm-boo-'stee-blehs*	fueling pit
fuel-oil (aceite combustible) ligero (m)	*ehl foo-'ehl oh-'yeel (ah-'see-ee-teh kohm-boo-'stee-bleh) lee-'heh-roh*	oil (light fuel)
fuel-oil pesado	*ehl foo-'ehl oh-'yeel peh-'sah-doh*	oil (heavy fuel)
fuente (f)	*lah 'fwehn-teh*	source
fuentes (fpl) de energía	*lahs 'fwehn-tehs deh eh-nehr-'hee-ah*	energy sources
gas (m)	*ehl gahs*	gas
gas líquido	*ehl gahs 'lee-kee-doh*	gas (liquid petroleum)
gas natural	*ehl gahs nah-too-'rahl*	gas (natural)
gasolina (f)	*lah gah-soh-'lee-nah*	fuel
gasolina de aviación	*lah gah-soh-'lee-nah deh ah-bee-ah-see-'ohn*	fuel (aviation)
gasolina normal	*lah gah-soh-'lee-nah nohr-'mahl*	gasoline (regular)
gasolina super	*lah gah-soh-'lee-nah soo-'pehr*	gasoline (super grade)
gasolinera (f)	*lah gah-soh-lee-'neh-rah*	service station

grúa (f)	*lah 'groo-ah*	crane
grúa giratoria	*lah 'groo-ah hee-rah-'toh-ree-ah*	crane (revolving)
industria petrolera (f)	*lah een-'doos-tree-ah peh-troh-'leh-rah*	oil industry
industria petrolera indígena	*lah een-'doos-tree-ah peh-troh-'leh-rah een-'dee-heh-nah*	oil industry (indigenous)
industria petrolera integrada	*lah een-'doos-tree-ah peh-troh-'leh-rah een-teh-'grah-dah*	oil industry (integrated)
instalación de climatización	*lah een-stah-lah-see-'ohn deh klee-mah-tee-sah-see-'ohn*	seawater desalination plant
instalación de destilación	*lah een-stah-lah-see-'ohn deh deh-stee-lah-see-'ohn*	distillation plant
localizar	*loh-kah-lee-'sahr*	locate (v)
lubricante para cilindros (m)	*ehl loo-bree-'kahn-teh 'pah-rah see-'leen-drohs*	oil (lubricating)
mezcla de recursos de energía (f)	*lah 'mehs-klah deh reh-'koor-sohs deh eh-nehr-'hee-ah*	energy (mix)
montecargas (m)	*ehl mohn-teh-'kahr-gahs*	elevator
nivel del mar (m)	*ehl nee-'behl dehl mahr*	sea level
oferta (f)	*lah oh-'fehr-tah*	supply
oleoducto (m)	*ehl oh-leh-oh-'dook-toh*	pipeline
Organización de Países Exportadores de Petróleo (OPEP) (f)	*lah ohr-gah-nee-sah-see-'ohn deh pah-'ee-sehs ehks-pohr-tah-'doh-rehs deh peh-'troh-leh-oh*	Organization of Petroleum-Exporting Countries (OPEC)
organización vertical	*lah ohr-gah-nee-sah-see-'ohn behr-tee-'kahl*	vertical integration
países exportadores de petróleo (mpl)	*lohs pah'ee-sehs ehks-pohr-tah-'doh-rehs deh peh-'troh-leh-oh*	oil exporting countries
países importadores de petróleo	*lohs pah'ee-sehs eem-pohr-tah-'doh-rehs deh peh-'troh-leh-oh*	oil importing countries
países importadores de petróleo en vías de desarrollo	*lohs pah'ee-sehs ehks-pohr-tah-'doh-rehs deh peh-'troh-leh-oh ehn 'bee-ahs deh dehs-ah-'rroh-yoh*	oil-importing developing countries (IODC)

perforación a poca distancia de la costa (f)	*lah pehr-foh-rah-see-'ohn ah 'poh-kah dees-'tahn-see-ah deh lah 'koh-stah*	offshore drilling
petróleo crudo (m)	*ehl peh-'troh-leh-oh 'kroo-doh*	crude oil
plataforma de perforación (f)	*lah plah-tah-'fohr-mah deh pehr-foh-rah-see-'ohn*	drilling rig
producción (f)	*lah proh-dook-see-'ohn*	output
recursos (mpl)	*lohs reh-'koor-sohs*	resources
reducción en el consumo (f)	*lah reh-dook-see-'ohn ehn ehl kohn-'soo-moh*	consumption reduction
refinería (f)	*lah reh-fee-neh-'ree-ah*	refinery
refinería doméstica	*lah reh-fee-neh-'ree-ah doh-mehs-tee-kah*	refinery (home-based)
refinería localizada en el país del consumidor	*lah reh-fee-neh-'ree-ah loh-kah-lee-'sah-dah ehn ehl pah-'ees dehl kohm-soo-mee-'dohr*	refinery (market based)
sitio de exploración (m)	*ehl 'see-tee-oh deh ehks-ploh-rah-see-'ohn*	exploration site
tamaño (m)	*ehl tah-'mah-nyoh*	size
tanque (m)	*ehl 'tahn-keh*	tank
tanque de carburante para helicópteros	*ehl 'tahn-keh deh kahr-boo-'rahn-teh 'pah-rah eh-lee-'kohp-teh-rohs*	tank (jet fuel)
tanque de reserva para agua salada	*ehl 'tahn-keh deh reh-'sehr-bah 'pah-rah 'ah-gwah sah-'lah-dah*	tank (salt water)
tanque para el agua potable	*ehl 'tahn-keh 'pah-rah ehl 'ah-gwah poh-'tah-bleh*	tank (drinking water)
tanque para el almacenamiento de cemento	*ehl 'tahn-keh 'pah-rah ehl ahl-mah-seh-nah-mee-'ehn-toh deh seh-'mehn-toh*	tank (cement storage)
tanquero (m)	*ehl tahn-'keh-roh*	tanker
tecnología (f)	*lah tehk-noh-loh-'hee-ah*	technology
torre de perforación (f)	*lah 'toh-rreh deh pehr-foh-rah-see-'ohn*	derrick
yacimiento petrolífero (m)	*ehl yah-see-mee-'ehn-toh peh-troh-'lee-feh-roh*	oil field

PHARMACEUTICALS

English to Spanish

anesthetic	el anastésico	*ehl ah-nah-'steh-tee-koh*
analgesic	el analgésico	*ehl ah-nahl-'heh-see-koh*
anti-inflammatory	el antiinflamatorio	*ehl ahn-tee-een-flah-mah-'toh-ree-oh*
anticholinergic	el anticolinérgico	*ehl ahn-tee-koh-lee-'nehr-hee-koh*
anticoagulant	el anticoagulante	*ehl ahn-tee-koh-ah-goo-'lahn-teh*
aspirin	la aspirina	*lah ahs-pee-'ree-nah*
barbiturates	los barbitúricos	*lohs bahr-bee-'too-ree-kohs*
bleed (v)	sangrar	*sahn-'grahr*
blood	la sangre	*lah 'sahn-greh*
botanic	la botánica	*lah boh-'tah-nee-kah*
calcium	el calcio	*ehl 'kahl-see-oh*
compounds	los compuestos	*lohs kohm-'pwehs-tohs*
content	el contenido	*ehl kohn-teh-'nee-doh*
cortisone	la cortisona	*lah kohr-tee-'soh-nah*
cough (v)	toser	*toh-'sehr*
cough drop	la pastilla para la tos	*lah pahs-'tee-yah 'pah-rah lah tohs*
cough syrup	el jarabe para la tos	*ehl hah-'rah-beh 'pah-rah lah tohs*
crude (adj)	crudo	*'kroo-doh*
density	la densidad	*lah dehn-see-'dahd*
diabetes	la diabetis	*lah dee-ah-'beh-tees*
digitalis	el digital, la digitalina	*ehl dee-hee-'tahl, lah dee-hee-tah-'lee-nah*
disease	la enfermedad	*lah ehn-fehr-meh-'dahd*
diuretic	el diurético	*ehl dee-oo-'reh-tee-koh*
dose	la dosis	*lah 'doh-sees*
dressing	el vendaje	*ehl behn-'dah-heh*
drop	la gota	*lah 'goh-tah*
drug	la droga	*lah 'droh-gah*

drugstore	la farmacia	*lah fahr-'mah-see-ah*
eyedrop	la gota para los ojos	*lah 'goh-tah 'pah-rah lohs 'oh-hohs*
ground (adj)	molido	*moh-'lee-doh*
hexachlorophene	el hexaclorofeno	*ehl ehk-sah-kloh-roh-'feh-noh*
hormone	la hormona	*lah ohr-'moh-nah*
hypertension	la hipertensión	*lah ee-pehr-tehn-see-'ohn*
injection	la inyección	*lah een-yehk-see-'ohn*
insulin	la insulina	*lah een-soo-'lee-nah*
iodine	el yodo	*ehl 'yoh-doh*
iron	el hierro	*ehl 'yeh-roh*
laboratory technician	el técnico de laboratorio	*ehl 'tehk-nee-koh deh lah-boh-rah-'toh-ree-oh*
laxative	el laxante	*ehl lahk-'sahn-teh*
medicine	la medicina	*lah meh-dee-'see-nah*
morphine	la morfina	*lah mohr-'fee-nah*
narcotic	el narcótico	*ehl nahr-'koh-tee-koh*
nitrate	el nitrato	*ehl nee-'trah-toh*
nitrite	el nitrito	*ehl nee-tree-toh*
ointment	el ungüento	*ehl oon-'gwehn-toh*
opium	el opio	*ehl 'oh-pee-oh*
organic (adj)	orgánico	*ohr-'gah-nee-koh*
pellet	la píldora	*lah 'peel-doh-rah*
pharmaceutical (adj)	farmacéutico	*fahr-mah-'seh-oo-tee-koh*
pharmacist	el farmacéutico	*ehl fahr-mah-'seh-oo-tee-koh*
phenol	el fenol	*ehl feh-'nohl*
physician	el médico	*ehl 'meh-dee-koh*
pill	la píldora	*lah 'peel-doh-rah*
prescription	la receta	*lah reh-'seh-tah*
purgative	el purgante	*ehl poor-'gahn-teh*
remedies	los remedios	*lohs reh-'meh-dee-ohs*
saccharin	la sacarina	*lah sah-kah-'ree-nah*
salts	las sales	*lahs 'sah-lehs*

salve	el ungüento, la pomada	*ehl oon-'gwehn-toh, lah poh-'mah-dah*
sedative	el sedante, el calmante	*ehl seh-'dahn-teh, ehl kahl-'mahn-teh*
serum	el suero	*ehl 'sweh-roh*
sinus	el seno	*ehl 'seh-noh*
sleeping pill	la píldora para dormir	*lah 'peel-doh-rah 'pah-rah dohr-'meer*
sneeze (v)	estornudar	*ehs-tohr-noo-'dahr*
starch	el almidón, la fécula	*ehl ahl-mee-'dohn, lah 'feh-koo-lah*
stimulant	el estimulante	*ehl ehs-tee-moo-'lahn-teh*
sulphamide	la sulfamide	*lah sool-fah-'mee-deh*
synthesis	la síntesis	*lah 'seen-teh-sees*
syringe	la jeringuilla, la jeringa	*lah heh-reen-'gee-yah, lah heh-'reen-gah*
tablet	la tableta, la pastilla	*lah tah-'bleh-tah, lah pah-'stee-yah*
thermometer	el termómetro	*ehl tehr-'moh-meh-troh*
toxicology	la toxicología	*lah tok-see-koh-loh-'hee-ah*
toxin	la toxina	*lah tok-'see-nah*
tranquilizer	el tranquilizante	*ehl trahn-kee-lee-'sahn-teh*
vaccine	la vacuna	*lah bah-'koo-nah*
vitamin	la vitamina	*lah bee-tah-'mee-nah*
zinc	el zinc, el cinc	*ehl seenk, ehl seenk*

Spanish to English

almidón (m)	*ehl ahl-mee-'dohn*	starch
analgésico (m)	*ehl ah-nahl-'heh-see-koh*	analgesic
anestésico (m)	*ehl ah-neh-'steh-tee-koh*	anesthetic
anticoagulante (m)	*ehl ahn-tee-koh-ah-goo-'lahn-teh*	anticoagulant
anticolinérgico (m)	*ehl ahn-tee-koh-lee-'nehr-hee-koh*	anticholinergic
antiinflamatorio (m)	*ehl ahn-tee-een-flah-mah-'toh-ree-oh*	anti-inflammatory
aspirina (f)	*lah ahs-pee-'ree-nah*	aspirin

barbitúricos (mpl)	*lohs bahr-bee-'too-ree-kohs*	barbiturates
botánica (f)	*lah boh-'tah-nee-kah*	botanic
calcio (m)	*ehl 'kahl-see-oh*	calcium
calmante (m)	*ehl kahl-'mahn-teh*	sedative
cinc (m)	*ehl seenk*	zinc
compuestos (mpl)	*lohs kohm-'pwehs-tohs*	compounds
contenido (m)	*ehl kohn-teh-'nee-doh*	content
cortisona (f)	*lah kohr-tee-'soh-nah*	cortisone
crudo	*'kroo-doh*	crude (adj)
densidad (f)	*lah dehn-see-'dahd*	density
diabetis (f)	*lah dee-ah-'beh-tees*	diabetes
digital (f)	*lah dee-hee-'tahl*	digitalis
digitalina (f)	*lah dee-hee-tah-'lee-nah*	digitalis
diurético (m)	*ehl dee-oo-'reh-tee-koh*	diuretic
dosis (f)	*lah 'doh-sees*	dose
droga (f)	*lah 'droh-gah*	drug
enfermedad (f)	*lah ehn-fehr-meh-'dahd*	disease
estimulante (m)	*ehl ehs-tee-moo-'lahn-teh*	stimulant
estornudar	*ehs-tohr-noo-'dahr*	sneeze (v)
farmacéutico	*fahr-mah-'seh-oo-tee-koh*	pharmaceutical (adj)
farmacéutico (m)	*ehl fahr-mah-'seh-oo-tee-koh*	pharmacist
farmacia (f)	*lah fahr-'mah-see-ah*	drugstore
fécula (f)	*lah 'feh-koo-lah*	starch
fenol (m)	*ehl feh-'nohl*	phenol
gota (f) para los ojos	*lah 'goh-tah 'pah-rah lohs 'oh-hohs*	eyedrop
hexaclorofeno (m)	*ehl ehk-sah-kloh-roh-'feh-noh*	hexachlorophene
hierro (m)	*ehl 'yeh-roh*	iron
hipertensión (f)	*lah ee-pehr-tehn-see-'ohn*	hypertension
hormona (f)	*lah ohr-'moh-nah*	hormone
insulina (f)	*lah een-soo-'lee-nah*	insulin
inyección (f)	*lah een-yehk-see-'ohn*	injection
jarabe (m) para la tos	*ehl hah-'rah-beh 'pah-rah lah tohs*	cough syrup

jeringa (f)	*lah heh-'reen-gah*	syringe
laxante (m)	*ehl lahk-'sahn-teh*	laxative
medicina (f)	*lah meh-dee-'see-nah*	medicine
médico (m)	*ehl 'meh-dee-koh*	physician
molido	*moh-'lee-doh*	ground (adj)
morfina (f)	*lah mohr-'fee-nah*	morphine
narcótico (m)	*ehl nahr-'koh-tee-koh*	narcotic
nitrato (m)	*ehl nee-'trah-toh*	nitrate
nitrito (m)	*ehl nee-tree-toh*	nitrite
opio (m)	*ehl 'oh-pee-oh*	opium
orgánico	*ohr-'gah-nee-koh*	organic (adj)
pastilla (f)	*lah pah-'stee-yah*	tablet
pastilla para la tos	*lah pahs-'tee-yah 'pah-rah lah tohs*	cough drop
píldora (f)	*lah 'peel-doh-rah*	pellet, pill
píldora para dormir	*lah 'peel-doh-rah 'pah-rah dohr-'meer*	sleeping pill
pomada (f)	*lah poh-'mah-dah*	salve
purgante (m)	*ehl poor-'gahn-teh*	purgative
receta (f)	*lah reh-'seh-tah*	prescription
remedios (mpl)	*lohs reh-'meh-dee-ohs*	remedies
sacarina (f)	*lah sah-kah-'ree-nah*	saccharin
sales (fpl)	*lahs 'sah-lehs*	salts
sangrar	*sahn-'grahr*	bleed (v)
sangre (f)	*lah 'sahn-greh*	blood
sedante (m)	*ehl seh-'dahn-teh*	sedative
seno (m)	*ehl 'seh-noh*	sinus
síntesis (f)	*lah 'seen-teh-sees*	synthesis
suero (m)	*ehl 'sweh-roh*	serum
sulfamide (f)	*lah sool-fah-'mee-deh*	sulphamide
tableta (f)	*lah tah-'bleh-tah*	tablet
técnico (m) de laboratorio	*ehl 'tehk-nee-koh deh lah-boh-rah-'oh-ree-oh*	laboratory technician
termómetro (m)	*ehl tehr-'moh-meh-troh*	thermometer
toser	*toh-'sehr*	cough (v)

toxicología (f)	*lah tok-see-koh-loh-'hee-ah*	toxicology
toxina (f)	*lah tok-'see-nah*	toxin
tranquilizante (m)	*ehl trahn-kee-lee-'sahn-teh*	tranquilizer
ungüento (m)	*ehl oon-'gwehn-toh*	ointment, salve
vacuna (f)	*lah bah-'koo-nah*	vaccine
vendaje (m)	*ehl behn-'dah-heh*	dressing
vitamina (f)	*lah bee-tah-'mee-nah*	vitamin
yodo (m)	*ehl 'yoh-doh*	iodine

PRINTING AND PUBLISHING

English to Spanish

acknowledgment	el reconocimiento, el agradecimiento	*ehl reh-koh-noh-see-mee-'ehn-toh, ehl ah-grah-deh-see-mee-'ehn-toh*
black and white (adj)	blanco y negro	*'blahn-koh ee 'neh-groh*
bleed (v)	desteñir	*dehs-teh-'nyeer*
blowup (v)	ampliar	*ahm-plee-'ahr*
boldface	la negrita	*lah neh-'gree-tah*
book	el libro	*ehl 'lee-broh*
capital	la mayúscula	*lah mah'yoos-koo-lah*
chapter	el capítulo	*ehl kah-'pee-too-loh*
coated paper	el papel cuché, el papel revestido	*ehl pah-'pehl koo-'cheh, ehl pah-'ehl reh-vehs-'tee-doh*
copy (text)	el ejemplar	*ehl eh-hehm-'plahr*
copy (v)	copiar	*koh-pee-'ahr*
copyright	el derecho de autor	*ehl deh-'reh-choh deh ow-'tohr*
cover	la cubierta	*lah koo-bee-'ehr-tah*
daily newspaper	el periódico, el diario	*ehl peh-ree-'oh-dee-koh, ehl dee-'ah-ree-oh*
dropout	la omisión, la eliminación	*lah oh-mee-see-'ohn, lah eh-lee-mee-nah-see-'ohn*
dummy	la maqueta	*lah mah-'keh-tah*
edit (v)	editar	*eh-dee-'tahr*
edition	la edición	*lah eh-dee-see-'ohn*
editor	el editor	*ehl eh-dee-'tohr*
engrave (v)	grabar	*grah-'bahr*
folio	la página	*lah 'pah-hee-nah*
font	el tipo de letra	*ehl tee-poh deh 'leh-trah*
four-color	los cuatro colores	*lohs 'kwah-trohs koh-'loh-rehs*
galley proof	la galerada	*lah gah-leh-'rah-dah*
glossy (adj)	lustroso, glaseado	*loos-'troh-soh, glah-see-'ah-doh*

grain	el grano	*ehl 'grah-noh*
grid	la cuadrícula	*lah kwah-dree-'koo-lah*
hardcover	la carpeta dura	*lah kahr-'peh-tah 'doo-rah*
headline	el titular	*ehl tee-too-'lahr*
inch	la pulgada	*lah pool-'gah-dah*
ink	la tinta	*lah 'teen-tah*
insert	el entredós, el encarte	*ehl ehn-treh-'dohs, ehl ehn-'kahr-teh*
italic (adj)	cursiva	*koor-'see-bah*
jacket (book)	la sobrecubierta	*lah soh-breh-koo-bee-'ehr-tah*
justify (v)	justificar	*hoos-tee-fee-'kahr*
layout	la composición, el trazado	*lah kohm-poh-see-see-'ohn, ehl trah-'sah-doh*
letterpress	el texto impreso, la impresión tipográfica	*ehl 'tehks-toh eem-'preh-soh, lah eem-preh-see-'ohn tee-poh-'grah-fee-kah*
line drawing	el dibujo lineal	*ehl dee-'boo-hoh lee-neh-'ahl*
lower case	la minúscula, la caja baja	*lah mee-'noos-koo-lah, lah 'kah-hah 'bah-hah*
newsprint	el papel de periódico	*ehl pah-'pehl deh peh-ree-'oh-dee-koh*
packing	el relleno	*ehl reh-'yeh-noh*
page makeup	la compaginación	*lah kohm-pah-hee-nah-see-'ohn*
pamphlet	el panfleto	*ehl pahn-'fleh-toh*
paper	el papel	*ehl pah-'pehl*
paperback	el libro en rústica	*ehl 'lee-broh ehn 'roos-tee-kah*
perfect binding	la encuadernación perfecta	*lah ehn-kwah-dehr-nah-see-'ohn pehr-'fehk-tah*
pica	el cícero	*ehl 'see-seh-roh*
plate	el estereotipo, la lámina, el grabado	*ehl eh-steh-reh-oh-'tee-poh, lah 'lah-mee-nah, ehl grah-'bah-doh*
point	el punto	*ehl 'poon-toh*
preface	el prólogo	*ehl 'proh-loh-goh*

press book	el libro impreso	*ehl 'lee-broh eem-'preh-soh*
print run	la tirada	*lah tee-'rah-dah*
printing	la impresión	*lah eem-preh-see-'ohn*
proofreading	la corrección de prueba	*lah koh-rehk-see-'ohn deh proo-'eh-bah*
publisher	el publicador	*ehl poo-blee-kah-'dohr*
ream	la resma	*lah 'rehs-mah*
register marks	las marcas registradas	*lahs 'mahr-kahs reh-hees-'trah-dahs*
scoring	el rayado	*ehl rah-'yah-doh*
screen	la pantalla, la trama	*lah pahn-'tah-yah, lah 'trah-mah*
sewn (adj)	sewn (adj)	*koh-'see-doh*
sheet	la hoja de papel	*lah 'oh-hah deh pah-'pehl*
size	el tamaño	*ehl tah-mah-nyoh*
softcover	la cubierta rústica	*lah koo-bee-'ehr-tah*
spine	el lomo	*ehl 'loh-moh*
stripping (v)	desmontar	*dehs-mohn-'tahr*
table of contents	el índice	*ehl 'een-dee-seh*
title	el título	*ehl 'tee-too-loh*
web offset	el cilindro de offset	*ehl see-'leen-droh deh ohf-'seht*

Spanish to English

agradecimiento (m)	*ehl ah-grah-deh-see-mee-'ehn-toh*	acknowledgment
ampliar	*ahm-plee-'ahr*	blowup (v)
blanco y negro	*'blahn-koh ee 'neh-groh*	black and white (adj)
caja (f) baja	*lah 'kah-hah 'bah-hah*	lower case
capítulo (m)	*ehl kah-'pee-too-loh*	chapter
carpeta (f) dura	*lah kahr-'peh-tah 'doo-rah*	hardcover
cícero (m)	*ehl 'see-seh-roh*	pica
cilindro (m) de offset	*ehl see-'leen-droh deh ohf-'seht*	web offset
compaginación (f)	*lah kohm-pah-hee-nah-see-'ohn*	page makeup
composición (f)	*lah kohm-poh-see-see-'ohn*	layout

copiar	*koh-pee-'ahr*	copy (v)
corrección (f) de prueba	*lah koh-rehk-see-ohn deh proo-'eh-bah*	proofreading
cosido	*koh-'see-doh*	sewn (adj)
cuadrícula (f)	*lah kwah-dree-'koo-lah*	grid
cuatro colores (mpl)	*lohs 'kwah-trohs koh-'loh-rehs*	four-color
cubierta (f)	*lah koo-bee-'ehr-tah*	cover
cubierta rústica	*lah koo-bee-'ehr-tah*	softcover
cursiva	*koor-'see-bah*	italic (adj)
derecho (m) de autor	*ehl deh-'reh-choh deh ow-t'ohr*	copyright
desmontar	*dehs-mohn-'tahr*	stripping (v)
desteñir	*dehs-teh-'nyeer*	bleed (v)
dibujo (m) lineal	*ehl dee-'boo-hoh lee-neh-'ahl*	line drawing
editar	*eh-dee-'tahr*	edit (v)
ejemplar (m)	*ehl eh-hehm-'plahr*	copy (text)
eliminación (f)	*lah eh-lee-mee-nah-see-'ohn*	dropout
encarte (m)	*ehl ehn-'kahr-teh*	insert
encuadernación (f) perfecta	*lah ehn-kwah-dehr-nah-see-'ohn pehr-'fehk-tah*	perfect binding
entredós (m)	*ehl ehn-treh-'dohs*	insert
estereoptipo (m)	*ehl eh-steh-reh-oh-'tee-poh*	plate
galerada (f)	*lah gah-leh-'rah-dah*	galley proof
glaseado	*glah-see-'ah-dohr*	glossy (adj)
grano (m)	*ehl 'grah-noh*	grain
hoja (f) de papel	*lah 'oh-hah deh pah-'pehl*	sheet
impresión (f)	*lah eem-preh-see-'ohn*	printing
impresión tipográfica	*lah eem-preh-see-'ohn tee-poh-'grah-fee-kah*	letterpress
índice (m)	*ehl 'een-dee-seh*	table of contents
justificar	*hoos-tee-fee-'kahr*	justify (v)
libro (m)	*ehl 'lee-broh*	book
libro en rústica	*ehl 'lee-broh ehn 'roos-tee-kah*	paperback
libro impreso	*ehl 'lee-broh eem-'preh-soh*	press book

lomo (m)	*ehl 'loh-moh*	spine
lustroso	*loos-'troh-soh*	glossy (adj)
maqueta (f)	*lah mah-'keh-tah*	dummy
marcas (fpl) registradas	*lahs 'mahr-kahs reh-hees-'trah-dahs*	register marks
mayúscula (m)	*lah mah 'yoos-koo-lah*	capital
minúscula (f)	*lah mee-'noos-koo-lah*	lower case
negrita (f)	*lah neh-'gree-tah*	boldface
omisión (f)	*lah oh-mee-see-'ohn*	dropout
página (f)	*lah 'pah-hee-nah*	folio
panfleto (m)	*ehl pahn-fleh-toh*	pamphlet
pantalla (f)	*lah pahn-'tah-yah*	screen
papel (m)	*ehl pah-'pehl*	paper
papel cuché	*ehl pah-'pehl koo-'cheh*	coated paper
papel revestido	*ehl pah-'pehl reh-vehs-'tee-doh*	coated paper
periódico (m)	*ehl peh-ree-'oh-dee-koh*	daily newspaper
prólogo (m)	*ehl 'proh-loh-goh*	preface
publicador (m)	*ehl poo-blee-kah-'dohr*	publisher
pulgada (f)	*lah pool-'gah-dah*	inch
punto (m)	*ehl 'poon-toh*	point
rayado (m)	*ehl rah-'yah-doh*	scoring
relleno (m)	*ehl reh-'yeh-noh*	packing
resma (f)	*lah 'rehs-mah*	ream
sobrecubierta (f)	*lah soh-breh-koo-bee-'ehr-tah*	jacket (book)
tamaño (m)	*ehl tah-mah-nyoh*	size
texto impreso (m)	*ehl 'tehks-toh eem-'preh-soh*	letterpress
tinta (f)	*lah 'teen-tah*	ink
tipo de letra (m)	*ehl tee-poh deh 'leh-trah*	font
título (m)	*ehl 'tee-too-loh*	title
tirada (f)	*lah tee-'rah-dah*	print run
titular (m)	*ehl tee-too-'lahr*	headline
trama (f)	*lah 'trah-mah*	screen
trazado (m)	*ehl trah-'sah-doh*	layout

WINEMAKING

English to Spanish

acid content	el contenido acídico	*ehl kohn-teh-'nee-doh ah-'see-dee-koh*
acre	el acre (0.4047 hectáreas)	*ehl 'ah-kreh (0.4047 ehk-'tah-reh-ahs)*
aging	el envejecimiento	*ehl ehn-beh-heh-see-mee-'ehn-toh*
alcoholic content	el contenido alcohólico, el porcentaje de alcohol	*ehl kohn-teh-'nee-doh ahl-koh-'oh-lee-koh, ehl -pohr-sehn-'tah-heh deh ahl-koh-'ohl*
batch	el lote, la serie	*ehl 'loh-teh, lah 'seh-ree-eh*
biological diacidizing	la diacidificación biológica	*lah dee-ah-see-dee-fee-kah-see-'ohn bee-oh-'loh-hee-kah*
blend (v)	mezclar	*mehs'klahr*
body	el cuerpo	*ehl 'kwehr-poh*
bottle	la botella	*lah boh-'teh-yah*
case	la caja	*lah 'kah-hah*
cask (225 litres)	el tonel, el barril	*ehl toh-'nehl, ehl bah-'rreel*
character	la cualidad, la condición	*lah kwah-lee-'dahd, lah kohn-dee-see-'ohn*
classified sparkling wine	el vino espumoso clasificado	*ehl 'bee-noh ehs-poo-'moh-soh klah-see-fee-'kah-doh*
clearing	la clarificación	*lah klah-ree-fee-kah-see-'ohn*
climate	el clima	*ehl 'klee-mah*
copper	el cobre	*ehl 'koh-breh*
cork	el corcho	*ehl 'kohr-choh*
corkscrew	el sacacorchos	*ehl sah-kah-'kohr-chohs*
country	el país	*ehl pah-'ees*
draw off (v)	sacar	*sah-'kahr*
dregs	las heces	*lahs 'eh-sehs*
drink (v)	beber	*beh-'behr*
dry wine	el vino seco	*ehl 'bee-noh 'seh-koh*
estate (or chateau)	la estancia, la viña	*lah ehs-'tahn-see-ah*

estate bottled	envasado en la viña	ehn-bah-'sah-doh ehn lah 'bee-nyah
fruity	el sabor a frutas	ehl sah-'bohr ah 'froo-tahs
grape	la uva	lah 'oo-bah
grape bunch	el racimo de uvas	ehl rah-'see-moh deh 'oo-bahs
grape harvest	la vendimia, la cosecha de uvas	lah behn-'dee-mee-ah, lah koh-'seh-chah deh 'oo-bahs
guaranteed classified vintage	la cosecha clasificada garantizada	lah koh-'seh-chah klah-see-fee-'kah-dah gah-rahn-tee-'sah-dah
hectare	la hectárea (2.47 acres)	lah ehk-'tah-reh-ah
label	la etiqueta	lah eh-tee-'keh-tah
liter	el litro	ehl 'lee-troh
magnum (2 bottles in one)	la botella de dos litros	lah boh-'teh-yah deh dohs 'lee-trohs
malolactic fermentation	la fermentación maloláctica	lah fehr-mehn-tah-see-'ohn mah-loh-'lahk-tee-kah
neck (of bottle)	el cuello, el gollete	ehl 'kweh-yoh, ehl goh-'yeh-teh
production	la producción	lah proh-dook-see-'ohn
ripe (adj)	maduro	mah-'doo-roh
skin (grape)	el hollejo	ehl oh-'yeh-hoh
sour (adj)	agrio	'ah-gree-oh
sparkling wine	el vino espumoso	ehl 'bee-noh ehs-poo-'moh-soh
stalking (v)	encañar	ehn-kah-'nyahr
sugar content	el contenido de azúcar	ehl kohn-teh-'nee-doh deh ah-'soo-kahr
tasting (wine tasting)	la degustación de vino	lah deh-goos-tah-see-'ohn deh 'bee-noh
temperature	la temperatura	lah tehm-peh-rah-'too-rah
type of vine	el tipo de vid, el tipo de parra	ehl 'tee-poh deh beed, ehl 'tee-poh deh 'pah-rrah
unfermented grape juice	el zumo de uva no fermentado	ehl 'soo-moh deh 'oo-bah noh fehr-mehn-'tah-doh
vat	la cuba, la tina	lah 'koo-bah, lah 'tee-nah
vine	la vid	lah beed

vineyard	la viña, el viñedo	*lah 'bee-nyah, ehl bee-'nyeh-doh*
vintage	la vendimia, la cosecha	*lah behn-'dee-mee-ah*
vintage year	el año de cosecha	*ehl 'ah-nyoh deh koh-'seh-chah*
vintner	el vinatero	*ehl bee-nah-'teh-roh*
vintry	la vinatería	*bee-nah-teh-'ree-ah*
wine	el vino	*ehl 'bee-noh*
wine cellar	la bodega	*lah boh-deh-gah*
wine cooperative	la cooperativa de vino	*lah koh-oh-peh-rah-'tee-bah deh 'bee-noh*
winegrower	el viticultor	*ehl bee-tee-kool-'tohr*
winemaker	el vinicultor	*ehl bee-nee-kool-'tohr*
winepress	el lagar	*ehl lah-'gahr*
wine steward	el sumiller	*ehl soo-mee-'yehr*
yeast	la levadura	*lah leh-bah-'doo-rah*
yield	la producción, el rendimiento	*lah proh-dook-see-'ohn, ehl rehn-dee-mee-'ehn-toh*

Spanish to English

acre (0.4047 hectaréas) (m)	*ehl 'ah-kreh (0.4047 ehk-'tah-reh-ahs)*	acre
agrio	*'ah-gree-oh*	sour (adj)
año (m) de cosecha	*ehl 'ah-nyoh deh koh-'seh-chah*	vintage year
barril (m)	*ehl bah-'rreel*	cask
beber	*beh-'behr*	drink (v)
biacidificación (f) biológica (f)	*lah dee-ah-see-dee-fee-kah-see-'ohn bee-oh-'loh-hee-kah*	biological diacidizing
bodega (f)	*lah boh-deh-gah*	wine cellar
botella (f)	*lah boh-'teh-yah*	bottle
botella de dos litros	*lah boh-t'eh-yah deh dohs 'lee-trohs*	magnum (2 bottles in one)
caja (f)	*lah 'kah-hah*	case
clarificación (f)	*lah klah-ree-fee-kah-see-'ohn*	clearing
clima (m)	*ehl 'klee-mah*	climate

cobre (m)	*ehl 'koh-breh*	copper
condición (f)	*lah kohn-dee-see-'ohn*	character
contenido acídico (m)	*ehl kohn-teh-'nee-doh ah-'see-dee-koh*	acid content
contenido alcohólico	*ehl kohn-teh-'nee-doh ahl-koh-'oh-lee-koh*	alcoholic content
contenido de azúcar	*ehl kohn-teh-'nee-doh deh ah-'soo-kahr*	sugar content
cooperativa (f) de vino	*lah koh-oh-peh-rah-'tee-bah deh 'bee-noh*	wine cooperative
corcho (m)	*ehl 'kohr-choh*	cork
cosecha de uvas	*lah koh-'seh-chah deh 'oo-bahs*	grape harvest
cualidad (f)	*lah kwah-lee-'dahd*	character
cuba (f)	*lah 'koo-bah*	vat
cuello (m)	*ehl 'kweh-yoh*	neck (of bottle)
cuerpo (m)	*ehl 'kwehr-poh*	body
degustación (f) de vino	*lah deh-goos-tah-see-'ohn deh 'bee-noh*	tasting (wine tasting)
encañar	*ehn-kah-'nyahr*	stalking (v)
envasado en la viña	*ehn-bah-'sah-doh ehn lah 'bee-nyah*	estate bottled
envejecimiento (m)	*ehl ehn-beh-heh-see-mee-'ehn-toh*	aging
estancia (f)	*lah ehs-'tahn-see-ah*	estate (or chateau)
etiqueta (f)	*lah eh-tee-'keh-tah*	label
fermentación maloláctica	*lah fehr-mehn-tah-see-'ohn mah-loh-l'ahk-tee-kah*	malolactic fermentation
gollete (m)	*ehl goh-'yeh-teh*	neck of bottle
heces (fpl)	*lahs 'eh-sehs*	dregs
hectárea (2.47 acres) (f)	*lah ehk-'tah-reh-ah*	hectare
hollejo (m)	*ehl oh-'yeh-hoh*	skin (grape)
lagar (m)	*ehl lah-'gahr*	winepress
levadura (f)	*lah leh-bah-'doo-rah*	yeast
litro (m)	*ehl 'lee-troh*	liter
lote (m)	*ehl 'loh-teh*	batch

maduro	*mah-'doo-roh*	ripe (adj)
mezclar	*mehs-'klahr*	blend (v)
país (m)	*ehl pah-'ees*	country
producción (f)	*lah proh-dook-see-'ohn*	production, yield
racimo (m) de uvas	*ehl rah-'see-moh-deh 'oo-bahs*	grape bunch
sabor	*ehl sah-'bohr*	body
sabor a frutas (m)	*ehl sah-'bohr ah-'froo-tahs*	fruity
sacacorcho (m)	*ehl sah-kah-'kohr-chohs*	corkscrew
sacar	*sah-'kahr*	draw off (v)
serie (f)	*lah 'seh-ree-eh*	batch
sumiller (m)	*ehl soo-mee-'yehr*	wine steward
temperatura (f)	*lah tehm-peh-rah-'too-rah*	temperature
tina (f)	*lah 'tee-nah*	vat
tipo de vid (m)	*ehl 'tee-poh deh beed*	type of vine
tonel (m)	*ehl toh-'nehl*	cask (225 litres)
uva (f)	*lah 'oo-bah*	grape
vendimia (f)	*lah behn-'dee-mee-ah*	grape harvest, vintage
vid (f)	*lah beed*	vine
vinatero (m)	*ehl bee-nah-'teh-roh*	vintner
viñedo (m)	*ehl bee-'nyeh-doh*	vineyard
vinicultor (m)	*ehl bee-nee-kool-'tohr*	winemaker
vino (m)	*ehl 'bee-noh*	wine
vino espumoso	*ehl 'bee-noh ehs-poo-'moh-soh*	sparkling wine
vino espumoso clasificado	*ehl 'bee-noh ehs-poo-'moh-soh klah-see-fee-'kah-doh*	classified sparkling wine
vino seco	*ehl 'bee-noh 'seh-koh*	dry wine
viticultor (m)	*ehl bee-tee-kool-'tohr*	winegrower

WORLD ENVIRONMENT

English to Spanish

acid rain	la lluvia ácida	*lah 'yoo-bee-ah 'ah-see-dah*
algae	las algas (f)	*lahs 'ahl-gahs*
amphibians	los anfibios	*lohs ahn-'fee-bee-ohs*
animal kingdom	el reino animal	*ehl 'reh-ee-noh ah-nee-'mahl*
arms	las armas	*lahs 'ahr-mahs*
atmosphere	la atmósfera	*lah aht-'mohs-feh-rah*
barrel	el barril	*ehl bah-'rreel*
basin	la cuenca	*lah 'kwehn-kah*
basin (marine)	la cuenca marina	*lah 'kwehn-kah mah-'ree-nah*
beach	la playa	*lah 'plah-yah*
biodiversity	la biodiversidad	*lah bee-oh-dee-behr-see-'dahd*
biological function	la función biológica	*lah foonk-see-'ohn bee-oh-'loh-hee-kah*
birds	las aves, los pájaros	*lahs 'ah-behs, lohs 'pah-hah-rohs*
burning	la incineración	*lah een-see-neh-rah-see-'ohn*
carbon monoxide	el monóxido de carbono	*ehl moh-'nohk-see-doh deh kahr-'boh-noh*
census	el censo	*ehl 'sehn-soh*
census (to take the)	levantar el censo	*leh-bahn-'tahr ehl 'sehn-soh*
chemical (adj)	químico	*'kee-mee-koh*
clouds	las nubes	*lahs 'noo-behs*
coal	el carbón	*ehl kahr-'bohn*
coast	la costa	*lah 'koh-stah*
coastal (adj)	costeño	*koh-'steh-nyoh*
compound	el compuesto	*ehl kohm-'pweh-stoh*
compound (chemical)	el compuesto químico	*ehl kohm-'pweh-stoh 'kee-mee-koh*
concentrations	las concentraciones	*lahs kohn-sehn-trah-see-'oh-nehs*

conservation	la conservación	*lah kohn-sehr-bah-see-'ohn*
consumption (of provisions)	el consumo	*ehl kohn-'soo-moh*
consumption (animal)	el consumo animal	*ehl kohn-'soo-moh ah-nee-'mahl*
consumption (human)	el consumo humano	*ehl kohn-'soo-moh oo-'mah-noh*
contaminate (v)	contaminar	*kohn-tah-mee-'nahr*
coral reef	el arrecife de coral	*ehl ah-rreh-'see-feh deh koh-'rahl*
crop	la cosecha	*lah koh-'seh-chah*
crop rotation	la rotación de las cosechas	*lah roh-tah-see-'ohn deh lahs koh-'seh-chahs*
crop rotation (improper)	la rotación impropia de las cosechas	*lah roh-tah-see-'ohn eem-'proh-pee-ah deh lahs koh-'seh-chahs*
cycle	el ciclo	*el 'see-kloh*
cycle (biological)	el ciclo biológico	*ehl 'see-kloh bee-oh-'loh-hee-koh*
dam	la represa	*lah reh-'preh-sah*
damage	el daño	*ehl 'dah-nyoh*
danger	el peligro	*ehl peh-'lee-groh*
death rate	la mortalidad	*lah mohr-tah-lee-'dahd*
death rate (infant)	la mortalidad infantil	*lah mohr-tah-lee-'dahd een-fahn-'teel*
defoliating agent	el agente desfoliante (m)	*ehl ah-'hehn-teh dehs-foh-lee-'ahn-teh*
deforestation	la deforestación, despoblación forestal	*lah deh-foh-reh-stah-see-'ohn, dehs-poh-blah-see-'ohn foh-reh-'stahl*
desert	el desierto	*ehl deh-see-'ehr-toh*
desertification	la desertificación	*lah deh-sehr-tee-fee-kah-see-'ohn*
destruction	la destrucción	*lah deh-strook-see-'ohn*
deterioration	el deterioro	*ehl deh-teh-ree-'oh-roh*
development	el desarrollo	*ehl deh-sah-'rroh-yoh*
development (economic)	el desarrollo económico	*ehl deh-sah-'rroh-yoh eh-koh-'noh-mee-koh*

development (urban)	el desarrollo urbano	*ehl deh-sah-'rroh-yoh oor-'bah-noh*
disappearance	la desaparición	*lah dehs-ah-pah-ree-see-'ohn*
disease	la enfermedad	*lah ehn-fehr-meh-'dahd*
disease (contagious)	contagiosa	*kohn-tah-hee-'oh-sah*
disease (deadly)	mortal	*mohr-'tahl*
disease (respiratory)	respiratoria	*reh-spee-rah-'toh-ree-ah*
distribute	distribuir	*dees-tree-boo-'eer*
diversion	el desvío	*ehl dehs-'bee-oh*
dolphin	el delfín (m)	*ehl dehl-'feen*
drought	la sequía	*lah seh-'kee-ah*
dry (adj)	seco	*'seh-koh*
Earth	Tierra	*tee-'eh-rrah*
earthquake	el temblor	*ehl tehm-'blohr*
ecosystem	el ecosistema	*ehl eh-koh-sees-'teh-mah*
elephant	el elefante (m)	*ehl eh-leh-'fahn-teh*
emissions	las emisiones	*lahs eh-mee-see-'oh-nehs*
emissions (toxic)	las emisiones tóxicas	*lahs eh-mee-see-'oh-nehs 'tohk-see-kahs*
environment	el medio ambiente (m) el hábitat (m)	*ehl 'meh-dee-oh ahm-bee-'ehn-teh, ehl 'ah-bee-taht*
erosion	la erosión	*lah eh-roh-see-'ohn*
ethanol	el etanol (m)	*ehl eh-tah-'nohl*
excess population	el exceso de población	*ehl ehk-'seh-soh deh poh-blah-see-'ohn*
exhaust (v)	agotar	*ah-goh-'tahr*
exhausted (adj)	agotado	*ah-goh-'tah-doh*
experiment	el experimento	*ehl ehks-peh-ree-'mehn-toh*
extinction	la extinción	*lah ehk-steenk-see-'ohn*
farming	el cultivo	*ehl kool-'tee-boh*
fauna and flora	la fauna y flora	*lah 'fah-oo-nah ee 'floh-rah*
felling (of a tree)	la tala	*lah 'tah-lah*
fellow man, fellow creature	los prójimos	*lohs 'proh-hee-mohs*

fertilizer	el fertilizante (m)	*ehl fehr-tee-lee-'sahn-teh*
filter	el filtro	*ehl 'feel-troh*
firmness	la firmeza	*lah feer-'meh-sah*
fish	los peces (m), el pez (sing.)	*lohs peh-sehs, ehl pehs*
frosts	las heladas	*lahs eh-'lah-dahs*
future generations	las generaciones futuras	*lahs heh-neh-rah-see-'oh-nehs foo-'too-rahs*
garbage	la basura	*lah bah-'soo-rrah*
gas	el gas	*ehl gahs*
global warming	el calentamiento global	*ehl kah-lehn-tah-mee-'ehn-toh gloh-'bahl*
gravitation of earth	la gravitación terrestre	*lah grah-bee-tah-see-'ohn teh-'rreh-streh*
green revolution	la revolución verde	*lah reh-boh-loo-see-'ohn 'behr-deh*
growing (adj)	creciente	*kreh-see-'ehn-teh*
guanaco	el guanaco	*ehl gwah-'nah-koh*
guarantee (v)	garantizar	*gah-rahn-tee-'sashr*
hole	el agujero	*ehl ah-goo-'heh-roh*
home heating	la calefacción casera	*lah kah-leh-fahk-see-'ohn kah-'seh-rah*
hunting	la caza	*lah 'kah-sah*
hunting (excessive)	la caza excesiva	*lah 'kah-hah ehk-seh-'see-bah*
hydrocarbons	los hidrocarburos	*lohs ee-droh-kahr-'boo-rohs*
imbalance	el desequilibrio	*ehl dehs-eh-kee-'lee-bree-oh*
incinerator	el incinerador	*ehl een-see-neh-rah-'dohr*
increase	el crecimiento	*ehl kreh-see-mee-'ehn-toh*
increase (demographic)	el crecimiento demográfico	*ehl kreh-see-mee-'ehn-toh deh-moh-'grah-fee-koh*
increase (economic)	el crecimiento económico	*ehl kreh-see-mee-'ehn-toh eh-koh-'noh-mee-koh*
invertebrate	el invertebrado	*ehl een-behr-teh-'brah-doh*
irrigation	el riego	*ehl ree-'eh-goh*
lagoon	la laguna	*lah lah-'goo-nah*
lake	el lago	*ehl 'lah-goh*
land	el terreno	*ehl teh-'rreh-noh*

lead	el plomo	*ehl 'ploh-moh*
leaf	la hoja	*lah 'oh-hah*
living beings	los seres vivos	*lohs 'seh-rehs 'bee-bohs*
mammal	el mamífero	*ehl mah-'mee-feh-roh*
mankind	la humanidad	*lah oo-mah-nee-'dahd*
marsh	el pantano	*ehl pahn-'tah-noh*
materials	los materiales (m)	*lohs mah-teh-ree-'ah-lehs*
means	los medios	*lohs 'meh-dee-ohs*
microorganism	el micro-organismo	*ehl mee-kroh-ohr-gah-'nees-moh*
migration	la migración	*lah mee-grah-see-'ohn*
natural beauty	la belleza natural	*lah bee-'yeh-sah nah-too-'rahl*
natural science	la ciencia natural	*lah see-'ehn-see-ah nah-too-'rahl*
nitrogen	el nigrógeno	*ehl nee-'troh-heh-noh*
nitrogen dioxide	el dióxido de nitrógeno	*ehl dee-'ohk-see-doh deh nee-'troh-heh-noh*
oil	el petróleo	*ehl peh-'troh-leh-oh*
oil (crude)	el crudo, el aceite	*ehl 'kroo-doh, ehl ah-'seh-ee-teh*
oil spill	el derrame de petróleo (m)	*ehl deh-'rrah-meh deh peh-'troh-leh-oh*
oxides	los óxidos el ozono	*lohs 'ohk-see-dohs*
ozone	el ozono	*ehl oh-'soh-noh*
ozone layer	la capa de ozono	*lah 'kah-pah de oh-'soh-noh*
park	el parque	*ehl 'pahr-keh*
park (national)	el parque nacional	*ehl pahr-keh nah-see-oh-'nahl*
park (protected)	el parque protegido	*ehl pahr-keh proh-teh-'hee-doh*
particle	la partícula	*lah pahr-'tee-koo-lah*
penguin	el pingüino	*ehl peen-'gwee-noh*
perish (v)	perecer	*peh-reh-'sehr*
phosphate	el fosfato	*ehl fohs-'fah-toh*
physical characteristics	las características físicas	*lahs kah-rehk-teh-'rees-tee-kahs 'fee-see-kahs*

Physical Quality of Life Index (PQLI)	Indice General de la Calidad de Vida	*'een-dee-seh heh-neh-'rahl deh lah kah-lee-'dahd deh 'bee-dah*
plague	la plaga	*lah 'plah-gah*
planet	el planeta (m)	*ehl plah-'neh-tah*
plankton	el planctón (m)	*ehl plahnk-'tohn*
plankton (sea)	el planctón marino	*ehl plahnk-'tohn mah-'ree-noh*
poison (v)	envenenar	*ehn-beh-neh-'nahr*
productivity	la productividad	*lah proh-dook-tee-bee-'dahd*
progress	el progreso	*ehl proh-'greh-soh*
radiation	la radiación	*lah rah-dee-ah-see-'ohn*
radioactive (adj)	radiactivo	*rah-dee-oh-ahk-'tee-boh*
rain forest	la pluvisilva	*lah ploo-bee-'seel-bah*
rains	las lluvias	*lahs 'yoo-bee-ahs*
reach (v)	alcanzar	*ahl-kahn-'sahr*
recycle	reciclar	*reh-see-'klahr*
recycling	reciclaje (m)	*reh-see-'klah-heh*
Red List of Threatened Animals	lista roja de animales amenazados	*'lees-tah 'roh-hah deh ah-nee-'mah-lehs ah-meh-nah-'sah-dohs*
refill	el relleno	*ehl reh-'yeh-noh*
refinery	la refinería	*lah reh-fee-neh-'ree-ah*
reptiles	los reptiles	*lohs rehp-'tee-lehs*
rhinoceros	el rinoceronte	*ehl ree-noh-seh-'rohn-teh*
river	el río	*ehl 'ree-oh*
search	la búsqueda	*lah 'boos-keh-dah*
seaweed	las algas (f)	*lahs 'ahl-gahs*
sediment	el sedimento	*ehl seh-dee-'mehn-toh*
semi-arid	semiárido	*seh-mee-'ah-ree-doh*
ship	el buque	*ehl 'boo-keh*
smog	el smog (m)	*ehl es-'mohg*
smog (urban)	el smog urbano	*ehl es-mohg oor-'bah-noh*
solar (adj)	solar	*soh-'lahr*
stratosphere	la estratosfera	*lah ehs-trah-tohs-'feh-rah*

stress	la tensión nerviosa	*lah tehn-see-'ohn nehr-bee-'oh-sah*
submit to	someterse a	*soh-meh-'tehr-seh ah*
surface	la superficie (f)	*lah soo-pehr-'fee-see-eh*
surface areas (land)	los suelos	*lohs 'sweh-lohs*
sustain	sostener	*sohs-teh-'nehr*
sustenance	el sustento	*ehl soos-'tehn-toh*
swamp	el pantano	*ehl pahn-'tah-noh*
swamp (mangrove)	el pantano manglar	*ehl pahn-'tah-noh mahn-'glahr*
tackle (fishing)	los avíos de pescar	*lohs ah-'bee-ohs deh pehs-'kahr*
temperature	la temperatura	*lah tehm-peh-rah-'too-rah*
threat	la amenaza	*lah ah-meh-'nah-sah*
threatened (adj)	amenazado	*ah-meh-nah-'sah-doh*
tourist area	la zona turística	*lah 'soh-nah too-'rees-tee-kah*
tree	el árbol	*ehl 'ahr-bohl*
tropics	los trópicos	*lohs 'troh-pee-kohs*
Union for the Conservation of Nature and Natural Resources	Unión para la Conservación de la ñaturaleza y los Recursos Naturales	*oo-nee-'ohn 'pah-rah lah kohn-sehr-bah-see-'ohn deh lah nah-too-rah-'leh-sah ee lohs reh-'koor-sohs nah-too-'rah-lehs*
vegetation	el vegetal (m)	*ehl beh-heh-'tahl*
vegetation (aquatic)	el vegetal acuático	*ehl beh-heh-'tahl ah-'kwah-tee-koh*
vehicle	el vehículo	*ehl beh-'ee-koo-loh*
vehicle (motorized)	el vehículo motorizado	*ehl beh-'ee-koo-loh moh-toh-ree-'sah-doh*
vessel (sea)	el buque	*ehl 'boo-keh*
warm (adj)	el cálido	*ehl 'kah-lee-doh*
warming effect	el efecto invernadero	*ehl eh-'fehk-toh een-behr-nah-'deh-roh*
waste	el desgaste	*ehl dehs-'gah-steh*
waters	las aguas	*lahs 'ah-gwahs*
waves (of sea)	las olas del mar	*lahs 'oh-lahs dehl mahr*

weapons	las armas	*lahs 'ahr-mahs*
weapons (atomic)	las armas atómicas	*lahs 'ahr-mahs ah-'toh-mee-kahs*
weight	el peso	*ehl 'peh-soh*
well (drilled)	el pozo	*ehl 'poh-soh*
well-being	el bienestar	*ehl bee-ehn-eh-'stahr*
well-being (economic)	el bienestar económico	*ehl bee-ehn-eh-'stahr eh-koh-'noh-mee-koh*
well-being (social)	el bienestar social	*ehl bee-ehn-eh-'stahr soh-see-'ah*
winds	el viento	*ehl bee-'ehn-toh*
work aesthetic (environment)	la estética laboral	*lah ehs-'teh-tee-kah lah-boh-'rahl*
work ethic	la ética laboral	*lah 'eh-tee-kah lah-boh-'rahl*
worry	la preocupación	*lah preh-oh-koo-pah-see-'ohn*

Spanish to English

aceite (m)	*ehl ah-'seh-ee-teh*	oil (crude)
agente desfoliante (m)	*ehl ah-'hehn-teh dehs-foh-lee-'ahn-teh*	defoliating agent
agotado	*ah-goh-'tah-doh*	exhausted (adj)
agotar	*ah-goh-'tahr*	exhaust (v)
aguas (fpl)	*lahs 'ah-gwahs*	waters
agujero (m)	*ehl ah-goo-'heh-roh*	hole
alcanzar	*ahl-kahn-'sahr*	reach (v)
algas (fpl)	*lahs 'ahl-gahs*	algae, seaweed
amenaza (f)	*lah ah-meh-'nah-sah*	threat
amenazado	*ah-meh-nah-'sah-doh*	threatened (adj)
anfibios (mpl)	*lohs ahn-'fee-bee-ohs*	amphibians
árbol (m)	*ehl 'ahr-bohl*	tree
armas (fpl)	*lahs 'ahr-mahs*	arms, weapons
armas atómicas	*lahs 'ahr-mahs ah-'toh-mee-kahs*	weapons (atomic)
arrecife de coral (m)	*ehl ah-rreh-'see-feh deh koh-'rahl*	coral reef

atmósfera (f)	*lah aht-'mohs-feh-rah*	atmosphere
aves (fpl)	*lahs 'ah-behs*	birds
avíos de pescar (mpl)	*lohs ah-'bee-ohs deh pehs-'kahr*	tackle (fishing)
barril (m)	*ehl bah-'rreel*	barrel
basura (f)	*lah bah-'soo-rrah*	garbage
belleza natural (f)	*lah bee-'yeh-sah nah-too-'rahl*	natural beauty
bienestar (m)	*ehl bee-ehn-eh-'stahr*	well-being
bienestar económico	*ehl bee-ehn-eh-'stahr ehl eh-koh-'noh-mee-koh*	well-being (economic)
bienestar social	*ehl bee-ehn-eh-'stahr soh-see-'ahl*	well-being (social)
biodiversidad (f)	*lah bee-oh-dee-behr-see-'dahd*	biodiversity
buque (m)	*ehl 'boo-keh*	ship, vessel (sea)
búsqueda (f)	*lah 'boos-keh-dah*	search
calefacción casera (f)	*lah kah-leh-fahk-see-'ohn kah-'seh-rah*	home heating
calentamiento global (m)	*ehl kah-lehn-tah-mee-'ehn-toh gloh-'bahl*	global warming
cálido	*'kah-lee-doh*	warm (adj)
capa de ozono (f)	*lah 'kah-pah de oh-'soh-noh*	ozone layer
características físicas (fpl)	*lahs kah-rehk-teh-'rees-tee-kahs 'fee-see-kahs*	physical characteristics
carbón (m)	*ehl kahr-'bohn*	coal
caza (f)	*lah 'kah-sah*	hunting
caza excesiva	*lah 'kah-hah ehk-seh-'see-bah*	hunting (excessive)
censo (m)	*ehl 'sehn-soh*	census
ciclo (m)	*ehl 'see-kloh*	cycle
ciclo biológico	*ehl 'see-kloh bee-oh-'loh-hee-koh*	cycle (biological)
ciencia natural (f)	*ciencia natural (f)*	natural science
compuesto (m)	*ehl kohm-'pweh-stoh*	compound
compuesto químico	*ehl kohm-'pweh-stoh 'kee-mee-koh*	compound (chemical)

concentraciones (fpl)	*lahs kohn-sehn-trah-see-'oh-nehs*	concentrations
conservación (f)	*lah kohn-sehr-bah-see-'ohn*	conservation
consumo (m)	*ehl kohn-'soo-moh*	consumption (of provisions)
consumo animal	*ehl kohn-'soo-moh ah-nee-'mahl*	consumption (animal)
consumo humano	*ehl kohn-'soo-moh oo-'mah-noh*	consumption (human)
contaminar	*kohn-tah-mee-'nahr*	contaminate (v)
cosecha (f)	*lah koh-'seh-chah*	crop
costa (f)	*lah 'koh-stah*	coast
costeño	*koh-'steh-nyoh*	coastal (adj)
creciente	*kreh-see-'ehn-teh*	growing (adj)
crecimiento (m)	*ehl kreh-see-mee-'ehn-toh*	increase
crecimiento demográfico	*ehl kreh-see-mee-'ehn-toh deh-moh-'grah-fee-koh*	increase (demographic)
crecimiento económico	*ehl kreh-see-mee-'ehn-toh eh-koh-'noh-mee-koh*	increase (economic)
crudo (m)	*ehl 'kroo-doh*	oil (crude)
cuenca (f)	*lah 'kwehn-kah*	basin
cuenca marina	*lah 'kwehn-kah mah-'ree-nah*	basin (marine)
cultivo (m)	*ehl kool-'tee-boh*	farming
daño (m)	*ehl 'dah-nyoh*	damage
deforestación (f)	*lah deh-foh-reh-stah-see-'ohn*	deforestation
delfín (m)	*ehl dehl-'feen*	dolphin
derrame de petróleo (m)	*ehl deh-'rrah-meh deh peh-'troh-leh-oh*	oil spill
desaparición (f)	*lah dehs-ah-pah-ree-see-'ohn*	disappearance
desarrollo (m)	*ehl deh-sah-'rroh-yoh*	development
desarrollo económico	*ehl deh-sah-'rroh-yoh eh-koh-'noh-mee-koh*	development (economic)
desarrollo urbano	*ehl deh-sah-'rroh-yoh oor-'bah-noh*	development (urban)
desequilibrio (m)	*ehl dehs-eh-kee-'lee-bree-oh*	imbalance

desertificación (f)	*lah deh-sehr-tee-fee-kah-see-'ohn*	desertification
desgaste (m)	*ehl dehs-'gah-steh*	waste
desierto (m)	*ehl deh-see-'ehr-toh*	desert
despoblación forestal (f)	*lah dehs-poh-blah-see-'ohn foh-reh-'stahl*	deforestation
destrucción (f)	*lah deh-strook-see-'ohn*	destruction
desvío (m)	*ehl dehs-'bee-oh*	diversion
deterioro (m)	*ehl deh-teh-ree-'oh-roh*	deterioration, spoilage
dióxido de nitrógeno (m)	*ehl dee-'ohk-see-doh deh nee-'troh-heh-noh*	nitrogen dioxide
distribuir	*dees-tree-boo-'eer*	distribute (v)
ecosistema (m)	*ehl eh-koh-sees-'teh-mah*	ecosystem
efecto invernadero (m)	*ehl eh-'fehk-toh een-behr-nah-'deh-roh*	warming effect
elefante (m)	*ehl eh-leh-'fahn-teh*	elephant
emisiones (fpl)	*eh-mee-see-'oh-nehs*	emissions
emisiones tóxicas	*lahs eh-mee-see-'oh-nehs 'tohk-see-kahs*	emissions (toxic)
enfermedad (f)	*lah ehn-fehr-meh-dahd*	disease
enfermedad contagiosa	*lah ehn-fehr-meh-'dahd kohn-tah-hee-'oh-sah*	disease (contagious)
enfermedad mortal	*lah ehn-fehr-meh-'dahd mohr-'tahl*	disease (deadly)
enfermedad respiratoria	*lah ehn-fehr-meh-'dahd reh-spee-rah-'toh-ree-ah*	disease (respiratory)
envenenar	*ehn-beh-neh-'nahr*	poison (v)
erosión	*eh-roh-see-'ohn*	erosion
estética laboral (f)	*lah ehs-'teh-tee-kah lah-boh-'rahl*	work aesthetic (environment)
estratósfera (f)	*lah ehs-trah-'tohs-feh-rah*	stratosphere
etanol (m)	*ehl eh-tah-'nohl*	ethanol
ética laboral (f)	*lah 'eh-tee-kah lah-boh-'rahl*	work ethic
exceso de población (m)	*ehl ehk-'seh-soh deh poh-blah-see-'ohn*	excess population
experimento (m)	*ehl ehks-peh-ree-'mehn-toh*	experiment
extinción (f)	*lah ehk-steenk-see-'ohn*	extinction

fauna y flora (f)	*lah 'fah-oo-nah ee 'floh-rah*	fauna and flora
fertilizante (m)	*ehl fehr-tee-lee-'sahn-teh*	fertilizer
filtro (m)	*ehl 'feel-troh*	filter
firmeza (f)	*lah feer-'meh-sah*	firmness
fosfato (m)	*ehl fohs-'fah-toh*	phosphate
función biológica (f)	*lah foonk-see-'ohn bee-oh-'loh-hee-kah*	biological function
garantizar	*gah-rahn-tee-'sashr*	guarantee (v)
gas (m)	*ehl gahs*	gas
generaciones futuras (fpl)	*lahs heh-neh-rah-see-'oh-nehs foo-'too-rahs*	future generations
gravitación terrestre (f)	*lah grah-bee-tah-see-'ohn teh-'rreh-streh*	gravitation of earth
guanaco (m)	*ehl gwah-'nah-koh*	guanaco
hábitat (m)	*ehl 'ah-bee-taht*	environment
heladas (fpl)	*lahs eh-'lah-dahs*	frosts
hidrocarburos (mpl)	*lohs ee-droh-kahr-'boo-rohs*	hydrocarbons
hoja (f)	*lah 'oh-hah*	leaf
hombre (m)	*ehl 'ohm-breh*	man, mankind
incineración (f)	*lah een-see-neh-rah-see-'ohn*	burning
incinerador (m)	*ehl een-see-neh-rah-'dohr*	incinerator
Indice General de la Calidad de Vida (m)	*ehl 'een-dee-seh heh-neh-'rahl deh lah kah-lee-'dahd deh 'bee-dah*	Physical Quality of Life Index (PQLI)
invertebrado (m)	*ehl een-behr-teh-'brah-doh*	invertebrate
lago (m)	*ehl 'lah-goh*	lake
laguna (f)	*lah lah-'goo-nah*	lagoon
levantar el censo	*leh-bahn-'tahr ehl 'sehn-soh*	census (to take the) (v)
lista roja de animales amenazados (f)	*lah 'lees-tah 'roh-hah deh ah-nee-'mah-lehs ah-meh-nah-'sah-dohs*	Red List of Threatened Animals
lluvia ácida (f)	*lah 'yoo-bee-ah 'ah-see-dah*	acid rain
lluvias (fpl)	*lahs 'yoo-bee-ahs*	rains
mamífero (m)	*ehl mah-'mee-feh-roh*	mammal
manglar (m)	*ehl mahn-'glahr*	swamp (mangrove)

materiales (mpl)	*lohs mah-teh-ree-'ah-lehs*	materials
medio ambiente (m)	*ehl 'meh-dee-oh ahm-bee-'ehn-teh*	environment
medios (mpl)	*lohs 'meh-dee-ohs*	means
micro-organismo (m)	*ehl mee-kroh-ohr-gah-'nees-moh*	microorganism
migración (f)	*lah mee-grah-see-'ohn*	migration
monóxido de carbono (m)	*ehl moh-'nohk-see-doh deh kahr-'boh-noh*	carbon monoxide
mortalidad (f)	*lah mohr-tah-lee-'dahd*	death rate
mortalidad infantil	*lah mohr-tah-lee-'dahd een-fahn-'teel*	death rate (infant)
nitrógeno (m)	*ehl nee-'troh-heh-noh*	nitrogen
nubes (fpl)	*lahs 'noo-behs*	clouds
olas del mar (fpl)	*lahs 'oh-lahs dehl mahr*	waves (of sea)
óxidos (mpl)	*lohs 'ohk-see-dohs*	oxides
ozono (m)	*ehl oh-'soh-noh*	ozone
pájaros (mpl)	*lohs 'pah-hah-rohs*	birds
pantano (m)	*ehl pahn-'tah-noh*	marsh, swamp
parque (m)	*ehl 'pahr-keh*	park
parque nacional	*ehl pahr-keh nah-see-oh-'nahl*	park (national)
parque protegido	*ehl pahr-keh proh-teh-'hee-doh*	park (protected)
partícula (f)	*lah pahr-'tee-koo-lah*	particle
peces (mpl)	*lohs 'peh-sehs*	fish
peligro (m)	*ehl peh-'lee-groh*	danger
perecer	*peh-reh-'sehr*	perish (v)
peso (m)	*ehl 'peh-soh*	weight
petróleo (m)	*ehl peh-'troh-leh-oh*	oil
pez (m.sing.)	*ehl pehs*	fish
pingüino (m)	*ehl peen-'gwee-noh*	penguin
plaga (f)	*lah 'plah-gah*	plague
plancton (m)	*ehl plahnk-'tohn*	plankton
plancton marino	*ehl plahnk-'tohn mah-'ree-noh*	plankton (sea)

planeta (m)	*ehl plah-'neh-tah*	planet
playa (f)	*lah 'plah-yah*	beach
plomo (m)	*ehl 'ploh-moh*	lead
pluvisilva (f)	*lah ploo-bee-'seel-bah*	rain forest
pozo (m)	*ehl 'poh-soh*	well (drilled)
preocupación (f)	*lah preh-oh-koo-pah-see-'ohn*	worry
productividad (f)	*lah proh-dook-tee-bee-'dahd*	productivity
progreso (m)	*ehl proh-'greh-soh*	progress
prójimos (mpl)	*lohs 'proh-hee-mohs*	fellow man, fellow creature
químico	*'kee-mee-koh*	chemical (adj)
radiación (f)	*lah rah-dee-ah-see-'ohn*	radiation
radiactivo	*rah-dee-oh-ahk-'tee-boh*	radioactive (adj)
reciclaje (m)	*ehl reh-see-'klah-heh*	recycling
reciclar	*reh-see-'klahr*	recycle (v)
refinería (f)	*lah reh-fee-neh-'ree-ah*	refinery
reino animal (m)	*ehl 'reh-ee-noh ah-nee-'mahl*	animal kingdom
relleno (m)	*ehl reh-'yeh-noh*	refill
represa (f)	*lah reh-'preh-sah*	dam
reptiles (mpl)	*lohs rehp-'tee-lehs*	reptiles
revolución verde (f)	*lah reh-boh-loo-see-'ohn 'behr-deh*	green revolution
riego (m)	*ehl ree-'eh-goh*	irrigation
rinoceronte (m)	*ehl ree-noh-seh-'rohn-teh*	rhinoceros
río (m)	*ehl 'ree-oh*	river
rotación de las cosechas (f)	*lah roh-tah-see-'ohn deh lahs koh-'seh-chahs*	crop rotation
rotación impropia de las cosechas	*lah roh-tah-see-'ohn eem-'proh-pee-ah deh lahs koh-'seh-chahs*	crop rotation (improper)
seco	*'seh-koh*	dry (adj)
sedimento (m)	*ehl seh-dee-'mehn-toh*	sediment
semiárido	*seh-mee-'ah-ree-doh*	semi-arid (adj)
sequía (f)	*lah seh-'kee-ah*	drought
seres vivos (mpl)	*lohs 'seh-rehs 'bee-bohs*	living beings

smog (m)	*ehl es-'mohg*	smog
smog urbano	*ehl es-'mohg oor-'bah-noh*	smog (urban)
solar	*soh-'lahr*	solar (adj)
someterse a	*soh-meh-'tehr-seh ah*	submit to (v)
sostener	*sohs-teh-'nehr*	sustain (v)
suelos (mpl)	*lohs 'sweh-lohs*	surface areas (land)
superficie (f)	*lah soo-pehr-'fee-see-eh*	surface
sustento (m)	*ehl soos-'tehn-toh*	sustenance
tala (f)	*lah 'tah-lah*	felling (of a tree)
temblor (m)	*ehl tehm-'blohr*	earthquake
temperatura (f)	*lah tehm-peh-rah-'too-rah*	temperature
tensión nerviosa (f)	*lah tehn-see-'ohn nehr-bee-'oh-sah*	stress
terreno (m)	*ehl teh-'rreh-noh*	land
Tierra (f)	*lah tee-'eh-rrah*	Earth
trópicos (m)	*lohs 'troh-pee-kohs*	tropics
Unión para la Conservación de la Naturaleza y los Recursos Naturales (f)	*lah oo-nee-'ohn 'pah-rah lah kohn-sehr-bah-see-'ohn deh lah nah-too-rah-'leh-sah ee lohs reh-'koor-sohs nah-too-'rah-lehs*	Union for the Conservation of Nature and Natural Resources
vegetal (m)	*ehl beh-heh-'tahl*	vegetation
vegetal acuático	*ehl beh-heh-'tahl ah-'kwah-tee-koh*	vegetation (aquatic)
vehículo (m)	*ehl beh-'ee-koo-loh*	vehicle
vehículo motorizado	*ehl beh-'ee-koo-loh moh-toh-ree-'sah-doh*	vehicle (motorized)
viento (m)	*ehl bee-'ehn-toh*	winds

V. GENERAL INFORMATION

ABBREVIATIONS

a.a.	always afloat	B/V	book value
a.a.r.	against all risks		
a/c	account	ca.	circa; centaire
A/C	account current	C.A.	chartered accountant
acct.	account	c.a.	current account
a.c.v.	actual cash value	C.A.D.	cash against documents
a.d.	after date		
a.f.b.	air freight bill	C.B.	cash book
agcy.	agency	C.B.D.	cash before delivery
agt.	agent	c.c.	carbon copy
a.m.t.	air mail transfer	c/d	carried down
a/o	account of	c.d.	cum dividend
A.P.	accounts payable	c/f	carried forward
A/P	authority to pay	cf.	compare
approx.	approximately	c & f	cost and freight
A.R.	accounts receivable	C/H	clearing house
a/r	all risks	C.H.	custom house
A/S, A.S.	account sales	ch. fwd.	charges forward
a/s	at sight	ch. pd.	charges paid
at. wt.	atomic weight	ch. ppd.	charges prepaid
av.	average	chq.	check, cheque
avdp.	avoirdupois	c.i.f.	cost, insurance, freight
a/w	actual weight		
a.w.b.	air waybill	c.i.f. & c.	cost, insurance, freight, and commission
bal.	balance		
bar.	barrel	c.i.f. & e.	cost, insurance, freight, and exchange
bbl.	barrel		
b/d	brought down		
B/E, b/e	bill of exchange	c.i.f. & i.	cost, insurance, freight, and interest
b/f	brought forward		
B.H.	bill of health		
bk.	bank	c.l.	car load
bkge.	brokerage	C/m	call of more
B/L	bill of lading	C/N	credit note
b/o	brought over	c/o	care of
B.P.	bills payable	co.	company
b.p.	by procuration	C.O.D.	cash on delivery
B.R.	bills receivable	comm.	commission
B/S	balance sheet	corp.	corporation
b.t.	berth terms	C.O.S.	cash on shipment
bu.	bushel	C.P.	carriage paid

C/P	charter party	ECU	European Currency Unit
c.p.d.	charters pay duties		
cpn.	corporation	E.E.T.	East European Time
cr.	credit; creditor	e.g.	for example
C/T	cable transfer	encl.	enclosure
c.t.l.	constructive total loss	end.	endorsement
		E. & O.E.	errors and omissions excepted
c.t.l.o.	constructive total loss only		
		e.o.m.	end of month
cum.	cumulative	e.o.h.p.	except otherwise herein provided
cum div.	cum dividend		
cum. pref.	cumulative preference	esp.	especially
		Esq.	Esquire
c/w	commercial weight	est.	established
C.W.O.	cash with order	ex	out
cwt.	hundredweight	ex cp.	ex coupon
		ex div.	ex dividend
D/A	documents against acceptance; deposit account	ex int.	ex interest
		ex n.	ex new (shares)
		ex stre.	ex store
DAP	documents against payment	ex whf.	ex wharf
db.	debenture	f.a.a.	free of all average
DCF	discounted cash flow	f.a.c.	fast as can
d/d	days after date; delivered	f.a.k.	freight all kinds
		f.a.q.	fair average quality; free alongside quay
deb.	debenture		
def.	deferred	f.a.s.	free alongside ship
dept.	department	f/c	for cash
d.f.	dead freight	f.c. & s.	free of capture and seizure
dft.	draft		
dft/a.	draft attached	f.c.s.r. & c.c.	free of capture, seizure, riots, and civil commotion
dft/c.	clean draft		
disc.	discount		
div.	dividend	F.D.	free delivery to dock
DL	dayletter	f.d.	free discharge
DLT	daily letter telegram	ff.	following; folios
D/N	debit note	f.g.a.	free of general average
D/O	delivery order		
do.	ditto	f.i.b.	free in bunker
doz.	dozen	f.i.o.	free in and out
D/P	documents against payment	f.i.t.	free in truck
		f.o.b.	free on board
dr.	debtor	f.o.c.	free of charge
Dr.	doctor	f.o.d.	free of damage
d/s, d.s.	days after sight	fol.	following; folio
d.w.	deadweight	f.o.q.	free on quay
D/W	dock warrant	f.o.r.	free on rail
dwt.	pennyweight	f.o.s.	free on steamer
dz.	dozen	f.o.t.	free on truck(s)

f.o.w.	free on wagons; free on wharf	I.O.U.	I owe you
F.P.	floating policy	J/A, j.a.	joint account
f.p.	fully paid	Jr.	junior
f.p.a.	free of particular average	KV	kilovolt
frt.	freight	KW	kilowatt
frt. pd.	freight paid	KWh	kilowatt hour
frt. ppd.	freight prepaid		
frt. fwd.	freight forward	L/C, l.c.	letter of credit
ft.	foot	LCD	telegram in the language of the country of destination
fwd.	forward		
f.x.	foreign exchange		
		LCO	telegram in the language of the country of origin
g.a.	general average		
g.b.o.	goods in bad order		
g.m.b.	good merchantable brand	ldg.	landing; loading
		l.t.	long ton
g.m.q.	good merchantable quality	Ltd.	limited
		l. tn.	long ton
G.M.T.	Greenwich Mean Time	m.	month
GNP	gross national product	m/a	my account
		max.	maximum
g.o.b.	good ordinary brand	M.D.	memorandum of deposit
gr.	gross		
GRT	gross register ton	M/D, m,d.	months after date
gr. wt.	gross weight	memo.	memorandum
GT	gross tonnage	Messrs.	plural of Mr.
		mfr.	manufacturer
h.c.	home consumption	min.	minimum
hgt.	height	MLR	minimum lending rate
hhd.	hogshead		
H.O.	head office	M.O.	money order
H.P.	hire purchase	m.o.	my order
HP	horsepower	mortg.	mortgage
ht.	height	M/P, m.p.	months after payment
IDP	integrated data processing	M/R	mate's receipt
		M/S, m.s.	months' sight
i.e.	that is	M.T.	mail transfer
I/F	insufficient funds	M/U	making-up price
i.h.p.	indicated horsepower		
imp.	import	n.	name; nominal
Inc.	incorporated	n/a	no account
incl.	inclusive	N/A	no advice
ins.	insurance	n.c.v.	no commercial value
int.	interest	n.d.	no date
inv.	invoice		

n.e.s.	not elsewhere specified	P/L	profit and loss
N/F	no funds	p.l.	partial loss
NL	night letter	P/N	promissory note
N/N	no noting	P.O.	post office; postal order
N/O	no orders	P.O.B.	post office box
no.	number	P.O.O.	post office order
n.o.e.	not otherwise enumerated	p.o.r.	pay on return
		pp.	pages
n.o.s.	not otherwise stated	p & p	postage and packing
nos.	numbers	p. pro	per procuration
NPV	no par value	ppd.	prepaid
nr.	number	ppt.	prompt
n.r.t.	net register ton	pref.	preference
N/S	not sufficient funds	prox.	proximo
NSF	not sufficient funds	P.S.	postscript
n. wt.	net weight	pt.	payment
		P.T.O., p.t.o.	please turn over
o/a	on account	ptly. pd.	partly paid
OCP	overseas common point	p.v.	par value
O/D, o/d	on demand; overdraft	qlty.	quality
o.e.	omissions excepted	qty.	quantity
o/h	overhead		
ono.	or nearest offer	r. & c.c.	riot and civil commotions
O/o	order of		
O.P.	open policy	R/D	refer to drawer
o.p.	out of print; overproof	R.D.C.	running down clause
		re	in regard to
O/R, o.r.	owner's risk	rec.	received; receipt
ord.	order; ordinary	recd.	received
O.S., o/s	out of stock	red.	redeemable
OT	overtime	ref.	reference
		reg.	registered
p.	page; per; premium	retd.	returned
P.A., p.a.	particular average; per annum	rev.	revenue
		R.O.D.	refused on delivery
P/A	power of attorney; private account	R.P.	reply paid
		r.p.s.	revolutions per second
PAL	phase alternation line		
pat. pend.	patent pending	RSVP	please reply
PAYE	pay as you earn	R.S.W.C.	right side up with care
p/c	petty cash		
p.c.	percent; price current	Ry	railway
pcl.	parcel		
pd.	paid	s.a.e.	stamped addressed envelope
pf.	preferred		
pfd.	preferred	S.A.V.	stock at valuation
pkg.	package	S/D	sea damaged

S/D, s.d.	sight draft	UGT	urgent
s.d.	without date	u.s.c.	under separate cover
SDR	special drawing rights	U/ws	underwriters
sgd.	signed	v.	volt
s. & h. ex	Sundays and holidays excepted	val.	value
		v.a.t.	value-added tax
shipt.	shipment	v.g.	very good
sig.	signature	VHF	very high frequency
S/LC, s. & l.c	sue and labor clause	v.h.r.	very highly recommended
S/N	shipping note		
s.o.	seller's option	w.	watt
s.o.p.	standard operating procedure	WA	with average
		W.B.	waybill
spt.	spot	w.c.	without charge
Sr.	senior	W.E.T.	West European Time
S.S., s.s.	steamship	wg.	weight guaranteed
s.t.	short ton	whse.	warehouse
ster.	sterling	w.o.g.	with other goods
St. Ex.	stock exchange	W.P.	weather permitting; without prejudice
stg.	sterling		
s.v.	sub voce	w.p.a.	with particular average
T.A.	telegraphic address	W.R.	war risk
T.B.	trial balance	W/R, wr.	warehouse receipt
tel.	telephone	W.W.D.	weather working day
temp.	temporary secretary	wt.	weight
T.L., t.l.	total loss		
T.L.O.	total loss only	x.c.	ex coupon
TM	multiple telegram	x.d.	ex dividend
T.O.	turn over	x.i.	ex interest
tr.	transfer	x.n.	ex new shares
TR	telegram to be called for	y.	year
TR, T/R	trust receipt	yd.	yard
TT, T.T.	telegraphic transfer (cable)	yr.	year
		yrly.	yearly
TX	Telex		

WEIGHTS AND MEASURES

U.S. UNIT	METRIC EQUIVALENT
mile	1.609 kilometers
yard	0.914 meters
foot	30.480 centimeters
inch	2.540 centimeters

U.S. UNIT	METRIC EQUIVALENT
square mile	2.590 square kilometers
acre	0.405 hectares
square yard	0.836 square meters
square foot	0.093 square meters
square inch	6.451 square centimeters
cubic yard	0.765 cubic meters
cubic foot	0.028 cubic meters
cubic inch	16.387 cubic centimeters
short ton	0.907 metric tons
long ton	1.016 metric tons
short hundredweight	45.359 kilograms
long hundredweight	50.802 kilograms
pound	0.453 kilograms
ounce	28.349 grams
gallon	3.785 liters
quart	0.946 liters
pint	0.473 liters
fluid ounce	29.573 milliliters
bushel	35.238 liters
peck	8.809 liters
quart	1.101 liters
pint	0.550 liters

TEMPERATURE AND CLIMATE

Temperature Conversion Chart

DEGREES CELSIUS	DEGREES FAHRENHEIT
–5	23
0	32
5	41
10	50
15	59
20	68
25	77
30	86
35	95
40	104

Average Temperatures for Major Cities

	JAN	APR	JULY	OCT
Barcelona	50°F (10°C)	60°F (15°C)	78°F (25°C)	67°F (18°C)
Madrid	42°F (6°C)	55°F (13°C)	80°F (27°C)	60°F (15°C)
Mexico City	55°F (12°C)	70°F (21°C)	70°F (21°C)	65°F (18°C)
San Juan	75°F (24°C)	80°F (26°C)	85°F (30°C)	84°F (29°C)
Bogotá	60°F (15°C)	62°F (12°C)	60°F (15°C)	60°F (16°C)
Buenos Aires	75°F (23°C)	65°F (18°C)	50°F (10°C)	60°F (16°C)
Caracas	68°F (20°C)	72°F (22°C)	70°F (21°C)	73°F (23°C)
Montevideo	75°F (23°C)	65°F (18°C)	50°F (10°C)	60°F (15°C)

COMMUNICATIONS CODES

Telephone

public phone	el teléfono público (ehl tel-EH-foh-noh POO-blee-koh)
telephone directory	la guía telefónica (lah GHEE-ah tel-eh-FOHN-ee-kah)
local call	la llamada local (lah yah-MAH-dah loh-KAHL)
long-distance call	la llamada a larga distancia (lah yah-MAH-dah ah LAHR-gah dees-TAHN-see-ah)
person-to-person call	la llamada de persona a persona (lah yah-MAH-dah deh pehr-SOHN-ah ah pehr-SOHN-ah)
collect call	la llamada a cobro revertido (lah yah-MAH-dah ah KOH-broh ray-behr-TEE-doh)

International Country Codes

Algeria	213	Denmark	45
Argentina	54	Dominican Republic	809
Australia	61	Ecuador	593
Austria	43	El Salvador	503
Belgium	32	Finland	358
Bolivia	591	France	33
Brazil	55	Germany	37
Canada	1	Gibraltar	350
Chile	56	Greece	30
Colombia	57	Guatemala	502
Costa Rica	506	Honduras	504
Curacao	599	Hong Kong	852

Hungary	36	Poland	48
Iceland	354	Portugal	351
India	91	Russia	7
Ireland	353	Saudi Arabia	966
Israel	972	Singapore	65
Italy	39	South Africa	27
Japan	81	South Korea	82
Kuwait	965	Spain	34
Luxembourg	352	Sri Lanka	94
Malta	356	Sweden	46
Mexico	52	Switzerland	41
Morocco	212	Taiwan	886
Netherlands	31	Thailand	255
New Zealand	64	Tunisia	216
Nicaragua	505	Turkey	90
Norway	47	United Kingdom	44
Panama	507	Uruguay	598
Paraguay	595	USA	1
Peru	51	Venezuela	58
Philippines	63		

Area Codes within Spain

Barcelona	93	Seville	954
Bilbao	94	Valencia	96
Madrid	91	Zaragoza	976

Area Codes within Mexico

Guadalajara	36	Monterrey	83
Mérida	992	Nuevo Laredo	871
Mexico City	5	Puebla	22

Area Codes for Other Major Cities

Bogotá	9	Lima	14
Buenos Aires	1	Montevideo	2
Caracas	2	San Juan	809

POSTAL SERVICES

In Spain

Post offices are separate from telegraph and telephone services. Post office hours are generally 9:00 AM–7:00 PM. The general delivery window at the Central Post Office in Madrid is open until midnight. Stamps may be bought at a post office, a tobacconist's, or at most hotels.

Madrid Central Post Office—Plaza de la Cibeles.

Barcelona Central Post Office—Vía Laytena 1 (open 24 hours).

Long-distance calls may be made from hotels (there is a surcharge) or public phones (knowledge of Spanish is essential!). Telex and cable facilities are standard in large hotels, or call 232-88-00 (Madrid) or 317-68-98 (Barcelona).

In Mexico

Post offices are separate from telegraph and telephone services. Post office hours are generally 9:00 AM–1:00 PM and 3:00 PM–7:00 PM.

Mexico City Central Post Office—Lázaro Cárdenas at Tacuba. Open 9:00 AM–midnight, Monday–Friday; 9:00 AM–Noon, Saturday.

Long-distance service in Mexico City is available in hotels or at Victoria 59 (8:00 AM–10:00 PM) and Victoria 14 (24 hours).

All telegrams are handled by Telégrafos Nacionales, Balderas y Colón, Mexico City or call 519-29-20.

Public telex is available at: Avenida Universidad y Xola, Balera 7, and at large hotels.

In Argentina

Postal, telegraph, and telephone services are controlled by the state-run Empresa Nacional de Correos y Telégrafos (ENCOTEL).

Buenos Aires Central Post Office—Sarmiento 151.

There are public telex booths at: Corrientes & Maipú; and Corrientes & L. N. Alem.

In Colombia

Bogotá Central Post Office—Edificio Avianca, Carrera 7, No. 16-69. Open 7:00 AM–10:00 PM, Monday–Saturday; 8:00 AM–1:30 PM, Sunday.

International Telephone—Empresa Nacional de Telecomunicaciones, Calle 17, No. 7-15.

Public telex at: Bogotá Hilton, Carrera 7; Tequendama Hotel, Carrera 10.

In Peru

Lima Central Post Office—Jirón Jamin at Plaza de Armes. Open 8 AM–7:15 PM, Monday–Friday; 8:00 AM–Noon, Saturday–Sunday.

Cables may be sent at: Hotel Bolívar, Plaza San Martín, Casilla 864; Hotel Crillón, Avenida Nicolás de Piérolla 589, Casilla 2981.

In Uruguay

Montevideo Central Post Office—Misiones and Buenos Aires.

Telexes are located in most commercial banks. Cables can be sent in Montevideo via: Western Telegraph Co. Ltd., Mercury House, Calle Cerrito 449 or All American Cables and Radio, Inc., Calle Zabala 1451.

In Venezuela

Caracas Central Post Office—Avenida Urdaneta and Carmelitos.

In Puerto Rico

San Juan Central Post Office—Franklin D. Roosevelt Avenue, Hato Rey, San Juan 00936.

TIME ZONES

The table on the following page gives the time differences among various countries and major cities of the world, based on Greenwich Mean Time. Remember that from April through October, Daylight Savings Time must be considered.

MAJOR HOLIDAYS

In Spain and Latin America

Date	Name	Countries
January 1	New Year's Day	All
January 6	Epiphany	Spain, Colombia, Uruguay, Puerto Rico
January 11	Birth of De Hostos	Puerto Rico
February 5	Anniversary of the Constitution	Mexico
March 19	St. Joseph's Day	Spain, Colombia, Venezuela
March 21	Birth of Benito Juárez	Mexico
March 22	Abolition of Slavery	Puerto Rico*
April 16	Birth of de Diego	Puerto Rico*
April 19	Declaration of Independence Day	Venezuela
	Landing of the 33 Orientales	Uruguay
May 1	Labor Day	All (except Puerto Rico)
May 5	Battle of Puebla	Mexico
May 18	Battle of Las Piedras	Uruguay
May 25	Liberty Day	Argentina
June 4	Army Day	Venezuela
June 19	Birth of General Artigos	Uruguay
June 20	Flag Day	Argentina
June 29	St. Peter & St. Paul Day	Colombia, Peru
July 4	Independence Day	Puerto Rico
	Election Day	Mexico
July 5	Independence Day	Venezuela
July 9	Independence Day	Argentina

July 17	Birth of Muñoz Rivera	Puerto Rico*
July 18	Anniversary of First Constitution	Uruguay
July 20	Independence Day	Colombia
July 24	Birth of Bolívar	Venezuela
July 25	St. James' Day	Spain
	Constitution Day	Puerto Rico
July 27	Birth of Barbosa	Puerto Rico
July 28, 29	Independence Days	Peru
August 6	Independence Day	Bolivia
August 7	Battle of Boyacá	Colombia
August 15	Assumption	Spain, Colombia
August 17	San Martín's Day	Argentina
August 25	Independence Day	Uruguay
August 30	Santa Rosa de Lima	Peru
September 1	Presidential Address	Mexico
September 7	Independence Day	Brazil
September 16	Independence Day	Mexico
September 18	Independence Day	Chile
October 12	Columbus Day (Day of La Raza)	All (except Mexico)
November 1	All Saints' Day	Spain, Argentina, Colombia, Peru, Venezuela
November 2	All Souls' Day	Mexico, Uruguay
November 11	Independence of Cartagena	Venezuela
November 20	Anniversary of the Revolution	Mexico
November 24	Veterans' Day	Puerto Rico
December 8	Immaculate Conception	All
December 25	Christmas	All
December 26	Boxing Day	Puerto Rico

Movable Holidays

February	Carnival Week (Week of Ash Wednesday)	Argentina, Brazil, Uruguay, Venezuela
March–April	Maundy Thursday	All (except Spain)
	Good Friday	All
	Corpus Christi (40 Days after Easter)	All (except Mexico).

N.B.: Puerto Rico celebrates Washington's Birthday, Memorial Day, Labor Day, and Thanksgiving with the United States.
* Puerto Rican half-holidays

CURRENCY INFORMATION

Major Commercial Banks

In Spain
Banking Hours: 8:30 AM–2:00 PM,
Monday–Friday; 8:30 AM–1:00 PM,
Saturday

Banco Central
Alcalá 49
Madrid 14

Banco Exterior de España
Alcalá 24
Madrid 14

Banco Popular Español
Alcalá 26
Madrid 14

In Mexico
Banking Hours: 9:00 AM–2:00 PM,
Monday–Friday

Banco Nacional de México, S.N.C.
Isabel la Católica 44
México, D.F.

Bancomer, S.N.C.
Avenida Universidad 1200
México, D.F.

Multibanco Comermex, S.N.C.
M. Ávila Camacho, Plaza
Comermex
México, D.F.

In Argentina
Banking Hours: 10:00 AM–5:00 PM,
Monday–Friday

Banco de la Nación Argentina
Bartolomé Mitre 326
1036 Buenos Aires

Banco de la Provincia de Buenos
Aires
Calle San Martín 137
1004 Buenos Aires

In Colombia
Banking Hours: 9:00 AM–3:00 PM,
Monday–Thursday; 9:00 AM–3:30
PM, Friday

Banco de Bogotá
Carrera 13, No M4-33
2645 Bogotá

Banco del Comercio
Calle 13, No. 8-52
Bogotá

In Peru
Banking Hours: 8:00 AM–noon,
Monday–Friday (January–March);
9:15 AM–12:45 PM, Monday–Friday
(April–December)

Banco de la Nación
Avenida Abancay
Casilla 1835
Lima

In Uruguay
Banking Hours: 1:00 PM–5:00 PM,
Monday–Friday

Banco Comercial
Cerrito 400
Montevideo

In Venezuela
Banking Hours: 8:30 AM–11:30 AM
and 2:00 PM–4:30 PM,
Monday–Friday

Banco Central de Venezuela
Avenida Urdaneta esq. Carmelitas
Caracas

In Puerto Rico
Banking Hours: 9:00 AM–2:30 PM,
Monday–Friday

Banco de Ponce
Avenida Muñoz Rivera 628
Hato Rey, San Juan

Major Currencies of the World

Andorra	French Franc
Argentina	Argentinian Peso
Austria	Schilling
Belgium	Belgian Franc
Bolivia	Boliviano
Brazil	Cruzeiro
Chile	Chilean Peso
Colombia	Colombian Peso
Costa Rica	Colon
Cuba	Peso
Denmark	Danish Krone
Dominican Republic	Peso
Ecuador	Sucre
El Salvador	Colon
Finland	Finmark
France	Franc
Germany	Mark
Greece	Drachma
Guatemala	Quetzal
Honduras	Lempira
Hungary	Forint
Iceland	Krone
Ireland	Punt
Italy	Lira
Liechtenstein	Swiss Franc
Luxembourg	Luxembourg Franc
Malta	Maltese Lira
Mexico	Mexican Peso
Monaco	French Franc
Netherlands	Guilder
Nicaragua	Cordoba
Norway	Norwegian Krone
Panama	Balboa
Paraguay	Guaraní
Peru	Nuevo Sol
Portugal	Escudo
Puerto Rico	U.S. Dollar
Russia	Ruble
Spain	Peseta
Sweden	Swedish Krone
Uruguay	Uruguayan Peso
Venezuela	Bolívar

MAJOR BUSINESS PERIODICALS

Newspapers

In Spain
ABC
Cinco Días

Diario 16
Iberian Daily Sun

El País
El Periódico
La Vanguardia

In Mexico
Diario de México
Esto
Excélsior
El Heraldo de México
El Nacional
Novedades
Ovaciones
La Prensa
El Sol de México
El Universal

In Venezuela
Daily Journal
El Diario
El Nacional
Ultimas Noticias
El Universal
2001

In Colombia
El Espacio
El Espectador
La República
El Tiempo

Magazines

In Spain
Dinero
Economía
El Economista
Actualidad Económica
El Financiero
Información Comercial Española

In Mexico
El Campo
Comercio
Intercambio Internacional
Negobancos (Negocios y Bancos)
Transformación
Visión

In Argentina
Economic Survey
El Economista
Mercado

In Peru
El Comercio
Expreso
Ojo
La República

In Uruguay
El Día
El Diario
La Mañana
El País

In Argentina
Ambito Financiero
Buenos Aires Herald
Alarín
Crónica
El Cronista Comercial
La Nación
La Prensa
La Razón

In Puerto Rico
El Día
El Imparcial
El Mundo
San Juan Star

Review of the River Plate
Técnica e Industria

In Colombia
Coyuntura Económica
Económica Colombiana
Síntesis Económica

In Peru
La Republica

In Uruguay
Boletín Comercial
Crónicas Económicas

In Venezuela
El Mundo
Economía Hoy

ANNUAL TRADE FAIRS

In Spain

This is a partial list of annual events. Changes may occur from year to year, as well as during the year, and it is advisable to consult local tourist offices and the Government Tourist Offices abroad for up-to-date information.

January	Ready-made Menswear—Barcelona
	International Tourism Fair—Madrid
February	International Security Safety—Madrid
	International Exhibition on Men's Fashion—Madrid
March	Ready-made Ladies' Wear—Barcelona
	International Food Fair—Barcelona
April	International Aerospace and Defense Exhibition—Barcelona
May	International Optical Instruments—Madrid
	International Municipal Equipment and Services—Madrid
June	International Trade Fair—Barcelona
September	International Image, Sound, and Electronic Show—Barcelona
	International Book Fair—Barcelona
	International Scientific, Medical and Technical Instruments—Madrid
October	International Electrification Fair—Madrid
November	International Business Equipment and Data Processing—Madrid

For additional information contact: Secretaria de Estado de Comercio, Comisaria de Ferias, Paseo de la Castellana 162,128046 Madrid (458-00-16).

In Latin America

For information about trade fairs contact the following national organizations:

Ferias y Exposiciones Mexicanas, A.C.
Manuel Ma. Contreras 133-116-121
México, D.F.
telex: 1772163

Dirección Nacional de Promoción Comercial
Departamento de Ferias y Exposiciones
Avenida Julio A. Roca 651, 5°P.
Sector 21 (1322)
Buenos Aires
telephone: 343-103; telex: 1622, 17065, 18055

Corporación de Ferias y Exposiciones, S.A.
Carrera 40, No. 226-67
Apdo. Aéreo 6843
Bogotá
telephone: 244-01-41; telex: 44553

Confederación de Cámaras de Comercio y Producción del Perú
Avenida Gregorio Escobedo 398
Lima 11
telephone: 633-434

Cámara Nacional de Comercio
Edif. de la Bolsa de Comercio
Misiones 1400
Montevideo
telephone: 952-500

Venezuelan Fairs and Exhibitions
  Commission (VENEXPO)
Avenida Guaicaiparo
Qta. Cantoralia
El Rosal
Caracas

Chamber of Commerce of Puerto
  Rico
Chamber of Commerce Buildings
Tetuán 100
P.O.B. 3789
San Juan 00904
telephone: 809-721-6060

TRAVEL TIMES

Note that in most parts of the world, official time is based on the 24-hour
clock. Train schedules and other official documents will use 13:00 through
23:00 to express the PM hours.

Airlines

In Spain
  Most international flights go through Barajas Airport (ten miles from
  Madrid) although some flights, especially from England and Western
  Europe, do go to Barcelona (El Prat de Llobregat—seven miles from down-
  town.)

  Iberia, the national airline, flies international and domestic routes. Also,
  TWA, American, United, and Delta.

  Iberia, Velázquez 130, Madrid, telephone: 91-262-67-31

In Mexico
  Benito Juárez International Airport is three miles from Mexico City.

  Aeroméxico, the national airline, flies international and domestic routes.
  Mexicana flies domestic routes and to the U.S., Central America, and the
  Caribbean.

  Aeroméxico, Paseo de la Reforma 445-PH, Col. Cuauhtémoc, 06500,
  México, D.F., telephone: 525-42-99.
  Mexicana, Baleras 36, 6°, Apdo. 901, 06050 México, D.F., telephone 585-
  31-48

In Argentina
  Ezeiza Airport is 22 miles from downtown Buenos Aires.

  Aerolíneas Argentinas, the national airline, is the major international and
  domestic carrier. Three other airlines fly mainly domestic routes and to near-
  by countries.

  Aerolíneas Argentinas, Paseo Colón 185, Buenos Aires, telephone: 302-081
  Austral Líneas Aéreas, Florida 234, Buenos Aires, telephone: 468-841
  LADE, Perú 710, Buenos Aires, telephone: 347-071
  LAPA, Lavalle 465, Buenos Aires, telephone: 393:8099.

Average Flying Times between Major Spanish-Speaking Cities (in hours)

	BOGOTÁ	BUENOS AIRES	CARACAS	LIMA	MEXICO CITY	MONTEVIDEO	SAN JUAN
Bogotá	—	8	2	3	4.5	NA	3
Buenos Aires	8	—	6.5	5.5	11.5	1	NA
Caracas	2	6.5	—	6	6	NA	1.5
Lima	3	5.5	6	—	5.5	NA	7
Madrid	12	14.5	9	16	13.5	15.5	8
Mexico City	4.5	11.5	6	5.5	—	NA	4.5
Montevideo	NA	1	NA	NA	NA	—	NA
Suan Juan	3	NA	1.5	7	4.5	NA	—

Approximate Flying Times to Key Spanish-Speaking Cities (in hours)

	BARCELONA	BOGOTÁ	BUENOS AIRES	CARACAS	LIMA	MADRID	MEXICO CITY	MONTEVIDEO	SAN JUAN
London	3.5	13	17	10	15	2	13	NA	8
Los Angeles	15	8	15	9	8.5	13	4	NA	9
New York	9.5	6.5	14	5	10	8	6	17	3.5
Montreal	9	NA	16	NA	9.5	7.5	4.5	NA	NA
Toronto	10	NA	15.5	NA	11	9	4.5	NA	7.5

In Colombia

El Dorado International Airport is ten miles outside Bogotá.

AVIANCA, the national airline, operates international and domestic routes. SAM is the main domestic airline.

AVIANCA, Avenida El Dorado 93-30, Bogotá.
SAM, Avenida Jiménez, No. 5-14, Bogotá.

In Peru

Jorge Chavez International Airport is ten miles from Lima.

Aeroperú, the main international carrier, also flies domestic routes. One other airline, Faucett, flies mainly domestic routes.

Aeroperú, Jirón Cailloma 818, No. 11, Apdo. 1414, Lima.
Faucett, Jirón Unión 926, Plaza San Martín, Apdo. 1429, Lima.

In Uruguay

Carrasco Airport is 13 miles from Montevideo.

Two airlines fly mainly domestic routes.

PLUNA, Colonía 102 1, Apdo. 1360, Montevideo, telephone: 912-772.
TAMU, Colonía 1021, Apdo. 1360, Montevideo, telephone: 912-772

In Venezuela

Simón Bolívar International Airport and Maiquetía Airport are both 13 miles from Caracas.

VIASA, the national airline, flies international routes;
AVENSA, also government-owned, flies domestic routes.

VIASA, Torre Viasa, Avenida Sur 25, Plaza Morelos, Apdo. 6857, Caracas.
AVENSA, Edif. Banco de la Construcción y de Oriente 1-11-15-16, esq. de Platanal, Avenida Urdaneta.

In Puerto Rico

Isla Verde International Airport is nine miles from San Juan.

Prinair flies domestic routes and to Caribbean destinations.

N.B. The largest international carrier in South America is the Brazilian national airline, VARIG.

Rail Travel

In Spain

Good service from Madrid to most major cities. Provincial service is of poorer quality. Some areas of the country have little or no service. RENFE, the train service, can be reached at 733-30-33 or 222-76-09 (Madrid), or 310-72-00 (Barcelona).

In Mexico
Train service in Mexico is generally good.

In Argentina
Argentina has an extensive train service. For information call 311-64-11 (Buenos Aires).

In Colombia
Train service in Colombia is operated by the Ferrocarriles Nacionales de Colombia. For information call 277-55-77 (Bogotá).

In Uruguay
A generally good network exists throughout the country with connections to Argentinian and Brazilian networks. For information call 98-95-51 (Montevideo).

In Venezuela
The Venezuelan train system is under construction. For information call 41-61-41 (Caracas).

TRAVEL TIPS

On the Plane

1. Be aware that the engine noise is less noticeable in the front part of the plane. Try to sleep. Some frequent travelers bring along earplugs, eye-shades, and slippers.
2. Wear comfortable, loose-fitting clothing.
3. Walk up and down the aisles, when permitted, at least five minutes every hour to maintain body circulation.
4. Limit alcohol intake—altitude heightens the intoxicating effect.
5. Avoid heavy foods and caffeine, which dehydrates the body.
6. Drink plenty of liquids and eat foods rich in potassium. Pressurized cabins cause dehydration.
7. Take it easy when you arrive. When possible, schedule your first important meeting according to your "at home" peak period.

Jet Lag

Disruption of the body's natural cycles can have a lingering effect on your well-being, so take the following precautions:

1. *Avoid loss of sleep* by taking a flight that will get you to your destination early in the evening, if at all possible . Get a good night's sleep at home the night before your departure.
2. *Rearrange your daily routine* and sleep schedule to harmonize with a normal body clock at your destination.

3. *Avoid stress and last-minute rush*. You're going to need all your strength.
4. *Rearrange your eating habits*. Start four days early—begin a diet of alternate days of feasting and fasting. "Feast" features high-protein breakfasts and lunches (to increase energy level and wakefulness) and high-carbohydrate dinners (to help induce sleep).

Driving

You need the following documents when driving in Spain: passport, international insurance certificate (green card), registration (log) book, and a valid driver's license. An international driving permit is desirable, but in Spain you can drive with an American license. A red warning triangle—for display on the road in case of accident—is mandatory, as is the use of seat belts outside of city limits.

Telephones

In most towns and cities, long-distance calls can be placed from telephone offices (usually distinct from post offices). Most hotels allow you to use their phones for long-distance and international calls even if you're not staying there. A small service charge is added. The inland telephone network is partly automatic, and direct dialing is available to many countries.

Shopping

Shops in Spain usually open around 9:00 AM and close between 8:00 and 8:30 PM. All close for lunch from 1:00 to 3:30 or 4:00 PM in summer. Few shops are open on Sunday or holidays.

Clothing Sizes

In Europe, clothing sizes vary from country to country, so be sure to try on the garment. For men, a suit size is "10" more than the U.S. size—thus, an American 40 is a European or Continental 50. For women, the conversion is your American size plus "28"—an American size 10 is therefore a Continental 38.

Drug Stores

Spanish drug stores don't stock the range of products that are found in the U.S. For cosmetics you'd go to a perfumería.

Film

Film sizes aren't always indicated the same way in Europe as in the U.S. Check carefully before purchasing.

Tipping

Tipping, of course, varies with the individual and the situation. The following amounts are typical: In hotels in Spain, the service charge is included; the porter, bellhop, and doorman usually receive 75 pesetas; a maid, 50 pesetas per week. Lavatory and hatcheck attendants, as well as ushers, receive 20–50 pesetas. Taxi drivers, hairdressers, and tourist guides often are tipped 10 percent.

MAJOR HOTELS

Madrid

Fenix
Plaza de Colón
Tel: 91/431-6700
Fax: 91/576-0661
Major credit cards accepted

Palace
Plaza de las Cortes, 7
Tel: 91/429-7551
Fax: 91/429-8266
5 stars
Major credit cards accepted
Restaurant

Ritz
Plaza de Lealtad, 5
Tel: 91/521-2857
Fax: 91/532-8776
5 stars
Major credit cards accepted
Restaurant

Santo Mauro
Zurbano, 36
Tel: 91/319-6900
Fax: 91/308-5477
Major credit cards accepted
Restaurant

Villa Real
Plaza de las Cortes, 10
Tel: 91/420-3767
Fax: 91/420-2547
4 stars
Major credit cards accepted

Plaza
Gran Via, 84
Tel: 91/247-1200
Fax: 91/248-2389
Major credit cards accepted
Rooftop pool
Restaurant

El Prado
Calle Prado, 11
Tel: 91/369-0234
Fax: 91/429-2829
Major credit cards accepted

Reina Victoria
Plaza del Angel, 7
4 stars
Major credit cards accepted

Villamagna
Paseo de la Castellana, 22
Tel: 91/576-7500
Fax: 91/575-9504
Major credit cards accepted
Restaurant

Barcelona

Avenida Palace
Gran Via, 605
Tel: 93/301-9600
Fax: 93/318-1234
Major credit cards accepted
Restaurant, Gym

Condes de Barcelona
Passeig de Gràcia, 75
Tel: 93/487-3737
Fax: 93/484-8700
4 stars
Major credit cards accepted
Pool, Restaurant

Ritz
Gran Via, 668
Tel: 93/318-5200
Fax: 93/318-0148
5 stars
Major credit cards accepted
Restaurant

Alexandra
Mallorca, 251
Tel: 93/487-0505
Fax: 93/488-0258
Major credit cards accepted
Restaurant

Colón
Av. Catedral, 7
Tel: 93/301-1404
Fax: 93/317-2915
4 stars
Major credit cards accepted
Restaurant

Majestic
Passeig de Gràcia, 70
Tel: 93/488-1717
Fax: 93/488-1880
4 stars
Major credit cards accepted
Rooftop pool, Gym, Restaurant

Princess Sofía
Plaça Piux XII, 4
Tel: 93/330-7111
Fax: 93/411-2106
Major credit cards accepted
Restaurants (3)
Pools (2)
Gym

Mexico City

Camino Real
Mariano Escobedo, 700
Tel: 545-6960
Major credit cards accepted
Pool, Restaurant

Maria Isabel Sheraton
Reforma, 325
Tel: 211-0001
Major credit cards accepted
Pool, Restaurant

Buenos Aires

Alvear Palace
Av. Alvear, 1891
Tel: 804-4031/45
Fax: 804-0034
Pool, Health Club, Restaurant

Plaza Hotel
Florida, 1005
Tel: 311-5011/29
Fax: 313-2912
Pool, Health Club, Restaurants

La Paz

Hotel Plaza
Av. 16 de Julio
Tel: 378-300
Pool, Restaurant

Rio de Janeiro

Inter-Continental Rio
Prefeito Mendes de Morais, 222
Tel: 322-2200
Pool, Tennis Courts, Restaurants

Santiago

Carrera
Teatinos, 180
Tel: 698-2011

Crowne Plaza Holiday Inn
Benardo O'Higgins, 136
Tel: 381-042
Pool, Tennis Courts, Nightclub

Bogotá

Tequendama Inter-Continental
Carrera, 10
Tel: 282-9066
Restaurants

Caracas

Caracas Hilton
Av. México
Tel: 574-1122
Fax: 575-0024
Pool, Tennis Courts, Gym,
Restaurants

Tamanaco Inter-Continental
Av. Principal Las Mercedes
Tel: 208-7000
Fax: 208-7116
Pool, Tennis Courts, Gym,
Restaurants

MAJOR RESTAURANTS

Madrid

Café de Oriente
Plaza de Oriente, 2
Tel: 91/541-3974
Major credit cards accepted
Reservations advised

Horcher—one star
Alfonso XII, 6
Tel: 91/532-3596
Major credit cards accepted
Reservations required

El Pescador—one star
Jose Ortega y Gasset, 75
Tel: 91/402-1290
MasterCard, Visa
Reservations advised

La Trainera
Lagasca, 60
Tel: 91/576-8035
MasterCard, Visa
Reservations advised

Zalacaín—two stars
Alvarez de Baena, 4
Tel: 91/561-5935
Major credit cards accepted
Reservations required

Gure-Etxea—one star
Plaza de Paja, 12
Tel: 91/265-6149
Major credit cards accepted
Reservations advised

Barcelona

Azulete—one star
Via Augusta, 281
Tel: 93/203-5943
Major credit cards accepted
Dinner reservations advised

Beltxenea—one star
Mallorca, 275
Tel: 93/215-3024
Major credit cards accepted
Reservations required

La Dama—one star
Diagonal, 423
Tel: 93/202-0686
Major credit cards accepted
Reservations required

Eldorado Petit—two stars
Dolors Monserdà, 51
Tel: 93/204-5151
Major credit cards accepted
Reservations required

Reno—one star
Tuset, 27
Tel: 93/200-1390
Major credit cards accepted
Reservations strongly advised

Mexico City

San Angel Inn
Palmas, 50
Tel: 548-6746
Major credit cards accepted
Reservations advised

El Parador de Jose Luis
Pink Zone, 17
Tel: 533-1840
Major credit cards accepted
Reservations advised

Buenos Aires

La Caballeriza
Dardo Rocha, 1740
Tel: 798-1596

La Cabaña
Entre Rios, 436
Tel: 381-2373

La Paz

La Carreta
Calle Batallon Colorado #32
Tel: 355-891

Rio de Janeiro

Le Bec Fin
Av. Copacabana, 178
Tel: 542-4097
Major credit cards accepted
Reservations suggested

Le Pré Catalon
Av. Atlantica, 4240
Tel: 521-3232
Major credit cards accepted

Santiago

Aquí Está Coco
La Concepción, 236
Tel: 491-214
Major credit cards accepted

Bogotá

Casa San Isidro
Teleferíco
Tel: 284-5700
Major credit cards accepted

Caracas

La Atarraya
Plaza El Venezolano
Tel: 545-8235
Major credit cards accepted

Lasserre
3rd Av., Los Palos Grandes
Tel: 283-4558
Major credit cards accepted

USEFUL ADDRESSES

In Spain

Oficina de Información de Turismo
Plaza España
Madrid

Consejo Superior de las Cámaras
  Oficiales de Comercio
  Claudio Coello
19 Madrid-19

American Chamber of Commerce
Eurobuilding, Oficina 9H
Padre Damián 23
Madrid-16
  or
Avenida Diagonal 477
Barcelona-36

Dirección General de Política
  Comercial (Foreign Trade)
Paseo de la Castellana 162
Madrid-16

In Mexico

Confederación de Cámaras
  Nacionales de Comercio, Servicios
  y Turismo (CONCAACO)
Balderas 144, No. 2 y 3
Apdo. 113 bis
Centro Cuauhtémoc
06079 México, D.F.

Cámara Nacional de Comercio de la
  Ciudad de México (CANACO)
Paseo de la Reforma 42
Apdo. 32005
06048 México, D.F.

Confederación de Cámaras
  Industriales de los Estados Unidos
  Mexicanos (CONCAMIN)
Manuel María Contreras 133, 8°
Col. Cuauhtémoc
06597 México, D.F.

National Association of Importers
  and Exporters
Monterrey 130
Col. Roma-Cuauhtémoc
06700 México, D.F.

Institute for Foreign Trade
Alfonso Reyes 30
Col. Condesa
06140 México, D.F.

In Argentina

Cámara Argentina de Comercio
Avenida Leandro N. Alem 36
1003 Buenos Aires

Cámara de Comercio, Industria y
  Producción de la Federación
Gremial del Comercio e Industria
Avenida Córdoba 1868
Rosario
Sante Fe

National Tourist Bureau
Ezeira Airport

In Brazil

Riotur
Rua da Assembléia, 10
Rio de Janeiro

In Chile

Sernatur
Providencia 1550
Santiago

In Colombia

Cámara de Comercio de Bogotá
Carrera 9, No. 16-21
Bogotá

INDERENA
Diagonal 3Y
Bogotá

In Peru

Cámara de Comercio de Lima
Avenida Abancay 291, Piso 2
Lima

Ministerio de Industria, Turismo e
  Integración
Calle 1 Oeste
Corpac
San Isidro
Lima 27

In Uruguay

Dirección Nacional de Turismo
Agraciada 1409, No. 4-6
Montevideo

In Venezuela

Federación Venezolana de Cámaras y
  Asociaciones de Comercio y
  Producción (FEDECÁMARAS)
Edif. Fedecámaras 5°
Avenida El Empalme
Urb. El Bosque
Apdo. 2568
Caracas

Cámara de Comercio de Caracas
Avenida Este 2, No. 215
Los Caobas
Caracas

Departamento de Turismo
Parque Central
Caracas

In Puerto Rio

Cámara de Comercio de Puerto Rico
P.O. Box 3789
San Juan 00904

MAPS

Maps of Europe, Spain, Barcelona, Madrid, Mexico, and Latin America,
which appear on the following pages, will be useful in doing business
in Spanish-speaking areas.

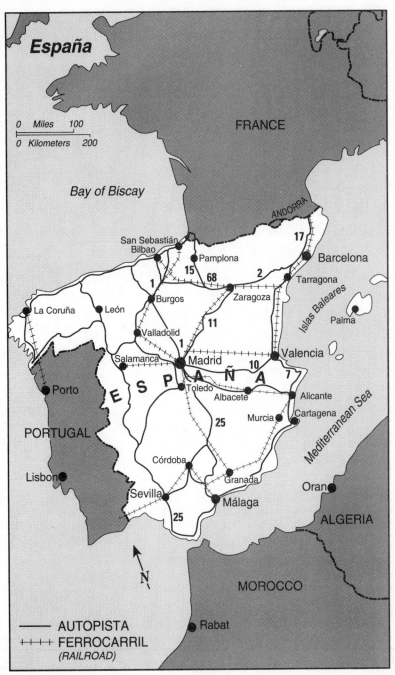

España

0 Miles 100
0 Kilometers 200

FRANCE

Bay of Biscay

ANDORRA

San Sebastián
Bilbao
Pamplona

17

Barcelona

15 68 2

Tarragona

1

Burgos Zaragoza

La Coruña León

Islas Baleares

Palma

11

Valladolid

Salamanca

1

Madrid

Valencia

10

E S P A Ñ A 7

Toledo
Albacete

Alicante

Porto

Murcia Cartagena

25

PORTUGAL

Córdoba

Lisbon

Granada

Oran

Sevilla Málaga

ALGERIA

25

N

MOROCCO

— AUTOPISTA
++++ FERROCARRIL
(RAILROAD)

Rabat

513

Europe

515

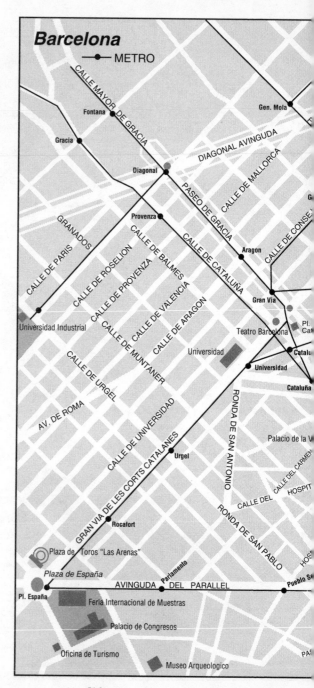

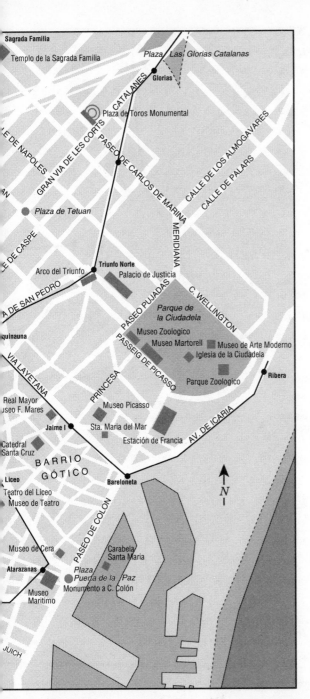

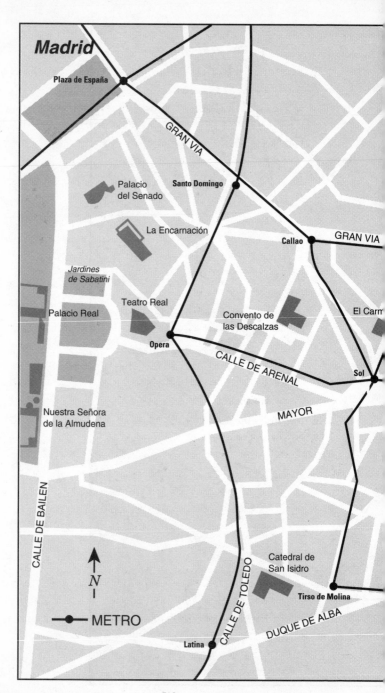

CALLE DE FUEN CARRAL

CALLE DE HORTALEZA

BARBARA DE BRAGANZA

Teatro Maria Guerrero

Chueca

Palacio del Duque de Sesto

PASEO DE RECOLETOS

Jose Antonio

CALLE DE ALCALA

Banco de España

Academia de Bellas Artes

Sevilla

PASEO DEL PRADO

Bolsa

CARRERA DE SAN JERONIMO

Congreso de los Diputados

CALLE DEL PRADO

Museo del Prado

CALLE DE LAS HUERTAS

LLE DE ATOCHA

A. Martin CALLE DE MORATIN

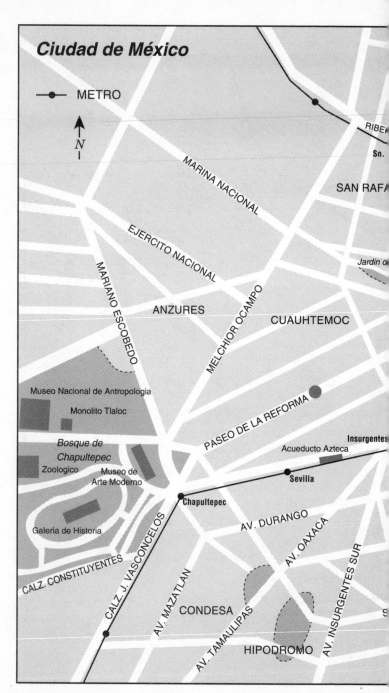

Ciudad de México

● METRO

N

MARINA NACIONAL

EJERCITO NACIONAL

MARIANO ESCOBEDO

ANZURES

MELCHIOR OCAMPO

CUAUHTEMOC

RIBE

Sn.

SAN RAFA

Jardin o

Museo Nacional de Antropologia

Monolito Tlaloc

PASEO DE LA REFORMA

Insurgentes

Acueducto Azteca

Bosque de Chapultepec

Zoologico

Museo de Arte Moderno

Sevilla

Galeria de Historia

Chapultepec

AV. DURANGO

CALZ. J. VASCONCELOS

AV. OAXACA

AV. INSURGENTES SUR

CALZ. CONSTITUYENTES

AV. MAZATLAN

CONDESA

AV. TAMAULIPAS

HIPODROMO

S

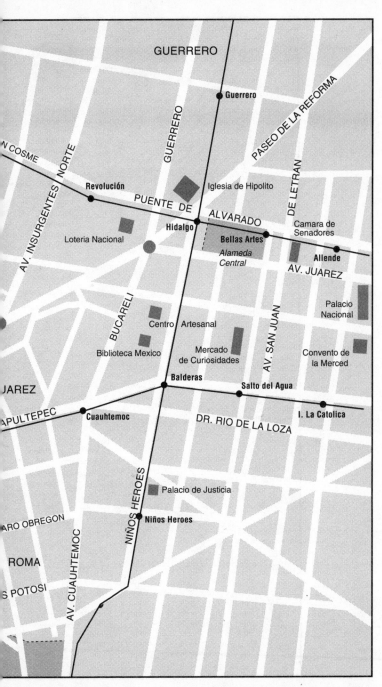

GUERRERO

Guerrero

PASEO DE LA REFORMA

N COSME

AV. INSURGENTES NORTE

GUERRERO

DE LETRAN

Revolución

Iglesia de Hipolito

PUENTE DE

ALVARADO

Hidalgo

Camara de
Senadores

Loteria Nacional

Bellas Artes

Alameda
Central

Allende

AV. JUAREZ

BUCARELI

Centro Artesanal

AV. SAN JUAN

Palacio
Nacional

Biblioteca Mexico

Mercado
de Curiosidades

Convento de
la Merced

Balderas

Salto del Agua

JUAREZ

I. La Catolica

APULTEPEC

Cuauhtemoc

DR. RIO DE LA LOZA

NIÑOS HEROES

Palacio de Justicia

ARO OBREGON

AV. CUAUHTEMOC

Niños Heroes

ROMA

S POTOSI

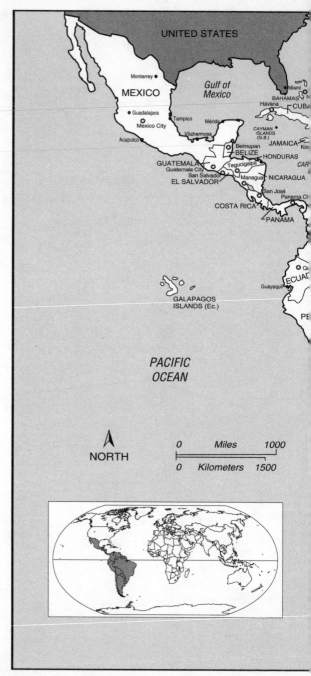

UNITED STATES

MEXICO

Monterrey

Gulf of
Mexico

Guadalajara

Tampico

Mexico City

Mérida

Vilahermosa

Acapulco

GUATEMALA

Guatemala City

San Salvador

EL SALVADOR

BELIZE

Belmopan

Tegucigalpa

Managua

San José

HONDURAS

NICARAGUA

COSTA RICA

Panama City

PANAMA

Miami

BAHAMAS

Havana

CUBA

CAYMAN
ISLANDS
(G.B.)

JAMAICA

Kin

CAR

ECUADOR

Qu

Guayaquil

PE

GALAPAGOS
ISLANDS (Ec.)

PACIFIC
OCEAN

NORTH

| 0 | Miles | 1000 |

| 0 | Kilometers | 1500 |

LATIN AMERICA

ATLANTIC
OCEAN

DOMINICAN
REPUBLIC
San Juan
PUERTO RICO
VIRGIN ISLANDS (U.S. & G.B.)
ANGUILLA (G.B.)
ANTIGUA & BARBUDA
Santo Domingo
Prince
ST. CHRISTOPHER & NEVIS
MONSERRAT (G.B.)
GUADELOUPE (Fr.)
DOMINICA
(Neth.)
THERLANDS
TILLES (Neth.)
MARTINIQUE (Fr.)
ST. LUCIA
ST. VINCENT & THE GRENADINES
BARBADOS
GRENADA
acaibo
TRINIDAD & TOBAGO
Caracas
Port-of-Spain
Ciudad
GUYANA
Bolívar
Georgetown
SURINAME
VENEZUELA
Paramaribo
a
FRENCH GUIANA (Fr.)
Cayenne
MBIA

Belém

Fortaleza

Recife

BRAZIL

Salvador

Brasilia

iticaca
BOLIVIA

Lake Poopo
La Paz
Sucre

PARAGUAY

Rio de Janeiro

CHILE

Asunción

San Paulo

Córdoba

Porto Alegre

Santiago
Rosario
URUGUAY

Valparaiso
Buenos Aires
Montevideo

ARGENTINA

Bahia Blanco

FALKLAND ISLANDS (G.B.)
Stanley
Strait of
Magellan
TIERRA DEL
FUEGO
S. GEORGIA ISLAND (G.B.)